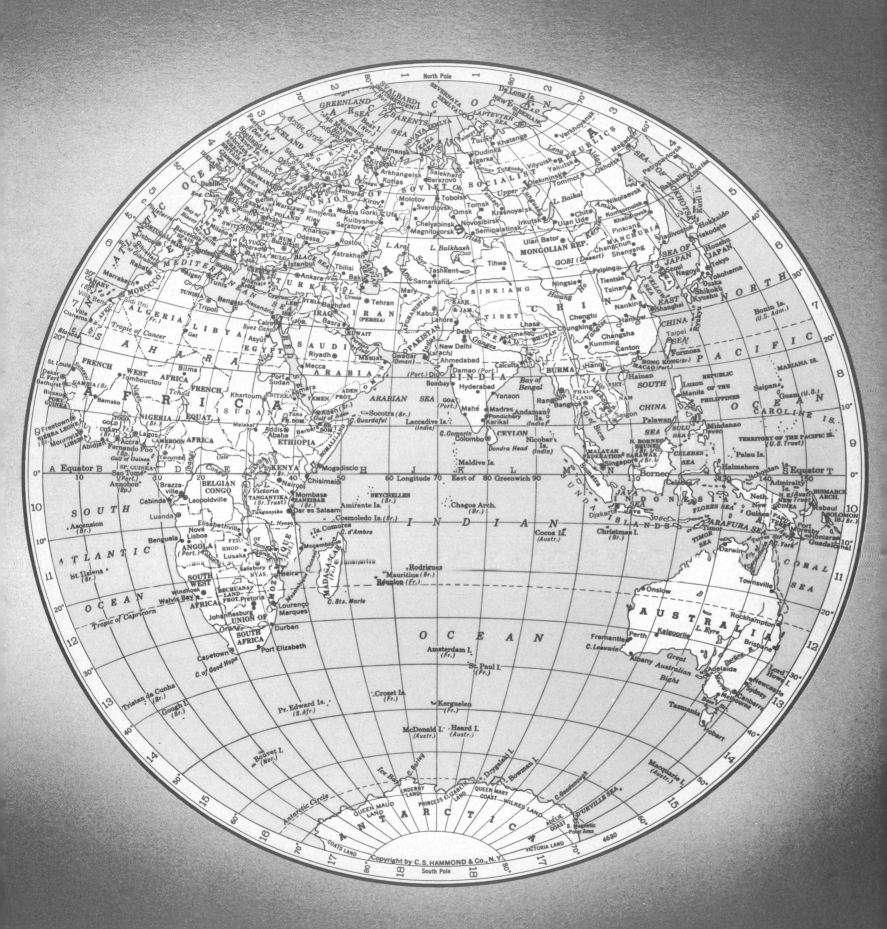

Eastern Hemisphere

HAMMOND'S
FAMILY REFERENCE
WORLD ATLAS

HANOVER HOUSE
GARDEN CITY   NEW YORK

Contents

SECTION ONE

Alphabetic List of Maps . . . . following Contents
Gazetteer-Index of the World 1-3
Index of Principal Cities of the World 4-5
Political Maps of the World 6-7
Political Maps of the Arctic and Antarctic 8
Political Maps of Europe and Individual Countries 9-24
Political Maps of Asia and Individual Countries 24-33
Political Map of Africa 34-35
Political Map of Australia 36
Political Map of the Pacific Ocean 37
Political Maps of North America and Individual Countries 38-44
Political Maps of the West Indies and South America 45-48
Political Maps of the Individual States of the United States and Possessions . . 49-96
Index of Cities and Towns of the United States 97-112
Illustrated Geography and Gazetteer of the World 113-154
World Distribution Maps 155-160

SECTION TWO — MAN'S STORY IN MAPS

The World at the Dawn of History 162
The Cradleland of Civilization 162
The Roman Empire 163
The Old World in the Middle Ages — 570-1400 A. D. 163
Voyages of Discovery — 1000-1522 164
The Modern Age — 1700 to the Present 164
European Empires in America in the 17th Century 165
The Thirteen Colonies about 1750 165
The United States in 1783 166
The American Revolution 166
Territorial Growth of the United States 167
Routes to the West 167
The States of the United States 168
The Confederate States of America 168
The United States Today 169
The United States and Overseas Possessions 169
Facts about Our Earth 170-171
What a Map Is 172
How to Use a Map 173
What Scale Means 174
Projection: Changing a Globe into a Flat Map 175
Contours: What they are and How to Use Them 176

List of Modern Maps

Name	Text Page	Map Ref.	& Page
Aden	152	E7	26
Afghanistan	152	J3	26
Africa, Political	137		34-35
Africa, Resource-Relief Map	...		237
Alabama, U.S.A.	...		49
Alaska	211		95
Albania	134	E5	21
Alberta, Canada	119		40
Algeria	138	G5	34
Andorra	134	G1	17
Anglo-Egyptian Sudan (Sudan)	138	M9	34
Angola	138	K14	35
Antarctica	...		8
Arabia	148		26
Arctic Ocean	...		8
Argentina	126		47
Arizona, U.S.A.	...		50
Arkansas, U.S.A.	...		51
Asia, Political	147		25
Asia, Resource-Relief Map	...		248
Australia, Political	145		36
Australia, Resource-Relief Map	...		245
Australian Capital Terr.		J7	36
Austria	134		20
Bahama Islands	119	C1	45
Bahrein Islands	152	F4	26
Balkan States	131		21
Barbados	119	G4	45
Basutoland	138	M17	35
Bechuanaland	138	L16	35
Belgian Congo	138	L12	35
Belgium	134		15
Bermuda	119	G2	45
Bhutan	152	F3	29
Bolivia	126	H7	46
Brazil	126		46
British Columbia, Canada	119		40
British Honduras	119	C2	39
Brunei	152	E5	31
Bulgaria	134	G4	21
Burma	152		30
California, U.S.A.	...		52
Cambodia	152	E4	30
Cameroons	138	J10	34
Cameroun	138	J10	34
Canada	119		40-41
Canal Zone	...		95
Cape Verde Islands	138	N5	6
Caroline Islands	145	E5	37
Central America	118		39
Ceylon	152		29
Channel Islands	128	E8	10
Chile	126		47
China	152		32
Colombia	126	F3	46
Colorado, U.S.A.	...		53
Comoro Islands	138	P14	35
Connecticut, U.S.A.	...		54
Cook Islands	145	K7	37
Costa Rica	119	E5	39
Cuba	119		48
Cyprus	152		28
Czechoslovakia	134		20
Damão	152	B4	29
Delaware, U.S.A.	...		65
Denmark	134		13
District of Columbia, U.S.A.	...	F5	65
Diu	152	B4	29
Dominican Republic	119	D6	48
East India Islands	150		31
Eastern Canada	115		41
Ecuador	126	E4	46
Egypt	138	M6	34
England	134		10
Eritrea	138	O8	34
Ethiopia	138	O9	34
Europe, Political	127		9
Europe, Resource-Relief Map	129		232
Faeröe Islands	129	D2	9
Falkland Islands	126	H14	47
Fiji	145	H7	37
Finland	134		13
Florida, U.S.A.	...		55
Formosa	152	K7	32
France	134		16
French Equatorial Africa	138	K10	34
French West Africa (see individual territories in Africa tables)	...	G8	34
Gambia	138	C9	34
Georgia, U.S.A.	...		56
Germany	134		14
Gibraltar	134	D4	17
Gilbert, Ellice and Phoenix Is.	145	H6	37
Gôa	152	B5	29
Gold Coast	138	F10	34
Great Britain	134	F3	9
Greece	135	F6	21
Greenland	119	D22	8
Guadeloupe	119	F3	45
Guam	145	E4	37
Guatemala	119	B3	39
Guiana, British	126	J2	46
Guiana, French	126	K3	46
Guiana, Neth. (Surinam)	126	J3	46
Guinea, Portuguese	139	C9	34
Guinea, Spanish	139	J11	35

Name	Text Page	Map Ref.	& Page
Haiti	119	C5	48
Hawaii	145		96
Holland (Netherlands)	135		15
Honduras	119	D3	39
Honduras, British	119	C2	39
Hong Kong	152	J7	32
Hungary	135		20
Iceland	135	C2	9
Idaho, U.S.A.	...		57
Illinois, U.S.A.	...		58
India	153		29
Indiana, U.S.A.	...		59
Indochina	150		30
Indonesia	153	F7	31
Iowa, U.S.A.	...		60
Iran (Persia)	153		27
Iraq	153		27
Ireland	135		12
Ireland, Northern	135	H2	12
Isle of Man	...	C3	10
Israel	153		24
Italy	135		18
Jamaica	119		48
Japan	153		33
Jordan	153		24
Kansas, U.S.A.	...		61
Kentucky, U.S.A.	...		62
Kenya	139	O11	35
Korea	153		33
Kuwait	153	E4	26
Laos	153	E3	30
Lebanon	153		28
Leeward Islands	119	G3	45
Liberia	139	E10	34
Libya	139	K6	34
Liechtenstein	135	J2	19
Louisiana, U.S.A.	...		63
Loyalty Islands	...	G8	37
Luxembourg	135		15
Macao	153	H7	32
Madagascar	139	R15	35
Maine, U.S.A.	...		64
Malayan Federation	153		30
Maldive Islands	153	L9	25
Malta	135	E7	18
Manitoba, Canada	119		40
Mariana Islands	145	E4	37
Maritime Provinces			41
Marquesas Is.	145	N6	37
Marshall Islands	145	H4	37
Martinique	119	-G4	45
Maryland, U.S.A.	...		65
Massachusetts, U.S.A.	...		66
Mauritius	139	S19	35
Mexico	117		44
Michigan, U.S.A.	...		67
Midway Island	...	J3	37
Minnesota, U.S.A.	...		68
Mississippi, U.S.A.	...		69
Missouri, U.S.A.	...		70
Monaco	135	G6	16
Mongolian Republic	153		32
Montana, U.S.A.	...		71
Morocco, French	139	E5	34
Morocco, Sp.	139	F5	34
Mozambique	139	O15	35
Nauru	145	G6	37
Near East	...		26
Nebraska, U.S.A.	...		72
Nepal	154	D3	29
Netherlands (Holland)	135		15
Netherlands Antilles	119	E4	45
Nevada, U.S.A.	...		73
New Brunswick, Canada	119	G4	41
New Caledonia	145	G8	37
New Guinea, Terr. of	146	B7	31
New Guinea, Netherlands	154	K6	31
New Hampshire, U.S.A.	...		74
New Hebrides Islands	145	G7	37
New Jersey, U.S.A.	...		75
New Mexico, U.S.A.	...		76
New South Wales, Australia	145	H6	36
New York, U.S.A.	...		77
New Zealand, Political	145		36
New Zealand, Resource-Relief Map..	...		245
Newfoundland, Canada	120	J4	41
Nicaragua	120	E4	39
Nigeria	139	H10	34
Niue, I.	146	K7	37
North America, Political	114		38
North America, Resource-Relief Map	...		217
North Borneo	154	F5	31
North Carolina, U.S.A.	...		78
North Dakota, U.S.A.	...		79
Northern Ireland	135	H2	12
Northern Rhodesia	139	M14	35
Northern Territory, Australia	146	F3	36
Northwest Territories, Canada	120		40
Norway	135		13
Nova Scotia, Canada	120	H4	41
Nyasaland Prot.	139	N14	35
Ohio, U.S.A.	...		80
Oklahoma, U.S.A.	...		81
Oman, Sultanate of	154	G5	26
Ontario, Canada	120		41
Oregon, U.S.A.	...		82
Pacific Ocean	144		37

Name	Text Page	Map Ref.	& Page
Pakistan	154	A3&F4	29
Palau Islands	146	D5	37
Panama	120	G6	39
Papua Territory	146	B7	31
Paraguay	126	J8	47
Pennsylvania, U.S.A.	...		83
Persia (Iran)	153		27
Peru	126	E5	46
Philippines, Republic of the	154	G4	31
Pitcairn Island	146	O8	37
Poland	136		17
Portugal	136		17
Portuguese India	152	B4,5	29
Prince Edward Island, Canada	120	H4	41
Principe and São Tomé	139	H11	35
Puerto Rico	120	G2	45
Québec, Canada	120		41
Queensland, Australia	146	G4	36
Réunion	139	R20	35
Rhode Island, U.S.A.	...		66
Ruanda-Urundi	140	M12	35
Rumania	136	G3	21
Russia	136		22-23
Ryukyu Islands	154	L7	33
St. Helena I.	140	E15	35
St. Pierre and Miquelon Is.	120	J4	41
Salvador, El	120	C4	39
Samoa, American	146	J7	37
Samoa, Western	146	J7	37
San Marino	136	D2	18
São Tomé and Principe	139	H11	35
Sarawak	154	E5	31
Saskatchewan, Canada	120		40
Saudi Arabia	153	D4	26
Scotland	135		11
Seychelles	140	J10	25
Siam (Thailand)	154		30
Sierre Leone	140	D10	34
Sikkim	154	E3	29
Singapore	154	F6	30
Society Islands	...	L7	37
Solomon Islands Prot.	146	F6	37
Somaliland, French	140	P9	34
Somaliland (Italian Tr.)	140	R10	34
Somaliland Prot.	140	R10	34
South America, Political	121		46-47
South America, Resource-Relief Map	...		224
South Australia, Australia	146	E5	36
South Carolina, U.S.A.	...		84
South Dakota, U.S.A.	...		85
South West Africa	...	K16	35
Southeast Asia			31
Southern Rhodesia	140	M15	35
Spain	136		17
Spanish Sahara	140	D6	34
Sudan	138	M9	34
Surinam (Netherlands Guiana)	126	J3	46
Swaziland	140	N17	35
Sweden	136		13
Switzerland	136		19
Syria	154		28
Tanganyika Territory	140	N13	35
Tangier, International Zone	140	E4	34
Tasmania, Australia	146	J8	36
Tennessee, U.S.A.	...		86
Texas, U.S.A.	...		87
Thailand (Siam)	154		30
Tibet, China	154	C5	32
Timor, Portuguese	154	H7	31
Togo (Fr. Trust)	140	G10	34
Togoland (Br. Trust)	140	G10	34
Tokelau (Union Group)	146	J6	37
Tonga (Friendly) Is.	146	J7	37
Trinidad and Tobago	120	G5	45
Trucial Oman	154	F5	26
Tuamotu (Low) Arch.	146	M7	37
Tunisia	140	H5	34
Turkey	136		28
Uganda Protectorate	140	N11	35
Union of South Africa	140	L18	35
Union of Soviet Socialist Republics..	136		22-23
United Kingdom	134	D3	9
United States of America	120		42-43
Uruguay	126	J10	47
Utah, U.S.A.	...		88
Vatican City	136	B6	18
Venezuela	126	G2	46
Vermont, U.S.A.	...		89
Victoria, Australia	146	G7	36
Vietnam	154	E3	30
Virgin Islands (U.S.A.)	120	H1	45
Virginia, U.S.A.	...		90
Wake Island	...	G4	37
Wales	134	D5	10
Washington, U.S.A.	...		91
West Indies	118		45
West Virginia, U.S.A.	...		92
Western Australia, Australia	146	C4	36
Western Canada	115		40
Windward Islands	120	G4	45
Wisconsin, U.S.A.	...		93
World	...		6-7
Wyoming, U.S.A.	...		94
Yemen	154	D7	26
Yugoslavia	136	C3	21
Yukon Territory, Canada	120		40
Zanzibar Prot.	140	P13	35

HAMMOND'S
WORLD ATLAS AND GAZETTEER

GAZETTEER-INDEX OF THE WORLD

This alphabetical list of grand divisions, countries, states, colonial possessions, etc., gives area, population, capital, seat of government or chief town, and index references and numbers of plates on which they are shown on the largest scale. The mother country of colonial possessions is indicated by abbreviations in parentheses. The index reference shows the square on the respective map in which the name of the country, state or colonial possession is located.

ABBREVIATIONS

Aust. = Australian.	I. = Island.	Pak. = Pakistan.	Trust. = Trust Territory.
Belg. = Belgian or Belgium.	Is. = Islands.	pen. = peninsula.	U.S.A. = United States of America.
Br. = British Commonwealth of Nations.	It. = Italian or Italy.	Port. = Portugal or Portuguese.	U. S. Adm. = U. S. Administration.
Dan. = Danish or Denmark.	Jap. = Japan or Japanese.	Rep. = Republic.	U. S. S. R. = Union of Soviet Socialist Republics.
E. = East.	Mand. = Mandate.	So. = South.	U. of So.
Fr. = France or French.	N. = North.	Sp. = Spain or Spanish.	Africa = Union of South Africa.
Gr. = Greece or Greek.	Neth. = Netherlands.	sq. mi. = square miles.	W. = West.
	N. Z. = New Zealand.	S. S. R. = Soviet Socialist Republic.	

Country	Area (Sq. Miles)	Population	Capital or Chief Town	Index Ref.	Plate No.
Aden (incl. Protectorate) (Br.)	112,000	650,000	Aden	E 7	26
Aden Colony	75	80,516	Aden	E 7	26
Admiralty Is. (Aust. Tr.)	820	13,000	Lorengau	E 6	37
Afghanistan	250,000	12,000,000	Kabul	J 3	26
Africa	11,850,000	190,000,000			34, 35
Alabama, U.S.A.	51,078	3,061,743	Montgomery	M 6	43
Alaska (U.S.A.)	571,065	128,643	Juneau	C 3	38
Albania	11,096	1,112,355	Tiranë	E 5	21
Alberta, Canada	248,800	939,501	Edmonton	G 4	40
Aleutian Islands (U.S.A.)	6,800	5,600		F 3	38
Algeria (Fr.)	851,284	8,681,785	Alger (Algiers)	G 5	34
Andaman Is. (India)	2,508	21,316	Port Blair	F 6	29
Andorra	191	5,265	Andorra la Vieja	G 1	17
Anglo-Egyptian Sudan	967,500	8,309,663	Khartoum	M 9	34
Angola (Port.)	481,351	4,094,000	Luanda	K14	35
Antarctica	5,500,000				8
Antigua (Br.) (incl. Barbuda and Redonda)	171	41,757	St. Johns	G 3	45
Antilles, Greater, Lesser				E 3	45
Arabia	1,000,000	10,700,000		D 5	26
Arctic Ocean					8
Argentina	1,078,266	16,108,573	Buenos Aires	H10	47
Arizona, U.S.A.	113,580	749,587	Phoenix	E 6	42
Arkansas, U.S.A.	52,725	1,909,511	Little Rock	K 6	43
Armenian S.S.R. (U.S.S.R.)	11,500	1,345,000	Yerevan (Erivan)	F 5	22
Ascension Island (Br.)	34	159	Georgetown	D13	35
Asia	16,500,000	1,301,000,000			25
Australia, Commonwealth of (Br.)	2,974,581	7,579,358	Canberra		36
Australian Capital Territory	939	16,905	Canberra	J 7	36
Austria	32,369	6,918,959	Wien (Vienna)	B-C 3	20
Azerbaidzhan S.S.R. (U.S.S.R.)	33,100	3,100,000	Baku	F 5	22
Azores Islands (Port.)	890	287,091	Ponta Delgada	B 4	34
Bahama Islands (Br.)	4,404	79,000	Nassau	C 1	45
Bahrein Islands (Br.)	213	109,650	Manama	F 4	26
Balearic Islands (Sp.)	1,936	422,127	Palma	H 3	17
Baluchistan (Pak.)	134,002	530,000	Quetta	A 3	29
Barbados (Br.)	166	192,800	Bridgetown	G 4	45
Barbuda and Redonda Is. (Br.)	63	979	Codrington	F-G 3	45
Basutoland (Br.)	11,716	563,854	Maseru	M17	35
Bechuanaland Prot. (Br.)	275,000	294,232	Mafeking	L16	35
Belgian Congo	902,274	11,121,463	Léopoldville	L12	35
Belgium	11,775	8,512,195	Bruxelles (Brussels)	E 7	15
Bermuda (Br.)	21	37,000	Hamilton	G 2	45
Bhutan	18,000	300,000	Bumthang	F 3	29
Bismarck Archipelago (Aust. Trust.)	19,660	145,000	Rabaul	E 6	37
Bolivia	412,777	3,019,031	La Paz, Sucre	G 7	46
Bonin Is. (U.S. Adm.)	76			E 3	37
Borneo	208,286			E 5	31
Brazil	3,286,170	52,645,479	Rio de Janeiro	K 6	46
British Columbia, Canada	359,279	1,165,210	Victoria	F 4	40
British Honduras	8,867	59,220	Belize	C 2	39
Brunei (Br.)	2,226	40,657	Brunei	E 5	31
Bulgaria	42,796	7,022,206	Sofiya	G 4	21
Burma	261,610	18,489,000	Rangoon	C 2	30
Byelorussian S.S.R. (White Russian S.S.R.) (U.S.S.R.)	80,100	7,220,000	Minsk	D 4	22
California, U.S.A.	156,803	10,586,223	Sacramento	C 5	42
Cambodia	69,884	3,748,000	Phnom Penh	E 4	30
Cameroons (Br. Trust.)	34,081	1,027,100	Lagos	J10	34
Cameroun (Fr. Trust.)	161,787	3,065,800	Yaoundé	J10	34
Canada	3,621,616	14,009,429	Ottawa		40, 41
Canal Zone (U.S.A.)	362	52,822	Balboa Heights	G 6	39
Canary Islands (Sp.)	2,894	776,912	Las Palmas, Santa Cruz	B 4	17
Cape of Good Hope, U. of So. Africa	277,169	4,053,848	Capetown	M18	35
Cape Verde Islands (Port.)	1,557	147,328	Praia	N 5	6
Caroline Islands (U.S. Trust.)	525	36,980	Moen, Ponape	E 5	37
Cayman Is., Jamaica (Br.)	104	6,670	Georgetown	B 3	45
Celebes	72,986	5,500,000	Makassar	G 6	31
Central America	217,813	8,918,547			39
Ceylon	25,332	6,657,339	Colombo	D 7	29
Channel Islands (Br.)	75	102,776	St. Helier	E 8	10
Chatham Islands (N.Z.)	372	505		J10	37
Chile	286,396	5,809,000	Santiago	F10	47
China	3,724,273	461,006,285	Peiping, Taipei		32
Christmas Island (Br.)	60	866		O11	25
Colombia	439,828	11,260,000	Bogotá	F 3	46
Colorado, U.S.A.	103,967	1,325,089	Denver	G 5	42
Comoro Is. (Is. Comores), (Fr.)	849	156,150	Dzaoudzi	P14	35
Connecticut, U.S.A.	4,899	2,007,280	Hartford	P 4	43
Cook Islands (N.Z.)	99	14,088	Avarua	K 7	37
Corsica (Corse), (Fr.)	3,367	267,873	Ajaccio	G 6	16
Costa Rica	19,238	800,875	San José	E 5	39
Cuba	42,857	5,348,000	Habana	48 & B 2	45
Curaçao (Neth. Antilles)	173	95,195	Willemstad	E 4	45
Cyprus (Br.)	3,572	450,114	Nicosia	E 5	28
Czechoslovakia	49,356	12,090,164	Praha (Prague)	D 2	20
Dahomey (Fr.)	42,471	1,476,000	Porto Novo	G10	34
Daito Is. (U.S. Adm.)	18	2,691		M 6	32
Damão (Port.)	213	63,521		B 4	29
Delaware, U.S.A.	1,978	318,085	Dover	P 5	43
Denmark	16,556	4,279,151	København (Copenhagen)	E 9	13
District of Columbia, U.S.A.	61	802,178	Washington	O 5	43
Diu (Port.)	12	19,731		B 4	29
Dominica (Br.)	305	53,900	Roseau	G 4	45
Dominican Republic	19,129	2,121,083	Ciudad Trujillo	D 6 48 & D 3	45
Ecuador approx.	115,000	3,076,933	Quito	E 4	46
Egypt	386,000	19,087,304	Cairo	M 6	34
England and Wales	58,340	43,744,924	London		10
Eritrea	15,754	1,086,000	Asmara	O 8	34
Estonia (Estonian S.S.R.), (U.S.S.R.)	17,400	1,000,000	Tallin (Tallinn)	D 4	22
Ethiopia (excl. Eritrea)	350,000	10,000,000	Addis Ababa	O 9	34
Europe	4,129,908	551,000,000			9
Faeröe Islands (Dan.)	540	29,178	Thorshavn	D 2	9
Falkland Islands (Br.) (incl. S. Georgia)	5,618	2,239	Port Stanley	H14	47
Fernando Póo (island), (Sp. Guinea)	800	17,249	Santa Isabel	H11	34
Fiji (Br.)	7,036	259,638	Suva	H 7	37
Finland	130,500	4,028,910	Helsinki	P 4	13
Florida, U.S.A.	54,262	2,771,305	Tallahassee	N 7	43
Formosa (Taiwan), (China)	13,885	6,126,000	Taipei	K 7	32
France	212,736	40,502,513	Paris		16
Franz Josef Land (Zemlya Frantsa Iosifa)				F 1	22
French Equatorial Africa	961,392	4,168,910	Brazzaville	K10	34
French Sudan	584,942	3,137,000	Bamako	F 8	34
French West Africa	1,814,852	16,377,000	Dakar	G 8	34

Country	Area (Sq. Miles)	Population	Capital or Chief Town	Index Ref.	Plate No.
*G*abon (Fr.)	90,733	423,904	Libreville	J12	35
Galápagos Islands, Ecuador	3,042	1,346	Pto. Baquerizo	D 7	46
Gambia (Br.)	4,003	278,858	Bathurst	C 9	34
Gambier Islands (Fr.)	6	1,569	Rikitea	N 8	37
Georgia, U.S.A.	58,518	3,444,578	Atlanta	N 6	43
Georgian S.S.R. (U.S.S.R.)	29,400	3,555,000	Tbilisi (Tiflis)	F 5	22
Germany, East (German Democratic Rep.)	41,535	18,488,316	Berlin		14
Germany, West (Federal Republic of)	35,914	50,579,878	Bonn		14
Gibraltar (Br.)	2	23,232		D 4	17
Gilbert, Ellice and Phoenix Islands	196	32,311	Bairiki	H 6	37
Gôa (Port.)	1,313	540,925	Pangim	B 5	29
Gold Coast (Ghana), (Br.)	78,803	3,735,682	Accra	F10	34
Great Britain and Northern Ireland	94,279	50,210,472	London	E 3	9
Greece	51,182	7,856,000	Athenai (Athens)	F 6	21
Greenland (Dan.)	839,999	21,412	Godthaab	D22	8
Grenada (Br.)	133	72,387	St. George's	G 4	45
Guadeloupe and Dependencies (Fr.)	688	278,864	Basse Terre	F 3	45
Guam (U.S.A.)	203	59,498	Agaña	E 4	37
Guatemala	45,452	2,787,030	Guatemala	B 3	39
Guiana, British	89,480	375,701	Georgetown	J 2	46
Guiana, French	35,135	25,499	Cayenne	K 3	46
Guiana, Netherlands (Surinam)	54,300	219,000	Paramaribo	J 3	46
Guinea, French	96,525	2,130,000	Conakry	D 9	34
Guinea, Portuguese	13,948	510,736	Bissau	C 9	34
Guinea, Spanish	10,830	161,032	Santa Isabel	J11	35
*H*aiti	10,714	3,111,973	Port-au-Prince	C 5 48 & D 3	45
Hawaii (U.S.A.)	6,420	499,794	Honolulu	L 3	37
Holland (Netherlands).land	12,883	9,625,499	's Gravenhage, Amsterdam	F 4	15
Honduras	45,000	1,505,465	Tegucigalpa	D 3	39
Honduras, British	8,867	59,220	Belize	C 2	39
Hong Kong (Br.)	391	1,857,000	Victoria	J 7	32
Hungary	35,875	9,204,799	Budapest	E 3	20
*I*celand	39,709	144,263	Reykjavík	C 2	9
Idaho, U.S.A.	82,808	588,637	Boise	E 3	42
Ifni (Sp.)	676	45,852	Sidi Ifni	D 6	34
Illinois, U.S.A.	55,947	8,712,176	Springfield	L 4	43
India	1,059,342	356,755,978	New Delhi		29
India, Portuguese	1,538	624,177	Pangim	B 4-5	29
Indiana, U.S.A.	36,205	3,934,224	Indianapolis	M 5	43
Indochina (Fr.)	285,927	26,876,510		E 3	30
Indonesia (East Indies)	735,286	79,260,000	Djakarta (Batavia)	F 7	31
Iowa, U.S.A.	55,986	2,621,073	Des Moines	K 4	43
Iran (Persia)	628,000	19,000,000	Tehran	H 4	27
Iraq (Mesopotamia)	116,600	4,799,500	Baghdad	C 4	27
Ireland (Eire)	26,601	2,958,878	Dublin (Baile Atha Cliath)		12
Ireland, Northern	5,238	1,369,579	Belfast	H 2	12
Isle of Man (Br.)	221	55,213	Douglas	C 3	10
Israel	7,978	1,554,000	Jerusalem		24
Italy	116,000	47,020,536	Roma (Rome)		18
Ivory Coast (Fr.)	183,397	2,066,000	Abidjan	E10	34
*J*amaica (Br.)	4,411	1,237,391	Kingston	48 & C 3	45
Jammu and Kashmir	92,780	4,021,616	Srinagar	C 2	29
Japan	142,272	83,199,637	Tokyo		33
Java and Madura	51,032	52,000,000	Djakarta	K 2	31
Jordan (Trans-Jordan)	34,750	1,250,000	Amman	D 4	24
*K*ansas, U.S.A.	82,113	1,905,299	Topeka	J 5	42
† Karikal, India (Fr.)	52	70,541	Karikal	D 6	29
Kashmir and Jammu	92,780	4,021,616	Srinagar	C 2	29
Kazakh S.S.R. (U.S.S.R.)	1,061,600	6,000,000	Alma-Ata	H 5	22
Kentucky, U.S.A.	40,109	2,944,806	Frankfort	M 5	43
Kenya (Br.)	219,730	5,377,393	Nairobi	O11	35
Kerguelen Arch. (Fr.)				T 8	6
Kirghiz S.S.R. (U.S.S.R.)	76,100	1,490,000	Frunze	J 5	22
Korea	85,228	29,291,000	Seoul, P'yongyang	C 4	33
Krētē (Crete), Greece	3,232	441,687	Erákleion	G 8	21
Kuria Muria Is. (Br.)		70		G 6	26
Kuril Is. (Chishima), (U.S.S.R.)	5,700	15,000	Severo-Kuril'sk	R 5	23
Kuwait	8,000	170,000	Al Kuwait	E 4	26
*L*accadive Islands (India)	746	18,393		B 6	29
Laos	89,343	1,200,000	Vientiane	E 3	30
Latvia (Latvian S.S.R.), (U.S.S.R.)	24,600	1,000,000	Riga	D 4	22
Lebanon	3,475	1,165,208	Beirut	F 6	28
Leeward Islands (Br.)	423	108,838	St. Johns	G 3	45
Liberia	43,000	1,600,000	Monrovia	E10	34
Libya	679,358	1,100,000	Tripoli, Benghazi	K 6	34
Liechtenstein	65	13,757	Vaduz	J 2	19
Lithuania (Lithuanian S.S.R.), (U.S.S.R.)	31,200	2,700,000	Vil'nyus (Vilna)	D 4	22
Louisiana, U.S.A.	45,177	2,683,516	Baton Rouge	K 7	43

Country	Area (Sq. Miles)	Population	Capital or Chief Town	Index Ref.	Plate No.
Loyalty Islands (Fr.)	800	11,854	Chépénéhé	G 8	37
Luxembourg	999	290,992	Luxembourg	J 9	15
*M*acao (Port.)	6	389,000	Macao	H 7	32
Madagascar (Fr.)	241,094	4,294,985	Tananarive	R15	35
Madeira Islands (Port.)	308	269,179	Funchal	A 2	17
Madura I.	1,752	2,444,000	Pamekasan	K 2	31
† Mahé, India	23	18,293	Mahé	C 6	29
Maine, U.S.A.	31,040	913,777	Augusta	R 3	43
Malayan Federation	50,690	4,908,086	Kuala Lumpur	E 6	30
Maldive Islands (Br.)	115	82,068	Malé	L 9	25
Malta (Br.)	122	305,991	Valletta	E 7	18
Manchuria (China)	412,801	36,903,000	Shenyang (Mukden)	K 2	32
Manitoba, Canada	219,723	776,541	Winnipeg	L 3	40
Mariana Islands (U.S. Trust.)	142	6,286	Garapan	E 4	37
Marquesas Is. (Fr.)	480	2,976	Atuona	N 6	37
Marshall Islands (U.S. Trust.)	61	11,033	Majuro	H 4	37
Martinique (Fr.)	425	261,595	Fort de France	G 4	45
Maryland, U.S.A.	9,887	2,343,001	Annapolis	O 5	43
Massachusetts, U.S.A.	7,907	4,690,514	Boston	P 4	43
Mauritania (Fr.)	328,185	523,900	St.-Louis	D 8	34
Mauritius (Br.)	720	432,468	Port Louis	S19	35
Mesopotamia (See Iraq)				D 4	27
México	760,373	25,581,250	México		44
Michigan, U.S.A.	57,022	6,371,766	Lansing	M 3	43
Midway Islands (U.S.A.)	2	437		J 3	37
Minnesota, U.S.A.	80,009	2,982,483	St. Paul	K 3	43
Mississippi, U.S.A.	47,420	2,178,914	Jackson	K 5	43
Missouri, U.S.A.	69,270	3,954,653	Jefferson City	K 5	43
Moldavian S.S.R. (U.S.S.R.)	13,100	2,660,000	Kishinev	D 5	22
Molucca Islands	30,168	544,302	Ternate	C 6	37
Monaco	370 Acres	19,242	Monaco	G 6	16
Mongolian Republic	625,946	2,000,000	Ulan Bator	F 2	32
Montana, U.S.A.	146,316	591,024	Helena	F 3	42
Montserrat (Br.)	32	14,333	Plymouth	G 3	45
Morocco	171,583	9,809,387	Rabat	E 5	34
Moyen Congo (Fr.)	175,676	675,400	Pointe Noire	J12	35
Mozambique (Port.)	297,731	5,730,930	Lourenço Marques	O15	35
*N*atal, U. of So. Africa	35,284	2,202,392	Pietermaritzburg	N17	35
Nauru (Austr.-N.Z.—Br. Tr. Terr.)	8	2,855		G 6	37
Nebraska, U.S.A.	76,653	1,325,510	Lincoln	H 4	42
Nepal	54,000	6,910,000	Katmandu	D 3	29
Netherlands (Holland).land	12,883	9,625,499	Amsterdam, 's Gravenhage	F 4	15
Netherlands Antilles	383	154,914	Willemstad	E 4	45
Nevada, U.S.A.	109,802	160,083	Carson City	D 5	42
New Britain (island), (Aust. Trust.)	14,600	105,000	Rabaul	F 6	37
New Brunswick, Canada	27,473	515,697	Fredericton	G 4	41
New Caledonia (Fr.)	7,201	61,250	Nouméa	G 8	37
Newfoundland, Canada	42,734	361,416	St. John's	J 4	41
New Guinea, Netherlands	161,514	1,000,000	Hollandia	K 6	31
New Guinea, Territory of (Aust. Trust.)	93,000	1,100,023	Port Moresby	B 7	31
New Hampshire, U.S.A.	9,024	533,242	Concord	R 3	43
New Hebrides Islands (Br. and Fr.)	5,700	48,538	Vila	G 7	37
New Ireland (island), (Aust. Trust.)	3,800	33,960	Kavieng	F 6	37
New Jersey, U.S.A.	7,522	4,835,329	Trenton	P 5	43
New Mexico, U.S.A.	121,511	681,187	Santa Fe	G 6	42
New South Wales, Australia	309,432	2,984,838	Sydney	H 6	36
New York, U.S.A.	47,929	14,830,192	Albany	P 4	43
New Zealand, Dominion of (Br.)	103,934	1,702,298	Wellington	M 7	36
Nicaragua	57,143	1,053,189	Managua	E 4	39
Nicobar Islands (India)	635	12,452	Port Blair	F 7	29
Nigeria (Br.)	338,593	24,300,000	Lagos	H10	34
Niger Colony (Fr.)	501,930	2,168,000	Niamey	H 8	34
Niue I. (Br.)	100	4,253	Alofi	K 7	37
Norfolk Island (Aust.)	13	942	Kingston	G 8	37
North America	9,124,000	216,400,000			38
North Borneo (Br.)	29,387	331,361	Jesselton	F 5	31
North Carolina, U.S.A.	49,142	4,061,929	Raleigh	O 6	43
North Dakota, U.S.A.	70,054	619,636	Bismarck	J 3	42
Northern Ireland (Br.)	5,238	1,369,579	Belfast	H 2	12
* Northern Rhodesia (Br.)	290,320	1,849,000	Lusaka	M14	35
Northern Territory, Algeria	80,117	7,864,792	Alger	G 4	34
Northern Territory, Aust.	523,620	10,868	Darwin	E 3	36
Northwest Territories, Canada	1,258,217	16,004	Ottawa	F 1	40
Norway	124,560	3,156,950	Oslo	F 6	13
Nova Scotia, Canada	20,743	642,584	Halifax	H 4	41
* Nyasaland Prot. (Br.)	36,829	2,178,013	Zomba	N14	35
*O*hio, U.S.A.	41,122	7,946,627	Columbus	N 4	43
Oklahoma, U.S.A.	69,283	2,233,351	Oklahoma City	J 6	42
Oman, Sultanate of	82,000	830,000	Masqat	J 5	26
Ontario, Canada	363,282	4,597,542	Toronto	C 3	41

† French territory ceded to India 1954.

*Member of Federation of Rhodesia and Nyasaland.

Country	Area (Sq. Miles)	Population	Capital or Chief Town	Index Ref.	Plate No.
Orange Free State, U. of South Africa	49,647	879,071	Bloemfontein	M17	35
Oregon, U.S.A.	96,350	1,521,341	Salem	C 4	42
Orkney Islands, Scotland	376	21,258	Kirkwall	J 1	11
Oubangui-Chari (Fr.)	239,382	1,068,400	Bangui	K10	34
*P*acific Islands (excl. Australia)	262,718	4,313,654			37
Pacific Islands, Terr. of the (U.S. Trust)	680	54,299		E-F 5	37
Pakistan	364,218	75,843,000	Karachi	A 3 & F 4	29
Palau Islands (U.S. Trust.)	189	6,596	Koror	D 5	37
Palestine					20
Panama (excl. Canal Zone)	28,575	801,290	Panamá	G 6	39
Papua Territory (Aust.)	90,540	282,072	Port Moresby	B 7	31
Paraguay	150,518	1,251,517	Asunción	J 8	47
Pennsylvania, U.S.A.	45,045	10,498,012	Harrisburg	O 4	43
Persia (Iran)	628,000	19,000,000	Tehran	H 4	27
Peru approx.	513,000	8,405,000	Lima	E 5	46
Philippines, Republic of the	115,600	19,234,182	Quezon City	H 4	31
Phoenix Is. (U.S. and Br.)	16	984	Canton I.	J 6	37
Pitcairn Island (Br.)	2	138		O 8	37
Poland	119,734	24,976,926	Warszawa (Warsaw)		24
†Pondichéry, India (Fr.)	112	222,566	Pondichéry	D 6	29
Portugal	35,413	8,490,455	Lisboa (Lisbon)	B 3	17
Prince Edward Island, Canada	2,184	98,429	Charlottetown	H 4	41
Principe and S. Tomé (Port.)	372	62,000	São Tomé	H11	35
Puerto Rico (U.S.A.)	3,423	2,210,703	San Juan	G 2	45
*Q*atar	5,000	31,000	Doha	F 4	26
Québec, Canada	523,860	4,055,681	Québec	G 3	41
Queensland, Australia	670,500	1,106,269	Brisbane	G 4	36
*R*éunion (Fr.)	970	242,067	St. Denis	R20	35
Rhode Island, U.S.A.	1,058	791,896	Providence	R 4	43
Rio de Oro (Sp.)	71,583	24,000	Villa Cisneros	D 7	34
Rio Muni (continental Sp. Guinea)	10,040	142,237	Bata	J11	35
Ruanda-Urundi (Belg. Tr.)	20,309	3,889,051	Usumbura	M12	35
Rumania	91,671	15,072,624	Bucureşti	G 3	21
Russian S.F.S.R. (U.S.S.R.)	6,501,500	111,000,000	Moskva (Moscow)	E 4	22
Ryukyu Islands (U.S. Adm.)	921	914,462	Naha	L 7	33
*S*aar	988	851,615	Saarbrücken	B 4	14
Saguia el Hamra (Sp.)	31,660	14,298	Aiún	D 6	34
St. Croix, Virgin Is. (U.S.A.)	80	12,103	Christiansted	H 2	45
St. Helena I. (Br.)	47	4,748	Jamestown	E15	35
St. John, Virgin Is. (U.S.A.)	20	749		H 1	45
St. Lucia (Br.)	233	70,113	Castries	G 4	45
St. Pierre and Miquelon Is. (Fr.)	93	4,354	St. Pierre	J 4	41
St. Thomas, Virgin Is. (U.S.A.)	32	13,813	Charlotte Amalie	G 1	45
St. Vincent (Br.)	150	61,647	Kingstown	G 4	45
Sakhalin (U.S.S.R.)	35,400	300,000	Yuzhno-Sakhalinsk	R 5	23
Salvador, El	13,176	1,858,656	San Salvador	C 4	39
Samoa, Western (N.Z. Tr.)	1,133	78,155	Apia	J 7	37
Samoa (U.S.A.)	*76	18,937	Pago Pago	J 7	37
San Marino	38	12,100	San Marino	D 2	18
Santa Cruz Islands (Br.)	375	5,000	Peu	G 6	37
Sarawak (Br.)	47,071	546,385	Kuching	E 5	31
Sardinia (Sardegna), (It.)	9,301	1,273,714	Cagliari	B 4	18
Saskatchewan, Canada	237,975	831,728	Regina	J 4	40
Saudi Arabia, Kingdom of	350,000	5,500,000	Riyadh, Mecca	D 4	26
Scotland	30,405	5,095,969	Edinburgh	H 1	11
Senegal (Fr.)	77,401	1,720,000	St. Louis	D 9	34
Seychelles (Br.)	157	34,637	Victoria	T 6	6
Shetland Islands, Scotland	550	19,343	Lerwick	L 3	11
Siam (Thailand)	200,148	17,324,581	Krung Thep (Bangkok)	D 3	30
Sicily (It.)	9,926	4,452,773	Palermo	D 6	18
Sierra Leone (Br.)	27,925	1,858,275	Freetown	D10	34
Sikkim	2,745	129,000	Gangtok	E 3	29
Singapore (Br.)	220	940,824	Singapore	F 6	30
Sinkiang, China	660,977	4,012,330	Tihwa (Urumchi)	C 3	32
Society Islands (Fr.)	650	41,798	Papeete	L 7	37
Socotra (Br.)	1,400	12,000	Tamrida	J 8	25
Solomon Islands (Aust. Tr.)	4,070	49,067	Sohano	F 6	37
Solomon Islands Prot. (Br.)	14,600	94,965	Honiara	F 6	37
Somaliland, French	8,492	44,800	Djibouti	P 9	34
Somaliland (Italian Tr.)	194,000	916,300	Mogadiscio	R10	34
Somaliland Prot. (Br.)	68,000	700,000	Hargeisa	R10	34
South America	6,894,000	109,500,000			46, 47
South Australia, Australia	280,070	646,073	Adelaide	E 5	36
South Carolina, U.S.A.	30,594	2,117,027	Columbia	N 6	43
South Dakota, U.S.A.	76,536	652,740	Pierre	J 3	42
*Southern Rhodesia (Br.)	150,333	1,794,000	Salisbury	M15	35
Southern Territories, Algeria	767,435	816,993	Alger	G 6	34

Country	Area (Sq. Miles)	Population	Capital or Chief Town	Index Ref.	Plate No.
South West Africa (U. of South Africa Mand.)	317,725	350,037	Windhoek	K16	35
Spain	195,258	27,909,009	Madrid		17
Spanish Sahara	103,243	38,298	Aiún	D 6	34
Spanish West Africa	103,919	84,150	Sidi Ifni	D 6	34
Sudan	967,500	8,309,663	Khartoum	M 9	34
Sumatra	164,148	12,000,000	Padang	C 6	31
Surinam (Netherlands Guiana)	54,300	219,000	Paramaribo	J 3	46
Svalbard, Norway (Spitsbergen)	24,294	1,539	Longyearbyen	C 2	13
Swaziland (Br.)	6,704	185,215	Mbabane	N17	35
Sweden	173,394	7,046,920	Stockholm	J 6	13
Switzerland	15,944	4,714,992	Bern		19
Syria	72,587	3,135,000	Dimishq (Damascus)	H 5	28
*T*adzhik S.S.R. (U.S.S.R.)	54,900	1,455,000	Stalinabad	J 6	22
Tahiti (island), (Fr.)	600	29,684	Papeete	M 7	37
Tanganyika Territory (Br. Trust.)	342,706	7,408,096	Dar es Salaam	N13	35
Tasmania, Australia	26,215	257,078	Hobart	J 8	36
Tchad (Fr.)	455,598	2,052,469	Fort Lamy	K 8	34
Tennessee, U.S.A.	41,961	3,291,718	Nashville	M 6	43
Texas, U.S.A.	263,644	7,711,194	Austin	J 7	42
Thailand (Siam)	200,148	17,324,581	Krung Thep	D 3	30
Tibet, China	469,413	2,000,000	Lhasa	C 5	32
Timor (Port.)	7,332	424,132	Dili	H 7	31
Timor Archipelago (Indon.)	24,450	1,657,376	Kupang	G 8	31
Togo (Fr. Trust.)	20,733	923,000	Lomé	G10	34
Togoland (Br. Trust.)	13,041	382,768	Accra	G10	34
Tokelau (Union Group) (N.Z. and U.S.)	4	1,388	Fakaofo	J 6	37
Tonga (Friendly) Is. (Br.)	269	46,870	Nukualofa	J 7	37
Transvaal, Union of South Africa	110,450	4,283,038	Pretoria	N17	35
Trinidad and Tobago (Br.)	1,980	557,970	Port of Spain	G 5	45
Tristan da Cunha (Br.)	38	230		N 7	6
Trucial Oman	12,000	95,000	Sharja	F 5	26
Tuamotu (Low) Arch. (Fr.)	332	5,127	Apataki	M 7	37
Tunisia	48,300	2,230,952	Tunis	H 5	34
Turkey	296,185	20,934,670	Ankara		28
Turkmen S.S.R. (U.S.S.R.)	187,200	1,170,000	Ashkhabad	G 6	22
Turks and Caicos Is., Jamaica (Br.)	202	6,138	Grand Turk	D 2	45
*U*ganda Protectorate (Br.)	80,301	4,959,196	Entebbe	N11	35
Ukrainian S.S.R. (U.S.S.R.)	220,600	40,500,000	Kiev	E 5	22
Union of South Africa	472,494	11,418,349	Capetown, Pretoria	L18	35
Union of Soviet Socialist Republics	8,570,600	191,595,000	Moskva (Moscow)		22, 23
United Kingdom	94,279	50,210,472	London	D 3	9
United States of America land	2,977,128	150,697,361	Washington		42, 43
land and water	3,022,387				
Upper (Haute) Volta (Fr.)		3,070,000	Ouagadougou	F 9	34
Uruguay	72,172	2,353,000	Montevideo	J10	47
Utah, U.S.A.	82,346	688,862	Salt Lake City	F 5	42
Uzbek S.S.R. (U.S.S.R.)	157,400	6,000,000	Tashkent	H 5	22
*V*atican City	109 Acres	1,010		B 6	18
Venezuela	352,143	4,985,716	Caracas	G 2	46
Vermont, U.S.A.	9,278	377,747	Montpelier	P 4	43
Victoria, Australia	87,884	2,054,701	Melbourne	G 7	36
Vietnam	126,700	21,928,510	Saigon	E 3	30
Virgin Islands (Br.)	58	6,508	Road Town	H 1	45
Virgin Islands (U.S.A.)	132	26,665	Charlotte Amalie	H 1	45
Virginia, U.S.A.	39,899	3,318,680	Richmond	O 5	43
Volcano Is. (U.S. Adm.)	29			E 3	37
*W*ake Island (U.S.A.)	3			G 4	37
Wales (excluding Monmouthshire)	7,466	2,172,339	Cardiff	D 5	10
Wallis and Futuna (Fr.)	75	6,700	Matautu	J 7	37
Walvis Bay (Br.)	430	2,263		J16	35
Washington, U.S.A.	66,977	2,378,963	Olympia	C 3	42
Western Australia, Australia	975,920	502,480	Perth	C 4	36
West Indies	90,000	17,000,000			45
West Virginia, U.S.A.	24,090	2,005,552	Charleston	N 5	43
White Russian S.S.R. (Byelorussian S.S.R.), (U.S.S.R.)	80,100	7,220,000	Minsk	D 4	22
Windward Islands	821	251,771	St. George's	G 4	45
Wisconsin, U.S.A.	54,715	3,434,575	Madison	L 3	43
World land area	57,500,000	2,200,000,000			6, 7
Wyoming, U.S.A.	97,506	290,529	Cheyenne	G 4	42
*Y*anaon, India (Fr.)	6½	5,833	Yanaon	D 5	29
Yap (U.S. Trust.)	87	2,560	Yap	D 5	37
Yemen	75,000	3,500,000	San'a	D 7	26
Yugoslavia	99,079	15,751,935	Beograd (Belgrade)	C 3	21
Yukon Territory, Canada	205,346	9,096	White Horse	C 1	40
*Z*anzibar Prot. (Br.)	1,020	264,162	Zanzibar	P13	35

*Member of Federation of Rhodesia and Nyasaland.

† French territory ceded to India 1954.

INDEX OF PRINCIPAL CITIES OF THE WORLD

This alphabetical list of cities gives statistics of population based on the latest official reports. Each line begins with the name of a place, followed by the name of the country or state, the population, the index reference and the plate number. Different forms of names have been included to a large extent in the index.

Capitals are designated by asterisks * † Including suburbs. ‡ No room on map for name.

Aachen (Aix-la-Chapelle), Ger., 129,967....B3 14
Aarhus, Den., 116,167....F8 13
Aberdeen, Scot., 182,714....N5 11
Accra,* G.C., 135,456....G11 34
Adana (Seyhan), Turk., 117,799....F4 28
Addis Ababa,* Ethiopia, 250,000....O10 34
Adelaide,* So. Aust., †382,604....D7 36
Aden,* Aden, 36,231....E7 26
Agaña,* Guam, 800....E4 37
Agra, India, 375,994....C3 29
Aguascalientes, Mex., 93,432....H6 44
Ahmadabad, India, 788,310....B4 29
Akron, Ohio, 274,605....N4 43
Albany,* N. Y., 134,995....O1 43
Aleppo (Haleb), Syria, 324,899....G4 28
Alessandria, It., 51,949....B2 18
Alexandria, Egypt, 925,081....M5 34
Alger (Algiers),* Alg., 315,210....G4 34
Al Kuwait,* Kuwait, 80,000....E4 26
Allahabad, India, 333,362....D3 29
Allentown, Pa., 106,756....P4 43
Amboina (Ambon), Indonesia, 17,334....H6 31
Amiens, Fr., 84,774....D3 16
Amman,* Jordan, 90,000....D4 24
Amoy, China, 138,032....J7 32
Amritsar, India, 320,465....B2 29
Amsterdam,* Neth., 803,847....B4 15
Ancona, It., 57,100....D3 18
Andizhan, U.S.S.R., 90,000....U2 23
Andorra la Vieja,* Andorra, 1,100....G1 17
Angers, Fr., 94,408....C4 16
Ankara (Angora),* Turk., 286,781....E3 28
Annapolis,* Md., 10,047....P5 43
Antwerpen (Antwerp, Anvers), Belg., 263,233....E6 15
Aomori, Jap., 106,417....K3 33
Apeldoorn, Neth., 83,449....H4 15
Apia,* W. Samoa....J7 37
Arkhangel'sk (Archangel), U.S.S.R., 300,000....F3 22
Arnhem, Neth., 97,350....H4 15
Asahigawa, Jap., 123,238....L2 33
Asmara,* Eritrea, 132,000....O9 34
Astrakhan', U.S.S.R., 300,000....F5 22
Asunción,* Para., 205,605....J9 47
Athēnai (Athens),* Gr., 487,045....G7 21
Atlanta,* Ga., 331,314....N6 43
Atlantic City, N. J., 61,657....P5 43
Auckland, N. Z., †263,370....L5 36
Augsburg, Ger., 184,712....D4 14
Augusta,* Me., 20,913....R3 43
Austin,* Tex., 132,459....J7 42
Avellaneda, Arg., 282,054....O12 47
Baghdad,* Iraq, 364,049....D4 27
Bahía Blanca, Arg., 93,122....H11 47
Bahia (Salvador), Braz., 395,993....N6 46
Baile Atha Cliath (Dublin),* Ireland, 506,635....J5 12
Baku, U.S.S.R., 800,000....G6 22
Baltimore, Md., 949,708....O5 43
Banaras, India, 375,175....D3 29
Bandjermasin, Borneo, Indon., 65,698....E6 31
Bandung, Java, Indon., 765,084....H2 31
Bangalore, India, 776,170....C6 29
Bangkok (Krung Thep),* Thai., 827,290....D4 30
Barcelona, Sp., 1,205,509....H2 17
Bari, It., 267,726....F4 18
Barnaul, U.S.S.R., 200,000....K4 22
Barnsley, Eng., 75,625....F4 10
Baroda, India, 211,413....B4 29
Barranquilla, Col., 235,000....F1 46
Barrow-in-Furness, Eng., 67,473....D3 10
Basel (Bâle, Basle) Switz., 183,543....E1 19
Batavia (Djakarta),* Java, Indon., 2,800,000....H1 31
Bath, England, 79,275....E6 10
Bathurst,* Gambia, 19,602....C9 34
Baton Rouge,* La., 125,629....L7 43
Batumi, U.S.S.R., 75,000....F5 22
Bayonne, N. J., 77,203....R5 43
Beirut,* Lebanon, 177,780....F6 28
Belém (Pará), Braz., 230,181....L4 46
Belfast,* No. Ire., 443,670....J2 12
Belize,* Br. Hond., 21,886....C2 39
Belo Horizonte, Braz., 346,207....M7 46
Benghazi, *Libya, 60,000....K5 34
Beograd (Belgrade),* Yugo., 388,246....E3 21
Berbera, Som. Prot., 20,000....R9 34
Berdichev, U.S.S.R., 66,306....D5 22
Bergamo, It., 73,534....B2 18
Bergen, Nor., 110,424....D6 13
Berkeley, Calif., 113,805....D8 42
Berlin,* Ger., 3,187,470....E2 14
Bern (Berne),* Switz., 146,499....D3 19
Besançon, Fr., 63,508....G4 16
Beuthen (Bytom), Pol., 93,179....B4 24
Béziers, Fr., 64,561....E6 16
Białystok, Poland, 56,759....F2 24
Bielefeld, Ger., 153,111....C2 14
Bilbao, Sp., 229,091....E1 17
Binghamton, N. Y., 80,674....P4 43
Binh Dinh, Vietnam, 75,000....F4 30
Birkenhead, Eng., 142,392....D4 10
Birmingham, Ala., 326,037....M6 43
Birmingham, Eng., 1,112,340....F5 10
Bismarck,* N. D., 18,640....H3 42
Blackburn, Eng., 111,217....E4 10
Blackpool, Eng., 147,131....D4 10
Blagoveshchensk, U.S.S.R., 58,761....O4 23
Bloemfontein,* O.F.S., †83,296....L17 35
Bobruysk, U.S.S.R., 80,000....D4 22
Bochum, Ger., 290,406....G4 14
Bogor, Java, Indon., 124,000....H2 31
Bogotá,* Col., 503,000....F3 46
Boise,* Idaho, 34,393....D4 42
Bologna, It., 338,710....C2 18
Bolton, Eng., 167,162....E4 10
Bombay, India, 2,840,011....B8 29
Bône (Bona), Alg., 102,823....H4 34

Bonn,* Ger., 111,287....B3 14
Bootle, Eng., 74,302....D4 10
Bordeaux, Fr., 253,751....C5 16
Boston,* Mass., 801,444....R2 43
Bottrop, Ger., 91,892....G4 14
Bournemouth, Eng., 144,726....F7 10
Bradford, Eng., 292,394....F4 10
Brăila, Rum., 95,514....H3 21
Brandenburg, Ger., 70,632....E2 14
Bratislava (Pressburg), Czech., 171,362....D2 20
Braunschweig (Brunswick), Ger., 223,263....D2 14
Brazzaville,* Fr. Equat. Afr., 63,023....J12 35
Bremen, Ger., 455,999....C2 14
Brescia, It., 141,633....C2 18
Breslau (Wrocław), Pol., 170,656....C3 24
Brest, Fr., 74,991....A3 16
Bridgeport, Conn., 158,709....O2 43
Bridgetown,* Barbados, 13,345....G4 45
Brighton, Eng., 156,440....G7 10
Brisbane,* Queen., †402,172....J5 36
Bristol, Eng., 442,281....E6 10
Brno (Brünn), Czech., 258,333....D2 20
Brockton, Mass., 62,860....R2 43
Brunei,* Brunei, 10,620....E4 31
Bruxelles (Brussel),* Belg., 1,299,925....F7 15
București (Bucharest),* Rum., 1,041,807....G3 21
Budapest,* Hung., 1,164,963....E3 20
Buenos Aires,* Arg., 3,000,371....O11 47
Buffalo, N. Y., 580,132....O4 43
Buitenzorg (Bogor), Java, Indon., 124,000....H2 31
Bursa (Brusa), Tur., 100,007....C2 28
Bydgoszcz (Bromberg), Pol., 134,614....D2 24
Bytom (Beuthen), Pol., 93,179....B4 24
Cádiz, Sp., 100,249....C4 17
Caen, Fr., 51,445....C3 16
Cagliari, Sardinia, It., 137,040....B5 18
Cairo (El Qahira),* Egypt, 2,100,506....N5 34
Calais, Fr., 50,048....D2 16
Calcutta, India, 2,549,790....E2 29
Calgary, Alta., 129,060....H4 40
Cali, Col., 153,000....E3 46
Calicut, India, 158,020....C6 29
Callao, Peru, 69,406....E6 46
Camagüey, Cuba, 80,509....B2 45
Cambridge, Eng., 81,463....H5 10
Cambridge, Mass., 120,740....R2 43
Camden, N. J., 124,555....P6 43
Campinas, Braz., 101,746....L8 47
Canberra,* Aust., 15,156....J7 36
Canton (Kwangchow), China, 1,413,460....H7 32
Canton, Ohio, 116,912....N4 43
Capetown,* U. of S. A., †470,930....C19 35
Caracas,* Venez., 487,903....G1 46
Cardiff, Wales, 243,627....E6 10
Carson City,* Nev., 3,082....D5 22
Cartagena, Col., 109,000....E1 46
Cartagena, Sp., 43,825....F4 17
Casablanca, Mor., 551,322....E5 34
Catania, Sicily, It., 297,773....E6 18
Cayenne,* Fr. Guiana, 10,961....K2 46
Ceará (Fortaleza), Braz., 213,604....N4 46
Cebu, P. I., 167,503....G3 31
Changchun (Hsinking), China, 605,279....K3 32
Changsha, China, 421,616....H6 32
Changteh, China, 50,000....H6 32
Charleston, S. C., 70,174....O6 43
Charleston,* W. Va., 73,501....N5 43
Charlotte, N. C., 134,042....N6 43
Chattanooga, Tenn., 131,041....M6 43
Chefoo, China, 227,000....K4 32
Chelyabinsk, U.S.S.R., 500,000....H4 122
Chemnitz, Ger., 250,188....E3 14
Chengtu, China, 620,302....F5 32
Cherbourg, Fr., 40,042....C3 16
Chernovtsy (Cernăuţi), U.S.S.R., 78,825....D5 22
Chesterfield, Eng., 68,540....F4 10
Cheyenne,* Wyo., 31,935....G4 42
Chicago, Ill., 3,620,962....L1 43
Chinkiang (Tantu), China, 216,781....K5 32
Chita, U.S.S.R., 150,000....N4 23
Chittagong, Pak., 269,000....F4 29
Chkalov, U.S.S.R., 200,000....G4 22
Cho Lon, Vietnam, 481,200....E5 30
Christchurch, N. Z., †150,047....L7 36
Chungking, China, 1,002,787....G6 32
Cincinnati, Ohio, 503,998....H1 42
Ciudad Trujillo,* Dom. Rep., 181,533....E3 45
Clermont-Ferrand, Fr., 108,090....E5 16
Cleveland, Ohio, 914,808....N4 43
Cluj (Kolozsvár), Rum., 117,915....F2 21
Coblenz (Koblenz), Ger., 64,961....B3 14
Cologne (Köln), Ger., 590,825....B3 14
Colombo,* Ceylon, 355,374....C7 29
Columbia,* S. C., 86,914....N6 43
Columbus,* Ohio, 375,901....N5 43
Concepción, Chile, 100,000....F11 47
Concord,* N. H., 27,988....P4 43
Constantine, Alg., 118,774....H4 34
Constantinople (Istanbul), Tur., 751,823....D6 28
Copenhagen (København),* Den., 765,580....G9 13
Córdoba, Arg., 351,644....G10 47
Córdoba (Cordova), Sp., 165,256....D4 17
Cork, Ire., 75,595....E8 12
Corpus Christi, Tex., 108,287....J8 42
Coruña, La, Sp., 133,844....B1 17
Coventry, Eng., 258,211....F5 10
Craiova, Rum., 84,574....F3 21
Cremona, It., 54,564....B2 18
Croydon, Eng., 249,592....G6 10
Curitiba, Braz., 141,349....L9 47
Cuttack, India, 102,091....E4 29
Częstochowa, Poland, 101,255....D3 24
Dacca, Pak., †401,000....F4 29
Dairen (Talien), China, 722,950....K4 32
Dakar,* Fr. W. Afr., 185,000....C9 34
Dallas, Tex., 434,462....J6 42
Damão, Port. India, 63,521....B4 29

Damascus (Dimishq),* Syria, 291,157....G6 28
Danzig (Gdańsk), Pol., 117,894....D1 24
Dar es Salaam,* Tang. Terr., 69,227....P13 35
Darlington, Eng., 84,861....F3 10
Darmstadt, Ger., 94,132....C4 14
Davao, P. I., 81,523....H4 31
Dayton, Ohio, 243,872....M5 43
Debrecen, Hung., 125,933....F3 20
Decatur, Ill., 66,269....L5 43
Delhi, india, 914,634....C3 29
Denver,* Colo., 415,786....G5 42
Derby, Eng., 141,264....F5 10
Des Moines,* Iowa, 177,965....K4 43
Dessau, Ger., 88,139....E3 14
Detroit, Mich., 1,849,568....M1 43
Dhahran, Saudi Arabia, 10,000....E4 26
Dijon, Fr., 100,664....F4 16
Dimishq (Damascus),* Syria, 291,157....G6 28
Djakarta, Java,* Indon., 2,800,000....H1 31
Djibouti,* Fr. Som., 17,500....P9 34
Djokjakarta, Java, Indon., 500,000....J2 31
Dnepropetrovsk, U.S.S.R., 500,000....E5 22
Doncaster, Eng., 81,896....G4 10
Dortmund, Ger., 500,150....H4 14
Dover,* Del., 6,223....P5 43
Dover, Eng., 35,217....J6 10
Dresden, Ger., 467,966....E3 14
Dublin (Baile Atha Cliath),* Ire., 506,635....J5 12
Duisburg, Ger., 408,877....F4 14
Duluth, Minn., 104,511....K3 43
Dundee, Scot., 177,333....K7 11
Dunedin, N. Z., †83,351....L7 36
Durban, Natal, 371,349....N18 35
Düsseldorf, Ger., 498,347....F5 14
Dzaudzhikau (Ordzhonikidze), U.S.S.R., 127,172....F5 22
Eastbourne, Eng., 57,801....H7 10
Edinburgh,* Scot., 466,770....K8 11
Edmonton,* Alta., 159,631....H4 40
Eindhoven, Neth., 134,527....G6 15
Elbląg (Elbing), Pol., 20,924....D1 24
Elizabeth, N. J., 112,817....R5 43
El Paso, Tex., 130,485....G7 42
Erfurt, Ger., 174,633....D3 14
Erie, Pa., 130,803....N4 43
Erivan (Yerevan), U.S.S.R., 255,000....F6 22
Essen, Ger., 605,125....G4 14
Evanston, Ill., 73,641....L1 43
Evansville, Ind., 128,636....M5 43
Exeter, Eng., 75,479....D7 10
Fall River, Mass., 111,963....R2 43
Ferrara, It., 134,181....C2 18
Fez, Mor., 200,946....F5 34
Firenze (Florence), It., 375,392....C3 18
Fiume (Rijeka), Yugo., 72,130....B3 21
Flensburg, Ger., 102,045....C1 14
Flint, Mich., 163,143....N4 43
Foochow (Minhow), China, 318,075....J6 32
Forli, It., 33,505....D2 18
Fortaleza (Ceará), Braz., 213,604....N4 46
Fort-de-France,* Mart., 66,006....G4 45
Fort Wayne, Ind., 133,607....M4 43
Fort Worth, Tex., 278,778....J6 42
Frankfort,* Ky., 11,916....M5 43
Frankfurt-am-Main, Ger., 523,923....C3 14
Frankfurt-an-der-Oder, Ger., 51,577....F2 14
Fredericton,* N. B., 16,018....G4 41
Freetown,* Sierra Leone, 64,576....D10 34
Freiburg, Ger., 109,822....B5 14
Fresno, Cal., 91,669....C5 42
Fukui, Jap., 100,691....G5 33
Fukuoka, Jap., 392,649....D7 33
Fürth, Ger., 99,503....D4 14
Fusan (Pusan), Korea, 473,619....D6 33
Galaţi, Rum., 80,411....H3 21
Galveston, Tex., 66,568....K7 43
Gander, Nfld., 3,000....K4 41
Gary, Ind., 133,911....L1 43
Gateshead, Eng., 115,017....F3 10
Gdańsk (Danzig), Pol., 117,894....D1 24
Gdynia, Poland, 77,829....D1 24
Gelsenkirchen, Ger., 310,108....G4 14
Genève (Geneva, Genf), Switz., 145,473....B4 19
Genova (Genoa), It., 678,200....B2 18
Gent (Gand, Ghent), Belg., 166,096....D6 15
Georgetown,* Br. Guiana, 73,509....J2 46
George Town (Penang), Mal. Fed., 189,068....C6 30
Gera, Ger., 89,212....E3 14
Gibraltar,* Gibr., 23,232....D4 17
Gifu, Jap., 211,845....H6 33
Gladbach (München-Gladbach), Ger., 122,388....B3 14
Glascow, Scot., 1,089,555....D2 11
Gliwice (Gleiwitz), Pol., 95,980....A4 24
Glendale, Cal., 95,702....D8 42
Gomel', U.S.S.R., 120,000....E4 22
Goose Airport (Goose Bay), Lab., Nfld., 1,000....H3 41
Gor'kiy (Nizhni Novgorod), U.S.S.R., 900,000....F4 22
Görlitz, Ger., 85,686....F3 14
Göteborg (Gothenburg), Swed., 353,991....G8 13
Granada, Sp., 153,256....E4 17
Grand Rapids, Mich., 176,515....M4 43
Graz, Austria, 226,271....C3 20
Great Yarmouth (Yarmouth), Eng., 51.105....J5 10
Greenock, Scot., 76,299....A2 11
Greenwich, Eng., 91,492....H6 10
Grenoble, Fr., 102,161....G5 16
Grimsby (Great Grimsby), Eng., 94,527....H4 10
Groningen, Neth., 132.021....K2 15
Groznyy, U.S.S.R., 172.468....F5 22
Guadalajara, Mex., 378,423....H6 44
Guatemala,* Guat., 284,233....B3 39
Guayaquil, Ecu., 262,624....D4 46
Győr, Hung., 57,190....D3 20
Haarlem, Neth., 156,856....F4 15

Habana (Havana),* Cuba, 659,883....A2 45
Hagen, Ger., 146,099....H4 14
Hague, The ('s Gravenhage),* Neth., 532,998....E4 15
Haifa, Israel, 155,000....B2 24
Haiphong, Vietnam, 143,000....E2 30
Hakodate, Jap., 228,994....K3 33
Haleb (Aleppo), Syria, 324,899....G4 28
Halifax, England, 98,376....F4 10
Halifax,* N. S., 85,589....H5 41
Halle, Ger., 222,505....E3 14
Hälsingborg (Helsingborg), Swed., 91,718....H8 13
Hamamatsu, Jap., 152,028....J6 33
Hamburg, Ger., 1,604,600....D2 14
Hamilton, Ont., 208,321....E5 41
Hammond, Ind., 87,594....L1 43
Hamtramck, Mich., 43,355....N1 43
Hangchow, China, 606,134....J5 32
Hankow, China, 749,952....H5 32
Hannover, Ger., 441,615....C2 14
Hanoi,* Vietnam, 237,150....E2 30
Hanyang, China, 100,000....H5 32
Harbin (Pinkiang), China, 760,000....L2 32
Harrisburg,* Pa., 89,544....O4 43
Hartford,* Conn., 177,397....O2 43
Hastings, Eng., 65,506....H7 10
Havre (Le Havre), Fr., 106,934....C3 16
Heidelberg, Ger., 115,750....C4 14
Heilbronn, Ger., 64,544....C4 14
Helena,* Mont., 17,581....E3 42
Helsinki (Helsingfors),* Fin., 371,662....O6 13
Herne, Ger., 112,249....G4 14
Hildesheim, Ger., 71,821....D2 14
Hilversum, Neth., 85,051....G4 15
Himeji, Jap., 212,100....G6 33
Hindenburg (Zabrze), Pol., 104,184....A4 24
Hiroshima, Jap., 285,712....E6 33
Hobart,* Tas., †76,567....H8 36
Hódmezővásárhely, Hung., 61,776....F3 20
Hollandia,* Neth. N. Guin....K6 31
Holyoke, Mass., 54,661....P1 43
Honiara,*Sol. Is. Prot....G6 37
Honolulu,* Hawaii, 248,034....L3 37
Houston, Tex., 596,163....K7 43
Howrah, India, 443,207....E2 29
Huddersfield, Eng., 129,021....F4 10
Hue, Vietnam, 407,000....E3 30
Hull, Que., 43,483....E4 41
Hull (Kingston-upon-Hull), Eng., 299,068....G4 10
Huntington, W. Va., 86,353....N5 43
Hyderabad, India, 1,085,074....C5 29
Hyderabad, Pak., 241,801....A3 29
Iaşi (Jassy), Rum., 94,075....H2 21
Ibadan, Nig., 335,500....G10 34
Ibagué, Col., 27,448....F3 46
Ichang, China, 107,940....H5 32
Inch'ŏn (Jinsen), Korea, 265,767....C5 33
Indianapolis,* Ind., 427,173....M5 43
Indore, India, 308,158....C4 29
Ipswich, Eng., 104,788....J5 10
Irkutsk, U.S.S.R., 300,000....M4 23
Irvington, N. J., 59,201....R5 43
Isfahan, Iran, 183,597....G4 27
Istanbul (Constantinople), Tur., 751,823....D6 28
Ivanovo, U.S.S.R., 300,000....E4 22
Ixelles, Belg., 90,711....C9 15
Izmir (Smyrna), Tur., 230,508....B3 28
Jackson,* Miss., 98,271....L6 43
Jacksonville, Fla., 204,517....N7 43
Jaffa, Israel, 94,310....B3 24
Jaipur, India, 291,187....C3 29
Jakarta (Djakarta),* Java, Indon., 2,800,000....H1 31
Jamshedpur, India, 219,377....E4 29
Jassy (Iaşi), Rum., 94,075....H2 21
Jefferson City,* Mo., 25,099....K5 43
Jena, Ger., 82,722....D3 14
Jersey City, N. J., 299,017....R5 43
Jerusalem, Jord. and *Israel, 120,000....C4 24
Jesselton,* N. Bor., 10,000....F4 31
Jinsen (Inch'ŏn), Korea, 265,767....C5 33
João Pessoa (Parahyba), Braz., 90,853....O5 46
Johannesburg, Transv., †762,910....M17 35
Juiz de Fora, Braz., 86,819....M8 46
Juneau,* Alaska, 5,956....E4 38
Kabul,* Afgh., 206,208....J3 26
Kagoshima, Jap., 229,462....E8 33
Kaifeng, China, 303,422....J5 32
Kaiserslautern, Ger., 62,395....B4 14
Kalamazoo, Mich., 57,704....M4 43
Kalgan, China, 151,234....J3 32
Kalinin, U.S.S.R., 300,000....E4 22
Kaliningrad (Königsberg), U.S.S.R., 150,000....C4 22
Kalisz, Poland, 48,092....D3 24
Kaluga, U.S.S.R., 89,484....E4 22
Kanazawa, Jap., 252,017....H5 33
Kandahar, Afgh., 77,186....A2 29
Kano, Nig., 98,000....H9 34
Kanpur, India, 704,536....D3 29
Kansas City, Kans., 129,553....K5 43
Kansas City, Mo., 456,622....K5 43
Karachi,* Pak., 1,006,416....A4 29
Karlsruhe, Ger., 198,014....C4 14
Kassel, Ger., 161,322....C3 14
Katmandu,* Nepal, 108,805....D3 29
Katowice, Poland, 128,290....B4 24
Kaunas, U.S.S.R., 105,370....D4 22
Kawasaki, Jap., 319,226....O2 33
Kazan', U.S.S.R., 500,000....G4 22
Kecskemét, Hung., 87,269....E3 20
Keijo (Seoul),* Korea, 1,446,019....C5 33
Kerch', U.S.S.R., 104,471....E5 22
Khabarovsk, U.S.S.R., 300,000....P5 23
Khar'kov, U.S.S.R., 900,000....E4 22
Khartoum,* Sudan, 75,000....N8 34
Kherson, U.S.S.R., 97,186....E5 22
Kiangtu, China, 127,392....K5 32
Kiel, Ger., 253,857....C1 14
Kielce, Poland, 49,960....E3 24
Kiev, U.S.S.R., 900,000....E4 22

Kingston,* Jam., 109,056....C3 45
Kingston-upon-Hull (Hull), Eng., 299,068....G4 10
Kingstown,* St. Vin., 4,831....G4 45
Kirin (Yungki), China, 239,325....L3 32
Kirov, U.S.S.R., 250,000....F4 22
Kirovabad, U.S.S.R., 110,000....F5 22
Kirovograd, U.S.S.R., 100,331....E5 22
Kishinev (Chişinău), U.S.S.R., 52,962....D5 22
Klaypeda (Klaipéda, Memel), U.S.S.R., 41,297....D4 22
Knoxville, Tenn., 124,769....N5 43
Kobe, Jap., 765,435....H7 33
København (Copenhagen),* Den., 765,580....G9 13
Koblenz (Coblenz), Ger., 64,961....B3 14
Kochi, Jap., 161,640....F7 33
Kofu, Jap., 121,645....J6 33
Kokand, U.S.S.R., 75,000....T2 23
Kokura, Jap., 199,397....E7 33
Kolhapur, India, 137,138....B5 29
Köln (Cologne), Ger., 590,825....B3 14
Kolomna, U.S.S.R., 75,139....E4 22
Kolozsvár (Cluj), Rum., 117,915....F2 21
Königsberg (Kaliningrad), U.S.S.R., 150,000....C4 22
Kostroma, U.S.S.R., 150,000....F4 22
Kozhikode (Calicut), India, 158,020....C6 29
Kraków, Poland, 299,396....E3 24
Krasnodar, U.S.S.R., 200,000....E5 22
Krasnoyarsk, U.S.S.R., 300,000....L4 23
Krefeld, Ger., 170,482....F4 14
Kremenchug, U.S.S.R., 89,553....E5 22
Krung Thep (Bangkok),* Thai., 827,290....D4 30
Kuala Lumpur,* Mal. Fed., 175,961....D7 30
Kuching,* Sara., 37,949....E5 31
Kükong, (Kiukiang), China, 137,106....H7 32
Kumamoto, Jap., 267,506....E7 33
Kunming, China, 255,462....F6 32
Kure, Jap., 187,775....F6 33
Kursk, U.S.S.R., 119,972....E4 22
Kurume, Jap., 100,997....E7 33
Kutaisi, U.S.S.R., 90,000....F5 22
Kuybyshev, U.S.S.R., 600,000....G4 22
Kyŏngsŏng (Seoul),* Korea, 1,446,019....C5 33
Kyoto, Jap., 1,101,854....J7 33
La Coruña, Sp., 133,844....B1 17
Lae, Territory N. G....B7 31
Lagos,* Nig., 174,200....G10 34
Lahore, Pak., 849,333....B2 29
Lanchow, China, 203,722....F4 32
Lansing,* Mich., 92,129....M4 43
La Paz,* Bol., 319,600....G7 46
La Spezia, It., 109,866....B2 18
Lausanne, Switz., 106,807....C3 19
Lawrence, Mass., 80,536....R1 43
Leeds, Eng., 504,954....F4 10
Leghorn (Livorno), It., 140,367....C3 18
Legnica (Liegnitz), Pol., 24,357....C3 24
Le Havre (Havre), Fr., 106,934....C3 16
Leicester, Eng., 285,061....G5 10
Leiden, Neth., 86,914....E4 15
Leipzig, Ger., 607,655....E3 14
Le Mans, Fr., 100,455....C3 16
Leninakan, U.S.S.R., 75,000....F5 22
Leningrad, U.S.S.R., 3,300,000....C2 22
León, Mex., 122,585....J6 44
León, Nicar., 31,008....D4 39
Léopoldville,* Belg. Cong., 83,363....K12 35
Lepaya (Liepája, Libau), U.S.S.R., 75,000....D4 22
Levallois-Perret, Fr., 61,681....A1 16
Liége, Belg., 156,208....H7 15
Lille (Lisle), Fr., 188,871....E2 16
Lima,* Peru, 520,528....E6 46
Limoges, Fr., 107,857....D5 16
Lincoln, Eng., 69,412....G4 10
Lincoln,* Neb., 98,884....J4 42
Linz, Aust., 185,177....C2 20
Lisboa (Lisbon),* Port., 783,919....A1 17
Little Rock,* Ark., 102,213....K6 43
Liverpool, Eng., 789,532....D4 10
Livorno (Leghorn), It., 140,367....C3 18
Ljubljana, Yugo., 120,944....B3 21
Łódź, Poland, 496,929....D3 24
London,* Eng., (administrative county and city), 3,348,336, (greater city), 8,346,137....G6 10
London, Ont., 95,343....D5 41
Long Beach, Calif., 250,767....D9 42
Long Xuyen, Vietnam, 148,000....E5 30
Los Alamos, N. Mex., 9,934....G6 42
Los Angeles, Calif., 1,970,358....D8 42
Louisville, Ky., 369,129....K5 43
Lourenço Marques,* Moz., 93,516....N17 35
Lowell, Mass., 97,249....A1 43
Luanda,* Angola, 61,396....J13 35
Lübeck, Ger., 237,860....D2 14
Lublin, Poland, 99,400....F3 24
Lucca, It., 32,896....C3 18
Lucknow, India, 497,594....D3 29
Ludwigshafen, Ger., 122,329....C4 14
Lungkiang (Tsitsihar), China, 174,675....L2 32
Lushun (Port Arthur), China, 141,291....K4 32
Luton, Eng., 110,370....G6 10
Luxembourg,* Lux., 61,996....J9 15
Luzern (Lucerne), Switz., 60,526....F2 19
L'vov (Lwów), U.S.S.R., 400,000....D4 22
Lynn, Mass., 99,738....R2 43
Lyon, Fr., 460,748....F5 16
McKeesport, Pa., 51,502....O4 43
Maastricht, Neth., 74,449....H7 15
Macao (Macau) (Port.), China, 389,000....H7 32
Maceió, Braz., 102.301....O5 46
Madison,* Wis., 96,056....L4 43

Madras, India, 1,429,985 ..... D6 29
Madrid,* Sp., 1,609,524 ..... F4 17
Madurai, India, 361,954 ..... C7 29
Maebashi, Jap., 97,394 ..... J5 33
Magdeburg, Ger., 236,326 ..... D2 14
Magnitogorsk, U.S.S.R., 200,000 ..... G4 22
Mainz, Ger., 87,046 ..... C4 14
Makassar (Macassar), Celebes, Indon., 400,000 ..... F7 31
Málaga, Sp., 261,162 ..... D4 17
Malden, Mass., 59,804 ..... R1 43
Malmö, Swed., 192,498 ..... H9 13
Managua,* Nicar., 107,444 ..... D4 39
Manaus (Manáos), Braz., 110,678 ..... H4 46
Manchester, Eng., 703,175 ..... E4 10
Manchester, N. H., 82,732 ..... R4 43
Mandalay, Burma, 163,243 ..... C2 30
Manila, P. I., 983,906 ..... G3 31
Manizales, Col., 51,025 ..... E2 46
Mannheim, Ger., 244,000 ..... C4 14
Maracaibo, Venez., 232,488 ..... F1 46
Maranhão, (São Luís), Braz., 81,432 ..... M4 46
Mariupol' (Zhdanov), U.S.S.R., 200,000 ..... E5 22
Marrakech (Marakesh, Morocco), Mor., 238,436 ..... E5 34
Marsala, Sicily, It., 24,650 ..... D6 18
Marseille, Fr., 636,264 ..... F6 16
Matsumoto, Jap., 86,005 ..... H5 33
Matsuyama, Jap., 163,859 ..... F7 33
Mecca,* Saudi Arabia, 90,000 ..... C5 26
Mechelen (Malines), Belg., 60,288 ..... F6 15
Medan, Sumatra, Indon., 500,000 ..... B5 31
Medellín, Col., 300,000 ..... E2 46
Meknès, Mor., 159,811 ..... E5 34
Melbourne,* Vic., †1,226,923 ..... L1 36
Memel (Klaypeda, Klaipéda), U.S.S.R., 41,297 ..... D4 22
Memphis, Tenn., 396,000 ..... L6 43
Mendoza, Arg., 105,328 ..... G10 47
Mérida, Mex., 144,793 ..... P6 44
Merthyr Tydfil, Wales, 61,093 ..... D6 10
Meshed, Iran, 190,653 ..... L2 27
Messina, Sicily, It., 218,593 ..... E5 18
Metz, Fr., 70,105 ..... G3 16
México (Mexico City),* Mex., 2,233,914 ..... L1 44
Miami, Fla., 249,276 ..... N8 43
Middlesbrough, Eng., 147,336 ..... F3 10
Milano (Milan), It., 1,264,402 ..... B2 18
Milwaukee, Wis., 637,392 ..... M4 43
Minhow (Foochow), China, 328,434 ..... J6 32
Minneapolis, Minn., 521,718 ..... K3 43
Minsk, U.S.S.R., 231,000 ..... D4 22
Miskolc, Hung., 109,433 ..... F2 20
Mobile, Ala., 129,009 ..... M7 43
Modena, It., 100,034 ..... C2 10
Mogadiscio (Mogadishu),* Somaliland, 74,000 ..... R11 35
Moji, Jap., 124,399 ..... E7 33
Molenbeek-Saint Jean, Belg., 63,922 ..... B9 15
Molotov (Perm), U.S.S.R., 450,000 ..... G4 22
Monterrey, Mex., 331,771 ..... J4 44
Montevideo,* Uru., 850,000 ..... K11 47
Montgomery,* Ala., 106,525 ..... M6 43
Montpelier,* Vt., 8,599 ..... P3 43
Montpellier, Fr., 93,102 ..... E6 16
Montreal, Que., 1,021,520 ..... F4 41
Montreuil-sous-Bois, Fr., 69,838 ..... B2 16
Monza, It., 58,503 ..... B2 18
Morioka, Jap., 117,578 ..... K4 33
Moskva (Moscow),* U.S.S.R., 4,500,000 ..... B4 22
Mosul, Iraq, 203,273 ..... C2 27
Motherwell, Scot., 68,137 ..... D2 11
Mt. Vernon, N. Y., 71,899 ..... S5 43
Mukden (Shenyang), China, 1,120,918 ..... K3 32
Mülheim, Ger., 148,606 ..... G4 14
Mulhouse, Fr., 87,655 ..... G4 16
Multan, Pak., 190,122 ..... B2 29
München (Munich), Ger., 831,017 ..... D4 14
Münster, Ger., 119,788 ..... B3 14
Murcia, Sp., 201,259 ..... F4 17
Murmansk, U.S.S.R., 150,000 ..... E3 22
Mysore, India, 244,334 ..... C6 29
Nagano, Jap., 101,426 ..... J5 33
Nagaoka, Jap., 66,818 ..... J5 33
Nagasaki, Jap., 241,805 ..... D7 33
Nagoya, Jap., 1,030,635 ..... H6 33
Nagpur, India, 449,441 ..... C4 29
Nairobi,* Kenya, 118,976 ..... O12 35
Nanchang, China, 258,692 ..... H6 32
Nancy, Fr., 113,477 ..... G3 16
Nanking, China, 1,137,430 ..... J5 32
Nanning (Yungning), China, 202,720 ..... G7 32
Nantes, Fr., 200,265 ..... C4 16
Napoli (Naples), It., 1,003,815 ..... E4 18
Nashville,* Tenn., 174,307 ..... M5 43
Nassau,* Bahama Is., 13,231 ..... C1 45
Neuilly-sur-Seine, Fr., 60,172 ..... A1 16
Neuss, Ger., 62,926 ..... F5 14
Newark, N. J., 438,776 ..... R5 43
New Bedford, Mass., 109,189 ..... R2 43
New Britain, Conn., 73,726 ..... P2 43
Newcastle, N. S. W., †127,188 ..... J6 36
Newcastle-on-Tyne, Eng., 291,723 ..... F2 10
New Delhi,* India, 279,063 ..... C3 29
New Haven, Conn., 164,443 ..... O2 43
New Orleans, La., 570,445 ..... L7 43
Newport, Eng., 105,285 ..... E6 10
New York, N. Y., 7,891,957 ..... R5 43
Niagara Falls, N. Y., 90,872 ..... O4 43
Nice, Fr., 211,165 ..... G6 16
Nictheroy (Niterói), Brazil, 174,535 ..... P14 47
Niigata, Jap., 220,901 ..... J5 33
Nijmegen, Neth., 106,523 ..... H5 15
Nikolaev, U.S.S.R., 200,000 ..... E5 22
Nîmes (Nismes), Fr., 91,667 ..... F6 16
Ninghsien (Ningpo), China, 249,633 ..... K6 32
Niterói, Braz., 174,535 ..... P14 47
Nizhni Novgorod (Gor'kiy), U.S.S.R., 900,000 ..... F4 22
Norfolk, Va., 213,513 ..... P5 43
Norrköping, Swed., 84,939 ..... K7 13
Northampton, Eng., 104,429 ..... G5 10
Nottingham, Eng., 306,008 ..... G5 10
Nouméa,* N. Cal., 10,466 ..... G8 37
Novara, It., 52,269 ..... B2 18
Novi Sad, Yugo., 77,127 ..... D3 21
Novocherkassk, U.S.S.R., 81,286 ..... F5 22
Novorossiysk, U.S.S.R., 95,280 ..... E5 22
Novosibirsk, U.S.S.R., 750,000 ..... K4 22
Nürnberg (Nuremberg), Ger., 360,017 ..... D4 14
Oak Ridge, Tenn., 30,229 ..... M5 43
Oakland, Cal., 384,575 ..... D8 42
Oberammergau, Ger., 5,101 ..... D5 14
Oberhausen, Ger., 202,343 ..... G4 14
Odense, Den., 100,940 ..... G9 13
Odessa, U.S.S.R., 600,000 ..... E5 23
Offenbach, Ger., 88,528 ..... C3 14
Oita, Jap., 94,455 ..... E7 33
Okayama, Jap., 162,904 ..... F6 33
Oklahoma City,* Okla., 243,504 ..... J6 42
Oldenburg, Ger., 121,643 ..... B2 14
Oldham, Eng., 121,212 ..... E4 10
Olomouc (Olmütz), Czech., 58,178 ..... D2 20
Olympia,* Wash., 15,819 ..... C3 42
Omaha, Neb., 251,117 ..... J4 42
Omdurman, Sudan, 126,650 ..... N8 34
Omsk, U.S.S.R., 500,000 ..... J4 22
Omuda, Jap., 191,978 ..... E7 33
Oporto (Porto), Port., 279,738 ..... B2 17
Oradea, Rum., 82,282 ..... E2 21
Oran, Alg., 256,661 ..... F4 34
Ordzhonikidze, U.S.S.R., 127,172 ..... F5 22
Orel, U.S.S.R., 110,567 ..... E4 22
Orléans, Fr., 70,240 ..... D3 16
Osaka, Jap., 1,956,136 ..... J8 33
Oslo,* Nor., 417,238 ..... D3 13
Osnabrück, Ger., 108,900 ..... C2 14
Ostrava, Czech., 171,064 ..... E2 20
Otaru, Jap., 178,330 ..... K2 33
Ottawa,* Canada, 202,045 ..... E4 41
Oxford, Eng., 98,675 ..... F6 10
Padova (Padua), It., 167,068 ..... C2 18
Pago Pago,* Amer. Samoa, 1,586 ..... J7 37
Paisley, Scot., 93,704 ..... C2 11
Palembang, Sumatra, Indon., 350,000 ..... D6 31
Palermo, Sicily, It., 482,594 ..... D5 18
Palmas, Las,* Can. Is., Sp., 138,441 ..... B4 17
Panamá,* Pan., 122,693 ..... H6 39
Paoting (Tsingyuen), China, 130,000 ..... H4 32
Papeete,* Tahiti, Soc. Is., 12,428 ..... M7 37
Pará (Belém), Braz., 230,181 ..... L4 46
Parahyba (João Pessoa), Braz., 90,853 ..... O5 46
Paramaribo,* Sur., 67,381 ..... K2 46
Paraná, Arg., 83,824 ..... J10 47
Paris,* France, 2,725,374 ..... E3 16
Greater, 4,775,711 ..... E3 16
Parma, It., 122,256 ..... C2 18
Pasadena, Cal., 104,577 ..... D8 42
Passaic, N. J., 57,702 ..... R5 43
Paterson, N. J., 139,336 ..... R5 43
Patna, India, 282,057 ..... E3 29
Pátrai (Patras), Gr., 79,338 ..... E6 21
Pécs, Hung., 78,612 ..... E3 20
Peiping (Peking),* China, 1,796,517 ..... J3 32
Peiraiévs (Piraeus), Gr., 210,722 ..... F7 21
Pelotas, Braz., 79,649 ..... K10 47
Penang (George Town), Mal. Fed., 189,068 ..... C6 30
Penza, U.S.S.R., 250,000 ..... F4 22
Peoria, Ill., 111,856 ..... L4 43
Perm (Molotov), U.S.S.R., 450,000 ..... G4 22
Pernambuco (Recife), Braz., 522,466 ..... O5 46
Perpignan, Fr., 74,984 ..... E6 16
Perth,* W. Aust. (with Fremantle), †272,586 ..... B2 36
Perugia, It., 31,839 ..... D3 18
Peshawar, Pak., 151,435 ..... B2 29
Pforzheim, Ger., 53,942 ..... C4 14
Philadelphia, Pa., 2,071,605 ..... R6 43
Phnom Penh,* Cambodia, 110,600 ..... E5 30
Phoenix,* Ariz., 106,818 ..... E6 42
Piacenza, It., 49,527 ..... B2 18
Pierre,* S. Dak., 5,715 ..... H3 42
Pilsen (Plzeň), Czech., 106,904 ..... B2 20
Pinkiang (Harbin), China, 760,000 ..... L2 32
Piraeus (Peiraiévs), Gr., 210,722 ..... F7 21
Pisa, It., 49,471 ..... C3 18
Pistoia, It., 29,532 ..... C3 18
Pittsburgh, Pa., 676,806 ..... O4 43
Plauen, Ger., 84,778 ..... E3 14
Ploeşti, Rum., 95,632 ..... H3 21
Plovdiv, Bul., 125,440 ..... G4 21
Plymouth, Eng., 208,985 ..... D7 10
Plzeň (Pilsen), Czech., 106,904 ..... B2 20
Pola (Pula), Yugo., 22,714 ..... A3 21
Poltava, U.S.S.R., 130,305 ..... E5 22
Pontiac, Mich., 73,681 ..... M1 43
Poole, Eng., 82,958 ..... E7 10
Poona, India, 485,486 ..... B5 29
Port Arthur (Lushun), China, 141,291 ..... K4 32
Port-au-Prince,* Haiti, 142,840 ..... D3 45
Port Elizabeth, C. of G. H., †147,544 ..... M18 35
Portland, Me., 77,634 ..... R4 43
Portland, Oreg., 373,628 ..... C3 42
Port Louis,* Mauritius, 57,466 ..... S19 35
Port Moresby,* Pap. Terr., Aust., 17,546 ..... B7 31
Porto (Oporto), Port., 279,738 ..... B2 17
Pôrto Alegre, Braz., 381,964 ..... L10 47
Port of Spain,* Trinidad, 92,793 ..... G5 45
Port Said, Egypt, 178,432 ..... N5 34
Portsmouth, Eng., 233,464 ..... G7 10
Poznań (Posen), Pol., 267,978 ..... C2 24
Praha (Prag, Prague),* Czech., 934,933 ..... C1 20
Preston, Eng., 119,243 ..... E4 10
Pretoria,* U. of S. A., †244,496 ..... M17 35
Providence,* R. I., 248,674 ..... P2 43
Pskov, U.S.S.R., 59,898 ..... D4 22
Puebla, Mex., 206,840 ..... N2 44
Pula (Pola), Yugo., 22,714 ..... A3 21
Pusan (Fusan), Korea, 473,619 ..... D6 33
P'yŏngyang (Heijo),* Korea, 342,551 ..... C4 33
Quebec,* Que., 164,016 ..... F4 41
Quetta, Pak., 83,892 ..... A2 29
Quezon City,* P. I., 107,977 ..... G3 31
Quincy, Mass., 83,835 ..... R2 43
Quito,* Ecu., 212,873 ..... E3 46
Rabat,* Mor., 161,461 ..... E5 34
Rabaul, New Brit., Bismarck Arch., Terr. N. G. F6 37
Racine, Wis., 71,193 ..... L4 43
Radom, Poland, 69,455 ..... E3 24
Raleigh,* N. C., 65,679 ..... O6 43
Rangoon,* Burma, 500,800 ..... C3 30
Ravenna, It., 31,251 ..... D2 18
Rawalpindi, Pak., 236,877 ..... B2 29
Reading, Eng., 114,176 ..... F6 10
Reading, Pa., 109,320 ..... P4 43
Recife (Pernambuco), Braz., 522,466 ..... O5 46
Recklinghausen, Ger., 104,857 ..... B3 14
Regensburg (Ratisbon), Ger., 116,997 ..... D4 14
Reggio di Calabria, It., 140,757 ..... E5 18
Reggio nell'Emilia, It., 106,107 ..... C2 18
Reims, Fr., 110,749 ..... E3 16
Remscheid, Ger., 102,929 ..... G5 14
Rennes, Fr., 113,781 ..... C3 16
Resht, Iran, 121,600 ..... F2 27
Reykjavik,* Ice., 56,096 ..... B2 9
Rheydt, Ger., 78,500 ..... B3 14
Rhondda, Wales, 111,357 ..... D6 10
Ribeirão Prêto, Braz., 65,081 ..... L8 46
Richland, Wash., 21,809 ..... D3 42
Richmond,* Va., 230,310 ..... O5 43
Riga, U.S.S.R., 390,000 ..... D4 22
Rijeka (Fiume), Yugo., 72,130 ..... B3 21
Rimini, It., 31,505 ..... D2 18
Rio de Janeiro,* Braz., 2,335,931 ..... P14 47
Riyadh,* Saudi Arabia, 80,000 ..... E5 26
Roanoke, Va., 91,921 ..... N5 43
Rochester, N. Y., 332,488 ..... O4 43
Rockford, Ill., 92,927 ..... L4 43
Roma (Rome),* It., 1,606,739 ..... D4 18
Rosario, Arg., 404,600 ..... I10 47
Rostock, Ger., 114,869 ..... D1 14
Rostov-na-Donu (Rostov on Don), U.S.S.R., 500,000 ..... F5 22
Rotherham, Eng., 82,334 ..... F4 10
Rotterdam, Neth., 646,248 ..... E5 15
Roubaix, Fr., 100,978 ..... E2 16
Rouen, Fr., 107,739 ..... D3 16
Ryazan', U.S.S.R., 95,358 ..... F4 22
Rybinsk (Shcherbakov), U.S.S.R., 150,000 ..... E4 22
Saarbrücken, Ger., 89,700 ..... B4 14
Sacramento,* Cal., 137,572 ..... C5 42
Saginaw, Mich., 92,918 ..... N4 43
Saharanpur, India, 148,116 ..... E5 30
Saïgon,* Vietnam, 697,800 ..... E5 30
St. Denis, Fr., 69,939 ..... B1 16
St. Étienne, Fr., 177,966 ..... F5 16
St. Gallen (Sankt Gallen), Switz., 68,011 ..... H2 19
St. Helens, Eng., 110,276 ..... E4 10
Saint John, New Brunswick, 50,779 ..... G4 41
St. John's,* Nfld., 52,873 ..... K4 41
St. Joseph, Mo., 78,588 ..... K5 43
St. Louis, Mo., 856,796 ..... G1 43
St. Paul,* Minn., 311,349 ..... K3 43
Sakai, Jap., 213,688 ..... H8 33
Salem,* Oreg., 43,140 ..... C3 42
Salerno, It., 41,925 ..... E4 18
Salisbury,* S. Rhod., 69,049 ..... N15 35
Salonika (Thessalonikë), Gr., 224,748 ..... F5 21
Salt Lake City,* Utah, 182,121 ..... F4 42
Salvador (Bahia), Brazil, 395,993 ..... N6 46
Samarkand, U.S.S.R., 150,000 ..... H6 22
San Antonio, Tex., 408,442 ..... J7 42
San Diego, Cal., 334,387 ..... D6 42
Sandakan, N. Bor., 15,000 ..... F4 31
San Francisco, Cal., 775,357 ..... D8 42
San Jose, Cal., 95,280 ..... D8 42
San José,* C. R., 83,242 ..... F5 39
San Juan,* P. R., 223,949 ..... G1 45
San Luis Potosí, Mex., 126,596 ..... J6 44
San Salvador,* El Sal., 112,731 ..... C4 39
Santa Ana, El Sal., 48,424 ..... C4 39
Santa Cruz de Tenerife,* Can. Is., Sp., 102,437 ..... B4 17
Santa Fé, Arg., 168,011 ..... H10 47
Santa Fe,* N. Mex., 27,998 ..... G6 42
Santander, Sp., 102,510 ..... D1 17
Santiago,* Chile, 1,120,000 ..... O10 47
Santiago de Cuba, Cuba, 118,266 ..... C3 45
Santos, Braz., 201,739 ..... L8 47
São Luís (Maranhão), Braz., 81,432 ..... M4 46
São Paulo, Braz., 2,041,716 ..... L8 47
Sapporo, Jap., 313,850 ..... K2 33
Saragossa (Zaragoza), Sp., 261,084 ..... F2 17
Sarajevo, Yugo., 118,158 ..... D4 21
Saratov, U.S.S.R., 500,000 ..... F4 22
Sasebo, Jap., 194,453 ..... D7 33
Sassari, Sardinia, It., 44,130 ..... B4 18
Savannah, Ga., 119,638 ..... N6 43
Savona, It., 57,354 ..... B2 18
Schaerbeek, Belg., 123,671 ..... C9 15
Schenectady, N. Y., 91,785 ..... O1 43
Schwerin, Ger., 88,164 ..... D2 14
Scranton, Pa., 125,536 ..... P4 43
Scutari (Üsküdar), Tur., 69,671 ..... D6 28
Seattle, Wash., 467,591 ..... C3 42
Semarang (Samarang), Java, Indon., 60,000 ..... J2 31
Sendai, Jap., 341,685 ..... K4 33
Seoul (Kyŏngsŏng, Keijo),* Korea, 1,446,019 ..... C5 33
Serpukhov, U.S.S.R., 90,766 ..... E4 22
Sevastopol', U.S.S.R., 111,946 ..... E5 22
Sevilla (Seville), Sp., 375,401 ..... D4 17
Seyhan (Adana), Tur., 117,799 ..... F4 28
's Gravenhage (The Hague),* Neth., 532,998 ..... E4 15
Shahjahanpur, India, 104,703 ..... D3 29
Shanghai, China, 4,447,015 ..... K5 32
Shasi, China, 113,526 ..... H5 32
Shcherbakov (Rybinsk), U.S.S.R., 150,000 ..... E4 22
Sheffield, Eng., 512,834 ..... F4 10
Shenyang (Mukden), China, 1,120,918 ..... K3 32
Sherbrooke, Que., 50,543 ..... F4 41
Shimonoseki, Jap., 193,572 ..... E6 33
Shizuoka, Jap., 238,629 ..... H6 33
Shreveport, La., 127,206 ..... K6 43
Shufu (Kashgar), China, 50,000 ..... C7 32
Siangtan, China, 82,589 ..... H6 32
Simferopol', U.S.S.R., 142,678 ..... E5 22
Singapore,* Sing., 679,659 ..... F6 30
Sioux City, Iowa, 83,991 ..... J4 42
Skopje (Skoplje, Usküb), Yugo., 91,557 ..... E5 21
Smolensk, U.S.S.R., 150,000 ..... E4 22
Smyrna (Izmir), Tur., 230,538 ..... B3 28
Sofiya (Sofia),* Bul., 434,888 ..... F4 21
Solingen, Ger., 147,782 ..... G5 14
Somerville, Mass., 102,351 ..... R1 43
Soochow (Wuhsien), China, 389,797 ..... K5 32
Sosnowiec, Poland, 77,853 ..... B4 24
Southampton, Eng., 178,326 ..... F7 10
South Bend, Ind., 115,911 ..... M4 43
Southend-on-Sea, Eng., 151,830 ..... H6 10
Southport, Eng., 84,057 ..... D4 10
South Shields, Eng., 106,605 ..... F3 10
Sovetsk (Tilsit), U.S.S.R., 57,244 ..... D4 22
Spezia, La, It., 109,866 ..... B2 18
Spokane, Wash., 161,721 ..... D3 42
Springfield,* Ill., 81,628 ..... L5 43
Springfield, Mass., 162,399 ..... P1 43
Springfield, Ohio, 78,508 ..... N4 43
Srinagar,* Kash., 207,787 ..... C2 29
Stalin (Varna), Bul., 77,792 ..... H4 21
Stalingrad, U.S.S.R., 400,000 ..... F5 22
Stalino, U.S.S.R., 462,395 ..... K1 23
Stanislav (Stanisławów), U.S.S.R., 60,256 ..... D5 22
Stettin (Szczecin), Pol., 72,948 ..... B2 24
Stockholm,* Swed., 745,936 ..... G1 13
Stockport, Eng., 141,660 ..... E4 10
Stockton-on-Tees, Eng., 74,024 ..... F3 10
Stoke-on-Trent, Eng., 275,095 ..... E4 10
Strasbourg, Fr., 175,515 ..... G3 16
Stuttgart, Ger., 401,045 ..... C4 14
Subotica, Yugo., 112,551 ..... D2 21
Sucre,* Bolivia, 35,000 ..... H7 46
Suez, Egypt, 108,250 ..... N6 34
Sunderland, Eng., 181,515 ..... F3 10
Surabaja, Java, Indon., 800,000 ..... K2 31
Surakarta, Java, Indon., 500,000 ..... J2 31
Suva,* Fiji Is., †23,513 ..... H7 37
Sverdlovsk, U.S.S.R., 600,000 ..... P6 23
Swansea, Wales, 160,832 ..... C6 10
Swatow, China, 168,154 ..... J7 32
Swindon, Eng., 68,932 ..... E6 10
Sydney,* N. S. W., †1,484,434 ..... L3 36
Syracuse, N. Y., 220,583 ..... O4 43
Syzran', U.S.S.R., 150,000 ..... F4 22
Szczecin (Stettin), Pol., 72,948 ..... B2 24
Szeged, Hung., 136,752 ..... E3 20
Tabriz, Iran, 258,865 ..... E2 27
Tacoma, Wash., 143,673 ..... C3 42
Taegu (Taikyu), Korea, 313,705 ..... D6 33
Taganrog, U.S.S.R., 150,000 ..... E5 22
Tainan, Formosa, China, 172,602 ..... J7 32
Taipei (Taihoku), *Formosa, China, 320,765 ..... K7 32
Taiyuan (Yangku), China, 304,550 ..... H4 32
Takamatsu, Jap., 124,545 ..... G6 33
Takaoka, Jap., 142,046 ..... H5 33
Talien (Dairen), China, 722,950 ..... K4 32
Tallahassee,* Fla., 27,237 ..... M7 43
Tallin (Tallinn, Reval, Revel), U.S.S.R., 190,000 ..... D4 22
Tambov, U.S.S.R., 150,000 ..... F4 22
Tampa, Fla., 124,681 ..... N8 43
Tampere, Fin., 89,071 ..... N6 13
Tampico, Mex., 94,221 ..... L5 44
Tananarive,* Mada., 165,477 ..... R15 35
Tangier, Mor., 150,000 ..... E4 34
Tanjore, India, 100,787 ..... C6 29
Tanta, Egypt, 139,965 ..... N5 34
Tantu (Chinkiang), China, 216,781 ..... K5 32
Taranto, It., 166,957 ..... F4 18
Tartu, U.S.S.R., 50,000 ..... D4 22
Tashkent, U.S.S.R., 600,000 ..... S1 23
Tbilisi (Tiflis), U.S.S.R., 540,000 ..... F5 22
Tegucigalpa,* Hon., 72,385 ..... D3 39
Tehran (Teheran),* Iran, 554,372 ..... G3 27
Tel Aviv, Israel, 300,000 ..... B3 24
Terni, It., 37,295 ..... D3 18
Thessalonikë (Salonika), Gr., 224,748 ..... F5 21
Tientsin, China, 1,707,670 ..... J4 32
Tiflis (Tbilisi), U.S.S.R., 540,000 ..... F5 22
Tilburg, Neth., 114,312 ..... G5 15
Tilsit (Sovetsk), U.S.S.R., 57,244 ..... D4 22
Timişoara (Temesvár), Rum., 111,987 ..... E3 21
Tiranë (Tirana),* Alb., 59,887 ..... E5 21
Tokushima, Jap., 121,416 ..... G7 33
Tokyo,* Jap., 5,385,071 ..... O2 33
Toledo, Ohio, 303,616 ..... M2 43
Tomsk, U.S.S.R., 150,000 ..... K4 22
Topeka,* Kans., 78,791 ..... K5 43
Torino (Turin), It., 711,492 ..... A2 18
Toronto,* Ont., 675,754 ..... E5 41
Torreón, Mex., 128,548 ..... H4 44
Toruń (Thorn), Poland, 68,085 ..... D2 24
Toulon, Fr., 125,742 ..... F6 16
Toulouse, Fr., 264,411 ..... D6 16
Tourcoing, Fr., 76,080 ..... E2 16
Tours, Fr., 80,044 ..... D4 16
Toyama, Jap., 154,484 ..... H5 33
Toyohashi, Jap., 145,855 ..... H6 33
Trapani, Sicily, It., 52,661 ..... D5 18
Trento, It., 37,290 ..... C1 18
Trenton,* N. J., 128,009 ..... R5 43
Treviso, It., 43,949 ..... D2 18
Trier (Treves), Ger., 74,709 ..... B4 14
Trieste, Italy, 261,935 ..... D2 18
Tripoli,* Libya, 128,714 ..... J5 34
Trois Rivières, Que., 46,074 ..... F4 41
Trondheim, Nor., 57,128 ..... F5 13
Troy, N. Y., 72,311 ..... O1 43
Troyes, Fr., 58,805 ..... F3 16
Tsinan, China, 391,420 ..... J4 32
Tsingtao, China, 759,057 ..... K4 32
Tsingyuen (Paoting), China, 130,000 ..... H4 32
Tsitsihar (Lungkiang), China, 174,675 ..... L2 32
Tsu, Jap., 76,077 ..... H6 33
Tucumán, Arg., 152,508 ..... H9 47
Tula, U.S.S.R., 300,000 ..... E4 22
Tulsa, Okla., 182,740 ..... K5 43
Tunis,* Tun., 364,593 ..... J4 34
Turin (Torino), It., 711,492 ..... A2 18
Tuticorin, India, 75,614 ..... C7 29
Tynemouth, Eng., 66,544 ..... F2 10
Udine, It., 54,638 ..... D1 18
Ufa, U.S.S.R., 300,000 ..... G4 22
Ujpest, Hung., 76,000 ..... E3 20
Ulan Bator (Urga),* Mong. Rep., 50,000 ..... G2 32
Ulm, Ger., 69,941 ..... C4 14
Ul'yanovsk, U.S.S.R., 200,000 ..... F4 22
Üsküb (Skoplje, Skopje), Yugo., 91,557 ..... E5 21
Üsküdar (Scutari), Tur., 69,671 ..... D6 28
Utica, N. Y., 101,531 ..... P4 43
Utrecht, Neth., 185,246 ..... G4 15
Utsonomiya, Jap., 107,210 ..... K5 33
Valencia, Sp., 509,175 ..... F3 17
Valletta,* Malta, 18,666 ..... E7 18
Valparaíso, Chile, 245,000 ..... N10 47
Vancouver, B. C., 344,833 ..... F5 40
Varna (Stalin), Bul., 77,792 ..... H4 21
Venezia (Venice), It., 315,291 ..... D2 18
Veracruz, Mex., 104,469 ..... Q2 44
Verona, It., 176,911 ..... C2 18
Versailles, Fr., 70,141 ..... A2 16
Vicenza, It., 48,279 ..... C2 18
Vichy, Fr., 29,370 ..... E4 16
Victoria,* Hong Kong, 859,400 ..... H7 32
Victoria,* Br. Col., 51,331 ..... F5 40
Vienna (Wien),* Austria, 1,760,784 ..... D2 20
Vientiane,* Laos, 10,000 ..... D3 30
Vigo, Sp., 43,116 ..... B1 17
Villeurbanne, Fr., 82,399 ..... F5 16
Vil'nyus (Vilna, Wilno), U.S.S.R., 163,000 ..... D4 22
Vinnitsa, U.S.S.R., 92,868 ..... D5 22
Vitebsk, U.S.S.R., 80,000 ..... E4 22
Vladivostok, U.S.S.R., 300,000 ..... P5 23
Vologda, U.S.S.R., 95,194 ..... F4 22
Voronezh, U.S.S.R., 300,000 ..... F4 22
Voroshilovgrad, U.S.S.R., 200,000 ..... P1 23
Vyborg (Viipuri), U.S.S.R., 71,944 ..... D3 22
Wakayama, Jap., 191,337 ..... G6 33
Wallasey, Eng., 101,331 ..... D4 10
Walsall, Eng., 114,514 ..... F5 10
Wanne-Eickel, Ger., 86,370 ..... G4 14
Warrington, Eng., 80,681 ..... E4 10
Warszawa (Warsaw),* Poland, 478,755 ..... E2 24
Washington, D. C.,* U. S. A., 802,178 ..... O5 43
Waterbury, Conn., 104,477 ..... O2 43
Wattenscheid, Ger., 67,116 ..... G4 14
Wellington,* N. Z., †173,520 ..... M6 36
Wenchow (Yungkia), China, 153,395 ..... K6 32
Wesermünde, Ger., 102,940 ..... C2 14
West Hartlepool, Eng., 72,597 ..... G3 10
Wichita, Kans., 168,279 ..... J5 42
Wien (Vienna),* Austria, 1,760,784 ..... D2 20
Wiesbaden, Ger., 218,255 ..... B3 14
Wigan, Eng., 84,546 ..... E4 10
Wilkes-Barre, Pa., 76,826 ..... P4 43
Willemstad,* Neth. Ant., 40,597 ..... E4 45
Wilmington, Del., 110,356 ..... P5 43
Wimbledon, Eng., 58,158 ..... G6 10
Windsor, Ont., 120,049 ..... D5 41
Winnipeg,* Man., 235,710 ..... L5 40
Winston-Salem, N. C., 87,811 ..... N5 43
Winterthur, Switz., 66,925 ..... G1 19
Witten, Ger., 76,351 ..... G4 14
Włocławek, Pol., 48,126 ..... D2 24
Wolverhampton, Eng., 162,669 ..... E5 10
Worcester, Eng., 59,700 ..... F5 10
Worcester, Mass., 203,486 ..... P1 43
Worms, Ger., 51,857 ..... C4 14
Wrocław (Breslau), Pol., 170,656 ..... C3 24
Wuchang, China, 199,012 ..... H5 32
Wuchow (Tsangwu), China, 206,986 ..... H7 32
Wuhsien (Soochow), China, 339,517 ..... K5 32
Wuhu, China, 203,550 ..... J5 32
Wuppertal, Ger., 362,125 ..... G4 14
Würzburg, Ger., 78,195 ..... D4 14
Yangku (Taiyuan), China, 304,550 ..... H4 32
Yarkand (Soche), China, 57,000 ..... C7 32
Yarmouth (Great Yarmouth), Eng., 51,105 ..... J5 10
Yaroslavl,' U.S.S.R., 300,000 ..... E4 22
Yawata, Jap., 210,051 ..... E7 33
Yerevan (Erivan), U.S.S.R., 255,000 ..... F6 22
Yokohama, Jap., 951,189 ..... O3 33
Yokosuka, Jap., 250,533 ..... O3 33
Yonkers, N. Y., 152,798 ..... R5 43
York, Eng., 105,336 ..... F4 10
York, Pa., 59,953 ..... O5 43
Youngstown, Ohio, 168,330 ..... N4 43
Yungki (Kirin), China, 239,325 ..... L3 32
Zabrze (Hindenburg), Pol., 104,184 ..... A4 24
Zagreb, Yugo., 290,417 ..... C3 21
Zaragoza (Saragossa), Sp., 261,084 ..... F2 17
Zhdanov (Mariupol'), U.S.S.R., 200,000 ..... E5 22
Zhitomir, U.S.S.R., 95,090 ..... D4 22
Zlatoust, U.S.S.R., 150,000 ..... G4 22
Zürich, Switz., 390,020 ..... F2 19
Zwickau, Ger., 122,862 ..... E3 14

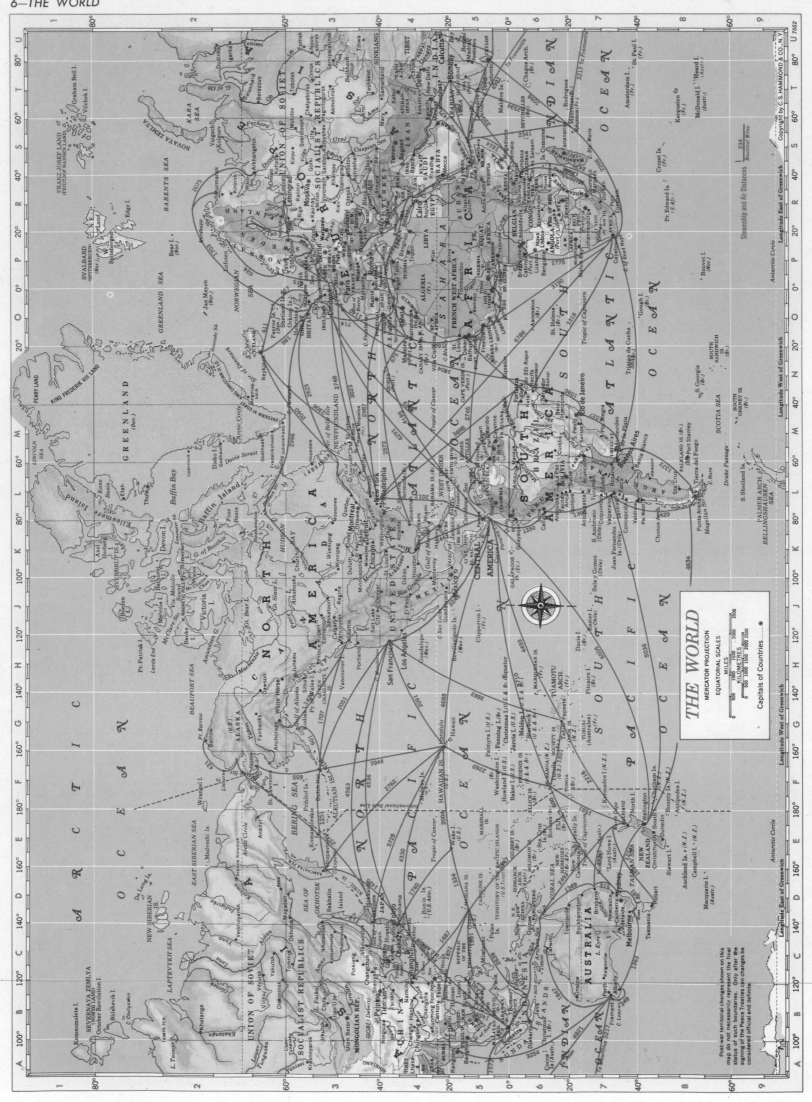

THE WORLD
MERCATOR PROJECTION
EQUATORIAL SCALES
MILES
0   500   1000   1500   2000   2500
0 500 1000 1500 2000 2500
KILOMETRES
Capitals of Countries ...... ●

Post-war territorial changes shown on this map do not necessarily represent the final status of such boundaries. Only after the signing of the Peace Treaties can changes be considered official and definite.

Steamship and Air Distances

234 Nautical Miles

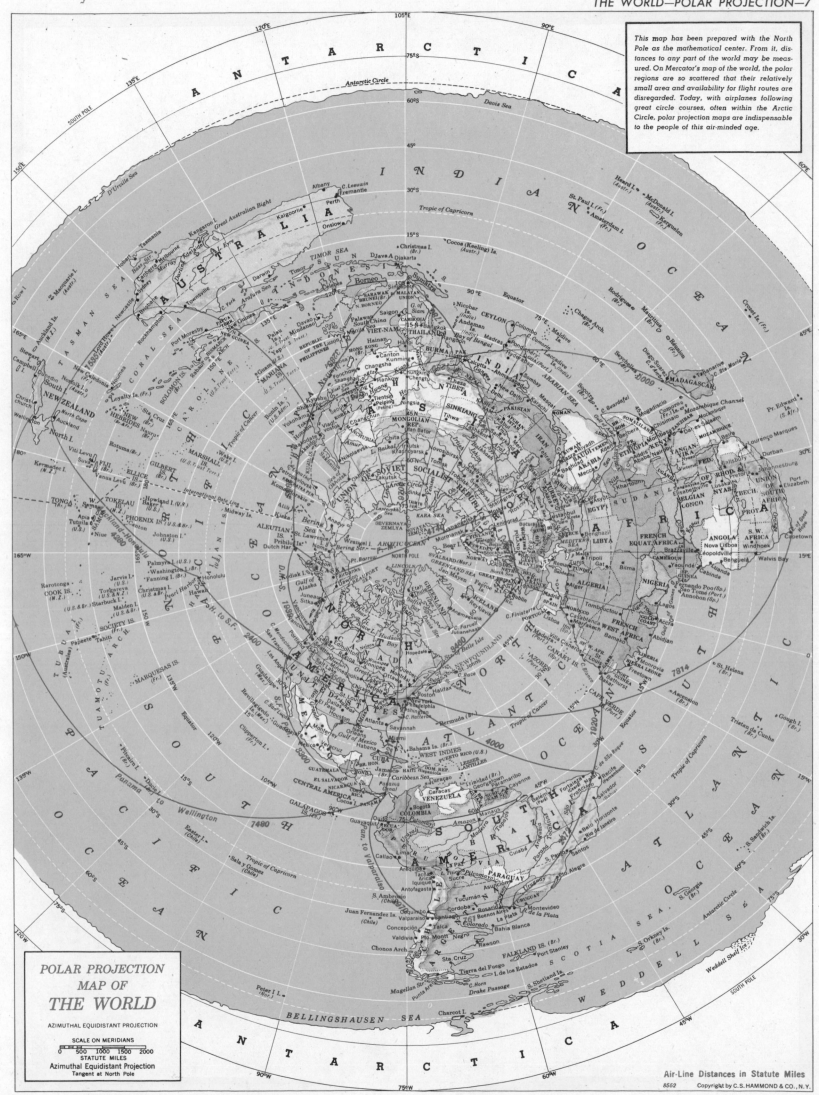

This map has been prepared with the North Pole as the mathematical center. From it, distances to any part of the world may be measured. On Mercator's map of the world, the polar regions are so scattered that their relatively small area and availability for flight routes are disregarded. Today, with airplanes following great circle courses, often within the Arctic Circle, polar projection maps are indispensable to the people of this air-minded age.

POLAR PROJECTION
MAP OF
THE WORLD

AZIMUTHAL EQUIDISTANT PROJECTION

SCALE ON MERIDIANS

0   500   1000   1500   2000
STATUTE MILES

Azimuthal Equidistant Projection
Tangent at North Pole

Air-Line Distances in Statute Miles

8552   Copyright by C.S. Hammond & CO., N.Y.

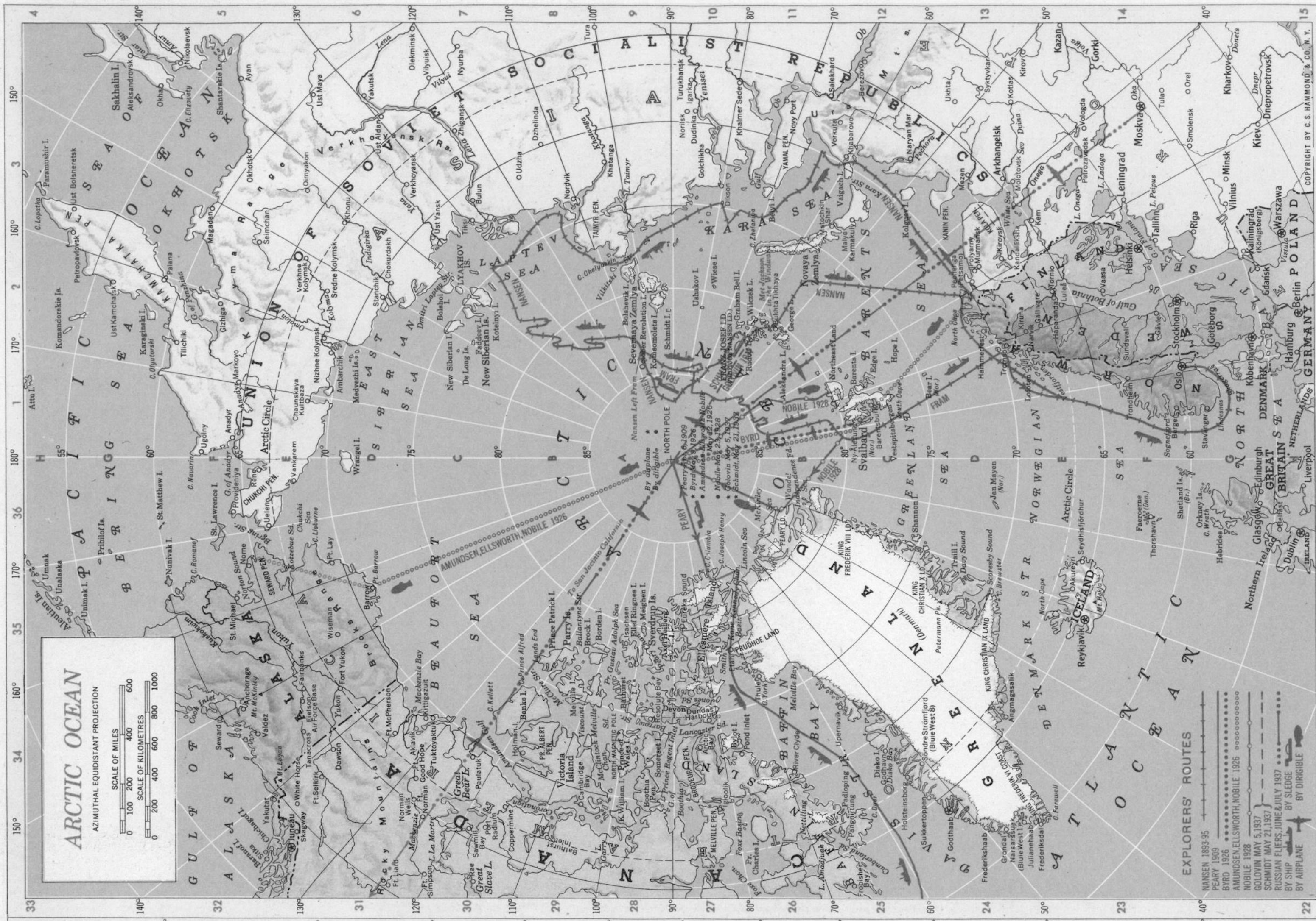

ARCTIC OCEAN
AZIMUTHAL EQUIDISTANT PROJECTION
SCALE OF MILES
0 100 200 400 600
SCALE OF KILOMETRES
0 200 400 600 800 1000
EXPLORERS' ROUTES
NANSEN 1893-95
PEARY 1909
BYRD 1926
AMUNDSEN, ELLSWORTH, NOBILE 1926
NOBILE 1928
GROMOV MAY 5, 1937
SCHMIDT MAY 21, 1937
RUSSIAN FLIERS JUNE & JULY 1937
BY SHIP
BY SLEDGE
BY AIRPLANE
BY DIRIGIBLE
COPYRIGHT BY C. S. HAMMOND & CO., N. Y.

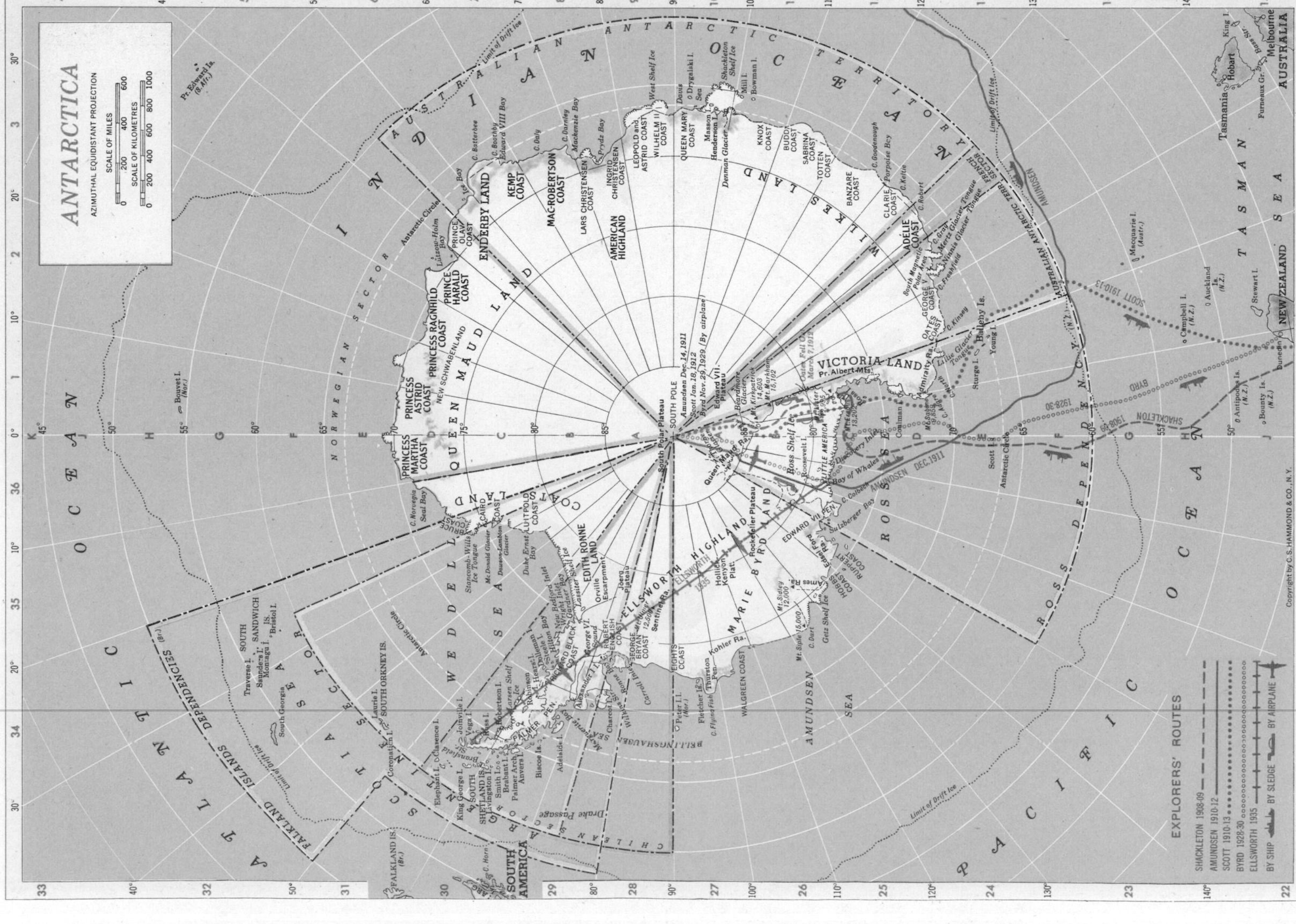

ANTARCTICA
AZIMUTHAL EQUIDISTANT PROJECTION
SCALE OF MILES
0 200 400 600
SCALE OF KILOMETRES
0 200 400 600 800 1000
EXPLORERS' ROUTES
SHACKLETON 1908-09
AMUNDSEN 1910-12
SCOTT 1910-13
BYRD 1928-30
ELLSWORTH 1935
BY SHIP
BY SLEDGE
BY AIRPLANE
Copyright by C.S. HAMMOND & CO., N.Y.

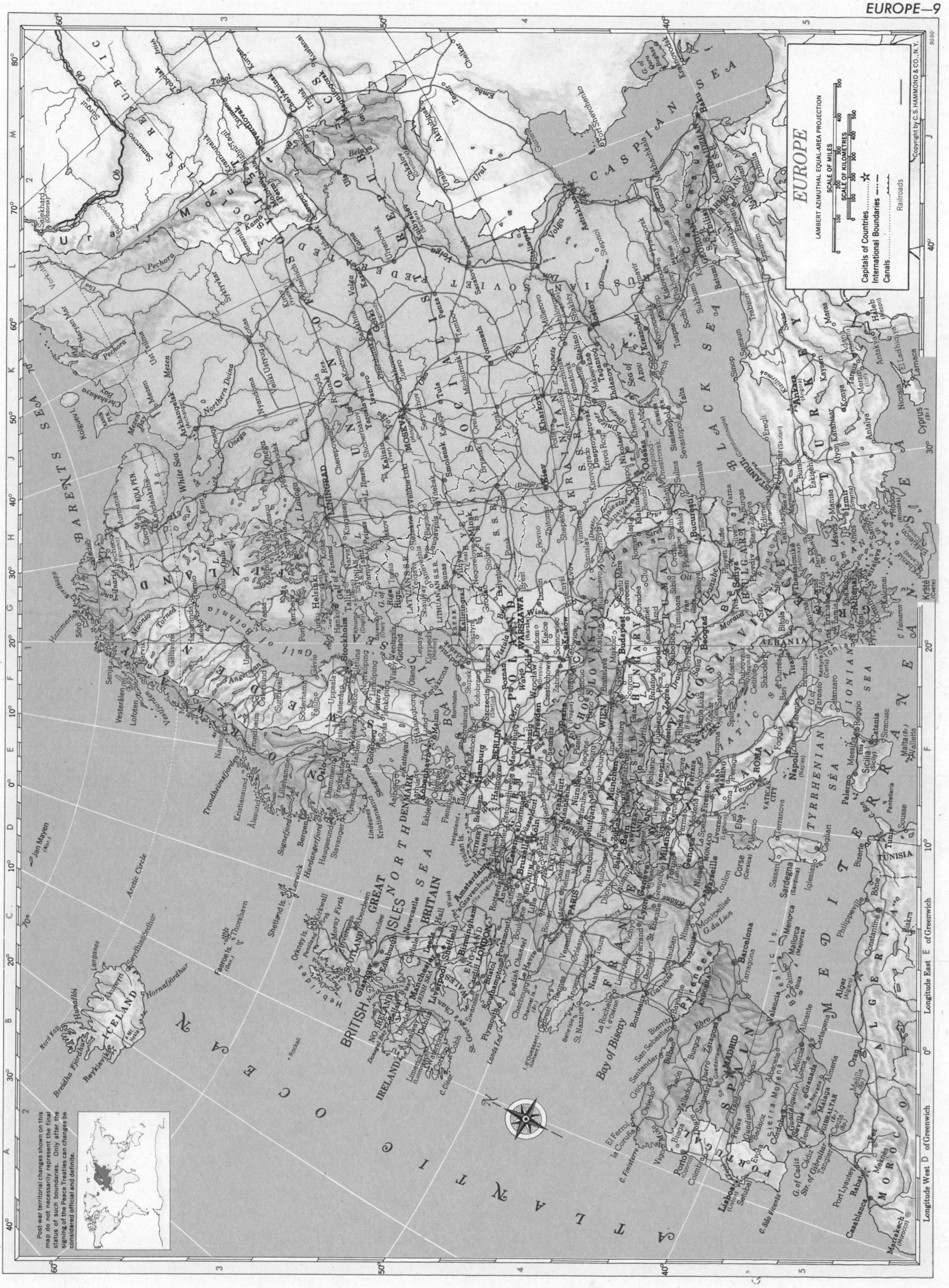

EUROPE

LAMBERT AZIMUTHAL EQUAL-AREA PROJECTION

SCALE OF MILES

SCALE OF KILOMETRES

Capitals of Countries........☆
International Boundaries.....
Canals.............................
Railroads

Post-war territorial changes shown on this map do not necessarily represent the final status of such boundaries. Only after the signing of the Peace Treaties can changes be considered official and definite.

ARCTIC OCEAN

BARENTS SEA

UNION OF SOVIET SOCIALIST REPUBLICS

CASPIAN SEA

BLACK SEA

TURKEY

MEDITERRANEAN SEA

ADRIATIC SEA

TYRRHENIAN SEA

IONIAN SEA

AEGEAN SEA

ATLANTIC OCEAN

NORTH SEA

GREAT BRITAIN

BRITISH ISLES

IRELAND

ICELAND

NORWAY

SWEDEN

FINLAND

DENMARK

GERMANY

POLAND

CZECHOSLOVAKIA

HUNGARY

RUMANIA

BULGARIA

YUGOSLAVIA

ALBANIA

ITALY

FRANCE

SPAIN

PORTUGAL

MOROCCO

ALGERIA

TUNISIA

MADRID

PARIS

ROMA

WIEN

WARSZAWA

BUDAPEST

BEOGRAD

MOSKVA

LENINGRAD

BERLIN

LONDON

Longitude West of Greenwich

Longitude East of Greenwich

ENGLAND and WALES

CONIC PROJECTION

SCALE OF MILES

0 10 20 40 60 80

SCALE OF KILOMETRES

0 10 20 40 60 80

Capitals of Countries ★   County Boundaries -----

Canals ....   Railroads _____

NORTH SEA

IRISH SEA

ST. GEORGE'S CHANNEL

NORTH CHANNEL

BRISTOL CHANNEL

ENGLISH CHANNEL

NORTHERN IRELAND

IRELAND

SCOTLAND

NORTHUMBERLAND

CUMBERLAND

DURHAM

WESTMORLAND

YORKSHIRE

NORTH RIDING

EAST RIDING

WEST RIDING

LINDSEY

KESTEVEN

HOLLAND

LANCASHIRE

CHESHIRE

DERBY

NOTTINGHAM

LINCOLN

NORFOLK

SUFFOLK

CAMBRIDGE

HUNTINGDON

BEDFORD

NORTHAMPTON

LEICESTER

RUTLAND

STAFFORD

SHROPSHIRE

WARWICK

WORCESTER

HEREFORD

GLOUCESTER

OXFORD

BUCKINGHAM

HERTFORD

ESSEX

MIDDLESEX

LONDON

KENT

SURREY

SUSSEX

EAST

WEST

HAMPSHIRE

BERKS

WILTS

SOMERSET

DORSET

DEVON

CORNWALL

MONMOUTH

GLAMORGAN

CARMARTHEN

PEMBROKE

CARDIGAN

BRECKNOCK

RADNOR

MONTGOMERY

MERIONETH

CAERNARVON

DENBIGH

FLINT

ANGLESEY

WALES

GLASGOW

Edinburgh

Newcastle

Liverpool

Manchester

Sheffield

Leeds

Bradford

Hull

Nottingham

Leicester

Birmingham

Coventry

Wolverhampton

Worcester

Gloucester

Bristol

Cardiff

Swansea

Oxford

Reading

LONDON

Southampton

Portsmouth

Brighton

Exeter

Plymouth

York

Lincoln

Norwich

Cambridge

Dublin

Belfast

CHANNEL ISLANDS

Guernsey

Jersey

FRANCE

Cherbourg

Le Havre

Rouen

Caen

Boulogne sur Mer

Calais

Copyright by C.S. HAMMOND & CO., N.Y.

Longitude West of Greenwich   Longitude East of Greenwich

3590

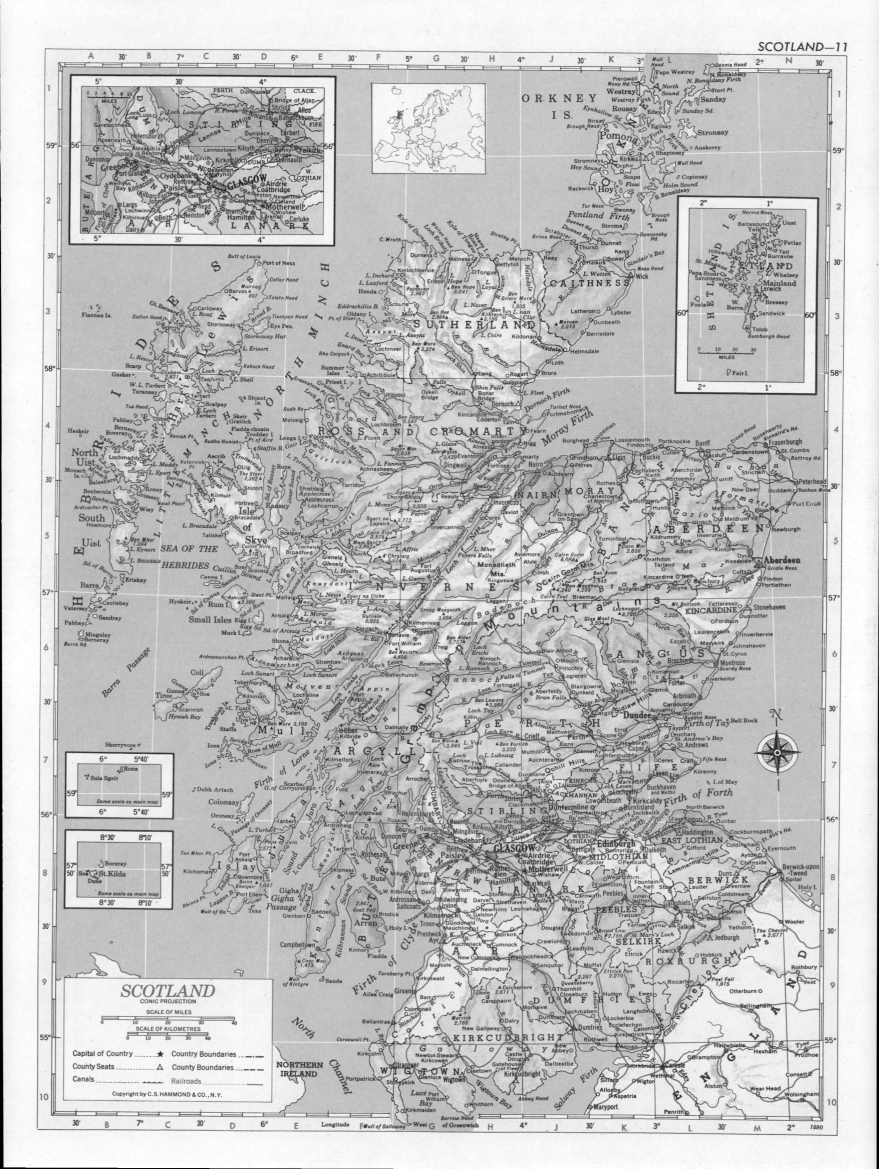

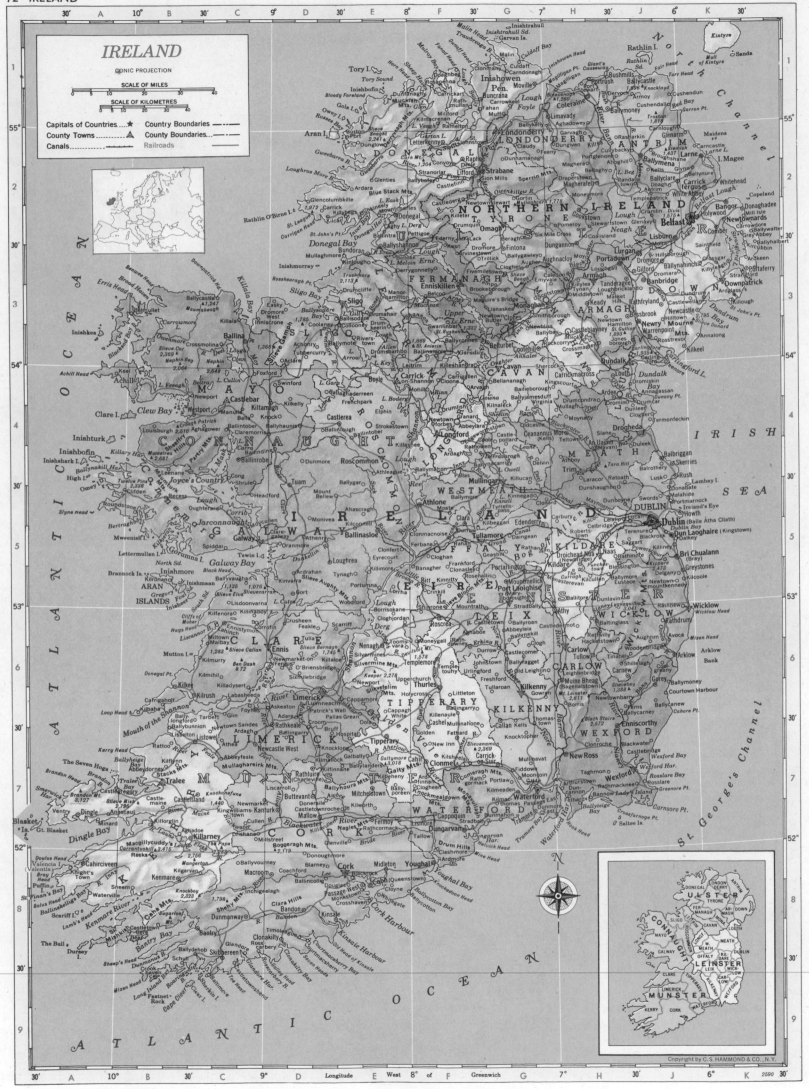

IRELAND

CONIC PROJECTION

SCALE OF MILES

SCALE OF KILOMETRES

Capitals of Countries ★   Country Boundaries -·-·-·-
County Towns △   County Boundaries -··-··-
Canals   Railroads

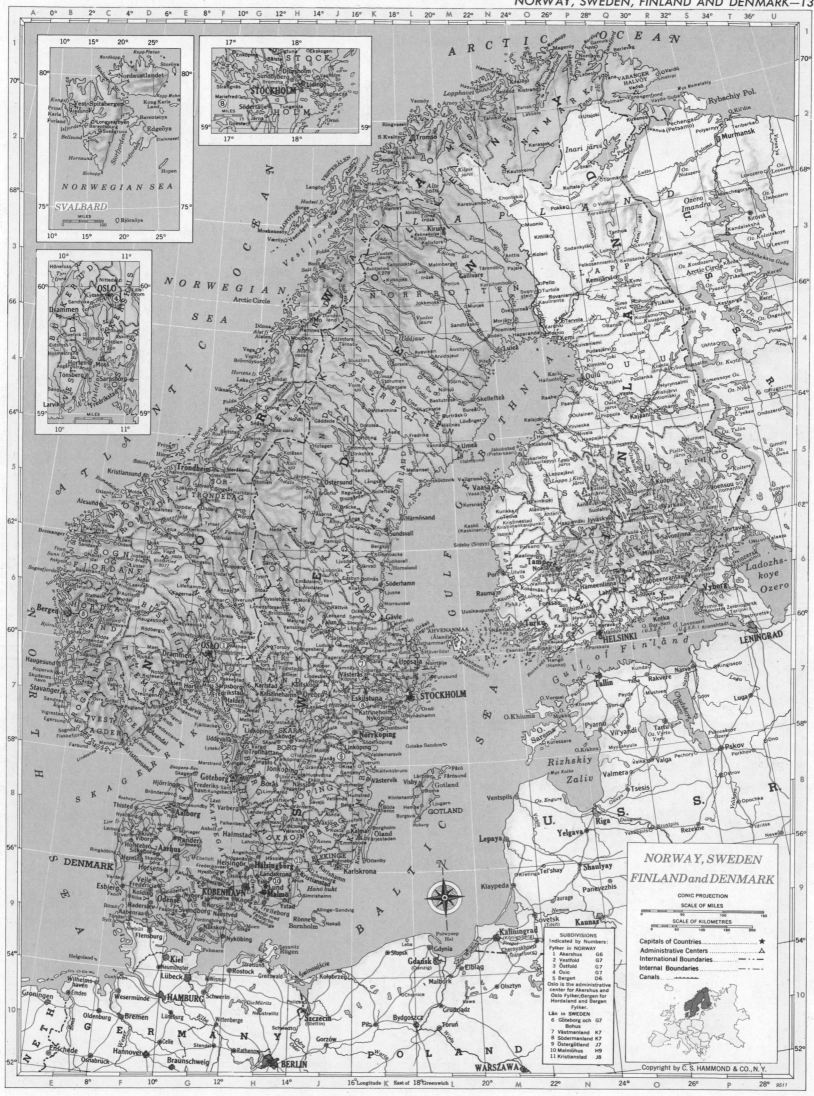

NORWAY, SWEDEN
FINLAND and DENMARK

CONIC PROJECTION

SCALE OF MILES

SCALE OF KILOMETRES

Capitals of Countries..............★
Administrative Centers............△
International Boundaries..........—·—·—
Internal Boundaries................—·—·—
Canals..................................

SUBDIVISIONS
Indicated by Numbers:
Fylker in NORWAY:
1 Akershus   G6
2 Vestfold   G7
3 Østfold   G7
4 Oslo   G7
5 Bergen   D6
Oslo is the administrative
center for Akershus and
Oslo Fylker; Bergen for
Hordaland and Bergen for
Fylker.

Län in SWEDEN
6 Göteborg och   G7
  Bohus
7 Västmanland   K7
8 Södermanland   K7
9 Östergötland   J7
10 Malmöhus   H9
11 Kristianstad   J8

Copyright by C. S. HAMMOND & CO., N.Y.

9511

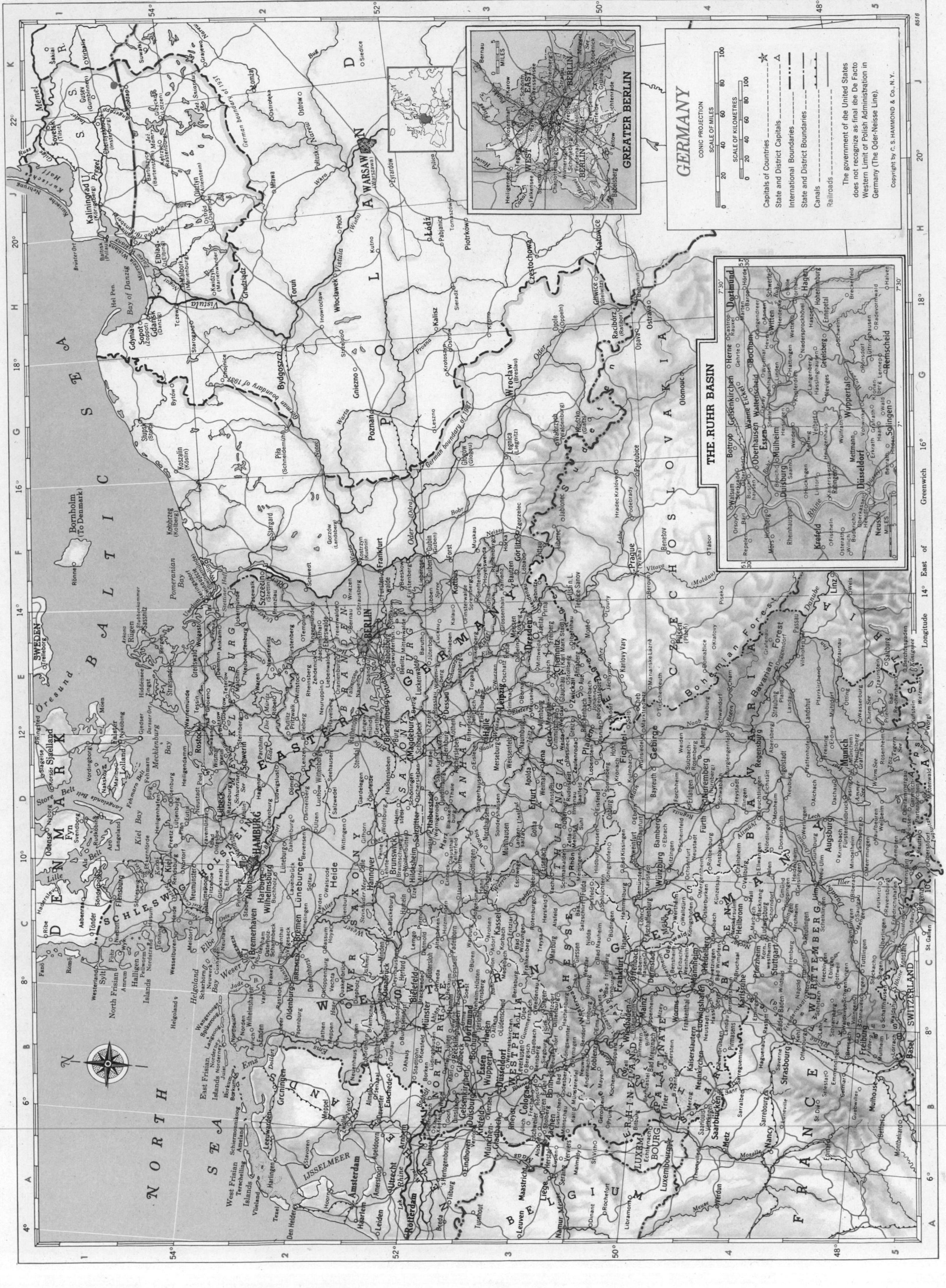

GERMANY
CONIC PROJECTION
SCALE OF MILES
SCALE OF KILOMETRES
Capitals of Countries
State and District Capitals
International Boundaries
State and District Boundaries
Canals
Railroads
The government of the United States does not recognize as final the De Facto Western Limit of Polish Administration in Germany (The Oder-Neisse Line).
Copyright by C. S. HAMMOND & Co., N.Y.
GREATER BERLIN
THE RUHR BASIN
NORTH SEA
BALTIC SEA
DENMARK
POLAND
CZECHOSLOVAKIA
FRANCE
SWITZERLAND
Longitude East of Greenwich

NETHERLANDS, BELGIUM
and LUXEMBOURG

CONIC PROJECTION

SCALE OF MILES

0 5 10   20   30   40

SCALE OF KILOMETRES

0 5 10   20   30   40   50

Capitals of Countries . . . . ★
Provincial Capitals . . . . ⌘
International Boundaries . . . . —·—·—
Provincial Boundaries . . . . —·—·—
Canals . . . .
Railroads . . . .

Elevations in Feet

AMSTERDAM

BRUXELLES

FRANCE

CONIC PROJECTION

SCALE OF MILES

0 20 40 60 80 100

SCALE OF KILOMETRES

0 20 40 60 80 100

Capitals of Countries .... ☆
Capitals of Departments .... △
International Boundaries .... — · —
Department Boundaries .... — · · —
Canals
Railroads

PARIS AND ENVIRONS

Maisons-Laffitte, Argenteuil, Gennevilliers, Colombes, Asnières, St:Denis, Aulnay-sous-Bois, Le Bourget, Drancy, St:Ouen, Aubervilliers, Nanterre, Levallois-Perret, Neuilly, Pantin, Bondy, Courbevoie, Puteaux, Suresnes, Bagnolet, Villemomble, Rueil, Malmaison, Boulogne-Billancourt, Montreuil, Vincennes, Le Chesnay, St:Cloud, Sèvres, Issy-les-Moulineaux, Meudon, Malakoff, Fontenay-sous-Bois, Champigny-sur-Marne, Versailles, Clamart, Montrouge, Ivry-sur-Seine, Charenton, le-Pont, St:Maur-des-Fossés, Sceaux, Bièvres, Villejuif, Vitry, Choisy-le-Roi, Maisons-Alfort

0 1 2 3 4 MILES

FORMER PROVINCES

English Channel, FLANDERS, ARTOIS, PICARDY, NORMANDY, MAINE, ISLE DE FRANCE, CHAMPAGNE, LORRAINE, ALSACE, BRITTANY, ANJOU, TOURAINE, ORLÉANAIS, BERRY, NIVERNAIS, BURGUNDY, FRANCHE COMTÉ, POITOU, AUNIS, MARCHE, BOURBONNAIS, LYONAIS, SAINTONGE, ANGOUMOIS, LIMOUSIN, AUVERGNE, DAUPHINÉ, GUYENNE, QUERCY, COMTAT, PROVENCE, GASCONY, LANGUEDOC, ROUSSILLON, BÉARN, Bay of Biscay, Mediterranean Sea

DEPT. DE LA CORSE

Same Scale as Main Map

C. Corse, Rogliano, G. de St-Florent, L'Île Rousse, Calvi, Calenzana, Bastia, M.¹ Cinto 8,891 m., Cervione, Corte, Bastelica, M.¹ l'Incudine 7,007, Vivario, Ajaccio, G.d' Ajaccio, Levie, Sartène, Bonifacio, Porto-Vecchio, Str. of Bonifacio

MEDITERRANEAN SEA

Departments and places (main map)

ENGLISH CHANNEL (La Manche), NORTH SEA, BAY OF BISCAY, MEDITERRANEAN SEA

Paris, London, Amsterdam, Rotterdam, Bruxelles, Luxembourg, Bern, Barcelona

SEINE-INFÉRIEURE, SOMME, PAS-DE-CALAIS, ARDENNES, OISE, AISNE, MARNE, MEUSE, MOSELLE, MEURTHE-ET-MOSELLE, CALVADOS, EURE, SEINE-ET-OISE, SEINE-ET-MARNE, AUBE, HAUTE-MARNE, VOSGES, HAUT-RHIN, BAS-RHIN, MANCHE, ORNE, EURE-ET-LOIR, LOIRET, YONNE, CÔTE-D'OR, HAUTE-SAÔNE, DOUBS, JURA, CÔTES-DU-NORD, ILLE-ET-VILAINE, MAYENNE, SARTHE, LOIR-ET-CHER, CHER, NIÈVRE, SAÔNE-ET-LOIRE, AIN, FINISTÈRE, MORBIHAN, LOIRE-INFÉRIEURE, MAINE-ET-LOIRE, INDRE-ET-LOIRE, INDRE, ALLIER, LOIRE, RHÔNE, HAUTE-SAVOIE, SAVOIE, VENDÉE, DEUX-SÈVRES, VIENNE, CREUSE, PUY-DE-DÔME, HAUTE-LOIRE, ISÈRE, HAUTES-ALPES, CHARENTE-MARITIME, CHARENTE, HAUTE-VIENNE, CORRÈZE, CANTAL, LOZÈRE, ARDÈCHE, DRÔME, BASSES-ALPES, ALPES-MARITIMES, GIRONDE, DORDOGNE, LOT, AVEYRON, GARD, VAUCLUSE, VAR, LANDES, LOT-ET-GARONNE, TARN-ET-GARONNE, TARN, HÉRAULT, BOUCHES-DU-RHÔNE, GERS, HAUTE-GARONNE, AUDE, PYRÉNÉES-ORIENTALES, BASSES-PYRÉNÉES, HAUTES-PYRÉNÉES, ARIÈGE, SWITZERLAND, SPAIN, ANDORRA, MONACO

The Franco-Italian boundary is shown in accordance with territorial provisions of the Italian Peace Treaty 1946-1947.

Copyright by C.S. HAMMOND & Co., N.Y.

55120

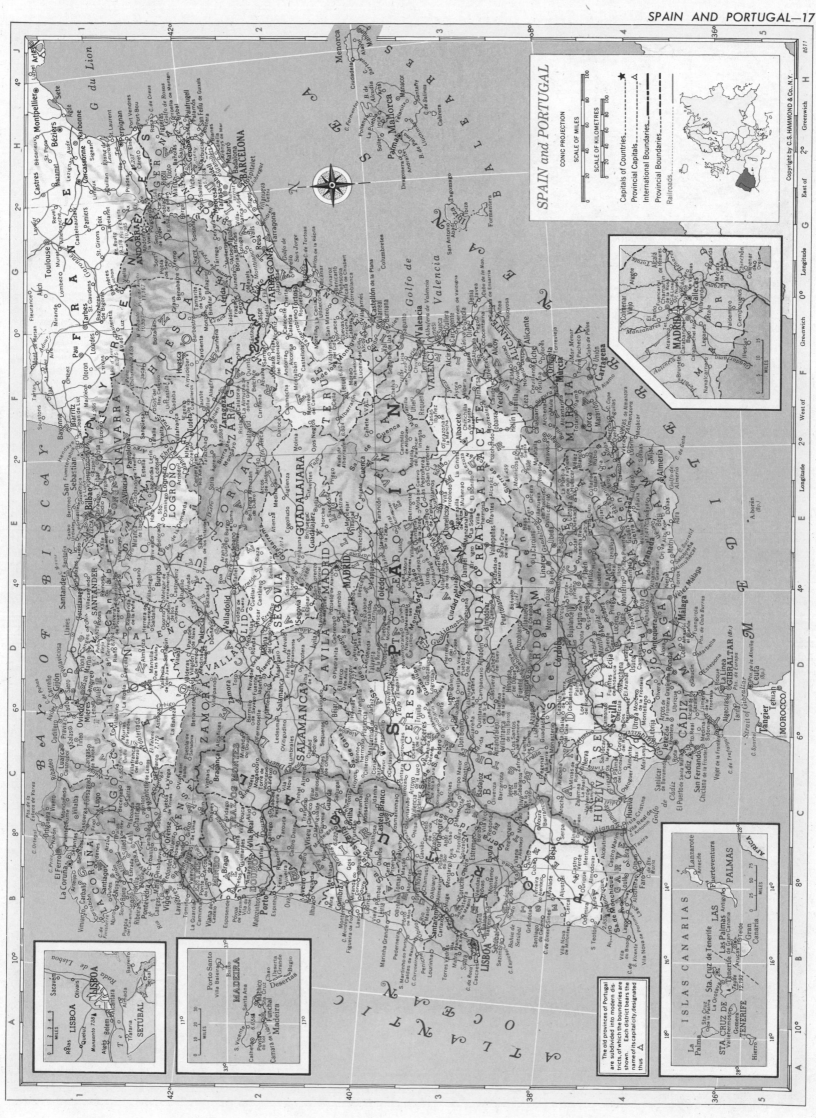

SPAIN and PORTUGAL

CONIC PROJECTION

SCALE OF MILES

SCALE OF KILOMETRES

Capitals of Countries............ ★
Provincial Capitals................. ⊙
International Boundaries.........
Provincial Boundaries.............
Railroads...............................

The old provinces of Portugal
are subdivided into modern districts, of which the boundaries are
shown. Each district bears the
name of its capital city, designated
thus ....△

ISLAS CANARIAS

LISBOA

MADEIRA

ITALY
CONIC PROJECTION
SCALE OF MILES
SCALE OF KILOMETERS

Capitals of Countries........★
Regional Capitals...........✠
Provincial Capitals.........△
International Boundaries.....
Regional Boundaries.........
Railroads...................

ITALY is divided for administrative purposes into
19 regions, shown on the map in separate colors.
The regions of Friuli-Venezia Giulia, Sardegna, Sicilia,
Trentino-Alto Adige and Valle d'Aosta enjoy special
autonomy.

The regions are subdivided into provinces bearing
the same names as their respective capitals, except:

PROVINCE	CAPITAL
IONIO	Taranto
MASSA E CARRARA	Massa
PESARO E URBINO	Pesaro

CITTÀ DEL VATICANO

PROVINCIA DI LATINA

Copyright by C.S. HAMMOND & Co., N.Y.

Longitude   East of   Greenwich

6511

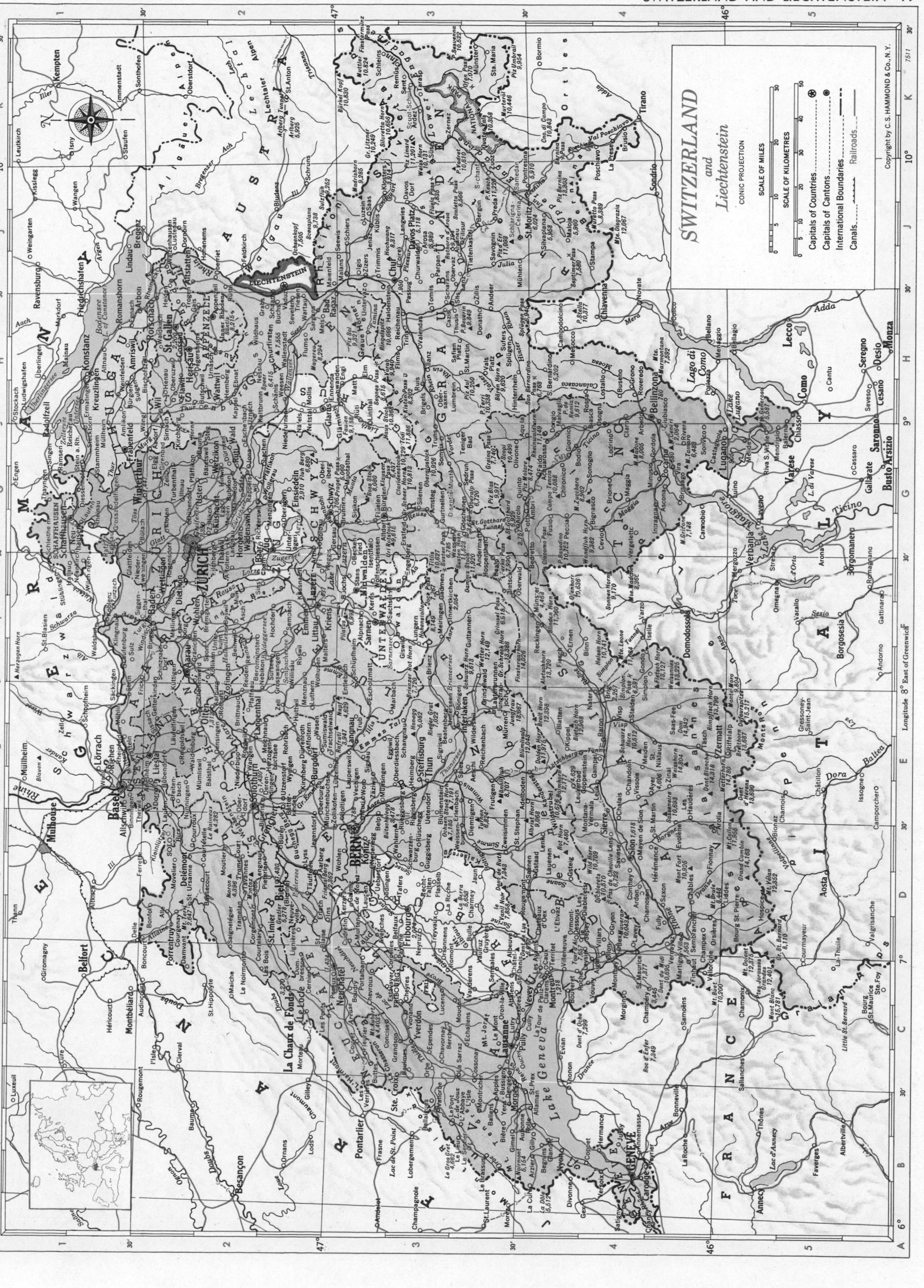

SWITZERLAND
and
Liechtenstein
CONIC PROJECTION

SCALE OF MILES

SCALE OF KILOMETRES

Capitals of Countries .... ⊛
Capitals of Cantons .... ◉
International Boundaries ....
Canals ....   Railroads ....

Copyright by C.S. HAMMOND & CO., N.Y.

AUSTRIA

LIECHTENSTEIN

GRAUBÜNDEN

TICINO

VALAIS

VAUD

FRIBOURG

BERN

ZÜRICH

ST. GALLEN

THURGAU

Lake Geneva

GENÈVE

Lausanne

BERN

ZÜRICH

Basel

Mulhouse

Lago di Como

Longitude 8° East of Greenwich

FRANCE

ITALY

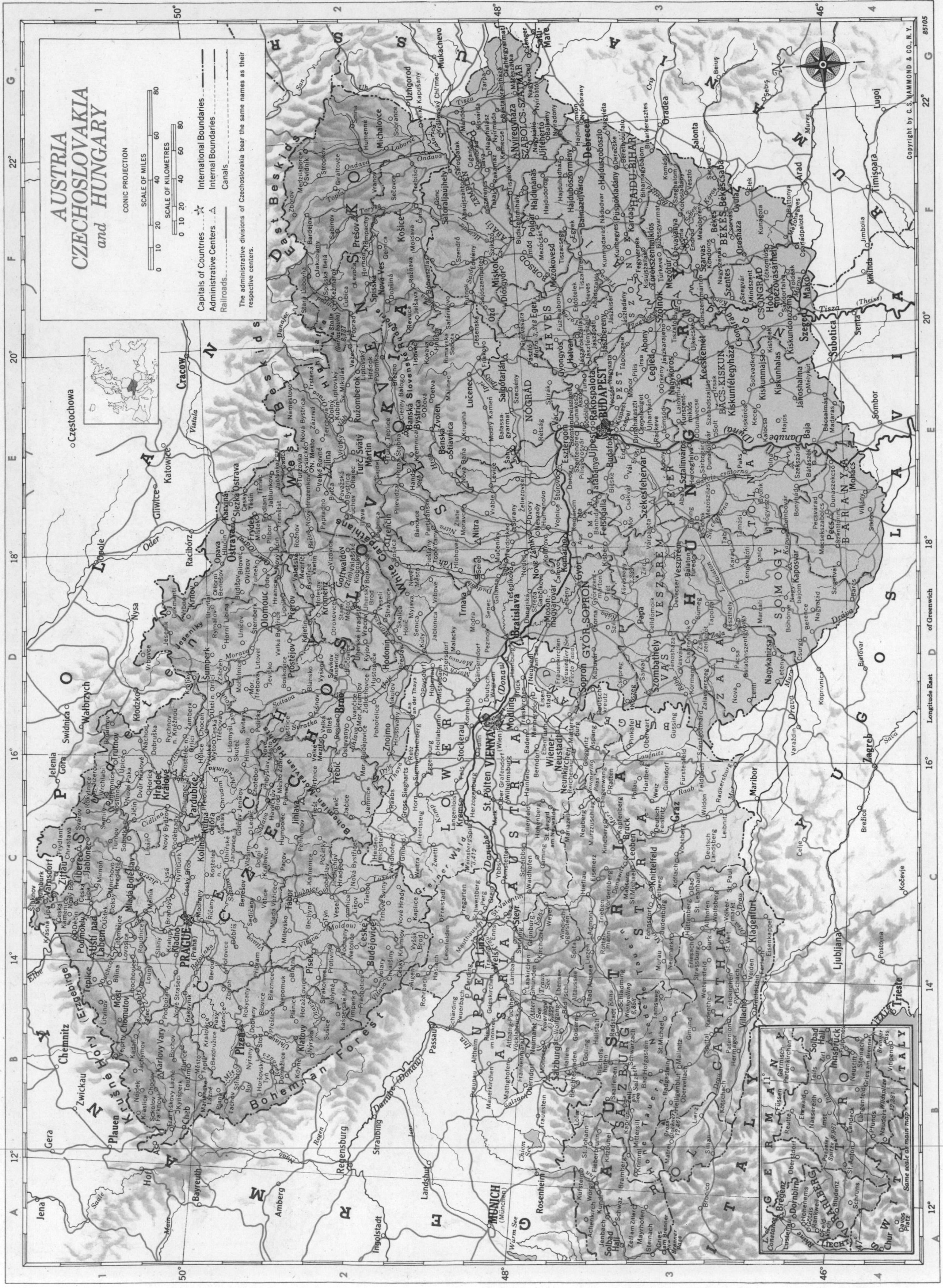

AUSTRIA CZECHOSLOVAKIA and HUNGARY

CONIC PROJECTION

SCALE OF MILES

SCALE OF KILOMETRES

Capitals of Countries ....★
Administrative Centers ......△
Railroads ....

International Boundaries ------
Internal Boundaries ——
Canals ——

The administrative divisions of Czechoslovakia bear the same names as their respective centers.

Copyright by C. S. HAMMOND & CO., N.Y.

(Map of Austria, Czechoslovakia and Hungary, with inset map of the Tyrol/Salzburg region in the lower right. Principal labels include: GERMANY, POLAND, U.S.S.R., CZECHOSLOVAKIA, SLOVAKIA, HUNGARY, AUSTRIA, YUGOSLAVIA, ITALY, STYRIA, CARINTHIA, LOWER AUSTRIA, UPPER AUSTRIA, SALZBURG, TYROL, VORARLBERG, Bohemian Forest, West Carpathians, Low Carpathians, Beskids, East Beskids. Cities include PRAGUE (Praha), VIENNA (Wien), BUDAPEST, Bratislava, Brno, Ostrava, Košice, Debrecen, Szeged, Munich (München), Linz, Graz, Salzburg, Innsbruck.)

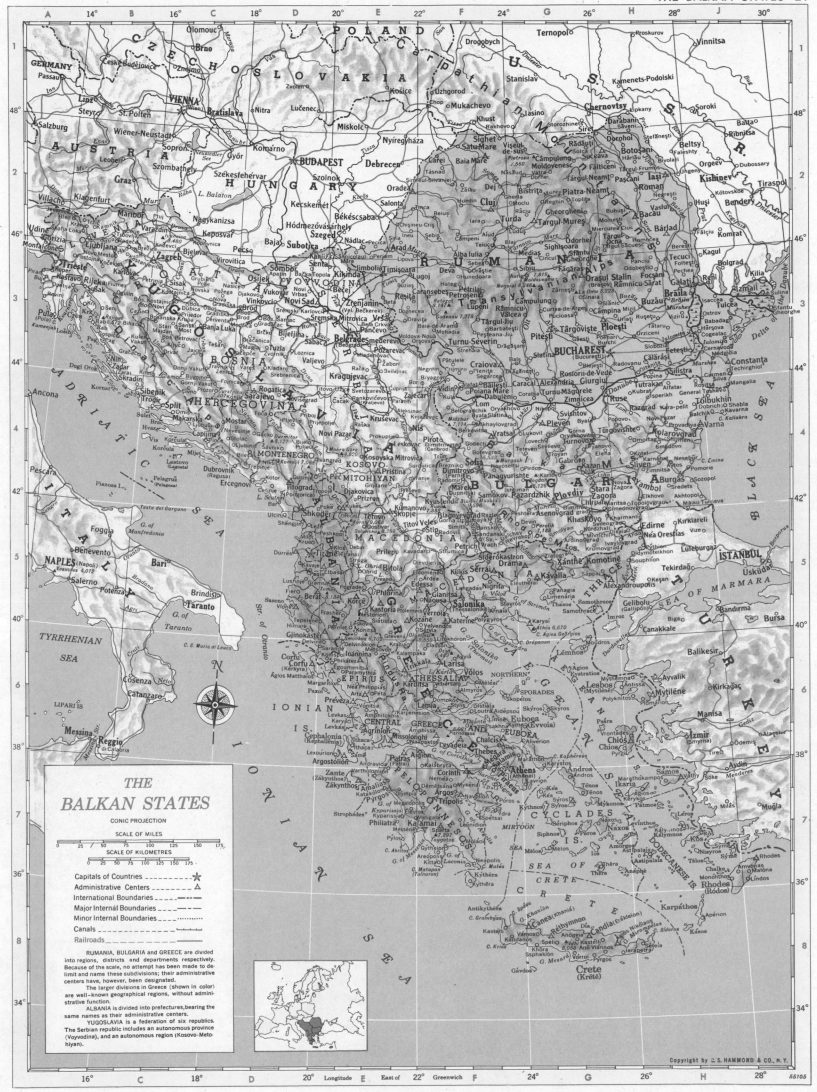

THE
BALKAN STATES

CONIC PROJECTION

SCALE OF MILES

0   25   50   75   100   125   150   175

SCALE OF KILOMETRES

0   25   50   75   100   125   150   175

Capitals of Countries _____ ☆
Administrative Centers _____ △
International Boundaries _____
Major Internal Boundaries _____
Minor Internal Boundaries _____
Canals _____
Railroads _____

RUMANIA, BULGARIA and GREECE are divided
into regions, districts and departments respectively.
Because of the scale, no attempt has been made to de-
limit and name these subdivisions; their administrative
centers have, however, been designated.
The larger divisions in Greece (shown in color)
are well-known geographical regions, without administrative function.
ALBANIA is divided into prefectures, bearing the
same names as their administrative centers.
YUGOSLAVIA is a federation of six republics.
The Serbian republic includes an autonomous province
(Voyvodina), and an autonomous region (Kosovo-Meto-
hiyan).

65105

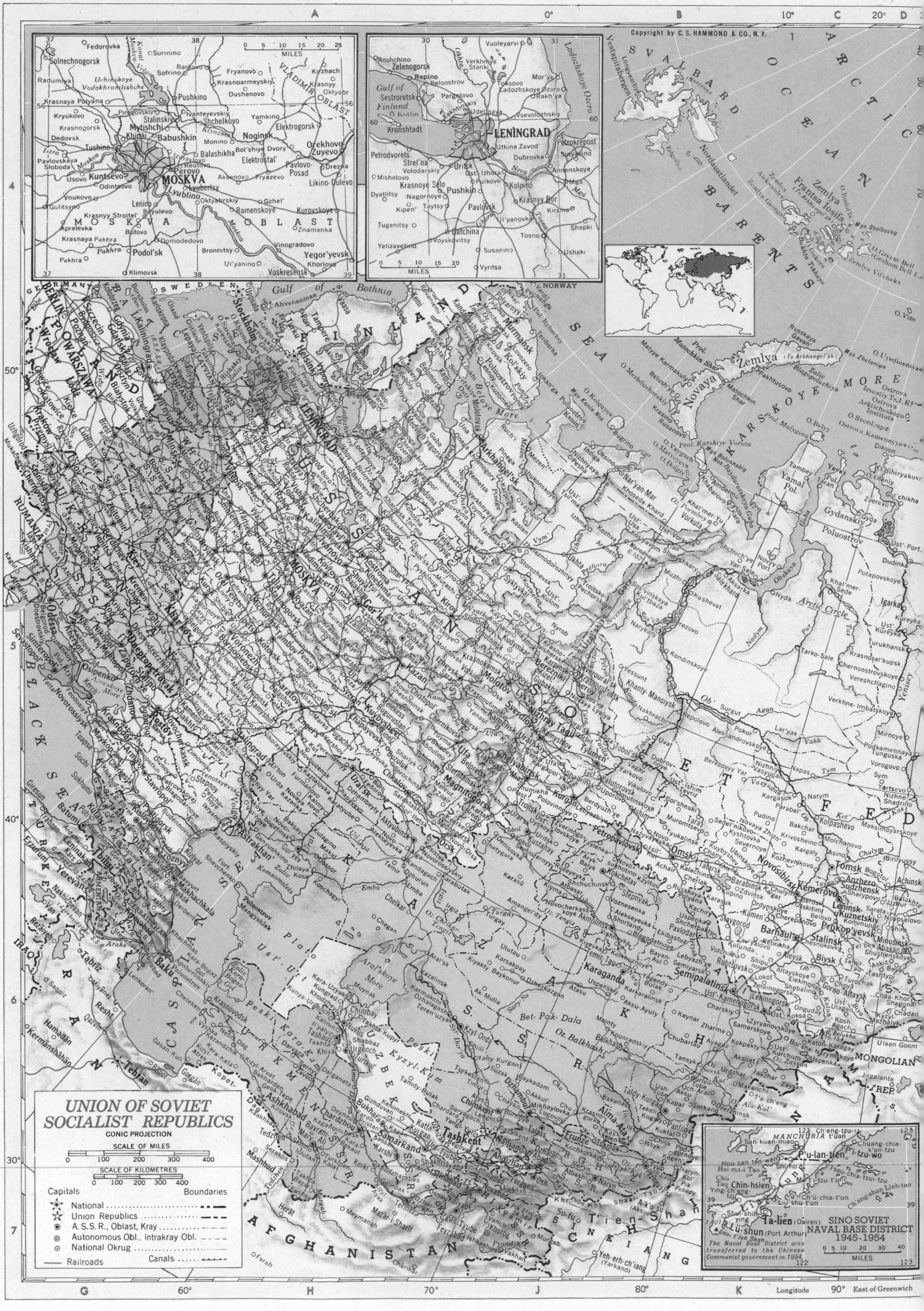

UNION OF SOVIET SOCIALIST REPUBLICS
CONIC PROJECTION
SCALE OF MILES
0 100 200 300 400
SCALE OF KILOMETRES
0 100 200 300 400
Capitals
Boundaries
National
Union Republics
A.S.S.R., Oblast, Kray
Autonomous Obl., Intrakray Obl.
National Okrug
Railroads
Canals
Copyright by C. S. HAMMOND & CO., N.Y.
MOSKVA
MOSKVA OBLAST
VLADIMIR OBLAST
LENINGRAD
Gulf of Finland
SINO SOVIET NAVAL BASE DISTRICT 1945-1954
The Naval Base District was transferred to the Chinese Communist government in 1954.
MANCHURIA
P'u-lan-tien
Ta-lien (Dairen)
Lü-shun (Port Arthur)
ARCTIC OCEAN
BARENTS SEA
KARSKOYE MORE
SVALBARD
Novaya Zemlya
Zemlya Frantsa Iosifa
Arctic Circle
BLACK SEA
CASPIAN SEA
Aral'skoye More
FINLAND
SWEDEN
NORWAY
POLAND
RUMANIA
TURKEY
IRAN
IRAQ
AFGHANISTAN
MONGOLIAN REP.
SINKIANG
Leningrad
Moskva
Kiev
Khar'kov
Stalingrad
Astrakhan'
Kazan'
Sverdlovsk
Chelyabinsk
Omsk
Novosibirsk
Tashkent
Alma-Ata
Frunze
Karaganda
Semipalatinsk
Arkhangel'sk
Murmansk
Tbilisi
Baku
Yerevan
Ashkhabad
Samarkand
Longitude
East of Greenwich

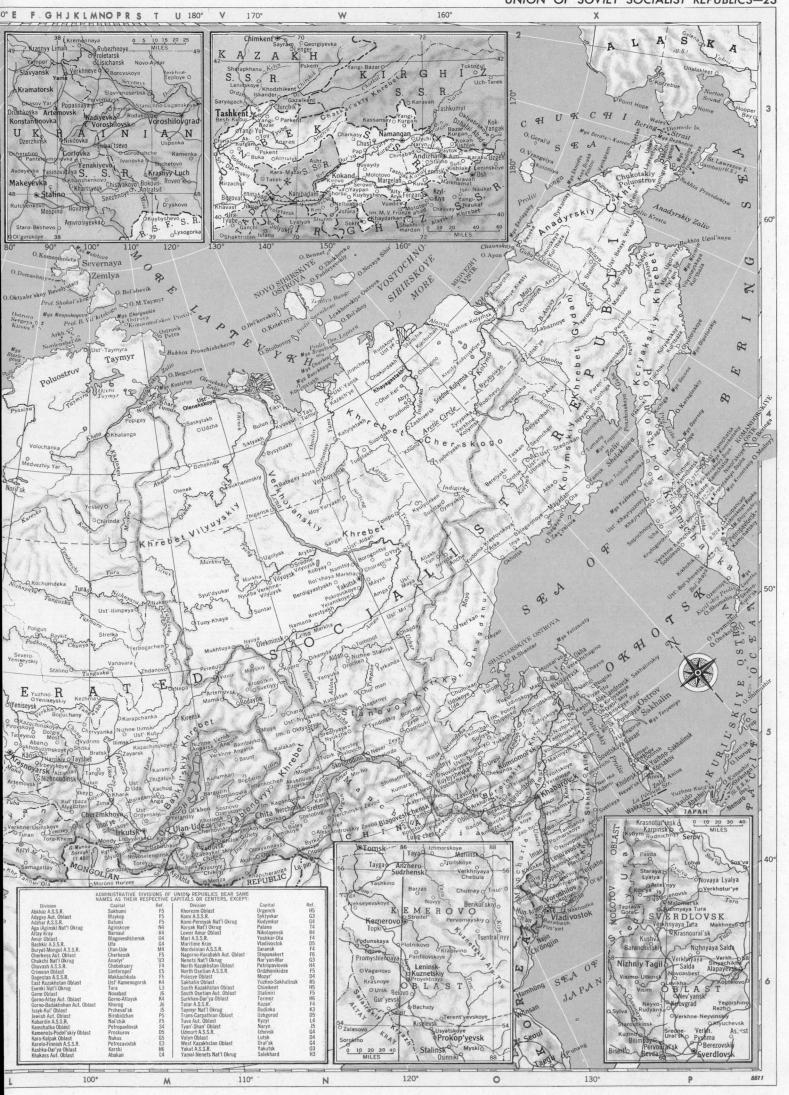

ADMINISTRATIVE DIVISIONS OF UNION REPUBLICS BEAR SAME
NAMES AS THEIR RESPECTIVE CAPITALS OR CENTERS, EXCEPT:

Division	Capital	Ref.	Division	Capital	Ref.
Abkhaz A.S.S.R.	Sukhumi	F5	Khorezm Oblast	Urgench	H5
Adygey Aut. Oblast	Maykop	F5	Komi A.S.S.R.	Syktyvkar	G3
Adzhar A.S.S.R.	Batumi	F5	Komi-Permyak Nat'l Okrug	Kudymkar	G4
Aga (Aginsk) Nat'l Okrug	Aginskoye	N4	Koryak Nat'l Okrug	Palana	T4
Altay Kray	Barnaul	K4	Lower Amur Oblast	Nikolayevsk	R4
Amur Oblast	Blagoveshchensk	O4	Mari A.S.S.R.	Yoshkar-Ola	F4
Bashkir A.S.S.R.	Ufa	G4	Maritime Kray	Vladivostok	O5
Buryat-Mongol A.S.S.R.	Ulan-Ude	M4	Mordvinian A.S.S.R.	Saransk	F4
Cherkess Aut. Oblast	Cherkessk	F5	Nagorno-Karabakh Aut. Oblast	Stepanakert	F6
Chukchi Nat'l Okrug	Anadyr'	U3	Nenets Nat'l Okrug	Nar'yan-Mar	G3
Chuvash A.S.S.R.	Cheboksary	F4	North Kazakhstan Oblast	Petropavlovsk	H4
Crimean Oblast	Simferopol	E5	North Osetian A.S.S.R.	Ordzhonikidze	F5
Dagestan A.S.S.R.	Makhachkala	F5	Polesye Oblast	Mozyr'	D4
East Kazakhstan Oblast	Ust'-Kamenogorsk	K4	Sakhalin Oblast	Yuzhno-Sakhalinsk	R5
Evenki Nat'l Okrug	Tura	L3	South Kazakhstan Oblast	Chimkent	H5
Garm Oblast	Novabad	J6	South Osetian Aut. Oblast	Stalinir	F5
Gorno-Altay Aut. Oblast	Gorno-Altaysk	K4	Surkhan-Dar'ya Oblast	Termez	H6
Gorno-Badakhshan Aut. Oblast	Khorog	J6	Tatar A.S.S.R.	Kazan'	F4
Issyk-Kul' Oblast	Przheval'sk	J5	Taymyr Nat'l Okrug	Dudinka	K3
Jewish Aut. Oblast	Birobidzhan	O4	Trans-Carpathian Oblast	Uzhgorod	D5
Kabardin A.S.S.R.	Nal'chik	F5	Tuva Aut. Oblast	Kyzyl	L4
Kamchatka Oblast	Petropavlovsk	S4	Tyan'-Shan' Oblast	Naryn	J5
Kamenets-Podol'skiy Oblast	Proskurov	D5	Udmurt A.S.S.R.	Izhevsk	G4
Kara-Kalpak A.S.S.R.	Nukus	G5	Volyn Oblast	Lutsk	D4
Karelo-Finnish A.S.S.R.	Petrozavodsk	E3	West Kazakhstan Oblast	Ural'sk	G4
Kashka-Dar'ya Oblast	Karshi	H6	Yakut A.S.S.R.	Yakutsk	O3
Khakass Aut. Oblast	Abakan	L4	Yamal-Nenets Nat'l Okrug	Salekhard	H3

8511

POLAND
CONIC PROJECTION
SCALE OF MILES
0 20 40 60 80 100
SCALE OF KILOMETRES
0 20 40 60 80 100 120 140 160

International Boundaries
Internal Boundaries
Capitals of Countries ⊛
Administrative Centers ⊙
Canals
Railroads

GLOSSARY

PRESENT POLISH	FORMER GERMAN	KEY
Brzeg	Brieg	C-3
Bytom	Beuthen	B-4
Elbląg	Elbing	D-1
Gdańsk	Danzig	D-1
Gliwice	Gleiwitz	A-4
Głogów	Glogau	C-3
Gorzów	Landsberg	B-2
Gubin	Guben	B-3
Jelenia Góra	Hirschberg	B-3
Kołobrzeg	Kolberg	B-2
Kostrzyń	Küstrin	B-2
Koszalin	Köslin	C-1
Legnica	Liegnitz	C-3
Malbork	Marienburg	D-2
Nysa	Neisse	C-3
Olsztyn	Allenstein	E-2
Opole	Oppeln	C-3
Piła	Schneidemühl	C-2
Racibórz	Ratibor	D-3
Słupsk	Stolp	C-1
Świdnica	Schweidnitz	B-3
Świnoujście	Swinemünde	B-2
Szczecin	Stettin	B-2
Wałbrzych	Waldenburg	B-3
Wrocław	Breslau	C-3
Zabrze	Hindenburg	D-3
Zielona Góra	Grünberg	B-2

Post-war territorial changes shown on this map do not necessarily represent the final status of such boundaries. Only after the signing of the Peace Treaties can changes be considered official and definite.

BALTIC SEA
POLISH BOUNDARIES
1938
1945

Copyright by C.S. HAMMOND & Co., N.Y.

45114

Israel and Jordan
CYLINDRICAL PROJECTION
SCALE OF MILES
SCALE OF KILOMETRES
Capitals of Countries ⊛
District Capitals ⊙
International Boundaries
District Boundaries
Sub-District Boundaries
Railroads

Israel is shown according to the terms of the Israeli-Jordanian and Israeli-Egyptian armistice agreements. The districts and sub-districts of the former Palestinian Mandate are shown for reference only and are not the present-day administrative divisions.

Copyright by C.S. HAMMOND & CO., N.Y.

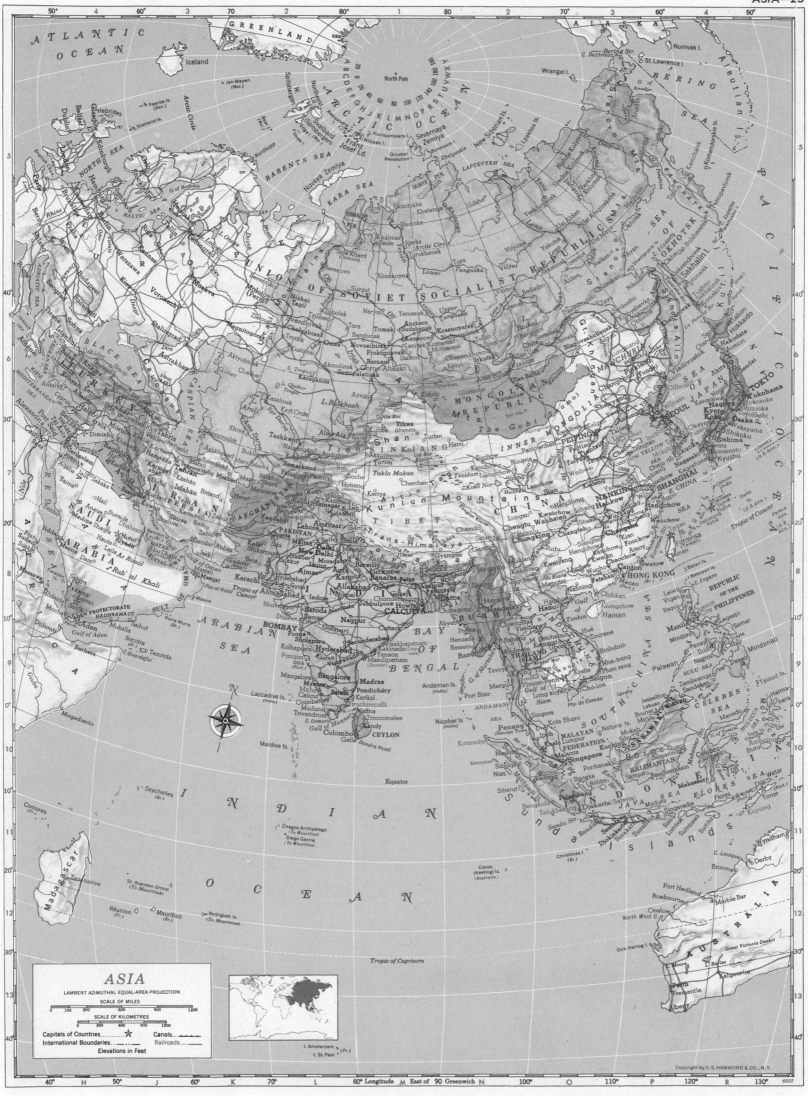

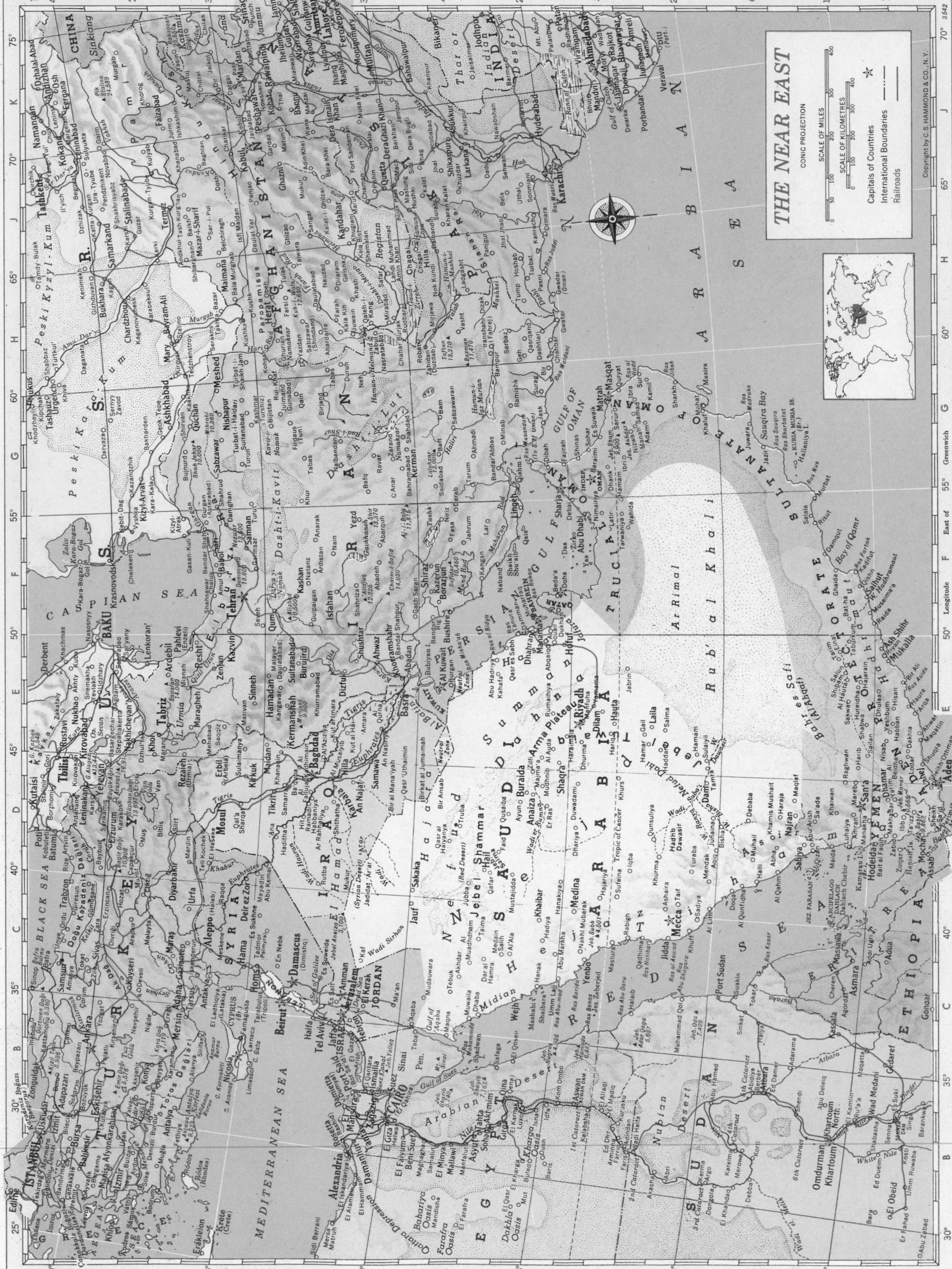

THE NEAR EAST

CONIC PROJECTION

SCALE OF MILES

SCALE OF KILOMETRES

Capitals of Countries ✶
International Boundaries ......
Railroads ———

Copyright by C. S. HAMMOND & CO., N.Y.

CHINA · U.S.S.R. · S.S.R. · AFGHANISTAN · PAKISTAN · INDIA · KASHMIR

IRAN · IRAQ · TURKEY · SYRIA · JORDAN · SAUDI ARABIA · YEMEN · OMAN

SULTANATE OF OMAN · TRUCIAL · QATAR · BAHREIN · KUWAIT

EGYPT · SUDAN · ETHIOPIA · ERITREA · CYPRUS · ISRAEL · LEBANON

CASPIAN SEA · BLACK SEA · MEDITERRANEAN SEA · ARABIAN SEA · RED SEA

GULF OF OMAN · PERSIAN GULF · AEGEAN SEA

Rub' al Khali · Ar Rimal · An Nefud · El Hamad · Nubian Desert · Arabian Desert

Baku · Tehran · Baghdad · Damascus · Beirut · Jerusalem · Amman · Cairo · Mecca · Medina · Aden · San'a · Khartoum · Istanbul · Ankara · Alexandria · Tabriz · Isfahan · Shiraz · Mosul · Basra · Kuwait · Riyadh · Karachi · Lahore · Kabul · Kandahar · Meshed · Tashkent · Samarkand

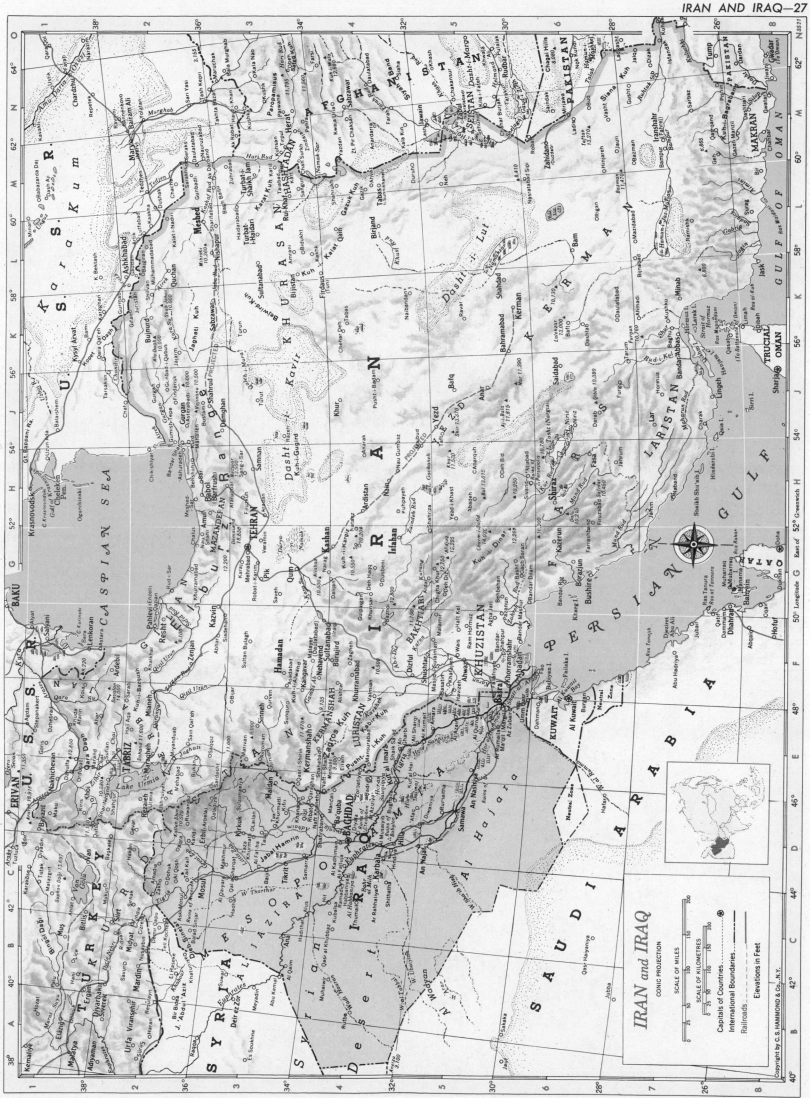

IRAN and IRAQ

CONIC PROJECTION

SCALE OF MILES

SCALE OF KILOMETRES

Capitals of Countries..........⊛
International Boundaries..........
Railroads..........
Elevations in Feet

Copyright by C.S. HAMMOND & CO., N.Y.

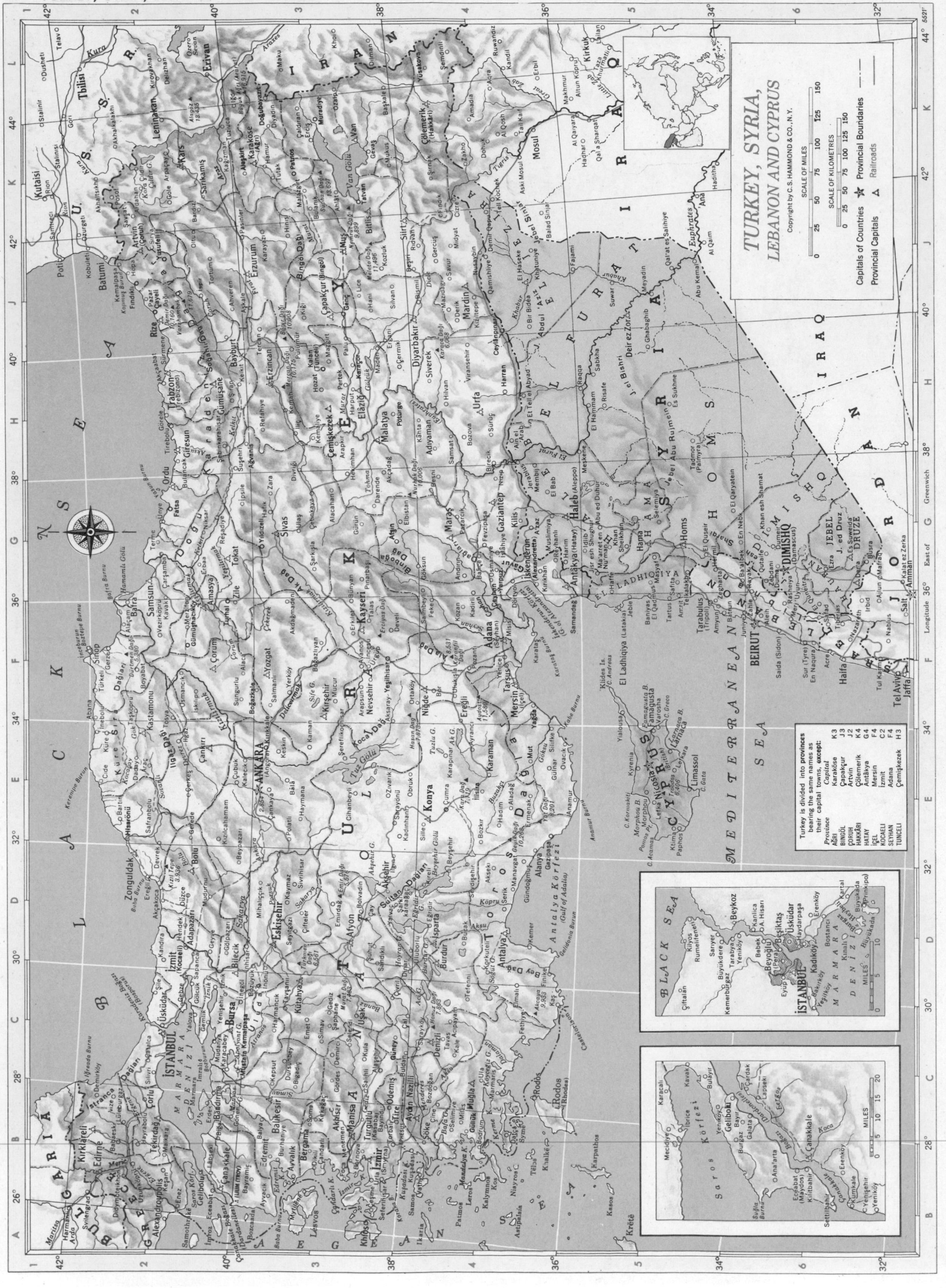

TURKEY, SYRIA, LEBANON AND CYPRUS

Copyright by C. S. HAMMOND & CO., N.Y.

SCALE OF MILES

0 25 50 75 100 125 150

SCALE OF KILOMETRES

0 25 50 75 100 125 150

★ Capitals of Countries   — Provincial Boundaries

☆ Provincial Capitals   ⊣ Railroads

Turkey is divided into provinces bearing the same names as their capital towns, except:

Province	Capital
AĞRI	Karaköse K3
BİNGÖL	Çapakçur J3
ÇORUH	Artvin J2
HAKKARİ	Çölemerik K4
HATAY	Antakya G4
İÇEL	Mersin F4
KOCAELİ	İzmit C2
SEYHAN	Adana F4
TUNCELİ	Çemişkezek H3

BLACK SEA

MEDITERRANEAN SEA

CYPRUS

U. S. S. R.

IRAN

IRAQ

SYRIA

LEBANON

TRANSJORDAN

BULGARIA

GREECE

EL FURAT

HAMA

HOMS

EL LADHIQIYA

JEBEL DRUZE

ANKARA

İSTANBUL

BEIRUT

DIMISHQ (Damascus)

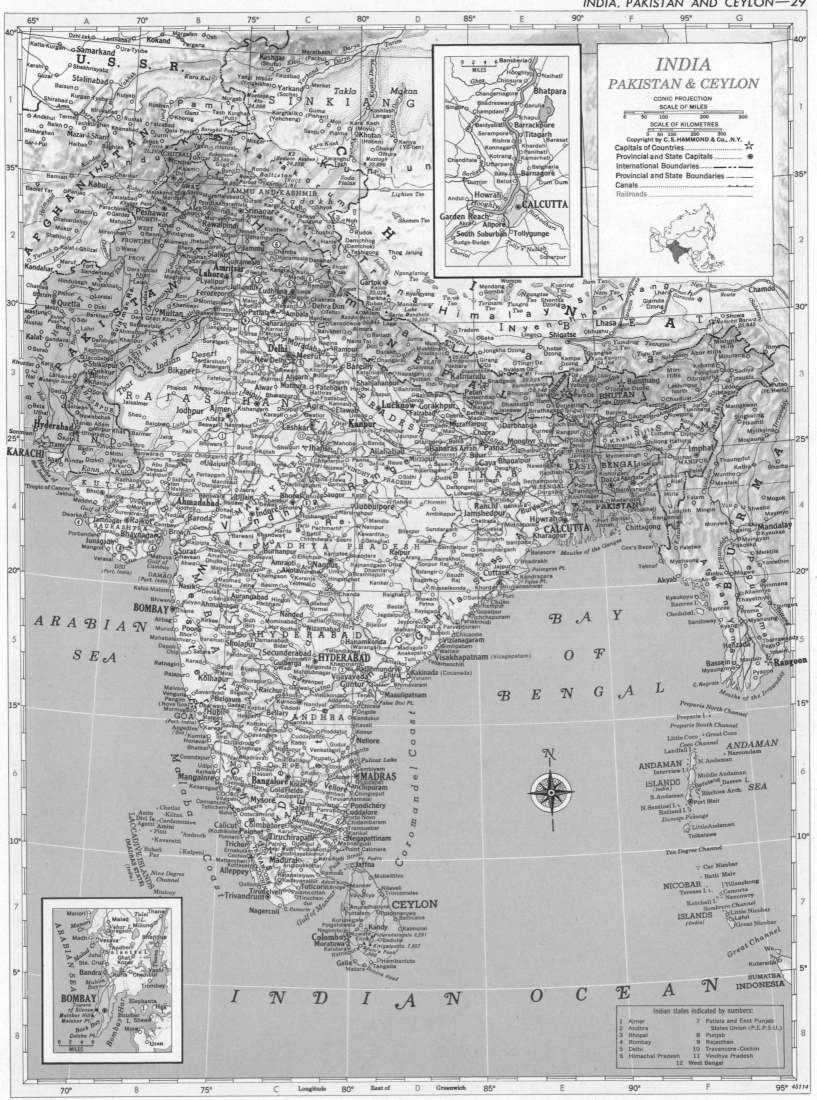

INDIA
PAKISTAN & CEYLON
CONIC PROJECTION
SCALE OF MILES
0   50   100   200   300
SCALE OF KILOMETRES
0   50 100   200   300
Copyright by C. S. HAMMOND & Co., N.Y.
Capitals of Countries............................☆
Provincial and State Capitals ....◉
International Boundaries............------
Provincial and State Boundaries....—·—·—
Canals...
Railroads ....

Indian states indicated by numbers:
1 Ajmer   7 Patiala and East Punjab
2 Andhra   States Union (P.E.P.S.U.)
3 Bhopal   8 Punjab
4 Bombay   9 Rajasthan
5 Delhi   10 Travancore-Cochin
6 Himachal Pradesh 11 Vindhya Pradesh
                     12 West Bengal

BURMA, THAILAND, INDOCHINA AND MALAYAN FEDERATION

CONIC PROJECTION

SCALE OF MILES

0   50   100   150   200

SCALE OF KILOMETRES

0 50 100   200   300

International Boundaries ....
Capitals of Countries ....⊛
Administrative Centers ....◉
Railroads

Copyright by C.S. HAMMOND & CO., N.Y.

0521

INDIA

BURMA

CHINA

THAILAND (SIAM)

CAMBODIA

ANNAM

COCHIN CHINA

TONKIN

HAINAN

SUMATRA

INDONESIA

MALAYAN FEDERATION

BAY OF BENGAL

ANDAMAN SEA

GULF OF SIAM

SOUTH CHINA SEA

GULF OF TONKIN

ANDAMAN IS. (India)

NICOBAR IS. (India)

Mandalay
Rangoon
Moulmein
Bassein
Akyab

KRUNG THEP (Bangkok)
Chiangmai
Luang Prabang
Vientiane
Hanoi
Haiphong
Hue
Tourane
Saigon
Cho Lon
Phnom Penh
Kunming

Kuala Lumpur
Penang (George Town)
Ipoh
Taiping

JOHORE
Johore Bahru
SINGAPORE
Singapore

Tropic of Cancer

Longitude 100° East of Greenwich

SOUTHEAST ASIA

LAMBERT AZIMUTHAL EQUAL-AREA PROJECTION

SCALE OF MILES

SCALE OF KILOMETRES

Capitals of Countries.............★
International Boundaries.............
Railroads.............

Copyright by C.S. HAMMOND & CO., N.Y.

JAVA

MILES
0 25 50

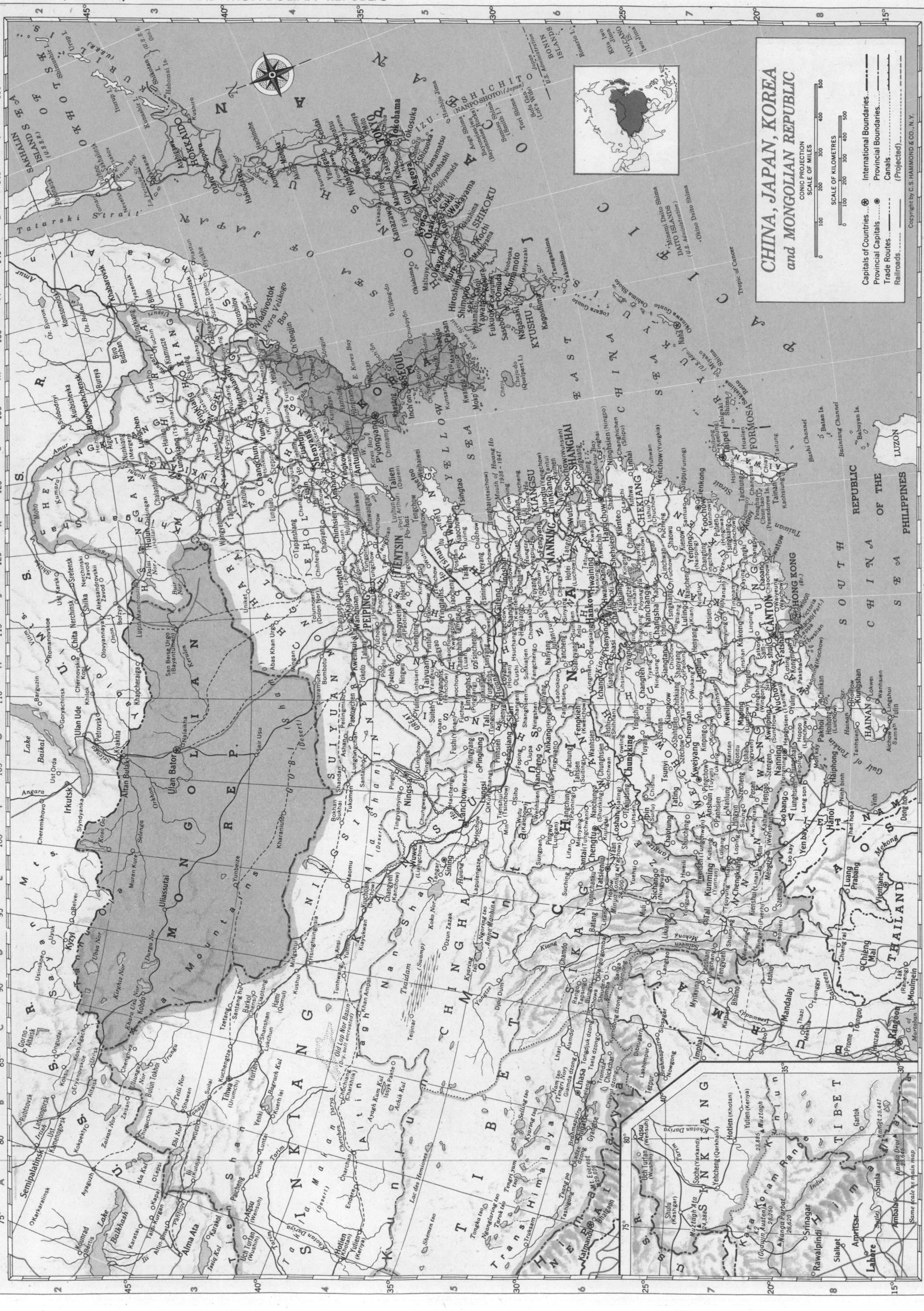

CHINA, JAPAN, KOREA and MONGOLIAN REPUBLIC

CONIC PROJECTION

SCALE OF MILES

SCALE OF KILOMETRES

Copyright by C. S. HAMMOND & CO., N.Y.

Capitals of Countries........ ⊛
Provincial Capitals........... ⊛
Trade Routes ....
Railroads ....

International Boundaries...— ·—·—
Provincial Boundaries....— · · —
Canals ....
(Projected) ....

MONGOLIAN REP.

Ulan Bator

S. S. R.

MANCHURIA

HEILUNGKIANG

SINKIANG

TIBET

CHINGHAI

SIKANG

YUNNAN

SZECHWAN

Chungking

Chengtu

PEIPING

TIENTSIN

SHANTUNG

HONAN

HUPEH

Hankow

KIANGSU

SHANGHAI

NANKING

CHEKIANG

FUKIEN

KWANGTUNG

CANTON

HONG KONG (Br.)

KWANGSI

KWEICHOW

KWEIYANG

HAINAN

FORMOSA

KOREA

SEOUL

Pyongyang

JAPAN

TOKYO

HOKKAIDO

KYUSHU

SHIKOKU

SAKHALIN ISLAND (U.S.S.R.)

SEA OF OKHOTSK

SEA OF JAPAN

YELLOW SEA

EAST CHINA SEA

SOUTH CHINA SEA

PACIFIC OCEAN

PHILIPPINES

LUZON

THAILAND

VIETNAM

LAOS

BURMA

Mandalay

Rangoon

Hanoi

Lhasa

Himalaya

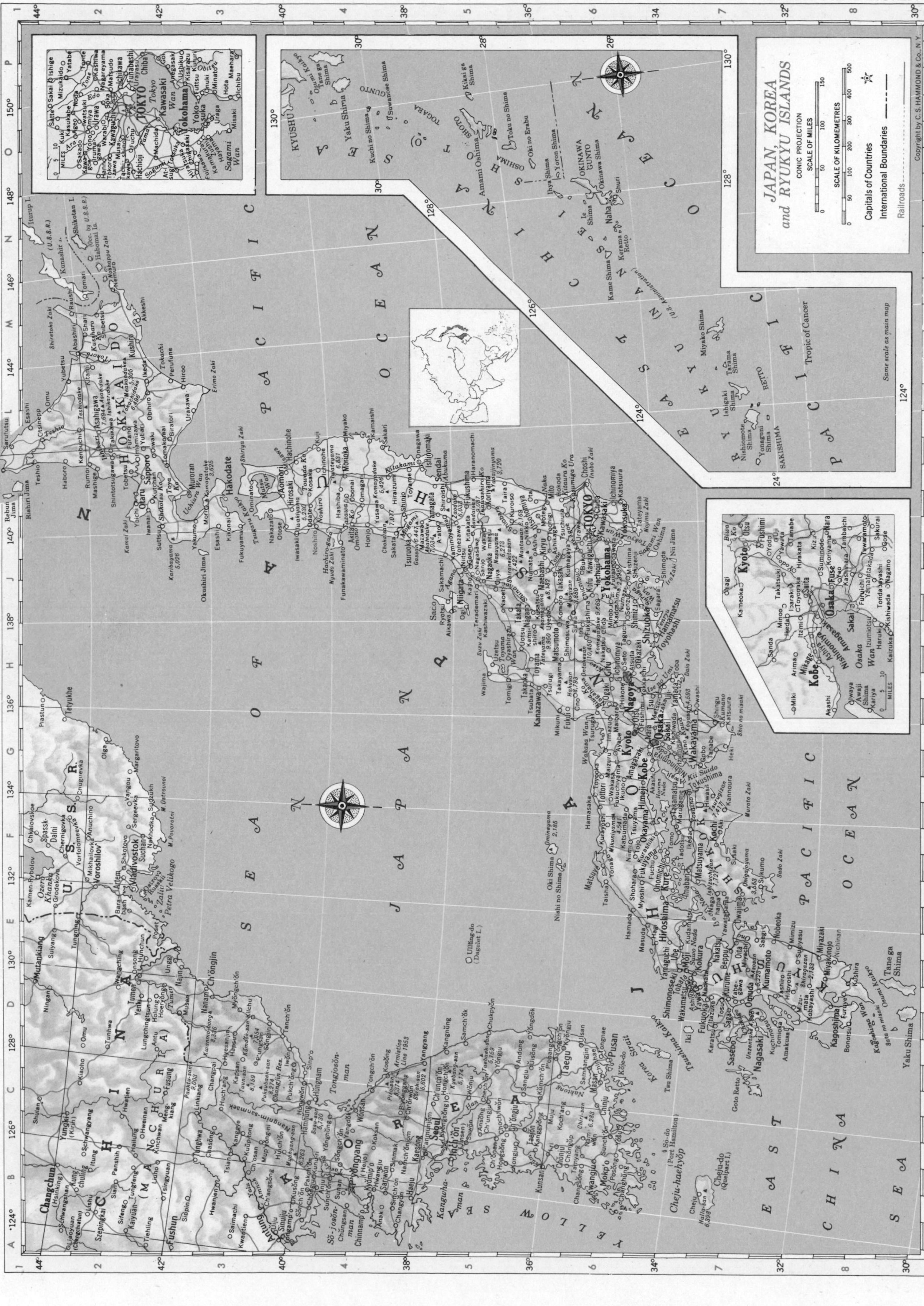

JAPAN, KOREA and RYUKYU ISLANDS

CONIC PROJECTION

SCALE OF MILES

0 50 100 150

SCALE OF KILOMETRES

0 100 200 300 400 500

Capitals of Countries
International Boundaries
Railroads

Same scale as main map

TOKYO

Yokohama

Kawasaki

Sagami Wan

KYUSHU

RYUKYU ISLANDS

OKINAWA GUNTO

Naha

Shuri

SAKISHIMA

Tropic of Cancer

KYOTO

Osaka

Kobe

Sakai

Nara

HOKKAIDO

Sapporo

Hakodate

Otaru

Muroran

Aomori

Akita

Sendai

Morioka

Yamagata

Niigata

Nagano

Nagoya

Shizuoka

Hamamatsu

Gifu

Kanazawa

Toyama

Matsumoto

Wakayama

Okayama

Hiroshima

Kure

Matsuyama

Kochi

Tokushima

Takamatsu

Yamaguchi

Shimonoseki

Kokura

Fukuoka

Nagasaki

Sasebo

Kumamoto

Oita

Beppu

Miyazaki

Kagoshima

Yaku Shima

Tane ga Shima

U. S. S. R.

Vladivostok

Voroshilov

CHINA

MANCHURIA

Changchun

Mukden

Fushun

KOREA

Seoul

Pyongyang

Pusan

Taegu

Kaesong

Inchon

Wonsan

Hamhung

Chongjin

Najin

SEA OF JAPAN

PACIFIC OCEAN

YELLOW SEA

EAST CHINA SEA

Cheju-do (Quelpart I.)

Ullung-do (Dagelet I.)

Tsushima Strait

Korea Strait

AFRICA
Northern Part
LAMBERT AZIMUTHAL EQUAL-AREA PROJECTION

SCALE OF MILES
0 100 200 400 600

SCALE OF KILOMETRES
0 100 200 400 600

⭐ Capitals of Countries
⊛ Capitals of Minor Divisions
International Boundaries
Boundaries of Colonies
Internal Boundaries
Canals — — — Wells
Railroads

NORTH ATLANTIC OCEAN

MEDITERRANEAN SEA

BLACK SEA

RED SEA

Persian Gulf

NORTH SEA

IRELAND
GREAT BRITAIN
London
FRANCE
Paris
GERMANY
Hamburg
Berlin
BELGIUM
LUX.
SWITZ.
POLAND
Warszawa
CZECHOSLOVAKIA
Praha
AUSTR.
Wien
HUNG.
Budapest
RUMANIA
Bucuresti
YUGOSLAVIA
Beograd
BULGARIA
Sofiya
ALBANIA
ITALY
Roma
Napoli
Sardegna
Sicilia
Corse
SPAIN
Madrid
Barcelona
PORTUGAL
Lisboa
ANDORRA
Is. Baleares

U. S. S. R.
Rostov
Kharkov
Kiev
Odessa
Dniepr
Sea of Azov

TURKEY
Ankara
Istanbul
Kréta
Athenai

SYRIA
Dimishq
LEBANON
Beirut
ISRAEL
Tel Aviv
JORDAN
Cyprus

IRAQ
Baghdad
Basra
Mosul
KUWAIT

IRAN
Tehran

SAUDI ARABIA
Riyadh
Dhahran
Mecca
Medina

YEMEN
ADEN PROT.
FR. SOMALILAND
Aden
Djibouti

ETHIOPIA
Addis Ababa
Gondar

ANGLO-EGYPTIAN SUDAN
Khartoum
Omdurman
KORDOFAN
DARFUR
BAHR EL GHAZAL
UPPER NILE

EGYPT
CAIRO
Alexandria
NORTHERN PROV.
Arabian Desert
Nubian Desert
Tropic of Cancer

LIBYA
Tripoli
Benghazi
Cyrenaica
Tripolitania
Fezzan

FRENCH EQUATORIAL AFRICA
TCHAD
OUBANGUI-CHARI

FRENCH WEST AFRICA
NIGER
SAHARA
TERR. DU SUD
Tombouctou
Gao

ALGERIA
Alger
Oran
Constantine

TUNISIA
Tunis

MOROCCO
Rabat
Casablanca
Marrakech
Fès

SPANISH MOROCCO
IFNI (Sp.)
SPANISH WEST AFRICA
RIO DE ORO

ISLAS CANARIAS (Sp.)
Madeira (Port.)
Azores (Port.)

NIGERIA
NORTHERN PROVINCES
Kano
Sokoto
Lagos

GOLD COAST
ASHANTI (GHANA)
TOGO
DAHOMEY
IVORY COAST
FRENCH GUINEA
PORT. GUINEA
GAMBIA
Bathurst
Dakar
St. Louis
SENEGAL
SIERRA LEONE
Freetown
LIBERIA
Monrovia

NORTHERN SOMALILAND
Tropic of Cancer

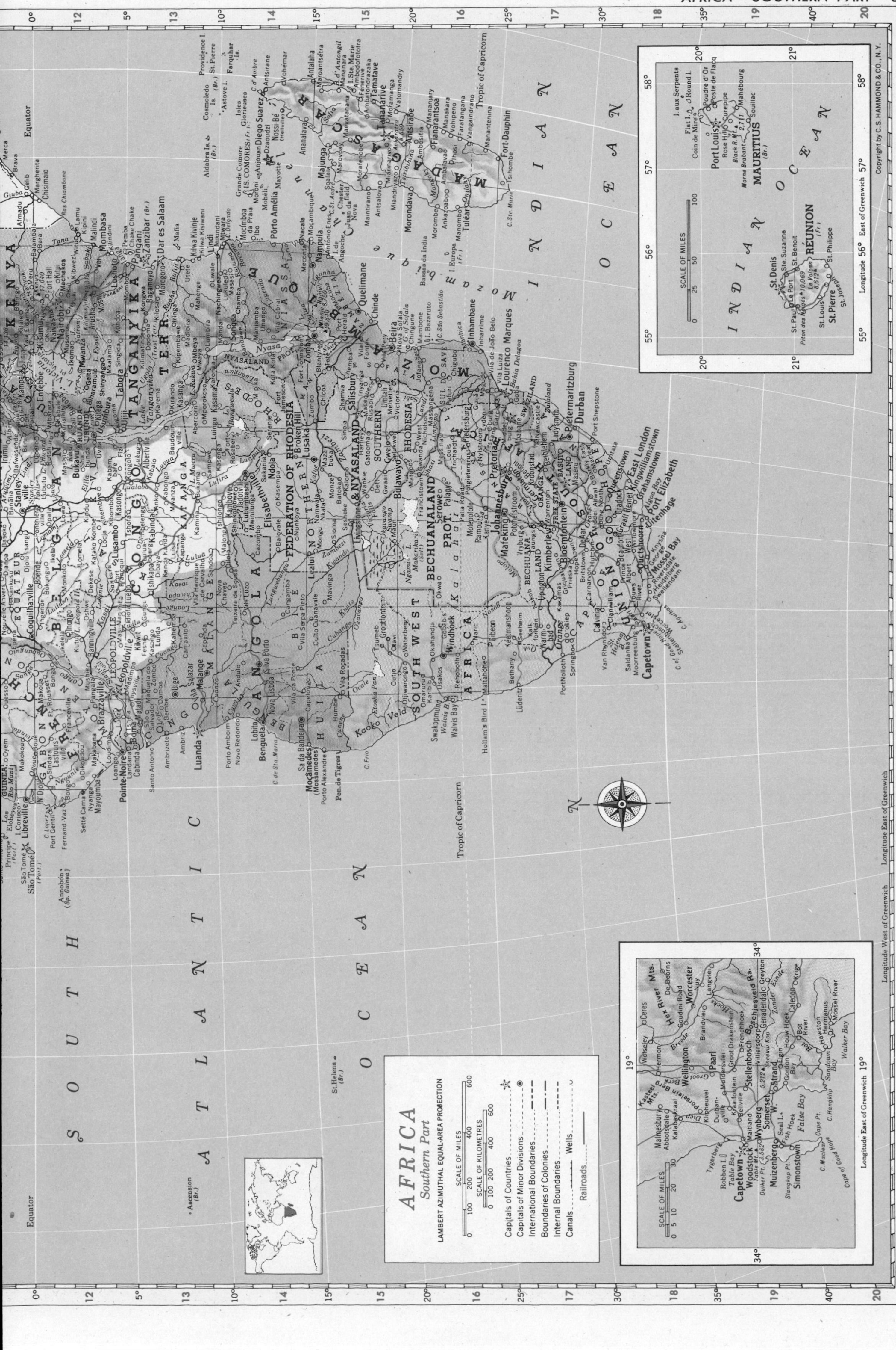

U 7642

AFRICA
Southern Part
LAMBERT AZIMUTHAL EQUAL-AREA PROJECTION

SCALE OF MILES
0   100   200   400   600

SCALE OF KILOMETRES
0   100 200   400   600

Capitals of Countries .... ✴
Capitals of Minor Divisions ...... ◉
International Boundaries .... ___
Boundaries of Colonies .... _·_·_
Internal Boundaries .... _··_··_
Canals .... Wells .... �
Railroads .... ▬▬▬

Copyright by C. S. HAMMOND & CO., N.Y.

MAURITIUS (Br.)
Port Louis
SCALE OF MILES
0   25   50   100

RÉUNION (Fr.)
St. Denis
Le Volcan 10,069
St. Pierre
St. Joseph

INDIAN OCEAN

KENYA
TANGANYIKA TERR.
BELGIAN CONGO
ANGOLA
NORTHERN RHODESIA
FEDERATION OF RHODESIA & NYASALAND
SOUTHERN RHODESIA
BECHUANALAND PROT.
SOUTH WEST AFRICA
UNION OF SOUTH AFRICA
MADAGASCAR
MOZAMBIQUE

Nairobi
Mombasa
Zanzibar
Dar es Salaam
Lourenço Marques
Salisbury
Bulawayo
Lusaka
Broken Hill
Elisabethville
Leopoldville
Brazzaville
Luanda
Benguela
Windhoek
Walvis Bay
Johannesburg
Pretoria
Bloemfontein
Kimberley
Durban
Pietermaritzburg
East London
Port Elizabeth
Capetown
Antananarive

Equator
Tropic of Capricorn

SOUTH ATLANTIC OCEAN

St. Helena (Br.)
Ascension (Br.)

SCALE OF MILES
0 5 10   20

Capetown
Worcester
Paarl
Stellenbosch
Wellington
Simonstown
Cape of Good Hope
Table Bay
False Bay

Hex River Mts.

Longitude East of Greenwich
Longitude West of Greenwich

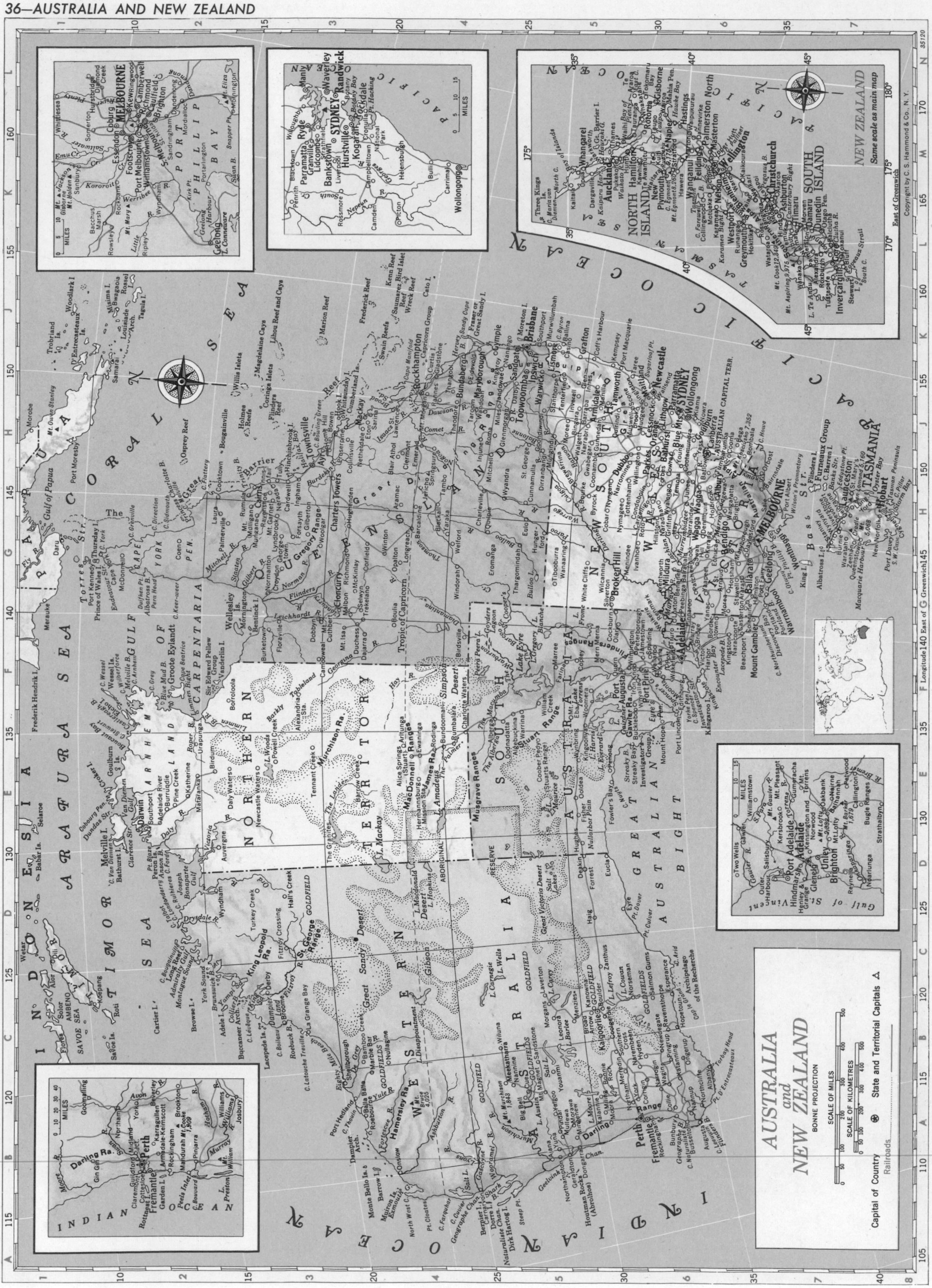

AUSTRALIA and NEW ZEALAND

BONNE PROJECTION

SCALE OF MILES

SCALE OF KILOMETRES

Capital of Country ⊕ State and Territorial Capitals ▲

Railroads

NEW ZEALAND
Same scale as main map

NORTH ISLAND

SOUTH ISLAND

Wellington
Auckland
Christchurch
Dunedin
Invercargill

PACIFIC OCEAN

TASMAN SEA

CORAL SEA

ARAFURA SEA

TIMOR SEA

INDONESIA

NEW GUINEA

PAPUA

Gulf of Papua

GULF OF CARPENTARIA

ARNHEM LAND

NORTHERN TERRITORY

QUEENSLAND

NEW SOUTH WALES

VICTORIA

SOUTH AUSTRALIA

WESTERN AUSTRALIA

TASMANIA

Great Dividing Range

Tropic of Capricorn

INDIAN OCEAN

GREAT AUSTRALIAN BIGHT

Darwin
Brisbane
SYDNEY
MELBOURNE
Adelaide
Perth
Hobart
Canberra

MELBOURNE

PORT PHILLIP BAY

SYDNEY

Wollongong

PACIFIC OCEAN

INDIAN OCEAN

Perth

Gulf of St Vincent

ADELAIDE

F Longitude 140 East of G Greenwich 145

Copyright by C. S. Hammond & Co., N.Y.

PACIFIC OCEAN

LAMBERT AZIMUTHAL EQUAL-AREA PROJECTION

Copyright by C. S. HAMMOND & Co., N.Y.

NAUTICAL MILES

STATUTE MILES

KILOMETRES

National and Dominion Capitals	⊛
Capitals of Colonies, Dependencies and Australian States and Territories	★
Administrative Centers	⊚
International Boundaries	
Internal Boundaries	
Railroads	
Distances Between Points	5444 (nautical miles)

NORTH AMERICA

UNITED STATES

MEXICO

Equator

Tropic of Cancer

Tropic of Capricorn

International Date Line

HAWAIIAN ISLANDS

TERRITORY OF HAWAII

Honolulu

POLYNESIA

MICRONESIA

MELANESIA

MARSHALL ISLANDS

CAROLINE ISLANDS

TERRITORY OF THE PACIFIC ISLANDS

GILBERT & ELLICE ISLANDS

PHOENIX IS.

LINE ISLANDS

MARQUESAS IS.

TUAMOTU ARCH.

SOCIETY IS.

FRENCH OCEANIA

AUSTRAL IS.

COOK ISLANDS

TONGA

FIJI ISLANDS

SAMOA

SOLOMON ISLANDS

NEW HEBRIDES

NEW CALEDONIA

SANTA CRUZ IS.

TERR. OF NEW GUINEA

NETH. NEW GUINEA

PHILIPPINE SEA

CHINA

JAPAN

Tokyo

SEA OF JAPAN

YELLOW SEA

EAST CHINA SEA

SOUTH CHINA SEA

REPUBLIC OF THE PHILIPPINES

VOLCANO ISLANDS

MARIANA ISLANDS

PALAU IS.

BONIN IS.

DAITO ISLANDS

INDONESIA

BORNEO

CELEBES SEA

FLORES SEA

BANDA SEA

ARAFURA SEA

TIMOR SEA

CORAL SEA

TASMAN SEA

AUSTRALIA

WESTERN AUSTRALIA

NORTHERN TERRITORY

QUEENSLAND

SOUTH AUSTRALIA

NEW SOUTH WALES

VICTORIA

TASMANIA

Sydney

Melbourne

Brisbane

NEW ZEALAND

NORTH ISLAND

SOUTH ISLAND

Wellington

Auckland

Christchurch

INDIAN OCEAN

San Francisco

Los Angeles

San Diego

Chatham Is.

Easter I.

Sala y Gomez I.

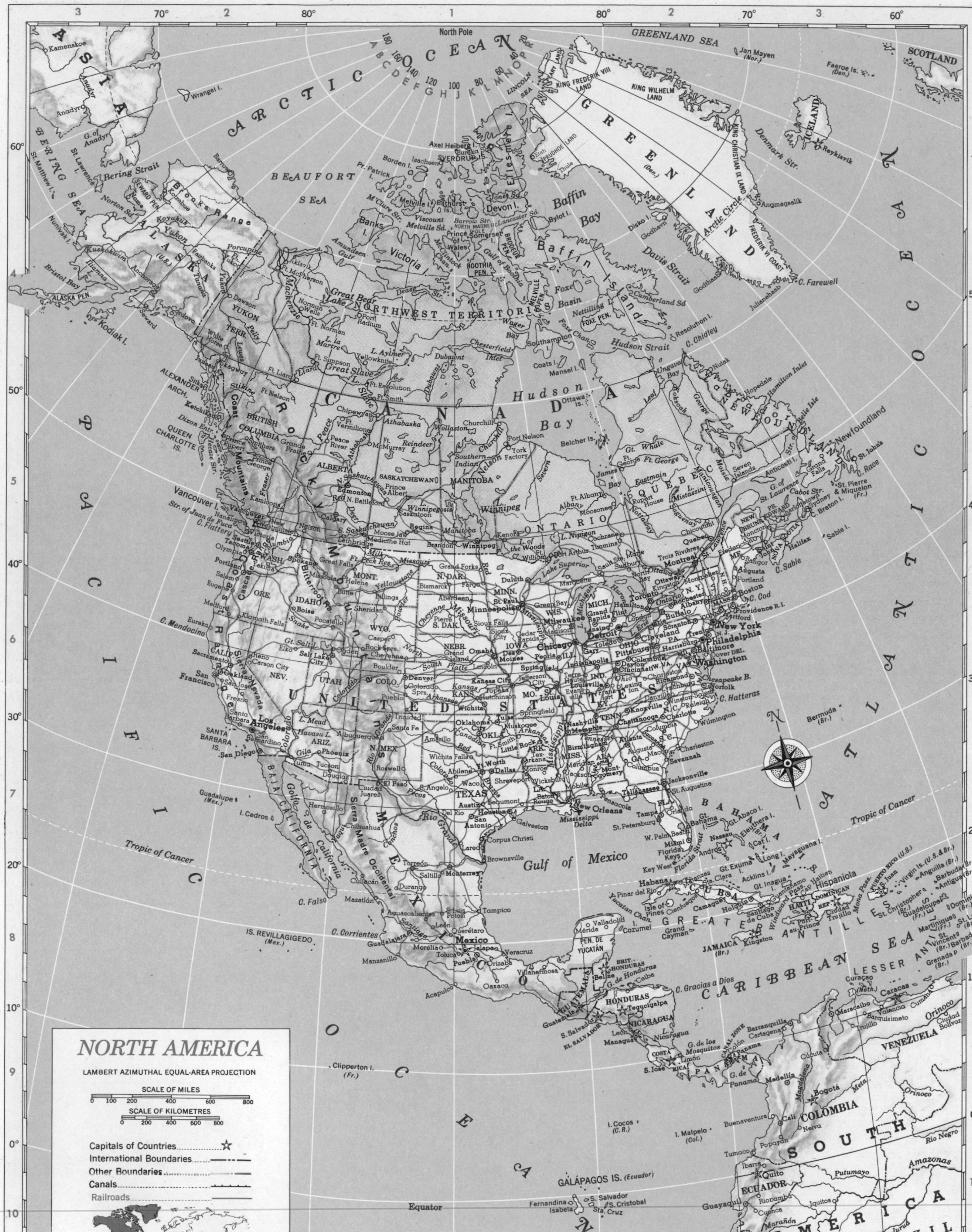

NORTH AMERICA

LAMBERT AZIMUTHAL EQUAL-AREA PROJECTION

SCALE OF MILES
0 100 200 400 600 800

SCALE OF KILOMETRES
0 200 400 600

Capitals of Countries .... ☆
International Boundaries ....
Other Boundaries ....
Canals ....
Railroads ....

Copyright by C.S. HAMMOND & Co., N.Y.

ARCTIC OCEAN

GREENLAND SEA

GREENLAND (Den.)

BEAUFORT SEA

ALASKA (U.S.)

CANADA

NORTHWEST TERRITORIES

YUKON TERR.

BRITISH COLUMBIA

ALBERTA

SASKATCHEWAN

MANITOBA

ONTARIO

QUEBEC

Baffin Island

Baffin Bay

Hudson Bay

Hudson Strait

UNITED STATES

WASH.
ORE.
IDAHO
MONT.
N. DAK.
S. DAK.
WYO.
NEBR.
NEV.
UTAH
COLO.
KANS.
OKLA.
CALIF.
ARIZ.
N. MEX.
TEXAS
MINN.
IOWA
MO.
ARK.
LA.
WIS.
MICH.
ILL.
IND.
OHIO
KY.
TENN.
MISS.
ALA.
GA.
FLA.
S.C.
N.C.
VA.
W. VA.
PA.
N.Y.
MD.

MEXICO

Gulf of Mexico

PACIFIC OCEAN

ATLANTIC OCEAN

CARIBBEAN SEA

GREATER ANTILLES

LESSER ANTILLES

BAHAMA IS.

CUBA

HAITI

DOMINICAN REP.

JAMAICA (Br.)

GUATEMALA
BRIT. HONDURAS
HONDURAS
EL SALVADOR
NICARAGUA
COSTA RICA
PANAMA

VENEZUELA

COLOMBIA

ECUADOR

PERU

BRAZIL

SOUTH AMERICA

Tropic of Cancer

Equator

GALÁPAGOS IS. (Ecuador)

Longitude West of Greenwich

North Pole

Tropic of Cancer

ASIA

BERING SEA

Bering Strait

ICELAND

SCOTLAND

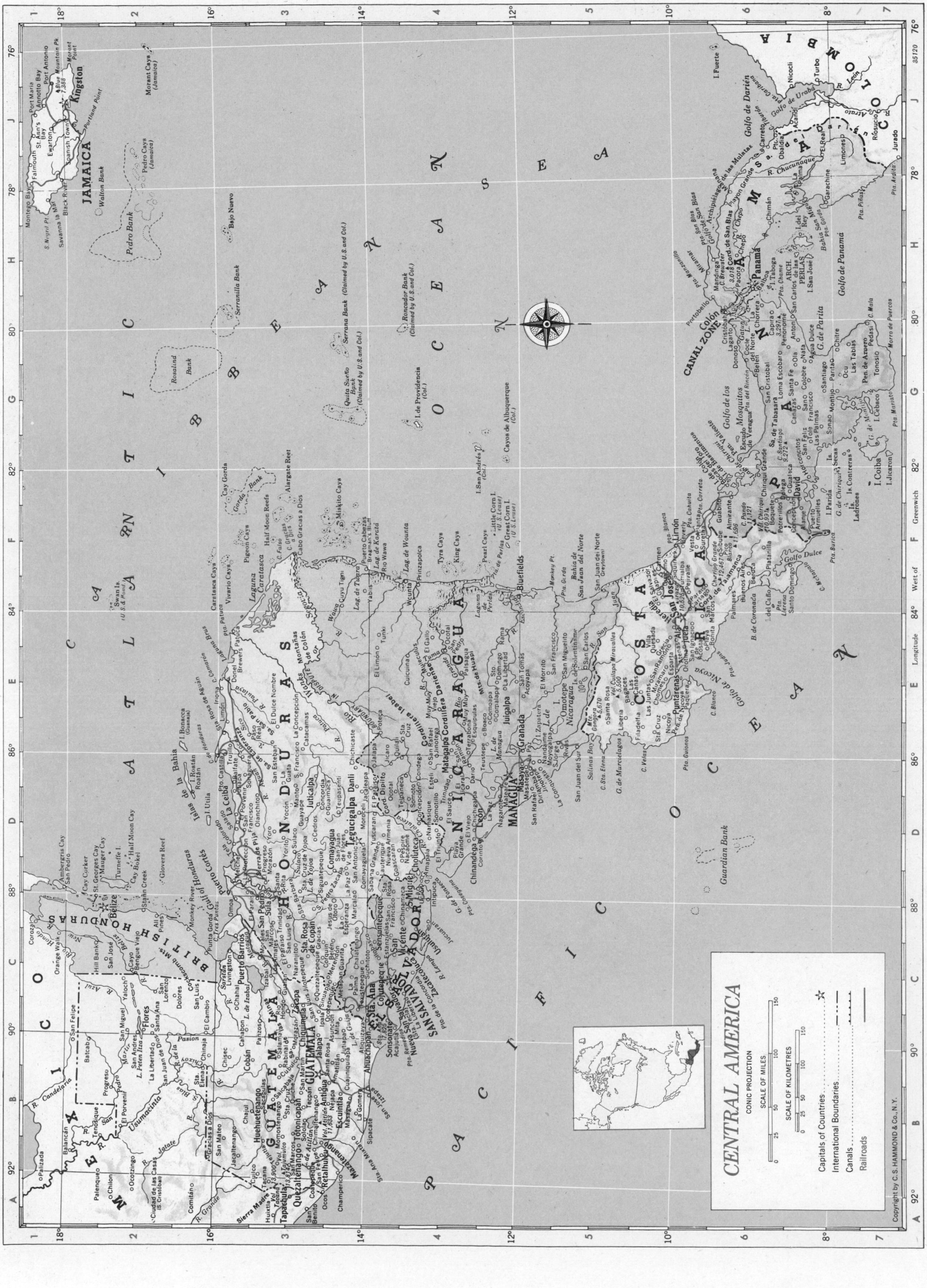

JAMAICA

MEXICO

BRITISH HONDURAS

GUATEMALA

EL SALVADOR

HONDURAS

NICARAGUA

COSTA RICA

PANAMA

COLOMBIA

CARIBBEAN SEA

ATLANTIC OCEAN

PACIFIC OCEAN

CANAL ZONE

Golfo de Panamá

Golfo de Darién

Golfo de Urabá

Golfo Dulce

Golfo de los Mosquitos

Gulf of Honduras

Kingston

Belize

Guatemala

San Salvador

Tegucigalpa

Managua

San José

Panamá

Colón

Islas de la Bahía

I. Roatán

I. Providencia (Col.)

I. San Andrés (Col.)

Cayos de Albuquerque (Col.)

Pedro Bank

Serranilla Bank

Serrana Bank (Claimed by U.S. and Col.)

Roncador Bank (Claimed by U.S. and Col.)

Quita Sueño Bank (Claimed by U.S. and Col.)

Rosalind Bank

Miskito Cays

Little Corn I. (U.S. Lease)

Great Corn I. (U.S. Lease)

Golfo de Nicoya

Lago de Nicaragua

Lago de Managua

CENTRAL AMERICA
CONIC PROJECTION

SCALE OF MILES

SCALE OF KILOMETRES

Capitals of Countries .... ⋆

International Boundaries .... ·—··—··

Canals ....

Railroads ....

Copyright by C. S. HAMMOND & Co., N.Y.

WESTERN CANADA

Copyright by C.S. HAMMOND & Co., N.Y.

SCALE OF MILES
0   50   100   200
SCALE OF KILOMETRES
0   50   100   200

Provincial and
Territorial Capitals .... ⊛
International Boundaries ....
Boundaries of Provinces ....
Railroads ....

NORTHWEST TERRITORIES

MACKENZIE DISTRICT

KEEWATIN DISTRICT

YUKON TERRITORY

BRITISH COLUMBIA

ALBERTA

SASKATCHEWAN

MANITOBA

ONTARIO

ALASKA

NORTH DAKOTA

SOUTH DAKOTA

MINNESOTA

MONTANA

IDAHO

WASHINGTON

HUDSON BAY

PACIFIC OCEAN

ALEXANDER ARCH.

WOOD BUFFALO NATIONAL PARK

Edmonton

Calgary

Regina

Winnipeg

Vancouver

Victoria

Duluth

115° Longitude West H of Greenwich 110°

EASTERN CANADA

CONIC PROJECTION

SCALE OF MILES

SCALE OF KILOMETRES

Capital of Canada ....
Capitals of Provinces ....
International Boundaries ....
Boundaries of Provinces ....
Canals ....
Railroads ....

ATLANTIC OCEAN

HUDSON BAY

JAMES BAY

UNGAVA BAY

Hudson Strait

NEWFOUNDLAND

QUEBEC

ONTARIO

NEW BRUNSWICK

NOVA SCOTIA

PRINCE EDWARD I.

Gulf of St. Lawrence

MANITOBA

MINN.

WISCONSIN

MICHIGAN

UNITED STATES

MASS.

N.H.

VT.

N.Y.

MAINE

Lake Superior

Lake Michigan

Lake Huron

Lake Erie

Lake Ontario

MONTREAL

Quebec

TORONTO

Ottawa

Halifax

St. Johns

DETROIT

CHICAGO

BOSTON

CLEVELAND

4521

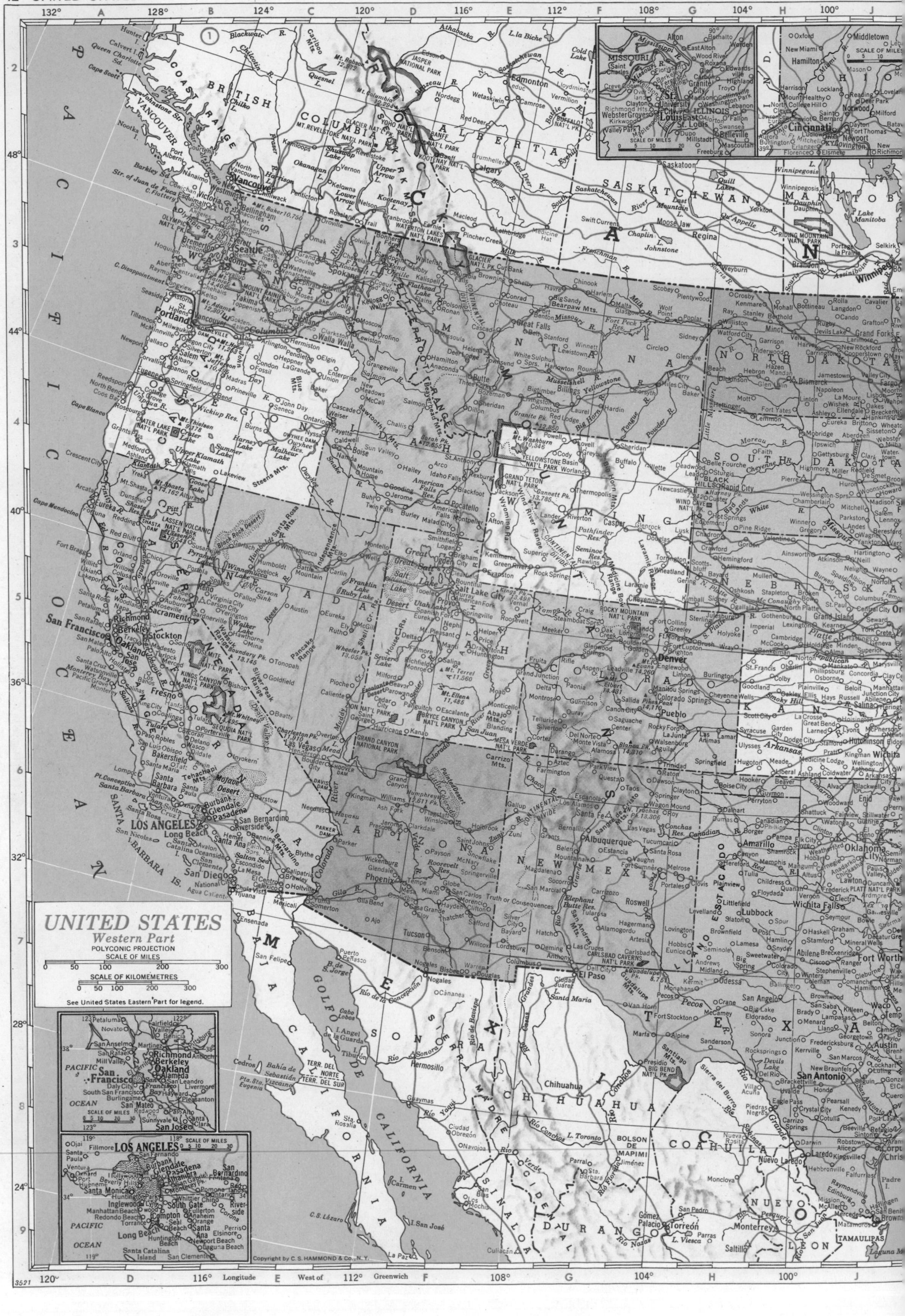

UNITED STATES
Western Part
POLYCONIC PROJECTION
SCALE OF MILES
0   50   100   200   300

SCALE OF KILOMETRES
0   50   100   200   300

See United States Eastern Part for legend.

MISSOURI

OHIO

PACIFIC OCEAN

San Francisco

Los Angeles

Copyright by C. S. HAMMOND & Co., N. Y.

3521

120°   116°   Longitude   E   West of   112°   Greenwich   F   108°   G   104°   H   100°   J

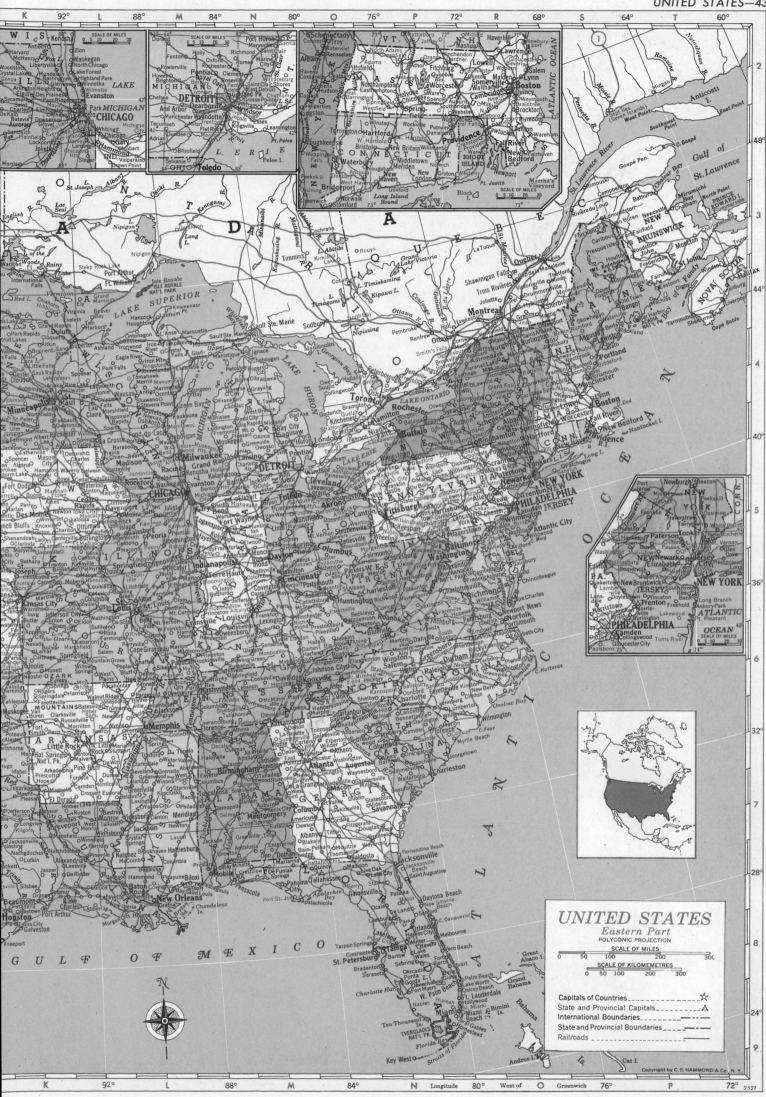

UNITED STATES
Eastern Part
POLYCONIC PROJECTION
SCALE OF MILES
SCALE OF KILOMEMETRES

Capitals of Countries
State and Provincial Capitals
International Boundaries
State and Provincial Boundaries
Railroads

Copyright by C. S. HAMMOND & Co., N.Y.

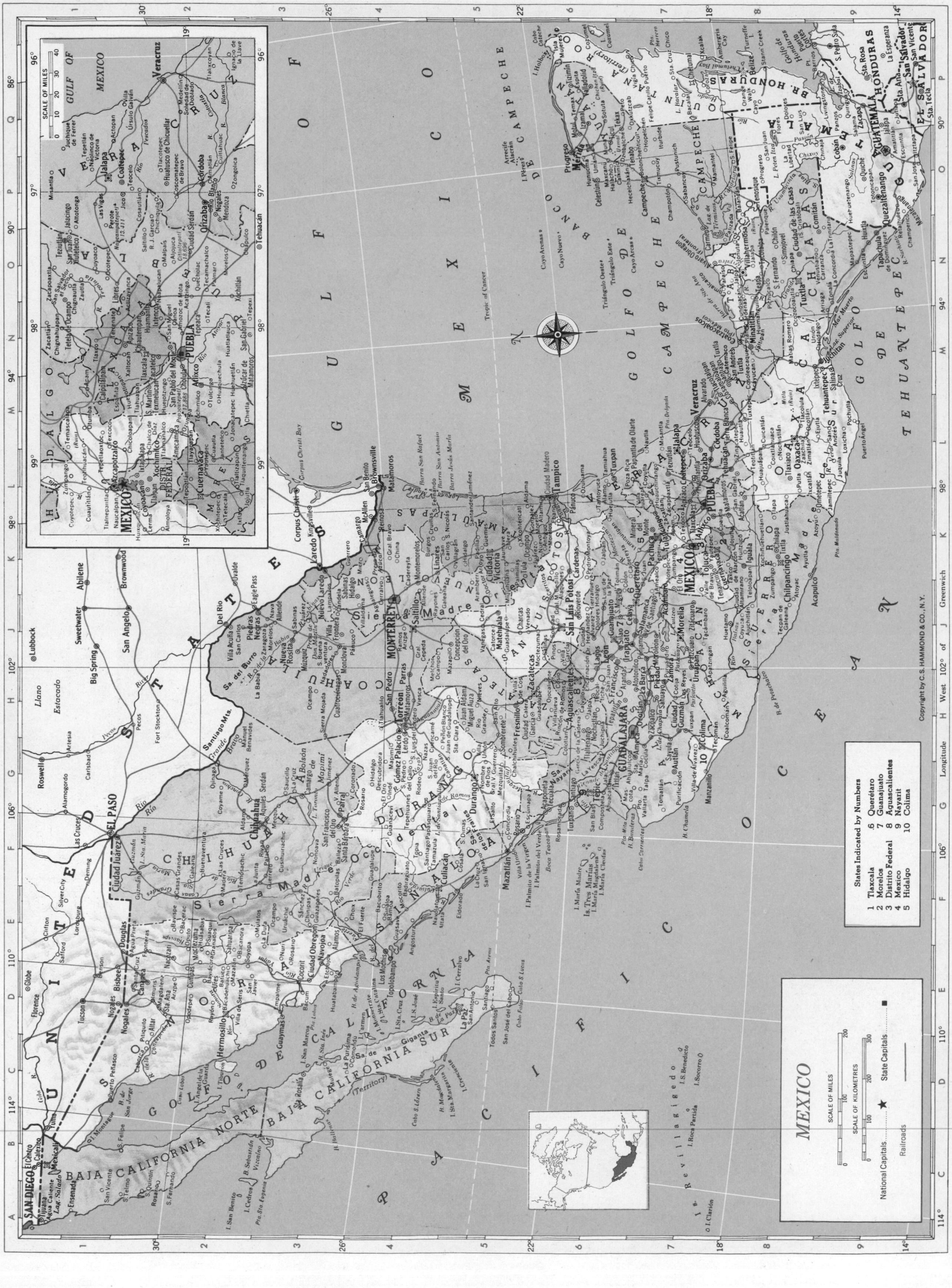

MEXICO

SCALE OF MILES

SCALE OF KILOMETRES

National Capitals ★
State Capitals ☆
Railroads ....

States Indicated by Numbers

1 Tlaxcala
2 Morelos
3 Distrito Federal
4 Mexico
5 Hidalgo
6 Querétaro
7 Guanajuato
8 Aguascalientes
9 Nayarit
10 Colima

Inset: Veracruz region

SCALE OF MILES

GULF OF MEXICO

VERA CRUZ
TLAXCALA
PUEBLA
HIDALGO
DISTRITO FEDERAL
MEXICO
MORELOS

Veracruz
Jalapa
Orizaba
Córdoba
Puebla
México
Cuernavaca

Copyright by C.S. HAMMOND & CO., N.Y.

West 102° of Greenwich

GULF OF MEXICO

GOLFO DE CAMPECHE

PACIFIC OCEAN

GOLFO DE TEHUANTEPEC

GULF OF CALIFORNIA

BAJA CALIFORNIA NORTE

BAJA CALIFORNIA SUR (Territory)

SONORA
CHIHUAHUA
COAHUILA
NUEVO LEON
TAMAULIPAS
DURANGO
SINALOA
ZACATECAS
SAN LUIS POTOSI
JALISCO
MICHOACAN
GUERRERO
OAXACA
VERACRUZ
CHIAPAS
TABASCO
CAMPECHE
YUCATAN
QUINTANA ROO (Territory)

UNITED STATES

GUATEMALA
BR. HONDURAS
HONDURAS
EL SALVADOR

Revillagigedo

Tropic of Cancer

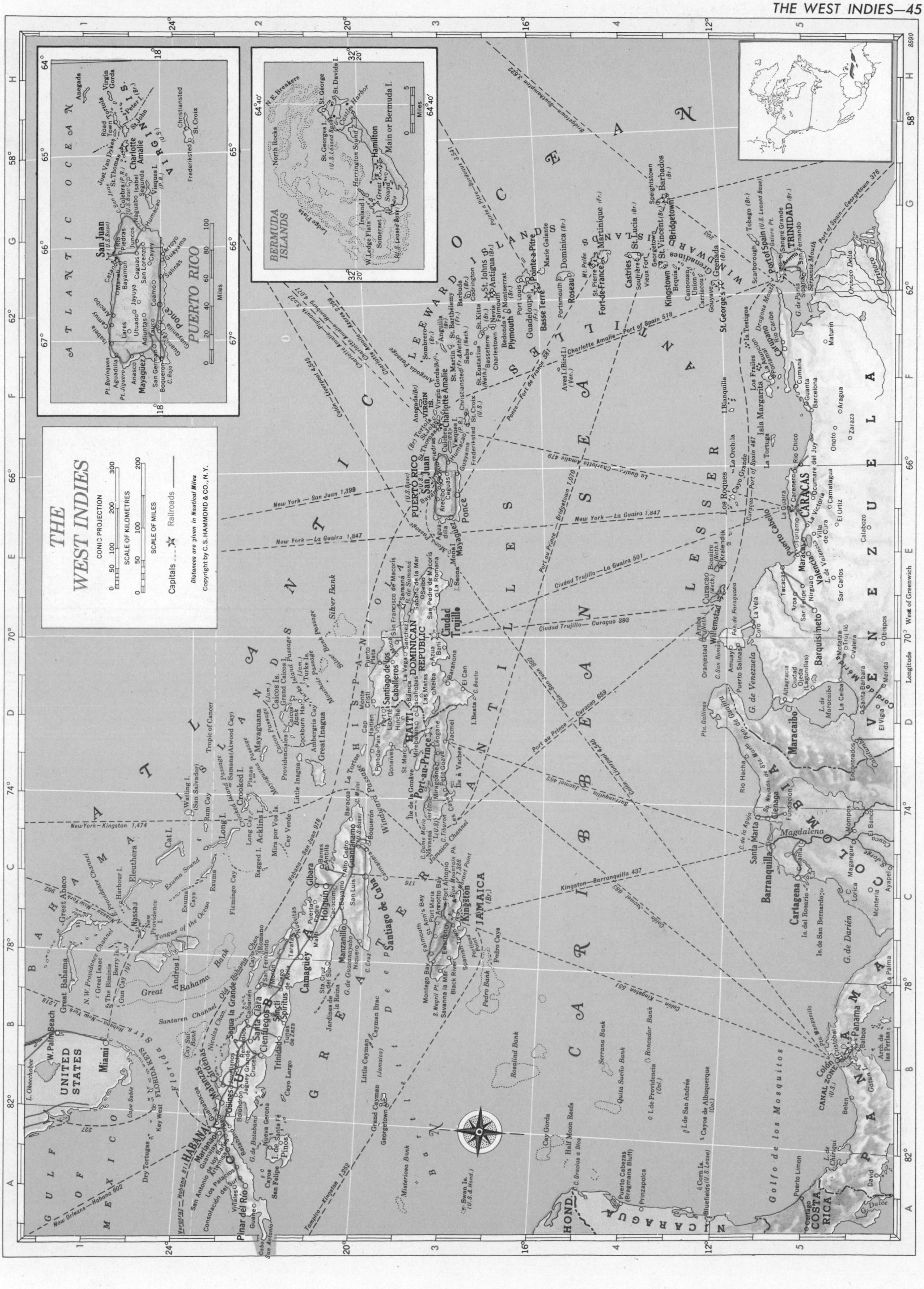

THE WEST INDIES

CONIC PROJECTION

SCALE OF KILOMETRES
0   50   100   200   300

SCALE OF MILES
0   50   100   200

Capitals ....★........ Railroads ....

Distances are given in Nautical Miles

Copyright by C. S. HAMMOND & CO., N. Y.

PUERTO RICO

San Juan (U.S.Base)

Mayagüez
Ponce

VIRGIN ISLANDS

BERMUDA ISLANDS

St. George
Hamilton

ATLANTIC OCEAN

CARIBBEAN SEA

GULF OF MEXICO

UNITED STATES

B A H A M A   I S L A N D S

Tropic of Cancer

GREATER ANTILLES

LESSER ANTILLES

LEEWARD ISLANDS

WINDWARD ISLANDS

CUBA
HABANA
Santiago de Cuba
Camagüey
Holguín
Cienfuegos

JAMAICA (Br.)
Kingston

HAITI
Port-au-Prince

DOMINICAN REPUBLIC
Ciudad Trujillo

PUERTO RICO (U.S.Base)
San Juan
Ponce

Guadeloupe (Fr.)
Martinique (Fr.)
St. Lucia (Br.)
Barbados (Br.)
Bridgetown
St. Vincent (Br.)
Grenada (Br.)
St. George's
TRINIDAD (Br.)
Port of Spain
Tobago (Br.)

VENEZUELA
CARACAS
Maracaibo
Valencia
Barquisimeto
Barcelona
Cumaná
Maturín

COLOMBIA
Barranquilla
Cartagena
Santa Marta

PANAMA
CANAL ZONE (U.S.)
Colón
Panamá
Balboa

COSTA RICA
NICARAGUA
HONDURAS

New York—San Juan 1,399
New York—La Guaira 1,847
New York—Kingston 1,474
Kingston—Barranquilla 437

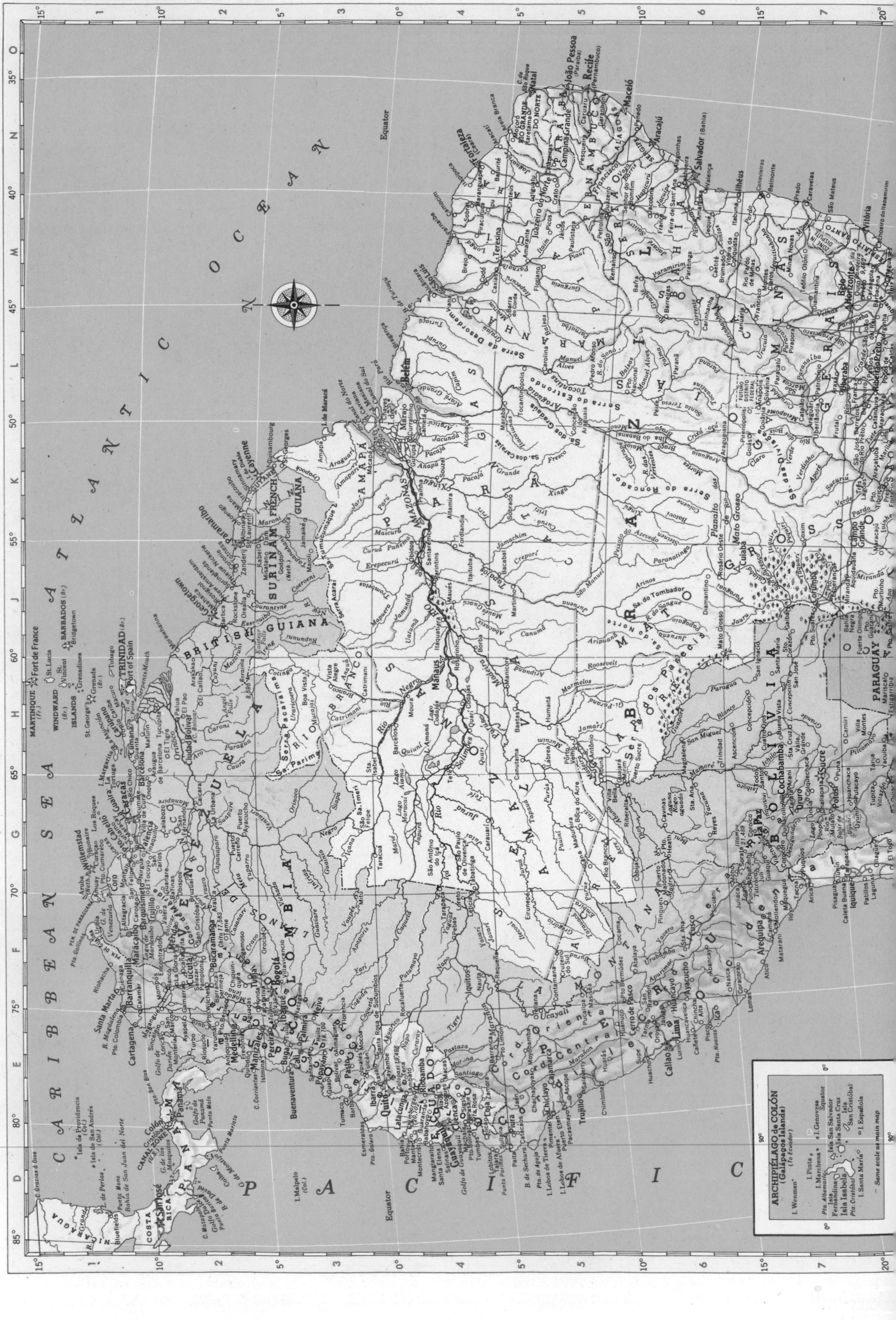

ATLANTIC OCEAN

PACIFIC OCEAN

CARIBBEAN SEA

Equator

VENEZUELA

COLOMBIA

ECUADOR

BRITISH GUIANA

SURINAM (Neth.)

FRENCH GUIANA

BRASIL

BOLIVIA

PERU

PARAGUAY

PANAMA

COSTA RICA

NICARAGUA

MARTINIQUE (Fr.)
WINDWARD ISLANDS (Br.)
BARBADOS (Br.)
TRINIDAD (Br.)

MATO GROSSO

MINAS GERAES

BAHIA

PERNAMBUCO

MARANHÃO

PARÁ

AMAZONAS

AMAPÁ

Bogotá
Medellín
Cali
Quito
Guayaquil
Lima
Callao
Caracas
Maracaibo
Barranquilla
Cartagena
Georgetown
Paramaribo
Cayenne
Belém
Manaus
Recife
Salvador (Bahia)
Natal
João Pessoa
Maceió
Fortaleza
Teresina
São Luiz
Cuiabá
Corumbá
La Paz
Sucre
Potosí
Cochabamba
Oruro

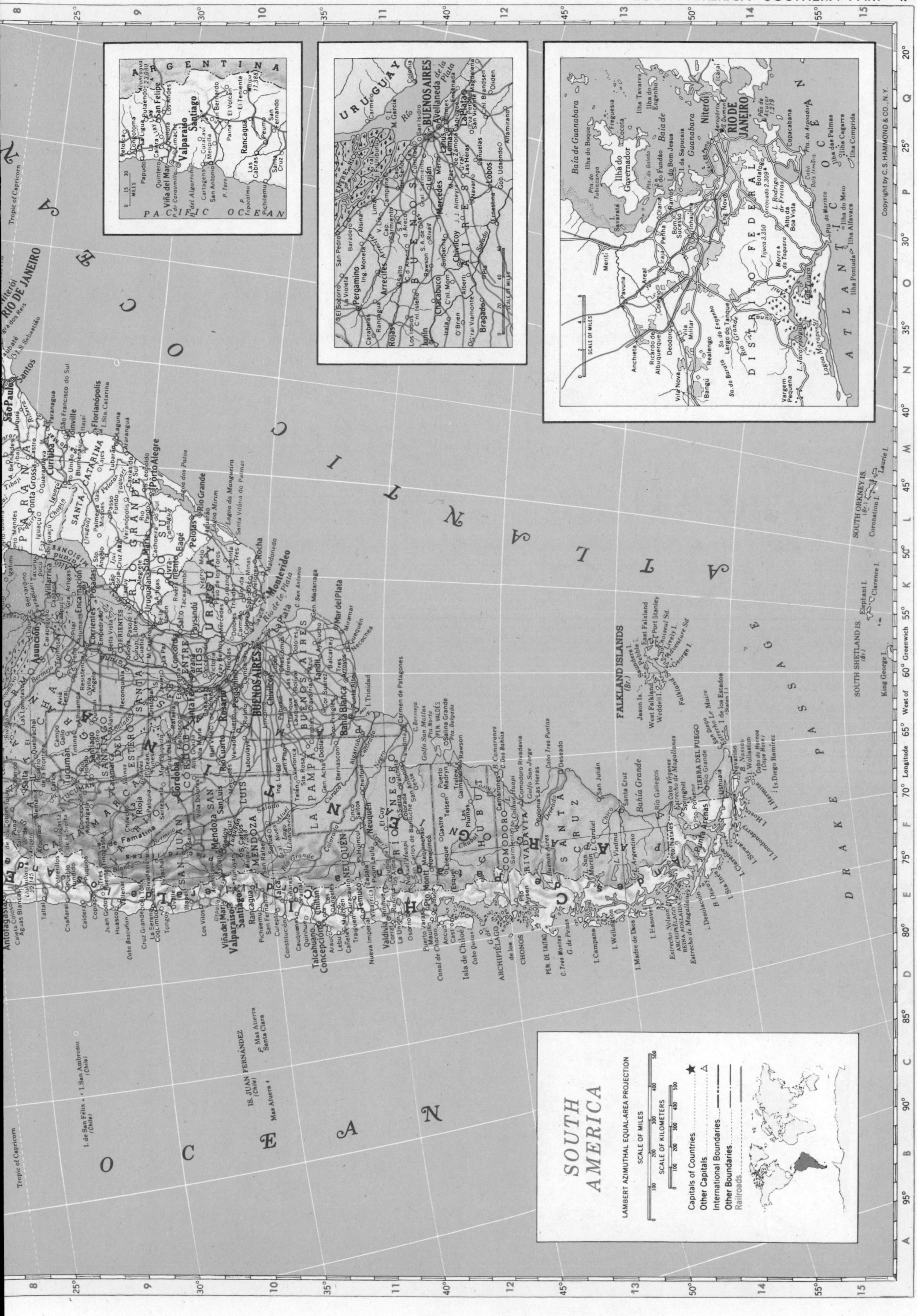

SOUTH AMERICA

LAMBERT AZIMUTHAL EQUAL-AREA PROJECTION

SCALE OF MILES
SCALE OF KILOMETERS

Capitals of Countries ....★
Other Capitals ....◬
International Boundaries ....
Other Boundaries ....
Railroads ....

ARGENTINA

URUGUAY

BUENOS AIRES

DISTRITO FEDERAL
RIO DE JANEIRO

ATLANTIC OCEAN

PACIFIC OCEAN

DRAKE PASSAGE

FALKLAND ISLANDS

SOUTH SHETLAND IS.

SOUTH ORKNEY IS.

TIERRA DEL FUEGO

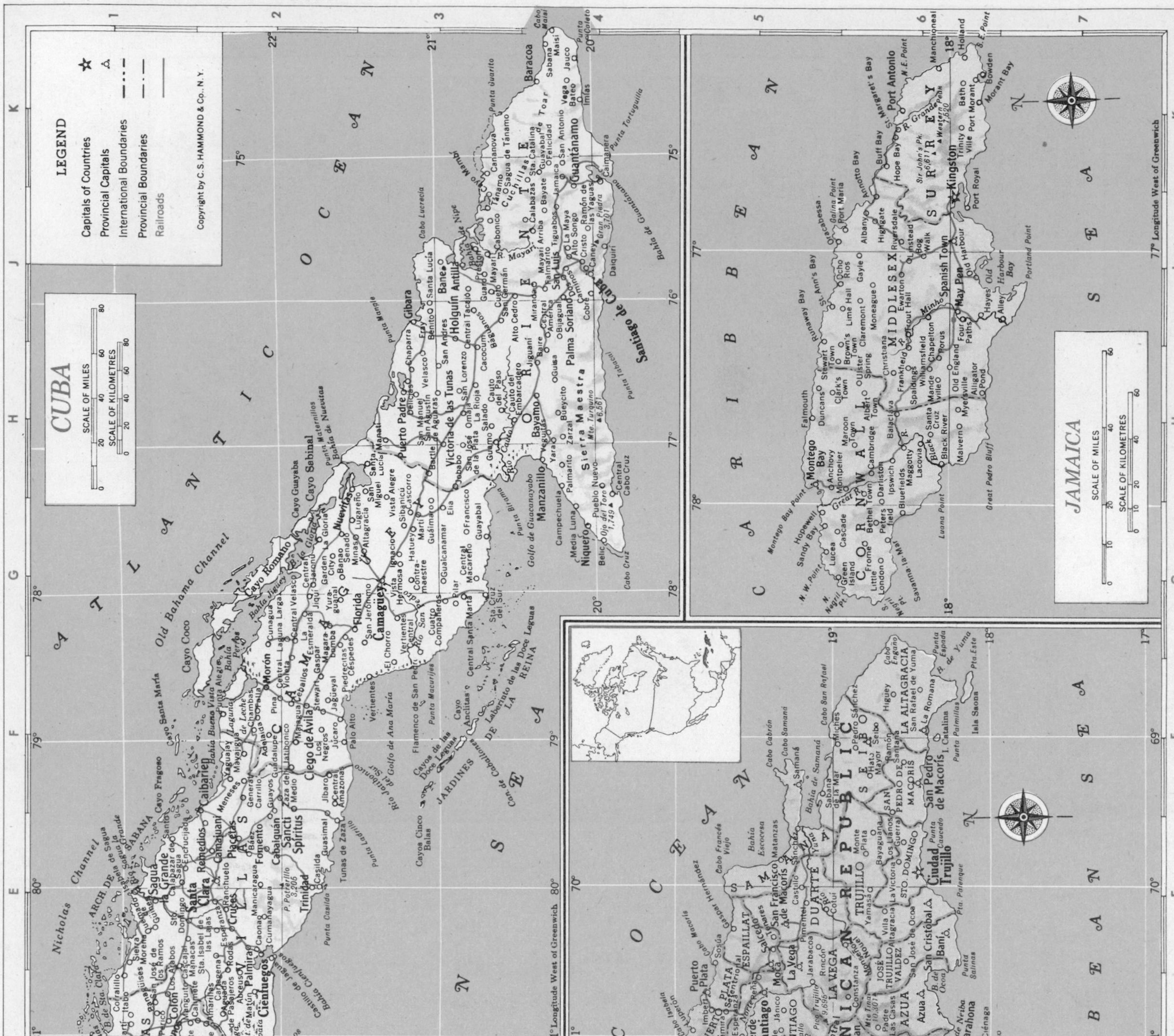

LEGEND

☆	Capitals of Countries
▲	Provincial Capitals
·–··–··	International Boundaries
·–·–·–	Provincial Boundaries
———	Railroads

Copyright by C. S. HAMMOND & Co., N.Y.

CUBA

SCALE OF MILES
SCALE OF KILOMETRES

JAMAICA

SCALE OF MILES
SCALE OF KILOMETRES

HISPANIOLA

SCALE OF MILES
SCALE OF KILOMETRES

ATLANTIC OCEAN

CARIBBEAN SEA

GULF OF MEXICO

Nicholas Channel

Old Bahama Channel

Windward Passage

Isla de Pinos (LA HABANA)

LA HABANA

Matanzas

Santa Clara

Cienfuegos

Camaguey

Santiago de Cuba

Sierra Maestra

Bayamo

Guantánamo

Holguín

Gibara

Puerto Padre

Victoria de las Tunas

Manzanillo

DOMINICAN REPUBLIC

SANTIAGO

STO. DOMINGO

Ciudad Trujillo

Puerto Plata

La Vega

San Pedro de Macorís

Barahona

Azua

HAITI

Port-au-Prince

Cap-Haïtien

Gonaïves

Les Cayes

Jérémie

Île de la Gonâve

Île de la Tortue

JAMAICA

Kingston

Spanish Town

Montego Bay

Port Antonio

CORNWALL

MIDDLESEX

SURREY

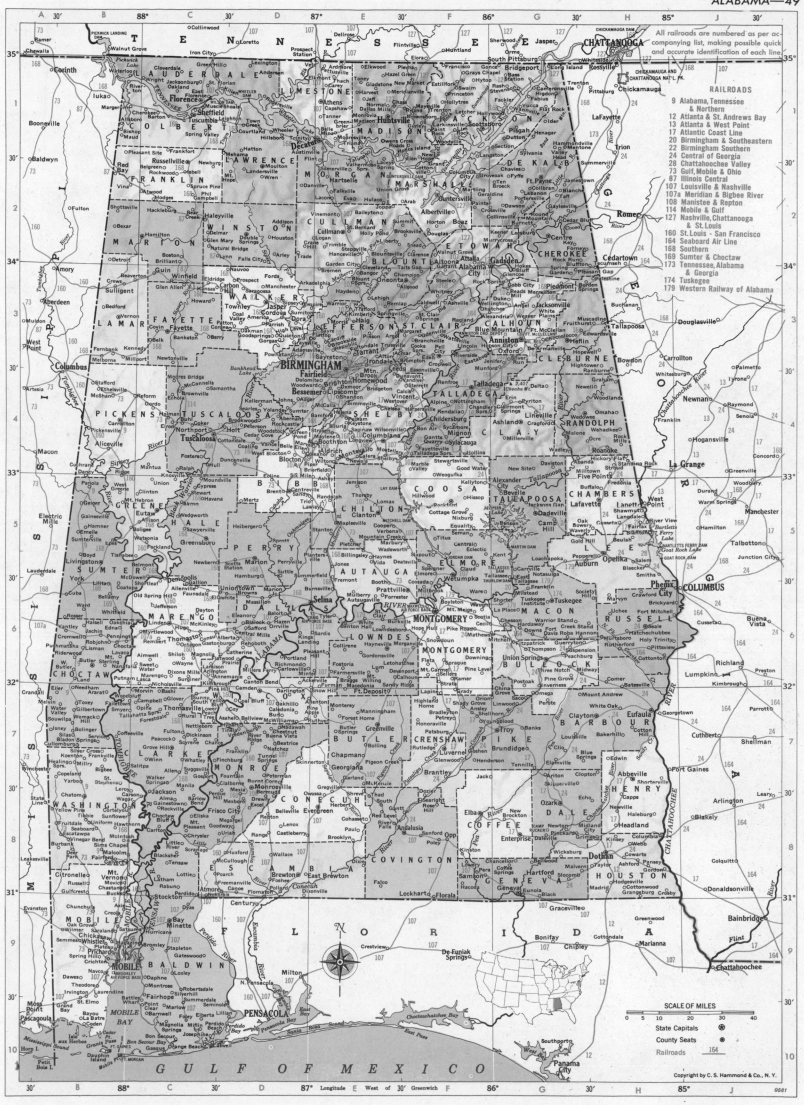

RAILROADS

All railroads are numbered as per accompanying list, making possible quick and accurate identification of each line.

9	Alabama, Tennessee & Northern
12	Atlanta & St. Andrews Bay
13	Atlanta & West Point
17	Atlantic Coast Line
20	Birmingham & Southeastern
22	Birmingham Southern
24	Central of Georgia
28	Chattahoochee Valley
73	Gulf, Mobile & Ohio
87	Illinois Central
107	Louisville & Nashville
107a	Meridian & Bigbee River
108	Manistee & Repton
114	Mobile & Gulf
127	Nashville, Chattanooga & St. Louis
160	St. Louis - San Francisco
164	Seaboard Air Line
168	Southern
169	Sumter & Choctaw
173	Tennessee, Alabama & Georgia
174	Tuskegee
179	Western Railway of Alabama

SCALE OF MILES

0 5 10 20 30 40

State Capitals ⊛
County Seats ⊙
Railroads 164

Copyright by C. S. Hammond & Co., N.Y.

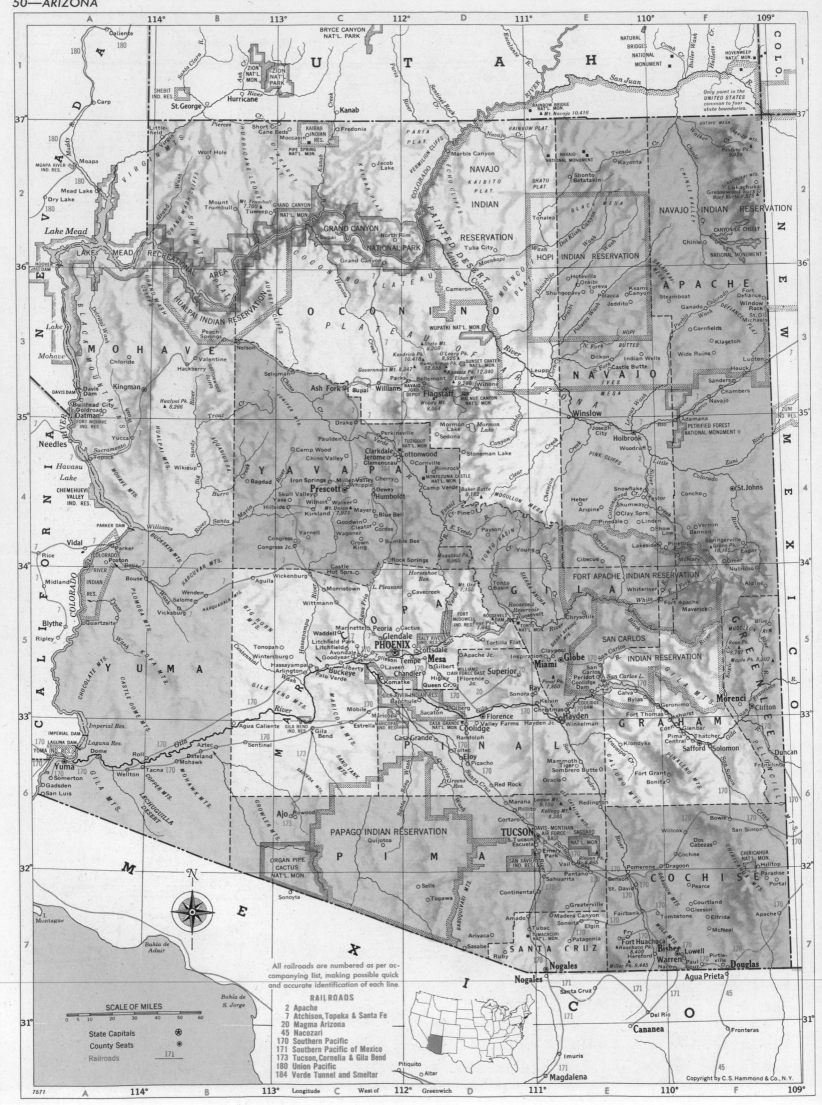

SCALE OF MILES
0 5 10 20 30 40 60

● State Capitals
◎ County Seats
—171— Railroads

All railroads are numbered as per accompanying list, making possible quick and accurate identification of each line.

RAILROADS

2 Apache
7 Atchison, Topeka & Santa Fe
20 Magma Arizona
45 Nacozari
170 Southern Pacific
171 Southern Pacific of Mexico
173 Tucson, Cornelia & Gila Bend
180 Union Pacific
184 Verde Tunnel and Smelter

Copyright by C.S. Hammond & Co., N.Y.

7571

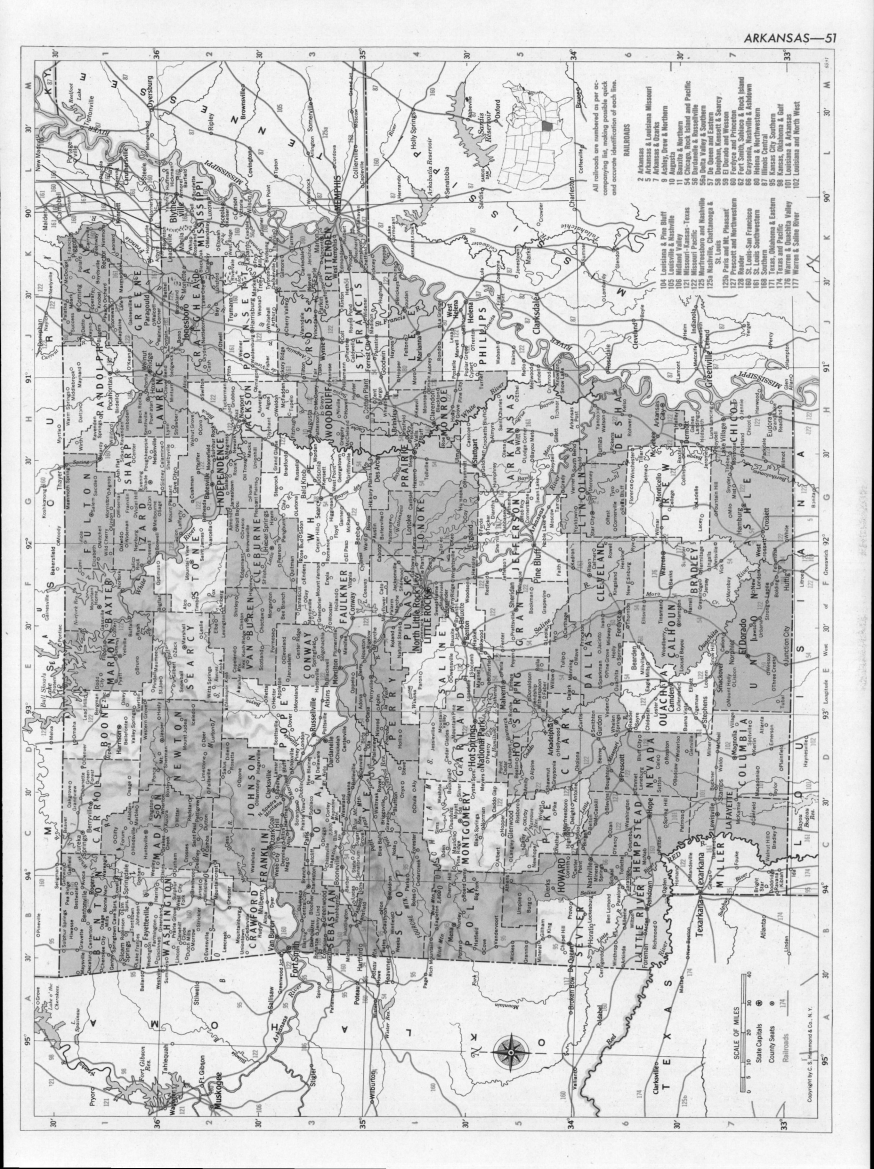

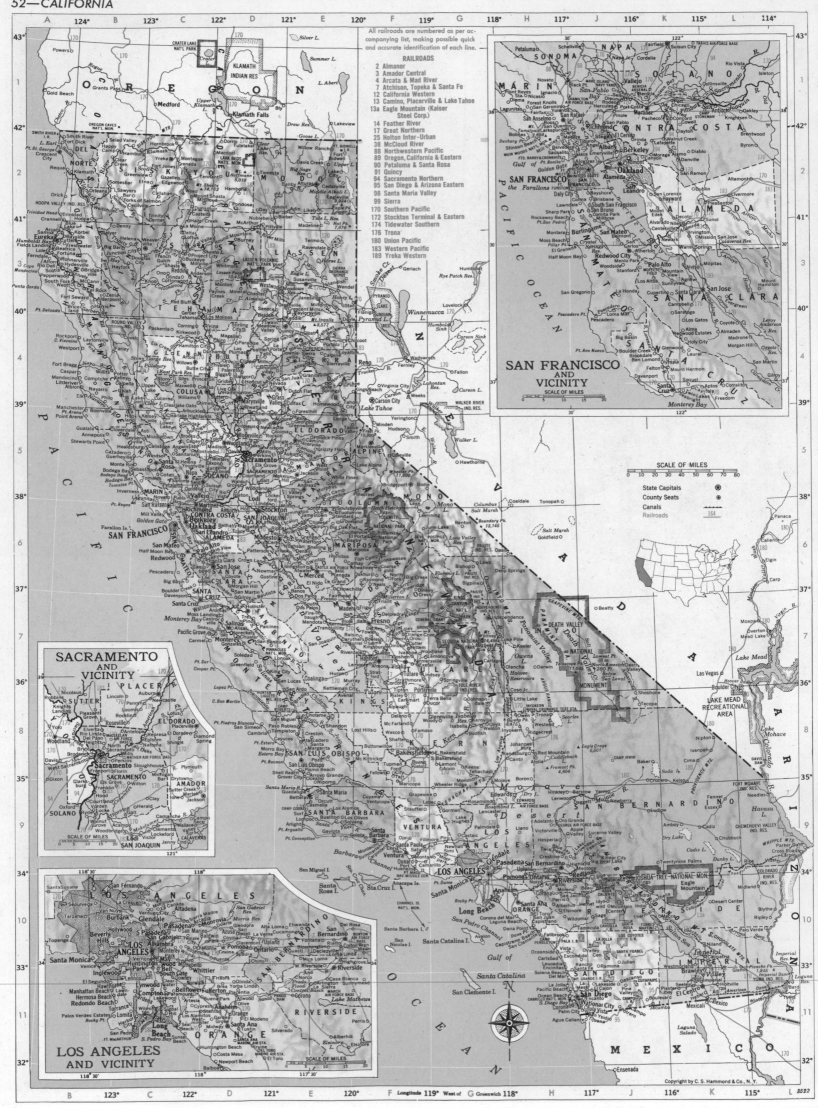

All railroads are numbered as per accompanying list, making possible quick and accurate identification of each line.

RAILROADS

2 Almanor
3 Amador Central
4 Arcata & Mad River
7 Atchison, Topeka & Santa Fe
12 California Western
13 Camino, Placerville & Lake Tahoe
13a Eagle Mountain (Kaiser Steel Corp.)
14 Feather River
17 Great Northern
25 Holton Inter-Urban
38 McCloud River
88 Northwestern Pacific
89 Oregon, California & Eastern
90 Petaluma & Santa Rosa
91 Quincy
94 Sacramento Northern
95 San Diego & Arizona Eastern
98 Santa Maria Valley
99 Sierra
170 Southern Pacific
172 Stockton Terminal & Eastern
174 Tidewater Southern
176 Trona
180 Union Pacific
183 Western Pacific
189 Yreka Western

SAN FRANCISCO AND VICINITY
SCALE OF MILES

SACRAMENTO AND VICINITY
SCALE OF MILES

LOS ANGELES AND VICINITY
SCALE OF MILES

SCALE OF MILES

State Capitals
County Seats
Canals
Railroads

Copyright by C. S. Hammond & Co., N. Y.

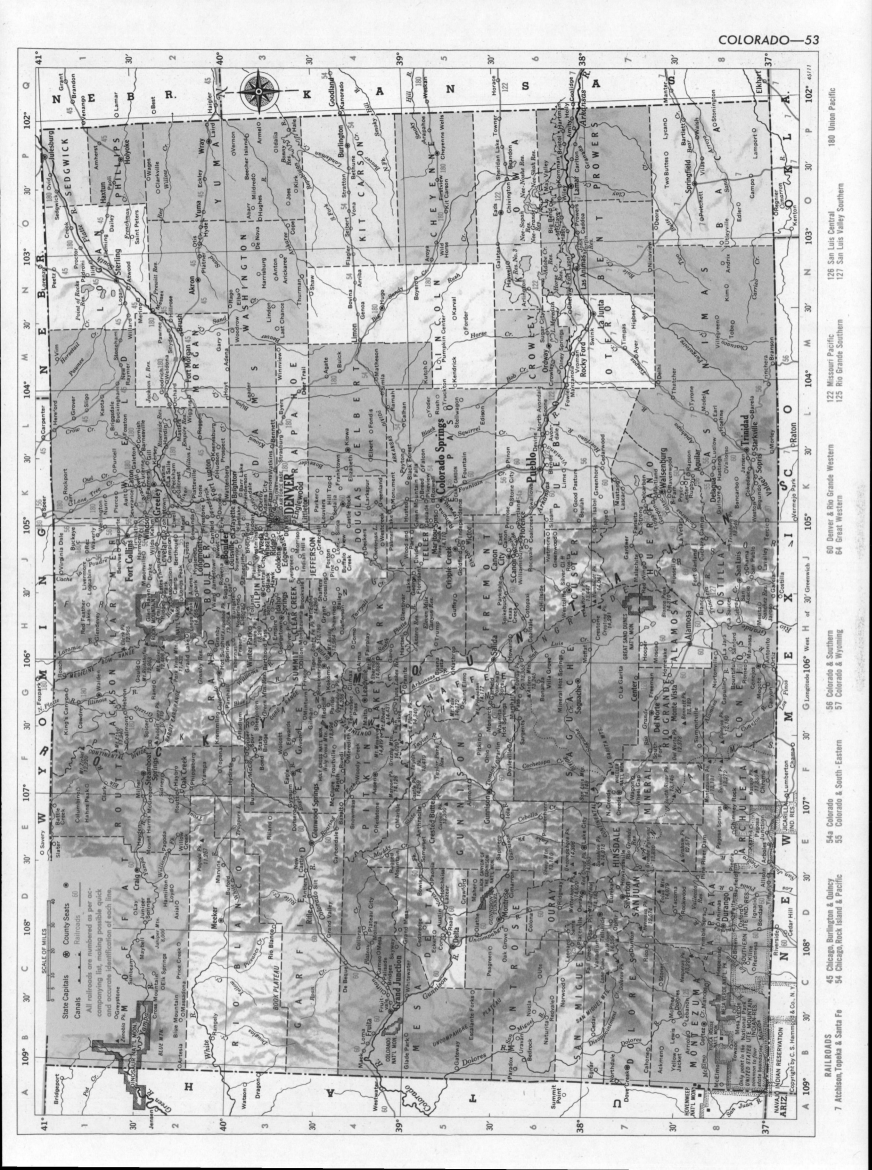

RAILROADS

7 Atchison, Topeka & Santa Fe
45 Chicago, Burlington & Quincy
54 Chicago, Rock Island & Pacific
54a Colorado
55 Colorado & South-Eastern
56 Colorado & Southern
57 Colorado & Wyoming
60 Denver & Rio Grande Western
64 Great Western
122 Missouri Pacific
125 Rio Grande Southern
126 San Luis Central
127 San Luis Valley Southern
180 Union Pacific

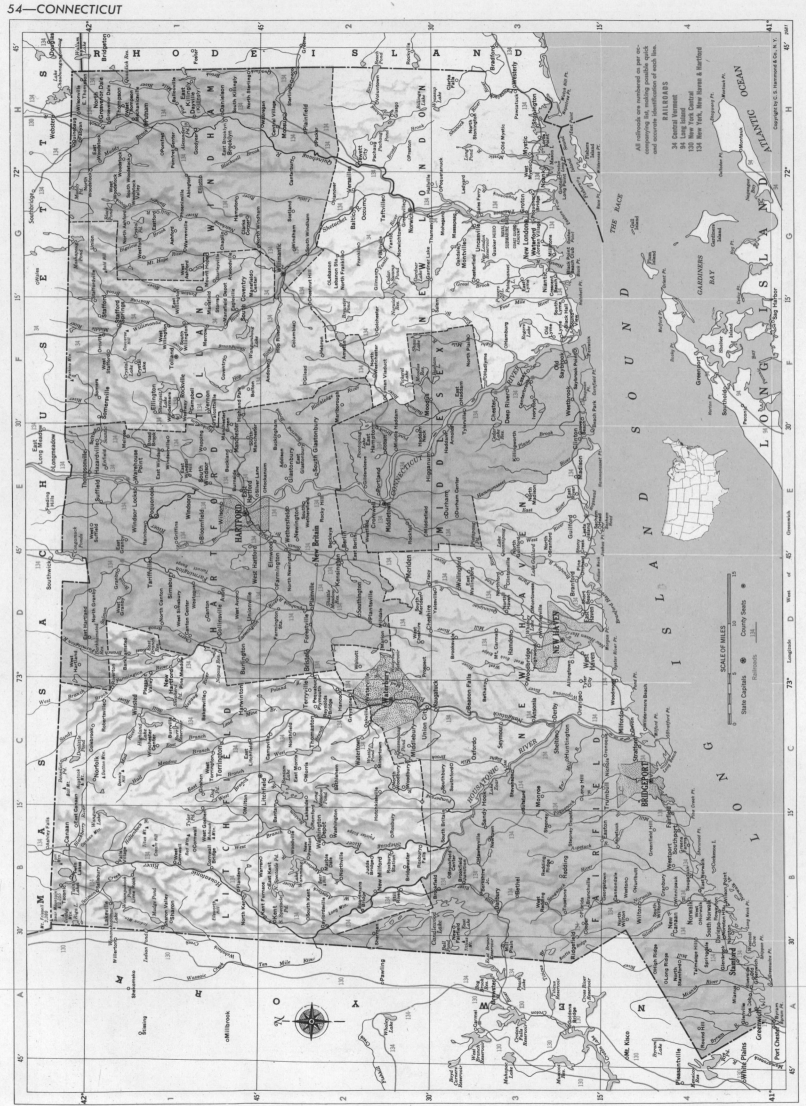

RAILROADS

All railroads are numbered as per accompanying list, making possible quick and accurate identification of each line.

34 Central Vermont
94 Long Island
130 New York Central
134 New York, New Haven & Hartford

SCALE OF MILES

⊛ State Capitals   ⊛ County Seats
────── Railroads   134

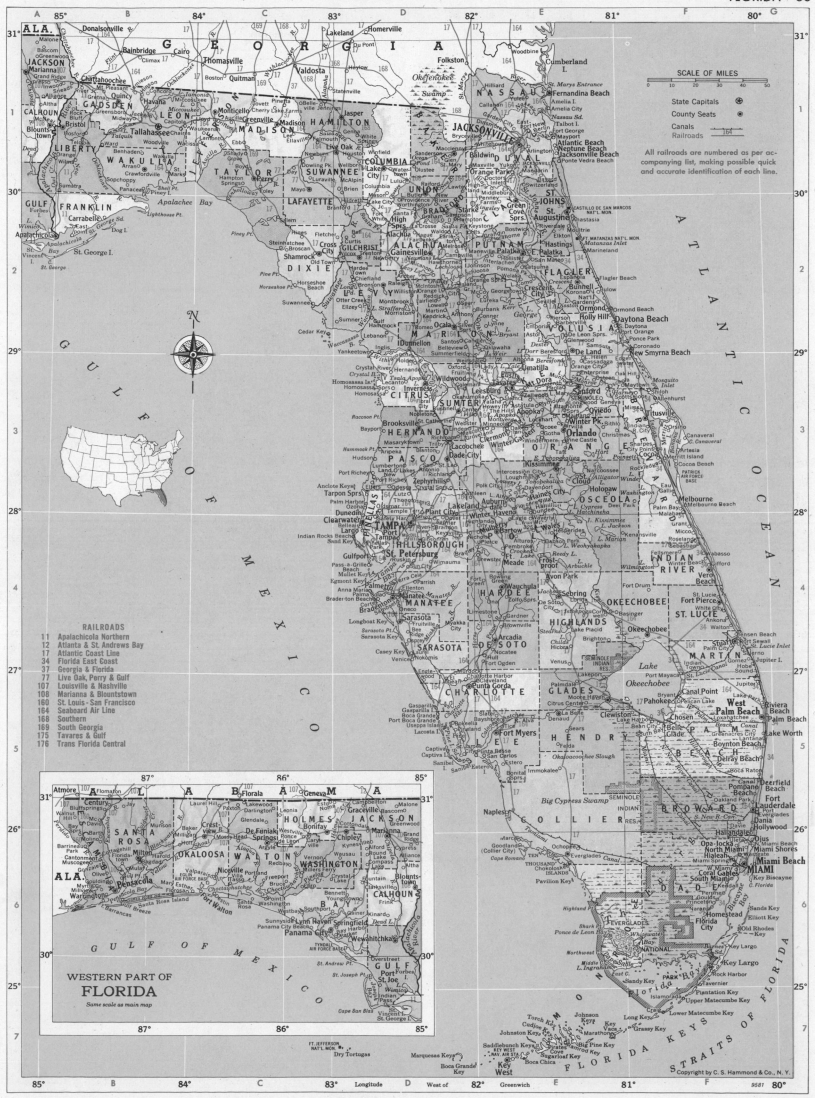

RAILROADS
11 Apalachicola Northern
12 Atlanta & St. Andrews Bay
17 Atlantic Coast Line
34 Florida East Coast
37 Georgia & Florida
77 Live Oak, Perry & Gulf
107 Louisville & Nashville
108 Marianna & Blountstown
160 St. Louis - San Francisco
164 Seaboard Air Line
168 Southern
169 South Georgia
175 Tavares & Gulf
176 Trans Florida Central

SCALE OF MILES

State Capitals
County Seats
Canals
Railroads

All railroads are numbered as per accompanying list, making possible quick and accurate identification of each line.

WESTERN PART OF
FLORIDA
Same scale as main map

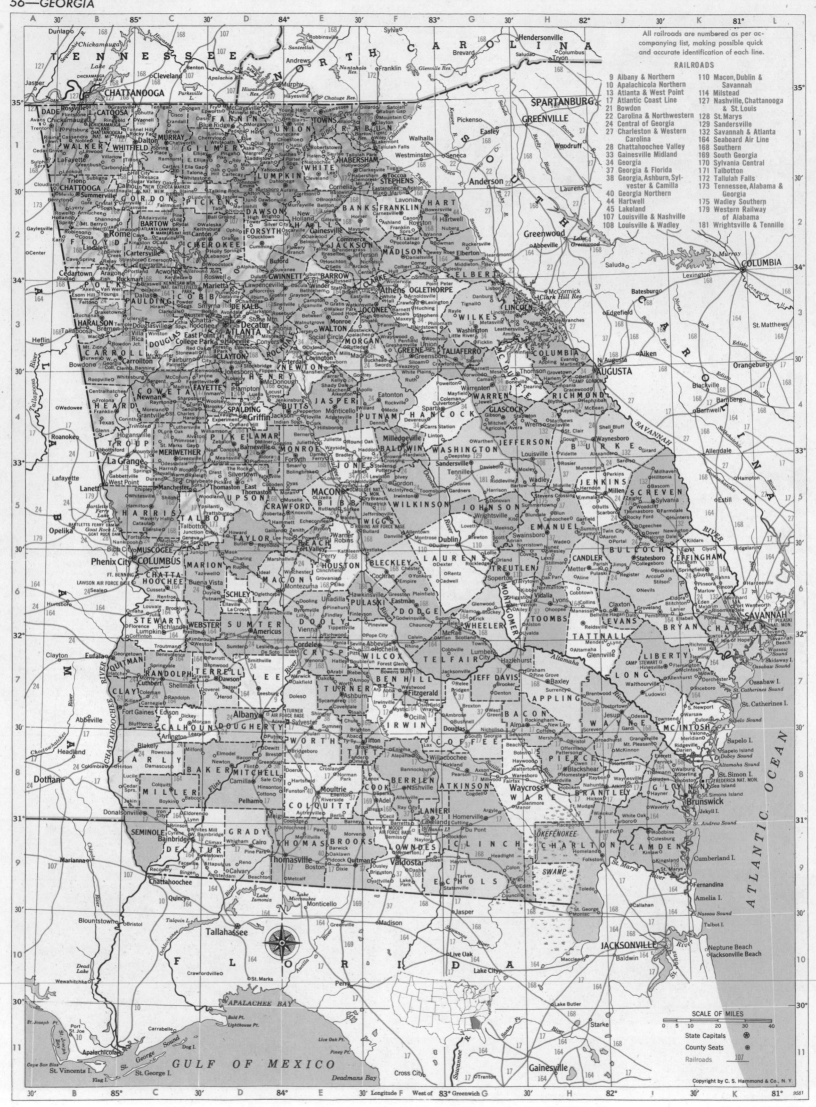

All railroads are numbered as per accompanying list, making possible quick and accurate identification of each line.

RAILROADS

9 Albany & Northern	110 Macon, Dublin & Savannah
10 Apalachicola Northern	114 Milstead
13 Atlanta & West Point	127 Nashville, Chattanooga & St. Louis
17 Atlantic Coast Line	128 St. Marys
21 Bowdon	129 Sandersville
22 Carolina & Northwestern	132 Savannah & Atlanta
24 Central of Georgia	164 Seaboard Air Line
27 Charleston & Western Carolina	168 Southern
28 Chattahoochee Valley	169 South Georgia
33 Chattahoochee Valley	170 Sylvania Central
33 Georgia	171 Talbotton
34 Georgia	172 Tallulah Falls
37 Georgia & Florida	173 Tennessee, Alabama & Georgia
38 Georgia, Ashburn, Sylvester & Camilla	175 Wadley Southern
40 Georgia Northern	179 Western Railway of Alabama
44 Hartwell	181 Wrightsville & Tennille
45 Lakeland	
107 Louisville & Nashville	
108 Louisville & Wadley	

SCALE OF MILES

State Capitals
County Seats
Railroads

Copyright by C. S. Hammond & Co., N.Y.

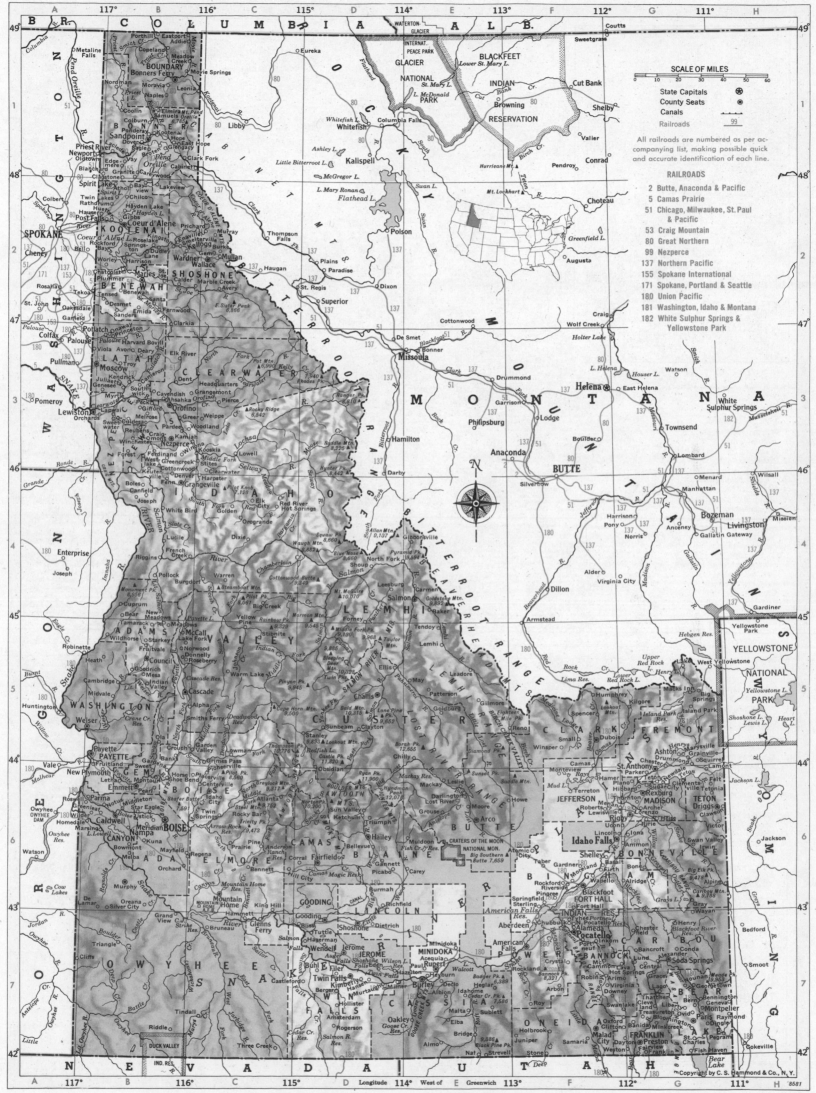

SCALE OF MILES

State Capitals ⊗
County Seats ⊙
Canals
Railroads

All railroads are numbered as per accompanying list, making possible quick and accurate identification of each line.

RAILROADS

2   Butte, Anaconda & Pacific
5   Camas Prairie
51 Chicago, Milwaukee, St. Paul & Pacific
53 Craig Mountain
80 Great Northern
99 Nezperce
137 Northern Pacific
155 Spokane International
171 Spokane, Portland & Seattle
180 Union Pacific
181 Washington, Idaho & Montana
182 White Sulphur Springs & Yellowstone Park

Copyright by C. S. Hammond & Co., N.Y.

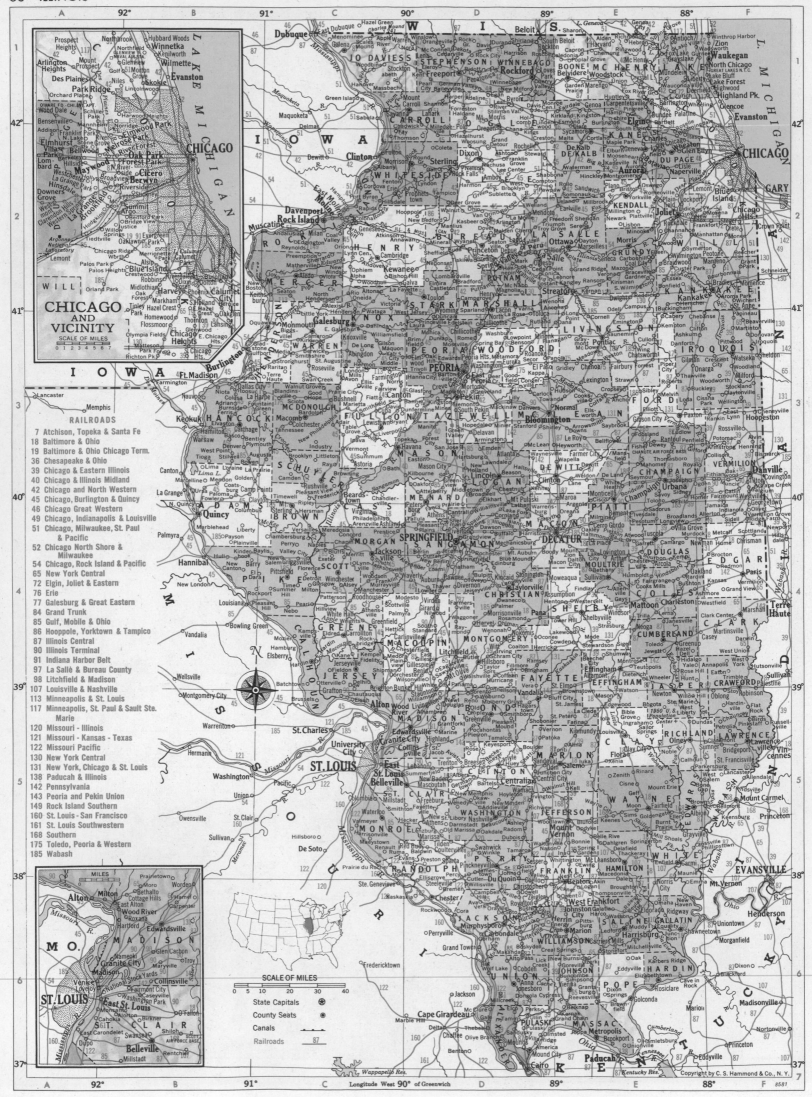

CHICAGO AND VICINITY
SCALE OF MILES
0 1 2 3 4 5 6 7

RAILROADS

7 Atchison, Topeka & Santa Fe
18 Baltimore & Ohio
19 Baltimore & Ohio Chicago Term.
36 Chesapeake & Ohio
39 Chicago & Eastern Illinois
40 Chicago & Illinois Midland
42 Chicago and North Western
45 Chicago, Burlington & Quincy
46 Chicago Great Western
49 Chicago, Indianapolis & Louisville
51 Chicago, Milwaukee, St. Paul
   & Pacific
52 Chicago North Shore & Milwaukee
54 Chicago, Rock Island & Pacific
65 New York Central
72 Elgin, Joliet & Eastern
76 Erie
77 Galesburg & Great Eastern
84 Grand Trunk
85 Gulf, Mobile & Ohio
86 Hooppole, Yorktown & Tampico
87 Illinois Central
90 Illinois Terminal
91 Indiana Harbor Belt
97 La Salle & Bureau County
107 Louisville & Nashville
113 Minneapolis & St. Louis
117 Minneapolis, St. Paul & Sault Ste.
   Marie
120 Missouri - Illinois
121 Missouri - Kansas - Texas
122 Missouri Pacific
130 New York Central
131 New York, Chicago & St. Louis
138 Paducah & Illinois
142 Pennsylvania
143 Peoria and Pekin Union
149 Rock Island Southern
160 St. Louis - San Francisco
161 St. Louis Southwestern
168 Southern
175 Toledo, Peoria & Western
185 Wabash

SCALE OF MILES
0 5 10   20   30   40

⊛ State Capitals
⊙ County Seats
   Canals
   Railroads   87

Longitude West 90° of Greenwich

Copyright by C. S. Hammond & Co., N. Y.

8581

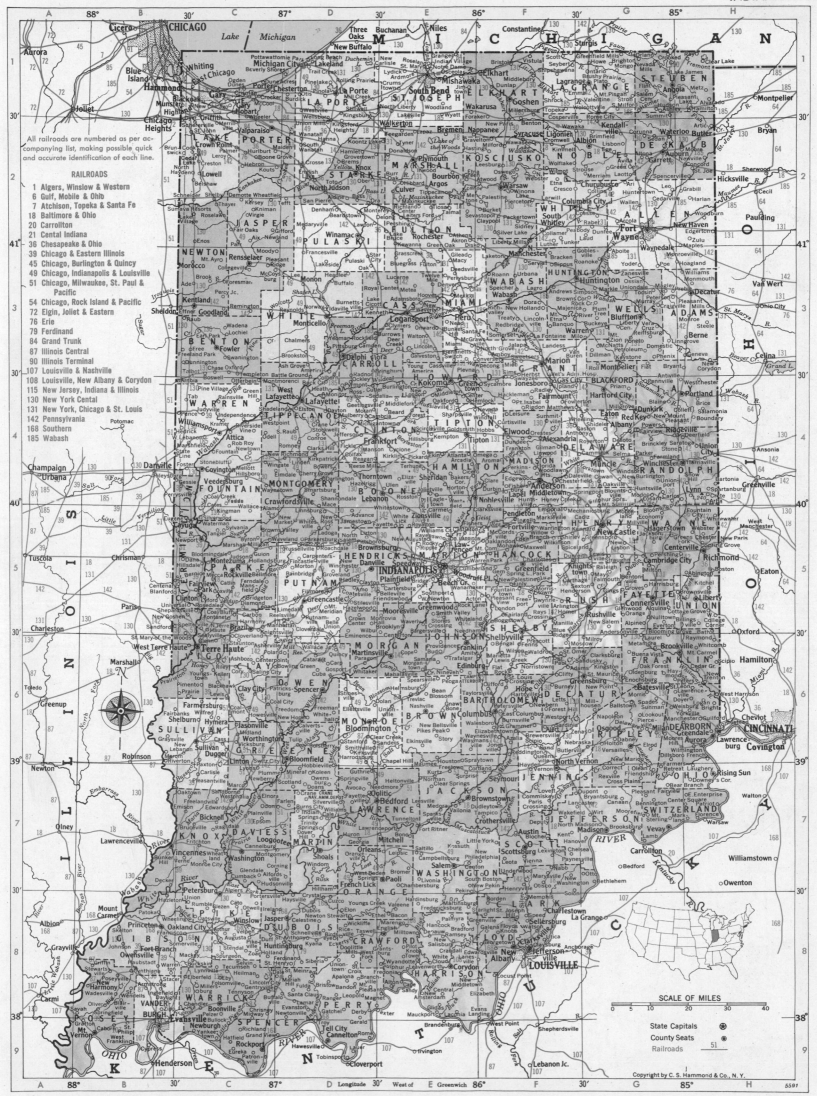

RAILROADS

1 Algers, Winslow & Western
6 Gulf, Mobile & Ohio
7 Atchison, Topeka & Santa Fe
18 Baltimore & Ohio
20 Carrollton
21 Cental Indiana
36 Chesapeake & Ohio
39 Chicago & Eastern Illinois
45 Chicago, Burlington & Quincy
49 Chicago, Indianapolis & Louisville
51 Chicago, Milwaukee, St. Paul & Pacific
54 Chicago, Rock Island & Pacific
72 Elgin, Joliet & Eastern
76 Erie
79 Ferdinand
84 Grand Trunk
87 Illinois Central
90 Illinois Terminal
107 Louisville & Nashville
108 Louisville, New Albany & Corydon
115 New Jersey, Indiana & Illinois
130 New York Central
131 New York, Chicago & St. Louis
142 Pennsylvania
168 Southern
185 Wabash

All railroads are numbered as per accompanying list, making possible quick and accurate identification of each line.

SCALE OF MILES
0 5 10 20 30 40

State Capitals ⊛
County Seats ⊙
Railroads 51

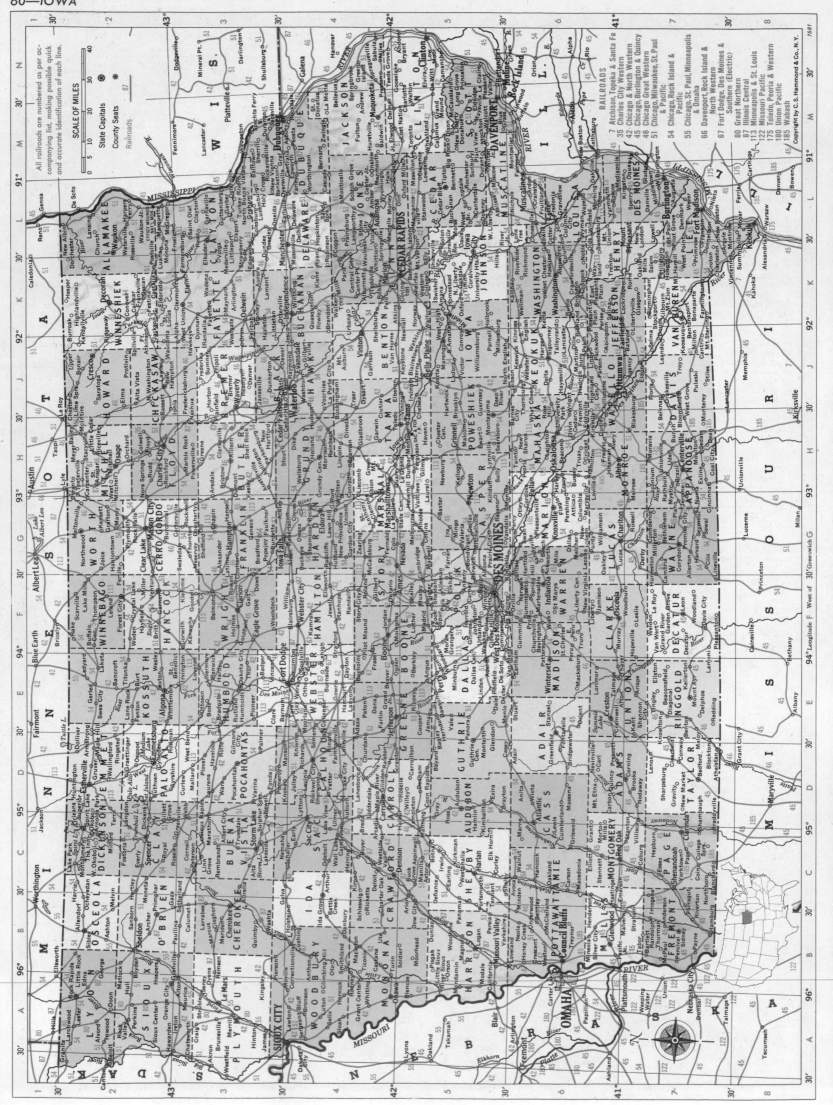

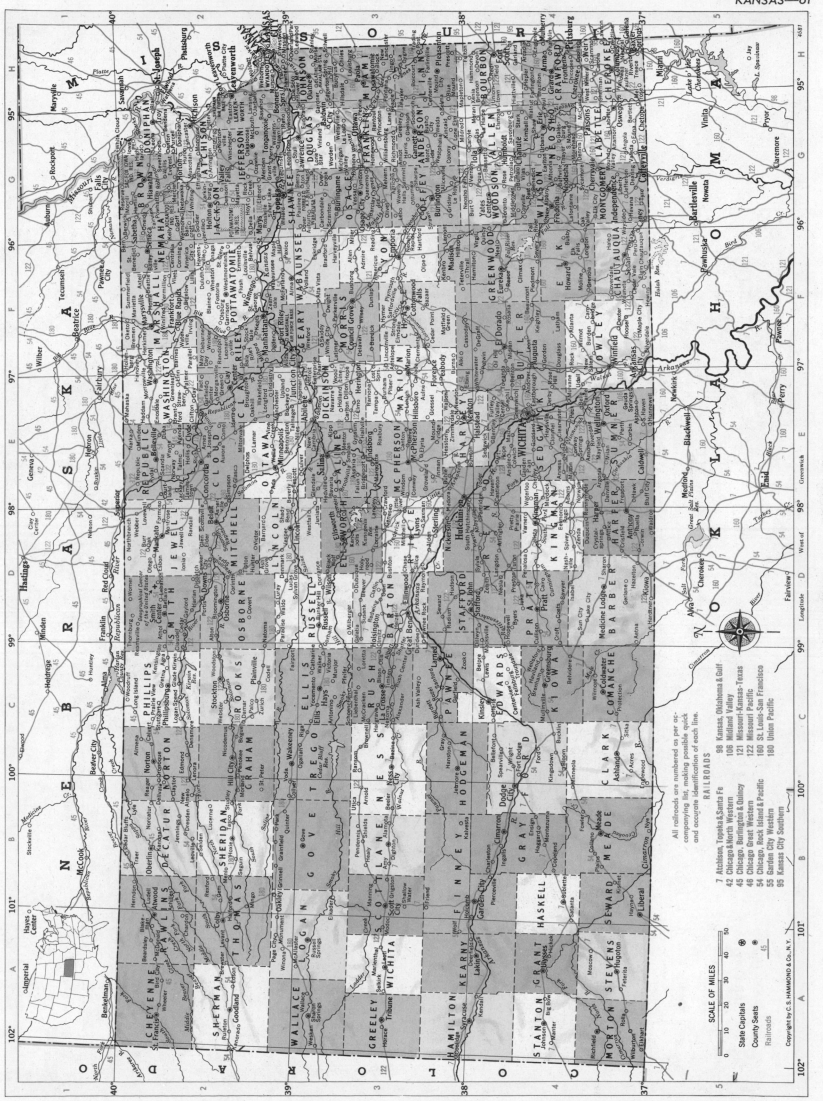

RAILROADS

All railroads are numbered as per accompanying list, making possible quick and accurate identification of each line.

7	Atchison, Topeka & Santa Fe	98	Kansas, Oklahoma & Gulf
42	Chicago & North Western	106	Midland Valley
45	Chicago, Burlington & Quincy	121	Missouri-Kansas-Texas
46	Chicago Great Western	122	Missouri Pacific
54	Chicago, Rock Island & Pacific	160	St. Louis-San Francisco
55	Garden City Western	180	Union Pacific
95	Kansas City Southern		

SCALE OF MILES

0 10 20 30 40 50

⊛ State Capitals
◉ County Seats
Railroads

Copyright by C. S. Hammond & Co., N.Y.

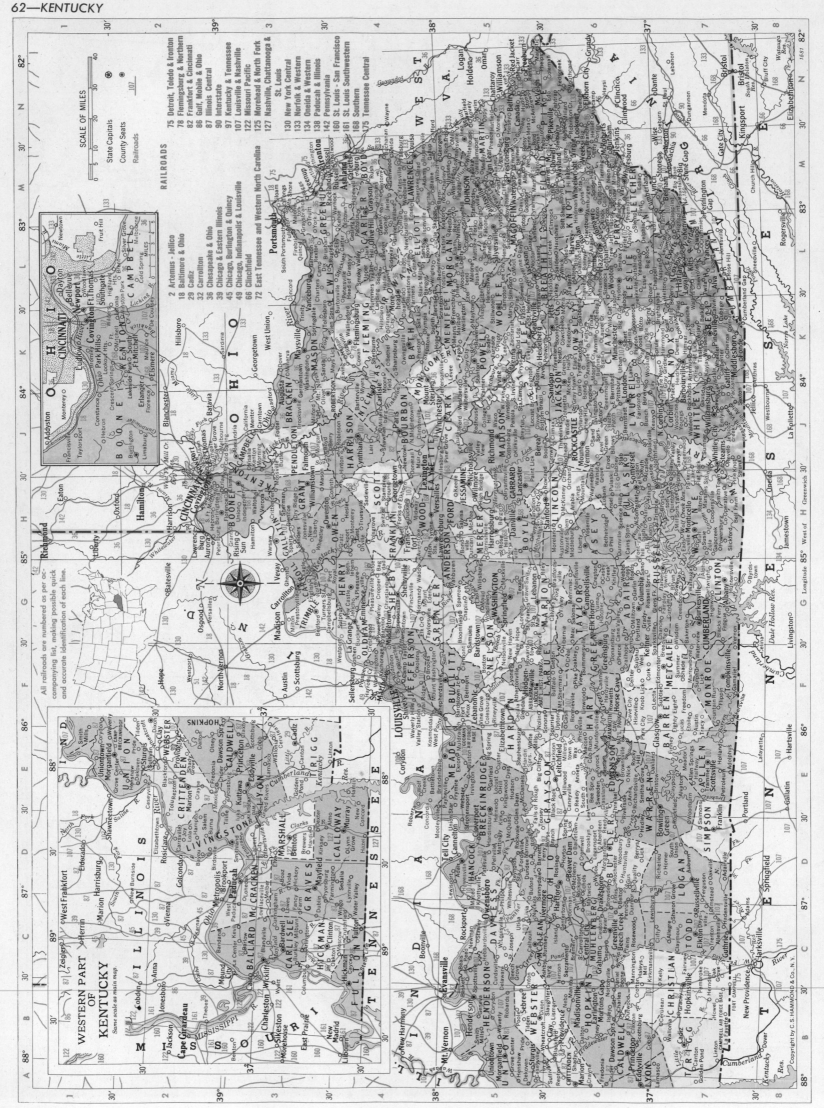

SCALE OF MILES

State Capitals
County Seats
Railroads

RAILROADS

2	Artemus - Jellico
18	Baltimore & Ohio
29	Cadiz
36	Carrollton
36	Chesapeake & Ohio
39	Chicago & Eastern Illinois
45	Chicago, Burlington & Quincy
49	Chicago, Indianapolis & Louisville
66	Clinchfield
72	East Tennessee and Western North Carolina
75	Detroit, Toledo & Ironton
78	Flemingsburg & Northern
82	Frankfort & Cincinnati
86	Gulf, Mobile & Ohio
87	Illinois Central
90	Interstate
97	Kentucky & Tennessee
107	Louisville & Nashville
122	Missouri Pacific
125	Morehead & North Fork
127	Nashville, Chattanooga & St. Louis
130	New York Central
134	Norfolk & Western
134	Oneida & Western
142	Paducah & Illinois
160	Pennsylvania
161	St. Louis - San Francisco
168	St. Louis Southwestern
168	Southern
175	Tennessee Central

All railroads are numbered as per accompanying list, making possible quick and accurate identification of each line.

WESTERN PART OF KENTUCKY
Same scale as main map.

Copyright by C. S. HAMMOND & Co., N.Y.

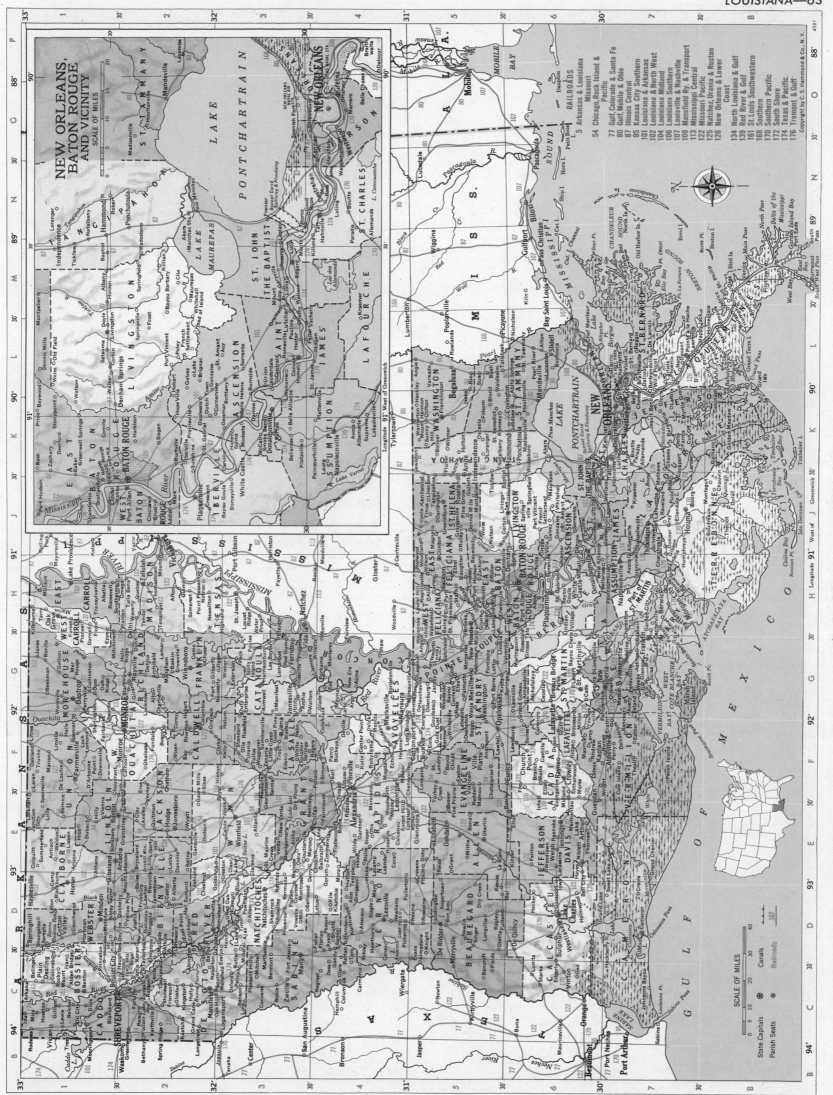

NEW ORLEANS,
BATON ROUGE
AND VICINITY

SCALE OF MILES

RAILROADS

Arkansas & Louisiana	5
Chicago, Rock Island &	
Pacific	54
Gulf, Colorado & Santa Fe	77
Gulf, Mobile & Ohio	80
Illinois Central	87
Kansas City Southern	95
Louisiana & Arkansas	101
Louisiana & North West	102
Louisiana Midland	104
Louisiana Southern	106
Louisville & Nashville	107
Mansfield Ry. & Transport	108
Mississippi Central	113
Missouri Pacific	122
Natchez, Urania & Ruston	125
New Orleans & Lower	
Coast	126
North Louisiana & Gulf	134
Red River & Gulf	139
St. Louis Southwestern	161
Southern	168
Southern Pacific	170
South Shore	172
Texas & Pacific	174
Tremont & Gulf	176

SCALE OF MILES

State Capitals
Parish Seats

Canals
Railroads

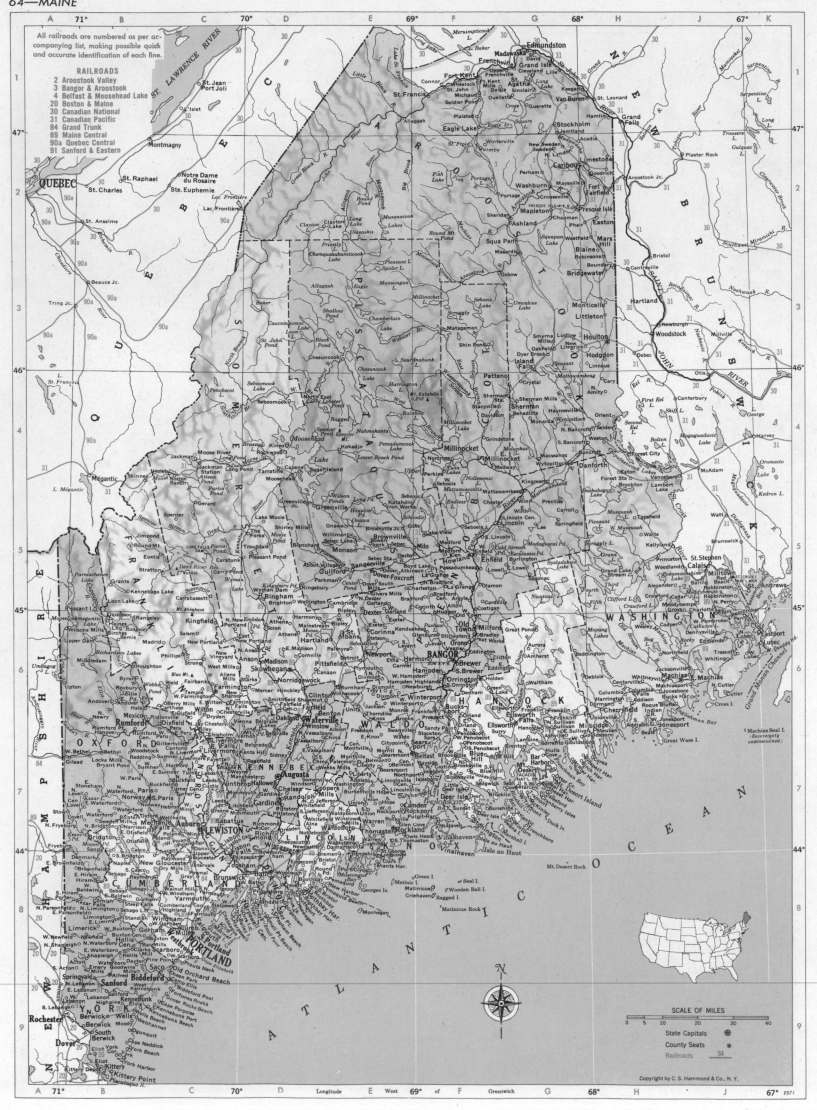

All railroads are numbered as per accompanying list, making possible quick and accurate identification of each line.

RAILROADS
- 2 Aroostook Valley
- 3 Bangor & Aroostook
- 4 Belfast & Moosehead Lake
- 20 Boston & Maine
- 30 Canadian National
- 31 Canadian Pacific
- 84 Grand Trunk
- 89 Maine Central
- 90a Quebec Central
- 91 Sanford & Eastern

SCALE OF MILES

State Capitals
County Seats
Railroads   84

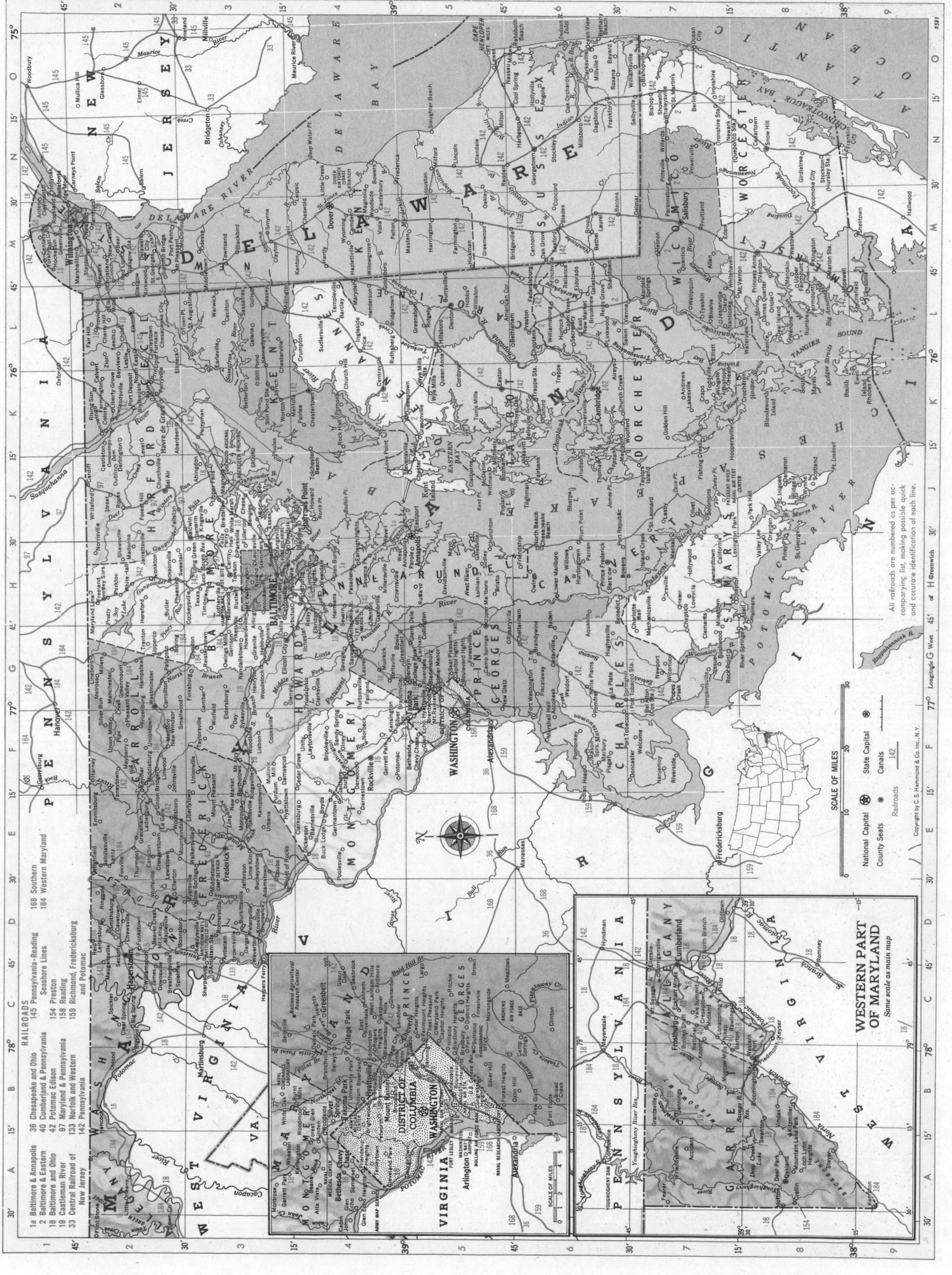

RAILROADS

1a Baltimore & Annapolis	36 Chesapeake and Ohio
2 Baltimore & Eastern	40 Cumberland & Pennsylvania
18 Baltimore and Ohio	42 Potomac Edison
19 Castleman River	97 Maryland & Pennsylvania
33 Central Railroad of New Jersey	133 Norfolk and Western
	142 Pennsylvania
145 Pennsylvania–Reading Seashore Lines	168 Southern
154 Preston	184 Western Maryland
158 Reading	
159 Richmond, Fredericksburg and Potomac	

All railroads are numbered as per accompanying list, making possible quick and accurate identification of each line.

SCALE OF MILES

National Capital ⊛
State Capital ⊛
County Seats ●
Canals 142
Railroads

Copyright by C.S. Hammond & Co. Inc., N.Y.

WESTERN PART OF MARYLAND
Same scale as main map

STATES AND REGIONS: NEW JERSEY, DELAWARE, PENNSYLVANIA, WEST VIRGINIA, VIRGINIA, MARYLAND, DISTRICT OF COLUMBIA, WASHINGTON

COUNTIES: KENT, SUSSEX, NEW CASTLE, CECIL, HARFORD, BALTIMORE, CARROLL, FREDERICK, MONTGOMERY, HOWARD, ANNE ARUNDEL, QUEEN ANNE'S, TALBOT, CAROLINE, DORCHESTER, WICOMICO, WORCESTER, SOMERSET, PRINCE GEORGES, CALVERT, CHARLES, ST. MARY'S, CUMBERLAND, ALLEGANY, GARRETT

WATER: DELAWARE BAY, CHESAPEAKE BAY, ATLANTIC OCEAN, EASTERN BAY, TANGIER SOUND, POTOMAC RIVER, SUSQUEHANNA RIVER, DELAWARE RIVER, CHINCOTEAGUE BAY

Major cities: Wilmington, Dover, Baltimore, Annapolis, Washington, Salisbury, Frederick, Hagerstown, Cumberland, Rockville

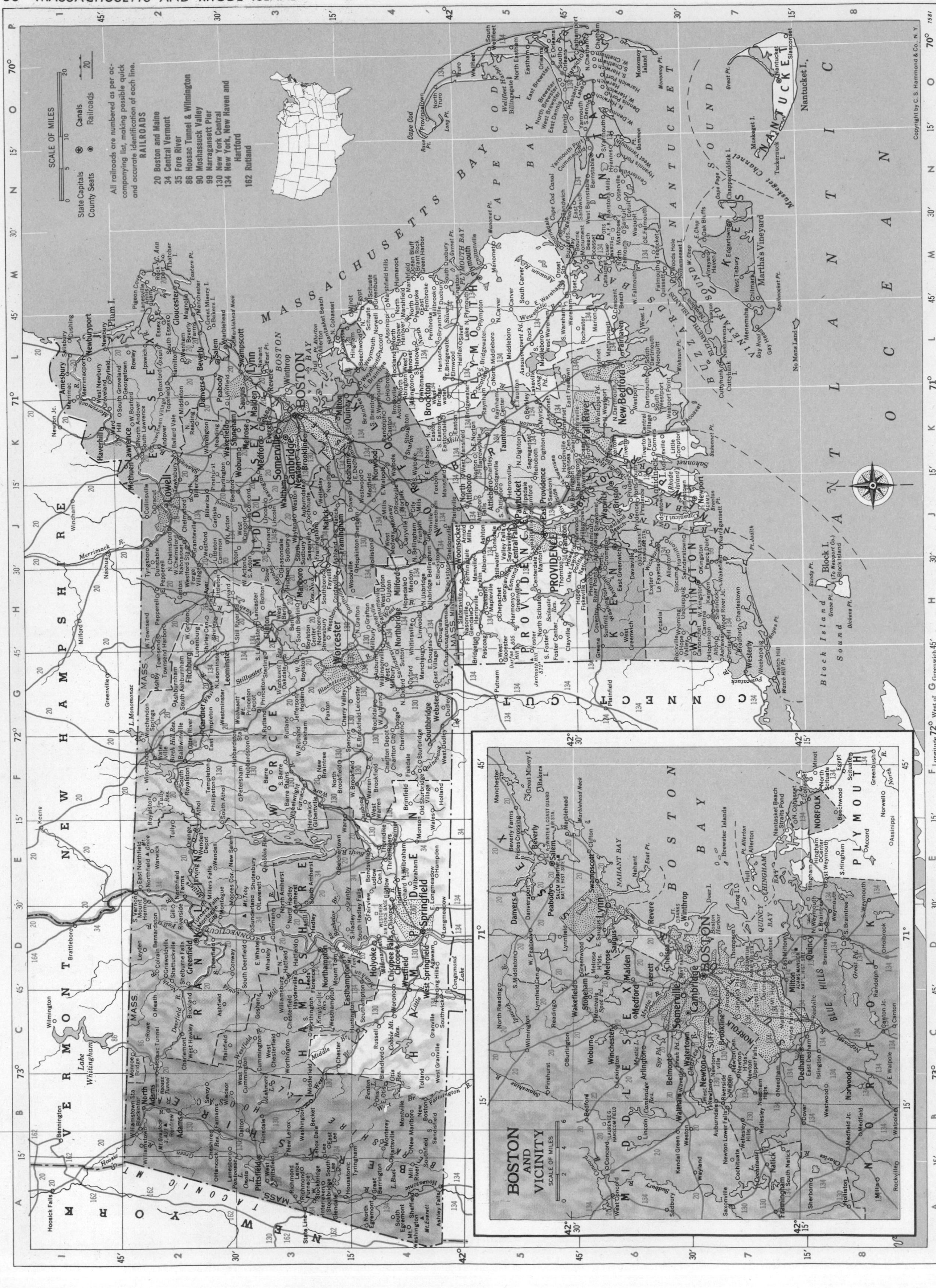

SCALE OF MILES

All railroads are numbered as per accompanying list, making possible quick and accurate identification of each line.

RAILROADS

- 20 Boston and Maine
- 34 Central Vermont
- 35 Fore River
- 86 Hoosac Tunnel & Wilmington
- 90 Moshassuck Valley
- 99 Narragansett Pier
- 130 New York Central
- 134 New York, New Haven and Hartford
- 162 Rutland

State Capitals
County Seats

Copyright by C. S. Hammond & Co., N. Y.

BOSTON AND VICINITY
SCALE OF MILES

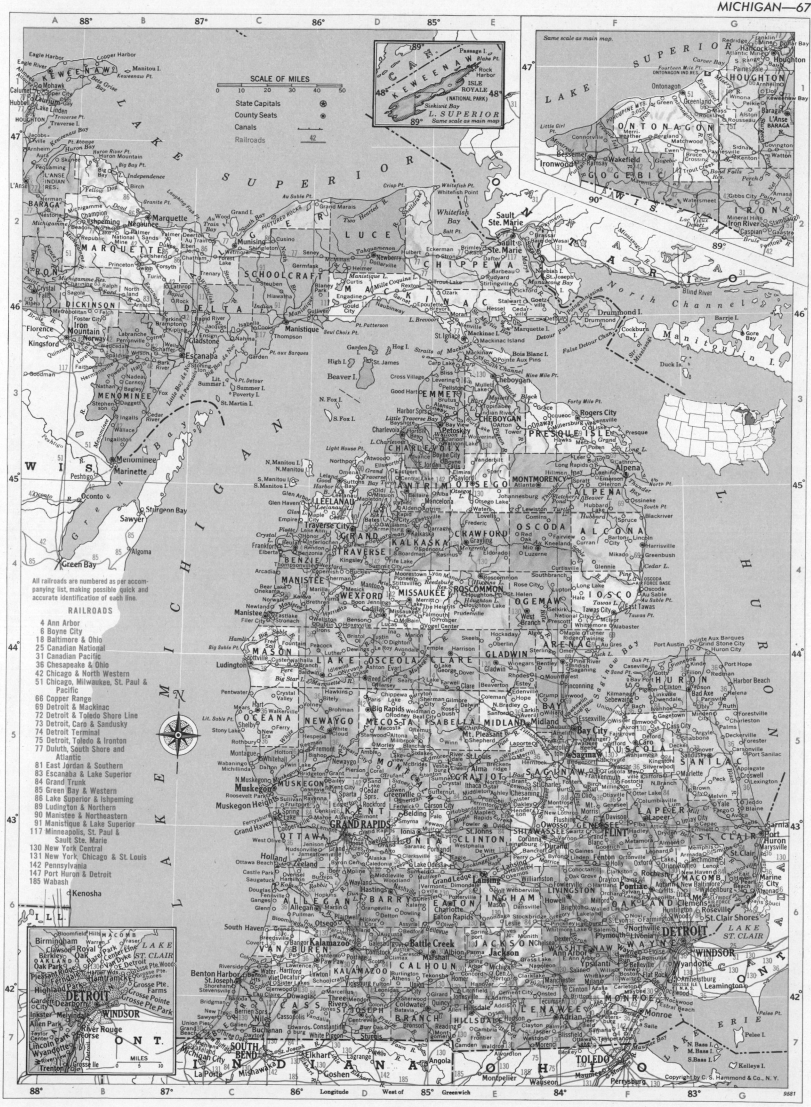

SCALE OF MILES

State Capitals
County Seats
Canals
Railroads

ISLE ROYALE (NATIONAL PARK)
L. SUPERIOR
Same scale as main map.

All railroads are numbered as per accompanying list, making possible quick and accurate identification of each line.

RAILROADS

4 Ann Arbor
6 Boyne City
18 Baltimore & Ohio
25 Canadian National
31 Canadian Pacific
36 Chesapeake & Ohio
42 Chicago & North Western
51 Chicago, Milwaukee, St. Paul & Pacific
66 Copper Range
69 Detroit & Mackinac
72 Detroit & Toledo Shore Line
73 Detroit, Caro & Sandusky
74 Detroit Terminal
75 Detroit, Toledo & Ironton
77 Duluth, South Shore and Atlantic
81 East Jordan & Southern
83 Escanaba & Lake Superior
84 Grand Trunk
85 Green Bay & Western
86 Lake Superior & Ishpeming
89 Ludington & Northern
90 Manistee & Northeastern
91 Manistique & Lake Superior
117 Minneapolis, St. Paul & Sault Ste. Marie
130 New York Central
131 New York, Chicago & St. Louis
142 Pennsylvania
147 Port Huron & Detroit
185 Wabash

Copyright by C. S. Hammond & Co., N.Y.

9581

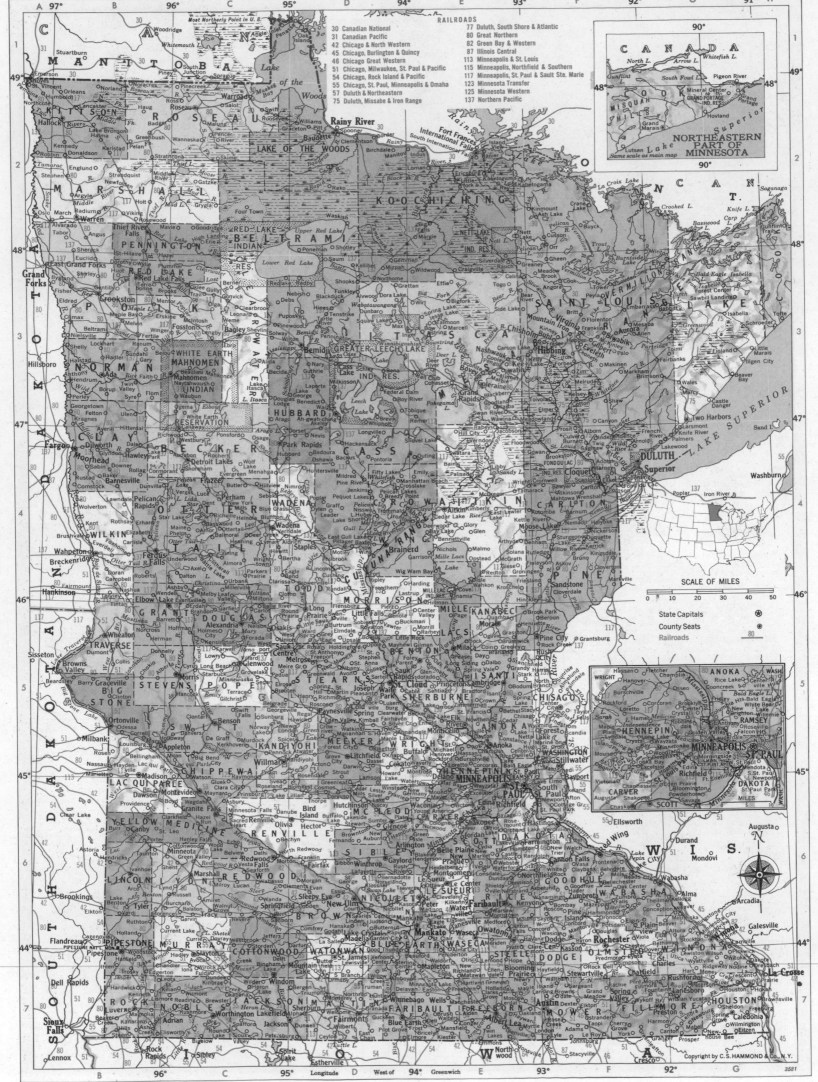

RAILROADS
30 Canadian National
31 Canadian Pacific
42 Chicago & North Western
45 Chicago, Burlington & Quincy
46 Chicago Great Western
51 Chicago, Milwaukee, St. Paul & Pacific
54 Chicago, Rock Island & Pacific
55 Chicago, St. Paul, Minneapolis & Omaha
57 Duluth & Northeastern
75 Duluth, Missabe & Iron Range
77 Duluth, South Shore & Atlantic
80 Great Northern
82 Green Bay & Western
87 Illinois Central
113 Minneapolis & St. Louis
115 Minneapolis, Northfield & Southern
117 Minneapolis, St. Paul & Sault Ste. Marie
123 Minnesota Transfer
125 Minnesota Western
137 Northern Pacific

NORTHEASTERN PART OF MINNESOTA
Same scale as main map

SCALE OF MILES
0 10 20 30 40 50

State Capitals
County Seats
Railroads

Copyright by C. S. HAMMOND & Co., N.Y.

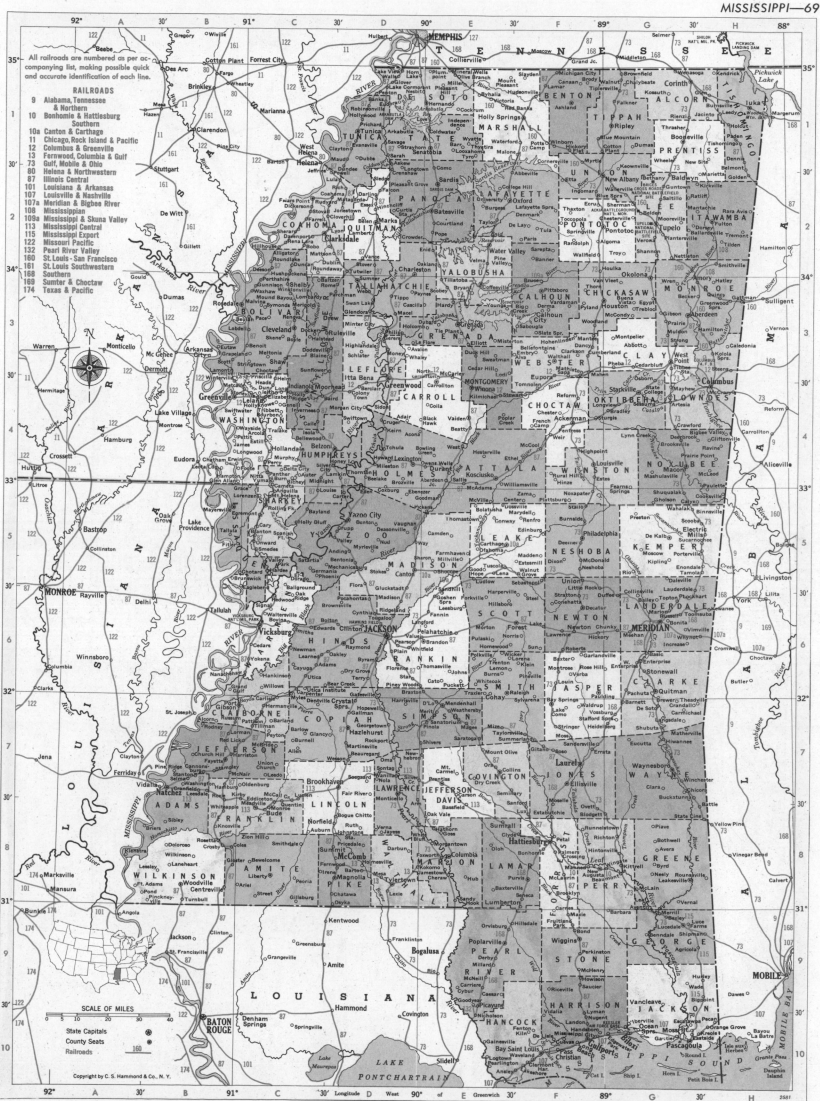

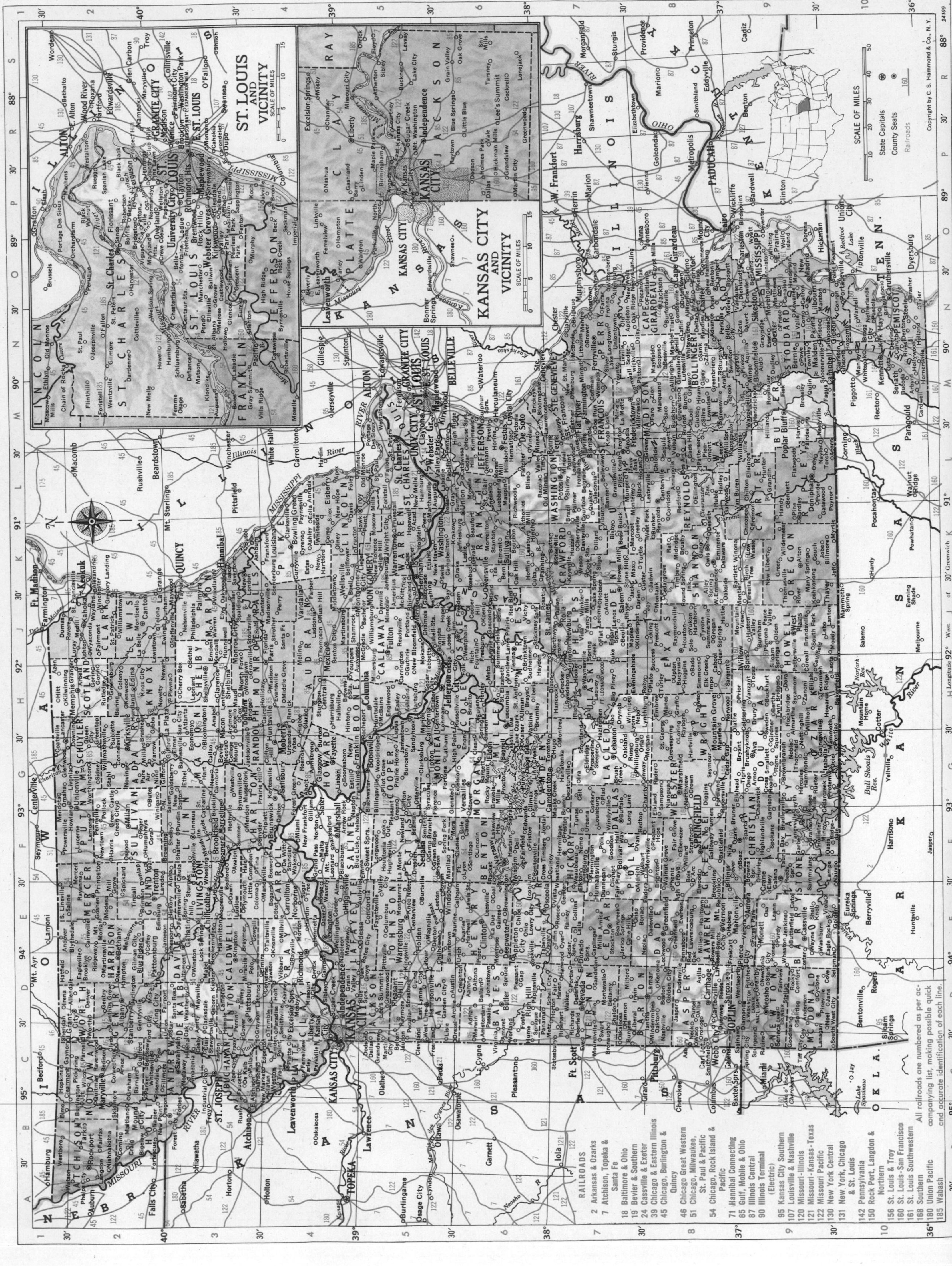

ST. LOUIS AND VICINITY
SCALE OF MILES

KANSAS CITY AND VICINITY
SCALE OF MILES

SCALE OF MILES

Copyright by C. S. Hammond & Co., N. Y.

State Capitals ⊛
County Seats ◉
Railroads

RAILROADS

1 Arkansas & Ozarks
2 Atchison, Topeka &
   Santa Fe
7 Baltimore & Ohio
18 Bevier & Southern
19 Cassville & Exeter
24 Chicago & Eastern Illinois
39 Chicago, Burlington &
   Quincy
45 Chicago, Milwaukee,
   St. Paul & Pacific
46 Chicago, Rock Island &
   Pacific
51 Gulf, Mobile & Ohio
54 Illinois Central
85 Illinois Terminal
   (Electric)
87 Kansas City Southern
90 Louisville & Nashville
107 Missouri-Illinois
120 Missouri-Kansas-Texas
121 Missouri Pacific
122 New York, Chicago
130 & St. Louis
131 Pennsylvania
142 Rock Port, Langdon &
150 Northern
156 St. Louis & Troy
160 St. Louis-San Francisco
161 St. Louis Southwestern
168 Southern
180 Union Pacific
185 Wabash

All railroads are numbered as per accompanying list, making possible quick
and accurate identification of each line.

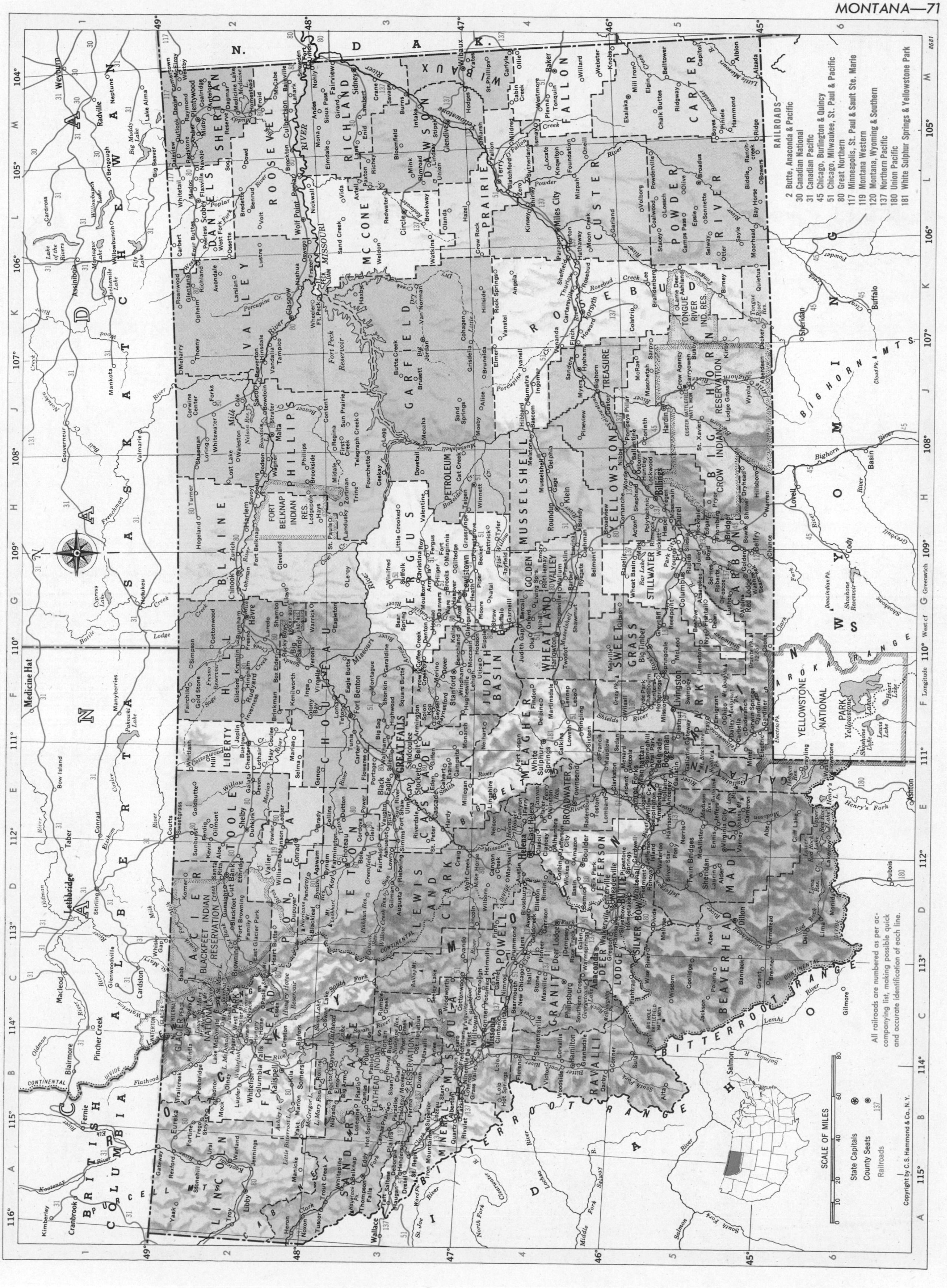

RAILROADS

2 Butte, Anaconda & Pacific
30 Canadian National
31 Canadian Pacific
45 Chicago, Burlington & Quincy
51 Chicago, Milwaukee, St. Paul & Pacific
80 Great Northern
117 Minneapolis, St. Paul & Sault Ste. Marie
119 Montana Western
120 Montana, Wyoming & Southern
137 Northern Pacific
180 Union Pacific
181 White Sulphur Springs & Yellowstone Park

All railroads are numbered as per accompanying list, making possible quick and accurate identification of each line.

SCALE OF MILES

State Capitals
County Seats
Railroads

Copyright by C. S. Hammond & Co., N.Y.

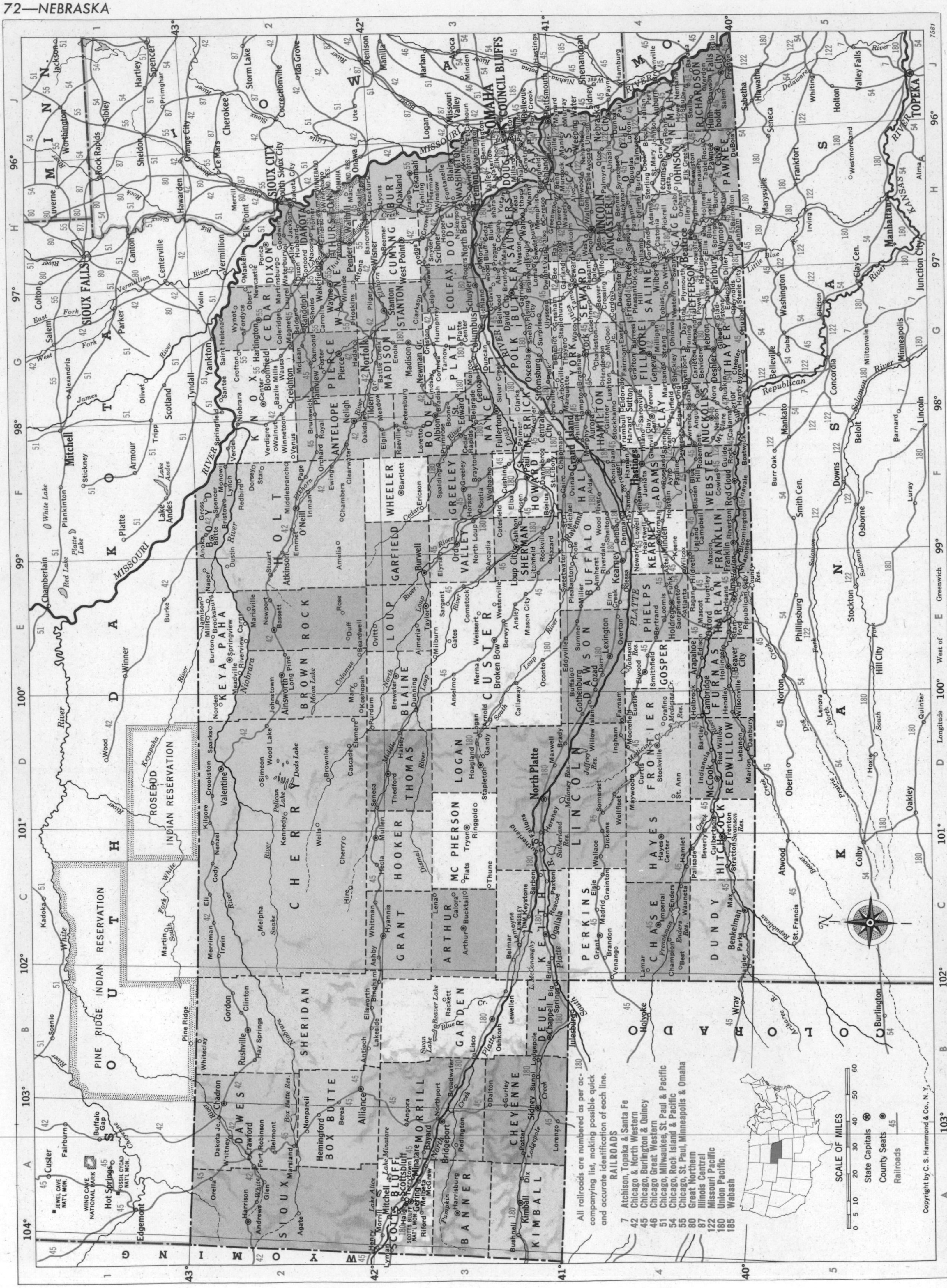

MINNESOTA

IOWA

MO.

SOUTH DAKOTA

WYOMING

COLORADO

KANSAS

NEBRASKA

OMAHA
COUNCIL BLUFFS
SIOUX CITY
SIOUX FALLS
TOPEKA
LINCOLN

PINE RIDGE INDIAN RESERVATION

ROSEBUD INDIAN RESERVATION

Counties:
SIOUX, DAWES, SHERIDAN, CHERRY, KEYA PAHA, BOYD, HOLT, BROWN, ROCK, KNOX, CEDAR, DIXON, DAKOTA, PIERCE, ANTELOPE, WAYNE, THURSTON, CUMING, BURT, MADISON, STANTON, WHEELER, GARFIELD, LOUP, BLAINE, THOMAS, HOOKER, GRANT, ARTHUR, McPHERSON, LOGAN, CUSTER, VALLEY, GREELEY, BOONE, PLATTE, COLFAX, DODGE, WASHINGTON, SAUNDERS, DOUGLAS, SARPY, BUTLER, POLK, NANCE, MERRICK, HOWARD, SHERMAN, BUFFALO, HALL, HAMILTON, YORK, SEWARD, LANCASTER, CASS, OTOE, SAUNDERS, BOX BUTTE, MORRILL, GARDEN, DEUEL, KEITH, LINCOLN, DAWSON, GOSPER, PHELPS, KEARNEY, ADAMS, CLAY, FILLMORE, SALINE, JOHNSON, NEMAHA, PAWNEE, RICHARDSON, GAGE, JEFFERSON, THAYER, NUCKOLLS, WEBSTER, FRANKLIN, HARLAN, FURNAS, RED WILLOW, HITCHCOCK, HAYES, FRONTIER, CHASE, DUNDY, PERKINS, CHEYENNE, KIMBALL, BANNER, SCOTTS BLUFF, SHERIDAN

WIND CAVE NATIONAL PARK
JEWEL CAVE NAT'L MON.
FOSSIL CYCAD NAT'L MON.

NORTH PLATTE

MISSOURI RIVER
PLATTE RIVER
NIOBRARA RIVER
REPUBLICAN RIVER
LOUP RIVER

RAILROADS
All railroads are numbered as per accompanying list, making possible quick and accurate identification of each line.

7   Atchison, Topeka & Santa Fe
42 Chicago & North Western
45 Chicago, Burlington & Quincy
46 Chicago Great Western
51 Chicago, Milwaukee, St. Paul & Pacific
54 Chicago, Rock Island & Pacific
55 Chicago, St. Paul, Minneapolis & Omaha
80 Great Northern
87 Illinois Central
122 Missouri Pacific
180 Union Pacific
185 Wabash

SCALE OF MILES
0 5 10 20 30 40 50 60

⊗ State Capitals
⊙ County Seats
— Railroads

Copyright by C. S. Hammond & Co., N. Y.

West of Greenwich
Longitude
104° 103° 102° 101° 100° 99° 98° 97° 96°
43° 42° 41° 40°

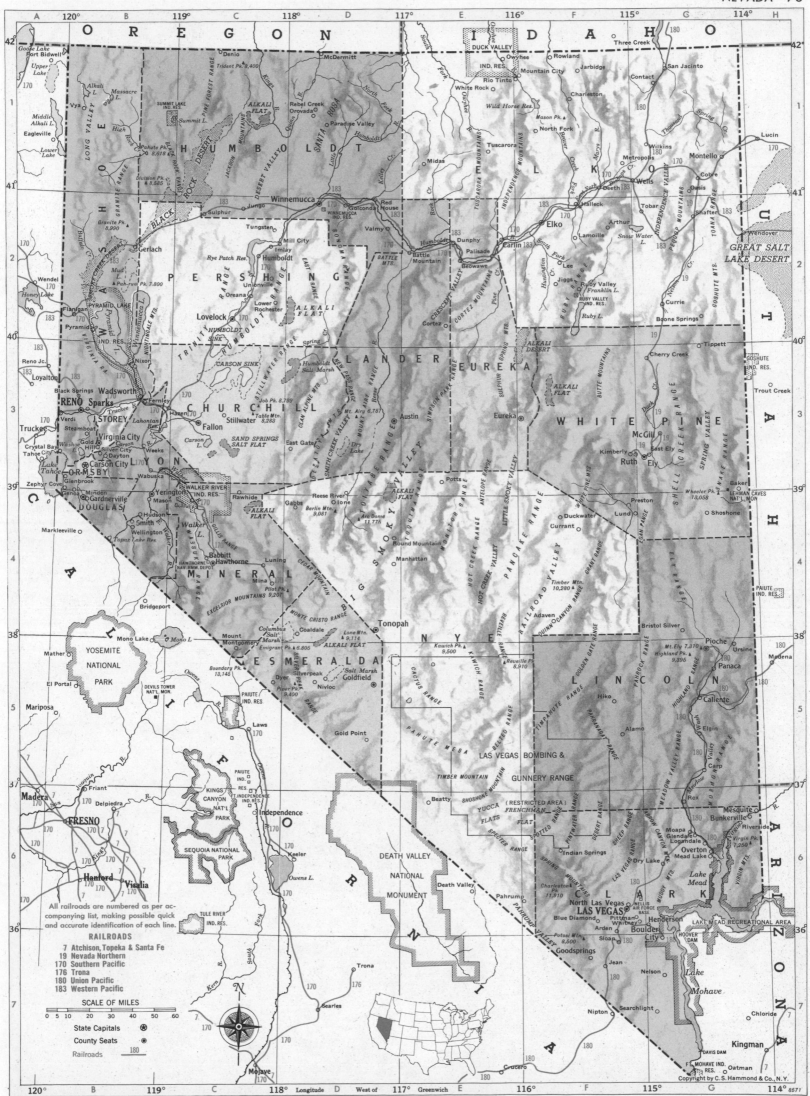

All railroads are numbered as per accompanying list, making possible quick and accurate identification of each line.

RAILROADS

7 Atchison, Topeka & Santa Fe
19 Nevada Northern
170 Southern Pacific
176 Trona
180 Union Pacific
183 Western Pacific

SCALE OF MILES
0 5 10 20 30 40 50 60

✪ State Capitals
⊛ County Seats
Railroads ___180___

Copyright by C. S. Hammond & Co., N.Y.

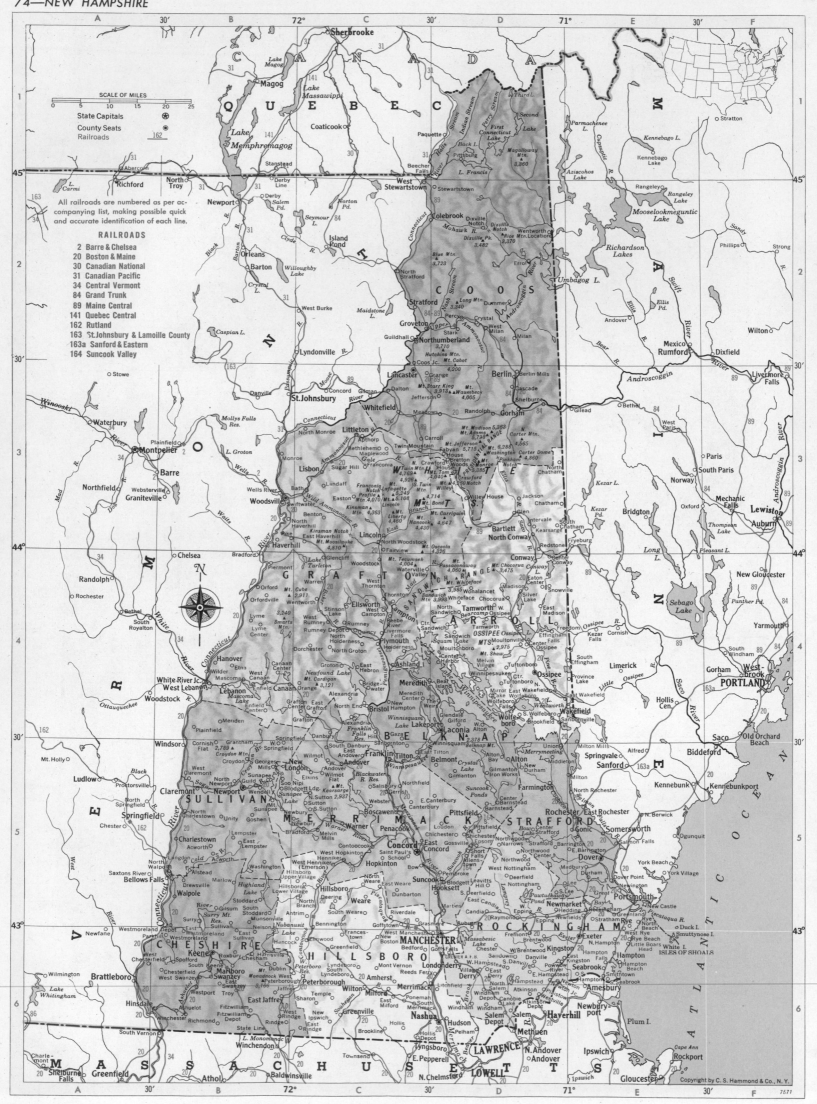

SCALE OF MILES
0 5 10 15 20 25

⊛ State Capitals
⊛ County Seats
Railroads ___162___

All railroads are numbered as per accompanying list, making possible quick and accurate identification of each line.

RAILROADS

2 Barre & Chelsea
20 Boston & Maine
30 Canadian National
31 Canadian Pacific
34 Central Vermont
84 Grand Trunk
89 Maine Central
141 Quebec Central
162 Rutland
163 St.Johnsbury & Lamoille County
163a Sanford & Eastern
164 Suncook Valley

Copyright by C. S. Hammond & Co., N. Y.

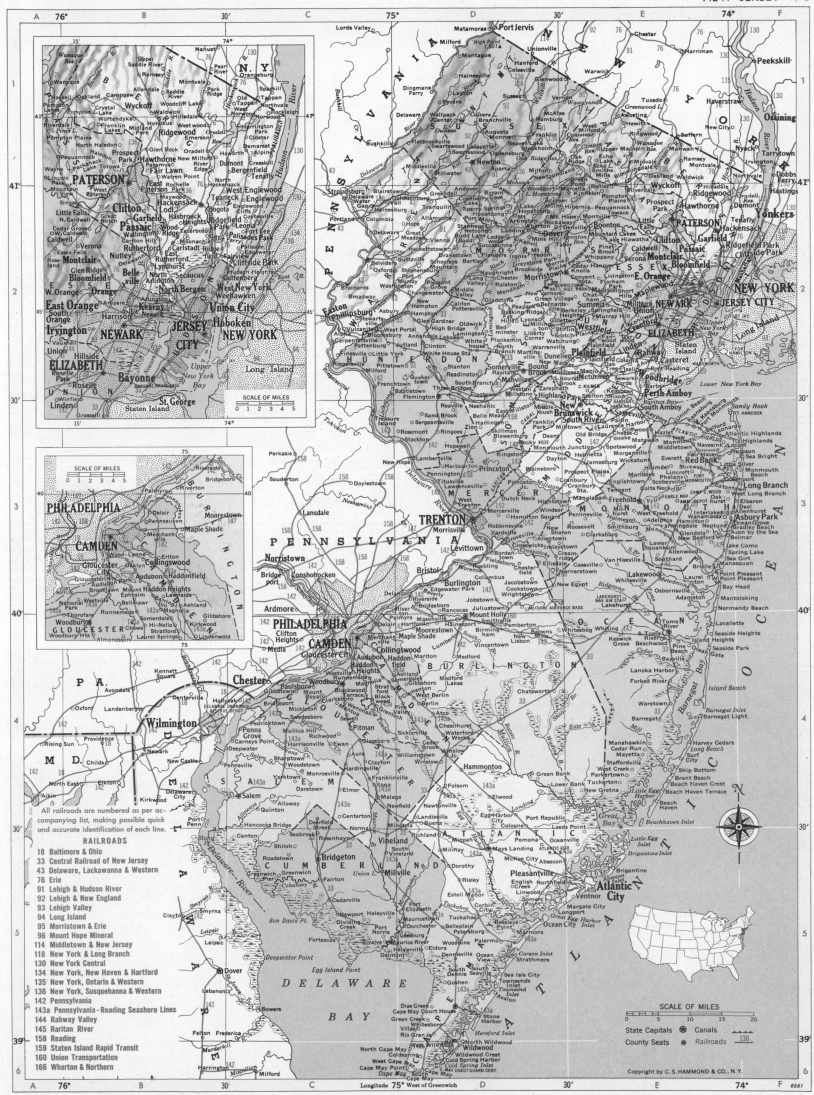

RAILROADS

18 Baltimore & Ohio
33 Central Railroad of New Jersey
43 Delaware, Lackawanna & Western
76 Erie
91 Lehigh & Hudson River
92 Lehigh & New England
93 Lehigh Valley
94 Long Island
95 Morristown & Erie
96 Mount Hope Mineral
114 Middletown & New Jersey
118 New York & Long Branch
130 New York Central
134 New York, New Haven & Hartford
135 New York, Ontario & Western
136 New York, Susquehanna & Western
142 Pennsylvania
143a Pennsylvania – Reading Seashore Lines
144 Rahway Valley
145 Raritan River
158 Reading
159 Staten Island Rapid Transit
160 Union Transportation
166 Wharton & Northern

All railroads are numbered as per accompanying list, making possible quick and accurate identification of each line.

SCALE OF MILES
0 5 10 15 20

State Capitals ⊛   Canals
County Seats ⊙   Railroads

Copyright by C. S. HAMMOND & CO., N.Y.

6581

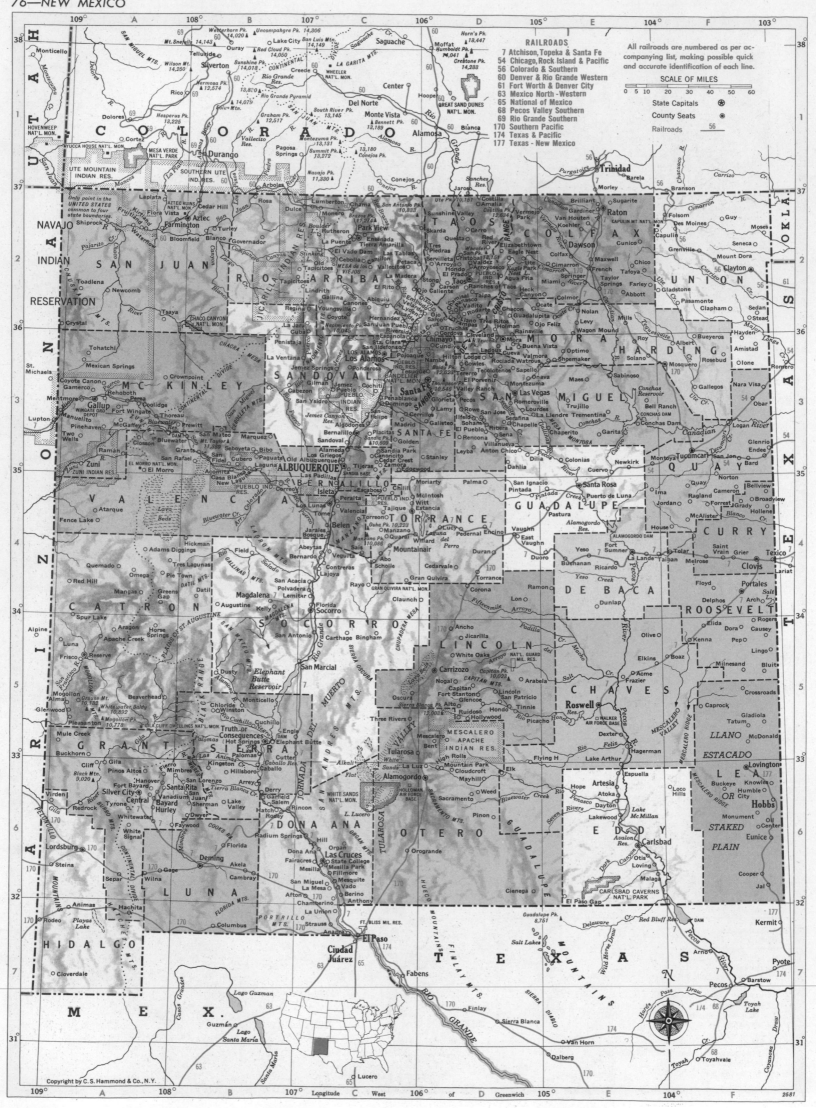

RAILROADS
7 Atchison, Topeka & Santa Fe
54 Chicago, Rock Island & Pacific
56 Colorado & Southern
60 Denver & Rio Grande Western
61 Fort Worth & Denver City
63 Mexico North-Western
65 National of Mexico
68 Pecos Valley Southern
69 Rio Grande Southern
170 Southern Pacific
174 Texas & Pacific
177 Texas-New Mexico

All railroads are numbered as per accompanying list, making possible quick and accurate identification of each line.

SCALE OF MILES
0 5 10   20   30   40   50   60

State Capitals ⊛
County Seats ⊚
Railroads —— 56 ——

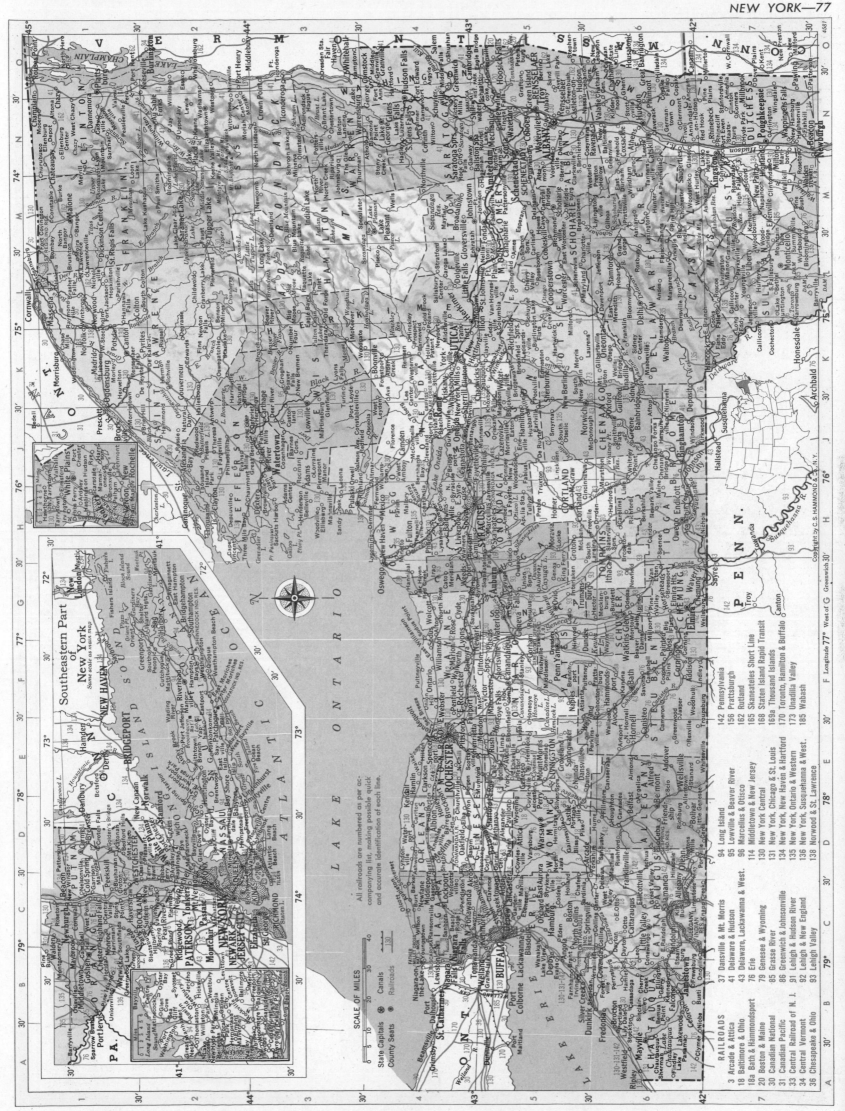

Southeastern Part of
New York
Same scale as main map

SCALE OF MILES

⊛ State Capitals
● County Seats

All railroads are numbered as per accompanying list, making possible quick
and accurate identification of each line.

RAILROADS

3	Arcade & Attica	94	Long Island
		95	Lowville & Beaver River
18	Baltimore & Ohio	96	Marcellus & Otisco
18a	Bath & Hammondsport	114	Middletown & New Jersey
20	Boston & Maine	130	New York Central
30	Canadian National	131	New York, Chicago & St. Louis
31	Canadian Pacific	134	New York, New Haven & Hartford
34	Central Railroad of N. J.	135	New York, Ontario & Western
34	Central Vermont	136	New York, Susquehanna & West.
36	Chesapeake & Ohio	138	Norwood & St. Lawrence
37	Dansville & Mt. Morris	142	Pennsylvania
41	Delaware & Hudson	156	Prattsburgh
43	Delaware, Lackawanna & West.	162	Rutland
79	Erie	165	Skaneateles Short Line
79	Genesee & Wyoming	168	Staten Island Rapid Transit
85	Grasse River	169a	Thousand Islands
86	Greenwich & Johnsonville	170	Toronto, Hamilton & Buffalo
91	Lehigh & Hudson River	173	Unadilla Valley
92	Lehigh & New England	185	Wabash
93	Lehigh Valley		

Copyright by C. S. HAMMOND & CO., N. Y.

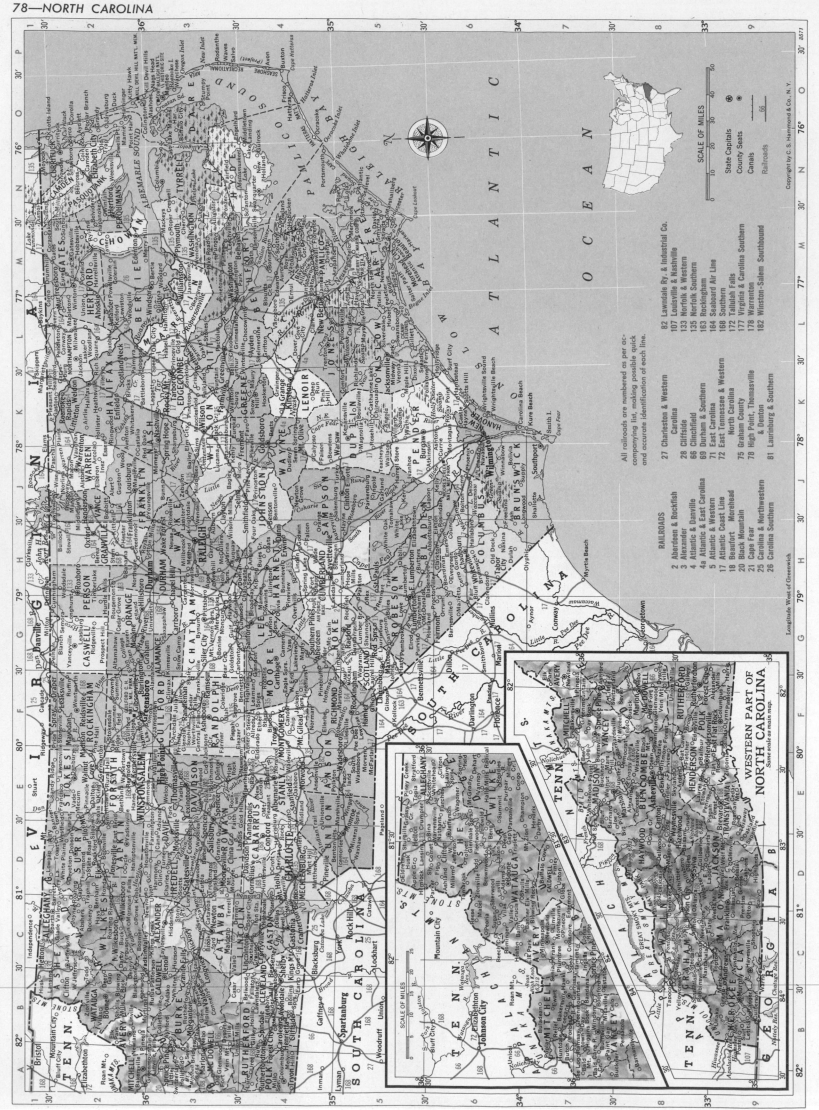

RAILROADS

2	Aberdeen & Rockfish		82	Lawndale Ry. & Industrial Co.
3	Alexander		107	Louisville & Nashville
4	Atlantic & Danville		133	Norfolk & Western
4a	Atlantic & East Carolina		135	Norfolk Southern
5	Atlantic & Western		163	Rockingham
17	Atlantic Coast Line		164	Seaboard Air Line
18	Beaufort Morehead		168	Southern
20	Black Mountain		172	Tallulah Falls
21	Cape Fear		177	Virginia & Carolina Southern
25	Carolina & Northwestern		178	Warrenton
26	Carolina Southern		182	Winston-Salem Southbound
27	Charleston & Rockfish Carolina			
28	Cliffside			
66	Clinchfield			
69	Durham & Southern			
71	East Carolina			
72	East Tennessee & Western North Carolina			
75	Graham County			
78	High Point, Thomasville & Denton			
81	Laurinburg & Southern			

All railroads are numbered as per accompanying list, making possible quick and accurate identification of each line.

SCALE OF MILES

⊗ State Capitals
⊙ County Seats
Canals
Railroads

WESTERN PART OF NORTH CAROLINA
Same scale as main map.

SCALE OF MILES

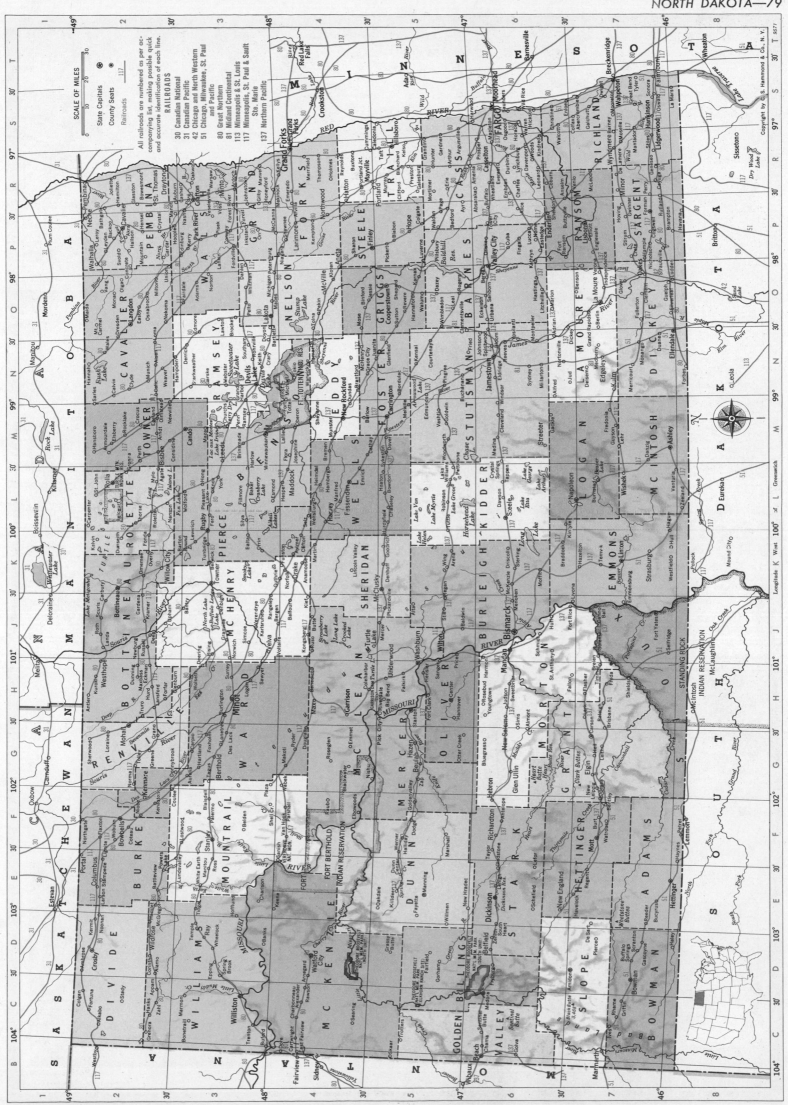

SCALE OF MILES

RAILROADS

All railroads are numbered as per accompanying list, making possible quick and accurate identification of each line.

30 Canadian National
31 Canadian Pacific
42 Chicago and North Western
51 Chicago, Milwaukee, St. Paul and Pacific
80 Great Northern
81 Midland Continental
113 Minneapolis & St. Louis
117 Minneapolis, St. Paul & Sault Ste. Marie
137 Northern Pacific

⊛ State Capitals
⊙ County Seats
Railroads 117

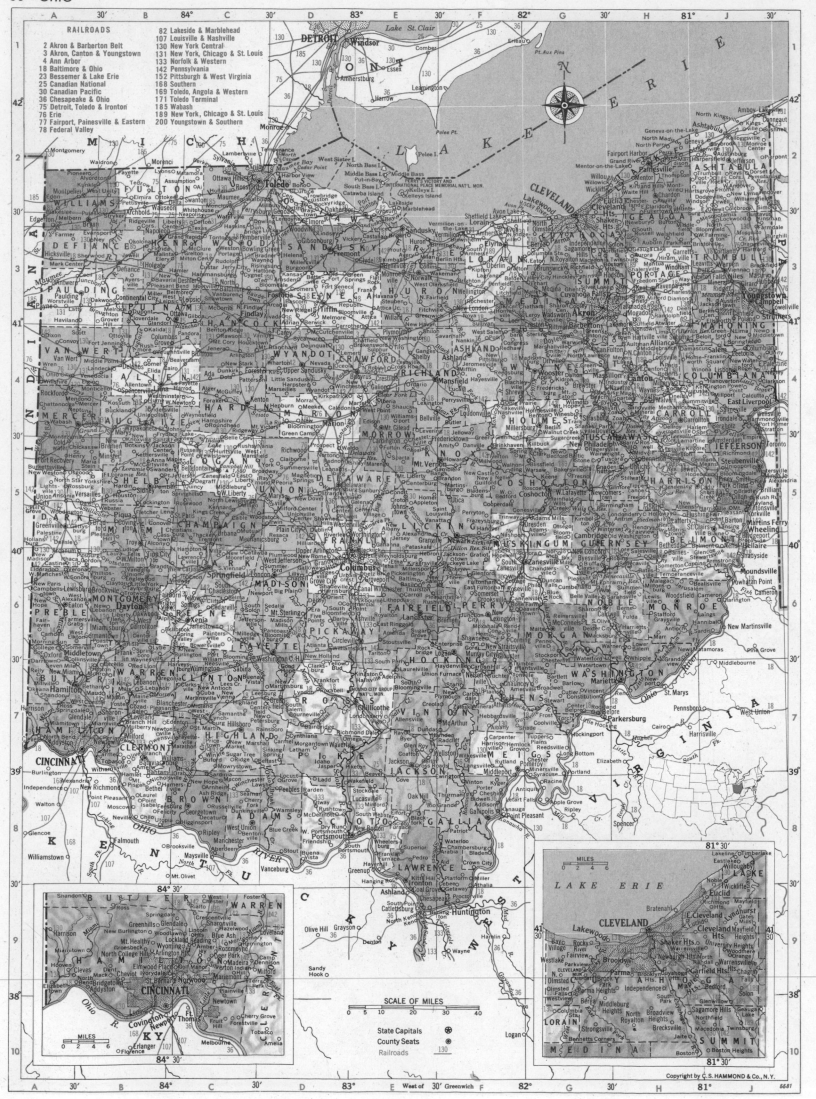

RAILROADS

2 Akron & Barberton Belt	82 Lakeside & Marblehead
3 Akron, Canton & Youngstown	107 Louisville & Nashville
4 Ann Arbor	130 New York Central
18 Baltimore & Ohio	131 New York, Chicago & St. Louis
23 Bessemer & Lake Erie	133 Norfolk & Western
25 Canadian National	142 Pennsylvania
30 Canadian Pacific	152 Pittsburgh & West Virginia
36 Chesapeake & Ohio	168 Southern
75 Detroit, Toledo & Ironton	169 Toledo, Angola & Western
76 Erie	171 Toledo Terminal
77 Fairport, Painesville & Eastern	185 Wabash
78 Federal Valley	189 New York, Chicago & St. Louis
	200 Youngstown & Southern

SCALE OF MILES

State Capitals ✵
County Seats ⊙
Railroads 130

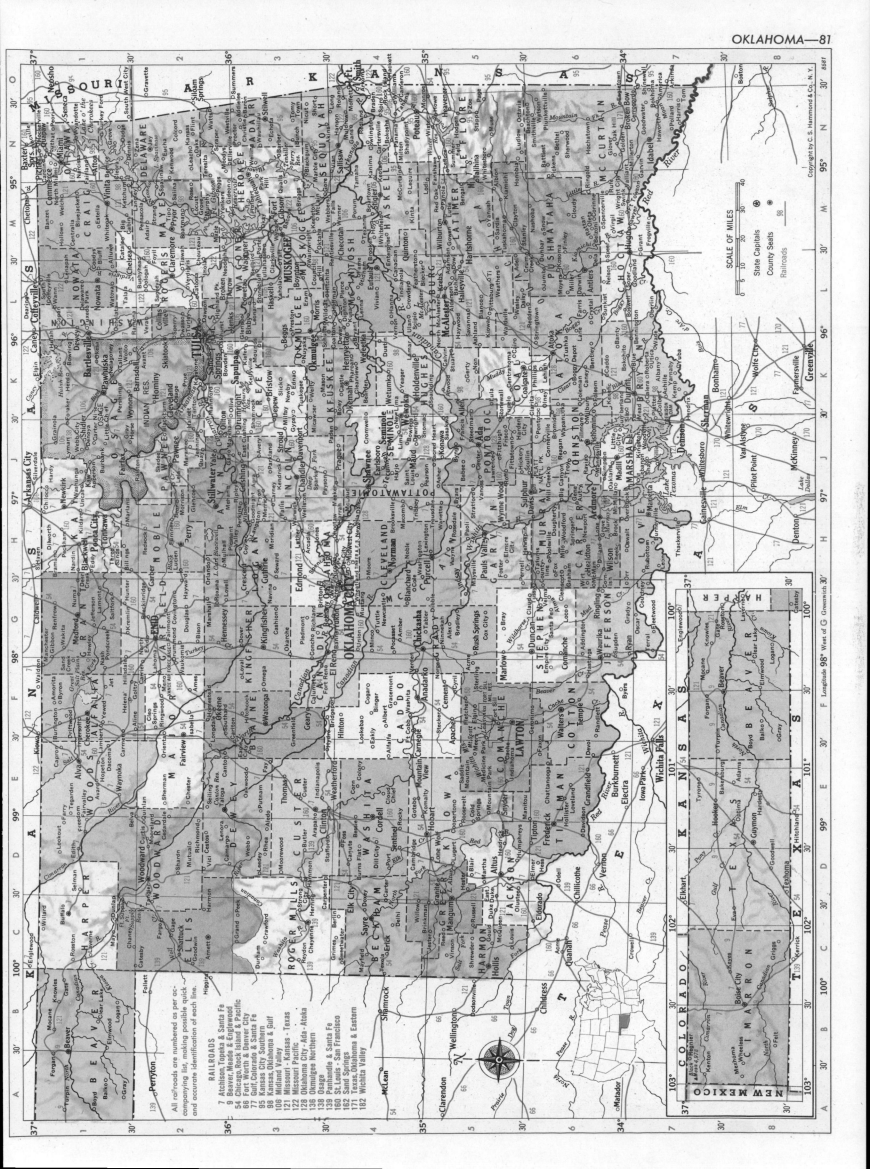

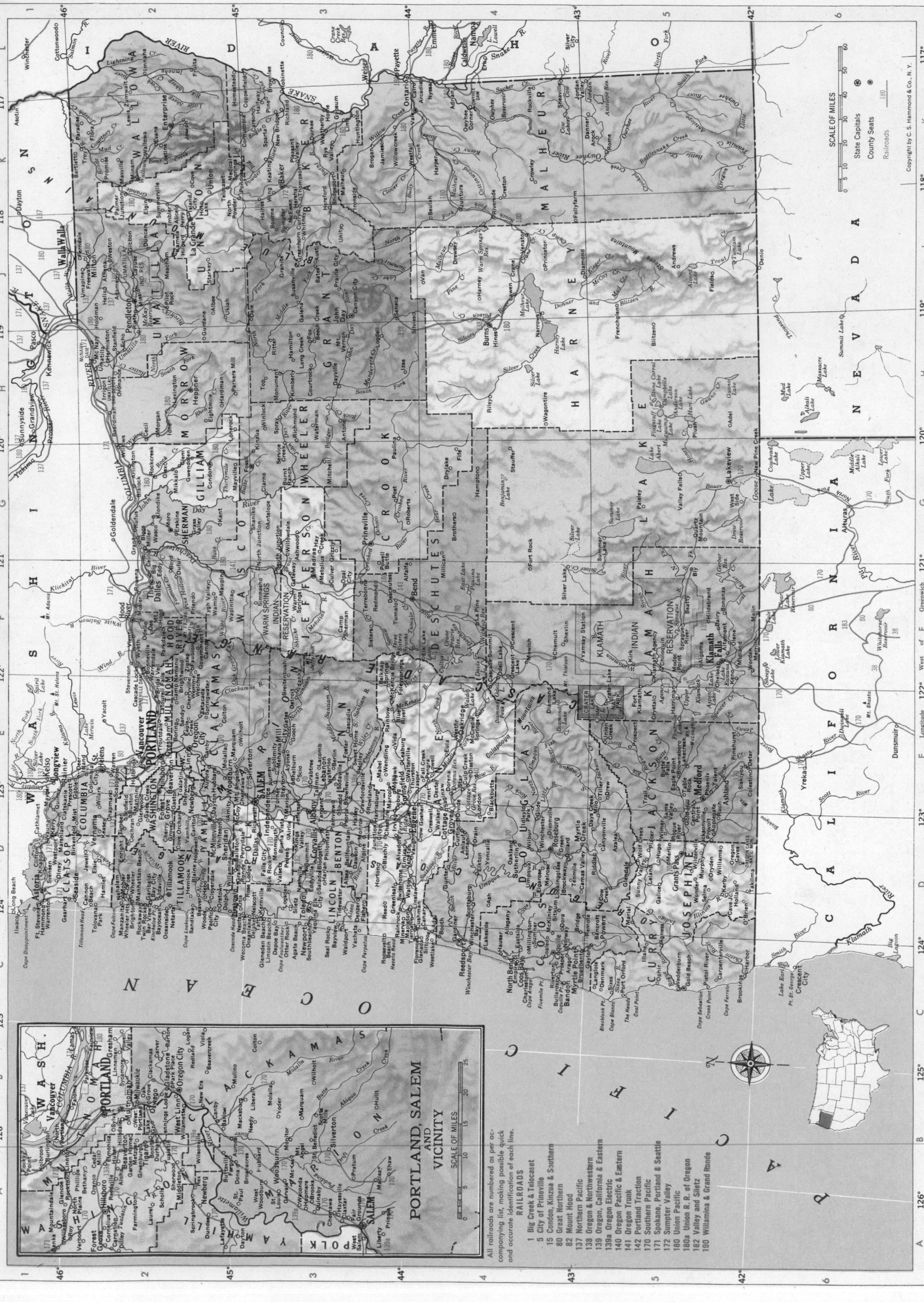

PORTLAND, SALEM AND VICINITY

SCALE OF MILES

RAILROADS

All railroads are numbered as per accompanying list, making possible quick and accurate identification of each line.

1 Big Creek & Telocaset
5 City of Prineville
15 Condon, Kinzua & Southern
80 Great Northern
82 Mount Hood
137 Northern Pacific
138 Oregon & Northwestern
139 Oregon, California & Eastern
139a Oregon Pacific & Eastern
140 Oregon Electric
141 Oregon Trunk
142 Portland Traction
170 Southern Pacific
171 Spokane, Portland & Seattle
172 Sumpter Valley
180 Union Pacific
180a Union R.R. of Oregon
182 Valley and Siletz
190 Willamina & Grand Ronde

SCALE OF MILES

State Capitals
County Seats
Railroads

Copyright by C. S. Hammond & Co., N.Y.

PACIFIC OCEAN

WASHINGTON
IDAHO
NEVADA
CALIFORNIA

CLATSOP
COLUMBIA
TILLAMOOK
WASHINGTON
MULTNOMAH
YAMHILL
CLACKAMAS
POLK
MARION
LINCOLN
BENTON
LINN
LANE
DOUGLAS
COOS
CURRY
JOSEPHINE
JACKSON
KLAMATH
LAKE
HARNEY
MALHEUR
DESCHUTES
CROOK
JEFFERSON
WHEELER
GRANT
BAKER
UNION
WALLOWA
UMATILLA
MORROW
GILLIAM
SHERMAN
WASCO
HOOD RIVER
WARM SPRINGS INDIAN RESERVATION
KLAMATH INDIAN RESERVATION

PORTLAND
SALEM

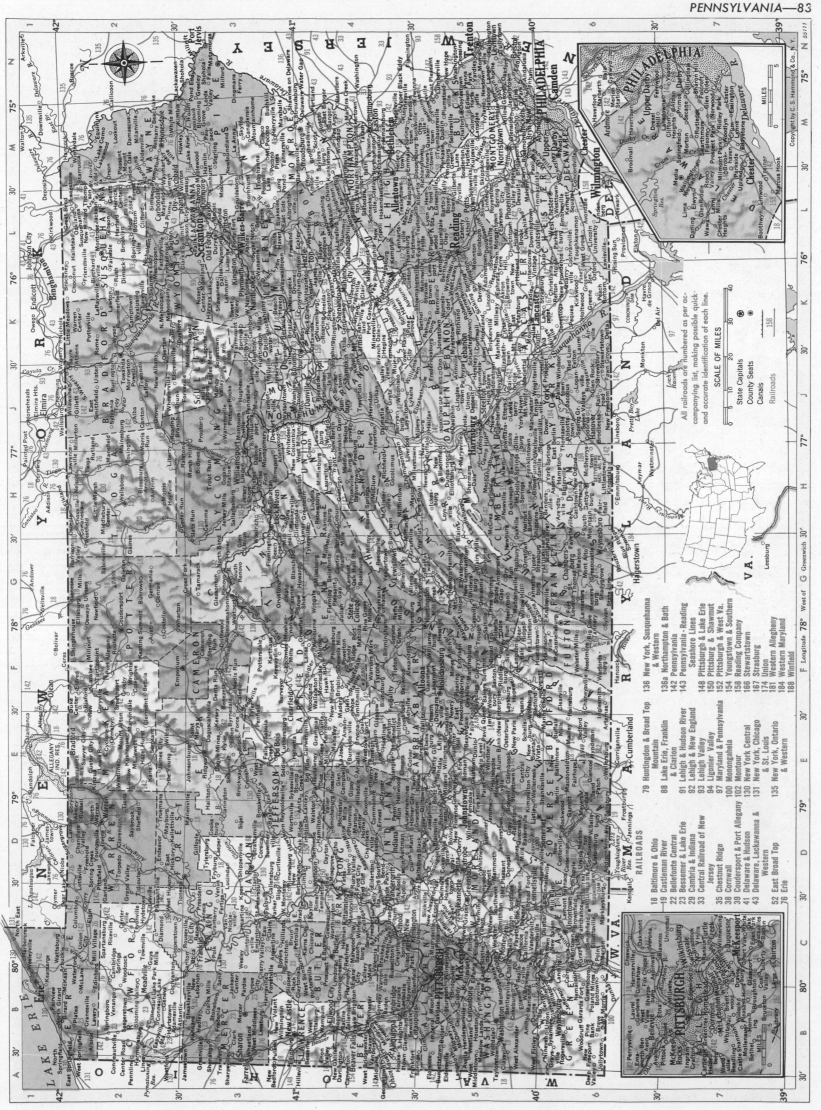

RAILROADS

18	Baltimore & Ohio
19	Castleman River
22	Bellefonte Central
23	Bessemer & Lake Erie
29	Cambria & Indiana
33	Central Railroad of New Jersey
35	Chestnut Ridge
38	Cornwall
39	Coudersport & Port Allegany
41	Delaware & Hudson
43	Delaware, Lackawanna & Western
52	East Broad Top
76	Erie
79	Huntingdon & Broad Top Mountain
88	Lake Erie, Franklin & Clarion
91	Lehigh & Hudson River
92	Lehigh & New England
93	Lehigh Valley
97	Ligonier Valley
100	Monongahela
102	Montour
130	New York Central
131	New York, Chicago & St. Louis
135	New York, Ontario & Western
136	New York, Susquehanna & Western
136a	Northampton & Bath
142	Pennsylvania
143	Pennsylvania-Reading Seashore Lines
148	Pittsburgh & Lake Erie
150	Pittsburg & Shawmut
152	Pittsburgh & West Va.
154	Youngstown & Southern
158	Reading Company
166	Stewartstown
167	Strasburg
174	Union
181	Western Allegheny
184	Western Maryland
188	Winfield

SCALE OF MILES

All railroads are numbered as per accompanying list, making possible quick and accurate identification of each line.

⊛ State Capitals
◉ County Seats
——— Canals
——158——— Railroads

Copyright by C. S. Hammond & Co., N.Y.

RAILROADS

All railroads are numbered as per accompanying list, making possible quick and accurate identification of each line.

No.	Railroad
2	Aberdeen & Rockfish
17	Atlantic Coast Line
21	Bennettsville & Cheraw
22	Blue Ridge
23	Buffalo, Union-Carolina
24	Carolina & Northwestern
25	Carolina Western
26	Central of Georgia
27	Charleston & Western Carolina
28	Cliffside
46	Clinchfield
47	Columbia, Newberry & Laurens
50	Edgmoor & Manetta
63	Gainesville Midland
66	Georgia
67	Georgia & Florida
71	Greenville & Northern
72	Hampton & Branchville
73	Hartwell
75	Lancaster & Chester
81	Laurinburg & Southern
108	Louisville & Wadley
110	Macon, Dublin & Savannah
115	Norfolk Southern
124	Pickens
128	Piedmont & Northern
133	Rockingham
139	Sandersville
162	Savannah & Atlanta
164	Seaboard Air Line
168	Southern
169	Sylvania Central
172	Tallulah Falls
173	Virginia & Carolina Southern
175	Wadley Southern
179	Ware Shoals
180	Winston - Salem Southbound
181	Wrightsville & Tennille

SCALE OF MILES
0 5 10 20 30 40

State Capitals
County Seats
Canals
Railroads

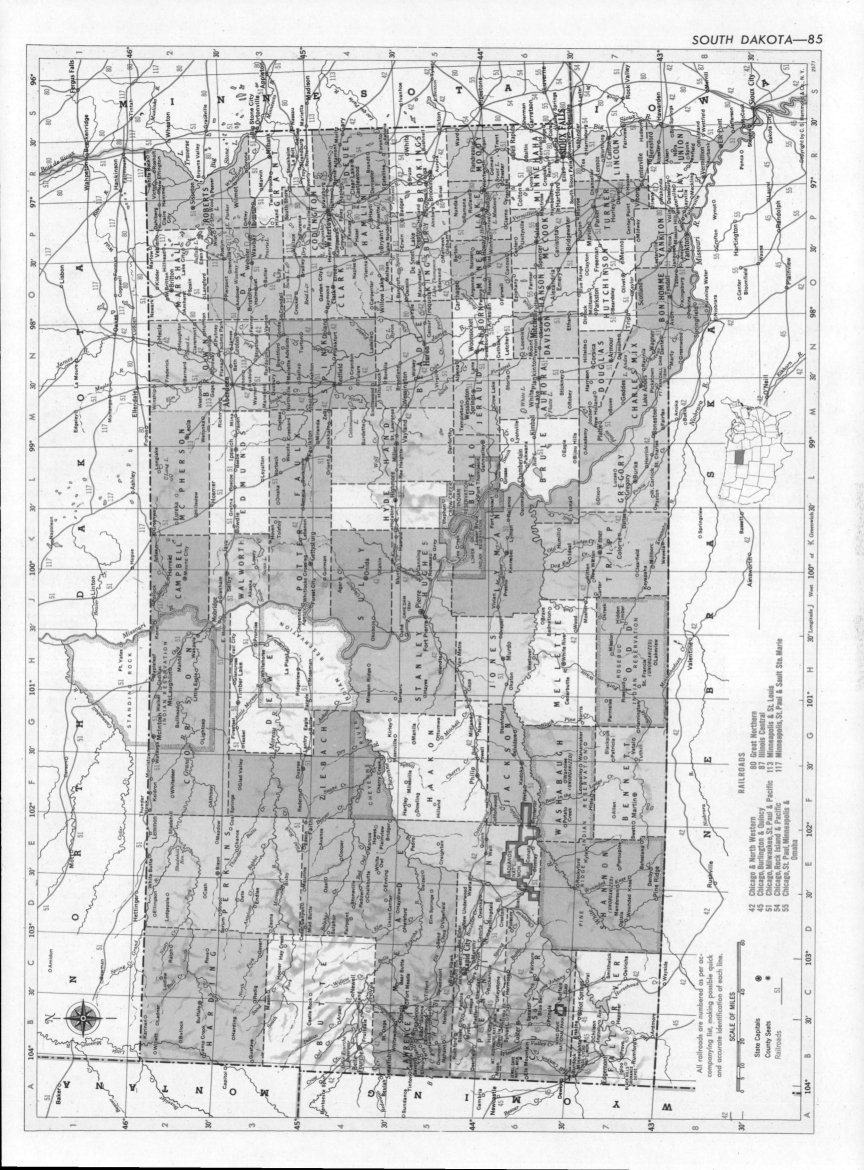

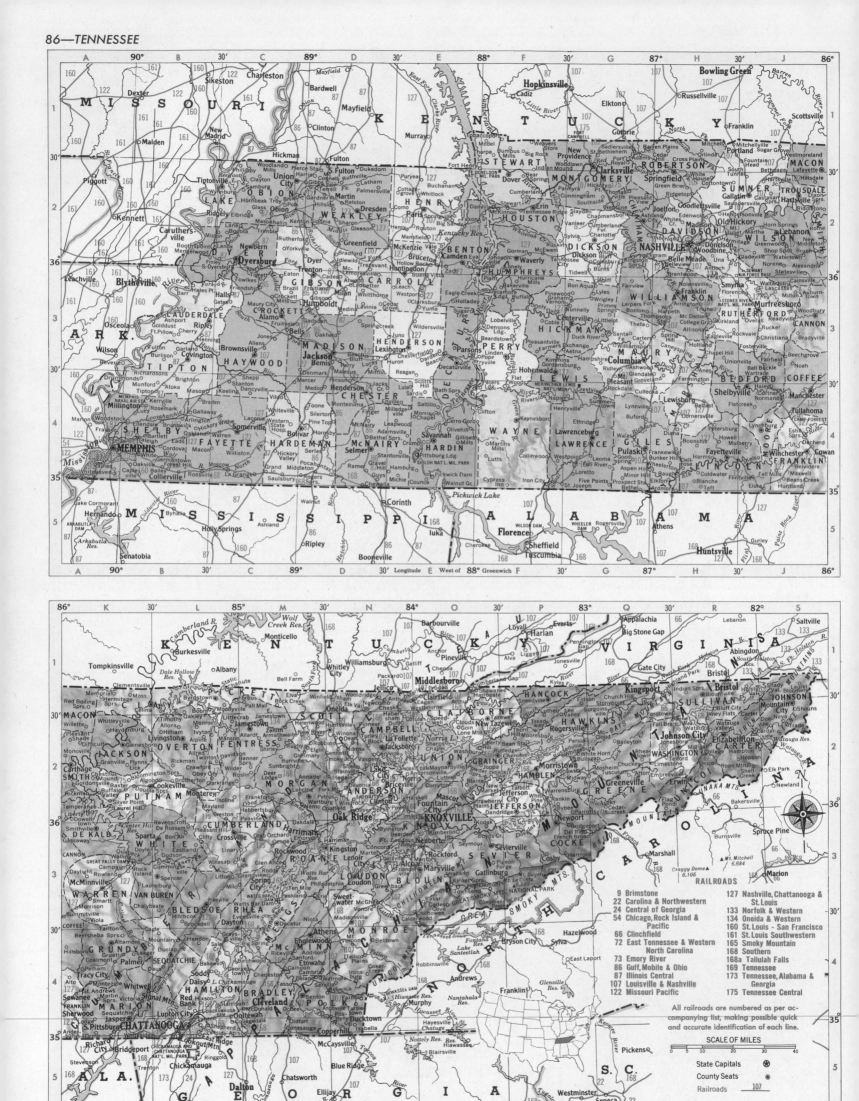

SCALE OF MILES

State Capitals ⊛
County Seats •
Railroads ——107——

RAILROADS

9 Brimstone	127 Nashville, Chattanooga &
22 Carolina & Northwestern	St. Louis
24 Central of Georgia	133 Norfolk & Western
54 Chicago, Rock Island &	134 Oneida & Western
Pacific	160 St. Louis - San Francisco
66 Clinchfield	161 St. Louis Southwestern
72 East Tennessee & Western	165 Smoky Mountain
North Carolina	168 Southern
73 Emory River	168a Tallulah Falls
86 Gulf, Mobile & Ohio	169 Tennessee
87 Illinois Central	173 Tennessee, Alabama &
107 Louisville & Nashville	Georgia
122 Missouri Pacific	175 Tennessee Central

All railroads are numbered as per accompanying list, making possible quick and accurate identification of each line.

Copyright by C.S. Hammond & Co., N.Y.

95111

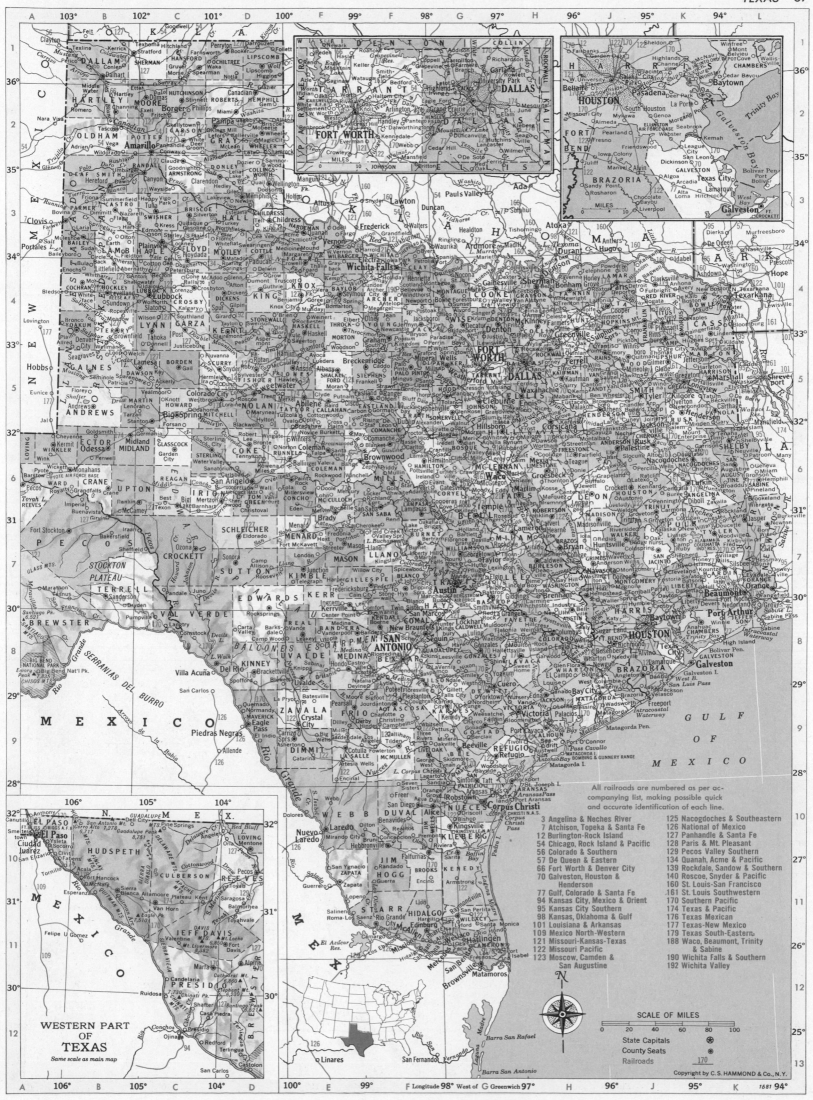

WESTERN PART
OF
TEXAS
Same scale as main map

All railroads are numbered as per accompanying list, making possible quick and accurate identification of each line.

3 Angelina & Neches River	125	Nacogdoches & Southeastern
7 Atchison, Topeka & Santa Fe	126	National of Mexico
12 Burlington-Rock Island	127	Panhandle & Santa Fe
54 Chicago, Rock Island & Pacific	128	Paris & Mt. Pleasant
56 Colorado & Southern	129	Pecos Valley Southern
57 De Queen & Eastern	134	Quanah, Acme & Pacific
66 Fort Worth & Denver City	139	Rockdale, Sandow & Southern
70 Galveston, Houston & Henderson	140	Roscoe, Snyder & Pacific
77 Gulf, Colorado & Santa Fe	160	St. Louis-San Francisco
94 Kansas City, Mexico & Orient	161	St. Louis Southwestern
95 Kansas City Southern	170	Southern Pacific
98 Kansas, Oklahoma & Gulf	174	Texas & Pacific
101 Louisiana & Arkansas	176	Texas Mexican
109 Mexico North-Western	177	Texas-New Mexico
121 Missouri-Kansas-Texas	179	Texas South-Eastern
122 Missouri Pacific	188	Waco, Beaumont, Trinity & Sabine
123 Moscow, Camden & San Augustine	190	Wichita Falls & Southern
	192	Wichita Valley

SCALE OF MILES

State Capitals
County Seats
Railroads

Copyright by C.S. HAMMOND & Co., N.Y.

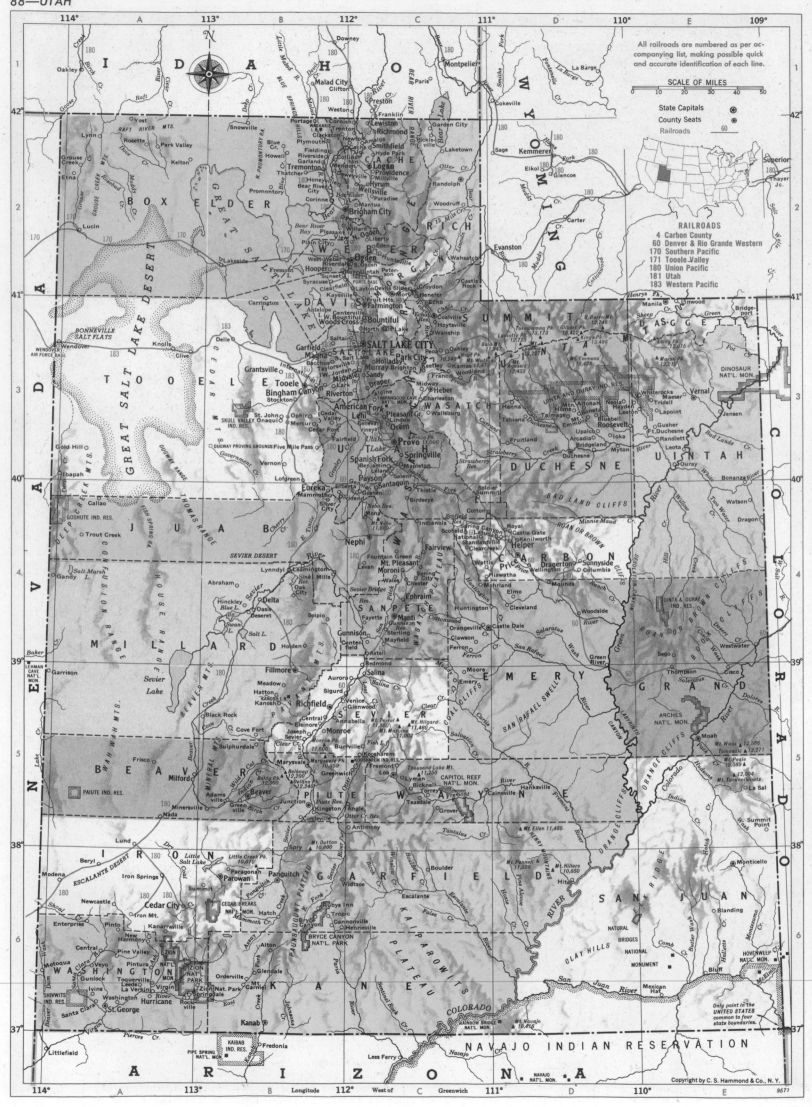

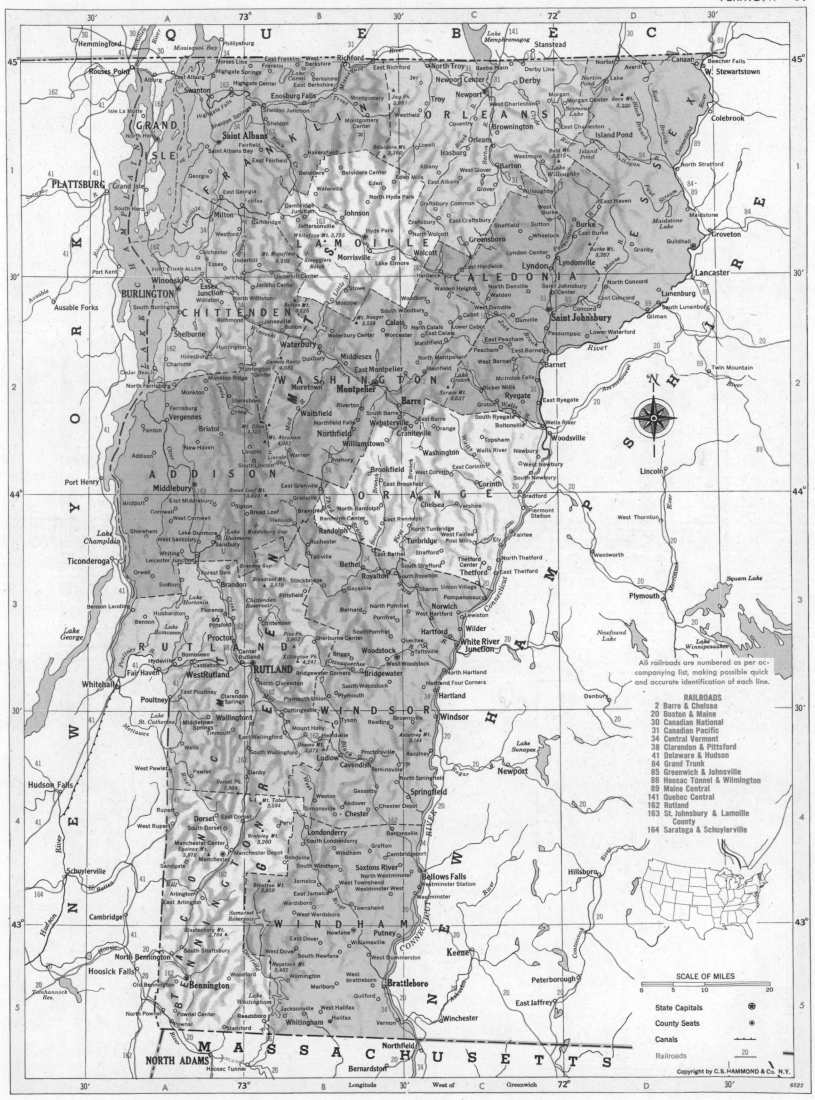

RAILROADS

- 2 Barre & Chelsea
- 20 Boston & Maine
- 30 Canadian National
- 31 Canadian Pacific
- 34 Central Vermont
- 38 Clarendon & Pittsford
- 41 Delaware & Hudson
- 84 Grand Trunk
- 85 Greenwich & Johnsville
- 86 Hoosac Tunnel & Wilmington
- 89 Maine Central
- 141 Quebec Central
- 162 Rutland
- 163 St. Johnsbury & Lamoille County
- 164 Saratoga & Schuylerville

All railroads are numbered as per accompanying list, making possible quick and accurate identification of each line.

SCALE OF MILES

State Capitals ⊛
County Seats ⊙
Canals
Railroads

Copyright by C.S. HAMMOND & Co. N.Y.

6522

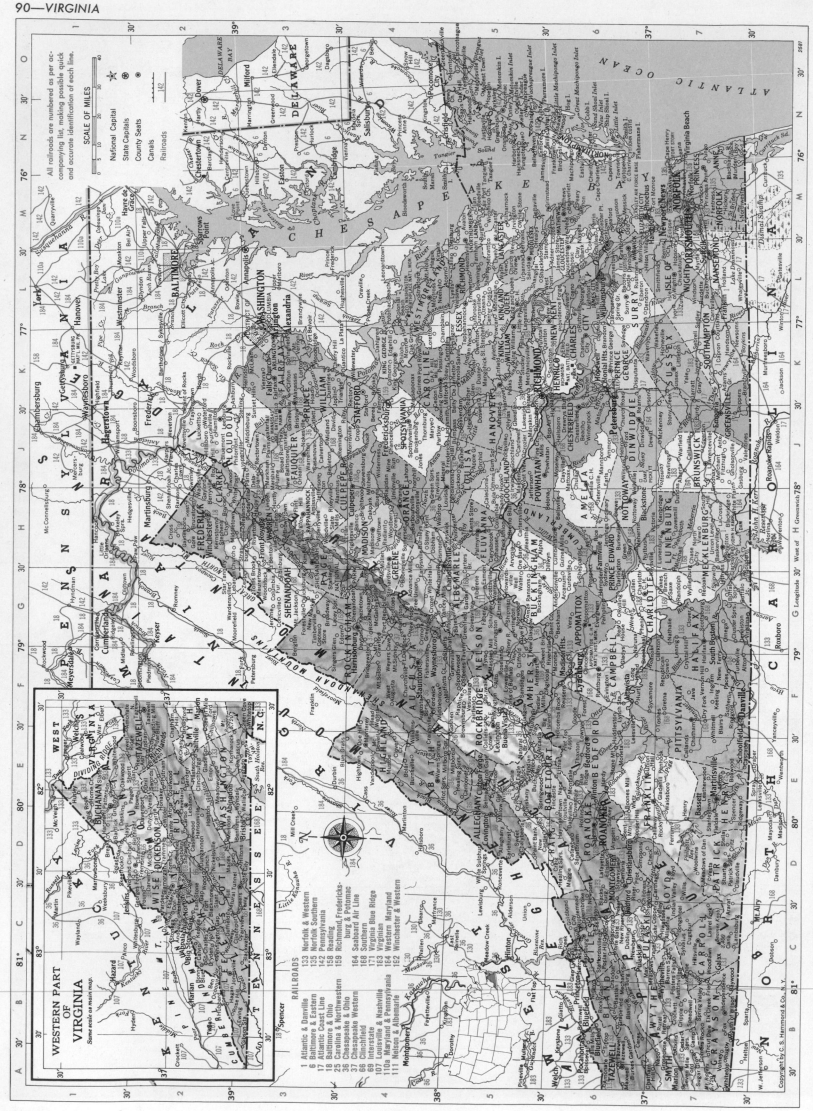

All railroads are numbered as per accompanying list, making possible quick and accurate identification of each line.

SCALE OF MILES

National Capital
State Capitals
County Seats
Canals
Railroads

RAILROADS

1 Atlantic & Danville
6 Baltimore & Eastern
17 Atlantic Coast Line
18 Baltimore & Ohio
25 Carolina & Northwestern
36 Chesapeake & Ohio
37 Chesapeake Western
66 Clinchfield
69 Interstate
107 Louisville & Nashville
110a Maryland & Pennsylvania
111 Nelson & Albemarle

133 Norfolk & Western
135 Norfolk Southern
142 Pennsylvania
158 Reading
159 Richmond, Fredericksburg & Potomac
164 Seaboard Air Line
168 Southern
171 Virginian
183 Virginia Blue Ridge
184 Western Maryland
192 Winchester & Western

WESTERN PART OF VIRGINIA
Some scale as main map.

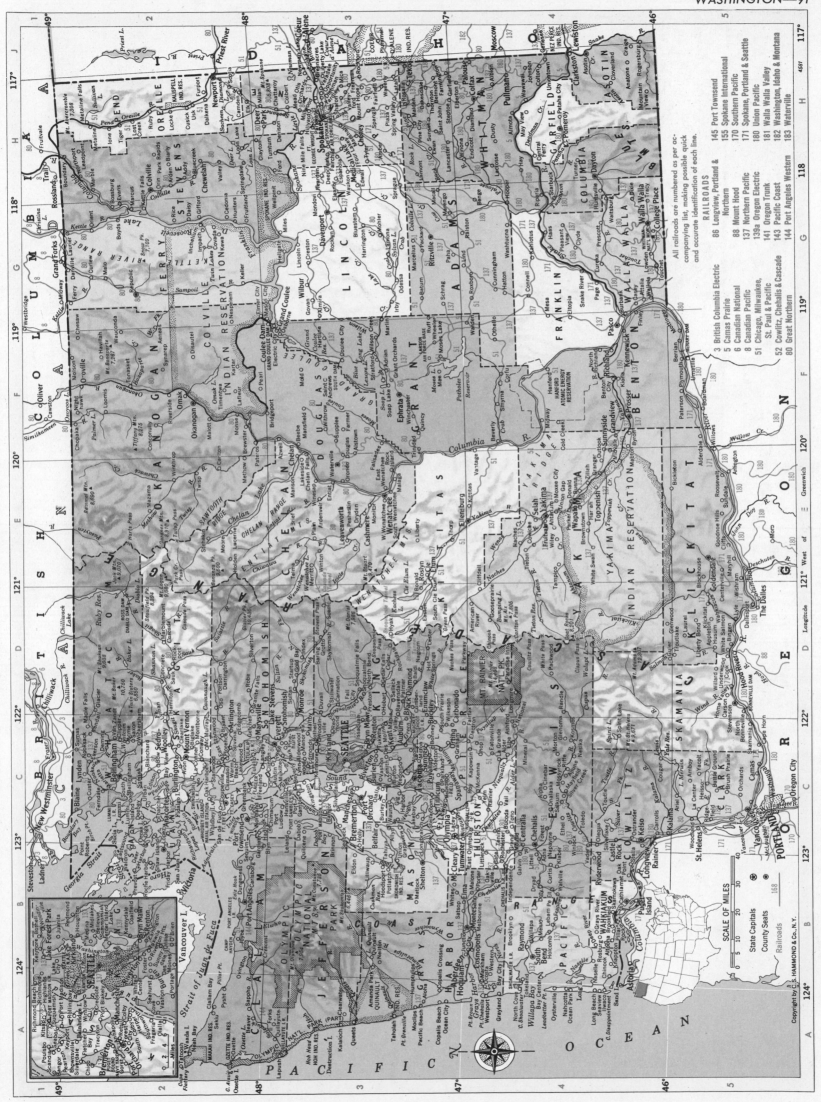

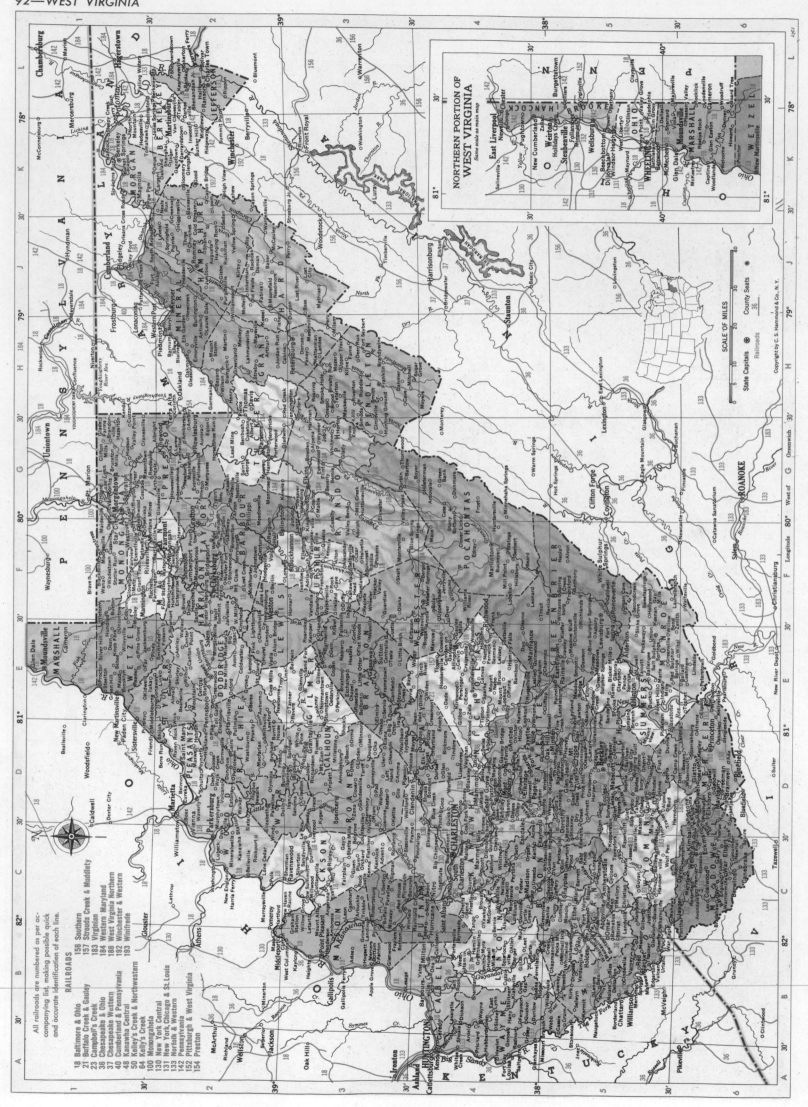

NORTHERN PORTION OF
WEST VIRGINIA
Same scale as main map

RAILROADS

All railroads are numbered as per accompanying list, making possible quick and accurate identification of each line.

18	Baltimore & Ohio	156	Southern
21	Buffalo Creek & Gauley	157	Strouds Creek & Muddlety
23	Campbell's Creek	183	Virginian
36	Chesapeake & Ohio	184	Western Maryland
37	Chesapeake Western	188	West Virginia Northern
40	Cumberland & Pennsylvania	192	Winchester & Western
48	Kanawha Central	193	Winifrede
50	Kelly's Creek		
64	Kelly's Creek & Northwestern		
100	Monongahela		
130	New York Central		
131	New York, Chicago & St. Louis		
133	Norfolk & Western		
142	Pennsylvania		
152	Pittsburgh & West Virginia		
154	Preston		

SCALE OF MILES

⊛ State Capitals ⊛ County Seats ——— Railroads

Copyright by C. S. Hammond & Co., N. Y.

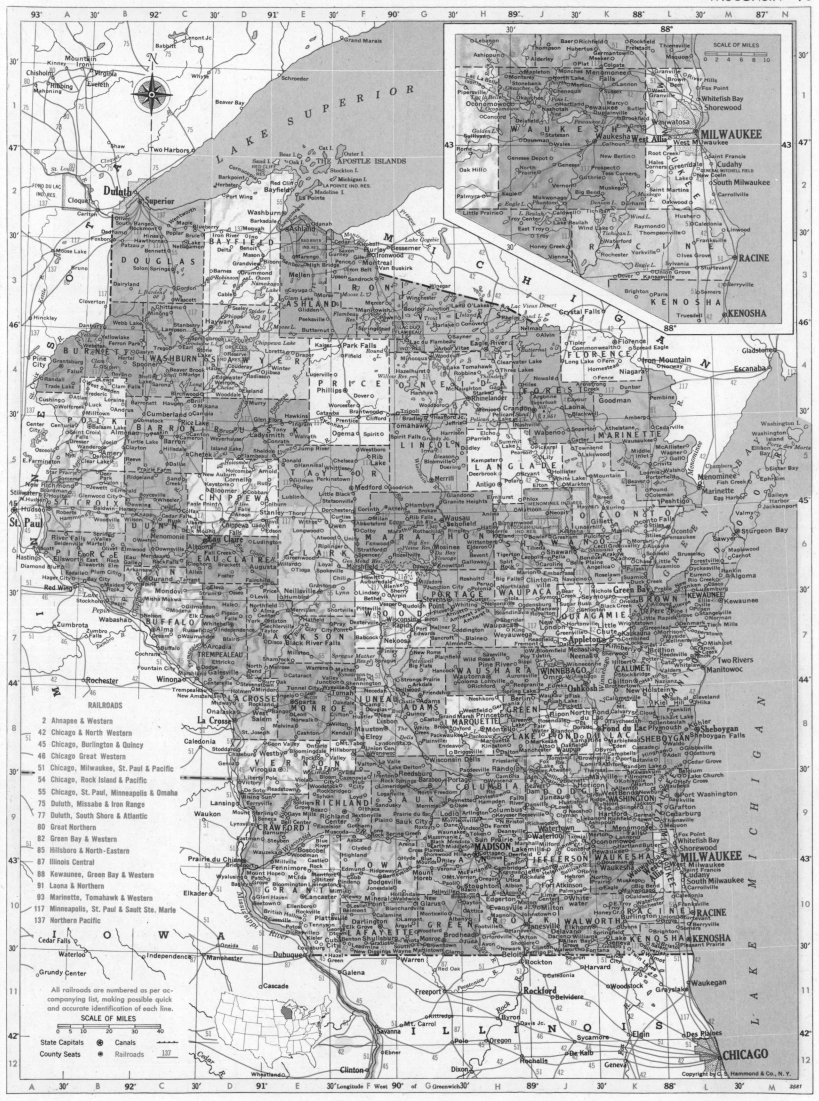

RAILROADS

2 Ahnapee & Western
42 Chicago & North Western
45 Chicago, Burlington & Quincy
46 Chicago Great Western
51 Chicago, Milwaukee, St. Paul & Pacific
54 Chicago, Rock Island & Pacific
55 Chicago, St. Paul, Minneapolis & Omaha
75 Duluth, Missabe & Iron Range
77 Duluth, South Shore & Atlantic
80 Great Northern
82 Green Bay & Western
85 Hillsboro & North-Eastern
87 Illinois Central
88 Kewaunee, Green Bay & Western
91 Laona & Northern
93 Marinette, Tomahawk & Western
117 Minneapolis, St. Paul & Sault Ste. Marie
137 Northern Pacific

All railroads are numbered as per accompanying list, making possible quick and accurate identification of each line.

SCALE OF MILES

State Capitals
County Seats

Canals
Railroads

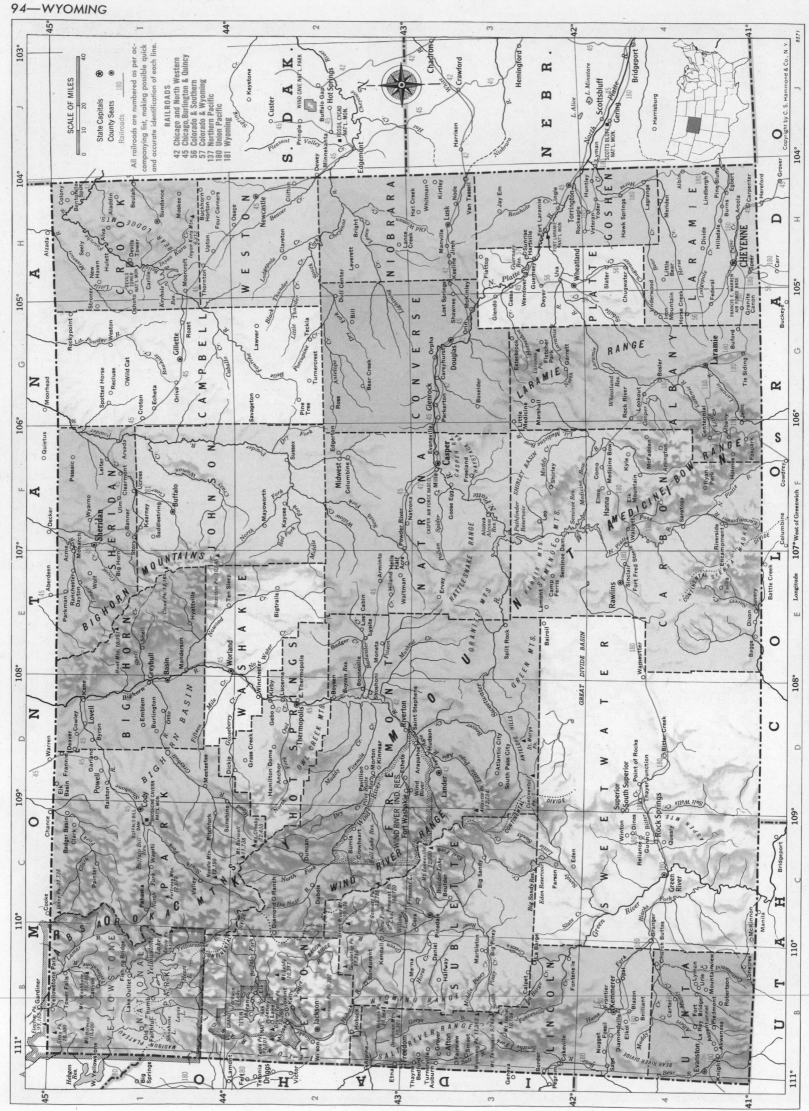

SCALE OF MILES

State Capitals ⊛
County Seats ◉

RAILROADS

All railroads are numbered as per accompanying list, making possible quick
and accurate identification of each line.

42 Chicago and North Western
45 Chicago, Burlington & Quincy
56 Colorado & Southern
57 Colorado & Southern
137 Northern Pacific
180 Union Pacific
181 Wyoming

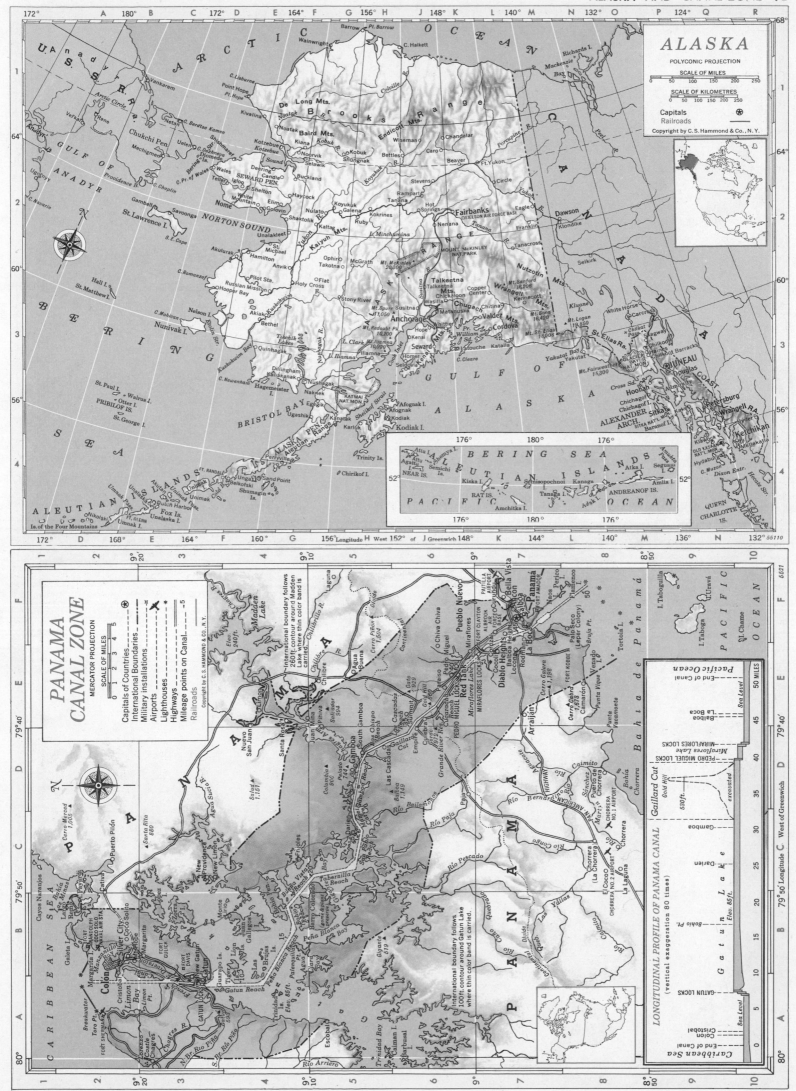

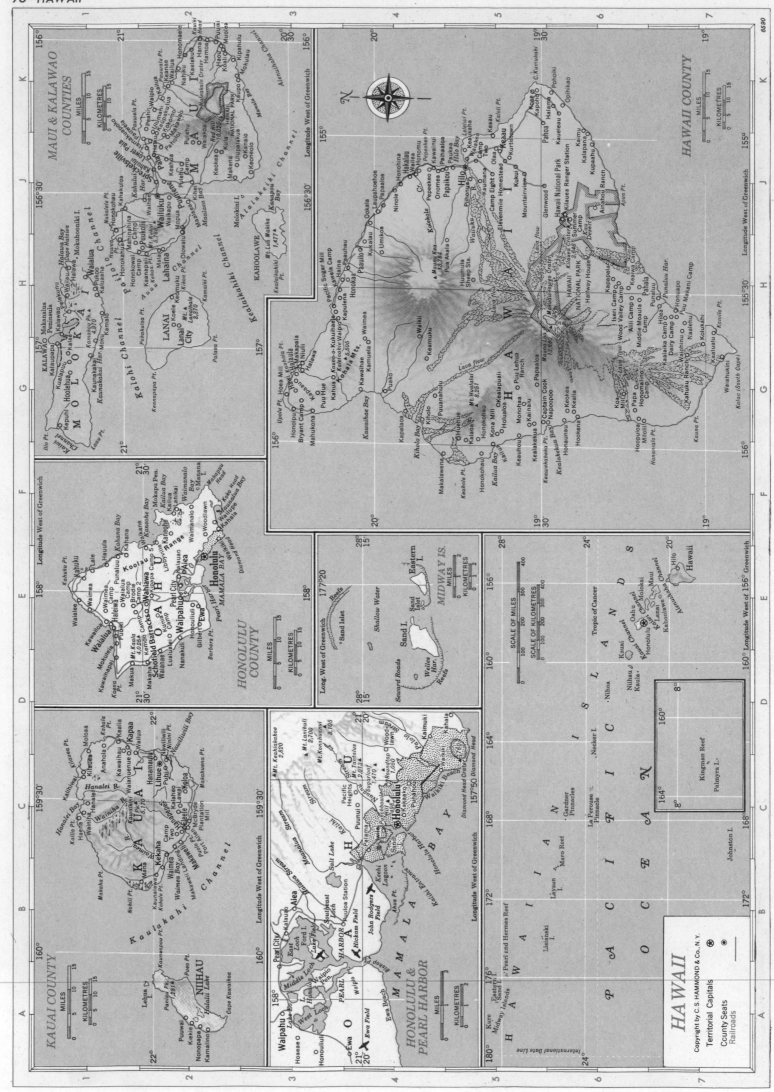

HAWAII

Copyright by C. S. HAMMOND & Co., N. Y.

Territorial Capitals ⊛
County Seats ⊙
Railroads ——————

Index of the
UNITED STATES

In this compilation the official population figures of incorporated places are given according to the latest (1950) Federal Census. The symbol □ denotes population of townships. For unincorporated places which are not separately enumerated by the Census, recent estimates supplied by local officials or other reliable authorities are given.

Following the place name is the abbreviated name of the state in which it is located, the population, the map reference and the page number on which it is to be found. Capitals of states are printed in capital letters.

Index Ref. — Plate No.

Abbeville, Ala., 2,162 ... H 7 49
Abbeville, La., 9,338 ... F 7 63
Abbeville, S. C., 5,395 ... D 3 84
Aberdeen, Idaho, 1,486 ... F 7 57
Aberdeen, Md., 2,944 ... K 2 65
Aberdeen, Miss., 5,290 ... H 3 69
Aberdeen, S. Dak., 21,051 ... M 3 85
Aberdeen, Wash., 19,653 ... B 4 91
Abilene, Kans., 5,775 ... E 3 61
Abilene, Tex., 45,570 ... E 5 87
Abingdon, Ill., 3,300 ... C 3 58
Abingdon, Va., 4,709 ... E 2 90
Abington, Mass., □7,152 ... L 4 66
Abiquiu, N. Mex., 680 ... C 2 76
Accoville, W. Va., 1,400 ... C 5 92
Ackerman, Miss., 1,463 ... F 4 69
Ackley, Iowa, 1,608 ... G 3 60
Acushnet, Mass., □4,401 ... L 6 66
Acworth, Ga., 1,466 ... C 2 56
Ada, Minn., 2,121 ... B 3 68
Ada, Ohio, 3,640 ... C 4 80
Ada, Okla., 15,595 ... J 5 81
Adairville, Ky., 800 ... D 7 62
Adams, Mass., □12,034 ... B 2 66
Adams, N. Y., 1,762 ... J 3 77
Adams, Wis., 1,425 ... G 8 93
Adamsville, R. I., 250 ... K 6 66
Adamsville, Tenn., 927 ... E 4 86
Addison, N. Y., 1,920 ... F 6 77
Addison, W. Va., 1,313 ... F 4 92
Addyston, Ohio, 1,651 ... A 7 80
Adel, Ga., 2,776 ... F 8 56
Adel, Iowa, 1,799 ... E 5 60
Adena, Ohio, 1,517 ... J 5 80
Adrian, Mich., 18,393 ... E 7 67
Adrian, Minn., 1,115 ... C 7 68
Afton, Okla., 1,252 ... N 1 81
Afton, Wyo., 1,319 ... B 3 94
Agawam, Mass., □10,166 ... D 5 66
Aguilar, Colo., 1,038 ... K 8 53
Ahoskie, N. C., 3,579 ... L 2 78
Aiea, Hawaii Territory 3,553 ... B 3 95
Aiken, S. C., 7,083 ... E 4 84
Ainsworth, Nebr., 2,150 ... E 2 72
Aitkin, Minn., 2,079 ... E 4 68
Ajo, Ariz., 5,817 ... C 6 50
Akron, Colo., 1,605 ... N 2 53
Akron, Ind., 946 ... E 2 59
Akron, Iowa, 1,251 ... A 3 60
Akron, N. Y., 2,481 ... B 4 77
Akron, Ohio, 274,605 ... G 3 80
Alachua, Fla., 1,116 ... D 2 55
Alameda, Calif., 64,430 ... J 2 52
Alameda, Idaho, 4,694 ... F 7 57
Alamo, Nev., 384 ... F 5 73
Alamo, Tenn., 1,501 ... C 3 86
Alamo, Tex., 3,017 ... G11 87
Alamogordo, N. Mex., 6,783 ... C 6 76
Alamo Heights, Tex., 8,000 ... F 8 87
Alamosa, Colo., 5,354 ... H 8 53
Albany, Calif., 17,590 ... J 2 52
Albany, Ga., 31,155 ... D 7 56
Albany, Ind., 1,846 ... G 4 59
Albany, Ky., 1,920 ... G 7 62
Albany, Minn., 1,196 ... D 5 68
Albany, Mo., 1,850 ... D 2 70
ALBANY, N. Y., 134,995 ... N 5 77
Albany, Oreg., 10,115 ... D 3 82
Albany, Tex., 2,241 ... E 5 87
Albany, Vt., 196 ... C 1 89
Albemarle, N. C., 11,798 ... E 4 78
Alberta, Va., 430 ... J 7 90
Albert Lea, Minn., 13,545 ... E 7 68
Alberton, Mont., 326 ... B 3 71
Albertville, Ala., 5,397 ... F 2 49
Albia, Iowa, 4,838 ... H 6 60
Albin, Wyo., 208 ... H 4 94
Albion, Idaho, 610 ... E 7 57
Albion, Ill., 2,287 ... E 5 58
Albion, Ind., 1,341 ... G 2 59
Albion, Mich., 10,406 ... E 6 67
Albion, Nebr., 2,132 ... F 3 72
Albion, N. Y., 4,850 ... D 4 77
Albuquerque, N. Mex., 96,815 ... C 3 86
Alburg, Vt., 563 ... A 1 89
Alcester, S. Dak., 585 ... R 7 85
Alcoa, Tenn., 6,355 ... N 3 76
Aldan, Pa., 3,430 ... M 6 83
Alderson, W. Va., 1,489 ... E 5 92
Aldrich, Ala., 1,000 ... E 4 49
Aledo, Ill., 2,919 ... C 2 58
Alexander City, Ala., 6,430 ... G 5 49
Alexandria, Ind., 5,147 ... F 4 59
Alexandria, La., 34,913 ... F 4 63
Alexandria, Minn., 6,319 ... C 5 68
Alexandria, S. Dak., 714 ... O 6 85
Alexandria, Va., 61,787 ... L 3 90
Alexandria Bay, N. Y., 1,688 ... J 2 77
Algoma, Wis., 3,384 ... M 6 93
Algona, Iowa, 5,415 ... E 2 60
Algonac, Mich., 2,639 ... G 6 67
Algood, Tenn., 729 ... K 2 86
Alhambra, Calif., 51,359 ... C10 52
Alice, Tex., 16,449 ... F10 87
Aliceville, Ala., 3,170 ... B 4 49
Aliquippa, Pa., 26,132 ... B 4 83
Alisal, Calif., 16,714 ... D 7 52
Allegan, Mich., 4,801 ... D 6 67
Allegany, N. Y., 1,738 ... C 6 77
Allen, Okla., 1,215 ... K 5 81
Allendale, S. C., 2,474 ... F 5 84
Allen Park, Mich., 12,329 ... B 7 67
Allenstown, N. H., □1,540 ... D 5 74
Allenton, R. I., 250 ... H 6 66
Allentown, Pa., 106,756 ... L 4 83
Alliance, Nebr., 7,891 ... A 2 72
Alliance, Ohio, 26,161 ... H 4 80
Alma, Ark., 1,228 ... B 3 51
Alma, Ga., 2,588 ... H 7 56
Alma, Mich., 8,341 ... E 5 67
Alma, Nebr., 1,768 ... E 4 72
Alma, Wis., 1,060 ... C 7 93
Aloha, Oreg., 50 ... E 2 82
Alpena, Mich., 13,135 ... F 3 67
Alpine, Tex., 5,261 ... D11 87
Alta, Iowa, 1,348 ... C 3 60
Altadena, Calif., 37,500 ... C10 52
Altamont, Ill., 1,580 ... E 4 58
Altavista, Va., 3,332 ... F 6 90
Alton, Ill., 32,550 ... C 5 58
Alton, Iowa, 1,038 ... A 3 60
Alton, N. H., □1,189 ... D 5 74
Altoona, Ala., 860 ... F 2 49
Altoona, Pa., 77,177 ... F 4 83
Altoona, Wis., 1,713 ... D 6 93
Alturas, Calif., 2,819 ... E 2 52
Altus, Okla., 9,735 ... D 5 81
Alva, Okla., 6,505 ... E 1 81
Alvin, Tex., 3,701 ... J 3 87
Amarillo, Tex., 74,246 ... C 2 87
Ambler, Pa., 4,565 ... M 5 83
Amboy, Ill., 2,128 ... D 2 58
Ambridge, Pa., 16,429 ... B 4 83
Amenia, N. Y., 1,300 ... N 7 77
American Falls, Idaho, 1,874 ... F 7 57
American Fork, Utah, 5,126 ... C 3 88
Americus, Ga., 11,389 ... D 6 56
Amery, Wis., 1,625 ... B 5 93
Ames, Iowa, 22,898 ... F 4 60
Amesbury, Mass., □10,851 ... L 1 66
Amherst, Mass., □10,856 ... D 3 66
Amherst, N. H., □1,461 ... C 6 74
Amherst, Ohio, 3,542 ... F 3 80
Amherst, Va., 1,038 ... F 5 90
Amherstdale, W. Va., 2,000 ... C 5 92
Amite, La., 2,804 ... K 5 63
Amity, Oreg., 672 ... D 2 82
Amityville, N. Y., 6,164 ... E 3 77
Ammon, Idaho, 447 ... G 6 57
Amory, Miss., 4,990 ... H 3 69
Amsterdam, N. Y., 32,240 ... M 5 77
Anaconda, Mont., 11,254 ... C 4 71
Anacortes, Wash., 6,919 ... C 2 91
Anadarko, Okla., 6,184 ... F 4 81
Anaheim, Calif., 14,556 ... D11 52
Anamoose, N. Dak., 542 ... K 4 79
Anamosa, Iowa, 3,910 ... L 4 60
Anchorage, Alaska Territory, 11,060 ... J 2 95
Andalusia, Ala., 9,162 ... E 8 49
Anderson, Ind., 46,820 ... F 4 59
Anderson, Mo., 1,073 ... D 9 70
Anderson, S. C., 19,770 ... C 3 84
Andover, Mass., □12,437 ... K 2 66
Andover, N. H., □1,057 ... C 5 74
Andover, N. Y., 1,351 ... E 6 77
Andrews, Ind., 1,083 ... F 3 59
Andrews, N. C., 1,397 ... C 9 78
Andrews, S. C., 2,702 ... K 5 84
Aneta, N. Dak., 469 ... O 4 79
Angleton, Tex., 3,399 ... J 8 87
Angola, Ind., 5,081 ... G 1 59
Angola, N. Y., 1,936 ... C 5 77
Animas, Colo., 2,500 ... D 8 53
Anita, Iowa, 1,112 ... D 6 60
Anna, Ill., 4,380 ... D 6 58
ANNAPOLIS, Md., 10,047 ... H 5 65
Ann Arbor, Mich., 48,251 ... F 6 67
Anniston, Ala., 31,066 ... G 3 49
Anoka, Minn., 7,396 ... E 5 68
Anson, Me., □2,199 ... D 6 64
Anson, Tex., 2,708 ... E 5 87
Ansonia, Conn., 18,706 ... C 3 54
Ansted, W. Va., 1,543 ... D 4 92
Anthony, Kans., 2,792 ... D 4 61
Anthony, N. Mex., 800 ... C 6 76
Anthony, R. I., 2,000 ... H 6 66
Antigo, Wis., 9,902 ... H 5 93
Antioch, Calif., 11,051 ... D 6 52
Antlers, Okla., 2,506 ... L 6 81
Antonito, Colo., 1,255 ... H 8 53
Antrim, N. H., □1,030 ... C 5 74
Apalachicola, Fla., 3,222 ... A 2 55
Apollo, Pa., 3,015 ... C 4 83
Apopka, Fla., 2,254 ... E 3 55
Appalachia, Va., 2,915 ... C 2 90
Appleton, Minn., 2,256 ... C 5 68
Appleton, Wis., 34,010 ... K 7 93
Appleton City, Mo., 1,150 ... D 6 70
Appomattox, Va., 1,094 ... G 6 90
Aransas Pass, Tex., 5,396 ... G10 87
Arapahoe, Nebr., 1,226 ... E 4 72
Arbor Terrace, Mo., 1,150 ... M 5 70
Arcade, N. Y., 1,818 ... D 5 77
Arcadia, Calif., 23,066 ... D10 52
Arcadia, Fla., 4,764 ... E 4 55
Arcadia, Ind., 1,073 ... E 4 59
Arcadia, La., 2,241 ... E 1 63
Arcadia, Wis., 1,949 ... C 7 93
Arcata, Calif., 3,729 ... A 3 52
Archbald, Pa., 6,304 ... M 2 83
Archbold, Ohio, 1,486 ... E 2 80
Archer City, Tex., 1,901 ... F 4 87
Arco, Idaho, 961 ... E 6 57
Arcola, Ill., 1,700 ... E 4 58
Arden, Nev., 43 ... F 6 73
Ardmore, Okla., 17,980 ... H 6 81
Ardmore, Pa. ... M 6 83
Ardsley, N. Y., 1,744 ... D 2 77
Argo, Ill. ... B 2 58
Argos, Ind., 1,284 ... E 2 59
Arkadelphia, Ark., 6,819 ... E 5 51
Arkansas City, Ark., 1,018 ... H 6 51
Arkansas City, Kans., 12,903 ... F 4 61
Arlington, Ga., 1,382 ... C 8 56
Arlington, Mass., □44,353 ... R10 66
Arlington, Minn., 1,313 ... D 6 68
Arlington, N. J., 16,000 ... B 2 75
Arlington, Oreg., 686 ... E 2 82
Arlington, S. Dak., 1,096 ... P 5 85
Arlington, Tenn., 463 ... B 4 86
Arlington, Tex., 7,692 ... F 2 87
Arlington, Vt., □1,463 ... A 4 89
Arlington, Va., 135,449 ... L 3 90
Arlington, Wash., 1,635 ... C 2 91
Arlington Heights, Ill., 8,768 ... A 1 58
Arlington Heights, Ohio, 1,312 ... C 9 80
Arma, Kans., 1,334 ... H 4 61
Armour, S. Dak., 900 ... N 7 85
Arnold, Nebr., 936 ... D 3 72
Arnold, Pa., 10,263 ... C 4 83
Artesia, N. Mex., 8,244 ... E 6 76
Arvada, Colo., 2,359 ... J 3 53
Asbury Park, N. J., 17,094 ... F 3 75
Ashaway, R. I., 1,022 ... H 7 66
Ashburn, Ga., 2,918 ... E 7 56
Ashdown, Ark., 2,738 ... B 6 51
Asheboro, N. C., 7,701 ... F 3 78
Asheville, N. C., 53,000 ... E 8 78
Ashford, Ala., 1,400 ... H 8 49
Ash Fork, Ariz., 800 ... C 3 50
Ash Grove, Mo., 970 ... E 8 70
Ashland, Ala., 1,593 ... G 4 49
Ashland, Kans., 1,493 ... C 4 61
Ashland, Ky., 31,131 ... M 4 62
Ashland, Me., □2,370 ... G 2 64
Ashland, Nebr., 1,713 ... H 3 72
Ashland, N. H., □1,599 ... C 4 74
Ashland, Ohio, 14,287 ... F 4 80
Ashland, Oreg., 7,739 ... E 5 82
Ashland, Pa., 6,192 ... K 4 83
Ashland, Va., 2,610 ... J 5 90
Ashland, Wis., 10,640 ... E 2 93
Ashland City, Tenn., 1,024 ... G 2 86
Ashley, N. Dak., 1,423 ... M 7 79
Ashley, Pa., 5,243 ... L 3 83
Ashtabula, Ohio, 23,696 ... J 2 80
Ashton, Idaho, 1,256 ... G 5 57
Ashton, R. I., 1,000 ... J 5 66
Asotin, Wash., 740 ... H 4 91
Aspen, Colo., 916 ... F 4 53
Aspinwall, Pa., 4,084 ... C 6 83
Astoria, Oreg., 12,331 ... D 1 82
Atascadero, Calif., 3,443 ... E 8 52
Atchison, Kans., 12,792 ... G 2 61
Athena, Oreg., 750 ... J 2 82
Athens, Ala., 5,720 ... E 1 49
Athens, Ga., 28,180 ... F 3 56
Athens, N. Y., 1,545 ... N 6 77
Athens, Ohio, 11,660 ... F 7 80
Athens, Pa., 4,430 ... K 2 83
Athens, Tenn., 8,618 ... M 4 86
Athens, Tex., 5,194 ... J 5 87
Atherton, Calif., 3,630 ... K 3 52
Athol, Mass., □11,554 ... F 2 66
Atkins, Ark., 1,291 ... E 3 51
Atkinson, Nebr., 1,713 ... F 2 72
ATLANTA, Ga., 331,314 ... D 3 56
Atlanta, Idaho, 300 ... C 6 57
Atlanta, Tex., 3,782 ... K 4 87
Atlantic, Iowa, 6,480 ... C 6 60
Atlantic City, N. J., 61,657 ... E 5 75
Atlantic Highlands, N. J., 3,083 ... F 3 75
Atmore, Ala., 5,720 ... C 8 49
Atoka, Okla., 2,653 ... K 6 81
Attalla, Ala., 7,537 ... F 2 49
Attica, Ind., 3,862 ... C 4 59
Attica, N. Y., 2,676 ... D 5 77
Attleboro, Mass., 23,809 ... J 5 66
Atwood, Kans., 1,613 ... B 2 61
Auburn, Ala., 12,939 ... G 5 49
Auburn, Calif., 4,653 ... E 5 52
Auburn, Ill., 1,963 ... D 4 58
Auburn, Ind., 5,879 ... H 2 59
Auburn, Ky., 994 ... D 7 62
Auburn, Me., 23,134 ... C 7 64
Auburn, Mass., □8,840 ... G 4 66
Auburn, Nebr., 3,422 ... J 4 72
Auburn, N. Y., 36,722 ... G 5 77
Auburn, Wash., 6,497 ... C 3 91
Auburn, Wyo., 400 ... A 3 94
Auburndale, Fla., 3,763 ... E 3 55
Audubon, Iowa, 2,808 ... D 5 60
Audubon, N. J., 9,531 ... C 4 75
Augusta, Ark., 2,317 ... H 3 51
Augusta, Ga., 71,508 ... J 4 56
Augusta, Kans., 4,483 ... F 4 61
Augusta, Ky., 1,599 ... J 3 62
AUGUSTA, Me., 20,913 ... D 7 64
Augusta, Mont., 475 ... D 3 71
Augusta, Wis., 1,459 ... D 6 93
Ault, Colo., 866 ... K 1 53
Aurora, Colo., 11,421 ... K 3 53
Aurora, Ill., 50,576 ... E 2 58
Aurora, Ind., 4,780 ... H 6 59
Aurora, Minn., 1,371 ... F 3 68
Aurora, Mo., 4,153 ... E 9 70
Aurora, Nebr., 2,455 ... F 4 72
Aurora, Utah, 614 ... B 5 88
Au Sable Forks, N. Y., 1,643 ... N 2 77
Austin, Minn., 23,100 ... F 7 68
Austin, Nev., 300 ... E 3 73
AUSTIN, Tex., 132,459 ... G 7 87
Austinville, Ala., 1,110 ... D 1 49
Ava, Mo., 1,611 ... G 9 70
Avalon, Pa., 6,463 ... B 6 83
Avoca, Iowa, 1,595 ... C 6 60
Avoca, Pa., 4,040 ... L 3 83
Avon, Conn., □3,171 ... D 1 54
Avon, N. Y., 2,412 ... E 5 77
Avon, Ohio, 2,773 ... F 3 80
Avon, S. Dak., 692 ... O 7 85
Avondale, Ariz., 2,505 ... C 5 50
Avon Lake, Ohio, 4,342 ... F 2 80
Avon Park, Fla., 4,612 ... E 4 55
Ayden, N. C., 2,282 ... L 4 78
Ayer, Mass., □5,740 ... H 2 66
Aynor, S. C., 551 ... K 4 84
Aztec, N. Mex., 885 ... B 2 76
Azusa, Calif., 11,042 ... D10 52
Babylon, N. Y., 6,015 ... D 2 77
Bad Axe, Mich., 2,973 ... G 5 67
Baggs, Wyo., 206 ... E 4 94
Bagley, Minn., 1,554 ... C 3 68
Bainbridge, Ga., 7,562 ... C 9 56
Bainbridge, N. Y., 1,505 ... J 6 77
Bainville, Mont., 356 ... M 2 71
Bairoil, Wyo., 300 ... E 3 94
Baird, Tex., 1,821 ... E 5 87
Baker, Mont., 1,772 ... M 4 71
Baker, Nev., 50 ... G 3 73
Baker, Oreg., 9,471 ... K 3 82
Bakersfield, Calif., 34,784 ... G 8 52
Bald Knob, Ark., 2,022 ... G 3 51
Baldwin, Fla., 1,048 ... E 1 55
Baldwin, La., 1,138 ... H 7 63
Baldwin, N. Y., 22,000 ... D 2 77
Baldwin City, Kans., 1,741 ... G 3 61
Baldwin Park, Calif., 28,000 ... D10 52
Baldwinsville, N. Y., 4,495 ... H 4 77
Baldwyn, Miss., 1,567 ... G 2 69
Ballinger, Tex., 5,302 ... E 6 87
Ballston Spa., N. Y., 4,937 ... N 5 77
Baltimore, Md., 949,708 ... H 3 65
Bamberg, S. C., 2,954 ... F 5 84
Bancroft, Idaho, 495 ... G 7 57
Bandon, Oreg., 1,251 ... C 4 82
Bangor, Me., 31,558 ... F 6 64
Bangor, Mich., 1,694 ... C 6 67
Bangor, Pa., 6,054 ... M 4 83
Banning, Calif., 7,034 ... J10 52
Bantam, Conn., 940 ... B 2 54
Baraboo, Wis., 7,264 ... G 9 93
Barberton, Ohio, 27,820 ... G 4 80
Barbourville, Ky., 2,926 ... K 7 62
Barboursville, W. Va., 1,943 ... B 4 92
Bardstown, Ky., 4,152 ... F 5 62
Bardwell, Ky., 1,033 ... C 3 62
Bar Harbor, Me., □3,864 ... G 7 64
Barnesboro, Pa., 3,442 ... E 4 83
Barnesville, Ga., 4,185 ... D 4 56
Barnesville, Minn., 1,593 ... B 4 68
Barnesville, Ohio, 4,665 ... H 6 80
Barnet, Vt., □1,425 ... C 2 89
Barnsdall, Okla., 1,708 ... K 1 81
Barnstable, Mass., □10,480 ... N 6 66
Barnwell, S. C., 2,005 ... F 5 84
Barre, Mass., □3,406 ... F 3 66
Barre, Vt., 10,922 ... C 2 89
Barrington, Ill., 4,209 ... E 1 58
Barrington, R. I., □8,246 ... J 6 66
Barron, Wis., 2,355 ... C 5 93
Bartlesville, Okla., 19,228 ... K 1 81
Bartlett, N. H., □1,074 ... D 3 74
Bartlett, Tenn., 489 ... B 4 86
Bartlett, Tex., 1,727 ... G 7 87
Barton, Md., 695 ... C 7 65
Barton, Vt., 1,267 ... C 1 89
Bartonville, Ill., 2,437 ... D 3 58
Bartow, Fla., 8,694 ... E 4 55
Basile, La., 1,572 ... E 6 63
Basin, Wyo., 1,220 ... D 1 94
Bassett, Nebr., 1,066 ... E 2 72
Bassett, Va., 3,421 ... E 7 90
Bastrop, La., 12,769 ... G 1 63
Bastrop, Tex., 3,176 ... G 7 87
Batavia, Ill., 5,838 ... E 2 58
Batavia, N. Y., 17,799 ... D 5 77
Batavia, Ohio, 1,445 ... B 7 80
Batesburg, S. C., 3,169 ... F 4 84
Batesville, Ark., 6,414 ... G 2 51
Batesville, Ind., 3,194 ... G 6 59
Batesville, Miss., 2,463 ... E 2 69
Bath, Me., 10,644 ... D 8 64
Bath, N. Y., 5,416 ... F 6 77
BATON ROUGE, La., 125,629 ... H 6 63
Battle Creek, Mich., 48,666 ... D 6 67
Battle Mountain, Nev., 850 ... E 2 73
Baudette, Minn., 929 ... D 2 68
Bauxite, Ark., 2,459 ... E 4 51

	Index Ref.	Plate No.
Baxley, Ga., 3,409	H 7	56
Baxter, Tenn., 861	K 2	86
Baxter Springs, Kans., 4,647	H 4	61
Bayard, Nebr., 1,869	A 3	72
Bayard, N. Mex., 2,119	A 6	76
Bay City, Mich., 52,523	F 5	67
Bay City, Oreg., 761	D 2	82
Bay City, Tex., 9,427	H 9	87
Bayfield, Wis., 1,153	E 2	93
Bay Minette, Ala., 3,732	C 9	49
Bayonne, N. J., 77,203	B 2	75
Bayport, Minn., 2,502	F 5	68
Bay Saint Louis, Miss., 4,621	F10	69
Bay Shore, N. Y., 9,665	E 2	77
Bay Springs, Miss., 1,302	F 7	69
Baytown, Tex., 22,983	K 2	87
Bay Village, Ohio, 6,917	G 9	80
Bayville, N. Y., 1,981	D 2	77
Beach, N. Dak., 1,461	B 6	79
Beacon, N. Y., 14,012	C 1	77
Bearden, Ark., 1,300	E 6	51
Beardstown, Ill., 6,080	C 3	58
Beatrice, Nebr., 11,813	H 4	72
Beatty, Nev., 485	E 6	73
Beattyville, Ky., 1,042	K 5	62
Beaufort, N. C., 3,212	M 5	78
Beaufort, S. C., 5,081	G 7	84
Beaumont, Calif., 3,152	J10	52
Beaumont, Tex., 94,014	K 7	87
Beaver, Okla., 1,495	F 7	81
Beaver, Pa., 6,360	B 4	83
Beaver, Utah, 1,685	B 5	88
Beaver City, Nebr., 913	E 4	72
Beaver Dam, Ky., 1,349	D 6	62
Beaver Dam, Wis., 11,867	J 9	93
Beaver Falls, Pa., 17,375	B 4	83
Beaverton, Oreg., 2,512	E 2	82
Beckley, W. Va., 19,397	D 5	92
Bedford, Ind., 12,562	E 7	59
Bedford, Iowa, 2,000	D 7	60
Bedford, Mass., □5,234	J 3	86
Bedford, N. H., □2,176	C 6	74
Bedford, Ohio, 9,105	J 9	80
Bedford, Pa., 3,521	F 5	83
Bedford, Va., 4,061	E 6	90
Bedford, Wyo., 268	A 3	94
Beebe, Ark., 1,192	G 3	51
Beech Grove, Ind., 5,685	E 5	59
Beeville, Tex., 9,348	G 9	87
Beggs, Okla., 1,214	L 3	81
Bel Air, Md., 2,578	J 2	65
Belchertown, Mass., □4,487	E 3	66
Belding, Mich., 4,436	D 5	67
Belen, N. Mex., 4,495	C 4	76
Belfast, Me., 5,960	E 7	64
Belfield, N. Dak., 1,051	D 6	79
Belfry, Mont., 200	H 5	71
Belgrade, Mont., 663	E 5	71
Belhaven, N. C., 2,528	M 3	78
Belington, W. Va., 1,699	G 2	92
Bell, Calif., 15,430	C11	52
Bellaire, Ohio, 12,573	J 6	80
Bellaire, Tex., 10,173	J 2	87
Bellefontaine, Ohio, 10,232	C 5	80
Bellefonte, Del., 1,472	N 1	65
Bellefonte, Pa., 5,651	G 4	83
Belle Fourche, S. Dak., 3,540	B 4	85
Belle Glade, Fla., 7,219	F 5	55
Belle Meade, Tenn., 2,831	H 2	86
Belle Plaine, Iowa, 3,056	J 5	60
Belle Plaine, Minn., 1,708	E 6	68
Bellerose, N. Y., 1,134	D 2	77
Belleville, Ill., 32,721	C 5	58
Belleville, Kans., 2,858	E 2	61
Belleville, Mich., 1,722	F 6	67
Belleville, N. J., 32,019	E 2	75
Bellevue, Idaho, 528	D 6	57
Bellevue, Iowa, 1,932	N 4	60
Bellevue, Ky., 9,040	H 2	62
Bellevue, Nebr., 3,858	J 3	72
Bellevue, Ohio, 6,906	E 3	80
Bellevue, Pa., 11,604	B 6	83
Bellflower, Calif., 40,000	C11	52
Bellingham, Wash., 34,112	C 2	91
Bells, Tenn., 1,225	C 3	86
Bellows Falls, Vt., 3,881	B 4	89
Bellwood, Ill., 8,746	A 2	58
Bellwood, Pa., 2,559	F 4	83
Belmar, N. J., 4,636	F 3	75
Belmond, Iowa, 2,169	F 3	60
Belmont, Mass., □27,381	R10	66
Belmont, N. H., □1,611	D 5	74
Belmont, N. Y., 1,211	E 6	77
Belmont, N. C., 5,330	D 4	78
Bel-Nor, Mo., 1,290	M 5	70
Beloit, Kans., 4,085	D 2	61
Beloit, Wis., 29,590	H10	93
Belpre, Ohio, 2,451	G 7	80
Belt, Mont., 702	F 3	71
Belton, Mo., 1,233	D 5	70
Belton, S. C., 3,371	C 2	84
Belton, Tex., 6,246	G 7	87
Belvedere, Calif., 800	H 2	52
Belvidere, Ill., 9,422	E 1	58
Belzoni, Miss., 4,071	C 4	69
Bemidji, Minn., 10,001	C 3	68
Benavides, Tex., 3,016	F10	87
Ben Avon, Pa., 2,465	B 6	83
Bend, Oreg., 11,409	F 3	82
Benham, Ky., 3,982	M 7	62
Benicia, Calif., 7,284	K 1	52
Benkelman, Nebr., 1,512	C 4	72
Benld, Ill., 2,093	D 4	58
Bennettsville, S. C., 5,140	J 2	84
Bennington, Vt., 8,002	A 5	89
Bensenville, Ill., 3,754	A 1	58
Benson, Ariz., 1,440	E 7	50
Benson, Minn., 3,398	C 5	68
Benson, N. C., 2,102	J 4	78
Bentleyville, Pa., 3,295	B 5	83
Benton, Ark., 6,277	E 4	51
Benton, Ill., 7,848	E 6	58
Benton, Ky., 1,980	D 3	62
Benton, Me., □1,421	D 6	64
Benton Harbor, Mich., 18,769	C 6	67
Bentonville, Ark., 2,942	B 1	51
Benwood, W. Va., 3,485	K 5	92
Beowawe, Nev., 175	E 2	73
Berea, Ky., 3,372	J 5	62
Berea, Ohio, 12,051	G 3	80
Beresford, S. Dak., 1,686	R 7	85
Bergenfield, N. J., 17,647	C 1	75
Berkeley, Calif., 113,805	K 2	52
Berkeley, Mo., 5,268	M 5	70
Berkeley Springs, W. Va., 1,213	K 1	92
Berkley, Mich., 17,931	B 6	67
Berlin, Conn., □7,470	E 2	54
Berlin, Md., 2,001	N 7	65
Berlin, N. H., 16,615	D 3	74
Berlin, Wis., 4,693	J 7	93
Bernalillo, N. Mex., 1,922	C 3	76
Bernardsville, N. J., 3,956	D 2	75
Berne, Ind., 2,277	H 3	59
Bernice, La., 1,524	E 1	63
Bernie, Mo., 1,308	N 9	70
Berrien Springs, Mich., 1,761	C 7	67
Berryville, Ark., 1,753	D 1	51
Berryville, Va., 1,401	H 2	90
Berthoud, Colo., 867	J 2	53
Berwick, La., 2,619	H 7	63
Berwick, Me., □2,166	B 9	64
Berwick, Pa., 14,010	K 3	83
Berwind, W. Va., 1,354	C 6	92
Berwyn, Ill., 51,280	B 2	58
Berwyn Heights, Md., 674	G 5	65
Bessemer, Ala., 28,445	D 4	49
Bessemer, Mich., 3,509	E 2	67
Bessemer City, N. C., 3,961	C 4	78
Bethany, Mo., 2,714	E 2	70
Bethany, Okla., 5,705	G 3	81
Bethany Beach, Del., 190	O 6	65
Bethel, Conn., □5,104	B 3	54
Bethel, Del., 271	M 6	65
Bethel, Me., □2,367	B 7	64
Bethel, N. C., 1,402	L 3	78
Bethel, Ohio, 1,932	B 8	80
Bethel, Pa., 11,324	B 7	83
Bethel, Vt., 1,534	B 3	89
Bethel Springs, Tenn., 623	D 4	86
Bethesda, Md.	F 5	65
Bethlehem, N. H., □882	C 3	74
Bethlehem, Pa., 66,340	M 4	83
Bethune, S. C., 639	H 3	84
Bettendorf, Iowa, 5,132	M 5	60
Beulah, N. Dak., 1,501	G 5	79
Beverly, Mass., 28,884	L 2	66
Beverly Hills, Calif., 29,032	B10	52
Bevier, Mo., 838	G 3	70
Bexley, Ohio, 12,378	E 6	80
Bibb City, Ga., 1,452	B 5	56
Bicknell, Ind., 4,572	C 7	59
Biddeford, Me., 20,836	B 9	64
Big Piney, Wyo., 206	B 3	94
Big Rapids, Mich., 6,736	D 5	67
Big Sandy, Mont., 743	G 2	71
Big Sandy, Tenn., 621	E 2	86
Big Spring, Tex., 17,286	C 5	87
Big Stone City, S. Dak., 829	R 3	85
Big Stone Gap, Va., 5,173	C 2	90
Bigtimber, Mont., 1,679	G 5	71
Billerica, Mass., □11,101	J 2	66
Billings, Mont., 31,834	H 5	71
Biloxi, Miss., 37,425	G10	69
Bingen, Wash., 736	D 5	91
Bingham, Me., □1,354	D 5	64
Binghamton, N. Y., 80,674	J 6	77
Bingham Canyon, Utah, 2,569	B 3	88
Bird Island, Minn., 1,333	D 6	68
Birdsboro, Pa., 3,158	L 5	83
Birmingham, Ala., 326,037	E 4	49
Birmingham, Mich., 15,467	B 6	67
Bisbee, Ariz., 3,801	F 7	50
Bishop, Calif., 2,891	G 6	52
Bishopville, S. C., 3,076	H 3	84
Bismarck, Mo., 1,244	L 7	70
BISMARCK, N. Dak., 18,640	J 6	79
Biwabik, Minn., 1,245	F 3	68
Bixby, Okla., 1,517	L 3	81
Black Eagle, Mont., 1,449	E 3	71
Blackfoot, Idaho, 5,180	F 6	57
Black River Falls, Wis., 2,824	E 7	93
Black Rock, Ark., 662	H 1	51
Blacksburg, S. C., 2,056	F 1	84
Blacksburg, Va., 3,358	D 6	90
Blackshear, Ga., 2,271	H 8	56
Blackstone, Mass., □4,968	H 4	66
Blackstone, Va., 3,536	H 6	90
Blackville, S. C., 1,294	F 5	84
Blackwell, Okla., 9,199	H 1	81
Bladensburg, Md., 2,899	G 5	65
Blades, Del., 789	M 8	65
Blaine, Wash., 1,693	C 2	91
Blair, Nebr., 3,815	H 3	72
Blairsville, Pa., 5,000	D 5	83
Blakely, Ga., 3,234	B 8	56
Blakely, Pa., 6,828	L 3	83
Blanchester, Ohio, 2,109	B 7	80
Blanding, Utah, 1,177	E 6	88
Blasdell, N. Y., 3,127	C 5	77
Blissfield, Mich., 2,365	F 7	67
Block Island, R. I., 848	H 8	66
Bloomer, Wis., 2,556	D 5	93
Bloomfield, Conn., □5,746	E 1	54
Bloomfield, Ind., 2,086	D 6	59
Bloomfield, Iowa, 2,688	J 7	60
Bloomfield, Mo., 1,382	M 9	70
Bloomfield, Nebr., 1,455	G 2	72
Bloomfield, N. J., 49,307	B 2	75
Bloomfield, N. Mex., 500	A 2	76
Bloomfield Hills, Mich., 1,468	F 6	67
Blooming Prairie, Minn., 1,442	F 7	68
Bloomington, Idaho, 302	G 7	57
Bloomington, Ill., 34,163	D 3	58
Bloomington, Ind., 28,163	D 6	59
Bloomsburg, Pa., 10,633	J 3	83
Blountstown, Fla., 2,118	A 1	55
Blue Diamond, Ky., 1,968	L 6	62
Blue Earth, Minn., 3,843	E 7	68
Bluefield, Va., 4,212	B 6	90
Bluefield, W. Va., 21,506	D 6	92
Blue Hill, Me., □1,308	F 7	64
Blue Island, Ill., 17,622	F 2	58
Blue Rapids, Kans., 1,430	F 2	61
Blue Ridge, Ga., 1,718	D 1	56
Bluff City, Tenn., 1,074	R 2	86
Bluffsprings, Fla., 100	B 5	55
Bluffton, Ind., 6,076	G 3	59
Bluffton, Ohio, 2,423	C 4	80
Blythe, Calif., 4,089	L10	52
Blytheville, Ark., 16,234	L 2	51
Boaz, Ala., 3,078	F 2	49
Bogalusa, La., 17,798	L 5	63
Bogota, N. J., 7,662	B 2	75
BOISE, Idaho, 34,393	B 6	57
Boise City, Okla., 1,902	B 8	81
Bolivar, Mo., 3,482	F 7	70
Bolivar, N. Y., 1,490	D 6	77
Bolivar, Tenn., 2,429	D 4	86
Bolton, Miss., 741	D 6	69
Bonesteel, S. Dak., 485	M 7	85
Bonham, Tex., 7,049	H 4	87
Bonifay, Fla., 2,252	C 5	55
Bonner, Mont., 250	C 4	71
Bonner Springs, Kans., 2,272	G 2	61
Bonners Ferry, Idaho, 1,776	B 1	57
Bonne Terre, Mo., 3,533	M 6	70
Boone, Iowa, 12,164	F 4	60
Boone, N. C., 2,973	B 2	78
Boones Mill, Va., 335	E 6	90
Booneville, Ark., 2,433	C 3	51
Booneville, Miss., 3,295	G 1	69
Boonsboro, Md., 1,071	D 2	65
Boonton, N. J., 7,163	E 2	75
Boonville, Ind., 5,092	C 8	59
Boonville, Mo., 6,686	G 5	70
Boonville, N. Y., 2,329	K 4	77
Boothbay, Me., □1,559	D 8	64
Boothbay Harbor, Me., □2,290	D 8	64
Boothton, Ala., 814	E 4	49
Bordentown, N. J., 5,497	D 3	75
Borger, Tex., 18,059	C 2	87
Boscawen, N. H., □1,857	C 5	74
Boscobel, Wis., 2,347	E 9	93
Bossier City, La., 15,470	C 1	63
Boston, Ga., 1,035	E 9	56
BOSTON, Mass., 801,444	K 3	66
Bothell, Wash., 1,019	C 3	91
Bottineau, N. Dak., 2,268	K 2	79
Boulder, Colo., 19,999	J 2	53
Boulder, Mont., 1,017	E 4	71
Boulder City, Nev., 3,903	G 7	73
Bound Brook, N. J., 8,374	D 2	75
Bountiful, Utah, 6,004	C 3	88
Bourbon, Ind., 1,404	E 2	59
Bovey, Minn., 1,320	E 3	68
Bovill, Idaho, 437	B 3	57
Bow, N. H., □1,062	C 5	74
Bowbells, N. Dak., 806	F 2	79
Bowdle, S. Dak., 788	K 3	85
Bowers, Del., 284	N 4	65
Bowie, Ariz., 300	F 6	50
Bowie, Md., 860	G 4	65
Bowie, Tex., 4,544	G 4	87
Bowling Green, Fla., 884	G 4	55
Bowling Green, Ky., 18,347	D 6	62
Bowling Green, Mo., 2,396	K 4	70
Bowling Green, Ohio, 12,005	C 3	80
Bowling Green, Va., 616	K 4	90
Bowman, N. Dak., 1,382	D 7	79
Bowman, S. C., 857	G 5	84
Boydton, Va., 501	H 7	90
Boyertown, Pa., 4,074	L 5	83
Boykins, Va., 811	K 7	90
Boyle, Miss., 799	C 3	69
Boyne City, Mich., 3,028	E 3	67
Boynton Beach, Fla., 2,542	F 5	55
Bozeman, Mont., 11,325	F 5	71
Brackenridge, Pa., 6,178	C 4	83
Brackettville, Tex., 1,858	D 8	87
Braddock, Pa., 16,488	C 7	83
Bradenton, Fla., 13,604	D 4	55
Bradford, Ohio, 2,055	B 5	80
Bradford, Pa., 17,354	E 2	83
Bradford, R. I., 1,024	H 7	66
Bradford, Tenn., 599	D 2	86
Bradford, Vt., 725	C 3	89
Bradley, Ill., 5,699	F 2	58
Bradley Beach, N. J., 3,911	F 3	75
Brady, Mont., 435	E 2	71
Brady, Tex., 5,944	E 6	87
Brainerd, Minn., 12,637	D 4	68
Braintree, Mass., □23,161	K 4	66
Bramwell, W. Va., 1,587	D 6	92
Branchville, S. C., 1,353	G 5	84
Brandon, Miss., 1,827	E 6	69
Brandon, Vt., 3,304	A 3	89
Branford, Conn., 2,552	D 3	54
Branson, Mo., 1,314	F 9	70
Brantley, Ala., 1,102	F 7	49
Bratenahl, Ohio, 1,240	H 9	80
Brattleboro, Vt., 11,522	B 5	89
Brawley, Calif., 11,922	K11	52
Braymer, Mo., 955	E 3	70
Brazil, Ind., 8,434	C 5	59
Brea, Calif., 3,208	D11	52
Breaux Bridge, La., 2,492	G 6	63
Breckenridge, Minn., 3,623	B 4	68
Breckenridge, Tex., 6,610	F 5	87
Brecksville, Ohio, 2,664	H10	80
Breese, Ill., 2,181	D 5	58
Bremen, Ga., 2,299	B 3	56
Bremen, Ind., 2,664	E 2	59
Bremerton, Wash., 27,678	C 3	91
Brenham, Tex., 6,941	H 7	87
Brentwood, Md., 3,523	G 5	65
Brentwood, Mo., 7,504	P 3	70
Brentwood, Pa., 12,535	B 7	83
Brevard, N. C., 3,908	E 9	78
Brewer, Me., 6,862	F 6	64
Brewster, N. Y., 1,810	D 1	77
Brewster, Ohio, 1,618	G 4	80
Brewton, Ala., 5,146	D 8	49
Briarcliff Manor, N. Y., 2,494	D 1	77
Bridgeport, Ala., 2,386	G 1	49
Bridgeport, Conn., 158,709	C 4	54
Bridgeport, Ill., 2,358	F 5	58
Bridgeport, Neb., 1,631	A 3	72
Bridgeport, Ohio, 4,309	J 5	80
Bridgeport, Pa., 5,827	M 5	83
Bridgeport, Tex., 2,049	G 4	87
Bridgeport, W. Va., 2,414	F 2	92
Bridger, Mont., 854	H 5	71
Bridgeton, N. J., 18,378	C 5	75
Bridgeton, R. I., 661	H 5	66
Bridgetown, Ohio, 1,500	B 9	80
Bridgeville, Del., 1,468	M 6	65
Bridgeville, Pa., 5,650	B 5	83
Bridgewater, Me., □1,279	G 3	64
Bridgewater, Mass., □9,512	K 5	66
Bridgewater, S. Dak., 748	P 6	85
Bridgewater, Va., 1,537	E 2	90
Bridgton, Me., □2,950	B 7	64
Brigham City, Utah, 6,790	C 2	88
Brighton, Ala., 1,689	E 4	49
Brighton, Colo., 4,336	K 3	53
Brighton, Mich., 1,861	F 6	67
Brightwaters, N. Y., 2,336	E 2	77
Brilliant, N. Mex., 225	E 2	76
Brilliant, Ohio, 2,066	J 5	80
Brillion, Wis., 1,390	L 7	93
Brinkley, Ark., 4,173	H 4	51
Bristol, Conn., 35,961	D 2	54
Bristol, Me., □1,476	E 8	64
Bristol, N. H., □1,586	C 4	74
Bristol, Pa., 12,710	N 5	83
Bristol, R. I., □12,320	J 6	66
Bristol, S. Dak., 647	O 3	85
Bristol, Tenn., 16,771	R 1	86
Bristol, Vt., 1,308	A 2	89
Bristol, Va., 15,954	D 3	90
Bristow, Okla., 5,400	K 3	81
Britt, Iowa, 1,908	F 2	60
Britton, S. Dak., 1,430	O 2	85
Broadalbin, N. Y., 1,400	M 4	77
Broadview, Ill., 5,196	A 2	58
Broadway, Va., 561	G 3	90
Brockport, N. Y., 4,748	D 4	77
Brockton, Mass., 62,860	K 3	66
Brockway, Pa., 2,650	E 3	83
Brocton, N. Y., 1,380	B 6	77
Brodhead, Ky., 808	J 6	62
Brodhead, Wis., 2,016	H10	93
Brodnax, Va., 499	J 7	90
Broken Arrow, Okla., 3,262	L 2	81
Broken Bow, Nebr., 3,396	E 3	72
Broken Bow, Okla., 1,838	N 7	81
Bromley, Ky., 980	H 2	62
Bronson, Mich., 2,106	D 7	67
Bronx, The (borough), N. Y., 1,451,277	D 2	77
Bronxville, N. Y., 6,778	D 2	77
Brookfield, Ill., 15,475	A 2	58
Brookfield, Mo., 5,810	F 3	70
Brookhaven, Miss., 7,801	D 7	69
Brookings, S. Dak., 7,764	R 5	85
Brookline, Mass., 57,589	K 3	66
Brooklyn, Conn., □2,652	H 1	54
Brooklyn, Iowa, 1,323	J 5	60
Brooklyn (borough), N. Y., 2,738,175	C 2	77
Brooklyn Center, Minn., 4,284	E 5	68
Brookneal, Va., 883	G 6	90
Brooksville, Fla., 1,818	D 3	55
Brooksville, Miss., 819	G 4	69
Brookville, Ind., 2,538	G 6	59
Brookville, Ohio, 1,908	B 6	80
Brookville, Pa., 4,274	D 3	83
Broussard, La., 1,237	G 6	63
Brownfield, Tex., 6,161	B 4	87
Browning, Mont., 1,691	C 2	71
Brownsburg, Ind., 1,578	E 5	59
Brownstown, Ind., 1,998	F 7	59
Browns Valley, Minn., 1,117	B 5	68
Brownsville, Oreg., 1,175	E 3	82
Brownsville, Pa., 7,643	C 5	83
Brownsville, Tenn., 4,711	C 3	86
Brownsville, Tex., 36,066	G12	87
Brownville, Me., □1,964	E 5	64
Brownwood, Tex., 20,181	F 6	87
Bruce, Miss., 1,719	F 2	69
Bruceton, Tenn., 1,204	E 2	86
Brundidge, Ala., 2,605	G 7	49
Brunson, S. C., 607	F 6	84
Brunswick, Ga., 17,954	K 8	56
Brunswick, Me., □10,996	C 8	64
Brunswick, Md., 3,752	D 3	65
Brunswick, Mo., 1,653	F 4	70
Brush, Colo., 2,431	M 2	53
Bryan, Ohio, 6,365	A 3	80
Bryan, Tex., 18,102	H 7	87
Bryant, S. Dak., 624	O 4	85
Bryn Mawr, Pa.	M 5	83
Bryson City, N. C., 1,499	D 8	78
Buchanan, Mich., 5,224	C 7	67
Buchanan, N. Y., 1,820	D 1	77
Buchanan, Va., 1,300	E 5	90
Buckeye, Ariz., 1,932	C 5	50
Buckeye, N. Mex., 227	F 6	76
Buckhannon, W. Va., 6,016	F 3	92
Buckhorn, N. Mex., 500	A 5	76
Buckley, Wash., 2,705	D 3	91
Bucksport, Me., □3,120	F 6	64
Bucyrus, Ohio, 10,327	E 4	80
Bude, Miss., 1,195	C 8	69
Buena Vista, Colo., 783	G 5	53
Buena Vista, Va., 5,214	F 5	90
Buffalo, Minn., 1,914	E 5	68
Buffalo, Mo., 1,213	F 7	70
Buffalo, N. Y., 580,132	C 5	77
Buffalo, Okla., 1,454	C 1	81
Buffalo, Wyo., 2,674	F 1	94
Buford, Ga., 3,812	E 2	56
Buhl, Idaho, 2,870	D 7	57
Buhl, Minn., 1,462	F 3	68
Bunkerville, Nev., 180	G 6	73
Bunkie, La., 4,666	F 5	63
Bunnel, Fla., 1,341	E 2	55
Burbank, Calif., 78,577	C10	52
Burgaw, N. C., 1,613	J 5	78
Burgin, Ky., 777	H 5	62
Burkburnett, Tex., 4,555	F 3	87
Burke, S. Dak., 829	L 7	85
Burkesville, Ky., 1,278	G 7	62
Burkeville, Va., 695	H 6	90
Burley, Idaho, 5,924	E 7	57
Burlingame, Calif., 19,886	J 2	52
Burlingame, Kans., 1,065	G 3	61
Burlington, Colo., 2,247	P 4	53
Burlington, Iowa, 30,613	L 7	60
Burlington, Kans., 2,304	G 3	61
Burlington, N. J., 12,051	D 3	75
Burlington, N. C., 24,560	F 2	78

Index Ref. Plate No.

Burlington, Vt., 33,155......A 2 89
Burlington, Wash., 2,350....C 2 91
Burlington, Wis., 4,780......K10 93
Burnet, Tex., 2,394...........F 7 87
Burnham, Pa., 2,954..........H 4 83
Burns, Oreg., 3,093............H 4 82
Burns, Wyo., 216...............H 4 94
Burnside, Ky., 615.............H 7 62
Burnsville, W. Va., 731.......E 3 92
Burwell, Nebr., 1,413.........E 3 72
Bushnell, Ill., 3,317...........C 3 58
Butler, Ind., 1,914.............H 2 59
Butler, Mo., 3,333..............D 6 70
Butler, N. J., 4,050............E 2 75
Butler, Pa., 23,482.............C 4 83
Butte, Mont., 33,251..........D 4 71
Buxton, Me., □2,009..........B 8 64
Byesville, Ohio, 2,236.........G 6 80
Byron, Wyo., 350...............D 1 94
Cabool, Mo., 1,245.............H 8 70
Cabot, Vt., 219..................C 2 89
Cadillac, Mich., 10,425........D 4 67
Cadiz, Ky., 1,280...............B 7 62
Cadiz, Ohio, 3,020..............J 5 80
Cairo, Ga., 5,575.................D 9 56
Cairo, Ill., 12,123...............D 6 58
Calais, Me., 4,589...............J 5 64
Caldwell, Idaho, 10,487.......B 6 57
Caldwell, Kans., 2,000.........E 4 61
Caldwell, N. J., 6,270..........E 2 75
Caldwell, Ohio, 1,767...........G 6 80
Caldwell, Tex., 2,109...........H 7 87
Caledonia, Minn., 2,243........G 7 68
Caledonia, N. Y., 1,683........E 5 77
Calera, Ala., 1,361..............E 4 49
Calexico, Calif., 6,433.........K11 52
Calhoun, Ga., 3,231.............C 2 56
Calhoun, Ky., 746................C 5 62
Calhoun City, Miss., 1,319..F 3 69
Calhoun Falls, S. C., 2,396.C 3 84
Caliente, Nev., 970..............G 5 73
California, Mo., 2,627..........G 5 70
California, Pa., 2,831...........C 5 83
Calipatria, Calif., 1,428.......K10 52
Calumet, Mich., 1,256..........A 1 67
Calumet, Minn., 854.............F 3 68
Calumet City, Ill., 15,799...B 2 58
Calvert, Tex., 2,548.............H 7 87
Camas, Wash., 4,725............C 5 91
Cambridge, Idaho, 354..........B 5 57
Cambridge, Md., 10,351........K 6 65
Cambridge, Mass., 120,740.K 3 66
Cambridge, Minn., 2,978.....E 5 68
Cambridge, Nebr., 1,352......D 4 72
Cambridge, N. Y., 1,692......O 4 77
Cambridge, Ohio, 14,739......G 5 80
Cambridge, Vt., 244.............B 1 89
Cambridge City, Ind.,
2,559..................................G 5 59
Camden, Ark., 11,372...........E 6 51
Camden, Del., 606...............M 4 65
Camden, Me., □3,670..........E 7 64
Camden, N. J., 124,555.......C 4 75
Camden, N. Y., 2,407...........J 4 77
Camden, S. C., 6,986...........G 3 84
Camden, Tenn., 2,029...........E 2 86
Cameron, Mo., 3,570............D 3 70
Cameron, S. C., 630..............G 4 84
Cameron, Tex., 5,052............H 7 87
Cameron, W. Va., 1,736........L 6 92
Camilla, Ga., 3,745...............D 8 56
Camillus, N. Y., 1,225...........H 4 77
Campbell, Mo., 1,931............M 9 70
Campbell, Ohio, 12,882.........J 3 80
Campbellsport, Wis., 1,254.K 8 93
Campbellsville, Ky., 3,477..G 6 62
Camp Hill, Ala., 1,296..........G 5 49
Camp Hill, Pa., 5,934............H 5 83
Campti, La., 1,014................D 3 63
Campton, N. H., □1,149.......C 4 74
Camp Verde, Ariz., 550........D 4 50
Canaan, N. H., □1,465..........B 4 74
Canadian, Tex., 2,700...........D 2 87
Canajoharie, N. Y., 2,761...L 5 77
Canandaigua, N. Y., 8,332..F 5 77
Canastota, N. Y., 4,458.........J 4 77
Canby, Minn., 2,173..............B 6 68
Canby, Oreg., 1,671..............E 2 82
Candia, N. H., □1,243..........D 5 74
Cando, N. Dak., 1,530..........M 2 79
Caney, Kans., 2,876..............G 4 61
Canisteo, N. Y., 2,625..........E 6 77
Canistota, S. Dak., 687.........P 6 85
Canjilon, N. Mex., 900..........C 2 76
Cannelton, Ind., 2,027..........D 9 59
Cannon, Del., 150..................M 6 65
Cannon Falls, Minn., 1,831.F 6 68
Canon City, Colo., 6,345......J 6 53
Canonsburg, Pa., 12,072......B 5 83
Canton, Conn., □3,613.........D 1 54
Canton, Ga., 2,716................D 2 56
Canton, Ill., 11,927...............C 3 58
Canton, Mass., □7,465.........K 4 66
Canton, Miss., 7,048..............D 5 69
Canton, Mo., 2,490................J 2 70
Canton, N. Y., 4,379..............K 1 77
Canton, N. C., 4,906..............E 8 78
Canton, Ohio, 116,912..........H 4 80

Canton, S. Dak., 2,530......R 7 85
Canyon, Tex., 4,364..........C 3 87
Cape Charles, Va., 2,427...M 6 90
Cape Girardeau, Mo.,
21,578..............................O 8 70
Capitan, N. Mex., 575......D 5 76
Capitol Heights, Md.,
2,729................................G 5 65
Carbondale, Ill., 10,921.....D 6 58
Carbondale, Pa., 16,296.....L 2 83
Carbon Hill, Ala., 2,179.....D 3 49
Cardington, Ohio, 1,465.....E 5 80
Cardwell, Mo., 952.........N10 70
Carencro, La., 1,587..........F 6 63
Carey, Ohio, 3,260............D 4 80
Caribou, Me., □9,923.........G 2 64
Carlin, Nev., 1,203............E 2 73
Carlinville, Ill., 5,116.......D 4 58
Carlisle, Ark., 1,396.........G 4 51
Carlisle, Ky., 1,524...........J 4 62
Carlisle, Pa., 16,812..........H 5 83
Carl Junction, Mo., 1,006..C 8 70
Carlsbad, N. Mex., 17,975..E 6 76
Carlstadt, N. J., 5,591........B 2 75
Carlton, Oreg., 1,081.........D 2 82
Carlyle, Ill., 2,669.............D 5 58
Carmel, Calif., 4,351..........D 7 52
Carmi, Ill., 5,574................E 5 58
Carnegie, Okla., 1,719........E 4 81
Carnegie, Pa., 12,105.........B 7 83
Caro, Mich., 3,464.............F 5 67
Carolina, R. I., 200............H 7 66
Carpinteria, Calif., 2,864....F 9 52
Carrabelle, Fla., 970..........B 2 55
Carrboro, N. C., 1,795........G 3 78
Carriers Mills, Ill., 2,252....E 6 58
Carrington, N. Dak., 2,101.M 5 79
Carrizo Springs, Tex.,
4,316................................E 9 87
Carrizozo, N. Mex., 1,389..D 5 76
Carroll, Iowa, 6,231...........D 4 60
Carrollton, Ga., 7,753.........C 3 56
Carrollton, Ill., 2,437..........C 4 58
Carrollton, Ky., 3,226..........G 3 62
Carrollton, Mo., 4,380.........E 4 70
Carrollton, Ohio, 2,658........J 4 80
Carson, N. Dak., 493...........G 7 79
CARSON CITY, Nev.,
3,082................................B 3 73
Carteret, N. J., 13,030.........E 2 75
Cartersville, Ga., 7,270........C 2 56
Carterville, Ill., 2,716..........D 6 58
Carterville, Mo., 1,552.........D 8 70
Carthage, Ill., 3,214.............B 3 58
Carthage, Ind., 1,065...........F 5 59
Carthage, Miss., 1,925.........E 5 69
Carthage, Mo., 11,188.........D 8 70
Carthage, N. Y., 4,420.........J 3 77
Carthage, N. C., 1,194.........F 4 78
Carthage, Tenn., 1,604.........K 2 86
Carthage, Tex., 4,750..........K 5 87
Caruthersville, Mo., 8,614..N10 70
Cary, N. C., 1,446...............H 3 78
Casa Grande, Ariz., 4,181..D 6 50
Cascade, Idaho, 943............C 5 57
Cascade, Iowa, 1,299...........L 4 60
Cascade, Mont., 447.............E 3 71
Cascade, N. H., 1,000...........D 3 74
Cascade Locks, Oreg., 733..F 2 82
Casey, Ill., 2,734...................F 4 58
Cashmere, Wash., 1,768.......E 3 91
Casper, Wyo., 23,673............F 3 94
Caspian, Mich., 1,608...........G 2 67
Cass City, Mich., 1,762.........F 5 67
Casselton, N. Dak., 1,373....R 6 79
Cass Lake, Minn., 1,936.......D 3 68
Cassopolis, Mich., 1,527.......D 7 67
Cassville, Mo., 1,441.............E 9 70
Castle Dale, Utah, 715..........D 4 88
Castlegate, Utah, 701............D 4 88
Castle Rock, Colo., 741.........K 4 53
Castle Rock, Wash., 1,255..B 4 91
Castle Shannon, Pa., 5,459.B 7 83
Castleton, Vt., □1,748..........A 3 89
Castleton on Hudson, N. Y.,
1,751................................N 5 77
Catasauqua, Pa., 4,923........M 4 83
Cathlamet, Wash., 501..........B 4 91
Catlettsburg, Ky., 4,750.......M 4 62
Catonsville, Md., 29,638.......H 3 65
Catskill, N. Y., 5,392.............N 6 77
Cattaraugus, N. Y., 1,190..C 6 77
Cavalier, N. Dak., 1,459.......P 2 79
Cave City, Ky., 1,119.............F 6 62
Cavendish, Vt., □1,374..........B 4 89
Cayce, S. C., 3,294................F 4 84
Cayuga, Ind., 1,022...............C 5 59
Cazenovia, N. Y., 1,946..........J 5 77
Cebolla, N. Mex., 1,000..........C 2 76
Cecilton, Md., 510..................L 3 65
Cedar Bluff, Va., 1,083..........E 2 90
Cedarburg, Wis., 2,810..........L 9 93
Cedar City, Utah, 6,106.........A 6 88
Cedaredge, Colo., 574............D 5 53
Cedar Falls, Iowa, 14,334......J 3 60
Cedar Grove, W. Va., 1,738.D 4 92
Cedarhurst, N. Y., 6,051.......D 2 77
Cedar Key, Fla., 900..............C 2 55

Cedar Rapids, Iowa,
72,296..............................K 5 60
Cedartown, Ga., 9,470.........B 2 56
Celina, Ohio, 5,703.............A 4 80
Celina, Tenn., 1,136............K 1 86
Celoron, N. Y., 1,555...........B 6 77
Center, Colo., 2,024.............G 7 53
Center, N. Dak., 492............H 5 79
Center, Tex., 4,323..............K 6 87
Centerdale, R. I.....................H 5 66
Centerfield, Utah, 601..........C 4 88
Center Line, Mich., 7,659....B 6 67
Centerville, Ala., 1,160........D 5 49
Centerville, Ind., 1,386.........H 5 59
Centerville, Iowa, 7,675.......H 7 60
Centerville, Md., 1,804.........K 4 65
Centerville, Mont., 1,800......D 4 71
Centerville, Pa., 5,845..........B 6 83
Centerville, S. Dak., 1,053..R 7 85
Centerville, Tenn., 1,532.....G 3 86
Centerville, Utah, 1,262.......C 3 88
Central, Ariz., 300................F 6 50
Central, N. Mex., 1,511.........A 6 76
Central, S. C., 1,263.............C 2 84
Central City, Ky., 4,110.......C 6 62
Central City, Nebr., 2,394..F 3 72
Central Falls, R. I., 23,550.J 5 66
Centralia, Ill., 13,863...........D 5 58
Centralia, Mo., 2,460............H 4 70
Centralia, Wash., 8,657........B 4 91
Central Point, Oreg., 1,667.E 5 82
Centre, Ala., 1,672...............G 2 49
Centreville, Miss., 2,025......B 8 69
Century, Fla., 1,350.............A 1 55
Ceredo, W. Va., 1,399...........A 4 92
Chadbourn, N. C., 2,103........H 6 78
Chadron, Nebr., 4,687..........B 2 72
Chadwicks, N. Y., 2,500........K 4 77
Chaffee, Mo., 3,134...............N 8 70
Chagrin Falls, Ohio, 3,085..J 9 80
Challis, Idaho, 728................D 5 57
Chama, N. Mex., 1,300..........C 2 76
Chamberlain, S. Dak.,
1,912................................L 6 85
Chambersburg, Pa., 17,212.G 6 83
Champaign, Ill., 39,563........F 3 58
Champlain, N. Y., 1,505........N 1 77
Chandler, Ariz., 3,799...........D 5 50
Chandler, Okla., 2,724...........J 3 81
Chanute, Kans., 10,109..........G 4 61
Chapel Hill, N. C., 9,177.......H 3 78
Chapman, Ala., 943................E 7 49
Chappell, Nebr., 1,297...........B 3 72
Chardon, Ohio, 2,478.............H 2 80
Chariton, Iowa, 5,320.............G 6 60
Charleroi, Pa., 9,872..............C 5 83
Charles City, Iowa, 10,305..H 2 60
Charleston, Ark., 968..............B 3 51
Charleston, Ill., 9,164.............E 4 58
Charleston, Miss., 2,629.........D 2 69
Charleston, Mo., 5,501...........O 9 70
Charleston, S. C., 70,174.......J 6 84
CHARLESTON, W. Va.,
73,501..............................C 4 92
Charlestown, Ind., 4,785.......F 8 59
Charlestown, N. H.,
□2,077.............................B 5 74
Charlestown, R. I., □1,598.H 7 66
Charles Town, W. Va.,
3,035................................L 2 92
Charlevoix, Mich., 2,695........D 3 67
Charlotte, Mich., 6,606...........E 6 67
Charlotte, N. C., 134,042.......D 4 78
Charlotte, Tenn., 478.............G 2 86
Charlotte Court House, Va.,
397...................................G 6 90
Charlottesville, Va., 25,969.H 4 90
Chase City, Va., 2,519............H 7 90
Chaska, Minn., 2,008.............E 6 68
Chatfield, Minn., 1,605...........F 7 68
Chatham, N. J., 7,391.............E 2 75
Chatham, N. Y., 2,304.............N 6 77
Chatham, Va., 1,456................F 7 90
Chattahoochee, Fla., 8,473.B 1 55
Chattanooga, Tenn.,
131,041............................L 4 86
Chauncey, Ohio, 1,016...........F 7 80
Cheboygan, Mich., 5,687.......E 3 67
Checotah, Okla., 2,638..........M 4 81
Cheektowaga, N. Y................C 5 77
Chehalis, Wash., 5,639..........C 4 91
Chelan, Wash., 2,157.............E 3 91
Chelmsford, Mass., □9,407.J 2 66
Chelsea, Me., □2,169.............D 7 64
Chelsea, Mass., 38,912..........L 3 66
Chelsea, Mich., 2,580.............E 6 67
Chelsea, Okla., 1,437..............L 1 81
Cheltenham, Pa., □22,854.M 5 83
Cheylan, W. Va., 1,500...........C 4 92
Chemawa, Oreg., 850.............E 2 82
Cheney, Wash., 2,797.............H 3 91
Cheneyville, La., 918..............F 4 63
Chepachet, R. I., 1,200...........H 5 66
Cheraw, S. C., 4,836...............J 2 84
Cherokee, Ala., 748................C 1 49
Cherokee, Iowa, 7,705............B 3 60
Cherokee, Kans., 849..............H 4 61
Cherokee, Okla., 2,635...........F 1 81

Cherry Creek, Nev., 75.......G 3 73
Cherryvale, Kans., 2,952....G 4 61
Cherryville, N. C., 3,492.....C 4 78
Chesaning, Mich., 2,264.....E 5 67
Chesapeake City, Md.,
1,154................................L 2 65
Cheshire, Conn., □6,295....D 3 54
Chesnee, S. C., 1,051.........E 1 84
Chester, Ill.......................D 6 58
Chester, Mont., 5,389.........F 2 71
Chester, Pa., 66,039...........M 6 83
Chester, S. C., 6,893...........F 2 84
Chester, Vt., 796.................B 4 89
Chester, W. Va., 3,758........L 4 92
Chesterfield, S. C., 1,530...H 2 84
Chesterton, Ind., 3,175........D 1 59
Chestertown, Md., 3,143.....K 4 65
Cheswold, Del., 292............M 4 65
Chetopa, Kans., 1,671..........G 4 61
Chetek, Wis., 1,585..............C 5 93
Cheverly, Md., 3,318............G 5 65
Cheviot, Ohio, 9,944............B 9 80
Chewelah, Wash., 1,683........H 2 91
CHEYENNE, Wyo., 31,935.H 4 94
Cheyenne Wells, Colo.,
1,154................................P 5 53
Chicago, Ill., 3,620,962.......F 2 58
Chicago Heights, Ill.,
24,551..............................F 2 58
Chickamauga, Ga., 1,747.....B 1 56
Chickasaw, Ala., 4,920.........B 9 49
Chickasha, Okla., 15,842.....G 4 81
Chico, Calif., 12,772.............D 4 52
Chicopee, Mass., 49,211.......D 4 66
Chicopee Falls, Mass.,
12,915..............................D 4 66
Childress, Tex., 7,619...........E 3 87
Chilhowie, Va., 1,022...........F 2 90
Chillicothe, Ill., 2,767..........D 3 58
Chillicothe, Mo., 8,694.........F 3 70
Chillicothe, Ohio, 20,133......E 7 80
Chiloquin, Oreg., 668............F 5 82
Chilton, Wis., 2,367..............K 7 93
Chimayo, N. Mex., 1,550......D 3 76
China, Me., □1,375...............E 7 64
China Grove, N. C., 1,491....D 3 78
Chincoteague, Va., 2,724......O 5 90
Chino, Calif., 5,784..............D10 52
Chino Valley, Ariz., 500........C 4 50
Chinook, Mont., 2,307...........G 2 71
Chipley, Fla., 2,959...............D 6 55
Chippewa Falls, Wis.,
11,088..............................D 6 93
Chisholm, Minn., 6,861.........F 3 68
Chloride, Ariz., 250...............A 3 50
Choteau, Mont., 1,618...........D 3 71
Chowchilla, Calif., 3,893.......E 6 52
Christiana, Del., 500.............M 2 65
Christiansburg, Va., 2,967..D 6 90
Christopher, Ill., 3,545..........D 6 58
Chugwater, Wyo., 283...........H 4 94
Chula Vista, Calif., 15,927..J11 52
Church Point, La., 2,897.......F 6 63
Churubusco, Ind., 1,232........G 2 59
Cibecue, Ariz., 35..................E 4 50
Cicero, Ill., 67,544..................B 2 58
Cimarron, Kans., 1,189..........B 4 61
Cimarron, N. Mex., 855.........E 2 76
Cincinnati, Ohio, 503,998....A 7 80
Circle, Mont., 856...................L 3 71
Circleville, Ohio, 8,723..........D 6 80
Circleville, Utah, 603.............B 5 88
Cisco, Tex., 5,230...................E 5 87
Citronelle, Ala., 1,350............B 8 49
Clairton, Pa., 19,652...............C 7 83
Clanton, Ala., 4,640................E 5 49
Clare, Mich., 2,440..................E 5 67
Claremont, Calif., 6,327........D10 52
Claremont, N. H., 12,811.....B 5 74
Claremore, Okla., 5,494........M 2 81
Clarence, Mo., 1,123..............H 3 70
Clarendon, Ark., 2,547...........H 4 51
Clarendon, Tex., 2,577...........C 3 87
Clarinda, Iowa, 5,086.............C 7 60
Clarion, Iowa, 3,150...............F 3 60
Clarion, Pa., 4,409..................D 3 83
Clark, S. Dak., 1,471..............O 4 85
Clarkdale, Ariz., 1,609...........C 4 50
Clarkfield, Minn., 1,012.........C 6 68
Clark Fork, Idaho, 387..........B 1 57
Clarksburg, W. Va., 32,014.F 2 92
Clarksdale, Miss., 16,539.....D 2 69
Clarkson, Nebr., 764..............G 3 72
Clarks Summit, Pa., 2,940..L 3 83
Clarkston, Utah, 526..............B 2 88
Clarkston, Wash., 5,617.........H 4 91
Clarksville, Ark., 4,343.........D 3 51
Clarksville, Ind., 5,905..........F 8 59
Clarksville, Iowa, 1,210.........H 3 60
Clarksville, Tenn., 16,246....G 1 86
Clarksville, Tex., 4,353..........K 4 87
Clarksville, Va., 1,035............H 7 90
Clatskanie, Oreg., 901...........D 1 82
Clawson, Mich., 5,196............B 6 67
Claxton, Ga., 1,923................J 6 56
Clay, Ky., 1,291.....................B 6 62
Clay Center, Kans., 4,528.....E 2 61
Clay City, Ind., 1,068.............C 6 59

Claymont, Del., 5,370........N 1 65
Claypool, Ariz., 1,200.........E 5 50
Clayton, Ala., 1,583............H 7 49
Clayton, Del., 825...............M 3 65
Clayton, Mo., 16,035...........M 5 70
Clayton, N. Mex., 3,515......F 2 76
Clayton, N. Y., 1,981...........H 2 77
Clayton, N. C., 2,229...........J 3 78
Clayville, R. I., 300..............H 5 66
Clearfield, Pa., 9,357...........F 3 83
Clearfield, Utah, 4,723.........C 2 88
Clear Lake, Iowa, 4,977.......G 2 60
Clear Lake, S. Dak., 1,105..R 4 85
Clearmont, Wyo., 225...........F 1 94
Clear Spring, Md., 558.........C 2 65
Clearwater, Fla., 15,581.......D 4 55
Cleburne, Tex., 12,905..........G 5 87
Cle Elum, Wash., 2,206.........E 3 91
Clemenceau, Ariz., 300.........C 4 50
Clendenin, W. Va., 1,475......D 3 92
Clermont, Fla., 2,168............E 3 55
Cleveland, Miss., 6,747.........C 3 69
Cleveland, Ohio, 914,808......G 2 80
Cleveland, Okla., 2,464.........K 2 81
Cleveland, Tenn., 12,605......M 4 86
Cleveland, Tex., 5,183...........K 7 87
Cleveland Heights, Ohio,
59,141..............................H 2 80
Cleves, Ohio, 1,981...............A 7 80
Clewiston, Fla., 2,499...........E 5 55
Cliffside Park, N. J.,
17,116..............................F 2 75
Clifton, Ariz., 3,466..............F 5 50
Clifton, N. J., 64,511............E 2 75
Clifton, S. C., 1,707..............E 2 84
Clifton, Tex., 1,837...............G 6 87
Clifton Forge, Va., 5,795.....E 5 90
Clifton Heights, Pa.,
7,549................................M 7 83
Clifton Springs, N. Y.,
1,838................................F 4 77
Clinton, Ark., 853..................F 2 51
Clinton, Ill., 5,945.................E 3 58
Clinton, Ind., 6,462...............C 5 59
Clinton, Iowa, 30,379............N 5 60
Clinton, Ky., 1,593................C 3 62
Clinton, La., 1,383.................J 5 63
Clinton, Me., □1,623.............E 6 64
Clinton, Mass., □12,287........H 3 66
Clinton, Miss., 2,255.............D 6 69
Clinton, Mo., 6,075...............E 6 70
Clinton, N. Y., 1,630..............K 4 77
Clinton, N. C., 4,414..............J 5 78
Clinton, Okla., 7,555..............D 3 81
Clinton, S. C., 7,168...............E 3 84
Clinton, Tenn., 3,712..............N 2 86
Clinton, Utah, 670..................B 2 88
Clintonville, Wis., 4,657........J 6 93
Clintwood, Va., 1,366.............D 1 90
Clio, Ala., 840.......................G 7 49
Clio, Mich., 1,963..................F 5 67
Clio, S. C., 837......................J 2 84
Cloquet, Minn., 7,685............F 4 68
Clover, S. C., 3,276................F 1 84
Cloverport, Ky., 1,357............D 5 62
Clovis, N. Mex., 17,318.........F 4 76
Clyde, Kans., 1,067................E 2 61
Clyde, N. Y., 2,492.................G 4 77
Clyde, Ohio, 4,083..................E 3 80
Clydepark, Mont., 280............F 5 71
Clymer, Pa., 2,500..................E 4 83
Coal City, Ill., 2,220...............E 2 58
Coaldale, Pa., 5,318...............L 4 83
Coalgate, Okla., 1,984............K 5 81
Coal Grove, Ohio, 2,492.........E 9 80
Coal Hill, Ark., 873................C 3 51
Coalinga, Calif., 5,539...........E 7 52
Coalville, Utah, 850................C 3 88
Coalwood, W. Va., 1,310........C 6 92
Coatesville, Pa., 13,826..........L 5 83
Cobleskill, N. Y., 3,208...........L 5 77
Coburg, Oreg., 693.................D 3 82
Cochran, Ga., 3,357...............F 6 56
Cocoa, Fla., 4,245..................F 3 55
Cody, Wyo., 3,872..................C 1 94
Coeburn, Va., 760..................D 2 90
Coeur d'Alene, Idaho,
12,198..............................B 2 57
Coffeyville, Kans., 17,113....G 4 61
Cohasset, Mass., □3,731......L 3 66
Cohoes, N. Y., 21,272...........N 5 77
Cokato, Minn., 1,403.............D 5 68
Cokeville, Wyo., 440..............B 3 94
Colby, Kans., 3,859...............A 2 61
Colchester, Conn., 1,522.......F 2 54
Colchester, Ill., 1,551............C 3 58
Colchester, Vt., □3,897.........A 1 89
Cold Spring, Minn., 1,488..D 5 68
Cold Spring, N. Y., 1,788..C 1 77
Coldwater, Kans., 1,208........C 4 61
Coldwater, Mich., 8,594........D 7 67
Coldwater, Miss., 949............E 1 69
Coldwater, Ohio, 2,217..........A 5 80
Colebrook, N. H., □2,116...D 2 74
Coleman, Tex., 6,530............E 6 87
Coleraine, Minn., 1,321.........E 3 68
Colfax, Iowa, 2,279...............G 5 60
Colfax, La., 1,651..................E 3 63

Index Ref. Plate No.

Colfax, Wash., 3,057 ..... H 4 91
College Park, Ga., 14,535 ..... C 3 56
College Park, Md., 11,170 ..... C 4 65
College Station, Tex.,
7,925 ..... H 7 87
Collierville, Tenn., 1,153 ..... B 4 86
Collindale, Pa., 8,443 ..... M 7 83
Collingswood, N. J., 15,800 ..... C 4 75
Collins, Miss., 1,293 ..... E 7 69
Collinsville, Ala., 1,023 ..... G 2 49
Collinsville, Ill., 11,862 ..... D 5 58
Collinsville, Mass., 1,500 ..... J 2 66
Collinsville, Okla., 2,011 ..... L 2 81
Colmar Manor, Md., 1,732 ..... G 5 65
Colonial Beach, Va., 1,464 ..... L 4 90
Colonial Heights, Va.,
6,077 ..... K 6 90
Colonie, N. Y., 2,068 ..... N 5 77
Colorado City, Tex., 6,774 ..... C 5 87
Colorado Springs, Colo.,
45,472 ..... K 5 53
Colquitt, Ga., 1,664 ..... C 8 56
Colton, Calif., 14,465 ..... H 9 52
Colton, S. Dak., 521 ..... R 6 85
Columbia, Ala., 849 ..... H 8 49
Columbia, Ill., 2,179 ..... C 5 58
Columbia, Ky., 2,167 ..... G 6 62
Columbia, La., 920 ..... F 2 63
Columbia, Miss., 6,124 ..... E 8 69
Columbia, Mo., 31,974 ..... H 5 70
Columbia, Pa., 11,993 ..... K 5 83
COLUMBIA, S. C., 86,914 ..... G 3 84
Columbia, Tenn., 10,911 ..... G 3 86
Columbia City, Ind., 4,745 ..... G 2 59
Columbia Falls, Mont.,
1,232 ..... C 2 71
Columbia Heights, Minn.,
8,175 ..... E 5 68
Columbiana, Ala., 1,761 ..... E 4 49
Columbiana, Ohio, 3,369 ..... J 4 80
Columbus, Ga., 79,611 ..... C 6 56
Columbus, Ind., 18,370 ..... E 6 59
Columbus, Kans., 3,490 ..... H 4 61
Columbus, Miss., 17,172 ..... H 3 69
Columbus, Mont., 1,097 ..... G 5 71
Columbus, Nebr., 8,884 ..... G 3 72
Columbus, N. Mex., 251 ..... B 7 76
Columbus, N. Dak., 525 ..... E 2 79
COLUMBUS, Ohio, 375,901 ..... E 6 80
Columbus, Tex., 2,878 ..... H 8 87
Columbus, Wis., 3,250 ..... H 9 93
Columbus Grove, Ohio,
1,936 ..... B 4 80
Colusa, Calif., 3,031 ..... C 4 52
Colville, Wash., 3,033 ..... H 2 91
Comanche, Okla., 2,083 ..... G 6 81
Comanche, Tex., 3,840 ..... F 6 87
Commerce, Ga., 3,351 ..... F 2 56
Commerce, Okla., 2,442 ..... M 1 81
Commerce, Tex., 5,889 ..... J 4 87
Como, Miss., 703 ..... E 1 69
Compton, Calif., 47,991 ..... C11 52
Concho, Ariz., 175 ..... F 4 50
Concord, Mass., □8,623 ..... J 3 66
CONCORD, N. H., 27,988 ..... C 5 74
Concord, N. C., 16,486 ..... D 4 78
Concord, Vt., 348 ..... D 2 89
Concordia, Kans., 7,175 ..... E 2 61
Concordia, Mo., 1,218 ..... E 5 70
Concrete, Wash., 760 ..... D 2 91
Condon, Oreg., 968 ..... G 2 82
Conneaut, Ohio, 10,230 ..... J 2 80
Connellsville, Pa., 13,293 ..... D 5 83
Connersville, Ind., 15,550 ..... G 5 59
Conover, N. C., 1,164 ..... C 3 78
Conrad, Mont., 1,865 ..... D 2 71
Conroe, Tex., 7,298 ..... J 7 87
Conshohocken, Pa., 10,922 ..... M 5 83
Constantine, Mich., 1,514 ..... D 7 67
Contact, Nev., 20 ..... G 1 73
Contoocook, N. H., 1,000 ..... C 5 74
Conway, Ark., 8,610 ..... F 3 51
Conway, N. H., □4,109 ..... D 4 74
Conyers, Ga., 2,003 ..... D 3 56
Cookeville, Tenn., 6,924 ..... K 2 86
Coolidge, Ariz., 4,603 ..... D 6 50
Coon Rapids, Iowa, 1,676 ..... D 5 60
Cooper, Tex., 2,350 ..... J 4 87
Coopers Mills, Me., 239 ..... D 7 64
Cooperstown, N. Y., 2,727 ..... L 5 77
Cooperstown, N. Dak.,
1,189 ..... O 5 79
Coplay, Pa., 2,994 ..... L 4 83
Copperhill, Tenn., 924 ..... N 4 86
Coquille, Oreg., 3,523 ..... C 4 82
Coral Gables, Fla., 19,837 ..... F 6 55
Coraopolis, Pa., 10,498 ..... B 4 83
Corbin, Ky., 7,744 ..... J 7 62
Corcoran, Calif., 3,150 ..... F 7 52
Cordele, Ga., 9,462 ..... E 6 56
Cordell, Okla., 2,920 ..... E 4 81
Cordova, Ala., 3,156 ..... D 3 49
Cordova, Alaska Territory,
1,141 ..... K 2 95
Corinna, Me., □1,752 ..... E 6 64
Corinth, Miss., 9,785 ..... H 1 69
Corinth, N. Y., 3,161 ..... N 4 77
Cornelia, Ga., 2,424 ..... F 1 56

Cornelius, N. C., 1,548 ..... D 4 78
Cornelius, Oreg., 998 ..... A 2 82
Cornell, Wis., 1,944 ..... D 5 93
Corning, Ark., 2,045 ..... J 1 51
Corning, Calif., 2,537 ..... C 4 52
Corning, Iowa, 2,104 ..... D 7 60
Corning, N. Y., 17,684 ..... F 6 77
Corning, Ohio, 1,215 ..... F 6 80
Cornwall, N. Y., 2,211 ..... C 1 77
Corona, Calif., 10,223 ..... E11 52
Coronado, Calif., 12,700 ..... H11 52
Corpus Christi, Tex.,
108,287 ..... G10 87
Correctionville, Iowa, 992 ..... B 4 60
Corry, Pa., 7,911 ..... C 2 83
Corsicana, Tex., 19,211 ..... H 5 87
Cortez, Colo., 2,680 ..... B 8 53
Cortland, N. Y., 18,152 ..... H 5 77
Corunna, Mich., 2,358 ..... E 6 67
Corvallis, Oreg., 16,207 ..... D 3 82
Corydon, Ind., 1,944 ..... E 8 59
Corydon, Iowa, 1,870 ..... G 7 60
Corydon, Ky., 742 ..... B 5 62
Cos Cob, Conn., 6,800 ..... A 4 54
Coshocton, Ohio, 11,675 ..... G 5 80
Cosmopolis, Wash., 1,164 ..... B 4 91
Costa Mesa, Calif., 11,844 ..... D11 52
Costilla, N. Mex., 300 ..... D 2 76
Cottage City, Md., 1,249 ..... G 5 65
Cottage Grove, Oreg.,
3,536 ..... D 4 82
Cottageville, S. C., 553 ..... H 6 84
Cotter, Ark., 1,089 ..... E 1 51
Cotton Plant, Ark., 1,838 ..... H 3 51
Cottonport, La., 1,534 ..... F 5 63
Cottonwood, Ariz., 1,326 ..... D 4 50
Cottonwood, Idaho, 689 ..... B 4 57
Cottonwood Falls, Kans.,
957 ..... F 3 61
Cotulla, Tex., 4,418 ..... E 9 87
Coudersport, Pa., 3,210 ..... G 2 83
Coulee City, Wash., 977 ..... F 3 91
Council, Idaho, 748 ..... B 5 57
Council Bluffs, Iowa,
45,429 ..... B 6 60
Council Grove, Kans.,
2,722 ..... F 3 61
Courtland, Va., 443 ..... K 7 90
Coushatta, La., 1,788 ..... D 2 63
Coventry, Conn., □4,043 ..... F 1 54
Coventry, R. I., □9,869 ..... H 6 66
Covina, Calif., 3,049 ..... D10 52
Covington, Ga., 5,192 ..... E 3 56
Covington, Ind., 2,235 ..... C 4 59
Covington, Ky., 64,452 ..... H 2 62
Covington, La., 5,113 ..... K 5 63
Covington, Ohio, 2,172 ..... B 5 80
Covington, Tenn., 4,379 ..... B 3 86
Covington, Va., 5,860 ..... D 5 90
Cowan, Tenn., 1,835 ..... J 4 86
Coweta, Okla., 1,601 ..... L 3 81
Cowley, Wyo., 463 ..... D 1 94
Cowpens, S. C., 1,879 ..... E 1 84
Coxsackie, N. Y., 2,722 ..... N 6 77
Cozad, Nebr., 2,910 ..... E 4 72
Crab Orchard, Ky., 757 ..... J 6 62
Crafton, Pa., 8,066 ..... B 7 83
Craig, Colo., 3,080 ..... D 2 53
Craigmont, Idaho, 594 ..... B 4 57
Crandon, Wis., 1,922 ..... J 4 93
Crane, Mo., 939 ..... E 9 70
Cranford, N. J., 18,602 ..... E 2 75
Cranston, R. I., 55,060 ..... J 5 66
Crawford, Nebr., 1,824 ..... A 2 72
Crawfordsville, Ind.,
12,851 ..... D 4 59
Creede, Colo., 503 ..... E 7 53
Creighton, Nebr., 1,401 ..... G 2 72
Crescent, Okla., 1,341 ..... G 3 81
Crescent City, Fla., 1,393 ..... E 2 55
Cresco, Iowa, 3,638 ..... J 2 60
Cresson, Pa., 2,569 ..... E 5 83
Crested Butte, Colo., 730 ..... E 5 53
Crestline, Ohio, 4,614 ..... E 4 80
Creston, Iowa, 8,317 ..... E 6 60
Crestview, Fla., 5,003 ..... C 6 55
Creswell, Oreg., 662 ..... D 4 82
Crete, Nebr., 3,692 ..... G 4 72
Creve Coeur, Ill., 5,499 ..... D 3 58
Crewe, Va., 2,030 ..... H 6 90
Cripple Creek, Colo., 853 ..... J 5 53
Crisfield, Md., 3,688 ..... L 9 65
Crockett, Tex., 5,932 ..... J 6 87
Cromwell, Conn., □4,286 ..... E 2 54
Crookston, Minn., 7,352 ..... B 3 68
Crooksville, Ohio, 2,960 ..... F 6 80
Crosby, Minn., 2,777 ..... E 4 68
Crosby, Miss., 1,152 ..... B 8 69
Crosby, N. Dak., 1,689 ..... D 2 79
Cross City, Fla., 1,522 ..... C 2 55
Crossett, Ark., 4,619 ..... G 7 51
Crossville, Tenn., 2,291 ..... L 3 86
Croswell, Mich., 1,775 ..... G 5 67
Crothersville, Ind., 1,276 ..... F 7 59
Croton on Hudson, N. Y.,
4,837 ..... C 1 77
Crowell, Tex., 1,912 ..... E 4 87
Crowley, La., 12,784 ..... F 6 63

Crown Point, Ind., 5,839 ..... C 2 59
Crystal, Minn., 5,713 ..... E 5 68
Crystal City, Mo., 3,499 ..... M 6 70
Crystal City, Tex., 7,198 ..... E 9 87
Crystal Falls, Mich., 2,316 ..... A 2 67
Crystal Lake, Ill., 4,832 ..... E 1 58
Crystal River, Fla., 1,026 ..... D 3 55
Crystal Springs, Miss.,
3,676 ..... C 7 69
Cuba, Mo., 1,301 ..... K 6 70
Cuba, N. Y., 1,783 ..... D 6 77
Cuba City, Wis., 1,333 ..... F10 93
Cucamonga, Calif., 1,255 ..... E10 52
Cudahy, Wis., 12,182 ..... L10 93
Cuero, Tex., 7,498 ..... G 8 87
Culbertson, Mont., 779 ..... M 2 71
Culbertson, Nebr., 770 ..... D 4 72
Cullendale, Ark., 3,225 ..... E 6 51
Cullman, Ala., 7,523 ..... E 2 49
Culpeper, Va., 2,527 ..... H 4 90
Culver, Ind., 1,563 ..... E 2 59
Culver City, Calif., 19,720 ..... B10 52
Cumberland, Ky., 4,249 ..... L 7 62
Cumberland Center, Me.,
1,987 ..... C 8 64
Cumberland, Md., 37,679 ..... D 7 65
Cumberland, Wis., 1,872 ..... C 4 93
Cumberland Gap, Tenn.,
403 ..... O 1 86
Custer, S. Dak., 2,017 ..... B 6 85
Curtis, Nebr., 964 ..... D 4 72
Curwensville, Pa., 3,332 ..... E 4 83
Cushing, Okla., 8,414 ..... J 3 81
Cut Bank, Mont., 3,721 ..... D 2 71
Cuthbert, Ga., 4,025 ..... C 7 56
Cuyahoga Falls, Ohio,
29,195 ..... G 3 80
Cynthiana, Ky., 4,847 ..... J 4 62
Dade City, Fla., 3,806 ..... D 3 55
Dadeville, Ala., 2,345 ..... G 5 49
Dagsboro, Del., 474 ..... N 6 65
Dahlonega, Ga., 2,152 ..... D 1 56
Dale, Pa., 3,310 ..... E 5 83
Dalhart, Tex., 5,918 ..... B 1 87
Dallas, Ga., 1,817 ..... C 3 56
Dallas, N. C., 2,454 ..... C 4 78
Dallas, Oreg., 4,793 ..... D 3 82
Dallas, Tex., 434,462 ..... H 2 87
Dallastown, Pa., 3,304 ..... J 6 83
Dalton, Ga., 15,968 ..... C 1 56
Dalton, Mass., □4,772 ..... B 3 66
Daly City, Calif., 15,191 ..... J 2 52
Damascus, Va., 1,726 ..... E 2 90
Danbury, Conn., 22,067 ..... B 2 54
Danby, Vt., □990 ..... A 4 89
Dandridge, Tenn., 690 ..... O 2 86
Danforth, Me., □1,174 ..... H 4 64
Dania, Fla., 4,540 ..... F 5 55
Danielson, Conn., 4,554 ..... H 1 54
Dannemora, N. Y., 4,122 ..... N 1 77
Dansville, N. Y., 5,253 ..... E 5 77
Dante, Va., 2,405 ..... D 2 90
Danvers, Mass., □15,720 ..... L 2 66
Danville, Ark., 829 ..... D 3 51
Danville, Ill., 37,864 ..... F 3 58
Danville, Ind., 2,802 ..... D 5 59
Danville, Ky., 8,686 ..... H 5 62
Danville, Pa., 6,994 ..... J 4 83
Danville, Vt., □1,312 ..... C 2 89
Danville, Va., 35,066 ..... F 7 90
Darby, Mont., 415 ..... B 4 71
Darby, Pa., 13,154 ..... M 7 83
Dardanelle, Ark., 1,772 ..... D 3 51
Darien, Conn., □11,767 ..... B 4 54
Darlington, S. C., 6,619 ..... J 3 84
Darlington, Wis., 2,174 ..... F10 93
Dartmouth, Mass.,
□11,115 ..... K 6 66
Davenport, Iowa, 74,549 ..... M 5 60
Davenport, Wash., 1,417 ..... G 3 91
David City, Nebr., 2,321 ..... G 3 72
Davidson, N. C., 2,423 ..... D 4 78
Davis, Okla., 1,928 ..... H 5 81
Davis, W. Va., 1,271 ..... H 2 92
Davison, Mich., 1,745 ..... F 5 67
Davy, W. Va., 1,650 ..... C 6 92
Dawson, Ga., 4,411 ..... D 7 56
Dawson, Minn., 1,834 ..... B 6 68
Dawson, N. Mex., 1,206 ..... E 2 76
Dawson Springs, Ky.,
2,374 ..... B 6 62
Dayton, Idaho, 287 ..... G 7 57
Dayton, Ky., 8,977 ..... J 2 62
Dayton, Nev., 300 ..... B 3 73
Dayton, Ohio, 243,872 ..... B 6 80
Dayton, Oreg., 719 ..... D 2 82
Dayton, Tenn., 3,191 ..... L 3 86
Dayton, Va., 788 ..... G 4 90
Dayton, Wash., 2,979 ..... H 4 91
Dayton, Wyo., 316 ..... E 1 94
Daytona Beach, Fla.,
30,187 ..... F 2 55
Deadwood, S. Dak., 3,288 ..... B 5 85
Dearborn, Mich., 94,994 ..... B 7 67
Deary, Idaho, 320 ..... B 3 57
Decatur, Ala., 19,974 ..... D 1 49
Decatur, Ga., 21,635 ..... D 3 56
Decatur, Ill., 66,269 ..... E 4 58

Decatur, Ind., 7,271 ..... H 3 59
Decatur, Mich., 1,664 ..... C 6 67
Decatur, Miss., 1,225 ..... F 6 69
Decatur, Nebr., 808 ..... H 3 72
Decatur, Tex., 2,922 ..... G 4 87
Decaturville, Tenn., 514 ..... E 3 86
Decherd, Tenn., 1,435 ..... J 4 86
Decorah, Iowa, 6,060 ..... K 2 60
Dedham, Mass., □18,487 ..... K 4 66
Deephaven, Minn., 1,823 ..... E 5 68
Deep River, Conn., □2,570 ..... F 3 54
Deepwater, Mo., 885 ..... E 6 70
Deerfield, Ill., 3,288 ..... F 1 58
Deerfield Beach, Fla.,
2,088 ..... F 5 55
Deer Isle, Me., □1,234 ..... F 7 64
Deer Lodge, Mont., 3,779 ..... D 4 71
Deer Park, Ohio, 7,241 ..... C 9 80
Deer Park, Wash., 1,167 ..... H 3 91
Deer River, Minn., 1,033 ..... E 3 68
Defiance, Ohio, 11,265 ..... B 3 80
De Funiak Springs, Fla.,
3,077 ..... C 6 55
De Kalb, Ill., 11,708 ..... E 2 58
De Kalb, Miss., 953 ..... G 5 69
De Land, Fla., 8,652 ..... E 2 55
Delano, Calif., 8,717 ..... F 8 52
Delano, Minn., 1,386 ..... E 5 68
Delavan, Wis., 4,007 ..... J10 93
Delaware, Ohio, 11,804 ..... E 5 80
Delaware City, Del.,
1,363 ..... M 2 65
Delcambre, La., 1,463 ..... F 7 63
De Leon, Tex., 2,241 ..... F 5 87
Delhi, La., 1,861 ..... G 2 63
Delhi, N. Y., 2,223 ..... L 6 77
Dell Rapids, S. Dak.,
1,650 ..... R 6 85
Delmar, Del., 1,015 ..... M 7 65
Delmar, Md., 1,328 ..... M 7 65
Del Norte, Colo., 2,048 ..... G 7 53
Delphi, Ind., 2,530 ..... D 3 59
Delphos, Ohio, 6,220 ..... B 4 80
Delray Beach, Fla., 6,312 ..... F 5 55
Del Rio, Tex., 14,211 ..... D 8 87
Delta, Colo., 4,097 ..... D 5 53
Delta, Ohio, 2,120 ..... B 2 80
Delta, Utah, 1,703 ..... B 4 88
Deming, N. Mex., 5,672 ..... B 6 76
Demopolis, Ala., 5,004 ..... C 6 49
Dendron, Va., 476 ..... L 6 90
Denham Springs, La.,
2,053 ..... J 5 63
Denison, Iowa, 4,554 ..... C 4 60
Denison, Tex., 17,504 ..... H 4 87
Denmark, S. C., 2,814 ..... F 5 84
Dennison, Ohio, 4,432 ..... H 5 80
Denton, Md., 1,806 ..... L 5 65
Denton, Mont., 435 ..... G 3 71
Denton, Tex., 21,378 ..... G 4 87
DENVER, Colo., 415,786 ..... K 3 53
De Pere, Wis., 8,146 ..... K 7 93
Depew, N. Y., 7,217 ..... C 5 77
Deposit, N. Y., 2,016 ..... K 6 77
Depue, Ill., 2,163 ..... D 2 58
De Queen, Ark., 3,015 ..... B 5 51
De Quincy, La., 3,837 ..... D 6 63
Derby, Conn., 10,259 ..... C 3 54
Derby, Vt., □2,245 ..... C 1 89
Derby Center, Vt., 383 ..... C 1 89
Derby Line, Vt., 767 ..... C 1 89
De Ridder, La., 5,799 ..... D 5 63
Dermott, Ark., 3,601 ..... H 6 51
Derry, N. H., □5,826 ..... D 6 74
Derry, Pa., 3,752 ..... D 5 83
Des Arc, Ark., 1,612 ..... G 4 51
Deshler, Nebr., 1,063 ..... G 4 72
Deshler, Ohio, 1,623 ..... C 3 80
Desloge, Mo., 1,957 ..... M 7 70
De Smet, S. Dak., 1,180 ..... O 5 85
DES MOINES, Iowa,
177,965 ..... F 5 60
Des Moines, N. Mex., 282 ..... F 2 76
De Soto, Mo., 5,357 ..... L 6 70
Des Plaines, Ill., 14,994 ..... F 1 58
Detroit, Mich., 1,849,568 ..... B 7 67
Detroit Lakes, Minn.,
5,787 ..... C 4 68
Devils Lake, N. Dak.,
6,427 ..... N 3 79
Dewey, Okla., 2,513 ..... L 1 81
De Witt, Ark., 2,843 ..... H 5 51
De Witt, Iowa, 2,644 ..... M 5 60
Dexter, Me., □4,126 ..... E 5 64
Dexter, Mo., 4,624 ..... N 9 70
Dexter, N. Mex., 784 ..... E 5 76
Dexter, N. Y., 1,038 ..... H 2 77
Diamondville, Wyo., 415 ..... B 4 94
Dickinson, N. Dak., 6,479 ..... E 6 79
Dickson City, Pa., 8,948 ..... L 3 83
Dickson, Tenn., 3,348 ..... G 2 86
Dierks, Ark., 1,253 ..... B 5 51
Dillon, Mont., 3,268 ..... D 5 71
Dillon, S. C., 5,171 ..... K 3 84
Dillonvale, Ohio, 1,407 ..... J 5 80
Dillwyn, Va., 556 ..... F 3 90
Dilworth, Minn., 1,429 ..... B 4 68
Dinuba, Calif., 4,971 ..... F 7 52

District Heights, Md.,
1,735 ..... G 5 65
Dixfield, Me., 2,022 ..... C 6 64
Dixon, Ill., 11,523 ..... D 2 58
Dixon, N. Mex., 1,250 ..... D 2 76
Dobbs Ferry, N. Y., 6,268 ..... D 2 77
Dodge Center, Minn.,
1,151 ..... F 6 68
Dodge City Kans.,
11,262 ..... C 4 61
Dodgeville, Wis., 2,532 ..... F10 93
Dodson, Mont., 330 ..... H 2 71
Doland, S. Dak., 535 ..... N 4 85
Dolgeville, N. Y., 3,204 ..... L 4 77
Dolores, Colo., 729 ..... C 8 53
Dolton, Ill., 5,558 ..... B 2 58
Donaldsonville, La., 4,150 ..... H 6 63
Donalsonville, Ga., 2,569 ..... C 8 56
Doniphan, Mo., 1,611 ..... L 9 70
Donna, Tex., 7,171 ..... F11 87
Donora, Pa., 12,186 ..... C 5 83
Dora, Ala., 984 ..... D 3 49
Dormont, Pa., 13,405 ..... B 5 83
Dos Cabezos, Ariz., 80 ..... F 6 50
Dothan, Ala., 21,584 ..... H 8 49
Douglas, Ariz., 9,442 ..... F 7 50
Douglas, Ga., 7,428 ..... G 8 56
Douglas, Wyo., 2,544 ..... G 3 94
Douglasville, Ga., 3,400 ..... C 3 56
DOVER, Del., 6,223 ..... M 4 65
Dover, N. H., 15,874 ..... E 5 74
Dover, N. J., 11,174 ..... D 2 75
Dover, Ohio, 9,852 ..... G 4 80
Dover-Foxcroft, Me.,
□4,218 ..... E 5 64
Dowagiac, Mich., 6,542 ..... D 6 67
Downers Grove, Ill., 11,886 ..... A 2 58
Downey, Calif., 35,000 ..... C11 52
Downey, Idaho, 748 ..... F 7 57
Downingtown, Pa., 4,948 ..... L 5 83
Downs, Kans., 1,221 ..... D 2 61
Doylestown, Ohio, 1,358 ..... J 3 80
Doylestown, Pa., 5,262 ..... M 5 83
Dracut, Mass., 8,666 ..... J 2 66
Dragerton, Utah, 3,453 ..... D 4 88
Drain, Oreg., 1,150 ..... D 4 82
Drake, N. Dak., 831 ..... K 4 79
Drakesboro, Ky., 1,102 ..... C 6 62
Drakes Branch, Va., 410 ..... F 4 90
Draper, Utah, 2,000 ..... C 3 88
Drayton, N. Dak., 875 ..... R 2 79
Dresden, Ohio, 1,310 ..... G 5 80
Dresden, Tenn., 1,509 ..... D 2 86
Drew, Miss., 1,681 ..... C 3 69
Driggs, Idaho, 941 ..... G 6 57
Drummond, Mont., 531 ..... C 4 71
Drumright, Okla., 5,028 ..... K 3 81
Dubach, La., 703 ..... E 1 63
Dublin, Ga., 10,232 ..... G 5 56
Dublin, Tex., 2,761 ..... F 5 87
Dublin, Va., 1,313 ..... C 6 90
Du Bois, Pa., 11,497 ..... E 3 83
Dubois, Idaho, 430 ..... F 5 57
Dubois, Wyo., 279 ..... C 2 94
Dubuque, Iowa, 49,671 ..... M 4 60
Duchesne, Utah, 804 ..... D 3 88
Duckwater, Nev., 5 ..... F 4 73
Dudley, Mass., □5,261 ..... G 4 66
Due West, S. C., 1,033 ..... D 3 84
Dugger, Ind., 1,204 ..... C 6 59
Duluth, Minn., 104,511 ..... G 4 68
Dumas, Ark., 2,912 ..... H 6 51
Dumas, Tex., 6,127 ..... C 2 87
Dumfries, Va., 1,300 ..... K 3 90
Dumont, N. J., 13,013 ..... F 2 75
Dunbar, W. Va., 8,032 ..... C 4 92
Duncan, Ariz., 941 ..... F 6 50
Duncan, Okla., 15,325 ..... G 5 81
Duncan, S. C., 599 ..... D 2 84
Dundee, Ill., 3,414 ..... E 1 58
Dundee, Mich., 1,975 ..... F 7 67
Dunedin, Fla., 3,202 ..... D 3 55
Dunellen, N. J., 6,291 ..... D 2 75
Dunkirk, Ind., 3,048 ..... G 4 59
Dunkirk, N. Y., 18,007 ..... B 5 77
Dunlap, Iowa, 1,409 ..... B 5 60
Dunlap, Tenn., 873 ..... L 4 86
Dunlo, Pa., 2,200 ..... E 5 83
Dunmore, Pa., 20,305 ..... L 3 83
Dunn, N. C., 6,316 ..... H 4 78
Dunnellon, Fla., 1,110 ..... D 2 55
Dunseith, N. Dak., 713 ..... K 2 79
Dunsmuir, Calif., 2,426 ..... C 2 52
Dupo, Ill., 2,239 ..... A 6 58
Dupont, Pa., 4,107 ..... L 3 83
Duquesne, Pa., 17,620 ..... C 7 83
Du Quoin, Ill., 7,147 ..... D 5 58
Durand, Mich., 3,194 ..... E 6 67
Durand, Wis., 1,961 ..... C 6 93
Durango, Colo., 7,459 ..... D 8 53
Durant, Miss., 2,311 ..... E 4 69
Durant, Okla., 10,541 ..... K 6 81
Durham, N. H., □4,770 ..... E 5 74
Durham, N. C., 71,311 ..... H 2 78
Duryea, Pa., 6,655 ..... L 3 83
Dutton, Mont., 431 ..... E 3 71
Dwight, Ill., 2,843 ..... E 2 58
Dyer, Ind., 1,556 ..... C 1 59

Index Ref. Plate No.
Dyer, Tenn., 1,864....D 2 86
Dyersburg, Tenn., 10,885..C 2 86
Dyersville, Iowa, 2,416....L 4 60
Eads, Colo., 1,015....O 6 53
Eagar, Ariz., 637....F 4 50
Eagle Grove, Iowa, 4,176...F 3 60
Eagle Lake, Fla., 1,060....E 4 55
Eagle Lake, Me., □1,516...F 1 64
Eagle Lake, Tex., 2,787....H 8 87
Eagle Pass, Tex., 7,276....D 9 87
Eagle River, Wis., 1,469....H 4 93
Earle, Ark., 2,375....K 3 51
Earlington, Ky., 2,753....B 6 62
Easley, S. C., 6,316....C 2 84
East Alton, Ill., 7,290....B 6 58
East Aurora, N. Y., 5,962...C 5 77
East Bakersfield, Calif., 38,177....G 8 52
East Bend, N. C., 475....D 2 78
East Braintree, Mass....L 4 66
East Brewton, Ala., 2,173...E 8 49
East Bridgewater, Mass., □4,412....L 4 66
East Canon, Colo., 761....J 6 53
East Chicago, Ind., 54,263...C 1 59
East Cleveland, Ohio, 40,047....H 9 80
East Concord, N. H....D 5 74
East Conemaugh, Pa., 4,101....E 5 83
East Dedham, Mass., 5,000....K 4 66
East Detroit, Mich., 21,461....B 6 67
East Dubuque, Ill., 1,697....C 1 58
East Ely, Nev., 1,000....G 3 73
East Gary, Ind., 5,635....C 1 59
East Grand Forks, Minn., 5,049....B 2 68
East Grand Rapids, Mich., 6,403....D 6 67
East Greenwich, R. I., □4,923....H 6 66
East Haddam, Conn., □2,554....F 3 54
East Hampton, Conn., □4,000....E 2 54
Easthampton, Mass., □10,694....D 3 66
East Hampton, N. Y., 1,737....G 2 77
East Hartford, Conn., □29,933....E 1 54
East Haven, Conn., □12,212....D 3 54
East Helena, Mont., 1,216..E 4 71
East Jaffrey, N. H., 1,866..B 6 74
East Jordan, Mich., 1,779..D 3 67
Eastlake, Ohio, 7,486....J 8 80
Eastland, Tex., 3,626....F 5 87
East Lansdowne, Pa., 3,527....M 7 83
East Lansing, Mich., 20,325....E 6 67
East Livermore, Me., 500...C 7 64
East Liverpool, Ohio, 24,217....J 4 80
East Lyme, Conn., □3,870....G 3 54
East McKeesport, Pa., 3,171....C 5 83
Eastman, Ga., 3,597....F 6 56
East Mauch Chunk, Pa., 3,132....L 4 83
East Millinocket, Me., □1,358....F 4 64
East Milton, Mass....R10 66
East Moline, Ill., 13,913....C 2 58
Easton, Me., □1,664....H 2 64
Easton, Md., 4,836....K 5 65
Easton, Mass., □6,244....K 4 66
Easton, Pa., 35,632....M 4 83
East Orange, N. J., 79,340..B 2 75
East Palatka, Fla., 1,367...E 2 55
East Palestine, Ohio, 5,159..J 4 80
East Paterson, N. J., 15,386....B 2 75
East Peoria, Ill., 8,698....D 3 58
East Pittsburgh, Pa., 5,259....C 7 83
East Point, Ga., 21,080....C 3 56
Eastport, Me., 3,123....J 6 64
Eastport, Md., 4,594....J 5 65
East Prairie, Mo., 3,033....O 9 70
East Providence, R. I., □35,871....J 5 66
East Rainelle, W. Va., 1,695....E 5 92
East Ridge, Tenn., 9,645....L 5 86
East Rochester, N. H., 1,100....E 5 74
East Rochester, N. Y., 7,022....F 4 77
East Rockaway, N. Y., 7,970....D 2 77
East Rutherford, N. J., 7,438....B 2 75
East St. Louis, Ill., 82,295..C 5 58
Eastside, Oreg., 890....C 4 82
East Spencer, N. C., 2,444..E 3 78
East Stroudsburg, Pa., 7,274....M 4 83
East Syracuse, N. Y., 4,766....H 4 77
East Tawas, Mich., 2,040...F 4 67
East Thomaston, Ga., 3,082....D 5 56
East Weymouth, Mass., 10,000....L 4 66
East Williston, N. Y., 1,734....D 2 77
East Windsor, Conn., □4,859....E 1 54
Eaton, Colo., 1,276....K 2 53
Eaton, Ind., 1,598....G 4 59
Eaton, Ohio, 4,242....A 6 80
Eaton Rapids, Mich., 3,509..E 6 67
Eatonton, Ga., 2,749....F 4 56
Eatonville, Wash., 1,048....C 4 91
Eau Gallie, Fla., 1,554....F 3 55
Eau Claire, S. C., 9,238....F 3 84
Eau Claire, Wis., 36,058....D 6 93
Ebensburg, Pa., 4,086....E 5 83
Eccles, W. Va., 1,885....D 5 92
Eckman, W. Va., 1,574....D 6 92
Ecorse, Mich., 17,948....B 7 67
Eddyville, Ky., 1,840....A 6 62
Eden, Idaho, 456....D 7 57
Edenton, N. C., 4,468....M 2 78
Edgefield, S. C., 2,815....E 4 84
Edgeley, N. Dak., 943....N 7 79
Edgemont, S. Dak., 1,158..B 7 85
Edge Moor, Del., 25....N 1 65
Edgerley, La., 500....C 6 63
Edgerton, Minn., 961....B 7 68
Edgerton, Wis., 3,507....H10 93
Edgerton, Wyo., 203....F 2 94
Edgewater, Colo., 2,580....J 3 53
Edgewater, N. J., 3,952....C 2 75
Edgewood, Pa., 5,292....B 7 83
Edina, Minn., 9,744....E 6 68
Edina, Mo., 1,607....H 2 70
Edinburg, Ind., 3,283....E 6 59
Edinburg, Tex., 12,383....F11 87
Edinburg, Va., 533....H 3 90
Edison, Ga., 1,247....C 7 56
Edmond, Okla., 6,086....G 3 81
Edmonds, Wash., 2,057....C 3 91
Edmonston, Md., 1,190....G 5 65
Edna, Tex., 3,855....H 9 87
Edwards, Miss., 1,002....C 6 69
Edwardsville, Ill., 8,776....D 5 58
Edwardsville, Pa., 6,686....L 3 83
Effingham, Ill., 6,892....E 4 58
Egg Harbor City, N. J., 3,838....D 4 75
Ekalaka, Mont., 904....M 5 71
Elba, Ala., 2,936....F 8 49
Elbert, W. Va., 1,565....C 6 92
Elberton, Ga., 6,772....F 2 56
Elbow Lake, Minn., 1,398..B 5 68
El Cajon, Calif., 5,600....J11 52
El Campo, Tex., 6,237....H 8 87
El Centro, Calif., 12,590....K11 52
El Cerrito, Calif., 18,111....J 2 52
Eldon, Iowa, 1,457....J 7 60
Eldon, Mo., 2,766....G 6 70
Eldora, Iowa, 3,107....G 4 60
El Dorado, Ark., 23,076....E 7 51
Eldorado, Ill., 4,500....E 6 58
El Dorado, Kans., 11,037...F 4 61
El Dorado Springs, Mo., 2,618....E 7 70
Electra, Tex., 4,970....F 4 87
Elgin, Ill., 44,223....E 1 58
Elgin, Nebr., 820....F 3 72
Elgin, N. Dak., 882....G 7 79
Elgin, Oreg., 1,223....H 2 82
Elgin, Tex., 3,168....G 7 87
Elida, N. Mex., 430....F 5 76
Eliot, Me., □2,509....B 9 64
Elizabeth, La., 1,113....E 5 63
Elizabeth, N. J., 112,817...E 2 75
Elizabeth, Pa., 2,615....C 5 83
Elizabeth City, N. C., 12,685....N 2 78
Elizabethton, Tenn., 10,754....R 2 86
Elizabethtown, Ky., 5,807..F 5 62
Elizabethtown, N. C., 1,611....H 5 78
Elizabethtown, Pa., 5,083..J 5 83
Elkader, Iowa, 1,584....L 3 60
Elk City, Okla., 7,962....D 4 81
Elkhart, Ind., 35,556....F 1 59
Elk Horn, Ky....G 6 62
Elkhorn, W. Va., 1,035....D 6 92
Elkhorn, Wis., 2,935....J10 93
Elkin, N. C., 2,842....D 2 78
Elkins, W. Va., 9,121....G 3 92
Elko, Nev., 5,393....F 2 73
Elk Point, S. Dak., 1,367...R 8 85
Elk River, Idaho, 312....B 3 57
Elk River, Minn., 1,399....E 5 68
Elkton, Ky., 1,312....C 7 62
Elkton, Md., 5,245....L 2 65
Elkton, S. Dak., 657....R 5 85
Elkton, Va., 1,361....G 4 90
Ellendale, Del., 321....N 5 65
Ellendale, N. Dak., 1,759...O 8 79
Ellensburg, Wash., 8,430....E 3 91
Ellenville, N. Y., 4,225....M 7 77
Ellijay, Ga., 1,527....C 1 56
Ellington, Conn., □3,099...F 1 54
Ellinwood, Kans., 2,569....D 3 61
Ellis, Kans., 2,649....C 3 61
Ellisville, Miss., 3,579....F 7 69
Elloree, S. C., 1,127....G 4 84
Ellsworth, Kans., 2,193....D 3 61
Ellsworth, Me., 3,936....G 6 64
Ellsworth, Wis., 1,475....B 6 93
Ellwood City, Pa., 12,945..B 4 83
Elma, Wash., 1,543....B 4 91
Elmhurst, Ill., 21,273....A 2 58
Elmira, N. Y., 49,716....G 6 77
Elmira Heights, N. Y., 5,009....G 6 77
Elmo, Wyo., 213....F 4 94
El Monte, Calif., 8,101....D10 52
Elmore, Minn., 1,074....D 7 68
Elmsford, N. Y., 3,147....D 1 77
Elmwood Park, Ill., 18,801.B 2 58
Elmwood Place, Ohio, 4,113....B 9 80
El Paso, Tex., 130,485....B10 87
El Reno, Okla., 10,991....F 3 81
El Rito, N. Mex., 1,200....C 2 76
Elroy, Wis., 1,654....F 8 93
Elsberry, Mo., 1,565....L 4 70
El Segundo, Calif., 8,011....B11 52
Elsinore, Utah, 657....B 5 88
Elsmere, Del., 5,314....M 2 65
Elsmere, Ky., 3,483....H 3 62
Elton, La., 1,434....E 6 63
Elvins, Mo., 1,977....M 7 70
Elwood, Ind., 11,362....F 4 59
Elwood, Kans., 1,020....H 2 61
Elwood, Utah, 393....B 2 88
Ely, Minn., 5,474....G 3 68
Ely, Nev., 3,558....G 3 73
Elyria, Ohio, 30,307....F 3 80
Emerson, Nebr., 784....H 2 72
Emery, Utah, 488....C 5 88
Emeryville, Calif., 2,521....J 2 52
Eminence, Ky., 1,462....G 4 62
Emmaus, Pa., 7,780....M 4 83
Emmetsburg, Iowa, 3,760...D 2 60
Emmett, Idaho, 3,067....B 6 57
Emmitsburg, Md., 1,261....E 2 65
Empire, Oreg., 2,261....C 4 82
Emporia, Kans., 15,669....F 3 61
Emporia, Va., 5,664....J 7 90
Emporium, Pa., 3,646....F 2 83
Emsworth, Pa., 3,128....B 6 83
Encampment, Wyo., 288....F 4 94
Encino, N. Mex., 408....D 4 76
Enderlin, N. Dak., 1,504....P 6 79
Endicott, N. Y., 20,050....H 6 77
Enfield, Conn., □15,464....E 1 54
Enfield, N. H., □1,612....B 4 74
Enfield, N. C., 2,361....K 2 78
England, Ark., 2,136....F 4 51
Englewood, Colo., 16,869....K 3 53
Englewood, N. J., 23,145....C 2 75
Englewood, Tenn., 1,545....M 4 86
Enid, Okla., 36,017....G 2 81
Ennis, Tex., 7,815....H 5 87
Enosburg Falls, Vt., 1,289....B 1 89
Ensenada, N. Mex., 400....C 2 76
Enterprise, Ala., 7,288....G 8 49
Enterprise, Miss., 691....G 6 69
Enterprise, Oreg., 1,718....K 2 82
Enterprise, Utah, 790....A 6 88
Enumclaw, Wash., 2,789....D 3 91
Ephraim, Utah, 1,987....C 4 88
Ephrata, Pa., 7,027....K 5 83
Ephrata, Wash., 4,589....F 3 91
Epping, N. H., □1,796....D 5 74
Erath, La., 1,514....F 7 63
Erick, Okla., 1,579....C 4 81
Erie, Colo., 937....K 2 53
Erie, Kans., 1,296....G 4 61
Erie, Pa., 130,803....B 1 83
Erin, Tenn., 858....F 2 86
Erlanger, Ky., 3,694....H 2 62
Erwin, Tenn., 3,387....R 2 86
Escalante, Utah, 773....C 6 88
Escanaba, Mich., 15,170....C 3 67
Escondido, Calif., 6,544....H10 52
Eskdale, W. Va....D 4 92
Esmond, R. I., 2,000....H 5 66
Espanola, N. Mex., 1,446..C 3 76
Essex, Conn., □3,491....F 3 54
Essex, Vt., □3,931....A 1 89
Essex Junction, Vt., 2,741....A 1 89
Essexville, Mich., 3,167....F 5 67
Estacada, Oreg., 850....E 2 82
Estancia, N. Mex., 916....D 4 76
Estelline, S. Dak., 760....R 4 85
Estes Park, Colo., 1,617....J 2 53
Estherville, Iowa, 6,719....D 2 60
Estill, S. C., 1,659....F 6 84
Ethel, Miss., 723....F 4 69
Ethel, W. Va., 1,032....C 5 92
Etna, Pa., 6,750....B 7 83
Etna, Wyo., 450....A 2 94
Etowah, Tenn., 3,261....M 4 86
Euclid, Ohio, 41,396....H 2 80
Eudora, Ark., 3,072....H 7 51
Eufaula, Ala., 6,906....H 7 49
Eufaula, Okla., 2,540....L 4 81
Eugene, Oreg., 35,879....D 3 82
Eunice, La., 8,184....F 6 63
Eunice, N. Mex., 2,352....F 6 76
Eupora, Miss., 1,338....F 3 69
Eureka, Calif., 23,058....A 3 52
Eureka, Kans., 3,958....F 4 61
Eureka, Mont., 929....B 2 71
Eureka, Nev., 500....E 3 73
Eureka, S. Dak., 1,576....K 2 85
Eureka, Utah, 1,318....B 4 88
Eureka Springs, Ark., 1,958....C 1 51
Eustis, Fla., 4,005....E 3 55
Eutaw, Ala., 2,348....C 5 49
Evans, Colo., 862....K 2 53
Evanston, Ill., 73,641....F 1 58
Evanston, Wyo., 3,863....B 4 94
Evansville, Ind., 128,636....C 9 59
Evansville, Wis., 2,531....H10 93
Evansville, Wyo., 393....F 3 94
Evart, Mich., 1,578....D 5 67
Evarts, Ky., 1,937....L 7 62
Eveleth, Minn., 5,872....F 3 68
Everett, Mass., 45,982....K 3 66
Everett, Wash., 33,849....C 3 91
Evergreen, Ala., 3,454....D 8 49
Evergreen Park, Ill., 10,531....B 2 58
Ewa, Hawaii Territory, 3,570....A 4 95
Excelsior, Minn., 1,763....E 6 68
Excelsior Springs, Mo., 5,888....D 4 70
Exeter, Calif., 4,078....F 7 52
Exeter, Nebr., 747....G 4 72
Exeter, N. H., □5,664....E 6 74
Exeter, R. I., □1,870....J 6 66
Exeter, Pa., 5,130....L 3 83
Exira, Iowa, 1,129....D 5 60
Fairbanks, Alaska Territory, 5,625....K 1 95
Fairborn, Ohio, 7,847....C 6 80
Fairburn, Ga., 1,889....C 3 56
Fairbury, Ill., 2,433....E 3 58
Fairbury, Nebr., 6,395....G 4 72
Fairfax, Calif., 2,198....H 2 52
Fairfax, Minn., 1,143....D 6 68
Fairfax, Okla., 2,017....J 1 81
Fairfax, S. C., 1,567....F 6 84
Fairfax, Va., 1,946....K 3 90
Fairfield, Ala., 13,177....E 3 49
Fairfield, Conn., □30,489..B 4 54
Fairfield, Idaho, 502....D 6 57
Fairfield, Ill., 5,576....E 5 58
Fairfield, Iowa, 7,299....K 7 60
Fairfield, Me., □5,811....D 6 64
Fairfield, Vt., □1,428....B 1 89
Fairhaven, Mass., □12,764....L 6 66
Fair Haven, Vt., 2,058....A 3 89
Fairhope, Ala., 3,354....C10 49
Fair Lawn, N. J., 23,885....B 1 75
Fairmont, Minn., 8,193....D 7 68
Fairmont, Nebr., 729....G 4 72
Fairmont, N. C., 2,319....G 6 78
Fairmont, W. Va., 29,346...F 2 92
Fairmont City, Ill., 2,284..B 6 58
Fairmont Heights, Md., 2,097....G 5 65
Fairmount, Ind., 2,646....F 4 59
Fairmount, N. Dak., 660....S 7 79
Fairplay, Colo., 476....H 4 53
Fairport, N. Y., 5,267....F 4 77
Fairport Harbor, Ohio, 4,519....H 2 80
Fairview, Idaho, 398....G 7 57
Fairview, Mont., 942....M 3 71
Fairview, N. J., 8,661....C 2 75
Fairview, Ohio, 9,311....G 9 80
Fairview, Okla., 2,411....E 2 81
Fairview, Utah, 974....C 4 88
Fairview, W. Va., 775....F 1 92
Fairview Park, Ind., 902....C 5 59
Falconer, N. Y., 3,292....B 6 77
Fallon, Nev., 2,400....C 3 73
Fall River, Mass., 111,963..K 6 66
Falls Church, Va., 7,535....K 3 90
Falls City, Nebr., 6,203....J 4 72
Falls City, Oreg., 853....D 3 82
Falmouth, Ky., 2,186....J 3 62
Falmouth, Me., □4,342....C 8 64
Falmouth, Mass., □8,662..M 6 66
Fargo, N. Dak., 38,256....S 6 79
Faribault, Minn., 16,028....E 6 68
Farmer City, Ill., 1,752....E 3 58
Farmersburg, Ind., 1,024....C 6 59
Farmersville, Tex., 1,955...H 4 87
Farmerville, La., 3,173....F 1 63
Farmingdale, N. Y., 4,492..D 2 77
Farmington, Conn., □7,026....D 2 54
Farmington, Del., 113....M 5 65
Farmington, Ill., 2,651....C 3 58
Farmington, Me., □4,677...C 6 64
Farmington, Mich., 2,325...F 6 67
Farmington, Minn., 1,916...E 6 68
Farmington, Mo., 4,490....M 7 70
Farmington, N. H., □3,454....D 5 74
Farmington, N. Mex., 3,637....A 2 76
Farmington, Utah, 1,468....C 3 88
Farmington, W. Va., 824....F 1 92
Farmville, N. C., 2,942....K 3 78
Farmville, Va., 4,375....H 6 90
Farrell, Pa., 13,644....A 3 83
Faulkton, S. Dak., 837....L 3 85
Fayette, Ala., 3,707....C 3 49
Fayette, Iowa, 1,469....K 3 60
Fayette, Miss., 1,498....B 7 69
Fayette, Mo., 3,144....G 4 70
Fayetteville, Ark., 17,071....B 1 51
Fayetteville, N. Y., 2,624...J 4 77
Fayetteville, N. C., 34,715..H 4 78
Fayetteville, Tenn., 5,447..H 4 86
Fayetteville, W. Va., 824..D 4 92
Federalsburg, Md., 1,878....L 6 65
Felton, Del., 455....M 4 65
Fennimore, Wis., 1,696....E10 93
Fenton, Mich., 4,226....F 6 67
Ferdinand, Ind., 1,252....D 8 59
Fergus Falls, Minn., 12,917....B 4 68
Ferguson, Mo., 11,573....M 5 70
Fernandina, Fla., 4,420....E 1 55
Ferndale, Mich., 29,675....B 6 67
Ferndale, Pa., 2,619....D 5 83
Ferndale, Wash., 979....C 2 91
Fernley, Nev., 650....B 3 73
Ferriday, La., 3,847....G 3 63
Ferrisburg, Vt., □1,387....A 2 89
Fertile, Minn., 890....B 3 68
Fessenden, N. Dak., 917....L 4 79
Festus, Mo., 5,199....M 6 70
Filer, Idaho, 1,425....D 7 57
Fillmore, Calif., 3,884....F 9 52
Fillmore, Utah, 1,890....B 5 88
Fincastle, Va., 405....E 6 90
Findlay, Ohio, 23,845....C 3 80
Finley, N. Dak., 671....P 4 79
Fitchburg, Mass., 42,691....G 2 66
Fitzgerald, Ga., 8,130....F 7 56
Flagstaff, Ariz., 7,663....D 3 50
Flandreau, S. Dak., 2,193...R 5 85
Flat River, Mo., 5,308....M 7 70
Flat Rock, Mich., 1,931....F 6 67
Fleming, Ky., 943....M 6 62
Flemingsburg, Ky., 1,502....K 4 62
Flint, Mich., 163,143....F 6 67
Flomaton, Ala., 2,713....D 8 49
Flora, Ill., 5,255....E 5 58
Flora, Ind., 1,657....E 3 59
Florala, Ala., 2,713....F 9 49
Floral Park, N. Y., 14,582..D 2 77
Florence, Ala., 23,879....C 1 49
Florence, Ariz., 1,776....D 5 50
Florence, Colo., 2,773....J 6 53
Florence, Kans., 1,009....E 3 61
Florence, Ky., 1,325....H 2 62
Florence, Oreg., 1,026....C 4 82
Florence, S. C., 22,513....J 3 84
Florissant, Mo., 3,737....P 2 70
Floyd, Va., 493....D 7 90
Floydada, Tex., 3,210....C 3 87
Flushing, Mich., 2,226....F 5 67
Foley, Ala., 1,301....C10 49
Foley, Minn., 1,089....E 5 68
Follansbee, W. Va., 4,435..K 5 92
Folsom, N. Mex., 206....F 2 76
Fonda, Iowa, 1,120....D 3 60
Fonda, N. Y., 1,026....M 5 77
Fond du Lac, Wis., 29,936..K 8 93
Ford City, Pa., 5,352....D 4 83
Fordyce, Ark., 3,754....E 6 51
Foreman, Ark., 907....B 6 51
Forest, Miss., 2,874....E 6 69
Forest City, Iowa, 2,766....F 2 60
Forest City, N. C., 4,971....B 4 78
Forest City, Pa., 3,122....L 2 83
Forester, Ark., 818....C 4 51
Forest Grove, Oreg., 4,343....D 2 82
Forest Hills, Pa., 6,301....C 5 83
Forest Lake, Minn., 1,766..F 5 68
Forest Park, Ill., 14,969....B 2 58
Forestville, Conn., 6,000....D 2 54
Forks, Wash., 1,120....A 3 91
Forman, N. Dak., 466....P 7 79
Fornfelt, Mo., 1,539....N 8 70
Forrest City, Ark., 7,607....J 4 51
Forsyth, Ga., 3,125....E 4 56
Forsyth, Mont., 1,906....K 4 71
Fort Atkinson, Wis., 6,280..J10 93
Fort Benton, Mont., 1,522..F 3 71
Fort Bragg, Calif., 3,826....B 4 52
Fort Bragg, N. C., 16,000..H 4 78
Fort Branch, Ind., 1,944....B 8 59

Index Ref. Plate No.

Fort Collins, Colo., 14,937..J 1 53
Fort Deposit, Ala., 1,358....E 7 49
Fort Dodge, Iowa, 25,115...E 3 60
Fort Edward, N. Y., 3,797..O 4 77
Fort Fairfield, Me., □5,791....H 2 64
Fort Gaines, Ga., 1,339......C 7 56
Fort Gibson, Okla., 1,496...M 3 81
Fort Huachuca, Ariz., 100..E 7 50
Fort Kent, Me., □5,343......F 1 64
Fort Laramie, Wyo., 300....H 3 94
Fort Lauderdale, Fla., 36,328....F 5 55
Fort Lee, N. J., 11,648......C 2 75
Fort Lewis, Wash., 35,000..C 3 91
Fort Lupton, Colo., 1,907..K 2 53
Fort Madison, Iowa, 14,954....L 7 60
Fort Meade, Fla., 2,803......E 4 55
Fort Mill., S. C., 3,204......G 2 84
Fort Mitchell, Ky., 372.......H 2 62
Fort Monroe, Va., 2,500....M 7 90
Fort Morgan, Colo., 5,315....M 2 53
Fort Myers, Fla., 13,195.....E 5 55
Fort Payne, Ala., 6,226......G 2 49
Fort Peck, Mont., 1,214.....K 2 71
Fort Pierce, Fla., 13,502....F 4 55
Fort Pierre, S. Dak., 951....J 5 85
Fort Plain, N. Y., 2,935......L 5 77
Fort Riley, Kans., 2,531.....F 2 61
Fort Scott, Kans., 10,335...H 4 61
Fort Smith, Ark., 47,942....B 3 51
Fort Stockton, Tex., 4,444..C 4 87
Fort Sumner, N. Mex., 1,982....E 4 76
Fort Thomas, Ky., 10,870...J 2 62
Fort Valley, Ga., 6,820.......E 5 56
Fortville, Ind., 1,786.........F 5 59
Fort Washakie, Wyo., 1,500....D 2 94
Fort Wayne, Ind., 133,607..G 2 59
Fort Worth, Tex., 278,778..E 2 87
Fort Yates, N. Dak., 825....J 7 79
Forty Fort, Pa., 6,173........L 3 83
Fossil, Oreg., 645............G 3 82
Fosston, Minn., 1,614.......C 3 68
Foster, R. I., □1,630.........H 5 66
Fostoria, Ohio, 14,351......D 3 80
Fountain, Colo., 713..........K 5 53
Fountain Green, Utah, 767....C 4 88
Fountain Hill, Pa., 5,456..M 4 83
Fountain Inn., S. C., 1,325....D 2 84
Fowler, Colo., 1,025..........L 6 53
Fowler, Ind., 2,117............C 3 59
Foxboro, Mass., □7,030.....J 4 66
Fox Lake, Wis., 1,153.........J 8 93
Fox Point, Wis., 2,585........L 9 93
Frackville, Pa., 6,541.........K 4 83
Framingham, Mass., □28,086....J 3 66
Frankford, Del., 615..........N 6 65
Frankfort, Ind., 15,028.......E 4 59
Frankfort, Kans., 1,237......F 2 61
FRANKFORT, Ky., 11,916..H 4 62
Frankfort, Mich., 1,858......C 4 67
Frankfort, N. Y., 3,844.......K 4 77
Franklin, Idaho, 467..........G 7 57
Franklin, Ind., 7,316..........E 6 59
Franklin, Ky., 4,343...........D 7 62
Franklin, La., 6,144...........G 7 63
Franklin, Mass., □8,037.....J 4 66
Franklin, Nebr., 1,602........F 4 72
Franklin, N. H., 6,552.......C 5 74
Franklin, N. J., 3,864.........D 1 75
Franklin, N. C., 1,975........C 9 78
Franklin, Ohio, 5,388.........B 6 80
Franklin, Pa., 10,006..........C 3 83
Franklin, Tenn., 5,475........H 3 86
Franklin, Va., 4,670...........L 7 90
Franklin Park, Ill., 8,899...A 2 58
Franklinton, La., 2,342.......K 5 63
Franklinton, N. C., 1,414....J 2 78
Franklinville, N. Y., 2,092..D 6 77
Frazee, Minn., 1,021..........C 4 68
Frederica, Del., 675...........N 4 65
Frederick, Colo., 599.........K 2 53
Frederick, Md., 18,142.......E 3 65
Frederick, Okla., 5,467......D 6 81
Fredericksburg, Tex., 3,854....E 7 87
Fredericksburg, Va., 12,158....J 4 90
Fredericktown, Mo., 3,696....M 7 70
Fredonia, Ariz., 350..........C 2 50
Fredonia, Kans., 3,257.......G 4 61
Fredonia, N. Y., 7,095.......B 6 77
Freedom, Pa., 3,000...........B 4 83
Freedom, Wyo., 510...........B 3 94
Freehold, N. J., 7,550.........E 3 75
Freeland, Pa., 5,909...........L 3 83
Freeman, S. Dak., 944........O 7 85
Freeman, W. Va., 400.........D 6 92
Freeport, Ill., 22,467.........D 1 58
Freeport, Me., □3,280.......C 8 64
Freeport, N. Y., 24,600......D 3 77
Freeport, Pa., 2,685...........C 4 83
Freeport, Tex., 6,012..........J 9 87
Freer, Tex., 2,280..............E 6 87
Freewater, Oreg., 1,489......J 2 82
Fremont, Mich., 3,056.......D 5 67
Fremont, Nebr., 14,762......H 3 72
Fremont, Ohio, 16,537........D 3 80
French Lick, Ind., 1,946....D 7 59
Frenchville, Me., □1,528....G 1 64
Fresno, Calif., 91,669.........F 7 52
Friars Point, Miss., 916.....C 2 69
Friday Harbor, Wash., 783....B 2 91
Friend, Nebr., 1,148...........G 4 72
Friendship, Tenn., 452........C 3 86
Friendsville, Md., 607........A 7 65
Fries, Va., 1,442...............B 7 90
Frisco City, Ala., 1,068......D 8 49
Froid, Mont., 555...............M 2 71
Fromberg, Mont., 442.........H 5 71
Frontenac, Kans., 1,569......H 4 61
Frontier, Wyo., 500............B 4 94
Front Royal, Va., 8,115......H 3 90
Frostburg, Md., 6,876.........C 7 65
Frostproof, Fla., 2,329........E 4 55
Fruita, Colo., 1,463............B 4 53
Fruitland, Md., 1,028.........M 7 65
Fruitland, N. Mex., 200......A 2 76
Fryeburg, Me., □1,926........B 8 64
Fulda, Minn., 1,149............C 7 68
Fullerton, Calif., 13,958.....D11 52
Fullerton, Md., 2,500..........J 3 65
Fullerton, Nebr., 1,520.......G 3 72
Fulton, Ill., 2,706...............C 2 53
Fulton, Ky., 3,224..............C 4 62
Fulton, Miss., 1,343...........H 2 69
Fulton, Mo., 10,052............J 5 70
Fulton, N. Y., 13,922..........H 4 77
Funkstown, Md., 879...........D 2 65
Fuquay Springs, N. C., 1,992....H 3 78
Gadsden, Ala., 55,725........G 2 49
Gadsden, Ariz., 250............A 6 50
Gaffney, S. C., 8,123...........E 1 84
Gainesboro, Tenn., 992.......K 2 86
Gainesville, Fla., 26,861.....D 2 55
Gainesville, Ga., 11,926......E 2 56
Gainesville, Tex., 11,246....G 4 87
Gaithersburg, Md., 1,755...F 4 65
Galax, Va., 5,248...............C 7 90
Galena, Ill., 4,648..............C 1 58
Galena, Kans., 4,029...........H 4 61
Galesburg, Ill., 31,425.......C 3 58
Galesville, Wis., 1,193........D 7 93
Galion, Ohio, 9,952.............E 4 80
Gallatin, Mo., 1,634...........D 3 70
Gallatin, Tenn., 5,107.........H 2 86
Gallipolis, Ohio, 7,871.......F 8 80
Gallitzin, Pa., 3,102...........E 5 83
Gallup, N. Mex., 9,133.......A 3 76
Galva, Ill., 2,886................D 2 58
Galveston, Tex., 66,568......L 3 87
Gardena, Calif., 14,405.......C11 52
Garden City, Kans., 10,905....B 4 61
Garden City, Mich., 9,012..B 7 67
Garden City, N. Y., 14,486....D 2 77
Gardiner, Me., 6,649..........D 7 64
Gardner, Mass., 19,581.......G 2 66
Gardnerville, Nev., 600.......B 4 73
Garfield, N. J., 27,500........E 2 75
Garfield, Utah, 2,079..........B 3 88
Garfield, Wash., 674...........H 3 91
Garfield Heights, Ohio, 21,662....H 9 80
Garibaldi, Oreg., 1,249.......D 2 82
Garland, Tex., 10,571..........H 1 87
Garland, Utah, 1,008...........B 2 88
Garner, Iowa, 1,696.............F 2 60
Garnett, Kans., 2,693..........G 3 61
Garretson, S. Dak., 745.......S 6 85
Garrett, Ind., 4,291.............G 2 59
Garrett Park, Md., 524........F 4 65
Garrettsville, Ohio, 1,504...H 3 80
Garrison, N. Dak., 1,890.....G 4 79
Garwood, N. J., 4,622.........E 2 75
Gary, Ind., 133,911..............C 1 59
Gary, S. Dak., 558...............S 4 85
Gary, W. Va., 1,600.............C 6 92
Gas City, Ind., 3,789...........F 4 59
Gassaway, W. Va., 1,306.....E 3 92
Gaston, Oreg., 368..............D 2 82
Gastonia, N. C., 23,069.......C 4 78
Gate City, Va., 2,126...........D 2 90
Gatesville, Tex., 3,856.........G 6 87
Gaylord, Mich., 2,271..........E 3 67
Gaylord, Minn., 1,229..........E 3 68
Geary, Okla., 1,614.............F 3 81
Gebo, Wyo., 200..................D 2 94
Geddes, S. Dak., 502...........M 7 85
Genesee, Idaho, 552............A 3 57
Geneseo, Ill., 4,325.............C 2 58
Geneseo, N. Y., 2,838..........E 3 77
Geneva, Ala., 3,579.............G 8 49
Geneva, Ill., 5,139...............E 2 58
Geneva, Ind., 999.................H 3 59
Geneva, Nebr., 2,031...........G 4 72
Geneseo, N. Y., 2,838..........E 3 77
Geneva, Ohio, 4,718.............J 2 80
Genoa, Nebr., 1,026.............G 3 72
Genoa, Ohio, 1,723..............D 2 80
George, Iowa, 1,210.............B 2 60
Georgetown, Del., 1,923.....N 6 65
Georgetown, Idaho, 404.....G 7 57
Georgetown, Ill., 3,294.......F 4 58
Georgetown, Ky., 5,516......J 4 62
Georgetown, Ohio, 2,200....C 8 80
Georgetown, S. C., 6,004..K 5 84
Georgetown, Tex., 4,951....G 7 87
Georgiana, Ala., 1,596........E 7 49
Georgiaville, R. I., 1,247....H 5 66
Geraldine, Mont., 374.........F 3 71
Gering, Nebr., 3,842...........A 3 72
Gerlach, Nev., 200...............B 2 73
Germantown, Ohio, 2,478...B 6 80
Germantown, Tenn., 408....B 4 86
Gervais, Oreg., 457.............A 3 82
Gettysburg, Pa., 7,046.......H 6 83
Gettysburg, S. Dak., 1,555....K 3 85
Giatto, W. Va., 550.............D 6 92
Gibbon, Nebr., 1,063..........F 4 72
Gibsland, La., 1,085...........D 1 63
Gibsonburg, Ohio, 2,281.....D 3 80
Gibson City, Ill., 3,029.......E 3 58
Gibsonville, N. C., 1,866....F 2 78
Giddings, Tex., 2,532..........H 7 87
Gideon, Mo., 1,754..............N10 70
Gig Harbor, Wash., 803.......C 3 91
Gila Bend, Ariz., 873...........C 6 50
Gilbert, Ariz., 1,114............D 5 50
Gilbert, Minn., 2,247...........F 3 68
Gilberton, Pa., 2,641...........K 4 83
Gilford, N. H., □1,251.........D 4 74
Gillespie, Ill., 4,105............D 4 58
Gillett, Ark., 774.................H 5 51
Gillett, Wis., 1,410..............K 6 93
Gillette, Wyo., 2,191............G 1 94
Gilmer, Tex., 4,096...............J 5 87
Gilroy, Calif., 4,951.............D 6 52
Girard, Kans., 2,426............H 4 61
Girard, Ohio, 10,113............J 3 80
Girardville, Pa., 3,864.........K 4 83
Glade Spring, Va., 827........E 2 90
Gladewater, Tex., 5,305.......K 5 87
Gladstone, Mich., 4,831.......C 3 67
Gladstone, Oreg., 2,434.......B 2 82
Gladwin, Mich., 1,878..........E 5 67
Glasgow, Ky., 7,025.............F 6 62
Glasgow, Mo., 1,440............G 4 70
Glasgow, Mont., 3,821.........K 2 71
Glasgow, Va., 810.................F 5 90
Glassboro, N. J., 5,867........C 4 75
Glassport, Pa., 8,707...........C 7 83
Glastonbury, Conn., □8,818....E 2 54
Gleason, Tenn., 1,063..........D 2 86
Glencoe, Ill., 6,980...............F 1 58
Glencoe, Minn., 2,801..........D 6 68
Glen Cove, N. Y., 15,130......D 2 77
Glendale, Ariz., 8,179..........C 5 50
Glendale, Calif., 95,702.......G 9 52
Glendale, Mo., 4,930............P 3 70
Glendale, Ohio, 2,402..........A 7 80
Glendale, Oreg., 871............D 5 82
Glendale, R. I., 243..............H 5 66
Glen Dale, W. Va., 1,467....K 6 92
Glendive, Mont., 5,254.......M 3 71
Glendo, Wyo., 215...............G 3 94
Glendora, Calif., 3,988.......D10 52
Glen Echo, Md., 356............F 5 65
Glen Ellyn, Ill., 9,524..........E 2 58
Glen Jean, W. Va., 1,600....D 5 92
Glen Lyon, Pa., 3,921..........K 3 83
Glenmora, La., 1,556...........E 5 63
Glenns Ferry, Idaho, 1,515....C 7 57
Glennville, Ga., 2,327..........J 7 56
Glen Olden, Pa., 6,450........M 7 83
Glen Ridge, N. J., 7,620......B 2 75
Glen Rock, N. J., 7,145........B 1 75
Glenrock, Wyo., 1,110.........G 3 94
Glens Falls, N. Y., 19,610..N 4 77
Glenside, Pa., 8,000............M 5 83
Glen Ullin, N. Dak., 1,324..G 6 79
Glenview, Ill., 6,142............B 1 58
Glenwood, Ark., 843............C 5 51
Glenwood, Iowa, 4,664........B 6 60
Glenwood, Minn., 2,666.......C 5 68
Glenwood Springs, Colo., 2,412....E 4 53
Globe, Ariz., 6,419..............E 5 50
Gloster, Miss., 1,467............C 8 69
Gloucester, Mass., 25,167..M 2 66
Gloucester City, N. J., 14,357....C 4 75
Glouster, Ohio, 2,327..........F 6 80
Glover, Vt., 228...................C 1 89
Gloversville, N. Y., 23,634....M 4 77
Goffstown, N. H., □5,638..C 5 74
Golconda, Nev., 350............D 2 73
Golden, Colo., 5,238.............J 3 53
Goldendale, Wash., 1,907...E 5 91
Golden Valley, Minn., 5,551....E 6 68
Goldfield, Nev., 275..............D 5 73
Gold Hill, Oreg., 619...........D 5 82
Goldsboro, N. C., 21,454....K 4 78
Gonic, N. H., 1,000.............E 5 74
Gonzales, La., 1,642............J 6 63
Gooding, Idaho, 3,099.........D 7 57
Goodland, Ind., 1,218..........C 3 59
Goodland, Kans., 4,690.......A 2 61
Goodrich, N. Dak., 448.......K 5 79
Goodsprings, Nev., 175........F 7 73
Good Water, Ala., 1,227.....G 4 49
Gordo, Ala., 952...................C 4 49
Gordon, Ga., 1,761...............F 5 56
Gordon, Nebr., 2,058...........B 2 72
Gordonsville, Va., 1,118......H 4 90
Gorham, Me., □4,742.........C 8 64
Gorham, N. H., □2,639.......D 3 74
Goshen, Ind., 13,003............F 1 59
Goshen, N. Y., 3,311............B 1 77
Goshen, Utah, 525...............C 4 88
Gothenburg, Nebr., 2,977....D 4 72
Gould, Ark., 1,076................H 6 51
Gouverneur, N. Y., 4,916...K 2 77
Gowanda, N. Y., 3,289........B 6 77
Gowrie, Iowa, 1,052.............E 4 60
Grace, Idaho, 761..................G 7 57
Graceville, Fla., 1,638..........D 5 55
Graceville, Minn., 962..........B 5 68
Grady, N. Mex., 130..............F 4 76
Grafton, Mass., □8,281.......H 4 66
Grafton, N. Dak., 4,901.......R 3 79
Grafton, W. Va., 7,365.........G 2 92
Grafton, Wis., 1,489.............L 9 93
Graham, N. C., 5,026...........G 2 78
Graham, Tex., 6,742.............F 4 87
Granby, Mo., 1,670...............D 9 70
Grand Canyon, Ariz., 1,001....C 2 50
Grand Coulee, Wash., 2,741....F 3 91
Granfield, Okla., 1,116.........E 6 81
Grand Forks, N. Dak., 26,836....S 4 79
Grand Haven, Mich., 9,536....C 5 67
Grand Island, Nebr., 22,682....F 4 72
Grand Isle, Me., □1,230....G 1 64
Grand Junction, Colo., 14,504....C 4 53
Grand Junction, Iowa, 1,036....E 4 60
Grand Junction, Tenn., 477....C 4 86
Grand Ledge, Mich., 4,506....E 6 67
Grand Marais, Minn., 1,078....H 3 68
Grand Prairie, Tex., 14,594....G 2 87
Grand Rapids, Mich., 176,515....D 5 67
Grand Rapids, Minn., 6,019....E 3 68
Grandview, Wash., 2,503....F 4 91
Grandview Heights, Ohio, 7,659....D 6 80
Grandville, Mich., 2,022.....D 6 67
Granger, Wash., 1,164..........E 4 91
Granger, Wyo., 122...............C 4 94
Grangeville, Idaho, 2,544....C 4 57
Granite City, Ill., 29,465.....C 5 58
Granite Falls, Minn., 2,511....C 6 68
Granite Falls, N. C., 2,286....C 3 78
Granite Falls, Wash., 635..D 2 91
Graniteville, Vt., 1,500.......C 2 89
Grant, Nebr., 1,091..............C 4 72
Grant City, Mo., 1,184.........D 1 70
Grants, N. Mex., 2,251........B 3 76
Grants Pass, Oreg., 8,116..D 5 82
Grantsville, Md., 461...........B 7 65
Grantsville, Utah, 1,537......B 3 88
Grantsville, W. Va., 959......D 3 92
Granville, N. Y., 2,826.........O 4 77
Granville, Ohio, 2,653..........E 5 80
Grass Creek, Wyo., 150........D 2 94
Grass Range, Mont., 234.....H 3 71
Grass Valley, Calif. 5,283....D 4 52
Gravette, Ark., 894...............B 1 51
Gray, Me., □1,631................C 8 64
Grayling, Mich., 2,066.........E 4 67
Grayson, Ky., 1,383.............M 4 62
Graysville, Tenn., 820..........L 4 86
Grayville, Ill., 2,461.............E 5 58
Great Barrington, Mass., □6,712....A 4 66
Great Bend, Kans., 12,655..D 3 61
Great Falls, Mont., 39,214..E 3 71
Great Falls, S. C., 3,533.......G 2 84
Great Neck, N. Y., 7,759.....D 2 77
Great Neck Estates, N. Y., 2,464....D 2 77
Great Neck Plaza, N. Y., 4,246....D 2 77
Greeley, Colo., 20,354.........K 2 53
Greeley, Nebr., 787...............F 3 72
Greeleyville, S. C., 600.........J 4 84
Green Bay, Wis., 52,735......L 6 93
Greenbelt, Md., 7,074...........G 5 65
Green Brier, Tenn., 890.......H 2 86
Greencastle, Ind., 6,888.......D 5 59
Green Cove Springs, Fla., 3,291....E 2 55
Greendale, Ind., 2,018..........H 6 59
Greendale, Wis., 2,752.........L10 93
Greene, Iowa, 1,347.............H 3 60
Greene, N. Y., 1,628.............J 6 77
Greene, R. I., 71...................G 6 66
Greeneville, Tenn., 8,721....Q 2 86
Greenfield, Iowa, 2,102........E 6 60
Greenfield, Ind., 6,159..........F 5 59
Greenfield, Mass., □17,349....D 2 66
Greenfield, Mo., 1,213..........E 8 70
Greenfield, Ohio, 4,862.........D 7 80
Greenfield, Tenn., 1,706.......D 2 86
Greenhills, Ohio, 3,005.........B 9 80
Green Island, N. Y.................N 5 77
Greenport, N. Y., 3,028.........F 1 77
Green River, Wyo., 3,187......C 4 94
Greensboro, Ala., 2,217........C 5 49
Greensboro, Ga., 2,688.........F 3 56
Greensboro, Md., 1,181.........L 5 65
Greensboro, N. C., 74,389..F 2 78
Greensburg, Ind., 6,599........G 6 59
Greensburg, Kans., 1,723.....C 4 61
Greensburg, Ky., 1,032.........F 6 62
Greensburg, Pa., 16,923.......D 5 83
Greentown, Ind., 1,160.........E 4 59
Greenup, Ill., 1,360...............E 4 58
Greenup, Ky., 1,276...............M 3 63
Greenville, Ala., 6,781..........E 7 49
Greenville, Del.......................M 1 65
Greenville, Fla., 1,163..........C 1 55
Greenville, Ill., 4,069...........D 5 58
Greenville, Ky., 2,661...........C 6 62
Greenville, Me., □1,889.......D 5 64
Greenville, Mich., 6,668.......D 5 67
Greenville, Miss., 29,936.....B 4 69
Greenville, N. H., □1,280....C 6 74
Greenville, N. C., 16,724......L 3 78
Greenville, Ohio, 8,859.........A 5 80
Greenville, Pa., 9,210............B 3 83
Greenville, R. I., 2,000..........H 5 66
Greenville, S. C., 58,161.......D 2 84
Greenville, Tex., 14,727........H 4 87
Greenwich, Conn., □40,835..A 4 54
Greenwich, N. Y., 2,212.........O 4 77
Greenwood, Ark., 1,634.........B 3 51
Greenwood, Del., 746............M 5 65
Greenwood, Ind., 3,066.........E 5 59
Greenwood, Miss., 18,061.....D 3 69
Greenwood, S. C., 13,806.....D 3 84
Greer, S. C., 5,050.................D 2 84
Gregory, S. Dak., 1,375........L 7 85
Grenada, Miss., 7,388...........E 3 69
Gresham, Oreg., 3,049..........E 2 82
Gretna, La., 13,813...............L 7 63
Gretna, Va., 803.....................F 7 90
Greybull, Wyo., 2,262............E 1 94
Gridley, Calif., 3,054.............D 4 52
Griffin, Ga., 13,982...............D 4 56
Griffith, Ind., 4,470...............C 1 59
Grinnell, Iowa, 6,828............H 5 60
Griswold, Iowa, 1,149............C 6 60
Groesbeck, Tex., 2,182..........H 6 87
Grosse Pointe, Mich., 6,283....B 7 67
Grosse Pointe Farms, Mich., 9,410....B 6 67
Grosse Pointe Park, Mich., 13,075....B 7 67
Grosse Pointe Woods, Mich., 10,381....B 6 67
Groton, Conn., 7,036.............G 3 54
Groton, N. Y., 2,150...............H 5 77
Groton, S. Dak., 1,084...........N 3 85
Groton, Vt., 435.....................C 2 89
Grottoes, Va., 908..................G 4 90
Grove City, Ohio, 2,339.........F 5 80
Grove City, Pa., 7,411...........B 3 83
Groveton, N. H., 1,918...........D 2 74
Grundy, Va., 1,947.................E 1 90
Grundy Center, Iowa, 2,135....H 4 60
Guernsey, Wyo., 721..............H 3 94
Gueydan, La., 2,041...............E 6 63
Guilford, Me., □1,842...........E 5 64
Guilford, N. Y., 557................K 6 77
Guin, Ala., 1,137....................C 3 49
Gulfport, Fla., 3,702..............D 4 55
Gulfport, Miss., 22,659.........F10 69
Gunnison, Colo., 2,770..........E 5 53
Gunnison, Utah, 1,144...........C 4 88
Guntersville, Ala., 5,253.......F 2 49
Gurdon, Ark., 2,390...............D 6 51
Guthrie, Ky., 1,253.................C 7 62
Guthrie, Okla., 10,113...........G 3 81
Guthrie Center, Iowa, 2,042....D 5 60

Index Ref. — *Plate No.*

Guttenberg, Iowa, 1,912 ..... L 3 60
Guttenberg, N. J., 5,566 ..... C 2 75
Guymon, Okla., 4,718 ..... D 8 81
Hackensack, N. J., 29,219 ..... F 2 75
Hackettstown, N. J., 3,894 ..... D 2 75
Haddonfield, N. J., 10,495 ..... D 4 75
Haddon Heights, N. J., 7,287 ..... C 4 75
Hagerman, Idaho, 520 ..... D 7 57
Hagerman, N. Mex., 1,024 ..... E 5 76
Hagerstown, Ind., 1,694 ..... G 5 59
Hagerstown, Md., 36,260 ..... C 2 65
Hailey, Idaho, 1,464 ..... D 6 57
Haileyville, Okla., 1,107 ..... L 5 81
Haines, Oreg., 321 ..... K 3 82
Haines City, Fla., 5,630 ..... E 3 55
Haledon, N. J., 6,204 ..... B 1 75
Haleyville, Ala., 3,331 ..... C 2 49
Halfway, Oreg., 312 ..... K 3 82
Halifax, Va., 791 ..... G 7 90
Hallandale, Fla., 3,886 ..... F 6 55
Hallock, Minn., 1,552 ..... A 2 68
Hallowell, Me., 3,404 ..... D 7 64
Halls, Tenn., 1,808 ..... C 3 86
Halstead, Kans., 1,328 ..... E 4 61
Hamburg, Ark., 2,655 ..... G 7 51
Hamburg, Iowa, 2,086 ..... B 7 60
Hamburg, N. Y., 6,938 ..... C 5 77
Hamburg, Pa., 3,805 ..... L 4 83
Hamden, Conn., □29,713 ..... D 3 54
Hamilton, Ala., 1,623 ..... C 2 49
Hamilton, Mo., 1,728 ..... E 3 70
Hamilton, Mont., 2,678 ..... C 4 71
Hamilton, N. Y., 3,507 ..... J 5 77
Hamilton, Ohio, 57,951 ..... A 7 80
Hamilton, Tex., 3,077 ..... G 6 87
Hamlet, N. C., 5,061 ..... F 5 78
Hamlin, Tex., 3,569 ..... E 5 87
Hamlin, W. Va., 841 ..... B 4 92
Hammond, Ind., 87,594 ..... B 1 59
Hammond, La., 8,010 ..... K 5 63
Hammond, Oreg., 522 ..... D 1 82
Hammonton, N. J., 8,411 ..... D 4 75
Hampden, Me., □3,608 ..... F 6 64
Hampstead, Md., 677 ..... G 2 65
Hampton, Iowa, 4,432 ..... G 3 60
Hampton, N. H., □2,847 ..... E 6 74
Hampton, S. C., 2,007 ..... F 6 84
Hampton, Va., 5,966 ..... M 6 90
Hamtramck, Mich., 43,355 ..... B 6 67
Hancock, Md., 963 ..... B 2 65
Hancock, Mich., 5,223 ..... G 1 67
Hancock, N. Y., 1,560 ..... K 7 77
Hanford, Calif., 10,028 ..... F 7 52
Hankinson, N. Dak., 1,409 ..... R 7 79
Hanna, Wyo., 1,326 ..... F 4 94
Hannibal, Mo., 20,444 ..... K 3 70
Hanover, N. H., □6,259 ..... B 4 74
Hanover, Pa., 14,048 ..... J 6 83
Hansen, Idaho, 463 ..... D 7 57
Hapeville, Ga., 8,560 ..... D 3 56
Harahan, La., 3,394 ..... N 4 63
Harbeson, Del., 142 ..... N 6 65
Harbor Beach, Mich., 2,349 ..... G 5 67
Harbor Springs, Mich., 1,626 ..... D 3 67
Hardeeville, S. C., 546 ..... G 7 84
Hardin, Mont., 2,306 ..... J 5 71
Hardinsburg, Ky., 902 ..... D 5 62
Hardwick, Vt., 1,696 ..... C 2 89
Harlan, Iowa, 3,915 ..... C 5 60
Harlan, Ky., 4,786 ..... L 7 62
Harlem, Mont., 1,107 ..... H 2 71
Harlingen, Tex., 23,229 ..... G11 87
Harlowton, Mont., 1,733 ..... G 4 71
Harmony, Minn., 1,022 ..... G 7 68
Harper, Kans., 1,672 ..... E 4 61
Harpswell Center, Me., 100 ..... D 8 64
Harriman, Tenn., 6,389 ..... M 3 86
Harrington, Del., 2,241 ..... M 5 65
Harrington, Wash., 620 ..... G 3 91
Harrisburg, Ark., 1,498 ..... J 2 51
Harrisburg, Ill., 10,999 ..... E 6 58
Harrisburg, Oreg., 862 ..... D 3 82
HARRISBURG, Pa., 89,544 ..... J 5 83
Harrison, Ark., 5,542 ..... D 1 51
Harrison, N. J., 13,490 ..... B 2 75
Harrison, N. Y. ..... J 1 77
Harrison, Ohio, 1,943 ..... A 7 80
Harrisonburg, Va., 10,810 ..... G 4 90
Harrisonville, Mo., 2,530 ..... D 5 70
Harrisville, R. I., 1,055 ..... H 5 66
Harrisville, W. Va., 1,387 ..... D 2 92
Harrodsburg, Ky., 5,262 ..... H 5 62
Hart, Mich., 2,172 ..... C 5 67
Hartford, Ala., 1,655 ..... G 8 49
Hartford, Ark., 865 ..... B 3 51
HARTFORD, Conn., 177,397 ..... E 1 54
Hartford, Ill., 1,909 ..... B 6 58
Hartford, Ky., 1,564 ..... D 6 62
Hartford, Mich., 1,838 ..... C 6 67
Hartford, S. Dak., 592 ..... P 6 85
Hartford, Vt., □5,827 ..... C 3 89
Hartford, Wis., 4,549 ..... K 9 93
Hartford City, Ind., 7,253 ..... G 4 59
Hartington, Nebr., 1,660 ..... G 2 72
Hartland, Me., □1,310 ..... E 6 64
Hartland, Vt., □1,559 ..... C 3 89
Hartley, Iowa, 1,611 ..... C 2 60
Hartly, Del., 139 ..... M 4 65
Hartselle, Ala., 3,429 ..... E 2 49
Hartshorne, Okla., 2,330 ..... M 5 81
Hartsville, S. C., 5,658 ..... H 3 84
Hartsville, Tenn., 1,130 ..... J 2 86
Hartville, Wyo., 229 ..... H 3 94
Hartwell, Ga., 2,964 ..... G 2 56
Harvard, Ill., 3,464 ..... E 1 58
Harvey, Ill., 20,683 ..... B 2 58
Harvey, N. Dak., 2,337 ..... K 4 79
Hasbrouck Heights, N. J., 9,181 ..... B 2 75
Haskell, Okla., 1,676 ..... L 3 81
Haskell, Tex., 3,836 ..... E 4 87
Hastings, Fla., 577 ..... E 2 55
Hastings, Mich., 6,096 ..... D 6 67
Hastings, Minn., 6,560 ..... F 6 68
Hastings, Nebr., 20,211 ..... F 4 72
Hastings on Hudson, N. Y., 7,565 ..... D 2 77
Hatboro, Pa., 4,788 ..... M 5 83
Hatch, N. Mex., 1,064 ..... B 6 76
Hattiesburg, Miss., 29,474 ..... F 8 69
Hatton, N. Dak., 991 ..... P 4 79
Havana, Fla., 1,634 ..... B 1 55
Havana, Ill., 4,379 ..... D 3 58
Haverford, Pa., □39,641 ..... M 6 83
Haverhill, Mass., 47,280 ..... K 1 66
Haverhill, N. H., □3,357 ..... B 3 74
Haverstraw, N. Y., 5,818 ..... C 1 77
Havre, Mont., 8,086 ..... G 2 71
Havre de Grace, Md., 7,809 ..... K 2 65
Hawarden, Iowa, 2,625 ..... A 3 60
Hawesville, Ky., 925 ..... D 5 62
Hawkinsville, Ga., 3,342 ..... E 6 56
Hawley, Minn., 1,196 ..... B 4 68
Hawthorne, Calif., 16,316 ..... C11 52
Hawthorne, Nev., 1,861 ..... C 4 73
Hawthorne, N. J., 14,816 ..... E 2 75
Hayden, Ariz., 1,494 ..... E 5 50
Hayden, Colo., 767 ..... E 2 53
Haynesville, La., 3,040 ..... D 1 63
Hays, Kans., 8,625 ..... C 3 61
Haysi, Va., 476 ..... D 1 90
Hay Springs, Nebr., 1,091 ..... B 2 72
Hayti, Mo., 3,302 ..... N10 70
Hayward, Calif., 14,272 ..... K 2 52
Hayward, Wis., 1,577 ..... D 4 93
Hazard, Ky., 6,985 ..... L 6 62
Hazel Park, Mich., 17,770 ..... B 6 67
Hazelton, Idaho, 429 ..... D 7 57
Hazelton, N. Dak., 453 ..... K 7 79
Hazelwood, N. C., 1,769 ..... D 8 78
Hazen, Ark., 1,270 ..... G 4 51
Hazen, Nev., 70 ..... C 3 73
Hazen, N. Dak., 1,230 ..... G 5 79
Hazlehurst, Ga., 2,687 ..... G 7 56
Hazlehurst, Miss., 3,397 ..... D 7 69
Hazleton, Pa., 35,491 ..... L 4 83
Headland, Ala., 2,091 ..... H 8 49
Healdsburg, Calif., 3,258 ..... B 5 52
Healdton, Okla., 2,578 ..... H 6 81
Hearne, Tex., 4,872 ..... H 7 87
Heath Springs, S. C., 694 ..... G 2 84
Heavener, Okla., 2,103 ..... N 5 81
Heber, Utah, 2,936 ..... C 3 88
Heber Springs, Ark., 2,109 ..... F 3 51
Hebron, Ind., 1,010 ..... C 2 59
Hebron, Md., 723 ..... M 7 65
Hebron, Nebr., 2,000 ..... G 4 72
Hebron, N. Dak., 1,412 ..... F 6 79
Hecla, S. Dak., 500 ..... N 2 85
Hector, Minn., 1,196 ..... D 6 68
Heflin, Ala., 1,982 ..... G 3 49
Helena, Ark., 11,236 ..... K 4 51
HELENA, Mont., 17,581 ..... E 4 71
Hellertown, Pa., 5,435 ..... M 4 83
Helper, Utah, 2,850 ..... D 4 88
Hemet, Calif., 3,386 ..... J10 52
Hempstead, N. Y., 29,135 ..... D 3 77
Hempstead, Tex., 1,395 ..... J 7 87
Henderson, Ky., 16,837 ..... C 5 62
Henderson, Nev., 3,643 ..... G 6 73
Henderson, N. C., 10,996 ..... J 2 78
Henderson, Tenn., 2,532 ..... D 4 86
Henderson, Tex., 6,833 ..... K 5 87
Hendersonville, N. C., 6,103 ..... F 8 78
Hennessey, Okla., 1,264 ..... G 2 81
Henniker, N. H., □1,675 ..... C 5 74
Henning, Minn., 1,004 ..... C 4 68
Henning, Tenn., 493 ..... B 3 86
Henrietta, Tex., 2,813 ..... F 4 87
Henry, Ill., 1,966 ..... D 2 58
Henryetta, Okla., 7,987 ..... K 4 81
Heppner, Oreg., 1,648 ..... H 2 82
Herculaneum, Mo., 1,603 ..... M 6 70
Hereford, Tex., 5,207 ..... B 3 87
Herington, Kans., 3,775 ..... E 3 61
Herkimer, N. Y., 9,400 ..... L 4 77
Hermann, Mo., 2,523 ..... K 5 70
Hermiston, Oreg., 3,804 ..... H 2 82
Hermosa Beach, Calif., 11,826 ..... B11 52
Hernando, Miss., 1,206 ..... E 1 69
Herndon, Va., 1,461 ..... K 3 90
Herreid, S. Dak., 633 ..... K 2 85
Herrin, Ill., 9,331 ..... E 6 58
Hertford, N. C., 2,096 ..... N 2 78
Hettinger, N. Dak., 1,762 ..... E 8 79
Heyburn, Idaho, 539 ..... E 7 57
Hialeah, Fla., 19,676 ..... F 6 55
Hiawatha, Kans., 3,294 ..... G 2 61
Hiawatha, Utah, 1,421 ..... C 4 88
Hibbing, Minn., 16,276 ..... F 3 68
Hickman, Ky., 2,037 ..... B 4 62
Hickory, Miss., 614 ..... G 6 69
Hickory, N. C., 14,755 ..... C 3 78
Hicksville, N. Y., 13,000 ..... D 2 77
Hicksville, Ohio, 2,629 ..... A 3 80
Higginsville, Mo., 3,428 ..... E 4 70
Highland, Ill., 4,283 ..... D 5 58
Highland, Ind., 5,878 ..... C 1 59
Highland, N. Y., 3,035 ..... M 7 77
Highland Falls, N. Y., 3,930 ..... C 1 77
Highland Heights, Ky., 1,569 ..... J 3 62
Highland Park, Ill., 16,808 ..... F 1 58
Highland Park, Mich., 46,393 ..... B 6 67
Highland Park, N. J., 9,721 ..... E 2 75
Highland Park, Tex., 11,405 ..... G 2 87
Highmore, S. Dak., 1,158 ..... L 4 85
High Point, N. C., 39,973 ..... E 3 78
High Ridge, Conn. ..... A 4 54
High Springs, Fla., 2,088 ..... D 2 55
Hightstown, N. J., 3,712 ..... D 3 75
Highwood, Ill., 3,813 ..... F 1 58
Hillburn, N. Y., 1,212 ..... C 2 77
Hill City, Kans., 1,432 ..... C 2 61
Hilliard, Fla., 607 ..... E 1 55
Hillsboro, Ill., 4,141 ..... D 4 58
Hillsboro, Kans., 2,150 ..... E 3 61
Hillsboro, N. H., □2,179 ..... C 5 74
Hillsboro, N. C., 1,329 ..... H 2 78
Hillsboro, N. Dak., 1,331 ..... S 5 79
Hillsboro, Ohio, 5,126 ..... C 7 80
Hillsboro, Oreg., 5,142 ..... E 2 82
Hillsboro, Tex., 8,363 ..... G 5 87
Hillsboro, Wis., 1,341 ..... F 8 93
Hillsdale, Mich., 7,297 ..... E 7 67
Hillsdale, N. J., 4,127 ..... E 2 75
Hillsgrove, R. I. ..... J 6 66
Hillside, N. J., 21,007 ..... B 2 75
Hillsville, Va., 764 ..... C 7 90
Hilo, Hawaii Territory, 27,019 ..... J 5 95
Hinckley, Utah, 589 ..... B 4 88
Hines, Oreg., 918 ..... H 4 82
Hingham, Mass., □10,665 ..... L 4 66
Hingham, Mont., 214 ..... F 2 71
Hinsdale, Ill., 8,676 ..... A 2 58
Hinsdale, N. H., □1,950 ..... B 6 74
Hinton, W. Va., 5,780 ..... E 5 92
Hobart, Ind., 10,244 ..... C 1 59
Hobart, Okla., 5,380 ..... E 5 81
Hobbs, N. Mex., 13,875 ..... F 6 70
Hoboken, N. J., 50,676 ..... C 2 75
Hockessin, Del., 1,200 ..... M 1 65
Hodge, La., 1,386 ..... E 2 63
Hodgenville, Ky., 1,695 ..... F 5 62
Hogansville, Ga., 3,769 ..... B 4 56
Hohenwald, Tenn., 1,703 ..... F 3 86
Hoisington, Kans., 4,012 ..... D 3 61
Holbrook, Ariz., 2,336 ..... E 4 50
Holden, Mass., □5,975 ..... G 3 66
Holden, Mo., 1,765 ..... E 5 70
Holden, W. Va., 2,000 ..... B 5 92
Holdenville, Okla., 6,192 ..... K 4 81
Holdrege, Nebr., 4,381 ..... E 4 72
Holladay, Utah, 3,100 ..... C 3 88
Holland, Mich., 15,858 ..... C 6 67
Hollandale, Miss., 2,346 ..... C 4 69
Holley, N. Y., 1,551 ..... D 4 77
Hollidaysburg, Pa., 6,483 ..... F 5 83
Hollidays Cove, W. Va. ..... K 5 92
Hollis, N. H., □1,196 ..... C 6 74
Hollis, Okla., 3,089 ..... C 5 81
Hollister, Calif., 4,903 ..... D 7 52
Holliston, Mass., □3,753 ..... J 4 66
Hollow Rock, Tenn., 397 ..... E 2 86
Holly, Colo., 1,236 ..... P 6 53
Holly, Mich., 2,663 ..... F 6 67
Holly Hill, Fla., 3,232 ..... E 2 55
Holly Hill, S. C., 1,116 ..... H 5 84
Hollyoak, Del., 1,450 ..... N 1 65
Holly Springs, Miss., 3,276 ..... E 1 69
Hollywood, Calif., 179,749 ..... C10 52
Hollywood, Fla., 14,351 ..... F 5 55
Holstein, Iowa, 1,336 ..... B 3 60
Holt, Ala., 2,400 ..... C 4 49
Holton, Kans., 2,705 ..... G 2 61
Holtville, Calif., 2,472 ..... K11 52
Holyoke, Colo., 1,558 ..... P 1 53
Holyoke, Mass., 54,661 ..... D 4 66
Homedale, Idaho, 1,411 ..... B 6 57
Homer, La., 4,749 ..... E 1 63
Homer, N. Y., 3,244 ..... H 5 77
Homerville, Ga., 1,787 ..... G 8 56
Homestead, Fla., 4,573 ..... F 6 55
Homestead, Pa., 10,046 ..... B 7 83
Homewood, Ala., 12,866 ..... E 4 49
Homewood, Ill., 5,887 ..... B 3 58
Hominy, Okla., 2,702 ..... K 2 81
Honaker, Va., 847 ..... E 1 90
Honea Path, S. C., 2,840 ..... D 3 84
Honeoye Falls, N. Y., 1,460 ..... F 5 77
Honesdale, Pa., 5,662 ..... M 2 83
Honey Grove, Tex., 2,340 ..... J 4 87
HONOLULU, Hawaii Territory, 245,612 ..... C 4 95
Hood River, Oreg., 3,701 ..... F 2 82
Hooker, Okla., 1,842 ..... E 7 81
Hooksett, N. H., □2,792 ..... C 5 74
Hooper, Nebr., 859 ..... H 3 72
Hoopeston, Ill., 5,992 ..... F 3 58
Hoosick Falls, N. Y., 4,297 ..... O 5 77
Hope, Ark., 8,605 ..... C 6 51
Hope, Ind., 1,215 ..... F 6 59
Hope, N. Mex., 186 ..... E 6 76
Hope, R. I., 800 ..... H 6 66
Hopedale, Mass., □3,479 ..... H 4 66
Hope Valley, R. I., 1,000 ..... G 6 66
Hopewell, Va., 10,219 ..... K 6 90
Hopkins, Minn., 7,595 ..... E 6 68
Hopkinsville, Ky., 12,526 ..... C 7 62
Hopkinton, N. H., □1,831 ..... C 5 74
Hopkinton, R. I., □3,676 ..... G 7 66
Hoquiam, Wash., 11,123 ..... B 4 91
Horatio, Ark., 776 ..... B 6 51
Horicon, Wis., 2,664 ..... J 9 93
Hornbeak, Tenn., 309 ..... C 2 86
Hornell, N. Y., 15,049 ..... E 6 77
Hornersville, Mo., 875 ..... M10 70
Horse Cave, Ky., 1,545 ..... F 6 62
Horseheads, N. Y., 3,606 ..... G 6 77
Horton, Kans., 2,354 ..... G 2 61
Hosmer, S. Dak., 533 ..... K 2 85
Hotchkiss, Colo., 715 ..... D 5 53
Hotevilla, Ariz., 572 ..... E 3 50
Hot Springs, Mont., 733 ..... B 3 71
Hot Springs, S. Dak., 5,030 ..... B 7 85
Hot Springs National Park, Ark., 29,307 ..... D 4 51
Houghton, Mich., 3,829 ..... A 1 67
Houlka, Miss., 545 ..... G 2 69
Houlton, Me., □8,377 ..... H 3 64
Houma, La., 11,505 ..... J 7 63
Houston, Del., 332 ..... N 5 65
Houston, Minn., 973 ..... G 7 68
Houston, Miss., 1,664 ..... F 3 69
Houston, Tex., 596,163 ..... J 2 87
Howard, S. Dak., 1,251 ..... P 5 85
Howell, Mich., 4,353 ..... F 6 67
Howells, Nebr., 784 ..... H 3 72
Hoxie, Ark., 1,855 ..... H 1 51
Hubbard, Ohio, 4,560 ..... J 3 80
Hubbard, Oreg., 493 ..... E 2 82
Hubbard, Tex., 1,768 ..... H 6 87
Hubbard Woods, Ill. ..... B 1 58
Hudson, Mass., □8,211 ..... H 3 66
Hudson, Mich., 2,773 ..... E 7 67
Hudson, N. H., □4,183 ..... D 6 74
Hudson, N. Y., 11,629 ..... N 6 77
Hudson, Ohio, 1,538 ..... H 3 80
Hudson, Wis., 3,435 ..... A 6 93
Hudson, Wyo., 293 ..... D 3 94
Hudson Falls, N. Y., 7,236 ..... O 4 77
Hughes, Ark., 1,686 ..... J 4 51
Hugo, Colo., 943 ..... N 4 53
Hugo, Okla., 5,984 ..... M 6 81
Hugoton, Kans., 2,781 ..... A 4 61
Hull, Iowa, 1,127 ..... A 2 60
Humboldt, Ariz., 350 ..... C 4 50
Humboldt, Iowa, 3,219 ..... E 3 60
Humboldt, Kans., 2,308 ..... G 4 61
Humboldt, Nebr., 1,404 ..... J 4 72
Humboldt, Tenn., 7,426 ..... D 3 86
Hummelstown, Pa., 3,789 ..... J 5 83
Humphrey, Nebr., 761 ..... G 3 72
Huntingburg, Ind., 4,056 ..... D 8 59
Huntingdon, Pa., 7,330 ..... G 5 83
Huntingdon, Tenn., 2,043 ..... E 2 86
Huntington, Ark., 744 ..... B 3 51
Huntington, Ind., 15,079 ..... G 3 59
Huntington, N. Y., 9,324 ..... E 2 77
Huntington, Oreg., 733 ..... K 3 82
Huntington, Utah, 1,029 ..... C 4 88
Huntington, W. Va., 86,353 ..... A 3 92
Huntington Beach, Calif., 5,237 ..... D11 52
Huntington Park, Calif., 29,450 ..... C11 52
Huntington Station, N. Y., 9,324 ..... E 2 77
Huntington Woods, Mich., 4,949 ..... F 6 67
Huntsville, Ala., 16,437 ..... E 1 49
Huntsville, Ark., 1,010 ..... C 1 51
Huntsville, Mo., 1,520 ..... H 3 70
Huntsville, Tex., 9,820 ..... J 7 87
Hurley, N. Mex., 2,079 ..... A 6 76
Hurley, S. Dak., 474 ..... P 7 85
Hurley, Wis., 3,034 ..... F 3 93
Hurlock, Md., 944 ..... L 6 65
Huron, Ohio, 2,515 ..... E 3 80
Huron, S. Dak., 12,788 ..... N 5 85
Hurricane, Utah, 1,271 ..... A 6 88
Hurricane, W. Va., 1,463 ..... B 4 92
Hurtsboro, Ala., 920 ..... H 6 49
Hutchinson, Kans, 33,575 ..... D 3 61
Hutchinson, Minn., 4,690 ..... D 6 68
Huttig, Ark., 1,038 ..... F 7 51
Hyannis, Mass., 4,235 ..... N 6 66
Hyattsville, Md., 12,308 ..... G 5 65
Hyde Park, N. Y., 1,059 ..... N 7 77
Hyde Park, Utah, 644 ..... C 2 88
Hyde Park, Vt., 440 ..... B 1 89
Hymera, Ind., 1,069 ..... C 6 59
Hyrum, Utah, 1,704 ..... C 2 88
Hysham, Mont., 410 ..... J 4 71
Iaeger, W. Va., 1,271 ..... C 6 92
Idabel, Okla., 4,671 ..... N 7 81
Ida Grove, Iowa, 2,202 ..... B 4 60
Idaho Falls, Idaho, 19,218 ..... F 6 57
Idaho Springs, Colo., 1,769 ..... H 3 53
Ignacio, Colo., 526 ..... D 8 53
Ilion, N. Y., 9,363 ..... K 5 77
Illmo, Mo., 1,247 ..... O 8 70
Ilwaco, Wash., 628 ..... A 4 91
Imlay, Nev., 250 ..... C 2 73
Imlay City, Mich., 1,654 ..... F 5 67
Imperial, Calif., 1,759 ..... K11 52
Imperial, Nebr., 1,563 ..... C 4 72
Independence, Iowa, 4,865 ..... K 4 60
Independence, Kans., 11,335 ..... G 4 61
Independence, La., 1,606 ..... K 5 63
Independence, Mo., 36,963 ..... D 4 70
Independence, Ohio, 3,105 ..... G 3 80
Independence, Oreg., 1,987 ..... D 3 82
Independence, Va., 486 ..... C 4 90
Independence, Wis., 1,088 ..... D 7 93
Indiana, Pa., 11,743 ..... D 4 83
INDIANAPOLIS, Ind., 427,173 ..... E 5 59
Indian Head, Md., 491 ..... F 6 65
Indianola, Iowa, 5,145 ..... F 6 60
Indianola, Miss., 4,369 ..... C 4 69
Indianola, Nebr., 738 ..... D 4 72
Indian Orchard, Mass., 10,000 ..... E 4 66
Indio, Calif., 5,300 ..... J 9 52
Inglewood, Calif., 46,185 ..... B11 52
Ingram, Pa., 4,236 ..... B 7 83
Inkster, Mich., 16,728 ..... B 7 67
Inman, S. C., 1,514 ..... D 1 84
Inspiration, Ariz., 500 ..... E 5 50
International Falls, Minn., 6,269 ..... E 2 68
Inverness, Fla., 1,471 ..... D 3 55
Inverness, Miss., 1,010 ..... C 4 69
Inwood, N. Y., 9,200 ..... D 2 77
Iola, Kans., 7,094 ..... G 4 61
Iona, Idaho, 502 ..... G 6 57
Ione, Wash., 714 ..... H 2 91
Ionia, Mich., 6,412 ..... D 6 67
Iota, La., 1,162 ..... E 6 63
Iowa City, Iowa, 27,212 ..... K 5 60
Iowa Falls, Iowa, 4,900 ..... G 3 60
Iowa Park, Tex., 2,110 ..... F 4 87
Ipswich, Mass., □6,895 ..... L 2 66
Ipswich, S. Dak., 1,058 ..... L 3 85
Irondale, Ala., 1,860 ..... E 3 49
Irondequoit, N. Y., □34,417 ..... E 4 77
Iron Gate, Va., 725 ..... E 5 90
Iron Mountain, Mich., 9,679 ..... B 3 67
Iron River, Mich., 4,048 ..... G 2 67
Ironton, Mo., 1,148 ..... L 7 70
Ironton, Ohio, 16,333 ..... E 8 80
Ironwood, Mich., 11,466 ..... E 2 67
Irvine, Ky., 3,259 ..... K 5 62
Irvington, Ky., 831 ..... E 5 62
Irvington, N. J., 59,201 ..... B 2 75
Irvington, N. Y., 3,657 ..... D 2 77
Irwin, Pa., 4,228 ..... C 5 83
Ishpeming, Mich., 8,962 ..... B 2 67
Island Falls, Me., □1,237 ..... G 3 64
Island Park, N. Y., 2,031 ..... D 2 77
Island Pond, Vt., 1,252 ..... D 1 89
Isleta, N. Mex., 1,400 ..... C 4 76
Isleton, Calif., 1,597 ..... D 5 52
Islip, N. Y., 5,254 ..... E 2 77
Issaquah, Wash., 955 ..... D 3 91
Itasca, Tex., 1,718 ..... G 5 87

Index Ref. Plate No.
Ithaca, Mich., 2,377.....E 5 67
Ithaca, N. Y., 29,257.....G 6 77
Itta Bena, Miss., 1,725.....D 4 69
Iuka, Miss., 1,527.....H 1 69
Iva, S. C., 1,164.....C 3 84
Jacksboro, Tex., 2,951.....F 4 87
Jackson, Ala., 3,072.....C 7 49
Jackson, Calif., 1,879.....E 5 52
Jackson, Ga., 2,053.....E 4 56
Jackson, Ky., 1,978.....L 5 62
Jackson, La., 6,772.....H 5 63
Jackson, Mich., 51,088.....E 6 67
Jackson, Minn., 3,313.....C 7 68
JACKSON, Miss., 98,271.....D 6 69
Jackson, Mo., 3,707.....N 8 70
Jackson, Ohio, 6,504.....E 7 80
Jackson, Tenn., 30,207.....D 3 86
Jackson, Wyo., 1,244.....B 2 94
Jacksonville, Ala., 4,751.....G 3 49
Jacksonville, Fla., 204,517.....E 1 55
Jacksonville, Ill., 20,387.....C 4 58
Jacksonville, Oreg., 1,193.....D 5 82
Jacksonville, Tex., 8,607.....J 5 87
Jacksonville, Vt., 220.....B 5 89
Jacksonville Beach, Fla., 6,430.....E 1 55
Jaffrey, N. H., □2,911.....B 6 74
Jal, N. Mex., 2,047.....F 6 76
Jamestown, N. Y., 43,354.....B 6 77
Jamestown, N. Dak., 10,697.....N 6 79
Jamestown, R. I., □2,068.....J 7 66
Jamestown, Tenn., 2,115.....M 2 86
Janesville, Minn., 1,287.....E 6 68
Janesville, Wis., 24,899.....J10 93
Jarbidge, Nev., 46.....F 1 73
Jarratt, Va., 574.....K 7 90
Jasonville, Ind., 2,937.....C 6 59
Jasper, Ala., 8,589.....D 3 49
Jasper, Fla., 2,327.....D 1 55
Jasper, Ind., 5,215.....D 8 59
Jasper, Tex., 4,403.....L 7 87
Jay, Me., □3,102.....C 6 64
Jeanerette, La., 4,692.....G 7 63
Jeannette, Pa., 16,172.....C 5 83
Jefferson, Ga., 2,040.....F 2 56
Jefferson, Iowa, 4,326.....E 4 60
Jefferson, Ohio, 1,844.....J 2 80
Jefferson, Oreg., 636.....D 3 82
Jefferson, Tex., 3,164.....K 5 87
Jefferson, Wis., 3,625.....J10 93
JEFFERSON CITY, Mo., 25,099.....H 5 70
Jefferson City, Tenn., 3,633.....P 2 86
Jeffersontown, Ky., 1,246.....F 4 62
Jeffersonville, Ind., 14,685.....F 8 59
Jeffersonville, Vt., 387.....B 1 89
Jellico, Tenn., 1,556.....N 1 86
Jemez Pueblo, N. Mex., 878.....C 3 76
Jena, La., 1,438.....F 3 63
Jenkins, Ky., 6,921.....M 6 62
Jenkintown, Pa., 5,130.....M 5 83
Jennings, La., 9,663.....E 6 63
Jennings, Mo., 15,282.....P 2 70
Jericho, Vt., □1,135.....B 2 89
Jermyn, Pa., 2,535.....L 2 83
Jerome, Ariz., 1,233.....C 4 50
Jerome, Idaho, 4,523.....D 7 57
Jersey City, N. J., 299,017.....F 2 75
Jersey Shore, Pa., 5,595.....H 3 83
Jerseyville, Ill., 5,792.....C 4 58
Jessup, Pa., 6,650.....L 3 83
Jesup, Ga., 4,605.....J 7 56
Jewell, Iowa, 1,158.....F 4 60
Jewett City, Conn., 3,702.....H 2 54
John Day, Oreg., 1,597.....J 3 82
Johnson, Vt., 900.....B 1 89
Johnsonburg, Pa., 4,567.....E 3 83
Johnson City, N. Y., 19,249.....J 6 77
Johnson City, Tenn., 27,864.....R 2 86
Johnston, S. C., 1,400.....E 4 84
Johnston City, Ill., 4,479.....E 6 58
Johnstown, Colo., 897.....K 2 53
Johnstown, N. Y., 10,923.....M 4 77
Johnstown, Pa., 63,232.....D 5 83
Joliet, Ill., 51,601.....E 2 58
Joliet, Mont., 410.....G 5 71
Jonesboro, Ark., 16,310.....J 2 51
Jonesboro, Ga., 1,741.....D 3 56
Jonesboro, Ind., 1,973.....F 4 59
Jonesboro, La., 3,097.....E 2 63
Jonesboro, Tenn., 1,126.....R 2 86
Jonesport, Me., □1,727.....H 6 64
Jonestown, Miss., 741.....D 2 69
Jonesville, La., 1,954.....G 3 63
Jonesville, Mich., 1,594.....E 6 67
Jonesville, N. C., 1,768.....D 2 78
Jonesville, S. C., 1,345.....E 2 84
Jonesville, Va., 597.....B 2 90
Joplin, Mo., 38,711.....C 8 70
Jordan, Minn., 1,494.....E 6 68
Jordan, N. Y., 1,295.....H 4 77

Index Ref. Plate No.
Joseph, Oreg., 666.....K 2 82
Joseph City, Ariz., 500.....E 4 50
Judith Gap, Mont., 175.....F 4 71
Judsonia, Ark., 1,122.....G 3 51
Julesburg, Colo., 1,951.....P 1 53
Juliaetta, Idaho, 365.....B 3 57
Junction, Tex., 2,471.....E 7 87
Junction City, Ark., 1,013.....E 7 51
Junction City, Kans., 13,462.....F 2 61
Junction City, Oreg., 1,475.....D 3 82
JUNEAU, Alaska Territory, 5,818.....N 3 95
Juneau, Wis., 1,444.....J 9 93
Kahoka, Mo., 1,847.....J 2 70
Kalama, Wash., 1,121.....C 4 91
Kalamazoo, Mich., 57,704.....D 6 67
Kalispell, Mont., 9,737.....B 2 71
Kamas, Utah, 721.....C 3 88
Kamiah, Idaho, 812.....C 3 57
Kanab, Utah, 1,287.....B 6 88
Kane, Pa., 5,706.....E 2 83
Kankakee, Ill., 25,856.....F 2 58
Kannapolis, N. C., 28,448.....E 4 78
Kanosh, Utah, 476.....B 5 88
Kansas City, Kans., 129,553.....H 2 61
Kansas City, Mo., 456,622.....C 5 70
Kapaa, Hawaii Territory, 2,828.....D 1 95
Kaplan, La., 4,562.....F 6 63
Kasson, Minn., 1,353.....F 6 68
Kaufman, Tex., 2,714.....H 5 87
Kaukauna, Wis., 8,337.....K 7 93
Kaycee, Wyo., 211.....F 2 94
Kayenta, Ariz., 100.....E 2 50
Kaysville, Utah, 1,898.....B 2 88
Keaau, Hawaii Territory, 2,509.....J 5 95
Keams Canyon, Ariz., 500.....E 3 50
Kearney, Nebr., 12,115.....E 4 72
Kearny, N. J., 39,952.....B 2 75
Keedysville, Md., 417.....D 3 65
Keene, N. H., 15,638.....B 6 74
Keeseville, N. Y., 1,977.....O 2 77
Keewatin, Minn., 1,807.....E 3 68
Kekaha, Hawaii Territory, 2,536.....B 2 95
Kellogg, Idaho, 4,913.....B 2 57
Kelso, Wash., 7,345.....C 4 91
Kemmerer, Wyo., 1,667.....B 4 94
Kenbridge, Va., 1,176.....H 7 90
Kendallville, Ind., 6,119.....G 2 59
Kendrick, Idaho, 409.....B 3 57
Kenedy, Tex., 4,234.....G 9 87
Kenilworth, Ill., 2,789.....B 1 58
Kenmare, N. Dak., 1,712.....G 2 79
Kenmore, N. Y., 20,066.....C 5 77
Kennebunk, Me., □4,273.....B 9 64
Kennebunk Port, Me., □1,522.....C 9 64
Kennedyville, Md., 180.....L 3 65
Kenner, La., 5,535.....K 6 63
Kennett, Mo., 8,685.....M10 70
Kennett Square, Pa., 3,699.....L 6 83
Kennewick, Wash., 10,106.....F 4 91
Kenosha, Wis., 54,368.....L10 93
Kenova, W. Va., 4,320.....A 4 92
Kensett, Ark., 829.....G 3 51
Kent, Ohio, 12,418.....H 3 80
Kent, Wash., 3,278.....C 3 91
Kentland, Ind., 1,633.....C 3 59
Kenton, Del., 211.....M 4 65
Kenton, Ohio, 8,479.....C 4 80
Kenton, Tenn., 899.....C 2 86
Kentwood, La., 2,417.....J 5 63
Kenyon, Minn., 1,651.....E 6 68
Keokuk, Iowa, 16,144.....L 7 60
Keota, Iowa, 1,145.....K 6 60
Kermit, Tex., 6,912.....B 6 87
Kermit, W. Va., 964.....B 5 92
Kernersville, N. C., 2,396.....E 2 78
Kerrville, Tex., 7,691.....E 7 87
Kershaw, S. C., 1,376.....G 2 84
Ketchikan, Alaska Territory, 5,202.....O 4 95
Kettle Falls, Wash., 714.....G 2 91
Kevin, Mont., 351.....E 2 71
Kewanee, Ill., 16,821.....C 2 58
Kewaunee, Wis., 2,583.....M 7 93
Keyport, N. J., 5,888.....E 3 75
Keyser, W. Va., 6,347.....J 2 92
Keystone, W. Va., 2,594.....D 6 92
Keysville, Va., 690.....H 6 90
Key West, Fla., 26,433.....E 7 55
Kiel, Wis., 2,129.....K 8 93
Kilgore, Tex., 9,638.....K 5 87
Kildeer, N. Dak., 698.....E 5 79
Killingly (Dayville), Conn., 1,105.....H 1 54
Kilmarnock, Va., 689.....M 5 90
Kimball, Nebr., 2,048.....A 3 72
Kimball, S. Dak., 952.....M 6 85
Kimball, W. Va., 1,359.....D 6 92
Kimberly, Idaho, 1,347.....D 7 57
Kimberly, Nev., 300.....F 3 73

Index Ref. Plate No.
Kimberly, Wis., 3,179.....K 7 93
Kinder, La., 2,003.....E 6 63
King City, Calif., 2,347.....D 7 52
King City, Mo., 1,031.....C 2 70
Kingfisher, Okla., 3,345.....G 3 81
Kingman, Ariz., 3,342.....A 3 50
Kingman, Kans., 3,200.....D 4 61
Kingsford, Mich., 5,038.....A 3 67
Kingsley, Iowa, 1,098.....B 3 60
Kings Mountain, N. C., 7,206.....C 4 78
Kings Park, N. Y., 10,960.....E 2 77
Kings Point, N. Y., 2,445.....E 2 77
Kingsport, Tenn., 19,571.....Q 1 86
Kingston, N. H., □1,283.....D 6 74
Kingston, N. Y., 28,817.....M 7 77
Kingston, Pa., 21,096.....L 3 83
Kingston, Tenn., 1,627.....N 3 86
Kingstree, S. C., 3,621.....J 4 84
Kingsville, Tex., 16,898.....G10 87
Kingwood, W. Va., 2,186.....G 2 92
Kinloch, Mo., 5,957.....P 2 70
Kinsley, Kans., 2,479.....C 4 61
Kinston, N. C., 18,336.....K 4 78
Kiowa, Kans., 1,561.....D 4 61
Kirkland, Wash., 4,713.....C 3 91
Kirksville, Mo., 11,110.....H 2 70
Kirkwood, Mo., 18,640.....L 5 70
Kissimmee, Fla., 4,310.....E 3 55
Kittanning, Pa., 7,731.....C 4 83
Kittery, Me., □8,380.....B 9 64
Kittitas, Wash., 586.....E 4 91
Kitzmiller, Md., 652.....B 8 65
Klamath Falls, Oreg., 15,875.....F 5 82
Knightstown, Ind., 2,486.....F 5 59
Knox, Ind., 3,034.....D 2 59
Knoxville, Ill., 2,209.....C 3 58
Knoxville, Iowa, 7,625.....G 6 60
Knoxville, Tenn., 124,769.....O 3 86
Kodiak, Alaska Territory, 1,623.....H 3 95
Kohler, Wis., 1,716.....K 8 93
Kokomo, Ind., 38,672.....E 4 59
Konawa, Okla., 2,707.....J 5 81
Kooskia, Idaho, 629.....C 3 57
Kosciusko, Miss., 6,753.....E 4 69
Krebs, Okla., 1,532.....L 5 81
Kremmling, Colo., 623.....G 2 53
Kulm, N. Dak., 707.....N 7 79
Kulpmont, Pa., 5,199.....J 4 83
Kuna, Idaho, 534.....B 6 57
Kuttawa, Ky., 794.....D 3 62
Kutztown, Pa., 3,110.....L 4 83
La Belle, Fla., 945.....E 5 55
Lackawanna, N. Y., 27,658.....C 5 77
Laconia, N. H., 14,745.....D 4 74
La Conner, Wash., 594.....C 2 91
Lacoochee, Fla., 1,792.....D 3 55
La Crosse, Kans., 1,769.....C 3 61
Lacrosse, Va., 675.....H 7 90
La Crosse, Wis., 47,535.....D 8 93
Ladoga, Ind., 912.....D 5 59
Ladue, Mo., 5,386.....P 3 70
Ladysmith, Wis., 3,924.....D 5 93
Lafayette, Ala., 2,353.....G 5 49
Lafayette, Colo., 2,090.....K 3 53
Lafayette, Ga., 4,884.....B 1 56
Lafayette, Ind., 35,568.....D 4 59
Lafayette, La., 33,541.....F 6 63
Lafayette, Oreg., 662.....A 2 82
La Fayette, R. I., 550.....J 6 66
La Follette, Tenn., 5,797.....N 2 86
La Grande, Oreg., 8,635.....J 2 82
La Grange, Ga., 25,025.....B 4 56
La Grange, Ill., 12,002.....A 2 58
Lagrange, Ind., 1,892.....G 1 59
La Grange, Ky., 1,558.....G 4 62
La Grange, Mo., 1,106.....J 2 70
La Grange, N. C., 1,852.....K 4 78
La Grange, Tex., 2,738.....G 8 87
La Grange, Wyo., 221.....H 4 94
La Grange Park, Ill., 6,176.....A 2 58
Laguna Beach, Calif., 6,661.....H10 52
La Habra, Calif., 4,961.....D11 52
Lahaina, Hawaii Territory, 5,217.....H 2 95
La Jara, Colo., 912.....H 8 53
La Jara, N. Mex., 2,500.....B 2 76
La Junta, Colo., 7,712.....M 7 53
Lake Alfred, Fla., 1,270.....E 3 55
Lake Andes, S. Dak., 1,851.....M 7 85
Lake Arthur, La., 2,849.....E 6 63
Lake Arthur, N. Mex., 380.....E 5 76
Lake Benton, Minn., 863.....B 6 68
Lake Butler, Fla., 1,040.....D 1 55
Lake Charles, La., 41,272.....D 6 63
Lake City, Ark., 783.....K 2 51
Lake City, Fla., 7,571.....D 1 55
Lake City, Iowa, 2,308.....D 4 60
Lake City, Minn., 3,457.....F 6 68
Lake City, S. C., 5,112.....J 4 84
Lake City, Tenn., 1,827.....N 2 86

Index Ref. Plate No.
Lake Crystal, Minn., 1,430.....D 6 68
Lakefield, Minn., 1,651.....C 7 68
Lake Forrest, Ill., 7,819.....F 1 58
Lake Geneva, Wis., 4,300.....K10 93
Lakeland, Fla., 30,851.....D 3 55
Lakeland, Ga., 1,551.....F 8 56
Lakeland, Ind., 2,172.....D 1 59
Lake Linden, Mich., 1,462.....A 1 67
Lake Mills, Iowa, 1,560.....F 2 60
Lakemills, Wis., 2,516.....J 9 93
Lakemore, Ohio, 2,463.....H 3 80
Lake Odessa, Mich., 1,596.....E 6 67
Lake Orion, Mich., 2,385.....F 6 67
Lake Placid, N. Y., 2,999.....N 2 77
Lakeport, N. H., 3,600.....D 4 74
Lake Preston, S. Dak., 957.....P 5 85
Lake Providence, La., 4,123.....H 1 63
Lakeside, Ky., 988.....H 2 62
Lake View, Iowa, 1,158.....C 4 60
Lakeview, Oreg., 2,831.....G 5 82
Lake Village, Ark., 2,484.....H 7 51
Lake Wales, Fla., 6,821.....E 4 55
Lakewood, N. J., 9,970.....E 3 75
Lakewood, N. Y., 3,013.....B 6 77
Lakewood, Ohio, 68,071.....G 2 80
Lake Worth, Fla., 11,777.....G 5 55
Lakota, N. Dak., 1,032.....O 3 79
Lamar, Colo., 6,829.....O 6 53
Lamar, Mo., 3,233.....D 8 70
Lamar, S. C., 958.....H 3 84
Lamarque, Tex., 7,359.....K 3 87
Lambert, Miss., 1,023.....D 2 69
Lamberton, Minn., 1,208.....C 6 68
Lambertville, N. J., 4,477.....D 3 75
La Mesa, Calif., 10,946.....H11 52
Lamesa, Tex., 10,704.....C 5 87
Lamoille, Nev., 200.....F 2 73
Lamoni, Iowa, 2,196.....F 7 60
La Moure, N. Dak., 1,010.....O 7 79
Lampasas, Tex., 4,869.....F 6 87
Lanai City, Hawaii Territory, 3,597.....H 2 95
Lancaster, Ky., 2,402.....H 5 62
Lancaster, N. H., □3,113.....C 3 74
Lancaster, N. Y., 8,665.....C 5 77
Lancaster, Ohio, 24,180.....E 6 80
Lancaster, Pa., 63,774.....K 5 83
Lancaster, S. C., 7,159.....G 2 84
Lancaster, Wis., 3,266.....E10 93
Lance Creek, Wyo., 2,000.....H 2 94
Lander, Wyo., 3,349.....D 3 94
Landis, N. C., 1,827.....D 3 78
Landrum, S. C., 1,333.....D 1 84
Lanesboro, Minn., 1,100.....G 7 68
Lanett, Ala., 7,434.....H 5 49
Langdon, N. Dak., 1,838.....O 2 79
Lansdale, Pa., 9,762.....M 5 83
Lansdowne, Pa., 12,169.....M 7 83
L'Anse, Mich., 2,376.....G 1 67
Lansford, Pa., 7,487.....L 4 83
Lansing, Ill., 8,682.....B 2 58
Lansing, Iowa, 1,536.....L 2 60
LANSING, Mich., 92,129.....E 6 67
Lapeer, Mich., 6,143.....F 5 67
Lapel, Ind., 1,389.....F 4 59
La Plata, Md., 780.....G 6 65
La Plata, Mo., 1,331.....H 2 70
La Porte, Ind., 20,414.....D 1 59
La Porte, Tex., 4,429.....K 2 87
La Porte City, Iowa, 1,770.....J 4 60
Lapwai, Idaho, 480.....B 3 57
Laramie, Wyo., 15,581.....G 4 94
Larchmont, N. Y., 6,330.....D 2 77
Laredo, Tex., 51,910.....E10 87
Largo, Fla., 1,547.....D 4 55
Larimore, N. Dak., 1,374.....P 4 79
Larksville, Pa., 6,360.....L 3 83
Larned, Kans., 4,447.....C 3 61
La Salle, Colo., 797.....K 2 53
La Salle, Ill., 12,083.....D 2 58
Las Animas, Colo., 3,223.....N 6 53
Las Cruces, N. Mex., 12,325.....C 6 76
Las Vegas, Nev., 24,624.....F 6 73
Las Vegas, N. Mex., 7,494.....D 3 76
Lathrop, Mo., 888.....D 3 70
Latrobe, Pa., 11,811.....D 5 83
Latta, S. C., 1,602.....K 3 84
Laurel, Del., 2,700.....M 6 65
Laurel, Md., 4,482.....G 4 65
Laurel, Miss., 25,038.....F 7 69
Laurel, Mont., 3,663.....H 5 71
Laurel, Nebr., 944.....G 2 72
Laureldale, Pa., 3,585.....L 5 83
Laurens, Iowa, 1,556.....D 3 60
Laurens, S. C., 8,658.....D 2 84
Laurinburg, N. C., 7,134.....F 5 78
Laurium, Mich., 3,211.....A 1 67
Lava Hot Springs, Idaho, 591.....G 7 57
Laveen, Ariz., 300.....C 5 50
La Verne, Calif., 4,198.....D10 52
La Veta, Colo., 701.....J 8 53
Lavonia, Ga., 1,766.....F 2 56

Index Ref. Plate No.
Lawrence, Ind., 1,951.....E 5 59
Lawrence, Kans., 23,531.....G 3 61
Lawrence, Mass., 80,536.....K 2 66
Lawrence, N. Y., 4,681.....D 2 77
Lawrenceburg, Ind., 4,806.....H 6 59
Lawrenceburg, Ky., 2,369.....H 4 62
Lawrenceburg, Tenn., 5,442.....G 4 86
Lawrenceville, Ga., 2,932.....E 2 56
Lawrenceville, Ill., 6,328.....F 5 58
Lawrenceville, Va., 2,239.....J 7 90
Lawton, Okla., 34,757.....F 5 81
Layton, Utah, 3,456.....B 2 88
Leachville, Ark., 1,230.....K 2 51
Lead, S. Dak., 6,422.....B 5 85
Leadville, Colo., 4,081.....G 4 53
Leakesville, Miss., 893.....G 8 69
Leaksville, N. C., 4,045.....F 2 78
Leavenworth, Kans., 20,579.....G 2 61
Leavenworth, Wash., 1,503.....E 3 91
Lebanon, Ill., 2,417.....D 5 58
Lebanon, Ind., 7,631.....D 4 59
Lebanon, Ky., 4,640.....G 5 62
Lebanon, Me., □1,499.....B 9 64
Lebanon, Mo., 6,808.....G 7 70
Lebanon, N. H., □8,495.....B 4 74
Lebanon, Ohio, 4,618.....B 7 80
Lebanon, Oreg., 5,873.....E 3 82
Lebanon, Pa., 28,156.....K 5 83
Lebanon, Tenn., 7,913.....J 2 86
Lebanon, Va., 672.....E 2 90
Lebanon Junction, Ky., 1,243.....F 5 62
Le Center, Minn., 1,314.....E 6 68
Lecompte, La., 1,443.....F 4 63
Lee, Mass., □4,820.....B 3 66
Leechburg, Pa., 4,042.....C 4 83
Leeds, Ala., 3,306.....E 3 49
Leeds, N. Dak., 778.....M 3 79
Leesburg, Fla., 7,395.....E 3 55
Leesburg, Va., 1,703.....J 2 90
Lee's Summit, Mo., 2,554.....D 5 70
Leesville, La., 4,670.....D 4 63
Leesville, S. C., 1,453.....F 4 84
Leetonia, Ohio, 2,565.....J 4 80
Lehi, Utah, 3,627.....C 3 88
Lehigh, Iowa, 881.....E 4 60
Lehighton, Pa., 6,565.....L 4 83
Lehr, N. Dak., 394.....M 7 79
Leicester, Mass., □6,029.....G 4 66
Leighton, Ala., 1,080.....D 1 49
Leipsic, Del., 253.....N 4 65
Leipsic, Ohio, 1,706.....C 3 80
Leitchfield, Ky., 1,312.....E 5 62
Leland, Miss., 4,736.....C 4 69
Le Mars, Iowa, 5,844.....A 3 60
Lemmon, S. Dak., 2,760.....E 2 85
Lemont, Ill., 2,757.....F 2 58
Lemoyne, Pa., 4,605.....J 5 83
Lennox, Calif., 25,000.....C11 52
Lennox, S. Dak., 1,218.....R 7 85
Lenoir, N. C., 7,888.....C 3 78
Lenoir City, Tenn., 5,159.....N 3 86
Lenox, Iowa, 1,171.....D 7 60
Leola, S. Dak., 772.....M 2 85
Leominster, Mass., 24,075.....G 2 66
Leon, Iowa, 2,139.....F 7 60
Leonardtown, Md., 1,017.....H 7 65
Leonia, N. J., 7,378.....C 2 75
Lepanto, Ark., 1,683.....K 2 51
Le Roy, N. Y., 4,721.....E 5 77
Leslie, Ark., 610.....F 2 51
Leslie, Mich., 1,543.....E 6 67
Lester, W. Va., 780.....D 5 92
Le Sueur, Minn., 2,713.....E 6 68
Levan, Utah, 521.....C 4 88
Levelland, Tex., 8,264.....B 4 87
Levy, Ark., 5,164.....F 4 51
Lewes, Del., 2,904.....O 5 65
Lewisburg, Pa., 5,268.....J 4 83
Lewisburg, Tenn., 5,164.....H 4 86
Lewisburg, W. Va., 2,192.....E 5 92
Lewiston, Idaho, 12,985.....A 3 57
Lewiston, Me., 40,974.....C 7 64
Lewiston, N. Y., 1,626.....B 4 77
Lewiston, Utah, 1,533.....C 2 88
Lewistown, Ill., 2,630.....C 3 58
Lewistown, Mont., 6,573.....G 3 71
Lewistown, Pa., 13,894.....G 4 83
Lewisville, Ark., 1,237.....D 7 51
Lewisville, Idaho, 402.....F 6 57
Lexington, Ky., 55,534.....J 4 62
Lexington, Mass., □17,335.....J 3 66
Lexington, Miss., 3,198.....E 4 69
Lexington, Mo., 5,074.....E 4 70
Lexington, Nebr., 5,068.....E 4 72
Lexington, N. C., 13,571.....E 3 78
Lexington, S. C., 1,081.....F 4 84
Lexington, Tenn., 3,566.....E 3 86
Lexington, Va., 5,976.....E 5 90
Libby, Mont., 2,401.....A 2 71
Liberal, Kans., 7,134.....B 4 61
Liberty, Ind., 1,730.....H 5 59

Index Plate Ref. No.

Liberty, Miss., 683..........C 8 69
Liberty, Mo., 4,709..........D 4 70
Liberty, N. Y., 4,658..........L 7 77
Liberty, S. C., 2,291..........C 2 84
Liberty, Tex., 4,163..........K 7 87
Libertyville, Ill., 5,425..........F 1 58
Lidgerwood, N. Dak., 1,147..........R 7 79
Ligonier, Ind., 2,375..........F 2 59
Lihue, Hawaii Territory, 4,254..........C 2 95
Lilbourn, Mo., 1,361..........N 9 70
Lima, Mont., 483..........D 6 71
Lima, Ohio, 50,246..........B 4 80
Limestone, Me., □2,427..........H 2 64
Limon, Colo., 1,471..........M 4 53
Lincoln, Calif., 2,410..........D 5 52
Lincoln, Del., 400..........N 5 65
Lincoln, Ill., 14,362..........D 3 58
Lincoln, Kans., 1,636..........D 2 61
Lincoln, Me., □4,030..........G 5 64
LINCOLN, Nebr., 98,884..........H 4 72
Lincoln, N. H., □1,415..........C 3 74
Lincoln Park, Mich., 29,310..........B 7 67
Lincolnton, N. C., 5,423..........C 4 78
Lind, Wash., 796..........G 4 91
Lindale, Ga., 2,834..........B 2 56
Linden, Ala., 1,363..........C 6 49
Linden, N. J., 30,644..........E 2 75
Linden, Tenn., 854..........F 3 86
Lindenhurst, N. Y., 8,644..........E 3 77
Lindon, Utah, 801..........C 3 88
Lindsay, Calif., 5,060..........G 7 52
Lindsay, Okla., 3,021..........G 5 81
Lindsborg, Kans., 2,383..........E 3 61
Lineville, Ala., 1,548..........G 4 49
Lingle, Wyo., 403..........H 3 94
Linton, Ind., 5,973..........C 6 59
Linton, N. Dak., 1,675..........K 7 79
Linwood, Pa..........L 7 83
Lipscomb, Ala., 2,550..........E 4 49
Lisbon, Me., □4,318..........C 7 64
Lisbon, N. H., □2,009..........C 3 74
Lisbon, N. Dak., 2,031..........P 7 79
Lisbon, Ohio, 3,293..........J 4 80
Lisbon Falls, Me., 2,155..........D 8 64
Litchfield, Conn., 1,174..........C 2 54
Litchfield, Ill., 7,208..........D 4 58
Litchfield, Minn., 4,608..........D 5 68
Lithonia, Ga., 1,534..........D 3 56
Lititz, Pa., 5,568..........K 5 83
Little Chute, Wis., 4,152..........K 7 93
Little Compton, R. I., □1,556..........K 6 66
Little Creek, Del., 266..........N 4 65
Little Falls, Minn., 6,717..........D 4 68
Little Falls, N. Y., 9,541..........L 4 77
Little Ferry, N. J., 4,955..........B 2 75
Littlefield, Tex., 6,540..........B 4 87
LITTLE ROCK, Ark., 102,213..........F 4 51
Littleton, Colo., 3,378..........K 3 53
Littleton, N. H., □4,817..........C 3 74
Little Valley, N. Y., 1,287..........C 6 77
Live Oak, Fla., 4,064..........D 1 55
Livermore, Calif., 4,364..........L 2 52
Livermore, Ky., 1,441..........C 6 62
Livermore, Me., □1,313..........C 7 64
Livermore Falls, Me., □3,359..........C 7 64
Liverpool, N. Y., 2,933..........H 4 77
Livingston, Ala., 1,681..........B 5 49
Livingston, Mont., 7,683..........F 5 71
Livingston, Tenn., 2,082..........L 2 86
Livingston, Tex., 2,865..........K 7 87
Livonia, Mich., 17,534..........F 6 67
Llano, Tex., 2,954..........F 7 87
Lockhart, Ala., 819..........F 8 49
Lockhart, Tex., 5,573..........G 8 87
Lock Haven, Pa., 11,381..........H 3 83
Lockland, Ohio, 5,736..........C 9 80
Lockport, Ill., 4,955..........F 2 58
Lockport, La., 1,388..........K 7 63
Lockport, N. Y., 25,133..........C 4 77
Lodge Grass, Mont., 536..........J 5 71
Lodi, Calif., 13,798..........D 5 52
Lodi, N. J., 15,392..........B 2 75
Lodi, Ohio, 1,523..........F 3 80
Lodi, Wis., 1,416..........G 9 93
Logan, Iowa, 1,550..........B 5 60
Logan, N. Mex., 500..........F 3 76
Logan, Ohio, 5,972..........F 6 80
Logan, Utah, 16,832..........C 2 88
Logan, W. Va., 5,079..........B 5 92
Logansport, Ind., 21,031..........E 3 59
Logansport, La., 1,270..........C 3 63
Lombard, Ill., 9,817..........A 2 58
Lomita, Calif., 10,000..........C11 52
Lompoc, Calif., 5,520..........E 9 52
Lonaconing, Md., 2,289..........C 7 65
London, Ky., 3,426..........J 6 62
London, Ohio, 5,222..........C 6 80
Londonderry, N. H., □1,640..........D 6 74
Long Beach, Calif., 250,767..........G10 52
Long Beach, Miss., 2,703..........F10 69
Long Beach, N. Y., 15,586..........D 3 77
Long Beach, Wash., 783..........A 4 91
Long Branch, N. J., 23,090..........F 3 75
Longmeadow, Mass., □6,508..........E 4 66
Longmont, Colo., 8,099..........J 2 53
Long Pine, Nebr., 567..........E 2 72
Long Prairie, Minn., 2,443..........D 5 68
Longview, N. C., 2,291..........C 3 78
Longview, Tex., 24,502..........K 5 87
Longview, Wash., 20,385..........B 4 91
Lonoke, Ark., 1,556..........G 4 51
Lonsdale, R. I., 2,500..........J 5 66
Loogootee, Ind., 2,424..........D 7 59
Lookout Mountain, Tenn., 1,675..........L 5 86
Lorain, Ohio, 51,202..........F 3 80
Lordsburg, N. Mex., 3,525..........A 6 76
Loris, S. C., 1,614..........L 3 84
Los Alamos, N. Mex., 9,934..........C 3 76
Los Angeles, Calif., 1,970,358..........G 9 52
Los Banos, Calif., 3,868..........E 6 52
Los Gatos, Calif., 4,907..........K 4 52
Los Lunas, N. Mex., 889..........C 4 76
Loudon, N. H., □1,012..........D 5 74
Loudon, Tenn., 3,567..........N 3 86
Loudonville, Ohio, 2,523..........F 4 80
Louisa, Ky., 2,015..........M 4 62
Louisburg, N. C., 2,545..........J 2 78
Louisiana, Mo., 4,389..........K 4 70
Louisville, Colo., 1,978..........J 3 53
Louisville, Ga., 2,231..........H 4 56
Louisville, Ky., 369,129..........F 4 62
Louisville, Miss., 5,282..........F 4 69
Louisville, Nebr., 1,014..........H 4 72
Louisville, Ohio, 3,801..........H 4 80
Loup City, Nebr., 1,508..........E 3 72
Lovejoy, Ill., 2,568..........C 5 58
Loveland, Colo., 6,773..........J 2 53
Loveland, Ohio, 2,149..........B 7 80
Lovell, Wyo., 2,508..........D 1 94
Lovelock, Nev., 1,605..........C 2 73
Lovington, N. Mex., 3,134..........F 6 76
Lowell, Ariz., 1,136..........F 7 50
Lowell, Ind., 1,621..........C 2 59
Lowell, Mass., 97,249..........J 2 66
Lowell, Mich., 2,191..........D 6 67
Lowell, N. C., 2,313..........C 4 78
Lowellville, Ohio, 2227..........J 3 80
Lower Merion, Pa., 39,566..........M 5 83
Lowville, N. Y., 3,671..........J 3 77
Loyall, Ky., 1,548..........L 7 62
Lubbock, Tex., 71,747..........C 4 87
Lubec, Me., □2,973..........J 6 64
Lucedale, Miss., 1,631..........G 9 69
Ludington, Mich., 9,506..........C 5 67
Ludlow, Ky., 6,374..........H 2 62
Ludlow, Mass., □8,660..........D 4 66
Ludlow, Vt., 1,678..........B 4 89
Lufkin, Tex., 15,135..........K 6 87
Luke, Md., 820..........B 8 65
Luling, Tex., 4,297..........G 8 87
Lumberport, W. Va., 1,198..........F 2 92
Lumberton, Miss., 1,803..........E 9 69
Lumberton, N. C., 9,186..........G 5 78
Lund, Nev., 365..........F 4 73
Lunenburg, Vt., □1,299..........D 2 89
Luray, Va., 2,731..........H 3 90
Lusk, Wyo., 2,089..........H 3 94
Lutcher, La., 2,198..........J 6 63
Luverne, Ala., 2,221..........F 7 49
Luverne, Minn., 3,650..........B 7 68
Luxora, Ark., 1,302..........L 2 51
Luzerne, Pa., 6,176..........L 3 83
Lykens, Pa., 2,735..........J 4 83
Lyme, N. H., □924..........B 4 74
Lynbrook, N. Y., 17,314..........D 3 77
Lynch, Ky., 3,970..........M 6 62
Lynchburg, Tenn., 401..........J 4 86
Lynchburg, Va., 47,727..........F 6 90
Lynden, Wash., 2,161..........C 2 91
Lyndhurst, N. J., □19,980..........B 2 75
Lyndhurst, Ohio, 7,359..........J 9 80
Lyndon, Vt., □3,360..........D 1 89
Lyndon Center, Vt., 321..........C 1 89
Lyndonville, Vt., 1,506..........D 1 89
Lynn, Ind., 1,149..........H 4 59
Lynn, Mass., 99,738..........L 3 66
Lynn Haven, Fla., 1,787..........C 6 55
Lynwood, Calif., 25,823..........C11 52
Lyons, Colo., 689..........J 2 53
Lyons, Ga., 2,799..........H 6 56
Lyons, Ill., 6,120..........B 2 58
Lyons, Kans., 4,545..........D 3 61
Lyons, Nebr., 1,011..........H 2 72
Lyons, N. Y., 4,217..........G 4 77
Maben, Miss., 616..........F 3 69
Mabscott, W. Va., 1,665..........D 5 92
Mc Adoo, Pa., 4,260..........L 4 83
Mc Alester, Okla., 17,878..........L 5 81
Mc Allen, Tex., 20,067..........F11 87
Mc Arthur, Ohio, 1,466..........F 7 80
Mc Bee, S. C., 420..........H 3 84
Mc Call, Idaho, 1,173..........B 5 57
Mc Camey, Tex., 3,121..........B 6 87
Mc Cammon, Idaho, 578..........F 7 57
Mc Caysville, Ga., 2,067..........D 1 56
Mc Clusky, N. Dak., 850..........K 5 79
Mc Coll, S. C., 2,688..........J 2 84
Mc Comb, Miss., 10,401..........C 8 69
Mc Connelsville, Ohio, 1,941..........G 6 80
Mc Cook, Nebr., 7,678..........D 4 72
Mc Cormick, S. C., 1,744..........D 4 84
Mc Crory, Ark., 1,115..........H 3 51
Mc Dermitt, Nev., 100..........D 1 73
Mc Donald, Pa., 3,543..........B 5 83
Mc Ewen, Tenn., 710..........F 2 86
Mc Gehee, Ark., 3,854..........H 6 51
Mc Gill, Nev., 2,297..........G 3 73
Mc Graw, N. Y., 1,197..........H 5 77
Mc Gregor, Iowa, 1,138..........L 2 60
Mc Gregor, Tex., 2,669..........G 5 87
Mc Henry, Ky., 511..........D 6 62
Machias, Me., □2,063..........J 6 64
Mc Intosh, Minn., 881..........C 3 68
Mc Intosh, S. Dak., 628..........G 2 85
Mack, Ohio, 870..........B 9 80
Mackay, Idaho, 760..........E 6 57
Mc Keesport, Pa., 51,502..........C 5 83
Mc Kees Rocks, Pa., 16,241..........B 7 83
Mc Kenney, Va., 476..........J 7 90
Mc Kenzie, Tenn., 3,774..........E 2 86
Mc Kinney, Tex., 10,560..........H 4 87
Mc Laughlin, S. Dak., 713..........H 2 85
Mc Leansboro, Ill., 3,008..........E 5 58
Mc Mechen, W. Va., 3,518..........K 6 92
Mc Minnville, Oreg., 6,635..........D 2 82
Mc Minnville, Tenn., 7,577..........K 3 86
Macomb, Ill., 10,592..........C 3 58
Macon, Ga., 70,272..........E 5 56
Macon, Miss., 2,241..........G 4 69
Macon, Mo., 4,152..........H 3 70
Mc Pherson, Kans., 8,689..........E 3 61
Mc Rae, Ga., 1,904..........G 6 56
Mc Ville, N. Dak., 626..........O 4 79
Madawaska, Me., 4,900..........G 1 64
Maddock, N. Dak., 741..........L 4 79
Madeira, Ohio, 2,689..........C 9 80
Madelia, Minn., 1,790..........D 6 68
Madera, Calif., 10,497..........E 7 52
Madill, Okla., 2,791..........J 6 81
Madison, Ark., 718..........J 3 51
Madison, Conn., □3,078..........E 3 54
Madison, Fla., 3,150..........C 1 55
Madison, Ga., 2,489..........F 3 56
Madison, Ill., 7,963..........C 5 58
Madison, Ind., 7,506..........G 7 59
Madison, Kans., 1,212..........F 3 61
Madison, Me., 3,639..........D 6 64
Madison, Minn., 2,303..........B 5 68
Madison, Nebr., 1,663..........G 3 72
Madison, N. J., 10,417..........E 2 75
Madison, N. C., 1,789..........F 2 78
Madison, S. Dak., 5,153..........P 5 85
Madison, W. Va., 2,025..........C 4 92
MADISON, Wis., 96,056..........H 9 93
Madison Heights, Va., 2,830..........F 6 90
Madisonville, Ky., 11,132..........C 6 62
Madisonville, La., 861..........K 6 63
Madisonville, Tenn., 1,487..........N 3 86
Madisonville, Tex., 2,393..........J 7 87
Madras, Oreg., 1,258..........F 3 82
Madrid, Iowa, 1,829..........F 5 60
Madrid, N. Mex., 477..........C 3 76
Magdalena, N. Mex., 1,297..........B 4 76
Magee, Miss., 1,738..........E 7 69
Magna, Utah, 3,502..........B 3 88
Magnolia, Ark., 6,918..........D 7 51
Magnolia, Del., 207..........M 4 65
Magnolia, Miss., 1,984..........D 8 69
Mahanoy City, Pa., 10,934..........K 4 83
Mahnomen, Minn., 1,464..........C 3 68
Maiden, N. C., 1,952..........C 3 78
Malad City, Idaho, 2,715..........F 7 57
Malden, Mass., 59,804..........K 3 66
Malden, Mo., 3,396..........M 9 70
Malin, Oreg., 592..........F 5 82
Malone, N. Y., 9,501..........M 1 77
Malta, Mont., 2,095..........J 2 71
Malvern, Ark., 8,072..........E 5 51
Malvern, Iowa, 1,263..........B 7 60
Malverne, N. Y., 8,086..........D 2 77
Mamaroneck, N. Y., 15,016..........D 2 77
Mammoth, W. Va., 1,000..........D 4 92
Mamou, La., 2,254..........F 5 63
Man, W. Va., 1,632..........C 5 92
Manassa, Colo., 832..........H 8 53
Manassas, Va., 1,804..........K 3 90
Manchester, Conn., □34,116..........F 1 54
Manchester, Ga., 4,036..........C 5 56
Manchester, Iowa, 3,987..........L 4 60
Manchester, Ky., 1,706..........K 6 62
Manchester, Md., 1,027..........G 2 65
Manchester, N. H., 82,732..........C 6 74
Manchester, N. Y., 1,262..........F 5 77
Manchester, Ohio, 2,281..........C 8 80
Manchester, Tenn., 2,341..........J 4 86
Manchester, Vt., 454..........A 4 89
Mancos, Colo., 785..........C 8 53
Mandan, N. Dak., 7,298..........J 6 79
Manderson, Wyo., 107..........E 1 94
Mandeville, La., 1,368..........L 6 63
Mangum, Okla., 4,271..........C 5 81
Manhattan, Kans., 19,056..........F 2 61
Manhattan, Mont., 716..........E 5 71
Manhattan, Nev., 125..........E 4 73
Manhattan (borough), N. Y., 1,960,101..........C 2 77
Manhattan Beach, Calif., 17,330..........B11 52
Manheim, Pa., 4,246..........K 5 83
Manila, Ark., 1,729..........K 2 51
Manistee, Mich., 8,642..........C 4 67
Manistique, Mich, 5,086..........C 3 67
Manitou Springs, Colo., 2,580..........J 5 53
Manitowoc, Wis., 27,598..........L 7 93
Mankato, Kans., 1,462..........D 2 61
Mankato, Minn., 18,809..........E 6 68
Manlius, N. Y., 1,742..........J 5 77
Manly, Iowa, 1,473..........G 2 60
Manning, Iowa, 1,801..........C 5 60
Manning, S. C., 2,775..........H 4 84
Mannington, W. Va., 3,241..........F 1 92
Mansfield, Ark., 869..........B 3 51
Mansfield, Conn., □10,008..........F 1 54
Mansfield, La., 4,440..........C 2 63
Mansfield, Mass., □7,184..........J 4 66
Mansfield, Mo., 963..........G 8 70
Mansfield, Ohio, 43,564..........F 4 80
Manson, Iowa, 1,622..........D 3 60
Mansura, La., 1,439..........F 4 63
Manteca, Calif., 3,804..........D 6 52
Manti, Utah, 2,051..........C 4 88
Manton, R. I., 2,500..........J 5 66
Manville, N. J., 8,597..........D 2 75
Manville, R. I., 3,429..........H 5 66
Manville, Wyo., 154..........H 3 94
Many, La., 1,681..........C 3 63
Manzano, N. Mex., 250..........C 4 76
Maple Heights, Ohio, 15,586..........H 9 80
Mapleton, Iowa, 1,857..........B 4 60
Mapleton, Me., □1,367..........G 2 64
Mapleton, Minn., 1,083..........D 7 68
Mapleton, Utah, 1,175..........C 3 88
Mapleville, R. I., 1,015..........H 5 66
Maplewood, Mo., 13,416..........M 5 70
Maplewood, N. J., □25,201..........E 2 75
Maquoketa, Iowa, 4,307..........M 4 60
Marblehead, Mass., 13,765..........S 9 66
Marceline, Mo., 3,172..........F 3 70
Marcellus, N. Y., 1,382..........H 5 77
Marcus, Iowa, 1,263..........B 3 60
Marcus Hook, Pa., 3,843..........L 7 83
Mardela Springs, Md., 428..........L 7 65
Marengo, Ill., 2,726..........E 1 58
Marengo, Iowa, 2,151..........J 5 60
Marfa, Tex., 3,603..........C12 87
Margate City, N. J., 4,715..........E 5 75
Marianna, Ark., 4,530..........J 4 51
Marianna, Fla., 5,845..........A 1 55
Marietta, Ga., 20,687..........C 3 56
Marietta, Ohio, 16,006..........G 7 80
Marietta, Okla., 1,875..........H 7 81
Marine City, Mich., 4,270..........G 6 67
Marinette, Wis., 14,178..........L 5 93
Marion, Ala., 2,822..........D 5 49
Marion, Ill., 10,459..........E 6 58
Marion, Ind., 30,081..........F 3 59
Marion, Iowa, 5,916..........K 4 60
Marion, Kans., 2,050..........F 3 61
Marion, Ky., 2,375..........A 6 62
Marion, N. Y., 800..........F 4 77
Marion, N. C., 2,740..........A 3 78
Marion, Ohio, 33,817..........D 4 80
Marion, S. C., 1,000..........K 3 84
Marion, S. Dak., 794..........P 7 85
Marion, Va., 6,982..........F 2 90
Marion, Wis., 1,118..........J 6 93
Marionville, Mo., 1,167..........F 9 70
Marked Tree, Ark., 2,878..........J 2 51
Marks, Miss., 2,209..........D 2 69
Marksville, La., 3,635..........G 4 63
Marlboro, Mass., 15,756..........H 3 66
Marlboro, N. H., □1,561..........B 6 74
Marlin, Tex., 7,099..........H 6 87
Marlinton, W. Va., 1,645..........F 4 92
Marlow, Okla., 3,399..........F 5 81
Marmarth, N. Dak., 469..........C 7 79
Marmet, W. Va., 2,515..........C 4 92
Marquette, Mich., 17,202..........B 2 67
Marseilles, Ill., 4,514..........E 2 58
Marshall, Ark., 1,189..........E 2 51
Marshall, Ill., 2,960..........F 4 58
Marshall, Mich., 5,777..........E 6 67
Marshall, Minn., 5,923..........C 6 68
Marshall, Mo., 8,850..........F 4 70
Marshall, Tex., 22,327..........K 5 87
Marshallton, Del., 1,600..........M 2 65
Marshalltown, Iowa, 19,821..........H 4 60
Marshfield, Mo., 1,925..........G 8 70
Marshfield, Vt., 274..........C 2 89
Marshfield, Wis., 12,394..........F 6 93
Mars Hill, Me., □2,060..........G 2 64
Mart, Tex., 2,269..........H 6 87
Martin, Ky., 1,170..........M 5 62
Martin, S. Dak., 989..........F 7 85
Martin, Tenn., 4,082..........D 2 86
Martinez, Calif., 8,268..........D 6 52
Martinsburg, W. Va., 15,621..........K 2 92
Martins Ferry, Ohio, 13,220..........J 5 80
Martinsville, Ind., 5,991..........D 6 59
Martinsville, Va., 17,251..........E 7 90
Marvell, Ark., 1,121..........J 4 51
Marysvale, Utah, 520..........B 5 88
Marysville, Calif., 7,826..........D 4 52
Marysville, Kans., 3,866..........F 2 61
Marysville, Mich., 2,534..........G 6 67
Marysville, Ohio, 4,256..........D 5 80
Marysville, Wash., 2,259..........C 2 91
Maryville, Mo., 6,834..........B 2 70
Maryville, Tenn., 7,742..........O 3 86
Mascoutah, Ill., 3,009..........D 5 58
Mason, Mich., 3,514..........E 6 67
Mason, Nev., 89..........B 4 73
Mason, Tenn., 414..........B 4 86
Mason, W. Va., 924..........B 2 92
Mason City, Ill., 2,004..........D 3 58
Mason City, Iowa, 27,980..........G 2 60
Masontown, Pa., 4,550..........C 6 83
Masontown, W. Va., 941..........G 1 92
Massena, N. Y., 13,137..........L 1 77
Massey, Md., 125..........L 3 65
Massillon, Ohio, 29,594..........H 4 80
Matewan, W. Va., 989..........B 5 92
Mathis, Tex., 4,050..........G 9 87
Matoaka, W. Va., 1,003..........D 6 92
Mattituck, N. Y., 1,089..........F 2 77
Mattoon, Ill., 17,547..........E 4 58
Mauch Chunk, Pa., 2,959..........L 4 83
Maud, Okla., 1,389..........J 4 81
Maumee, Ohio, 5,548..........C 2 80
Maury City, Tenn., 553..........C 3 86
Mauston, Wis., 3,171..........F 8 93
Maxton, N. C., 1,974..........G 5 78
Maxwell, N. Mex., 404..........E 2 76
Maybeury, W. Va., 1,000..........D 6 92
Mayer, Ariz., 500..........C 4 50
Mayfield, Ky., 8,990..........C 3 62
Mayfield, Pa., 2,373..........L 2 83
Mayfield Heights, Ohio, 5,807..........J 9 80
Maynard, Mass., □6,978..........J 3 66
Mayo, Fla., 697..........C 1 55
Mayodan, N. C., 2,246..........F 2 78
Maysville, Ky., 8,632..........K 3 62
Maysville, Mo., 973..........D 3 70
Mayville, N. Y., 1,492..........A 6 77
Mayville, N. Dak., 1,790..........R 4 79
Mayville, Wis., 3,010..........K 9 93
Maywood, Calif., 13,292..........C11 52
Maywood, Ill., 27,473..........A 2 58
Maywood, N. J., 8,667..........B 2 75
Meade, Kans., 1,763..........B 4 61
Meaderville, Mont., 250..........D 4 71
Meadowview, Va., 722..........E 2 90
Meadville, Pa., 18,972..........B 2 83
Mebane, N. C., 2,068..........G 2 78
Mechanic Falls, Me., □2,061..........C 7 64
Mechanicsburg, Ohio, 1,920..........C 5 80
Mechanisburg, Pa., 6,786..........H 5 83
Mechanicsville, N. Y., 7,385..........N 5 77
Media, Pa., 5,726..........M 6 83
Medfield, Mass., □4,549..........J 4 66
Medford, Mass., 66,113..........K 3 66
Medford, Okla., 1,305..........G 1 81
Medford, Oreg., 17,305..........E 5 82
Medford, Wis., 2,799..........F 5 93
Medical Lake, Wash., 4,488..........H 3 91
Medicine Bow, Wyo., 328..........F 4 94
Medicine Lake, Mont., 454..........M 2 71
Medicine Lodge, Kans., 2,288..........D 4 61
Medina, N. Y., 6,179..........D 4 77
Medina, N. Dak., 564..........M 6 79
Medina, Ohio, 5,097..........G 3 80

	Index Ref.	Plate No.
Medina, Tenn., 690	D 3	86
Medway, Mass., □3,744	J 4	66
Meeker, Colo., 1,658	D 2	53
Meeteetse, Wyo., 404	D 1	94
Melbourne, Fla., 4,223	F 3	55
Melcher, Iowa, 898	G 6	60
Mellen, Wis., 1,306	E 3	93
Melrose, Mass., 26,988	K 3	66
Melrose, Minn., 2,106	D 5	68
Melrose, N. Mex., 936	F 4	76
Melrose Park, Ill., 13,366	A 2	58
Melstone, Mont., 195	J 4	71
Melville, La., 1,901	G 5	63
Melvindale, Mich., 9,483	B 7	67
Memphis, Mo., 2,035	H 2	70
Memphis, Tenn., 396,000	B 4	86
Memphis, Tex., 3,810	D 3	87
Mena, Ark., 4,445	B 4	51
Menan, Idaho, 430	F 6	57
Menands, N. Y., 2,453	N 5	77
Menard, Tex., 2,685	E 4	87
Menasha, Wis., 12,385	K 7	93
Mendenhall, Miss., 1,539	E 7	69
Mendota, Ill., 5,129	D 2	58
Menlo Park, Calif., 13,587	J 3	52
Menno, S. Dak., 868	P 7	85
Menominee, Mich., 11,151	B 3	67
Menomonee Falls, Wis., 2,469	K 9	93
Menomonie, Wis., 8,245	C 6	93
Mentor, Ohio, 2,383	H 2	80
Merced, Calif., 15,278	E 6	52
Mercedes, Tex., 10,081	F12	87
Merchantville, N. J., 4,183	C 4	75
Meredith, N. H., □2,222	C 4	74
Meriden, Conn., 44,088	D 2	54
Meridian, Idaho, 1,810	B 6	57
Meridian, Miss., 41,893	G 6	69
Merigold, Miss., 682	C 3	69
Merion Station, Pa., 2,000	M 6	83
Merkel, Tex., 2,338	E 5	87
Merrill, Oreg., 835	F 5	82
Merrill, Wis., 8,951	G 5	93
Merrimack, N. H., □1,908	C 6	74
Merryville, La., 1,383	C 5	63
Mesa, Ariz., 16,790	D 5	50
Mesilla Park, N. Mex., 2,000	C 6	76
Mesquite, Nev., 540	G 6	73
Methuen, Mass., 24,447	K 2	66
Metropolis, Ill., 6,093	E 6	58
Metter, Ga., 2,091	H 6	56
Metuchen, N. J., 9,879	E 2	75
Mexia, Tex., 6,627	H 6	87
Mexico, Me., □4,762	B 6	64
Mexico, Mo., 11,623	J 4	70
Mexico, N. Y., 1,398	H 4	77
Meyersdale, Pa., 3,137	D 6	83
Miami, Ariz., 4,329	E 5	50
Miami, Fla., 249,276	F 6	55
Miami, Okla., 11,801	N 1	81
Miami Beach, Fla., 46,282	F 6	55
Miamisburg, Ohio, 6,329	B 6	80
Miami Shores, Fla., 5,086	F 6	55
Miami Springs, Fla., 5,108	F 6	55
Michigan, N. Dak., 486	O 3	79
Michigan City, Ind., 28,395	C 1	59
Midas, Nev., 100	E 1	73
Middleboro, Mass., □10,164	L 5	66
Middlebourne, W. Va., 741	E 1	92
Middleburg, Va., 663	J 3	90
Middlebury, Conn., □3,310	C 2	54
Middlebury, Vt., 3,614	A 2	89
Middleport, N. Y., 1,641	C 4	77
Middleport, Ohio, 3,446	G 5	80
Middlesboro, Ky., 14,482	K 7	62
Middlesex, N. J., 5,943	E 2	75
Middleton, Idaho, 496	B 6	57
Middleton, Tenn., 362	D 4	86
Middleton, Wis., 2,110	G 9	93
Middletown, Conn., 29,711	E 2	54
Middletown, Del., 1,755	M 3	65
Middletown, Ind., 1,731	F 4	59
Middletown, Md., 936	E 3	65
Middletown, N. Y., 22,586	B 1	77
Middletown, Ohio, 33,695	A 6	80
Middletown, Pa., 9,184	J 5	83
Middletown, R. I., □7,382	J 6	66
Midland, Md., 889	C 7	65
Midland, Mich., 14,285	E 5	67
Midland, Pa., 6,491	A 4	83
Midland, Tex., 21,713	C 6	87
Midland Park, N. J., 5,164	B 1	75
Midlothian, Ill., 3,216	B 2	58
Midvale, Utah, 3,996	B 3	88
Midway, Fla., 500	B 1	55
Midway, Ky., 950	H 4	62
Midway, Utah, 711	C 3	88
Midwest, Wyo., 2,000	F 2	94
Midwest City, Okla., 10,166	H 4	81
Milaca, Minn., 1,917	E 5	68
Milan, Ind., 1,014	G 6	59
Milan, Mich., 2,768	F 6	67
Milan, Mo., 1,972	F 2	70
Milan, Tenn., 4,938	D 3	86
Milbank, S. Dak., 2,982	R 3	85
Miles City, Mont., 9,243	L 4	71
Milford, Conn., □26,870	C 4	54
Milford, Del., 5,179	N 5	65
Milford, Iowa, 1,375	C 2	60
Milford, Me., □1,435	F 6	64
Milford, Mass., □15,442	H 4	66
Milford, Mich., 1,924	F 6	67
Milford, N. H., □4,159	C 6	74
Milford, Ohio, 2,448	B 7	80
Milford, Utah, 1,673	A 5	88
Millbridge, Me., 1,365	H 6	64
Millbrook, N. Y., 1,568	N 7	77
Millburn, N. J., □14,560	E 2	75
Millbury, Mass., □8,347	G 4	66
Mill City, Oreg., 1,792	E 3	82
Milledgeville, Ga., 8,835	F 4	56
Millen, Ga., 3,449	J 5	56
Miller, S. Dak., 1,916	L 4	85
Millersburg, Ky., 828	J 4	62
Millersburg, Ohio, 2,398	F 4	80
Millersburg, Pa., 2,861	J 4	83
Millington, Tenn., 4,696	B 4	86
Millinocket, Me., □5,890	F 4	64
Mills, Wyo., 866	F 3	94
Millsboro, Del., 470	N 6	65
Milltown, Mont., 750	C 4	71
Milltown, N. J., 3,786	E 3	75
Millvale, Pa., 7,287	B 7	83
Mill Valley, Calif., 7,331	H 2	52
Millville, Del., 270	O 6	65
Millville, N. J., 16,041	C 5	75
Millwood, Wash., 1,240	H 3	91
Milnor, N. Dak., 674	R 7	79
Milo, Me., □2,898	F 5	64
Milton, Del., 1,321	N 5	65
Milton, Fla., 2,040	B 6	55
Milton, Mass., □22,395	K 3	66
Milton, N. H., 1,510	D 5	74
Milton, Oreg., 2,362	J 2	82
Milton, Pa., 8,578	J 3	83
Milton, Vt., 739	A 1	89
Milton, Wash., 1,374	C 3	91
Milton, W. Va., 1,552	B 4	92
Milton, Wis., 1,549	J10	93
Milwaukee, Wis., 637,392	L 9	93
Milwaukie, Oreg., 5,253	B 2	82
Mina, Nev., 274	C 4	73
Minatare, Nebr., 890	A 3	72
Minden, La., 9,787	D 1	63
Minden, Nebr., 2,120	F 4	72
Minden, Nev., 250	B 4	73
Mineola, N. Y., 14,831	D 2	77
Mineola, Tex., 3,626	J 5	87
Mineral, Va., 414	J 4	90
Mineral Point, Wis., 2,285	F10	93
Mineral Wells, Tex., 7,801	G 5	87
Minersville, Pa., 7,783	K 4	83
Minersville, Utah, 593	A 5	88
Minerva, Ohio, 3,280	H 4	80
Mingo Jc., Ohio, 4,464	J 5	80
Minneapolis, Kans., 1,801	E 2	61
Minneapolis, Minn., 521,718	E 6	68
Minneota, Minn., 1,274	C 6	68
Minnewaukan, N. Dak., 443	M 3	79
Minonk, Ill., 1,955	D 3	58
Minot, N. Dak., 22,032	H 3	79
Minster, Ohio, 1,728	B 5	80
Minto, N. Dak., 592	R 3	79
Minturn, Colo., 509	G 3	53
Mishawaka, Ind., 32,913	E 1	59
Mission, Tex., 10,765	F12	87
Missoula, Mont., 22,485	C 4	71
Missouri Valley, Iowa, 3,546	B 5	60
Mitchell, Ind., 3,245	E 7	59
Mitchell, Nebr., 2,101	A 3	72
Mitchell, S. Dak., 12,123	N 6	85
Moab, Utah, 1,274	E 5	88
Moberly, Mo., 13,115	H 4	70
Mobile, Ala., 129,009	C 9	49
Mobridge, S. Dak., 3,753	J 2	85
Mocksville, N. C., 1,909	D 3	78
Modesto, Calif., 17,389	D 6	52
Mogadore, Ohio, 1,818	H 3	80
Mohall, N. Dak., 1,073	G 2	79
Mohawk, N. Y., 3,196	L 4	77
Molalla, Oreg., 1,497	E 2	82
Moline, Ill., 37,397	C 2	58
Momence, Ill., 2,644	F 2	58
Monaca, Pa., 7,415	B 4	83
Monahans, Tex., 6,311	B 6	87
Moncks Corner, S. C., 1,818	H 5	84
Mondovi, Wis., 2,285	C 6	93
Monero, N. Mex., 207	C 2	76
Monessen, Pa., 17,896	C 5	83
Monett, Mo., 4,771	E 9	70
Monette, Ark., 1,114	K 2	51
Monmouth, Ill., 10,193	C 3	58
Monmouth, Me., □1,683	D 7	64
Monmouth, Oreg., 1,956	D 3	82
Monon, Ind., 1,439	D 3	59
Monona, Iowa, 1,436	L 2	60
Monona, Wis., 2,544	H 9	93
Monongah, W. Va., 1,622	F 2	92
Monongahela, Pa., 8,922	B 5	83
Monroe, Ga., 4,542	E 3	56
Monroe, Iowa, 1,108	G 5	60
Monroe, La., 38,572	F 1	63
Monroe, Mich., 21,467	F 7	67
Monroe, N. Y., 1,753	B 1	77
Monroe, N. C., 10,140	E 5	78
Monroe, Utah, 1,214	B 5	88
Monroe, Wash., 1,556	D 3	91
Monroe, Wis., 7,037	G10	93
Monroe City, Mo., 2,093	J 3	70
Monroeville, Ala., 2,772	D 7	49
Monroeville, Ind., 1,150	H 3	59
Monrovia, Calif., 20,186	D10	52
Montague, Mass., □7,812	E 2	66
Monson, Mass., □6,125	E 4	66
Montclair, N. J., 43,297	E 2	75
Montebello, Calif., 21,735	C11	52
Montello, Nev., 350	G 1	73
Montello, Wis., 1,069	H 8	93
Monterey, Calif., 16,205	D 7	52
Monterey, Tenn., 2,043	L 2	86
Monterey Park, Calif., 20,395	C10	52
Montesano, Wash., 2,328	B 3	91
Montevallo, Ala., 2,150	E 4	49
Montevideo, Minn., 5,459	C 6	68
Monte Vista, Colo., 3,272	G 7	53
Montezuma, Ga., 2,921	E 6	56
Montezuma, Ind., 1,220	C 5	59
Montezuma, Iowa, 1,460	J 5	60
Montezuma, N. Mex., 1,200	D 3	76
MONTGOMERY, Ala., 106,525	F 6	49
Montgomery, Minn., 1,913	E 6	68
Montgomery, W. Va., 3,484	D 4	92
Montgomery, Vt., □1,091	B 1	89
Montgomery City, Mo., 1,679	J 4	70
Monticello, Ark., 4,501	G 6	51
Monticello, Fla., 2,264	C 1	55
Monticello, Ga., 1,918	E 4	56
Monticello, Ill., 2,612	E 3	58
Monticello, Ind., 3,467	D 3	59
Monticello, Iowa, 2,888	L 4	60
Monticello, Ky., 2,934	H 7	62
Monticello, Me., □1,284	H 3	64
Monticello, Minn., 1,231	E 5	68
Monticello, Miss., 1,382	D 7	69
Monticello, N. Y., 4,223	L 7	77
Monticello, Utah, 1,172	E 6	88
Montour Falls, N. Y., 1,457	G 6	77
Montoursville, Pa., 3,293	J 3	83
Montpelier, Idaho, 2,682	G 7	57
Montpelier, Ind., 1,826	G 3	59
Montpelier, Ohio, 3,867	A 2	80
MONTPELIER, Vt., 8,599	B 2	89
Montreal, Wis., 1,439	F 3	93
Montrose, Colo., 4,964	D 6	53
Montville, Conn., □4,766	G 3	54
Moorcroft, Wyo., 517	H 1	94
Moorefield, W. Va., 1,405	J 2	92
Moorestown, N. J., 9,175	D 4	75
Mooresville, Ind., 2,264	E 5	59
Mooresville, N. C., 7,120	D 3	78
Moorhead, Minn., 14,870	B 4	68
Moorhead, Miss., 1,749	D 4	69
Mooringsport, La., 709	B 1	63
Moose Lake, Minn., 1,603	F 4	68
Moosic, Pa., 3,965	L 3	83
Moosup, Conn., 2,909	H 2	54
Mora, Minn., 2,018	E 5	68
Mora, N. Mex., 1,750	D 3	76
Moravia, N. Y., 1,480	H 5	77
Moreauville, La., 835	G 4	63
Morehead, Ky., 3,102	L 4	62
Morehead City, N. C., 5,144	M 5	78
Morehouse, Mo., 1,635	N 9	70
Morenci, Ariz., 6,541	F 5	50
Morenci, Mich., 1,983	E 7	67
Morgan, Utah, 1,064	C 2	88
Morgan City, La., 9,759	H 7	63
Morganfield, Ky., 3,257	B 5	62
Morganton, N. C., 8,311	B 3	78
Morgantown, Ky., 850	D 6	62
Morgantown, W. Va., 25,525	G 1	92
Morningside, Minn., 1,699	E 5	68
Morocco, Ind., 1,141	C 3	59
Moroni, Utah, 1,076	C 4	88
Morrill, Nebr., 849	A 3	72
Morrilton, Ark., 5,483	E 3	51
Morris, Ill., 6,926	E 2	58
Morris, Minn., 3,811	B 5	68
Morris, Okla., 1,122	L 3	81
Morrison, Ill., 3,531	C 2	58
Morristown, N. J., 17,124	D 2	75
Morristown, Tenn., 13,019	P 2	86
Morrisville, Pa., 6,787	N 5	83
Morrisville, Vt., 1,995	B 1	89
Morton, Ill., 3,693	D 3	58
Morton, Minn., 794	D 6	68
Morton, Miss., 1,664	E 6	69
Morton, Wash., 1,140	C 4	91
Morton Grove, Ill., 3,926	B 1	58
Mortons Gap, Ky., 1,081	C 6	62
Moscow, Idaho, 10,593	A 3	57
Mosinee, Wis., 1,453	G 6	93
Mosquero, N. Mex., 583	F 3	76
Moss Point, Miss., 3,872	G10	69
Mott, N. Dak., 1,583	F 7	79
Moulton, Iowa, 985	H 7	60
Moultrie, Ga., 11,639	E 8	56
Mound, Minn., 2,061	E 6	68
Mound Bayou, Miss., 1,328	C 3	69
Mound City, Ill., 2,167	D 6	58
Mound City, Mo., 1,412	B 2	70
Mounds, Ill., 2,001	D 6	58
Moundsville, W. Va., 14,772	K 6	92
Moundville, Ala., 901	C 5	49
Mountainair, N. Mex., 1,418	C 4	76
Mountain City, Nev., 180	F 1	73
Mountain City, Tenn., 1,405	S 2	86
Mountain Grove, Mo., 3,106	H 8	70
Mountain Home, Ark., 2,217	F 1	51
Mountain Home, Idaho, 1,887	C 6	57
Mountain Iron, Minn., 1,377	F 3	68
Mountain Lake, Minn., 1,733	D 7	68
Mountain Lake Park, 891	A 8	65
Mountain View, Calif., 6,563	K 3	52
Mountain View, Colo., 878	J 3	53
Mount Airy, Md., 1,061	F 3	65
Mount Airy, N. C., 7,192	D 1	78
Mount Angel, Oreg., 1,315	E 2	82
Mount Ayr, Iowa, 1,793	E 7	60
Mount Carmel, Ill., 8,732	F 5	58
Mount Carmel, Pa., 14,222	K 4	83
Mount Carroll, Ill., 1,950	D 1	58
Mount Clemens, Mich., 17,027	G 6	67
Mount Desert, Me., □1,776	G 7	64
Mount Dora, Fla., 3,028	E 3	55
Mount Gilead, Ohio, 2,351	E 4	80
Mount Healthy, Ohio, 5,533	B 9	80
Mount Holly, N. J., 8,206	D 4	75
Mount Holly, N. C., 2,241	D 4	78
Mount Hope, W. Va., 2,588	D 5	92
Mount Horeb, Wis., 1,716	G 9	93
Mount Jackson, Va., 732	G 3	90
Mount Joy, Pa., 3,006	K 5	83
Mount Kisco, N. Y., 5,907	D 1	77
Mount Lebanon, Pa., □26,604	B 7	83
Mount Morris, Ill., 2,709	D 1	58
Mount Morris, Mich., 2,890	F 5	67
Mount Morris, N. Y., 3,450	E 5	77
Mount Olive, Ill., 2,401	D 4	58
Mount Olive, Miss., 827	E 7	69
Mount Olive, N. C., 3,732	K 4	78
Mount Oliver, Pa., 6,646	B 5	83
Mount Penn, Pa., 3,635	L 5	83
Mount Pleasant, Del., 87	M 2	65
Mount Pleasant, Iowa, 5,843	K 7	60
Mount Pleasant, Mich., 11,393	E 5	67
Mount Pleasant, Pa., 5,883	D 5	83
Mount Pleasant, S. C., 1,857	J 6	84
Mount Pleasant, Tenn., 2,931	G 3	86
Mount Pleasant, Tex., 6,342	K 4	87
Mount Pleasant, Utah, 2,030	C 4	88
Mount Rainier, Md., 10,989	G 5	65
Mount Savage, Md., 2,094	C 7	65
Mount Shasta, Calif., 1,909	C 2	52
Mount Sterling, Ill., 2,246	C 4	58
Mount Sterling, Ky., 5,294	K 4	62
Mount Union, Pa., 4,690	G 5	83
Mount Vernon, Ala., 2,300	B 8	49
Mount Vernon, Ill., 15,600	E 5	58
Mount Vernon, Ind., 6,150	B 9	59
Mount Vernon, Iowa, 2,320	L 5	60
Mount Vernon, Ky., 1,106	J 6	62
Mount Vernon, Mo., 2,057	E 8	70
Mount Vernon, N. Y., 71,899	D 2	77
Mount Vernon, Ohio, 12,185	E 5	80
Mount Vernon, Wash., 5,230	C 2	91
Mulberry, Ark., 952	B 2	51
Mulberry, Fla., 2,024	E 4	55
Mulberry, Kans., 779	H 4	61
Mullan, Idaho, 2,036	C 2	57
Mullens, W. Va., 3,470	D 5	92
Mullins, S. C., 4,916	K 3	84
Multnomah, Oreg., 5,000	E 2	82
Muncie, Ind., 58,479	G 4	59
Munford, Tenn., 976	B 4	86
Munfordville, Ky., 894	F 6	62
Munhall, Pa., 16,437	C 7	83
Munising, Mich., 4,339	F 5	67
Munsey Park, N. Y., 2,048	D 2	77
Munster, Ind., 4,753	B 1	59
Murdo, S. Dak., 739	H 6	85
Murfreesboro, Ark., 1,079	C 5	51
Murfreesboro, N. C., 2,140	M 2	78
Murfreesboro, Tenn., 13,052	J 3	86
Murphy, N. C., 2,433	C 9	78
Murphysboro, Ill., 9,241	D 6	58
Murray, Ky., 6,035	D 3	62
Murray, Utah, 9,006	C 3	88
Muscatine, Iowa, 19,041	L 6	60
Muscle Shoals, Ala., 1,937	C 1	49
Muskegon, Mich., 48,429	C 5	67
Muskegon Heights, Mich., 18,828	C 5	67
Muskogee, Okla., 37,289	M 3	81
Myrtle Creek, Oreg., 1,781	D 4	82
Myrtle Beach, S. C., 3,345	L 4	84
Myrtle Point, Oreg., 2,033	C 4	82
Mystic, Conn., 2,266	H 3	54
Mystic, Iowa, 1,233	H 7	60
Naches, Wash., 633	E 4	91
Naco, Ariz., 400	F 7	50
Nacogdoches, Tex., 12,327	J 6	87
Nambe, N. Mex., 500	D 3	76
Nameoki, Ill.	C 5	58
Nampa, Idaho, 16,185	B 6	57
Nanticoke, Md., 650	L 7	65
Nanticoke, Pa., 20,160	K 3	83
Nantucket, Mass., □3,484	O 7	66
Nanty Glo, Pa., 5,425	E 5	83
Napa, Calif., 13,579	C 5	52
Naperville, Ill., 7,013	E 2	58
Naples, Fla., 1,465	E 5	55
Napoleon, N. Dak., 1,070	L 6	79
Napoleon, Ohio, 5,335	B 3	80
Napoleonville, La., 1,260	H 7	63
Nappanee, Ind., 3,393	F 2	59
Narberth, Pa., 5,407	M 6	83
Narragansett, R. I., □2,288	J 7	66
Narrows, Va., 2,520	C 6	90
Nashua, Iowa, 1,609	J 3	60
Nashua, Mont., 691	K 2	71
Nashua, N. H., 34,669	C 6	74
Nashville, Ark., 3,548	C 6	51
Nashville, Ga., 3,414	F 8	56
Nashville, Ill., 2,432	D 5	58
Nashville, Mich., 1,374	D 6	67
NASHVILLE, Tenn., 174,307	H 2	86
Nashwauk, Minn., 2,029	E 3	68
Nasonville, R. I., 677	H 5	66
Nassau, Del., 120	O 6	65
Natchez, Miss., 22,740	B 7	69
Natchitoches, La., 9,914	D 3	63
Natick, Mass., □19,838	J 3	66
Natick, R. I., 2,000	H 6	66
National City, Calif., 21,199	J11	52
Naugatuck, Conn., 17,455	C 3	54
Navarre, Ohio, 1,763	H 4	80
Navasota, Tex., 5,188	J 7	87
Nazareth, Pa., 5,830	M 4	83
Nebraska City, Nebr., 6,872	J 4	72
Neche, N. Dak., 615	R 2	79

Index Ref. Plate No.

Needham, Mass., □16,313...R10 66
Needles, Calif., 4,051...L 9 52
Neenah, Wis., 12,437...K 7 93
Negaunee, Mich., 6,472...B 2 67
Neihart, Mont., 289...F 4 71
Neillsville, Wis., 2,663...E 6 93
Nekoosa, Wis., 2,352...G 7 93
Neligh, Nebr., 1,822...F 2 72
Nelson, Nebr., 806...F 4 72
Nelsonville, Ohio, 4,845...F 7 80
Neodesha, Kans., 3,723...G 4 61
Neon, Ky., 1,055...M 6 62
Neosho, Mo., 5,790...D 9 70
Nephi, Utah, 2,990...C 4 88
Neptune, N. J., 3,073...E 3 75
Neptune Beach, Fla., 1,767...E 1 55
Nesquehoning, Pa., 4,034...L 4 83
Ness City, Kans., 1,612...C 3 61
Nettleton, Ark., 1,382...J 2 51
Nettleton, Miss., 1,204...G 2 69
Nevada, Iowa, 3,763...G 5 60
Nevada, Mo., 8,009...D 7 70
Nevada City, Calif., 2,505...D 4 52
New Albany, Ind., 29,436...F 8 59
New Albany, Miss., 3,680...F 2 69
Newark, Ark., 913...H 2 51
Newark, Del., 6,731...M 2 65
Newark, N. J., 438,776...E 2 75
Newark, N. Y., 10,295...G 4 77
Newark, Ohio, 34,275...F 5 80
Newaygo, Mich., 1,385...D 5 67
New Baltimore, Mich., 2,043...G 6 67
New Bedford, Mass., 109,189...L 6 66
Newberg, Oreg., 3,946...E 2 82
New Bern, N. C., 15,812...L 4 78
Newbern, Tenn., 1,734...C 2 86
Newberry, Mich., 2,802...D 2 67
Newberry, S. C., 7,546...E 3 84
New Boston, Ohio, 4,754...E 8 80
New Braunfels, Tex., 12,210...F 8 87
New Bremen, Ohio, 1,546...B 5 80
New Brighton, Pa., 9,535...B 4 83
New Britain, Conn., 73,726...D 2 54
New Brockton, Ala., 1,055...G 8 49
New Brunswick, N. J., 38,811...E 3 75
Newburg, Mo., 949...J 7 70
Newburgh, Ind., 1,324...C 9 59
Newburgh, N. Y., 31,956...C 1 77
Newburgh Hts., O., 3,689...H 9 80
Newbury, Vt., □1,667...C 2 89
Newburyport, Mass., 14,111...L 1 66
New Canaan, Conn., □8,001...A 4 54
New Castle, Del., 5,396...M 2 65
New Castle, Ind., 18,271...G 5 59
New Castle, Pa., 48,834...B 3 83
Newcastle, Wyo., 3,395...H 2 94
Newcomerstown, Ohio, 4,514...G 5 80
New Cumberland, Pa., 6,204...J 5 83
New Cumberland, W. Va., 2,119...K 4 92
Newdale, Idaho, 312...G 6 57
Newell, S. Dak., 784...C 4 85
Newell, W. Va., 2,101...K 4 92
New England, N. Dak., 1,117...E 6 79
Newfane, Vt., 156...B 5 89
New Franklin, Mo., 1,060...G 4 70
New Glarus, Wis., 1,224...G10 93
New Gloucester, Me., □2,628...C 8 64
New Hampton, Iowa, 3,323...J 2 60
New Harmony, Ind., 1,360...B 8 59
New Hartford, N. Y., 1,947...K 4 77
New Haven, Conn., 164,443...D 3 54
New Haven, Ind., 2,336...H 2 59
New Haven, Mo., 1,009...K 5 70
New Holland, Ga., 1,618...E 2 56
New Holstein, Wis., 1,831...L 8 93
New Hyde Park, N. Y., 7,349...D 2 77
New Iberia, La., 16,467...G 6 63
Newington, Conn., □9,110...E 2 54
New Ipswich, N. H., □1,147...C 6 74
New Kensington, Pa., 25,146...C 4 83
Newkirk, Okla., 2,201...J 1 81
New Lexington, Ohio, 4,233...F 6 80
New Lisbon, Wis., 1,482...F 8 93
New London, Conn., 30,551...G 3 54
New London, Iowa, 1,510...L 7 60
New London, Mo., 858...J 3 70
New London, N. H., □1,484...C 5 74
New London, Ohio, 2,023...H 2 80
New London, Wis., 4,922...J 7 93
New Madrid, Mo., 2,726...O 9 70
Newman Grove, Nebr., 1,004...G 3 72
Newmarket, N. H., □2,709...E 5 74
New Market, Va., 701...G 3 90
New Martinsville, W. Va., 4,084...E 1 92
New Miami, Ohio, 1,860...A 7 80
New Milford, Conn., □5,799...B 2 54
New Milford, N. J., 6,006...B 1 75
Newnan, Ga., 8,218...C 4 56
New Orleans, La., 570,445...L 7 63
New Paltz, N. Y., 2,285...M 7 77
New Philadelphia, Ohio, 12,948...G 5 80
New Plymouth, Idaho, 942...B 6 57
Newport, Ark., 6,254...H 2 51
Newport, Del., 1,171...M 2 65
Newport, Ky., 31,044...J 2 62
Newport, Me., □2,190...E 6 64
Newport, N. H., □5,131...B 5 74
Newport, Oreg., 3,241...C 3 82
Newport, R. I., 37,564...J 7 66
Newport, Tenn., 3,892...P 3 86
Newport, Vt., 5,217...C 1 89
Newport, Wash., 1,385...H 2 91
Newport Beach, Calif., 12,120...D11 52
Newport Center, Vt., 235...C 1 89
Newport News, Va., 42,358...M 7 90
New Port Richey, Fla., 1,512...D 3 55
New Prague, Minn., 1,915...E 6 68
New Richmond, Ohio, 1,960...B 8 80
New Richmond, Wis., 2,886...B 5 93
New Roads, La., 2,818...H 5 63
New Rochelle, N. Y., 59,725...D 2 77
New Rockford, N. Dak., 2,185...N 4 79
New Salem, N. Dak., 942...H 6 79
New Sharon, Iowa, 1,089...H 6 60
New Smyrna Beach, Fla., 5,775...F 2 55
New Straitsville, Ohio, 1,122...F 6 80
Newton, Ill., 2,780...E 5 58
Newton, Iowa, 11,723...G 5 60
Newton, Kans., 11,590...E 3 61
Newton, Mass., 81,994...K 3 66
Newton, Miss., 2,912...F 6 99
Newton, N. H., □1,173...D 6 74
Newton, N. J., 5,781...D 1 75
Newton, N. C., 6,039...C 3 78
Newton, Utah, 497...B 2 88
Newton Falls, Ohio, 4,451...J 3 80
New Ulm, Minn., 9,348...D 6 68
New Windsor, Md., 707...F 2 65
New York (greater), N. Y., 7,891,957...C 2 77
New York Mills, N. Y., 3,366...K 4 77
Nezperce, Idaho, 543...B 3 57
Niagara, Wis., 2,022...K 4 93
Niagara Falls, N. Y., 90,872...C 4 77
Niceville, Fla., 2,497...C 6 55
Nicholasville, Ky., 3,406...H 5 62
Nickerson, Kans., 1,013...E 3 61
Niles, Ill., 3,587...A 1 58
Niles, Mich., 13,145...C 7 67
Niles, Ohio, 16,773...J 3 80
Ninety-Six, S. C., 1,556...D 3 84
Niota, Tenn., 956...M 3 86
Nitro, W. Va., 3,314...C 4 92
Nixon, Tex., 1,875...G 8 87
Noank, Conn., 1,149...G 3 54
Noblesville, Ind., 6,567...F 4 59
Nocona, Tex., 3,022...G 4 87
Nogales, Ariz., 6,153...E 7 50
Nokomis, Ill., 2,544...D 4 58
Nome, Alaska Territory, 1,852...E 1 95
Noonan, N. Dak., 551...D 2 79
Nora Springs, Iowa, 1,257...H 2 60
Norborne, Mo., 1,114...E 4 70
Norfield, Miss., 123...C 8 69
Norfolk, Nebr., 11,335...G 2 72
Norfolk, Va., 213,513...M 7 90
Normal, Ill., 9,772...E 3 58
Norman, Okla., 27,006...H 4 81
Normandy, Mo., 2,306...P 3 70
Noroton Heights, Conn., 3,918...A 4 54
Norridgewock, Me., □1,784...D 6 64
Norristown, Pa., 38,126...M 5 83
North, S. C., 954...F 4 84
North Adams, Mass., 21,567...B 2 63
Northampton, Mass., 29,063...D 3 66
Northampton, Pa., 9,332...M 4 83
North Andover, Mass., □8,485...K 2 66
North Arlington, N. J., 15,970...B 2 75
North Atlanta, Ga., 5,930...D 3 56
North Attleboro, Mass., □12,146...J 5 66
North Augusta, S. C., 3,659...E 4 84
North Baltimore, Ohio, 2,771...C 3 80
North Bellevernon, Pa., 3,147...C 5 83
North Bend, Nebr., 906...H 3 72
North Bend, Oreg., 6,099...C 4 82
North Bend, Wash., 787...D 3 91
North Bennington, Vt., 1,327...A 5 89
North Bergen, N. J., □41,560...B 2 75
North Berwick, Me., □1,655...B 9 64
North Bonneville, Wash., 564...C 5 91
North Braddock, Pa., 14,724...C 7 83
North Brentwood, Md., 833...G 5 65
Northbridge, Mass., □10,476...H 4 66
North Canton, Ohio, 4,032...H 4 80
North Chicago, Ill., 8,628...F 1 58
North College Hill, Ohio, 7,921...B 9 80
North Collins, N. Y., 1,325...C 5 77
North Conway, N. H., 1,200...D 3 74
North East, Md., 1,517...L 2 65
North East, Pa., 4,247...C 1 83
Northfield, Minn., 7,487...E 6 68
Northfield, N. H., □1,561...C 5 74
Northfield, N. J., 3,498...D 5 75
Northfield, Vt., 2,262...B 2 89
North Fond du Lac, Wis., 2,291...K 8 93
North Grosvenor Dale, Conn., 2,232...H 1 54
North Haven, Conn., □9,444...D 3 54
North Judson, Ind., 1,705...D 2 59
North Kansas City, Mo., 3,886...C 4 70
North Las Vegas, Nev., 3,875...F 6 73
North Liberty, Ind., 1,165...E 1 59
North Little Rock, Ark., 44,097...F 4 51
North Manchester, Ind., 3,977...F 3 977
North Mankato, Minn., 4,788...D 6 68
North Miami, Fla., 10,734...F 6 55
North Muskegon, Mich., 2,424...C 5 67
North Ogden, Utah, 1,105...C 2 88
North Olmsted, Ohio, 6,604...G 3 80
North Pelham, N. Y., 5,046...D 2 77
North Plainfield, N. J., 12,766...E 2 75
North Platte, Nebr., 15,433...D 3 72
Northport, Ala., 3,885...C 4 49
Northport, N. Y., 3,859...E 2 77
North Powder, Oreg., 403...K 2 82
North Royalton, Ohio, 3,939...G 3 80
North Sacramento, Calif., 6,029...D 4 52
North Saint Paul, Minn., 4,248...F 5 68
North Scituate, R. I., 1,000...H 5 66
North Syracuse, N. Y., 3,356...H 4 77
North Tarrytown, N. Y., 8,740...D 2 77
North Tazewell, Va., 816...C 3 90
North Tiverton, R. I., 4,000...K 6 66
North Tonawanda, N. Y., 24,731...C 4 77
North Troy, Vt., 1,075...C 1 89
Northumberland, N. H., □2,779...C 2 74
Northumberland, Pa., 4,207...J 4 83
North Vernon, Ind., 3,488...F 6 59
Northville, Mich., 3,240...F 6 67
North Walpole, N. H., 1,000...B 5 74
North Westminster, Vt., 404...B 4 89
North Weymouth, Mass., 700...D 8 66
North Wilkesboro, N. C., 4,379...C 2 78
Northwood, Iowa, 1,767...G 2 60
Northwood, N. Dak., 1,182...P 4 79
Norton, Kans., 3,060...C 2 61
Norton, Va., 4,315...C 2 90
Nortonville, Ky., 909...B 6 62
Norwalk, Calif., 6,300...C11 52
Norwalk, Conn., 49,460...B 4 54
Norwalk, Ohio, 9,775...E 3 80
Norway, Me., □3,811...B 7 64
Norway, Mich., 3,258...B 3 67
Norwich, Conn., 23,429...G 2 54
Norwich, N. Y., 8,816...J 5 77
Norwich, Vt., □1,532...C 3 89
Norwood, Mass., 16,632...K 4 66
Norwood, N. Y., 1,995...L 1 77
Norwood, N. C., 1,735...E 4 78
Norwood, Ohio, 35,001...D 6 80
Norwood, R. I., 2,300...J 6 66
Norwood, Pa., 5,246...M 7 83
Notasulga, Ala., 816...G 5 49
Nowata, Okla., 3,965...L 1 81
Nutley, N. J., 26,992...B 2 75
Nutrioso, Ariz., 100...F 5 50
Nutter Fort, W. Va., 2,285...F 2 92
Nyack, N. Y., 5,889...C 2 77
Nyssa, Oreg., 2,525...K 4 82
Oak Creek, Colo., 1,488...F 2 53
Oakdale, Calif., 4,064...E 6 52
Oakdale, La., 5,598...E 5 63
Oakdale, Tenn., 718...M 3 86
Oakes, N. Dak., 1,774...O 7 79
Oakesdale, Wash., 576...H 3 91
Oakfield, N. Y., 1,781...D 4 77
Oakglen, Ill., 3,840...B 3 58
Oak Grove, La., 1,796...H 1 63
Oakharbor, Ohio, 2,370...D 2 80
Oak Hill, Ohio, 1,615...E 8 80
Oak Hill, W. Va., 4,518...D 5 92
Oakland, Calif., 384,575...J 2 52
Oakland, Iowa, 1,296...C 6 60
Oakland, Me., □2,679...D 5 64
Oakland, Md., 1,640...A 8 65
Oakland, Nebr., 1,456...H 3 72
Oakland, Oreg., 829...D 4 82
Oakland, R. I., 226...H 5 66
Oakland Beach, R. I....J 6 66
Oakland City, Ind., 3,539...C 8 59
Oaklawn, Ill., 8,751...B 2 58
Oakley, Idaho, 684...D 7 57
Oakley, Kans., 1,915...B 2 61
Oaklyn, N. J., 4,889...B 3 75
Oakman, Ala., 1,022...D 3 49
Oakmont, Pa., 7,264...M 7 83
Oak Park, Ill., 63,529...B 2 58
Oakridge, Oreg., 1,562...E 4 82
Oak Ridge, Tenn., 30,229...N 2 86
Oakwood, Ohio, 9,691...B 6 80
Oatman, Ariz., 600...A 3 50
Oberlin, Kans., 2,019...B 2 61
Oberlin, La., 1,544...E 5 63
Oberlin, Ohio, 7,062...F 3 80
Ocala, Fla., 11,744...D 2 55
Ocean City, Md., 1,234...O 7 65
Ocean City, N. J., 6,040...D 5 75
Oceanport, N. J., 7,588...E 3 75
Oceanside, Calif., 12,881...H10 52
Ocean Springs, Miss., 3,058...G10 69
Ocean View, Del., 450...O 6 65
Ocilla, Ga., 2,697...F 7 56
Oconomowoc, Wis., 5,345...J 9 93
Oconto, Wis., 5,055...L 6 93
Oconto Falls, Wis., 2,050...K 6 93
Odebolt, Iowa, 1,279...C 4 60
Odessa, Del., 467...M 3 65
Odessa, Mo., 1,969...E 5 70
Odessa, Tex., 29,495...B 6 87
Odessa, Wash., 1,127...G 3 91
Odin, Ill., 1,341...D 5 58
Odon, Ind., 1,177...C 7 59
Oelwein, Iowa, 7,858...K 3 60
O'Fallon, Ill., 3,022...B 6 58
Ogallala, Nebr., 3,456...C 3 72
Ogden, Iowa, 1,486...E 4 60
Ogden, Utah, 57,112...C 2 88
Ogdensburg, N. Y., 16,166...K 1 77
Oglesby, Ill., 3,922...D 2 58
Oglethorpe, Ga., 1,204...D 6 56
Oil City, Pa., 19,581...C 3 83
Oildale, Calif., 16,615...F 7 52
Oilton, Okla., 1,109...J 2 81
Ojo Caliente, N. Mex....D 2 76
Okanogan, Wash., 2,013...F 2 91
Okeechobee, Fla., 1,849...F 4 55
Okemah, Okla., 3,454...K 4 81
OKLAHOMA CITY, Okla., 243,504...H 4 81
Okmulgee, Okla., 18,317...K 3 81
Okolona, Miss., 2,167...G 2 69
Ola, Ark., 880...D 3 51
Olathe, Colo., 810...D 5 53
Olathe, Kans., 5,593...H 3 61
Old Bennington, Vt., 198...A 5 89
Old Forge, Pa., 9,749...L 3 83
Old Greenwich, Conn., 5,348...A 4 54
Old Hickory, Tenn., 10,000...H 2 86
Old Lyme, Conn., □2,141...F 3 54
Old Orchard Beach, Me., □4,707...C 8 64
Old Saybrook, Conn., □2,499...F 3 54
Old Town, Me., 8,261...F 6 64
Old Westbury, N. Y., 1,160...D 2 77
Olean, N. Y., 22,884...D 6 77
Olive Hill, Ky., 1,351...L 4 62
Olivette, Mo., 1,761...M 5 70
Olivia, Minn., 2,012...C 6 68
Olmos Park, Tex., 2,841...F 8 87
Olney, Ill., 8,612...E 5 58
Olney, Tex., 3,765...F 4 87
OLYMPIA, Wash., 15,819...C 3 91
Olyphant, Pa., 7,047...L 3 83
Omaha, Nebr., 251,117...J 3 72
Omak, Wash., 3,791...F 2 91
Omar, W. Va., 1,575...C 5 92
Omega, N. Mex., 30...A 4 76
Omro, Wis., 1,470...J 7 93
Onalaska, Wis., 2,561...D 8 93
Onancock, Va., 1,353...N 5 90
Onarga, Ill., 1,455...F 3 58
Onawa, Iowa, 3,498...A 4 60
Onaway, Mich., 1,421...E 3 67
Oneida, N. Y., 11,325...J 4 77
Oneida, Tenn., 1,304...N 1 86
O'Neill, Nebr., 3,027...F 2 72
Oneonta, Ala., 2,802...E 3 49
Oneonta, N. Y., 13,564...K 6 77
Onida, S. Dak., 822...J 4 85
Ontario, Calif., 22,872...D10 52
Ontario, N. Y., 800...F 4 77
Ontario, Oreg., 4,465...K 3 82
Ontonagon, Mich., 2,307...F 1 67
Oolitic, Ind., 1,125...E 7 59
Opelika, Ala., 12,295...H 5 49
Opelousas, La., 11,659...F 5 63
Opheim, Mont., 383...K 2 71
Opp, Ala., 5,240...F 8 49
Oradell, N. J., 3,665...B 1 75
Oran, Mo., 1,156...N 8 70
Orange, Calif., 10,027...D11 52
Orange, Conn., □3,032...C 3 54
Orange, Mass., □5,894...E 2 66
Orange, N. J., 38,037...E 2 75
Orange, Tex., 21,174...L 7 87
Orange, Va., 2,571...H 4 90
Orangeburg, S. C., 15,332...G 4 84
Orange City, Iowa, 2,166...A 2 60
Orangeville, Utah, 589...C 4 88
Orchard, Colo., 956...L 2 53
Orchard Park, N. Y., 2,054...C 5 77
Ord, Nebr., 2,239...F 3 72
Ordway, Colo., 1,290...M 6 53
Oregon, Ill., 3,205...D 1 58
Oregon, Mo., 870...B 3 70
Oregon, Wis., 1,341...H10 93
Oregon City, Oreg., 7,682...E 2 82
Orem, Utah, 8,351...C 3 88
Orlando, Fla., 52,367...F 3 55
Orleans, Ind., 1,531...D 7 59
Orleans, Vt., 1,261...C 1 89
Ormond, Fla., 3,418...E 2 55
Orofino, Idaho, 1,656...B 3 57
Orono, Me., □7,504...F 6 64
Oroville, Calif., 5,387...D 4 52
Oroville, Wash., 1,500...F 2 91
Orrington, Me., □1,895...F 6 64
Orrville, Ohio, 5,153...G 4 80
Orting, Wash., 1,299...C 3 91
Ortonville, Minn., 2,577...B 5 68
Osage, Iowa, 3,436...H 2 60
Osage City, Kans., 1,919...G 3 61
Osakis, Minn., 1,488...C 5 68
Osawatomie, Kans., 4,347...G 3 61
Osborne, Kans., 2,068...D 2 61
Osceola, Ark., 5,006...K 2 51
Osceola, Iowa, 3,422...F 6 60
Osceola, Mo., 1,082...E 6 70
Osceola, Nebr., 1,098...G 3 72
Osgood, Ind., 1,228...G 6 59
Oshkosh, Nebr., 1,124...B 3 72
Oshkosh, Wis., 41,084...K 7 93
Oskaloosa, Iowa, 11,124...H 6 60
Osseo, Wis., 1,126...D 6 93
Ossining, N. Y., 16,098...D 1 77
Ossipee, N. H., □1,412...D 4 74
Oswego, Kans., 1,997...G 4 61
Oswego, N. Y., 22,647...G 4 77
Oswego, Oreg., 3,316...B 2 82
Osyka, Miss., 724...C 8 69
Otsego, Mich., 3,990...D 6 67
Ottawa, Ill., 16,957...E 2 58
Ottawa, Kans., 10,081...G 3 61
Ottawa, Ohio, 2,962...B 3 80

Index Ref. Plate No.

Ottawa Hills, Ohio, 2,333...C 2 80
Ottumwa, Iowa, 33,631......H 6 60
Ouray, Colo., 2,103........D 6 53
Outlook, Mont., 235........M 2 71
Overland, Mo., 11,566......P 3 70
Overton, Nev., 750.........G 6 73
Overton, Tex., 2,001.......K 5 87
Ovid, Colo., 664...........P 1 53
Ovid, Mich., 1,410.........E 5 67
Oviedo, Fla., 1,601........E 3 55
Owatonna, Minn., 10,191...E 6 68
Owego, N. Y., 5,350........H 6 77
Owen, Wis., 1,034..........E 6 93
Owensboro, Ky., 33,651.....C 5 62
Owensville, Ind., 1,110....B 8 59
Owensville, Mo., 1,946.....J 6 70
Owenton, Ky., 1,249........H 3 62
Owingsville, Ky., 929......K 4 62
Owosso, Mich., 15,948......E 5 67
Oxford, Ala., 1,697........G 3 49
Oxford, Kans., 798.........E 4 61
Oxford, Me., □1,569........C 7 64
Oxford, Md., 757...........K 6 65
Oxford, Mich., 2,305.......F 6 67
Oxford, Miss., 3,956.......F 2 69
Oxford, Nebr., 1,270.......E 4 72
Oxford, N. Y., 1,811.......J 6 77
Oxford, N. C., 6,685.......H 2 78
Oxford, Ohio, 6,944........A 6 80
Oxford, Pa., 3,091.........K 6 83
Oxnard, Calif., 21,567.....F 9 52
Oyster Bay, N. Y., 5,215....D 2 77
Ozark, Ala., 5,238.........G 8 49
Ozark, Ark., 1,757.........C 3 51
Ozark, Mo., 1,087..........F 8 70
Pacific, Mo., 1,985........L 6 70
Pacific Grove, Calif.,
9,623......................C 7 52
Paden City, W. Va., 2,588..E 1 92
Paducah, Ky., 32,828.......C 3 62
Paducah, Tex., 2,952.......D 4 87
Page, W. Va., 800..........D 4 92
Pageland, S. C., 1,925.....H 2 84
Paguate, N. Mex., 500......B 3 76
Pagosa Springs, Colo.,
1,379......................E 8 53
Pahokee, Fla., 4,472.......F 5 55
Pahrump, Nev., 120.........E 6 73
Paia, Hawaii Territory,
4,272......................J 2 95
Painesville, Ohio, 14,432....H 2 80
Painted Post, N. Y.,
2,405......................F 6 77
Paintsville, Ky., 4,309.....M 5 62
Palacios, Tex., 2,799......H 9 87
Palatine, Ill., 4,079......E 1 58
Palatka, Fla., 9,176.......E 2 55
Palestine, Tex., 12,503....J 6 87
Palisade, Colo., 861.......C 4 53
Palisade, Nev., 53.........E 2 73
Palisades Park, N. J.,
9,635......................C 2 75
Palm Beach, Fla., 3,886.....G 5 55
Palmdale, Calif., 3,300....G 9 52
Palmer, Mass., □9,533......E 4 66
Palmer, Tenn., 871.........K 4 86
Palmerton, Pa., 6,646......L 4 83
Palmetto, Fla., 4,103......D 4 55
Palm Springs, Calif.,
7,660......................J10 52
Palmyra, Mo., 2,295........J 3 70
Palmyra, N. J., 5,802......D 4 75
Palmyra, N. Y., 3,034......F 4 77
Palmyra, Pa., 5,910........J 5 83
Palo Alto, Calif., 25,475.....K 3 52
Palouse, Wash., 1,036......H 4 91
Palo Verde, Ariz...........C 5 50
Pampa, Tex., 16,583........D 2 87
Pana, Ill., 6,178...........D 4 58
Panaca, Nev., 499..........G 5 73
Panama City, Fla., 25,814..C 6 55
Panguitch, Utah, 1,501.....B 6 88
Panora, Iowa, 1,062........E 5 60
Paola, Kans., 3,972........H 3 61
Paoli, Ind., 2,575.........E 7 59
Paoli, Pa., 2,039..........M 5 83
Paonia, Colo., 1,257.......D 5 53
Paradise Valley, Nev., 95...D 1 73
Paragould, Ark., 9,668.....J 1 51
Pardeeville, Wis., 1,112...H 8 93
Paris, Ark., 3,731.........C 3 51
Paris, Idaho, 774..........G 7 57
Paris, Ill., 9,460..........F 4 58
Paris, Ky., 6,912..........J 4 62
Paris, Me., □4,358.........C 7 64
Paris, Mo., 1,407..........J 4 70
Paris, Tenn., 8,826........E 2 86
Paris, Tex., 21,643........J 4 87
Park City, Utah, 2,254.....C 3 88
Parker, Ariz., 1,201.......A 4 50
Parker, Idaho, 306.........G 6 57
Parker, S. Dak., 1,148.....P 7 85
Parkersburg, Iowa, 1,300...H 3 60
Parkersburg, W. Va.,
40,492.....................D 2 92
Park Falls, Wis., 2,924....E 4 93
Park Hills, Ky., 2,577.....H 2 62
Parkin, Ark., 1,414........J 3 51

Park Rapids, Minn., 3,027..D 4 68
Park Ridge, Ill., 16,602...A 1 58
Park River, N. Dak.,
1,692......................P 3 79
Parksley, Va., 883.........N 5 90
Parkston, S. Dak., 1,354...N 7 85
Park View, N. Mex., 300....C 2 76
Parma, Idaho, 1,369........B 6 57
Parma, Mo., 1,163..........N 9 70
Parma, Ohio, 28,897........J 3 80
Parma Heights, Ohio,
3,901......................G 9 80
Parowan, Utah, 1,455.......B 6 88
Parrish, Ala., 757.........D 3 49
Parshall, N. Dak., 935.....F 4 79
Parsons, Kans., 14,750.....G 4 61
Parsons, Tenn., 1,640......E 3 86
Parsons, W. Va., 2,009.....G 2 92
Pasadena, Calif., 104,577...H 9 52
Pasadena, Tex., 22,483.....K 2 87
Pascagoula, Miss., 10,805..H10 69
Pasco, Wash., 10,228.......F 4 91
Pascoag, R. I., 1,760......H 5 66
Paso Robles, Calif., 4,835..E 8 52
Passaic, N. J., 57,702......E 2 75
Pass Christian, Miss.,
3,383......................F10 69
Patagonia, Ariz., 700......E 7 50
Patchogue, N. Y., 7,361....E 2 77
Paterson, N. J., 139,336....E 2 75
Patten, Me., □1,536........F 4 64
Patterson, La., 1,938......H 7 63
Patton, Pa., 3,148.........E 4 83
Pattonsburg, Mo., 883......D 2 70
Paul, Idaho, 560...........E 7 57
Paulding, Ohio, 2,352......A 3 80
Paullina, Iowa, 1,289......B 3 60
Paulsboro, N. J., 7,842....C 4 75
Pauls Valley, Okla., 6,896..H 5 81
Pavillion, Wyo., 241.......D 2 94
Pawhuska, Okla., 5,331.....K 1 81
Pawling, N. Y., 1,430......N 7 77
Pawnee, Okla., 2,861.......J 2 81
Pawnee City, Nebr.,
1,606......................H 4 72
Paw Paw, Mich., 2,382......D 6 67
Paw Paw, W. Va., 820.......K 1 92
Pawtucket, R. I., 81,436....J 5 66
Paxton, Ill., 3,795........E 3 58
Payette, Idaho, 4,032......B 5 57
Paynesville, Minn., 1,503...D 5 68
Payson, Utah, 3,998........C 3 88
Peabody, Kans., 1,194......E 3 61
Peabody, Mass., 22,645.....L 2 66
Peace Dale, R. I., 2,177....J 7 66
Pearl River, N. Y..........C 2 77
Pearsall, Tex., 4,481......E 9 87
Pearson, Ga., 1,402........G 8 56
Pecos, Tex., 8,054.........D10 87
Peebles, Ohio, 1,498.......D 8 80
Peekskill, N. Y., 17,731....D 1 77
Pe Ell, Wash., 787.........B 4 91
Pekin, Ill., 21,858........D 3 58
Pelahatchee, Miss., 861....E 6 69
Pelham, Ga., 4,365.........D 8 56
Pelham, N. H., □1,317......D 6 74
Pelham, N. Y., 1,843.......D 2 77
Pelham Manor, N. Y.,
5,306......................D 2 77
Pelican Rapids, Minn.,
1,676......................C 2 68
Pella, Iowa, 4,427.........H 6 60
Pell City, Ala., 1,189.....F 3 49
Pelzer, S. C., 2,692.......C 2 84
Pembroke, Ga., 1,171.......J 6 56
Pembroke, N. H., □3,094...D 5 74
Penacook, N. H., 3,100.....C 5 74
Pen Argyl, Pa., 3,878......M 4 83
Penbrook, Pa., 3,691.......J 5 83
Pender, Nebr., 1,167.......H 2 72
Pendleton, Ind., 2,082.....F 5 59
Pendleton, Oreg., 11,774....J 2 82
Pendleton, S. C., 1,432....C 2 84
Penfield, N. Y., 1,013.....F 4 77
Pennsauken, N. J.,
□22,767....................C 4 75
Pennington Gap, Va.,
2,090......................C 2 90
Pennsboro, W. Va., 1,753...E 2 92
Penns Grove, N. J., 6,669..C 4 75
Penn Yan, N. Y., 5,481.....F 5 77
Pensacola, Fla., 43,749....B 6 55
Peoria, Ariz., 2,000.......C 5 50
Peoria, Ill., 111,856......D 3 58
Peoria Heights, Ill., 5,425..D 3 58
Pepperell, Mass., □3,460...H 2 66
Perham, Minn., 1,926.......C 4 68
Perkasie, Pa., 4,358.......M 5 83
Perkinsville, Vt., 142.....C 4 89
Perry, Fla., 2,797.........C 1 55
Perry, Ga., 3,849..........E 6 56
Perry, Iowa, 6,174.........E 5 60
Perry, N. Y., 4,533........D 5 77
Perry, Okla., 5,137........H 2 81
Perrysburg, Ohio, 4,006....C 2 80
Perryton, Tex., 4,417......D 1 87
Perryville, Md., 679.......K 2 65
Perryville, Mo., 4,591.....M 7 70

Perth Amboy, N. J.,
41,330.....................E 2 75
Peru, Ill., 8,653...........D 2 58
Peru, Ind., 13,308.........E 3 59
Peru, Nebr., 1,265.........J 4 72
Peshtigo, Wis., 2,279......L 5 93
Petaluma, Calif., 10,315....C 5 52
Peterborough, N. H.,
□2,556.....................C 6 74
Petersburg, Alaska
Territory, 1,605...........N 3 95
Petersburg, Ill., 2,325.....D 3 58
Petersburg, Ind., 3,035....C 7 59
Petersburg, Tenn., 497.....H 4 86
Petersburg, Va., 35,054....J 6 90
Petersburg, W. Va., 1,898..H 2 92
Petoskey, Mich., 6,468.....E 3 67
Pewaukee, Wis., 1,792......K 9 93
Pharr, Tex., 8,690.........F11 87
Phelps, N. Y., 1,650.......F 5 77
Phenix City, Ala., 23,305...H 6 49
Philadelphia, Miss., 4,472..F 5 69
Philadelphia, Pa.,
2,071,605..................N 6 83
Philip, S. Dak., 810.......F 5 85
Philippi, W. Va., 2,531....F 2 92
Philipsburg, Mont., 1,048...C 4 71
Philipsburg, Pa., 3,988....F 4 83
Phillips, Wis., 1,775......F 4 93
Phillipsburg, Kans., 2,589..C 2 61
Phillipsburg, N. J., 18,919..C 2 75
Philmont, N. Y., 1,792.....N 6 77
Philomath, Oreg., 1,289....D 3 82
Phoebus, Va., 3,694........M 6 90
PHOENIX, Ariz., 106,818...C 5 50
Phoenix, Ill., 3,606.......B 2 58
Phoenix, N. Y., 1,917......H 4 77
Phoenix, Oreg., 746........E 5 82
Phoenixville, Pa., 12,932....L 5 83
Picayune, Miss., 6,707.....E 9 69
Picher, Okla., 3,951.......N 1 81
Pickens, Miss., 638........D 5 69
Pickens, S. C., 1,961......C 2 84
Piedmont, Ala., 4,498......G 3 49
Piedmont, Calif., 10,132....J 2 52
Piedmont, Mo., 1,548.......L 8 70
Piedmont, S. C., 2,673.....D 2 84
Piedmont, W. Va., 2,565....J 1 92
Pierce, Idaho, 544.........C 3 57
Pierce, Nebr., 1,167.......G 2 72
Pierce City, Mo., 1,156....E 9 70
Piermont, N. Y., 1,897.....C 2 77
PIERRE, S. Dak., 5,715.....J 5 85
Piggott, Ark., 2,558.......K 1 51
Pikesville, Md., 15,000....G 3 65
Pikeville, Ky., 5,154......M 6 62
Pikeville, Tenn., 882......L 3 86
Pilot Rock, Oreg., 847.....J 2 82
Pima, Ariz., 824...........F 6 50
Pinckneyville, Ill., 3,299...D 5 58
Pine Bluff, Ark., 37,162....F 5 51
Pine Bluffs, Wyo., 846.....H 4 94
Pine City, Minn., 1,937....F 5 68
Pinedale, Wyo., 770........C 3 94
Pine Grove, W. Va., 877....E 1 92
Pine Island, Minn., 1,298...F 6 68
Pine Lawn, Mo., 6,425......P 3 70
Pineville, Ky., 3,890......K 7 62
Pineville, La., 6,423......F 4 63
Pineville, W. Va., 1,082....C 5 92
Pipestone, Minn., 5,269....B 6 68
Piqua, Ohio, 17,447........B 5 80
Pisgah, Ala., 217..........G 1 49
Pitcairn, Pa., 5,857.......C 5 83
Pitman, N. J., 6,960.......C 4 75
Pittsburg, Calif., 12,763...K 1 52
Pittsburg, Kans., 19,341...H 4 61
Pittsburg, Tex., 3,142.....J 4 87
Pittsburgh, Pa., 676,806...B 5 83
Pittsfield, Ill., 3,564.....C 4 58
Pittsfield, Me., □3,909....E 6 64
Pittsfield, Mass., 55,348...B 3 66
Pittsfield, N. H., □2,321...D 5 74
Pittsford, N. Y., 1,668....E 4 77
Pittsford, Vt., 622........A 3 89
Pittston, Pa., 15,012......L 3 83
Placerville, Calif., 3,749...E 5 52
Plain City, Ohio, 1,715....D 5 80
Plain Dealing, La., 1,321...C 1 63
Plainfield, Conn., □8,071...H 2 54
Plainfield, Ill., 1,764.....E 2 58
Plainfield, N. H., □1,011...B 4 74
Plainfield, N. J., 42,366...E 2 75
Plainfield, Vt., 604.......C 2 89
Plains, Mont., 714..........B 3 71
Plains, Pa., □12,541.......L 3 83
Plainview, Minn., 1,524....F 6 68
Plainview, Nebr., 1,427....G 2 72
Plainview, Tex., 14,044....C 3 87
Plainville, Conn., □9,994...D 2 54
Plainville, Kans., 2,082....C 2 61
Plainwell, Mich., 2,767....D 6 67
Plaistow, N. H., □2,082....D 6 74
Plankinton, S. Dak., 754....N 6 85
Plano, Ill., 2,154..........E 2 58
Plant City, Fla., 9,230....D 3 55
Plaquemine, La., 5,747.....H 6 63
Platte, S. Dak., 1,069......M 7 85

Platteville, Colo., 570.....K 2 53
Platteville, Wis., 5,751....E10 93
Plattsburg, Mo., 1,655.....D 3 70
Plattsburg, N. Y., 17,738...O 1 77
Plattsmouth, Nebr., 4,874..H 4 72
Pleasant Grove, Ala.,
1,802......................E 3 49
Pleasant Grove, Utah,
3,195......................C 3 88
Pleasant Hill, La., 856.....C 3 63
Pleasant Hill, Mo., 2,200...D 5 70
Pleasanton, Kans., 1,178....H 3 61
Pleasanton, Tex., 2,913....F 9 87
Pleasant Ridge, Mich.,
3,594......................B 6 67
Pleasantville, N. J.,
11,938.....................D 5 75
Pleasantville, N. Y., 4,861..D 1 77
Plentywood, Mont., 1,862..M 2 71
Plevna, Mont., 247.........M 4 71
Plummer, Idaho, 395........B 2 57
Plymouth, Conn., □6,771...C 2 54
Plymouth, Ind., 6,704......E 2 59
Plymouth, Mass.,
□13,608....................M 5 66
Plymouth, Mich., 6,637.....B 6 67
Plymouth, N. H., □3,039...C 4 74
Plymouth, N. C., 4,486.....M 3 78
Plymouth, Ohio, 1,510......E 4 80
Plymouth, Pa., 13,021......K 3 83
Plymouth, Wis., 4,543......L 8 93
Pocahontas, Ark., 3,840....H 1 51
Pocahontas, Iowa, 1,949....D 3 60
Pocahontas, Va., 2,410.....B 6 90
Pocatello, Idaho, 26,131....F 7 57
Pocomoke City, Md.,
3,191......................M 8 65
Point of Rocks, Md., 361...E 3 65
Point Pleasant, W. Va.,
4,596......................B 3 92
Polacca, Ariz..............E 3 50
Poland, Me., □1,503........C 7 64
Polk, Pa., 4,004...........C 3 83
Polo, Ill., 2,242..........D 2 58
Polson, Mont., 2,280.......B 3 71
Pomeroy, Ohio, 3,656.......G 7 80
Pomeroy, Wash., 1,775......H 4 91
Pomona, Calif., 35,405.....D10 52
Pompano Beach, Fla.,
5,682......................F 5 55
Pompton Lakes, N. J.,
4,654......................A 1 75
Ponca, Nebr., 893..........H 2 72
Ponca City, Okla., 20,180...H 1 81
Ponchatoula, La., 4,090....K 6 63
Pontiac, Ill., 8,990........E 3 58
Pontiac, Mich., 73,681.....F 6 67
Pontotoc, Miss., 1,596.....F 2 69
Poplar, Mont., 1,169.......L 2 71
Poplar Bluff, Mo., 15,064..L 9 70
Poplarville, Miss., 1,852....F 9 69
Portage, Pa., 4,371........E 5 83
Portage, Wis., 7,334.......H 8 93
Portageville, Mo., 2,662....N10 70
Portal, N. Dak., 409.......E 2 79
Portales, N. Mex., 8,112....F 4 76
Port Allen, La., 3,097.....H 6 63
Port Angeles, Wash.,
11,233.....................B 2 91
Port Arthur, Tex., 57,530..K 8 87
Port Barre, La., 1,066.....G 5 63
Port Carbon, Pa., 3,024....K 4 83
Port Chester, N. Y.,
23,970.....................D 1 77
Port Clinton, Ohio, 5,541...E 2 80
Port Deposit, Md., 1,139...K 2 65
Port Dickinson, N. Y.,
2,199......................J 6 77
Port Edwards, Wis.,
1,336......................G 7 93
Porter, Ind., 1,458........C 1 59
Porterdale, Ga., 3,207.....E 3 56
Porterville, Calif., 6,904....F 7 52
Port Gibson, Miss., 2,920...B 7 69
Port Henry, N. Y., 1,831....O 2 77
Port Huron, Mich., 35,725..G 6 67
Port Jefferson, N. Y.,
3,296......................E 2 77
Port Jervis, N. Y., 9,372....A 1 77
Portland, Conn., □5,186....E 2 54
Portland, Ind., 7,064......H 4 59
Portland, Me., 77,634......C 8 64
Portland, Mich., 2,807.....E 6 67
Portland, Oreg., 373,628....E 2 82
Portland, Tenn., 1,660.....H 1 86
Port Lavaca, Tex., 5,599....H 9 87
Port Neches, Tex., 5,448....K 7 87
Port Orchard, Wash.,
2,320......................C 3 91
Port Orford, Oreg., 674....C 5 82
Port Saint Joe, Fla.,
2,752......................D 6 55
Portsmouth, N. H.,
18,830.....................E 5 74
Portsmouth, Ohio, 36,798...D 8 80
Portsmouth, R. I.,
□6,578.....................K 6 66
Portsmouth, Va., 80,039....M 7 90

Port Tampa, Fla., 1,497....D 4 55
Port Townsend, Wash.,
6,888......................C 2 91
Port Vue, Pa., 4,756.......C 7 83
Port Washington, N. Y.,
15,000.....................D 2 77
Port Washington, Wis.,
4,755......................L 9 93
Post, Tex., 3,141..........C 4 87
Post Falls, Idaho, 1,069....B 2 57
Postville, Iowa, 1,343......K 2 60
Poteau, Okla., 4,776.......N 4 81
Poteet, Tex., 2,487........F 8 87
Potlatch, Idaho, 1,024.....B 3 57
Potosi, Mo., 2,359.........L 7 70
Potsdam, N. Y., 7,491......K 1 77
Potter Hill, R. I., 400....G 7 66
Pottstown, Pa., 22,589.....L 5 83
Pottsville, Pa., 23,640....K 4 83
Poughkeepsie, N. Y.,
41,023.....................N 7 77
Poulsbo, Wash., 1,014......C 3 91
Poultney, Vt., 1,685.......A 3 89
Powell, Wyo., 3,804........D 1 94
Powers, Oreg., 895.........C 5 82
Powhatan Point, Ohio,
2,135......................J 6 80
Pownal, Vt., □1,453........A 5 89
Prague, Okla., 1,546.......J 4 81
Prairie City, Oreg., 822....J 3 82
Prairie du Chien, Wis.,
5,392......................D 9 93
Pratt, Kans., 7,523........D 4 61
Prattville, Ala., 4,385.....E 6 49
Prentiss, Miss., 1,212.....E 7 69
Prescott, Ariz., 6,764.....C 4 50
Prescott, Ark., 3,960......D 6 51
Presho, S. Dak., 712.......J 6 85
Presque Isle, Me., □9,954..G 2 64
Preston, Conn., □1,775.....H 2 54
Preston, Idaho, 4,045......G 7 57
Preston, Minn., 1,399......G 7 68
Preston, Nev., 45..........F 4 73
Prestonsburg, Ky., 3,585...M 5 62
Price, Utah, 6,010.........D 4 88
Prichard, Ala., 19,014.....B 9 49
Priest River, Idaho, 1,592..B 1 57
Princess Anne, Md., 1,407..L 8 65
Princeton, Ill., 5,765......D 2 58
Princeton, Ind., 7,673.....B 8 59
Princeton, Ky., 5,388......B 6 62
Princeton, Minn., 2,108....E 5 68
Princeton, Mo., 1,506......F 2 70
Princeton, N. J., 12,230....D 3 75
Princeton, W. Va., 8,279...D 6 92
Princeton, Wis., 1,371.....H 8 93
Prineville, Oreg., 3,233....G 3 82
Proctor, Minn., 2,693......F 4 68
Proctor, Vt., 1,813........B 3 89
Proctorsville, Vt., 549....B 4 89
Prophetstown, Ill., 1,691...D 2 58
Prospect Park, N. J.,
5,242......................E 2 75
Prospect Park, Pa.,
5,834......................M 7 83
Prosperity, S. C., 699.....E 3 84
Prosser, Wash., 2,636......F 4 91
Providence, Ky., 3,905.....B 6 62
PROVIDENCE, R. I.,
248,674....................J 5 66
Providence, Utah, 1,055....C 2 88
Provincetown, Mass.,
□3,795.....................O 4 66
Provo, Utah, 28,937........C 3 88
Pryor, Okla., 4,486........M 2 81
Pueblo, Colo., 63,685......K 6 53
Pulaski, N. Y., 2,033......H 3 77
Pulaski, Tenn., 5,762......G 4 86
Pulaski, Va., 9,202........C 6 90
Pullman, Wash., 12,022.....H 4 91
Punta Gorda, Fla., 1,915....E 5 55
Punxsutawney, Pa., 8,969..E 4 83
Purcell, Okla., 3,546......H 4 81
Purcellville, Va., 945.....J 2 90
Purvis, Miss., 1,270.......F 8 69
Putnam, Conn., 8,181.......H 1 54
Puunene, Hawaii
Territory, 4,456...........J 2 95
Puyallup, Wash., 10,010....C 3 91
Quakertown, Pa., 5,673.....M 5 83
Quanah, Tex., 4,589........E 3 87
Quantico, Md., 250.........M 7 65
Quantico, Va., 1,240.......K 3 90
Quealy, Wyo., 147..........C 4 94
Queens, (borough) N. Y.,
1,550,849..................D 2 77
Quincy, Fla., 6,505........B 1 55
Quincy, Ill., 41,450.......B 4 58
Quincy, Mass., 83,835......L 3 66
Quincy, Mich., 1,527.......E 7 67
Quinton, Okla., 951........M 4 81
Quitman, Ga., 4,769........F 9 56
Quitman, Miss., 1,817......G 6 69
Raceland, Ky., 1,001.......M 3 62
Racine, Wis., 71,193.......L10 93
Radford, Va., 9,026........C 6 90
Raeford, N. C., 2,030......G 5 78
Ragland, Ala., 1,008.......F 3 49

Index Ref. Plate No.
Rahway, N. J., 21,290........E 2 75
Rainelle, W. Va., 853........E 6 92
Rainier, Oreg., 1,285..........E 1 82
Raleigh, Miss., 580............E 6 69
RALEIGH, N. C., 65,679....H 3 78
Ralston, Nebr., 1,300.........H 3 72
Ramsey, N. J., 4,670..........E 1 75
Ranchester, Wyo., 251.........E 1 94
Randleman, N. C., 2,066....F 3 78
Randolph, Me., □1,733......D 7 64
Randolph, Nebr., 1,029.......G 2 72
Randolph, N. Y., 1,455.......C 6 77
Randolph, Utah, 562..........C 2 88
Randolph, Wis., 1,350.........J 8 93
Rangeley, Me., □1,228.......B 6 64
Ranger, Texas, 3,989.........F 5 87
Rankin, Pa., 6,941..............C 7 83
Ranson, W. Va., 1,436.........L 2 92
Rantoul, Ill., 6,387.............E 3 58
Rapid City, S. Dak., 25,310..........C 5 85
Raritan, N. J., 5,131..........D 2 75
Rathdrum, Idaho, 610.........A 2 57
Raton, N. Mex., 8,241..........E 2 76
Ravena, N. Y., 2,006..........N 6 77
Ravenna, Ky., 979.............K 5 62
Ravenna, Nebr., 1,451.........F 3 72
Ravenna, Ohio, 9,857.........H 3 80
Ravenswood, W. Va., 1,175..........C 3 92
Rawlins, Wyo., 7,415..........E 4 94
Ray, Ariz., 2,000................E 5 50
Ray, N. Dak., 721...............D 3 79
Raymond, N. H., □1,428....D 5 74
Raymond, Wash., 4,110.......B 4 91
Raymondville, Tex., 9,136..G11 87
Rayne, La., 3,138..............F 6 63
Rayville, La., 3,138............G 1 63
Reading, Mass., □14,006...K 2 66
Reading, Ohio, 7,836..........C 9 80
Reading, Pa., 109,320........L 5 83
Readsboro, Vt., 654............B 5 89
Rector, Ark., 1,855..............K 1 51
Red Bank, N. J., 12,473.......E 3 75
Red Bay, Ala., 1,805............B 2 49
Red Bluff, Calif., 4,905........C 3 52
Redcliff, Colo., 556.............G 4 53
Red Cloud, Nebr., 1,744.......F 4 72
Redding, Calif., 10,256.........C 3 52
Redfield, S. Dak., 2,655......M 4 85
Red Jacket, W. Va., 1,575..........B 5 92
Red Lake Falls, Minn., 1,733..........B 5 68
Redlands, Calif., 18,429......H 9 52
Red Lion, Pa., 5,119............J 6 83
Red Lodge, Mont., 2,730....G 5 71
Redmond, Oreg., 2,956.........F 3 82
Redmond, Utah, 600............C 4 88
Redmond, Wash., 573...........C 3 91
Red Oak, Iowa, 6,526.........C 6 60
Redondo Beach, Calif., 25,226..........B 11 52
Red Springs, N. C., 2,245...G 5 78
Red Wing, Minn., 10,645....F 6 68
Redwood City, Calif., 25,544..........C 6 52
Redwood Falls, Minn., 3,813..........C 6 68
Reed City, Mich., 2,241......D 5 67
Reedley, Calif., 4,135.........F 7 52
Reedsburg, Wis., 4,072........G 8 93
Reedsport, Oreg., 2,288.......C 4 82
Reform, Ala., 1,141............C 4 49
Refugio, Tex., 4,666...........G 9 87
Rehoboth Beach, Del., 1,794..........O 6 65
Reidsville, N. C., 11,708......F 2 78
Reinbeck, Iowa, 1,460.........H 4 60
Reisterstown, Md., 1,500...G 3 65
Reliance, Wyo., 700.............C 4 94
Remsen, Iowa, 1,280............B 3 60
Reno, Nev., 32,497...............B 3 73
Renovo, Pa., 3,751...............G 3 83
Rensselaer, Ind., 4,072........C 3 59
Rensselaer, N. Y., 10,856...N 5 77
Renton, Wash., 16,039........C 3 91
Renville, Minn., 1,323..........C 6 68
Republic, Wash., 895..........G 2 91
Revere, Mass., 36,763.........L 3 66
Rexburg, Idaho, 4,253.........G 6 57
Reynoldsville, Pa., 3,569...D 3 83
Rhinebeck, N. Y., 1,923......N 7 77
Rhinelander, Wis., 8,774....H 4 93
Rhodell, W. Va., 829............D 5 92
Rialto, Calif., 3,156............E10 52
Rib Lake, Wis., 853..............F 5 93
Rice Lake, Wis., 6,898........C 4 93
Richardton, N. Dak., 721...F 6 79
Richfield, Idaho, 429..........D 6 57
Richfield, Minn., 17,502.......E 6 68
Richfield, Utah, 4,212..........B 5 88
Rich Hill, Mo., 1,820...........D 6 70
Richland, Ga., 1,571............C 6 56
Richland, Wash., 21,809......F 4 91
Richland Center, Wis., 4,608..........F 9 93
Richlands, Va., 4,648.........E 1 90

Index Ref. Plate No.
Richmond, Calif., 99,545.....J 2 52
Richmond, Ind., 39,539.......H 5 59
Richmond, Ky., 10,268........J 5 62
Richmond, Me., □2,217......D 7 64
Richmond, Mich., 2,025.......G 6 67
Richmond, Mo., 4,299..........E 4 70
Richmond, (borough) N. Y., 191,955..........C 3 77
Richmond, Tex., 2,030.........J 8 87
Richmond, Utah, 1,091........C 2 88
Richmond, Vt., 731..............A 2 89
RICHMOND, Va., 230,310..........K 5 90
Richmond Heights, Mo., 15,045..........P 3 70
Richton, Miss., 1,158..........G 8 69
Richwood, Ohio, 1,866........D 5 80
Richwood, W. Va., 5,321....F 4 92
Ridgefield, Conn., □4,356..A 3 54
Ridgefield, N. J., 8,312......B 2 75
Ridgefield, Wash., 762........C 5 91
Ridgefield Park, N. J., 11,993..........F 2 75
Ridgeland, S. C., 1,078........G 7 84
Ridgeley, W. Va., 1,754.......J 1 92
Ridgely, Md., 834................L 5 65
Ridgeside, Tenn., 337..........L 4 86
Ridge Spring, S. C., 598....E 4 84
Ridgeville, Ind., 950............G 4 59
Ridgeway, Va., 440.............H 7 90
Ridgewood, N. J., 17,481....E 2 75
Ridgway, Pa., 6,244............E 3 83
Ridley Park, Pa., 4,921.......M 7 83
Rifle, Colo., 1,525...............D 3 53
Ripley, Miss., 2,383............F 1 69
Ripley, Ohio, 1,792..............C 8 80
Ripley, Tenn., 3,318............B 3 86
Ripon, Wis., 5,619................J 8 93
Ririe, Idaho, 527..................F 6 57
Rising Sun, Ind., 1,930........H 7 59
Rising Sun, Md., 668..........K 2 65
Rison, Ark., 953....................F 6 51
Rittman, Ohio, 3,810............G 4 80
Ritzville, Wash., 2,145..........G 3 91
Riverdale, Ill., 5,840............B 2 58
Riverdale, Md., 5,530...........G 5 65
River Edge, N. J., 9,204.....B 1 75
River Falls, Wis., 3,877.......A 6 93
River Forest, Ill., 10,823....B 2 58
River Grove, Ill., 4,839........A 2 58
Riverhead, N. Y., 4,892........F 2 77
River Oaks, Tex., 7,097........E 2 87
River Rouge, Mich., 20,549..........B 7 67
Riverside, Calif., 46,764.....H10 52
Riverside, Ill., 9,153............B 2 58
Riverton, Utah, 1,666...........B 3 88
Riverton, Wyo., 4,142...........D 2 94
Rives, Tenn., 413..................C 2 86
Rivesville, W. Va., 1,343.....F 1 92
Riviera Beach, Fla., 4,065..F 5 55
Roanoke, Ala., 5,392............H 4 49
Roanoke, Va., 91,921...........D 6 90
Roanoke Rapids, N. C., 8,156..........K 2 78
Roaring Spring, Pa., 2,771..........F 5 83
Robbinsdale, Minn., 11,289..........E 5 68
Roberts, Idaho, 341.............F 6 57
Robinson, Ill., 6,407.............F 5 58
Robstown, Tex., 7,278..........G10 87
Rochelle, Ga., 1,097............F 7 56
Rochelle, Ill., 5,449..............D 2 58
Rochester, Ind., 4,673..........E 2 59
Rochester, Mich., 4,279.......F 6 67
Rochester, Minn., 29,885.....F 7 68
Rochester, N. H., 13,776.....D 5 74
Rochester, N. Y., 332,488...E 4 77
Rochester, Pa., 7,179...........B 4 83
Rockaway, N. J., 3,812........D 2 75
Rockdale, Tex., 2,321...........G 7 87
Rock Falls, Ill., 7,983............D 2 58
Rockford, Ill., 92,927............D 1 58
Rockford, Mich., 1,937..........D 5 67
Rock Hall, Md., 786..............K 4 65
Rock Hill, Mo., 3,847............D 3 70
Rock Hill, S. C., 24,502.......F 2 84
Rockingham, N. C., 3,356...F 5 78
Rock Island, Ill., 48,710.......C 2 58
Rockland, Del., 350..............M 1 65
Rockland, Me., 9,234............E 7 64
Rockland, Mass., □8,960....L 4 66
Rockmart, Ga., 3,821...........C 2 56
Rockport, Ind., 2,493...........C 9 59
Rockport, Me., □1,656........E 7 64
Rockport, Mass., □4,231...M 2 66
Rockport, Mo., 1,511.............B 2 70
Rockport, Tex., 2,266............H 9 87
Rock Rapids, Iowa, 2,640...A 2 60
Rock River, Wyo., 424...........G 4 94
Rock Springs, Wyo., 10,857..........C 4 94
Rockvale, Colo., 380.............J 6 53
Rock Valley, Iowa, 1,581....A 2 60
Rockville, Conn., 8,016........F 1 54
Rockville, Ind., 2,467...........C 5 59
Rockville, Md., 6,934...........F 4 65

Index Ref. Plate No.
Rockville Center, N. Y., 22,362..........D 3 77
Rockwell City, Iowa, 2,333..D 4 60
Rockwood, Tenn., 4,272......M 3 86
Rocky Ford, Colo., 4,087....M 6 53
Rocky Hill, Conn., □5,108..E 2 54
Rocky Mount, N. C., 27,697..........K 3 78
Rockymount, Va., 1,432......E 7 90
Rocky River, Ohio, 11,237...G 2 80
Rogers, Ark., 4,962.............B 1 51
Rogers City, Mich., 3,873...F 3 67
Rogersville, Tenn., 2,545....P 2 86
Rogue River, Oreg., 590.....D 5 82
Rolette, N. Dak., 451...........L 2 79
Rolfe, Iowa, 997...................E 3 60
Rolla, Mo., 9,354..................J 7 70
Rolla, N. Dak., 1,176............L 2 79
Rolling Fork, Miss., 1,229..C 5 69
Roma-Los Saenz, Tex., 1,576..........E11 87
Rome, Ga., 29,615...............B 2 56
Rome, N. Y., 41,682............K 4 77
Romeo, Mich., 2,985............F 6 67
Romney, W. Va., 2,059.........J 2 92
Ronan, Mont., 1,251.............C 3 71
Ronceverte, W. Va., 2,301..F 5 92
Roodhouse, Ill., 2,368..........C 4 58
Roosevelt, Utah, 1,628.........D 3 88
Rosalia, Wash., 660.............H 3 91
Roscoe, S. Dak., 726............L 3 85
Roseau, Minn., 2,231...........C 2 68
Rosebud, Tex., 1,730...........G 6 87
Roseburg, Oreg., 8,390.......D 4 82
Rosedale, Miss., 2,197.........C 3 69
Roseland, La., 1,038...........K 5 63
Roselle, N. J., 17,681...........B 2 75
Roselle Park, N. J., 11,537..........B 2 75
Rosenberg, Tex., 6,210........J 8 87
Roseton, N. Y., 350...............C 1 77
Roseville, Calif., 8,723.........D 5 52
Roseville, Mich., 15,816.......G 6 67
Roseville, Ohio, 1,808...........F 6 80
Roslyn, N. Y., 1,612..............B 2 77
Roslyn, Wash., 1,537............E 3 91
Ross, Calif., 2,179................H 2 52
Rossford, Ohio, 3,963...........C 2 80
Rossville, Ga., 3,892............B 1 56
Rossville, Ill., 1,382..............F 3 58
Roswell, Ga., 2,123..............D 2 56
Roswell, N. Mex., 25,738....E 5 76
Rotan, Tex., 3,163................D 5 87
Round Mountain, Nev., 305..........D 4 73
Roundup, Mont., 2,856.........H 4 71
Rouses Point, N. Y., 2,001..O 1 77
Rowayton, Conn., 3,200.......B 4 54
Rowlesburg, W. Va., 1,299..G 2 92
Rowood, Ariz., 50.................C 6 50
Roxboro, N. C., 4,321...........H 2 78
Roy, N. Mex., 1,074.............E 3 76
Roy, Utah, 3,723..................B 2 88
Royal Oak, Mich., 46,898...B 6 67
Royersford, Pa., 3,862.........L 5 83
Royston, Ga., 2,039.............F 2 56
Ruby Valley, Nev., 200.........F 2 73
Rudyard, Mont., 521.............F 2 71
Rugby, N. Dak., 2,907..........L 3 79
Ruleville, Miss., 1,521..........D 3 69
Rulo, Nebr., 639.....................J 4 72
Rumford, Me., □9,954..........B 6 64
Rumford, R. I., 10,000...........J 5 66
Rupert, Idaho, 3,098.............E 7 57
Rural Retreat, Va., 478........B 7 90
Rush City, Minn., 1,175........F 5 68
Rushford, Minn., 1,270..........G 7 68
Rush Springs, Okla., 1,402..........G 5 81
Rushville, Ill., 2,682..............C 3 58
Rushville, Ind., 6,761............G 5 59
Rushville, Nebr., 1,266.........B 2 72
Rusk, Tex., 6,598..................J 6 87
Russell, Kans., 6,483...........D 3 61
Russell, Ky., 1,681...............M 3 62
Russellville, Ala., 6,012.......C 2 49
Russellville, Ark., 8,166.......E 3 51
Russellville, Ky., 4,529........D 7 62
Ruston, La., 10,372..............E 2 63
Ruston, Wash., 838..............C 3 91
Ruth, Nev., 1,244..................F 3 73
Rutherford, N. J., 17,411....B 2 75
Rutherford, Tenn., 994.........C 2 86
Rutherfordton, N. C., 3,146..........A 4 78
Rutland, Vt., 17,659.............B 3 89
Ryan, Okla., 1,019...............G 6 81
Rye, N. H., □1,982..............E 5 74
Rye, N. Y., 11,721................D 2 77
Ryegate, Mont., 339.............G 4 71
Sabattus, Me., 1,216............C 7 64
Sabetha, Kans., 2,173.........G 2 61
Sabina, Ohio, 1,696..............C 7 80
Sac City, Iowa, 3,170...........D 4 60
Sackets Harbor, N. Y., 1,247..........H 3 77
Saco, Me., 10,324.................C 8 64
Saco, Mont., 539...................J 2 71

Index Ref. Plate No.
SACRAMENTO, Calif., 137,572..........D 5 52
Safford, Ariz., 3,756.............F 6 50
Sag Harbor, N. Y., 2,373...G 1 77
Saginaw, Mich., 98,918......F 5 67
Saguache, Colo., 1,024.......G 6 53
Saint Agatha, Me., □1,512..........G 1 64
Saint Albans, Vt., 8,552.......A 1 89
Saint Albans, W. Va., 9,870..........C 4 92
Saint Anthony, Idaho, 2,695..........G 5 57
Saint Augustine, Fla., 13,555..........E 2 55
Saint Bernard, Ohio, 7,066..B 9 80
Saint Charles, Idaho, 363....G 7 57
Saint Charles, Ill., 6,709......E 2 58
Saint Charles, Mich., 1,469..........E 5 67
Saint Charles, Minn., 1,548..........F 7 68
Saint Charles, Mo., 14,314..L 5 70
Saint Charles, Va., 550.......C 2 90
Saint Clair, Mich., 4,098......G 6 67
Saint Clair, Mo., 1,779.........L 6 70
Saint Clair, Pa., 5,856..........K 4 83
Saint Clair Shores, Mich., 19,823..........G 6 67
Saint Clairsville, Ohio, 3,040..........J 5 80
Saint Cloud, Fla., 3,001.......E 3 55
Saint Cloud, Minn., 28,410..D 5 68
Saint Croix Falls, Wis., 1,065..........A 5 93
Saint David, Ariz., 750........E 7 50
Saint Edward, Nebr., 917...G 3 72
Sainte Genevieve, Mo., 3,992..........N 7 70
Saint Elmo, Ill., 1,716...........E 4 58
Saint Francis, Kans., 1,892..A 2 61
Saint Francis, Me., □1,384..........F 1 64
Saint Francisville, La., 936..........H 5 63
Saint Francois, Mo., 292.....M 7 70
Saint George, Me., □1,482..........E 7 64
Saint George, Utah, 4,562...A 6 88
Saint Helens, Oreg., 4,711..E 2 82
Saint Ignace, Mich., 2,946..E 3 67
Saint Ignatius, Mont., 781..C 3 71
Saint James, Minn., 3,861...D 7 68
Saint James, Mo., 1,811......J 6 70
Saint John, Kans., 1,735......D 3 61
Saint John, N. Dak., 451.......L 2 79
Saint Johns, Ariz., 1,469.....F 4 50
Saint Johns, Mich., 4,954....E 6 67
Saint Johnsbury, Vt., 7,370..........D 2 89
Saint Johnsville, N. Y., 2,210..........L 5 77
Saint Joseph, La., 1,218.....H 3 63
Saint Joseph, Mich., 10,223..........C 6 67
Saint Joseph, Minn., 1,246..........D 5 68
Saint Joseph, Mo., 78,588...B 3 70
Saint Louis, Mich., 3,347....E 5 67
Saint Louis, Mo., 856,796...M 5 70
Saint Louis Park, Minn., 22,644..........E 6 68
Saint Maries, Idaho, 2,220..B 2 57
Saint Martinville, La., 4,614..........G 6 63
Saint Marys, Kans., 1,201...G 2 61
Saint Marys, Ohio, 6,208......B 4 80
Saint Marys, Pa., 7,846........E 3 83
Saint Marys, W. Va., 2,196..........D 2 92
Saint Mathews, S. C., 2,351..........G 4 84
Saint Michaels, Ariz., 120..F 3 50
Saint Paris, Ohio, 1,422......C 5 80
SAINT PAUL, Minn., 311,349..........F 6 68
Saint Paul, Nebr., 1,676.....F 3 72
Saint Paul, Va., 1,014.........D 2 90
Saint Paul Park, Minn., 2,438..........F 5 68
Saint Pauls, N. C., 2,251....H 5 78
Saint Peter, Minn., 7,754....D 6 68
Saint Petersburg, Fla., 96,738..........D 4 55
Saint Thomas, N. Dak., 566..........P 2 79
Salamanca, N. Y., 8,861....C 6 77
Salem, Ill., 6,159..................F 5 58
Salem, Ind., 3,271................E 7 59
Salem, Mass., 41,880..........L 2 66
Salem, Mo., 3,611.................J 7 70
Salem, N. H., □4,805..........D 6 74
Salem, N. J., 9,050..............C 4 75
Salem, N. Y., 1,067..............O 4 77
Salem, Ohio, 12,754.............J 4 80
SALEM, Oreg., 43,140.........E 3 82
Salem, S. Dak., 1,119..........P 6 85
Salem, Utah, 781..................C 3 88

Index Ref. Plate No.
Salem, Va., 6,823................D 6 90
Salem, W. Va., 2,578.........E 2 92
Salem Depot, N. H., 1,637..........D 6 74
Salida, Colo., 4,553.............H 6 53
Salina, Kans., 26,176..........E 3 61
Salina, Utah, 1,789...............C 5 88
Salinas, Calif., 13,917.........D 7 52
Saline, Mich., 1,533.............F 6 67
Salineville, Ohio, 2,018........J 4 80
Salisbury, Conn., □3,132...B 1 54
Salisbury, Md., 15,141.........M 7 65
Salisbury, Mo., 1,676..........G 4 70
Salisbury, N. C., 20,102......D 3 78
Sallisaw, Okla., 2,885..........N 4 81
Salmon, Idaho, 2,648...........E 4 57
Salmon Falls, N. H., 1,290..........E 5 74
SALT LAKE CITY, Utah, 182,121..........C 3 88
Saltville, Va., 2,678.............E 2 90
Saluda, S. C., 1,594.............E 3 84
Salyersville, Ky., 1,174........L 5 62
Samson, Ala., 2,204.............F 8 49
San Angelo, Tex., 52,093...D 6 87
San Anselmo, Calif., 9,188..........H 2 52
San Antonio, Tex., 408,442..........F 8 87
San Benito, Tex., 13,271....G12 87
San Bernardino, Calif., 63,058..........E10 52
Sanborn, Iowa, 1,337...........B 2 60
San Bruno, Calif., 12,478....J 2 52
San Carlos, Ariz., 3,000......E 5 50
San Carlos, Calif., 14,371....J 3 52
Sandcoulee, Mont., 500........E 3 71
Sandersville, Ga., 4,480.......G 5 56
San Diego, Calif., 334,387..H11 52
San Diego, Tex., 4,397.........F10 87
Sandpoint, Idaho, 4,265.......B 1 57
Sand Springs, Okla., 6,994..........K 2 81
Sandstone, Minn., 1,097......F 4 68
Sandusky, Mich., 1,819.......G 5 67
Sandusky, Ohio, 29,375.......E 3 80
Sandwich, Ill., 3,027...........E 2 58
Sandwich, Mass., □2,418...N 5 66
Sandy, Oreg., 1,003.............E 2 82
Sandy, Utah, 2,095...............C 3 88
San Felipe, N. Mex., 500...C 3 76
San Fernando, Calif., 12,992..........C10 52
Sanford, Fla., 11,935...........E 3 55
Sanford, Me., □15,177.........B 9 64
Sanford, N. C., 10,013.........G 4 78
San Francisco, Calif., 775,357..........H 2 52
San Gabriel, Calif., 20,343..........C10 52
San Ildefonso, N. Mex., 400..........C 3 76
Sanish, N. Dak., 507............E 4 79
San Jose, Calif., 95,280.......L 3 52
San Juan, Tex., 3,413..........F11 87
San Leandro, Calif., 27,542..........J 2 52
San Luis, Colo., 1,239..........J 8 53
San Luis Obispo, Calif., 14,180..........E 8 52
San Marcos, Tex., 9,980......F 8 87
San Marino, Calif., 11,230..........D10 52
San Mateo, Calif., 41,782....J 3 52
San Pablo, Calif., 14,511.....J 2 52
San Rafael, Calif., 13,848...J 1 52
San Saba, Tex., 3,400..........F 6 87
San Simon, Ariz., 175..........F 6 50
Santa Ana, Calif., 45,533...D11 52
Santa Barbara, Calif., 44,913..........F 9 52
Santa Clara, Calif., 11,702..........K 3 52
Santa Cruz, Calif., 21,970..K 4 52
SANTE FE, N. Mex., 27,998..........C 3 76
Santa Maria, Calif., 10,440..........E 9 52
Santa Monica, Calif., 71,595..........B10 52
Santa Paula, Calif., 11,049..........F 9 52
Santaquin, Utah, 1,214......C 4 88
Santa Rita, N. Mex., 2,135..........B 6 76
Santa Rosa, Calif., 17,902..C 5 52
Santa Rosa, N. Mex., 2,199..........E 4 76
Sapulpa, Okla., 13,031.......K 3 81
Saranac Lake, N. Y., 6,913..........M 2 77
Sarasota, Fla., 18,896.........D 4 55
Saratoga, Wyo., 926.............F 4 94
Saratoga Springs, N. Y., 15,473..........N 4 77
Sarcoxie, Mo., 1,042...........D 8 70
Sardis, Miss., 1,913............E 2 69
Sargent, Nebr., 818.............E 3 72

Index Ref. Plate No.

Saugerties, N. Y., 3,907....M 6 77
Saugus, Mass., □17,162....L 3 66
Sauk Centre, Minn., 3,140..D 5 68
Sauk City, Wis., 1,755....G 9 93
Sauk Rapids, Minn., 3,410..D 5 68
Sault Sainte Marie, Mich., 17,912....E 2 67
Sausalito, Calif., 4,828....H 2 52
Savanna, Ill., 5,058....C 1 58
Savannah, Ga., 119,638....K 6 56
Savannah, Mo., 2,332....C 3 70
Savannah, Tenn., 1,698....E 4 86
Saxtons River, Vt., 715....B 4 89
Saylesville, R. I., 3,500....J 5 66
Sayre, Okla., 3,362....C 4 81
Sayre, Pa., 7,735....K 2 83
Sayreville, N. J., 10,338....E 3 75
Sayville, N. Y., 4,251....E 2 77
Scarboro, Me., □4,600....C 8 64
Scarbro, W. Va., 244....D 5 92
Scarsdale, N. Y., 13,156....D 2 77
Schenectady, N. Y., 91,785....M 5 77
Schofield, Wis., 1,948....G 6 93
Schoolfield, Va....E 7 90
Schulenburg, Tex., 2,005....H 8 87
Schuyler, Nebr., 2,883....G 3 72
Schuylerville, N. Y., 1,314..N 4 77
Schuylkill Haven, Pa., 6,597....K 4 83
Scio, Oreg., 448....E 3 82
Scipio, Utah, 491....B 4 88
Scituate, Mass., □5,993....M 4 66
Scotia, N. Y., 7,812....N 5 77
Scotland, S. Dak., 1,188....O 7 85
Scotland Neck, N. C., 2,730....L 2 78
Scott City, Kans., 3,204....A 3 61
Scottdale, Pa., 6,249....C 5 83
Scottsbluff, Nebr., 12,858..A 3 72
Scottsboro, Ala., 4,731....G 1 49
Scottsburg, Ind., 2,953....F 7 59
Scottsdale, Ariz., 2,032....D 5 50
Scottsville, Ky., 2,060....E 7 62
Scranton, Pa., 125,536....L 3 83
Scribner, Nebr., 913....H 3 72
Seabrook, N. H., □1,788....E 6 74
Sea Cliff, N. Y., 4,868....D 2 77
Seaford, Del., 3,087....M 6 65
Seagraves, Tex., 2,101....B 5 87
Searchlight, Nev., 229....G 7 73
Searcy, Ark., 6,024....G 3 51
Searsport, Me., □1,457....F 7 64
Seaside, Calif., 10,226....D 7 52
Seaside, Oreg., 3,886....D 2 82
Seattle, Wash., 467,591....C 3 91
Sebastopol, Calif., 2,601....C 5 52
Sebewaing, Mich., 1,911....F 5 67
Sebree, Ky., 1,158....B 5 62
Sebring, Fla., 5,006....E 4 55
Sebring, Ohio, 4,045....H 4 80
Secaucus, N. J., 9,750....B 2 75
Seco, Ky., 644....M 6 62
Sedalia, Mo., 20,354....F 5 70
Sedan, Kans., 1,640....F 4 61
Sedro Woolley, Wash., 3,299....C 2 91
Seekonk, Mass., □6,104....J 4 66
Seguin, Tex., 9,733....G 8 87
Selah, Wash., 2,489....E 4 91
Selby, S. Dak., 706....K 2 85
Selbyville, Del., 1,086....N 7 65
Seligman, Ariz., 1,000....C 3 50
Sellersburg, Ind., 1,664....F 8 59
Selma, Ala., 22,840....E 6 49
Selma, Calif., 5,964....F 7 52
Selma, N. C., 2,639....J 3 78
Selmer, Tenn., 1,759....D 4 86
Seminole, Okla., 11,863....J 4 81
Senath, Mo., 1,528....M10 70
Senatobia, Miss., 2,108....E 1 69
Seneca, Kans., 1,911....F 2 61
Seneca, Mo., 1,195....C 9 70
Seneca, S. C., 3,649....C 2 84
Seneca Falls, N. Y., 6,634..G 5 77
Sequim, Wash., 1,044....B 2 91
Sesser, Ill., 2,086....D 5 58
Sevierville, Tenn., 1,620....P 3 86
Seward, Alaska Territory, 2,063....J 2 95
Seward, Nebr., 3,154....H 4 72
Sewickley, Pa., 5,836....B 4 83
Seymour, Conn., □7,832....C 3 54
Seymour, Ind., 9,629....F 7 59
Seymour, Iowa, 1,223....G 7 60
Seymour, Tex., 3,779....E 4 87
Seymour, Wis., 1,760....K 6 93
Shadyside, Ohio, 4,433....J 6 80
Shaker Heights, Ohio, 28,222....H 3 80
Shakopee, Minn., 3,185....E 6 68
Shamokin, Pa., 16,879....J 4 83
Shamrock, Tex., 3,322....D 2 87
Shannock, R. I., 300....H 7 66
Sharon, Mass., □4,847....K 4 66
Sharon, Pa., 26,454....B 3 83
Sharon, Tenn., 880....D 2 86
Sharon Hill, Pa., 5,464....N 7 82
Sharples, W. Va., 465....C 5 92
Sharpsburg, Md., 866....D 3 65
Sharpsburg, Pa., 7,296....B 6 83
Sharpsville, Pa., 5,414....A 3 83
Sharptown, Md., 680....M 6 65
Shattuck, Okla., 1,692....C 2 81
Shaw, Miss., 1,892....C 3 69
Shawano, Wis., 5,894....J 6 93
Shawnee, Okla., 22,948....J 4 81
Shawneetown, Ill., 1,917....E 6 58
Sheboygan, Wis., 42,365....L 8 93
Sheboygan Falls, Wis., 3,599....L 8 93
Sheffield, Ala., 10,767....C 1 49
Sheffield, Iowa, 1,163....G 3 60
Sheffield, Pa., 2,087....D 2 83
Shelbina, Mo., 2,113....H 3 70
Shelburn, Ind., 1,412....C 6 59
Shelby, Mich., 1,500....C 5 67
Shelby, Miss., 2,148....C 3 69
Shelby, Mont., 3,058....E 2 71
Shelby, N. C., 15,508....C 4 78
Shelby, Ohio, 7,971....E 4 80
Shelbyville, Ill., 4,462....E 4 58
Shelbyville, Ind., 11,734....F 6 59
Shelbyville, Ky., 4,403....G 4 62
Shelbyville, Tenn., 9,456....H 4 86
Sheldon, Iowa, 4,001....B 2 60
Sheldon, Vt., □1,352....B 1 89
Shelley, Idaho, 1,856....F 6 57
Shelton, Conn., 12,694....C 3 54
Shelton, Nebr., 1,032....F 4 72
Shelton, Wash., 5,045....B 3 91
Shenandoah, Iowa, 6,938....C 7 60
Shenandoah, Pa., 15,704....K 4 83
Shenandoah, Va., 1,903....H 3 90
Shepherdstown, W. Va., 1,173....L 2 92
Shepherdsville, Ky., 953....F 5 62
Sherburn, Minn., 1,221....D 7 68
Sheridan, Ark., 1,893....F 5 51
Sheridan, Ind., 1,965....E 4 59
Sheridan, Mont., 572....D 5 71
Sheridan, Oreg., 1,922....D 2 82
Sheridan, Wyo., 11,500....F 1 94
Sherman, Tex., 20,150....H 4 87
Sherrill, N. Y., 2,236....K 4 77
Sherwood, Oreg., 575....E 2 82
Shillington, Pa., 5,059....K 5 83
Shinnston, W. Va., 2,793....F 2 92
Shippensburg, Pa., 5,722....H 5 83
Shiprock, N. Mex., 250....A 2 76
Shively, Ky., 2,401....F 4 62
Shoals, Ind., 1,039....D 7 59
Shorewood, Wis., 16,199....L 9 93
Shorewood Hills, Wis., 1,594....H 9 93
Shortsville, N. Y., 1,314....F 5 77
Shoshone, Idaho, 1,420....D 7 57
Shoshoni, Wyo., 891....D 2 94
Shreveport, La., 127,206....C 1 63
Shrewsbury, Mass., □10,594....H 3 66
Shrewsbury, Mo., 3,382....P 3 70
Shullsburg, Wis., 1,306....F10 93
Sibley, Iowa, 2,559....B 2 60
Sidney, Iowa, 1,132....B 7 60
Sidney, Mont., 3,987....M 3 71
Sidney, Nebr., 4,912....B 3 72
Sidney, N. Y., 4,815....K 6 77
Sidney, Ohio, 11,491....B 5 80
Sierra Madre, Calif., 7,273....D10 52
Signal Hill, Calif., 4,040....C11 52
Signal Mountain, Tenn., 1,786....L 4 86
Sigourney, Iowa, 2,343....J 6 60
Sikeston, Mo., 11,640....N 9 70
Siler City, N. C., 2,501....G 3 78
Siloam Springs, Ark., 3,270....A 1 51
Silsbee, Tex., 3,179....K 7 87
Silver City, Nev., 200....B 3 73
Silver City, N. Mex., 7,022....A 6 76
Silver Creek, N. Y., 3,068....B 5 77
Silverpeak, Nev., 63....D 5 73
Silver Spring, Md....F 4 65
Silverton, Colo., 1,375....D 7 53
Silverton, Ohio, 4,827....C 9 80
Silverton, Oreg., 3,146....E 2 82
Silvertown, Ga., 3,387....D 5 56
Silis, Ill., 3,055....C 2 58
Simmesport, La., 1,510....G 5 63
Simms, Mont., 250....E 3 71
Simpsonville, S. C., 1,529..D 2 84
Simsbury, Conn., □4,822....D 1 54
Sinclair, Wyo., 775....E 4 94
Sinton, Tex., 4,254....G 9 87
Sioux Center, Iowa, 1,860..A 2 60
Sioux City, Iowa, 83,991....A 3 60
Sioux Falls, S. Dak., 52,696....R 6 85
Sioux Rapids, Iowa, 1,010..C 3 60
Sisseton, S. Dak., 2,871....R 2 85
Sisterville, W. Va., 2,313....D 1 92
Sitka, Alaska Territory, 2,080....N 3 95
Skagway, Alaska Territory, 761....N 3 95
Skaneateles, N. Y., 2,331....H 5 77
Skiatook, Okla., 1,734....K 2 81
Skokie, Ill., 14,832....B 1 58
Skowhegan, Me., □7,422....D 6 64
Skull Valley, Ariz., 250....C 4 50
Slater, Mo., 2,836....G 4 70
Slatersville, R. I., 1,780....H 4 66
Slatington, Pa., 4,343....L 4 83
Slaton, Tex., 5,036....C 4 87
Slayton, Minn., 1,887....C 7 68
Sleepy Eye, Minn., 3,278....D 6 68
Slidell, La., 3,464....L 6 63
Sloan, Nev., 200....F 7 73
Sloan, N. Y., 4,698....C 5 77
Sloatsburg, N. Y., 2,018....C 1 77
Smackover, Ark., 2,495....E 7 51
Smithers, W. Va., 2,208....D 4 92
Smithfield, N. C., 5,574....J 3 78
Smithfield, Utah, 2,383....C 2 88
Smithfield, Va., 1,180....L 7 90
Smithsburg, Md., 641....D 2 65
Smithville, Tenn., 1,558....K 3 86
Smithville, Tex., 3,379....G 7 87
Smoot, Wyo., 280....B 3 94
Smyrna, Del., 2,346....M 3 65
Smyrna, Ga., 2,005....D 3 56
Smyrna, Tenn., 1,544....H 3 86
Snohomish, Wash., 3,094....D 3 91
Snoqualmie, Wash., 806....D 3 91
Snowflake, Ariz., 929....E 4 50
Snow Hill, Md., 2,091....N 8 65
Snyder, Okla., 1,646....E 5 81
Snyder, Tex., 12,010....D 5 87
Soap Lake, Wash., 2,091....F 3 91
Society Hill, S. C., 645....J 3 84
Socorro, N. Mex., 4,334....C 4 76
Soda Springs, Idaho, 1,329....G 7 57
Sodus, N. Y., 1,588....G 4 77
Solomon, Ariz., 700....F 6 50
Solon, Ohio, 2,570....H 3 80
Solvay, N. Y., 7,868....H 4 77
Somers, Conn., □2,631....F 1 54
Somers, Mont., 750....B 2 71
Somerset, Ky., 7,097....H 6 62
Somerset, Md., 430....F 5 65
Somerset, Mass., □8,566....K 5 66
Somerset, Ohio, 1,383....F 6 80
Somerset, Pa., 5,936....D 6 83
Somersworth, N. H., 6,927....E 5 74
Somerton, Ariz., 1,825....A 6 50
Somerville, Mass., 102,351....K 3 66
Somerville, N. J., 11,571....D 2 75
Somerville, Tenn., 1,760....C 4 86
Sonora, Ariz., 1,821....D 5 50
Sonora, Calif., 2,448....E 6 52
Sonora, Tex., 2,633....D 7 87
Soperton, Ga., 1,667....G 6 56
Sophia, W. Va., 1,430....D 5 92
Sopris, Colo., 1,330....K 8 53
Souderton, Pa., 4,521....M 5 83
South Amboy, N. J., 8,422....E 3 75
Southampton, N. Y., 3,701....G 2 77
South Bakersfield, Calif., 12,120....F 7 52
South Beloit, Ill., 3,221....E 1 58
South Bend, Ind., 115,911..E 1 59
South Bend, Wash., 1,857..B 4 91
South Berwick, Me., □2,646....B 9 64
South Boston, Va., 6,057....G 7 90
South Braintree, Mass., 5,600....L 4 66
South Brewer, Me....F 6 64
Southbridge, Mass., □17,519....F 4 66
South Burlington, Vt., 3,279....A 2 89
South Canon, Colo., 1,588..J 6 53
South Charleston, W. Va., 16,686....C 4 92
South Chicago Heights, Ill., 2,129....B 3 58
Southern Pines, N. C., 4,272....G 4 78
South Euclid, Ohio, 15,432....H 9 80
South Fork, Pa., 2,616....E 5 83
South Fulton, Tenn., 2,119....D 2 86
South Gate, Calif., 51,116....C11 52
Southgate, Ky., 1,903....J 2 62
South Glens Falls, N. Y., 3,645....N 4 77
South Hadley, Mass., □10,145....D 4 66
South Haven, Mich., 5,629..C 6 67
South Hill, Va., 2,153....H 7 90
South Holland, Ill., 3,247....B 2 58
Southington, Conn., □13,061....D 2 54
South Jordan, Utah, 1,048....C 3 88
South Milwaukee, Wis., 12,855....L10 93
South Norfolk, Va., 10,434....M 7 90
South Norwalk, Conn., 18,000....B 4 54
South Nyack, N. Y., 3,102..C 2 77
South Ogden, Utah, 3,763..C 2 88
South Orange, N. J., 15,230....B 2 75
South Paris, Me., 2,067....B 7 64
South Pasadena, Calif., 16,935....C10 52
South Pittsburg, Tenn., 2,573....K 4 86
South Plainfield, N. J., 8,008....E 2 75
Southport, N. C., 1,748....J 7 78
South Portland, Me., 21,866....C 8 64
South River, N. J., 11,308..E 3 75
South Royalton, Vt., 700....C 3 89
South Ryegate, Vt., 340....C 3 89
South Saint Paul, Minn., 15,909....E 6 68
South Salt Lake, Utah, 7,704....C 3 88
South San Francisco, Calif., 19,351....J 2 52
South Sioux City, Nebr., 5,557....H 2 72
South Sioux Falls, S. Dak., 1,586....R 6 85
South Superior, Wyo., 780....D 4 94
South West Fargo, N. Dak., 1,032....S 6 79
Southwest Greensburg, Pa., 3,144....C 5 83
South West Harbor, Me., □1,534....G 7 64
South Weymouth, Mass....L 4 66
South Whitley, Ind., 1,299..F 2 59
South Williamsport, Pa., 6,364....J 3 83
South Windham, Me., 1,569....C 8 64
South Windsor, Conn., □4,066....E 1 54
South Zanesville, Ohio, 1,477....F 6 80
Spalding, Nebr., 713....F 3 72
Spangler, Pa., 3,013....E 4 83
Spanish Fork, Utah, 5,230..C 3 88
Sparkman, Ark., 964....E 6 51
Sparks, Nev., 8,203....B 3 73
Sparrows Point, Md., 12,000....J 4 65
Sparta, Ga., 1,954....G 4 56
Sparta, Ill., 3,576....D 5 58
Sparta, Mich., 2,327....D 5 67
Sparta, Tenn., 4,299....K 3 86
Sparta, Wis., 5,893....E 8 93
Spartanburg, S. C., 36,795....D 1 84
Spearfish, S. Dak., 2,755....B 5 85
Speedway, Ind., 5,498....E 5 59
Spencer, Ind., 2,394....D 6 59
Spencer, Iowa, 7,446....C 2 60
Spencer, Mass., □7,027....F 3 66
Spencer, N. C., 3,242....D 3 78
Spencer, S. Dak., 552....O 6 85
Spencer, Tenn., 721....L 3 86
Spencer, W. Va., 2,587....D 3 92
Spencerport, N. Y., 1,595..E 4 77
Spencerville, Ohio, 1,826....B 4 80
Spindale, N. C., 3,891....B 4 78
Spirit Lake, Idaho, 823....A 2 57
Spirit Lake, Iowa, 2,467....D 1 60
Spokane, Wash., 161,721....H 3 91
Spooner, Wis., 2,597....C 4 93
Sprague, Wash., 598....G 3 91
Spray, N. C., 5,542....F 1 78
Spreckelsville, Hawaii Territory, 2,634....J 1 95
Spring City, Pa., 3,258....L 5 83
Spring City, Tenn., 1,725..M 3 86
Spring City, Utah, 703....C 4 88
Springdale, Ark., 5,835....B 1 51
Springdale, Conn., 5,280....A 4 54
Springdale, Pa., 4,939....C 4 83
Springer, N. Mex., 1,558....E 2 76
Springerville, Ariz., 689....F 4 50
Springfield, Colo., 2,041....O 8 53
Springfield, Fla., 1,084....D 6 55
SPRINGFIELD, Ill., 81,628....D 4 58
Springfield, Ky., 2,032....G 5 62
Springfield, Mass., 162,399....D 4 66
Springfield, Minn., 2,574..C 6 68
Springfield, Mo., 66,731....F 8 70
Springfield, Ohio, 78,508...C 6 80
Springfield, Oreg., 10,807....E 3 82
Springfield, S. C., 782....F 4 84
Springfield, S. Dak., 801..N 8 85
Springfield, Tenn., 6,506....H 2 86
Springfield, Vt., 4,940....B 4 89
Spring Grove, Minn., 1,093....G 7 68
Springhill, La., 3,383....D 1 63
Spring Hill, Tenn., 541....H 3 86
Spring Lake, Mich., 1,824..C 5 67
Springvale, Me., 2,745....B 9 64
Spring Valley, Ill., 4,916....D 2 58
Spring Valley, Minn., 2,467....F 7 68
Spring Valley, N. Y., 4,500....C 2 77
Springville, N. Y., 3,322....C 5 77
Springville, Utah, 6,475....C 3 88
Spruce Pine, N. C., 2,280...A 3 78
Spur, Tex., 2,183....D 4 87
Stafford, Conn., □6,471....F 1 54
Stafford, Kans., 2,005....D 4 61
Stafford Springs, Conn., 3,396....F 1 54
Stambaugh, Mich., 1,969...G 2 67
Stamford, Conn., 74,293....A 4 54
Stamford, Tex., 5,819....E 5 87
Stamps, Ark., 2,552....D 7 51
Stanberry, Mo., 1,651....C 2 70
Standish, Me., □1,786....B 8 64
Stanford, Ky., 1,861....H 5 62
Stanford, Mont., 542....F 3 71
Stanley, N. Dak., 1,486....F 3 79
Stanley, Wis., 2,014....E 6 93
Stanton, Nebr., 1,403....G 3 72
Stanton, Tenn., 503....C 4 86
Stanwood, Wash., 710....C 2 91
Staples, Minn., 2,782....D 4 68
Starbuck, Minn., 1,143....C 5 68
Star City, Ark., 1,296....G 6 51
Star City, W. Va., 1,205....F 1 92
Starke, Fla., 2,944....D 2 55
Starkville, Miss., 7,107....G 4 69
State Center, Iowa, 1,040..G 4 60
State College, Pa., 17,227..G 4 83
Statesboro, Ga., 6,097....J 6 56
Statesville, N. C., 16,901....D 3 78
Staunton, Ill., 4,047....D 5 58
Staunton, Va., 19,927....F 4 90
Stayton, Oreg., 1,507....E 3 82
Steamboat Springs, Colo., 1,913....F 2 53
Steele, Mo., 2,360....N10 70
Steele, N. Dak., 762....L 6 79
Steelton, Pa., 12,574....J 5 83
Steelville, Mo., 1,157....K 7 70
Steger, Ill., 4,358....F 2 58
Steilacoom, Wash., 1,233...C 3 91
Stephens, Ark., 1,283....E 7 51
Stephens City, Va., 676....H 2 90
Stephenville, Tex., 7,155....F 5 87
Sterling, Colo., 7,534....N 1 53
Sterling, Ill., 12,817....D 2 58
Sterling, Kans., 2,243....D 3 61
Steubenville, Ohio, 35,872..J 5 80
Stevenson, Ala., 927....G 1 49
Stevenson, Wash., 584....D 5 91
Stevens Point, Wis., 16,564....H 6 93
Stevensville, Mont., 772....C 4 71
Stewart Manor, N. Y., 1,879....D 2 77
Stewartstown, N. H., □970....D 2 74
Stewartville, Minn., 1,193..F 7 68
Stickney, Ill., 3,317....B 2 58
Stigler, Okla., 2,125....M 4 81
Stillwater, Minn., 7,674....F 5 68
Stillwater, Nev., 9....C 3 73
Stillwater, Okla., 20,238....H 2 81
Stillwater, R. I....H 5 66
Stilwell, Okla., 1,813....N 3 81
Stockett, Mont., 300....E 3 71
Stockton, Calif., 70,853....D 6 52
Stockton, Ill., 1,445....C 1 58
Stoneham, Mass., □13,299....K 3 66
Stone Mountain, Ga., 1,899....D 3 56
Stonewall, Miss., 1,015....G 6 69
Stonington, Me., □1,660....F 7 64
Stony Creek, Va., 482....K 7 90
Storm Lake, Iowa, 6,954....C 3 60
Story City, Iowa, 1,545....F 4 60
Stoughton, Mass., □11,146....K 4 66
Stoughton, Wis., 4,833....H10 93
Stowe, Pa., 2,524....L 5 83
Stowe, Vt., 556....B 2 89
Strasburg, N. Dak., 733....K 7 79
Strasburg, Ohio, 1,366....G 4 80
Strasburg, Va., 2,022....H 3 90
Stratford, Conn., □33,428..C 4 54
Stratford, N. H., □973....C 2 74
Stratton, Colo., 720....O 4 53
Strawberry Point, Iowa, 1,247....K 3 60
Streator, Ill., 16,469....E 2 58
Streeter, N. Dak., 602....M 6 79
Strong, Ark., 893....F 7 51

INDEX OF CITIES AND TOWNS OF THE UNITED STATES

111

Index Ref. Plate No.

Strongsville, Ohio, 3,504....G10 80
Stroud, Okla., 2,450....J 3 81
Stroudsburg, Pa., 6,361....M 4 83
Struthers, Ohio, 11,941....J 3 80
Stuart, Fla., 2,912....F 4 55
Stuart, Iowa, 1,500....E 5 60
Stuart, Va., 849....D 7 90
Sturgeon Bay, Wis., 7,054....M 6 93
Sturgis, Ky., 2,222....B 5 62
Sturgis, Mich., 7,786....D 7 67
Sturgis, S. Dak., 3,471....C 5 85
Stuttgart, Ark., 7,276....H 4 51
Suffern, N. Y., 4,010....C 2 77
Suffolk, Va., 12,339....L 7 90
Sugar City, Idaho, 684....G 6 57
Sugar City, Colo., 527....M 6 53
Sugar Creek, Mo., 1,858....D 4 70
Sulligent, Ala., 1,209....B 3 49
Sullivan, Ill., 3,470....E 4 58
Sullivan, Ind., 5,423....C 6 59
Sullivan, Mo., 3,019....K 6 70
Sulphur, La., 5,996....E 2 63
Sulphur, Okla., 4,389....J 5 81
Sulphur Springs, Tex., 8,991....J 4 87
Sultan, Wash., 814....D 3 91
Sumas, Wash., 658....C 2 91
Summerton, S. C., 1,419....H 4 84
Summerville, Ga., 3,973....B 2 56
Summerville, S. C., 3,312....H 5 84
Summit, Ill., 8,957....F 2 58
Summit, Miss., 1,558....C 8 69
Summit, N. J., 17,929....E 2 75
Summit Hill, Pa., 4,294....L 4 83
Summitville, Ind., 1,061....F 4 59
Sumner, Wash., 2,816....C 3 91
Sumpter, Oreg., 146....J 3 82
Sumter, S. C., 20,185....H 4 84
Sunapee, N. H., □1,108....B 5 74
Sunburst, Mont., 845....D 2 71
Sunbury, Pa., 15,570....J 4 83
Sundance, Wyo., 893....H 1 94
Sunnyside, Wash., 4,194....F 4 91
Sunnyvale, Calif., 9,829....K 3 52
Sun Prairie, Wis., 2,263....H 9 93
Sunrise, Wyo., 450....H 3 94
Superior, Ariz., 4,500....D 5 50
Superior, Nebr., 3,227....G 4 72
Superior, Wis., 35,325....B 2 93
Superior, Wyo., 1,580....D 4 94
Susquehanna, Pa., 2,646....L 2 83
Sutherland, Nebr., 856....C 3 72
Sutherlin, Oreg., 2,230....D 4 82
Sutton, Nebr., 1,353....G 4 72
Sutton, W. Va., 1,070....E 3 92
Swainsboro, Ga., 4,300....H 5 56
Swampscott, Mass., □11,580....L 3 66
Swansea, Mass., □6,121....K 6 66
Swansea, S. C., 762....F 4 84
Swanton, Ohio, 1,740....C 2 80
Swanzey, N. H., □2,806....B 6 74
Swarthmore, Pa., 4,825....M 7 83
Sweet Home, Oreg., 3,603....E 3 82
Sweet Springs, Mo., 1,439....F 5 70
Sweetwater, Tenn., 4,199....N 3 86
Sweetwater, Tex., 13,619....D 5 87
Swissvale, Pa., 16,488....C 7 83
Swoyerville, Pa., 7,795....L 3 83
Sycamore, Ill., 5,912....E 2 58
Sykesville, Md., 941....F 3 65
Sylacauga, Ala., 9,606....F 4 49
Sylva, N. C., 1,382....D 8 78
Sylvania, Ga., 2,939....J 5 56
Sylvania, Ohio, 2,433....C 2 80
Sylvester, Ga., 2,623....E 7 56
Syracuse, Ind., 1,453....F 2 59
Syracuse, Kans., 2,075....A 4 61
Syracuse, Nebr., 1,097....H 4 72
Syracuse, N. Y., 220,583....H 4 77
Syracuse, Utah, 837....B 2 88
Tabor City, N. C., 2,033....H 6 78
Tacoma, Wash., 143,673....C 3 91
Taft, Calif., 3,707....F 7 52
Taft, Tex., 2,978....G 9 87
Tahlequah, Okla., 4,750....M 3 81
Tahoka, Tex., 2,848....C 4 87
Takoma Park, Md., 13,341....G 5 65
Talent, Oreg., 739....E 5 82
Talladega, Ala., 13,134....F 4 49
TALLAHASSEE, Fla., 27,237....B 1 55
Tallapoosa, Ga., 2,826....B 3 56
Tallmadge, Ohio, 5,821....H 3 80
Tallulah, La., 7,758....H 2 63
Tama, Iowa, 2,930....H 5 60
Tamaqua, Pa., 11,508....L 4 83
Tampa, Fla., 124,681....D 4 55
Tamworth, N. H., □1,025....D 4 74
Taneytown, Md., 1,420....F 2 65
Tangier, Va., 915....M 5 90
Taos, N. Mex., 1,815....D 2 76
Tappahannock, Va., 1,011....L 5 90
Tarboro, N. C., 8,120....K 3 78
Tarentum, Pa., 9,540....C 4 83
Tarkio, Mo., 2,221....B 2 70
Tarpon Springs, Fla., 4,323....D 3 55
Tarrant, Ala., 7,571....E 3 49
Tarrytown, N. Y., 8,851....D 2 77
Taunton, Mass., 40,109....K 5 66
Tavares, Fla., 1,763....E 3 55
Taylor, Pa., 7,176....L 3 83
Taylor, Tex., 9,071....G 7 87
Taylorville, Ill., 9,188....D 4 58
Taylorsville, Ky., 888....G 4 62
Tazewell, Va., 1,347....B 6 90
Teague, Tex., 2,925....H 6 87
Teaneck, N. J., □33,772....B 2 75
Tecumseh, Mich., 4,020....E 7 67
Tecumseh, Nebr., 1,930....H 4 72
Tecumseh, Okla., 2,275....J 4 81
Tekamah, Nebr., 1,914....H 3 72
Tekoa, Wash., 1,189....H 3 91
Tell City, Ind., 5,735....D 9 59
Tellico Plains, Tenn., 833....N 4 86
Telluride, Colo., 1,101....D 7 53
Tempe, Ariz., 7,684....D 5 50
Temple, Okla., 1,442....F 6 81
Temple, Tex., 25,467....G 6 87
Templeton, Mass., □4,757....F 2 66
Tenafly, N. J., 9,651....F 2 75
Tenille, Ga., 1,713....G 8 56
Tenino, Wash., 969....C 4 91
Ten Sleep, Wyo., 289....E 1 94
Terra Alta, W. Va., 1,649....G 2 92
Terre Haute, Ind., 64,214....C 6 59
Terrell, Tex., 11,544....H 5 87
Teton, Idaho, 463....G 6 57
Tewksbury, Mass., □7,505....J 2 66
Texarkana, Ark., 15,875....C 7 51
Texarkana, Tex., 24,753....L 4 87
Texas City, Tex., 16,620....K 3 87
Texico, N. Mex., 691....F 4 76
Thatcher, Ariz., 1,284....F 6 50
Thayer, Mo., 1,639....K 9 70
The Dalles, Oreg., 7,676....F 2 82
The Plains, Va., 405....J 3 90
Thermopolis, Wyo., 2,870....D 2 94
Thibodaux, La., 7,730....J 7 63
Thief River Falls, Minn., 6,926....C 2 68
Thomas, W. Va., 1,146....H 2 92
Thomaston, Conn., □4,896....C 2 54
Thomaston, Ga., 6,580....D 5 56
Thomaston, Me., □2,810....E 7 64
Thomaston, N. Y., 2,045....D 2 77
Thomasville, Ala., 2,425....C 7 49
Thomasville, Ga., 14,424....D 9 56
Thomasville, N. C., 11,154....E 3 78
Thompson, Conn., □5,585....H 1 54
Thompson Falls, Mont., 851....A 3 71
Thompsonville, Conn., 9,633....E 1 54
Thomson, Ga., 3,489....H 4 56
Thorntown, Ind., 1,380....D 4 59
Thorp, Wis., 1,383....E 6 93
Three Forks, Mont., 1,114....E 5 71
Three Oaks, Mich., 1,572....C 7 67
Three Rivers, Mich., 6,785....D 7 67
Throop, Pa., 5,861....L 3 83
Thurmont, Md., 1,676....E 2 65
Ticonderoga, N. Y., 3,517....N 3 77
Tierra Amarilla, N. Mex., 800....C 2 76
Tiffin, Ohio, 18,952....D 3 80
Tifton, Ga., 6,831....F 8 56
Tigard, Oreg., 800....A 2 82
Tilden, Nebr., 1,033....G 2 72
Tillamook, Oreg., 3,685....D 2 82
Tilton, N. H., □2,085....C 5 74
Tiltonsville, Ohio, 2,202....J 5 80
Timmonsville, S. C., 2,001....J 3 84
Tioga, La., 338....F 4 63
Tipton, Mo., 1,234....G 5 70
Tipton, Ind., 5,633....E 4 59
Tipton, Iowa, 2,633....L 5 60
Tiptonville, Tenn., 1,953....B 2 86
Titusville, Fla., 2,604....F 3 55
Titusville, Pa., 8,923....C 2 83
Tiverton, R. I., □5,659....K 6 66
Tiverton, Four Corners, R. I., 12....K 6 66
Toadlena, N. Mex., 500....A 2 76
Toccoa, Ga., 6,781....F 1 56
Toledo, Iowa, 2,106....H 4 60
Toledo, Ohio, 303,616....D 2 80
Toledo, Oreg., 2,323....D 3 82
Toledo, Wash., 602....C 4 91
Tolleson, Ariz., 3,042....C 5 50
Toluca, Ill., 1,419....D 2 58
Tomah, Wis., 4,760....F 8 93
Tomahawk, Wis., 3,534....G 5 93
Tombstone, Ariz., 910....F 7 50
Tompkinsville, Ky., 1,859....F 7 62
Tonasket, Wash., 957....F 2 91
Tonawanda, N. Y., 14,617....B 4 77
Tonganoxie, Kans., 1,138....H 2 61
Tonkawa, Okla., 3,643....H 1 81
Tonopah, Nev., 1,375....D 4 73
Tooele, Utah, 7,269....B 3 88
TOPEKA, Kans., 78,791....G 2 61
Toppenish, Wash., 5,265....E 4 91
Topsham, Me., □2,626....C 8 64
Toronto, Ohio, 7,253....J 5 80
Torrance, Calif., 22,241....C11 52
Torreon, N. Mex., 100....C 4 76
Torrington, Conn., 27,820....C 1 54
Torrington, Wyo., 3,247....H 3 94
Totowa, N. J., 6,045....E 2 75
Towanda, Pa., 4,069....J 2 83
Towner, N. Dak., 955....K 3 79
Townley, Ala., 660....D 3 49
Townsend, Del., 441....M 3 65
Townshend, Vt., 178....B 4 89
Towson, Md., 11,000....H 3 65
Tracy, Calif., 8,410....D 6 52
Tracy, Minn., 3,020....C 6 68
Traer, Iowa, 1,627....J 4 60
Trafford, Pa., 3,965....C 5 83
Traverse City, Mich., 16,794....D 4 67
Trenton, Mich., 6,222....B 7 67
Trenton, Mo., 6,157....E 2 70
Trenton, Nebr., 1,239....C 4 72
TRENTON, N. J., 128,009....D 3 75
Trenton, Tenn., 3,868....D 3 86
Trenton, Utah, 451....B 2 88
Trezevant, Tenn., 765....D 2 86
Trimble, Tenn., 674....C 2 86
Trinidad, Colo., 12,204....L 8 53
Trion, Ga., 3,028....B 1 56
Tripp, S. Dak., 913....O 7 85
Troy, Ala., 8,555....G 7 49
Troy, Idaho, 531....B 3 57
Troy, Kans., 977....G 2 61
Troy, Mo., 1,738....K 5 70
Troy, Mont., 770....A 2 71
Troy, N. H., □1,360....B 6 74
Troy, N. Y., 72,311....N 5 77
Troy, Ohio, 10,661....B 5 80
Troy, Tenn., 519....C 2 86
Troy, Vt., □1,786....C 1 89
Truchas, N. Mex., 750....D 2 76
Truman, Minn., 1,106....D 7 68
Trumann, Ark., 3,744....K 2 51
Trumbull, Conn., □8,641....C 4 54
Truth or Consequences, N. Mex., 4,563....B 5 76
Tryon, N. C., 1,985....A 4 78
Tuckahoe, N. Y., 5,991....D 2 77
Tucson, Ariz., 45,485....D 6 50
Tucumcari, N. Mex., 8,419....F 3 76
Tulare, Calif., 12,445....F 7 52
Tularosa, N. Mex., 1,642....C 5 76
Tullahoma, Tenn., 7,562....J 4 86
Tulsa, Okla., 182,740....K 2 81
Tumwater, Wash., 2,725....C 4 91
Tunica, Miss., 1,354....D 1 69
Tupelo, Miss., 11,527....G 2 69
Tupper Lake, N. Y., 5,441....M 2 77
Turlock, Calif., 6,235....E 6 52
Turner, Me., □1,712....C 7 64
Turner, Oreg., 610....E 3 82
Turners Falls, Mass., 5,179....D 2 66
Turtle Creek, Pa., 12,363....C 7 83
Turtle Lake, N. Dak., 839....J 4 79
Tuscaloosa, Ala., 46,396....C 4 49
Tuscarora, Nev., 30....E 1 73
Tuscola, Ill., 2,960....E 4 58
Tuscumbia, Ala., 6,734....C 1 49
Tuskegee, Ala., 6,712....G 6 49
Twin Bridges, Mont., 497....D 5 71
Twin Falls, Idaho, 17,600....D 7 57
Two Harbors, Minn., 4,400....G 3 68
Two Rivers, Wis., 10,243....L 7 93
Tyler, Tex., 38,968....J 5 87
Tylertown, Miss., 1,331....D 8 69
Tyndall, S. Dak., 1,292....O 8 85
Tyrone, Pa., 8,214....F 4 83
Ucon, Idaho, 356....G 6 57
Uhrichsville, Ohio, 6,614....H 5 80
Ukiah, Calif., 6,120....B 4 52
Umatilla, Fla., 1,312....E 3 55
Umatilla, Oreg., 883....H 2 82
Underwood, N. Dak., 1,061....H 5 79
Union, Miss., 1,559....F 5 69
Union, Mo., 2,917....L 6 70
Union, N. J., □38,004....E 2 75
Union, S. C., 9,730....E 2 84
Union Bridge, Md., 840....F 2 65
Union City, Conn., 5,000....C 2 54
Union City, Ind., 3,572....H 4 59
Union City, Mich., 1,564....D 6 67
Union City, N. J., 55,537....B 2 75
Union City, Ohio, 1,622....A 5 80
Union City, Pa., 3,911....C 2 83
Union City, Tenn., 7,665....C 2 86
Union Gap, Wash., 1,766....E 4 91
Union Point, Ga., 1,724....G 3 56
Union Springs, Ala., 3,232....G 6 49
Uniontown, Ala., 1,798....C 6 49
Uniontown, Ky., 1,054....B 5 62
Uniontown, Pa., 20,471....C 6 83
Unionville, Mo., 2,050....F 1 70
University City, Mo., 39,892....M 5 70
University Heights, Ohio, 11,566....J 9 80
University Park, Md., 2,205....G 5 65
University Park, Tex., 24,275....H 2 87
Upland, Calif., 9,203....D10 52
Upper Arlington, Ohio, 9,024....D 6 80
Upper Darby, Pa., □84,951....M 6 83
Upper Marlboro, Md., 702....H 5 65
Upper Sandusky, Ohio, 4,397....D 4 80
Upton, Wyo., 951....H 1 94
Urbana, Ill., 22,835....E 3 58
Urbana, Ohio, 9,335....C 5 58
Urbanna, Va., 505....L 5 90
Ustick, Idaho, 200....B 6 57
Utica, N. Y., 101,531....K 4 77
Utica, Ohio, 1,510....F 5 80
Uvalde, Tex., 8,674....E 8 87
Uxbridge, Mass., □7,007....H 4 66
Valdese, N. C., 2,730....B 3 78
Valdez, Alaska Territory, 560....K 2 95
Valdosta, Ga., 20,046....F 9 56
Valentine, Nebr., 2,700....D 2 72
Valier, Mont., 710....D 2 71
Vallecitos, N. Mex., 400....C 2 76
Vallejo, Calif., 26,038....K 1 52
Valley, Nebr., 1,113....H 3 72
Valley City, N. Dak., 6,851....O 6 79
Valley Falls, Kans., 1,139....G 2 61
Valley Falls, R. I., 2,500....J 5 66
Valley Park, Mo., 2,956....L 5 70
Valley Stream, N. Y., 26,854....D 2 77
Valmy, Nev., 75....D 2 73
Valparaiso, Ind., 12,028....C 2 59
Van Buren, Ark., 6,413....B 3 51
Van Buren, Me., □5,094....H 1 64
Vanceburg, Ky., 1,528....L 3 62
Vancouver, Wash., 41,664....C 5 91
Vandalia, Ill., 5,471....D 5 58
Vandalia, Mo., 2,624....J 4 70
Vandergrift, Pa., 9,424....D 4 83
Van Lear, Ky., 1,096....M 5 62
Van Wert, Ohio, 10,364....A 4 80
Varnville, S. C., 1,180....F 6 84
Vassalboro, Me., □2,261....D 7 64
Vassar, Mich., 2,530....F 5 67
Veedersburg, Ind., 1,719....C 4 59
Velarde, N. Mex., 600....C 2 76
Velva, N. Dak., 1,170....J 3 79
Venice, Ill., 6,226....A 6 58
Ventnor, N. J., 8,185....E 5 75
Ventura, Calif., 16,534....F 9 52
Vergennes, Vt., 1,736....A 2 89
Vermilion, Ohio, 2,214....F 3 80
Vermillion, S. Dak., 5,337....R 8 85
Vernal, Utah, 2,845....E 3 88
Vernon, Conn., □10,115....F 1 54
Vernon, Tex., 12,651....E 3 87
Vernonia, Oreg., 1,521....D 2 82
Vero Beach, Fla., 4,746....F 4 55
Verona, N. J., 10,921....E 2 75
Verona, Pa., 4,235....C 6 83
Versailles, Ky., 2,760....H 4 62
Versailles, Mo., 1,929....G 6 70
Versailles, Ohio, 1,810....A 5 80
Vevay, Ind., 1,309....G 7 59
Viborg, S. Dak., 644....P 7 85
Vicksburg, Mich., 2,171....D 6 67
Vicksburg, Miss., 27,948....C 6 69
Victor, Colo., 684....J 5 53
Victoria, Tex., 16,126....H 9 87
Victoria, Va., 1,607....H 6 90
Vidalia, Ga., 5,819....H 6 56
Vidalia, La., 1,641....H 3 63
Vienna, Ga., 2,202....E 6 56
Vienna, Va., 2,029....K 3 90
Vienna, W. Va., 6,020....D 2 92
Villa Park, Ill., 8,821....A 2 58
Villa Rica, Ga., 1,703....C 3 56
Ville Platte, La., 6,633....F 5 63
Villisca, Iowa, 1,838....D 7 60
Vinalhaven, Me., □1,427....F 7 64
Vincennes, Ind., 18,831....C 7 59
Vincent, Ala., 1,140....F 4 49
Vine Grove, Ky., 1,252....F 5 62
Vineland, N. J., 8,155....C 5 75
Vinita, Okla., 5,518....M 1 81
Vinton, Iowa, 4,307....J 4 60
Vinton, La., 2,597....D 6 63
Vinton, Va., 3,629....E 6 90
Viola, Del., 134....M 4 65
Virden, N. Mex., 146....A 6 76
Virginia, Minn., 12,486....F 3 68
Virginia Beach, Va., 5,390....N 7 90
Virginia City, Mont., 323....E 5 71
Virginia City, Nev., 800....B 3 73
Viroqua, Wis., 3,795....E 8 93
Visalia, Calif., 11,749....F 7 52
Vivian, La., 2,426....C 1 63
Volga, S. Dak., 578....R 5 85
Wabash, Ind., 10,621....F 3 59
Wabasha, Minn., 2,468....F 6 68
Wachapreague, Va., 551....N 5 90
Waco, Tex., 84,706....G 6 87
Waconia, Minn., 1,569....E 6 68
Wadena, Minn., 3,958....C 4 68
Wadesboro, N. C., 3,408....E 5 78
Wadsworth, Nev., 275....B 3 73
Wadsworth, Ohio, 7,966....G 3 80
Wagner, S. Dak., 1,528....N 7 85
Wagoner, Okla., 4,395....M 3 81
Wagon Mound, N. Mex., 1,120....E 2 76
Wahiawa, Hawaii Territory, 8,341....E 2 95
Wahoo, Nebr., 3,128....H 3 72
Wahpeton, N. Dak., 5,125....S 7 79
Waialua, Hawaii Territory, 2,512....E 1 95
Wailuku, Hawaii Territory, 7,411....J 2 95
Waipahu, Hawaii Territory, 7,162....A 3 95
Waite Park, Minn., 1,639....D 5 68
Waitsburg, Wash., 1,015....G 4 91
Wakarusa, Ind., 1,143....F 1 59
Wakeeney, Kans., 2,446....C 2 61
Wakefield, Mass., □19,633....K 3 66
Wakefield, Mich., 3,344....F 2 67
Wakefield, Nebr., 1,027....H 2 72
Wakefield, N. H., □1,267....D 4 74
Wakefield, R. I., 3,047....H 7 66
Wakefield, Va., 949....K 7 90
Wake Forest, N. C., 3,704....H 3 78
Walden, Colo., 696....G 1 53
Walden, N. Y., 4,559....B 1 77
Waldo, Ark., 1,491....D 7 51
Waldoboro, Me., □2,536....E 7 64
Waldport, Oreg., 689....C 3 82
Waldron, Ark., 1,292....B 4 51
Walhalla, N. Dak., 1,463....P 2 79
Walhalla, S. C., 3,104....B 2 84
Walker, Minn., 1,192....D 3 68
Walkersville, Md., 761....E 3 65
Walkerton, Ind., 2,102....E 2 59
Walkerville, Mont., 1,631....D 4 71
Wallace, Idaho, 3,140....B 2 57
Walla Walla, Wash., 24,102....G 4 91
Wallingford, Conn., 11,994....D 3 54
Wallingford, Vt., 1,482....B 4 89
Wallington, N. J., 8,910....B 2 75
Wallins Creek, Ky., 525....L 7 62
Wallowa, Oreg., 1,055....K 2 82
Walnut Ridge, Ark., 3,106....J 1 51
Walpole, Mass., □9,109....J 4 66
Walpole, N. H., □2,536....B 5 74
Walsenburg, Colo., 5,596....K 7 53
Walterboro, S. C., 4,616....G 6 84
Walters, Okla., 2,743....F 6 81
Waltham, Mass., 47,187....J 3 66
Walthill, Nebr., 958....H 2 72
Walton, Ky., 1,358....H 3 62
Walton, N. Y., 3,947....K 6 77
Wamac, Ill., 1,429....D 5 58
Wamego, Kans., 1,869....F 2 61
Wamsutter, Wyo., 103....E 4 94
Wanaque, N. J., 4,222....A 2 75
Wapakoneta, Ohio, 5,797....B 4 80
Wapello, Iowa, 1,755....L 6 60
Wappingers Falls, N. Y., 3,490....N 7 77
War, W. Va., 3,992....C 6 92
Wardner, Idaho, 772....B 2 57
Ware, Mass., □7,517....E 3 66
Wareham, Mass., □7,569....M 5 66
Ware Shoals, S. C., 3,032....D 3 84
Warner, N. H., □1,080....C 5 74
Warner Robins, Ga., 7,986....E 5 56
Warren, Ariz., 2,610....F 7 50
Warren, Ark., 2,615....F 6 51
Warren, Ind., 1,247....G 3 59
Warren, Me., □1,576....E 7 64
Warren, Mass., □3,406....F 4 66
Warren, Minn., 1,779....B 2 68
Warren, Ohio, 49,856....J 3 80
Warren, Pa., 14,849....D 2 83
Warren, R. I., 8,513....J 6 66
Warrensburg, Mo., 6,857....E 5 70
Warrenton, Mo., 1,584....K 5 70
Warrenton, Oreg., 1,896....D 1 82
Warrington, Fla., 13,570....A 1 55
Warrior, Ala., 1,384....E 3 49
Warroad, Minn., 1,276....C 2 68
Warsaw, Ill., 2,022....B 3 58
Warsaw, Ind., 6,625....F 2 59
Warsaw, Ky., 829....H 3 62

	Index Ref.	Plate No.
Warsaw, N. Y., 3,713	D 5	77
Warsaw, N. C., 1,598	J 4	78
Wartrace, Tenn., 545	J 3	86
Warwick, N. Y., 2,674	B 1	77
Warwick, R. I., 43,028	J 6	66
Waseca, Minn., 4,927	E 6	68
Washburn, Me., □1,913	G 2	64
Washburn, N. Dak., 913	J 5	79
Washburn, Wis., 2,070	E 2	93
WASHINGTON, D. C., 802,178	F 5	65
Washington, Ga., 3,802	G 3	56
Washington, Ill., 4,285	D 3	58
Washington, Ind., 10,987	C 7	59
Washington, Iowa, 5,902	K 6	60
Washington, Kans., 1,527	F 2	61
Washington, Mo., 6,850	K 5	70
Washington, N. J., 4,802	D 2	75
Washington, N. C., 9,698	M 3	78
Washington, Pa., 26,280	B 5	83
Washington, R. I., 2,800	H 6	66
Washington Court House, Ohio, 10,560	D 6	80
Washington Park, Ill., 5,840	B 6	58
Watch Hill, R. I., 750	G 7	66
Waterbury, Conn., 104,477	C 2	54
Waterbury, Vt., 3,153	B 2	89
Waterford, Conn., □9,100	G 3	54
Waterford, N. Y., 2,968	N 5	77
Waterloo, Ill., 2,821	C 5	58
Waterloo, Ind., 1,414	G 2	59
Waterloo, Iowa, 65,198	J 4	60
Waterloo, N. Y., 4,438	G 5	77
Waterloo, Wis., 1,667	J 9	93
Watertown, Conn., □10,699	C 2	54
Watertown, Mass., □37,329	R10	66
Watertown, N. Y., 34,350	J 3	77
Watertown, S. Dak., 12,699	P 4	85
Watertown, Tenn., 933	J 2	86
Watertown, Wis., 12,417	J 9	93
Water Valley, Miss., 3,113	E 2	69
Waterville, Me., 18,287	D 6	64
Waterville, Minn., 1,627	E 6	68
Waterville, N. Y., 1,634	K 5	77
Waterville, Wash., 1,013	E 3	91
Watervliet, N. Y., 15,197	N 5	77
Watford City, N. Dak., 1,371	D 4	79
Watkins Glen, N. Y., 3,052	G 6	77
Watonga, Okla., 3,249	F 3	81
Watseka, Ill., 4,235	F 3	58
Watsonville, Calif., 11,572	D 7	52
Waubay, S. Dak., 879	P 3	85
Wauchula, Fla., 2,872	E 4	55
Waukegan, Ill., 38,946	F 1	58
Waukesha, Wis., 21,233	K 9	93
Waukon, Iowa, 3,158	L 2	60
Waupaca, Wis., 3,921	J 7	93
Waupun, Wis., 6,725	J 8	93
Waurika, Okla., 2,327	G 6	81
Wausau, Wis., 30,414	G 6	93
Wauseon, Ohio, 3,494	D 1	80
Wauwatosa, Wis., 33,324	K 9	93
Waverly, Iowa, 5,124	H 3	60
Waverly, N. Y., 6,037	G 6	77
Waverly, Ohio, 1,679	D 7	80
Waverly, Tenn., 1,892	F 2	86
Waxahachie, Tex., 11,204	H 5	87
Waycross, Ga., 18,999	H 8	56
Wayland, Ky., 1,807	M 6	62
Wayland, Mass., □4,407	J 3	66
Wayland, N. Y., 1,834	E 5	77
Wayne, Mich., 9,409	F 6	67
Wayne, Nebr., 3,595	G 2	72
Wayne, Pa., 6,000	M 6	83
Wayne, W. Va., 1,257	B 4	92
Waynesboro, Ga., 4,461	J 4	56
Waynesboro, Pa., 10,334	G 6	83
Waynesboro, Tenn., 1,147	F 4	86
Waynesboro, Va., 12,357	F 4	90
Waynesburg, Pa., 5,514	B 6	83
Waynesville, N. C., 5,295	E 8	78
Waynoka, Okla., 2,018	E 1	81
Wayzata, Minn., 1,791	E 6	68
Weare, N. H., □1,345	C 5	74
Weatherford, Okla., 3,529	E 4	81
Weatherford, Tex., 8,093	G 5	87
Webb City, Mo., 6,919	C 8	70
Webster, Mass., □13,194	G 4	66
Webster, N. Y., 1,773	F 4	77
Webster, S. Dak., 2,503	P 3	85
Webster City, Iowa, 7,611	F 4	60
Webster Groves, Mo., 23,390	L 5	70
Websterville, Vt., 975	B 2	89
Weedsport, N. Y., 1,588	G 4	77
Weehawken, N. J., □14,380	B 2	75
Weekapaug, R. I., 200	G 7	66
Weeksbury, Ky., 1,340	M 6	62
Weeping Water, Nebr., 1,070	H 4	72
Weir, Kans., 819	H 4	61
Weirton, W. Va., 24,005	K 5	92
Weiser, Idaho, 3,961	B 5	57
Welch, W. Va., 6,603	C 6	92
Weldon, N. C., 2,295	K 2	78
Weleetka, Okla., 1,548	K 4	81
Wellesley, Mass., □20,549	Q10	66
Wellesley Hills, Mass	Q10	66
Wellington, Kans., 7,747	E 4	61
Wellington, Ohio, 2,992	E 3	80
Wellington, Tex., 3,676	E 3	87
Wellington, Utah, 845	D 4	88
Wells, Me., □2,321	B 9	64
Wells, Minn., 2,475	E 7	68
Wells, Nev., 947	G 1	73
Wellsboro, Pa., 4,215	H 2	83
Wellsburg, W. Va., 5,787	K 5	92
Wells River, Vt., 570	C 2	89
Wellston, Mo., 9,396	P 3	70
Wellston, Ohio, 5,691	F 7	80
Wellsville, N. Y., 6,402	E 6	77
Wellsville, Ohio, 7,854	J 4	80
Welsh, La., 2,416	E 6	63
Wenatchee, Wash., 13,072	E 3	91
Weslaco, Tex., 7,514	G11	87
West Allis, Wis., 42,959	K 9	93
West Barnet, Vt., 88	C 2	89
West Barrington, R. I., 4,250	J 6	66
West Bend, Wis., 6,849	K 9	93
West Blocton, Ala., 1,280	D 4	49
Westboro, Mass., □7,378	H 3	66
West Branch, Mich., 2,098	E 4	67
Westbrook, Me., 12,284	C 8	64
West Burke, Vt., 414	D 1	89
West Burlington, Iowa, 1,614	L 7	60
Westbury, N. Y., 7,112	D 2	77
Westby, Mont., 396	M 2	71
Westby, Wis., 1,491	E 8	93
West Caldwell, N. J., 4,666	E 2	75
West Carrollton, Ohio, 2,876	B 6	80
West Carthage, N. Y., 2,000	J 3	77
West Chester, Pa., 15,168	L 6	83
West Chicago, Ill., 3,973	E 2	58
West Columbia, S. C., 4,373	F 4	84
West Des Moines, Iowa, 5,615	F 5	60
West Englewood, N. J., 14,000	C 2	75
Westerly, R. I., □12,380	G 7	66
Western Port, Md., 3,431	B 8	65
Western Springs, Ill., 6,364	A 2	58
Westerville, Ohio, 4,112	D 5	80
Westfield, Mass., 20,962	C 4	66
Westfield, N. J., 21,243	E 2	75
Westfield, N. Y., 3,663	A 6	77
Westford, Mass., □4,262	J 2	66
West Frankfort, Ill., 11,384	E 6	58
West Greenwich, R. I., □847	H 6	66
West Hartford, Conn., □44,402	E 1	54
West Haven, Conn., □32,010	D 3	54
West Haverstraw, N. Y., 3,099	C 1	77
West Hazleton, Pa. 6,988	K 4	83
West Helena, Ark., 6,103	J 4	51
Westhope, N. Dak., 575	H 2	79
West Jefferson, Ohio, 1,647	D 6	80
West Lafayette, Ind., 11,873	D 4	59
Westlake, Ohio, 4,912	G 9	80
West Lebanon, N. H., 1,737	B 4	74
West Liberty, Iowa, 1,866	L 5	60
West Linn, Oreg., 2,945	E 2	82
West Memphis, Ark., 9,112	K 3	51
West Mifflin, Pa., 17,985	C 7	83
West Milwaukee, Wis., 5,429	L 9	93
Westminster, Md., 6,140	G 2	65
Westminster, S. C., 2,219	B 2	84
Westminster, Vt., 298	B 4	89
West Monroe, La., 10,302	F 1	63
Westmont, Ill., 3,402	A 1	58
West New York, N. J., 37,683	C 2	75
Weston, Idaho, 382	F 7	57
Weston, Mass., □5,026	J 3	66
Weston, Oreg., 679	J 2	82
Weston, W. Va., 8,945	E 2	92
West Orange, N. J., 28,605	A 2	75
Westover, Md., 400	M 8	65
Westover, W. Va., 4,318	G 1	92
West Palm Beach, Fla., 43,162	F 5	55
West Paterson, N. J., 3,931	B 2	75
West Pittston, Pa., 7,230	L 3	83
West Plains, Mo., 4,918	J 9	70
West Point, Ga., 4,076	B 5	56
West Point, Ky., 1,669	F 5	62
West Point, Miss., 6,432	G 3	69
Westpoint, Nebr., 2,658	H 3	72
West Point, N. Y., 5,000	C 1	77
West Point, Va., 1,919	L 5	90
Westport, Conn., □11,667	B 4	54
Westport, Mass., □4,989	K 6	66
West Reading, Pa., 5,072	L 5	83
West Rutland, Vt., □2,487	A 3	89
West Saint Paul, Minn., 7,955	E 6	68
West Salem, Wis., 1,376	D 8	93
West Springfield, Mass., □20,438	D 4	66
West Terre Haute, Ind., 3,357	B 6	59
West Union, Iowa, 2,141	K 3	60
West University Place, Tex., 17,074	J 8	87
West View, Pa., 7,581	B 6	83
Westville, Ill., 3,196	F 3	58
Westville, N. J., 4,731	C 4	75
Westwego, La., 8,328	K 7	63
Westwood, Calif., 3,618	D 3	52
Westwood, N. J., 6,766	B 1	75
West York, Pa., 5,756	J 6	83
Wethersfield, Conn., □12,533	E 2	54
Wetumka, Okla., 2,025	K 4	81
Wetumpka, Ala., 3,813	F 5	49
Wewahitchka, Fla., 1,289	D 6	55
Wewoka, Okla., 6,747	K 4	81
Weymouth, Mass., □32,690	L 4	66
Wharton, N. J., 3,853	D 2	75
Wharton, Tex., 4,450	J 8	87
What Cheer, Iowa, 1,119	J 6	60
Wheatland, Wyo., 2,286	H 3	94
Wheaton, Ill., 11,638	E 2	58
Wheaton, Minn., 1,948	B 5	68
Wheat Ridge, Colo., 7,000	J 3	53
Wheeling, W. Va., 58,891	K 5	92
Wheelwright, Ky., 2,037	M 6	62
Whistler, Ala	B 9	49
White, S. Dak., 525	R 5	85
White Bear Lake, Minn., 3,646	E 5	68
White Bluff, Tenn., 506	G 2	86
Whitefield, N. H., □1,677	C 3	74
Whitefish, Mont., 3,268	B 2	71
Whitefish Bay, Wis., 14,665	L 9	93
White Hall, Ill., 3,082	C 4	58
Whitehall, Mich., 1,819	C 5	67
Whitehall, Mont., 929	E 5	71
Whitehall, Pa., 7,342	B 7	83
White Pine, Tenn., 780	P 2	86
White Plains, N. Y., 43,466	D 2	77
Whiteriver, Ariz., 950	E 5	50
White River, S. Dak., 465	H 6	85
White River Junction, Vt., 2,365	C 3	89
White Salmon, Wash., 1,353	D 5	91
Whitesboro, N. Y., 3,902	K 4	77
Whitesburg, Ky., 1,393	M 6	62
White Settlement, Tex., 10,827	E 2	87
White Sulphur Springs, Mont., 1,025	E 4	71
White Sulphur Springs, W. Va., 2,643	F 5	92
Whiteville, N. C., 4,238	H 6	78
Whiteville, Tenn., 794	C 4	86
Whitewater, Wis., 5,101	J10	93
Whiting, Ind., 9,669	C 1	59
Whitinsville, Mass., 5,662	H 4	66
Whitman, Mass., □8,413	L 4	66
Whitmire, S. C., 3,006	E 3	84
Whittier, Calif., 23,820	D11	52
Wibaux, Mont., 739	M 3	71
Wichita, Kans., 168,279	E 4	61
Wichita Falls, Tex., 68,042	F 4	87
Wickenburg, Ariz., 1,736	C 5	50
Wickliffe, Ky., 1,019	B 3	62
Wickliffe, Ohio, 5,002	G 2	80
Wilber, Nebr., 1,356	G 4	72
Wilburton, Okla., 1,939	M 5	81
Wilder, Idaho, 555	B 6	57
Wildwood, Fla., 2,019	D 3	55
Wildwood, N. J., 5,475	D 6	75
Wilkes-Barre, Pa., 76,826	L 3	83
Wilkesboro, N. C., 1,370	C 2	78
Wilkins, S. C., 150	G 7	84
Wilkinsburg, Pa., 31,418	C 7	83
Willamina, Oreg., 1,082	D 2	82
Willard, Ohio, 4,744	G 2	80
Willard, Utah, 548	C 2	88
Wilcox, Ariz., 1,266	F 6	50
Williams, Ariz., 2,152	C 3	50
Williamsburg, Iowa, 1,183	K 5	60
Williamsburg, Ky., 3,348	J 7	62
Williamsburg, Va., 6,735	L 6	90
Williamson, N. Y., 1,520	F 4	77
Williamson, W. Va., 8,624	B 5	92
Williamsport, Ind., 1,241	C 4	59
Williamsport, Md., 1,890	C 2	65
Williamsport, Pa., 45,047	H 3	83
Williamston, N. C., 4,975	M 3	78
Williamston, S. C., 2,782	C 2	84
Williamstown, Ky., 1,466	H 3	62
Williamstown, Mass., □6,194	A 2	66
Williamstown, Vt., 1,600	B 2	89
Williamstown, W. Va., 2,001	C 2	92
Williamsville, N. Y., 4,649	C 5	77
Willimansett, Mass., 9,474	D 4	66
Willimantic, Conn., 13,586	G 2	54
Williston, N. Dak., 7,378	C 3	79
Williston, S. C., 896	F 5	84
Williston Park, N. Y., 7,505	D 2	77
Willmar, Minn., 9,410	C 5	68
Willow Grove, Pa	M 5	83
Willow Run, Mich., 11,365	F 6	67
Willows, Calif., 3,019	C 4	52
Wilmerding, Pa., 5,325	C 5	83
Wilmette, Ill., 18,162	B 1	58
Wilmington, Del., 110,356	M 2	65
Wilmington, Ill., 3,354	E 2	58
Wilmington, Mass., □7,039	K 2	66
Wilmington, N. C., 45,043	J 6	78
Wilmington, Ohio, 7,387	C 7	80
Wilmington, Vt., 571	B 5	89
Wilmore, Ky., 2,337	H 5	62
Wilsall, Mont., 300	F 5	71
Wilson, Ark., 1,301	K 2	51
Wilson, Kans., 1,039	D 3	61
Wilson, N. C., 23,010	K 3	78
Wilson, Okla., 1,832	H 6	81
Wilson, Pa., 8,159	M 4	83
Wilton, Conn., □4,558	B 4	54
Wilton, Me., □3,455	C 6	64
Wilton, N. H., □1,952	C 6	74
Wilton, N. Dak., 796	J 5	79
Wilton Junction, Iowa, 1,446	M 5	60
Winamac, Ind., 2,166	D 2	59
Winchendon, Mass., □6,585	F 2	66
Winchester Center, Conn	C 1	54
Winchester, Idaho, 488	B 3	57
Winchester, Ind., 5,467	G 4	59
Winchester, Ky., 9,226	J 4	62
Winchester, Mass., □15,509	R10	66
Winchester, N. H., □2,388	B 6	74
Winchester, Tenn., 3,974	J 4	86
Winchester, Va., 13,841	H 2	90
Windber, Pa., 8,010	E 5	83
Winder, Ga., 4,604	E 3	56
Windham, Conn., □15,884	G 2	54
Windom, Minn., 3,165	D 7	68
Windsor, Colo., 1,548	J 2	53
Windsor, Conn., □11,833	E 1	54
Windsor, Mo., 2,429	E 5	70
Windsor, N. C., 1,781	L 2	78
Windsor, Vt., 3,467	C 4	89
Windsor, Va., 451	L 7	90
Windsor Locks, Conn., □5,221	E 1	54
Winfield, Ala., 2,108	C 3	49
Winfield, Kans., 10,264	F 4	61
Winifred, Mont., 217	G 3	71
Winkelman, Ariz., 548	E 6	50
Winlock, Wash., 878	C 4	91
Winnebago, Minn., 2,127	D 7	68
Winnebago, Nebr., 684	H 2	72
Winnemucca, Nev., 2,847	D 2	73
Winner, S. Dak., 3,252	K 7	85
Winnetka, Ill., 12,105	B 1	58
Winnett, Mont., 407	H 3	71
Winnfield, La., 5,629	E 3	63
Winnsboro, La., 3,655	G 2	63
Winnsboro, S. C., 3,267	F 3	84
Winnsboro, Tex., 2,512	J 5	87
Winona, Minn., 25,031	G 6	68
Winona, Miss., 3,441	E 4	69
Winooski, Vt., 6,734	A 1	89
Winslow, Ariz., 6,518	E 3	50
Winslow, Ind., 1,322	C 8	59
Winsted, Conn., 8,781	C 1	54
Winston-Salem, N. C., 87,811	E 2	78
Winter Garden, Fla., 3,503	E 3	55
Winter Haven, Fla., 8,605	E 3	55
Winter Park, Fla., 8,250	E 3	55
Winterport, Me., □1,694	F 6	64
Winters, Tex., 2,676	E 6	87
Winterset, Iowa, 3,570	E 6	60
Winthrop, Mass., □19,496	L 3	66
Winthrop, Minn., 1,251	D 6	68
Winton, Pa., 6,280	M 3	83
Wiscasset, Me., □1,584	D 7	64
Wisconsin Dells, Wis., 1,957	G 8	93
Wisconsin Rapids, Wis., 13,496	G 7	93
Wishek, N. Dak., 1,241	L 7	79
Woburn, Mass., 20,492	K 3	66
Wolfeboro, N. H., □2,581	D 4	74
Wolf Point, Mont., 2,557	L 2	71
Woodbridge, Conn., □2,822	C 3	54
Woodbridge, N. J., □35,758	E 2	75
Woodburn, Oreg., 2,395	E 2	82
Woodbury, N. J., 10,931	C 4	75
Woodbury, Tenn., 1,000	J 3	86
Woodland, Calif., 9,386	D 5	52
Wood-Lynne, N. J., 2,776	B 3	75
Wood River, Ill., 10,190	C 5	58
Wood River, Nebr., 858	F 4	72
Woodruff, S. C., 3,831	E 2	84
Woodruff Place, Ind., 1,557	E 5	59
Woodsboro, Md., 427	E 2	65
Woodsfield, Ohio, 2,410	H 6	80
Woodside, Del., 157	M 4	65
Woodstock, Ill., 7,192	E 1	58
Woodstock, N. H., □894	C 4	74
Woodstock, Vt., 1,326	B 3	89
Woodstock, Va., 1,816	G 3	90
Woodward, Okla., 5,915	D 2	81
Woonsocket, R. I., 50,211	J 5	66
Woonsocket, S. Dak., 1,051	N 5	85
Wooster, Ohio, 14,005	G 4	80
Worcester, Mass., 203,486	G 3	66
Worland, Wyo., 4,202	E 1	94
Worthington, Ind., 1,627	C 6	59
Worthington, Ky., 1,000	F 4	62
Worthington, Minn., 7,923	C 7	68
Worthington, Ohio, 2,141	E 5	80
Worton, Md., 150	K 2	65
Wrangell, Alaska Territory	O 3	95
Wray, Colo., 2,198	P 2	53
Wrens, Ga., 1,380	H 4	56
Wrentham, Mass., □5,341	J 4	66
Wrightsville, Ga., 1,750	G 5	56
Wyandotte, Mich., 36,846	B 7	67
Wymore, Nebr., 2,258	H 4	72
Wyndmere, N. Dak., 627	R 7	79
Wynne, Ark., 4,142	J 3	51
Wynne Wood, Okla., 2,423	H 5	81
Wyoming, Del., 911	M 4	65
Wyoming, Ohio, 5,582	C 9	80
Wyoming, Pa., 4,511	L 3	83
Wyoming, R. I., 315	H 6	66
Wyomissing, Pa., 4,187	K 5	83
Wytheville, Va., 5,513	C 7	90
Xenia, Ohio, 12,877	E 5	80
Yakima, Wash., 38,486	E 4	91
Yale, Okla., 1,359	J 2	81
Yamhill, Oreg., 539	D 2	82
Yankton, S. Dak., 7,709	P 8	85
Yaphank, N. Y., 1,200	E 2	77
Yarmouth, Me., □2,669	C 8	64
Yates Center, Kans., 2,178	G 4	61
Yazoo City, Miss., 9,746	C 5	69
Yeadon, Pa., 11,068	N 7	83
Yellow Springs, Ohio, 2,896	C 6	80
Yemassee, S. C., 712	G 6	84
Yerington, Nev., 1,157	B 4	73
Yoakum, Tex., 5,231	G 8	87
Yonkers, N. Y., 152,798	C 2	77
York, Me., 2,000	A 9	64
York, Nebr., 6,178	G 4	72
York, Pa., 59,953	J 6	83
York, S. C., 4,181	F 1	84
York Harbor, Me., 750	B 9	64
Yorklyn, Del., 500	M 1	65
Yorktown, Tex., 2,596	G 9	87
Yorktown, Va., 384	M 6	90
Yorkville, N. Y., 3,528	K 4	77
Yorkville, Ohio, 1,854	J 5	80
Youngstown, Ohio, 168,330	J 3	80
Ypsilanti, Mich., 18,302	F 6	67
Yukon, Okla., 1,990	G 3	81
Yuma, Ariz., 9,145	A 6	50
Yuma, Colo., 1,908	O 2	53
Zanesville, Ohio, 40,517	G 6	80
Zeeland, Mich., 3,075	D 6	67
Zeeland, N. Dak., 484	L 8	79
Zeigler, Ill., 2,516	D 6	58
Zephyrhills, Fla., 1,826	D 3	55
Zion, Ill., 8,950	F 1	58
Zionsville, Ind., 1,536	E 5	59
Zumbrota, Minn., 1,686	F 6	68
Zwolle, La., 1,555	C 3	63

Illustrated Geography and Gazetteer

of

THE WORLD

Introduction

THE HEADLINE EVENTS of the last half-century have made the average American acutely curious of the vast world beyond the national borders of the American homeland. Constant repetition has tended to make this thought a cliché, yet it is one of the most significant truths of our times. This new national concern for the external world and its problems is one of the hopeful signs pointing to a better future for mankind. However, no matter how well-intentioned our concern for international relations may be it is of no value unless it is grounded on an intelligent appreciation of the great diversity of social, economic and political forms extant throughout the globe.

One of the main roads to a better knowledge of this fascinating planet is a thorough indoctrination in the golden lore of geography. This science is not a narrow and limited scholarly discipline but a universal department of knowledge drawing on the sum total of man's explorations in the field of thought. The very pervasiveness of earth science makes it intriguing reading for the average non-specialist. At the same time that it entertains, it also builds a permanent edifice of information for the general reader. As more individuals discover this golden key to understanding the tumultuous happenings of the day, our collective actions in the field of enlightened citizenship will gain immeasurably in effectiveness.

On the following pages the editors have presented a treasure-trove of information on the world's nations, resources, peoples and governments. Salient facts regarding the many countries of our Mother Earth have been arranged in easily-found tabular form. This arrangement by tables makes comparison between political units a simple task. Striking photographs lend a sense of immediacy to the equally engaging text descriptions of countries and continents. Highlighting the gazetteer and geography are the colorful Resource-Relief maps which locate at a glance the major relief and resource features of the continental land masses.

Alaska Development Board

Salmon fishing is the chief enterprise in Alaska. These small fleets play a vital part in providing tons of fish for the industry.

Canadian National Railroads

Ragged peaks and stoney crags form the watercourse for Emperor Falls in British Columbia.

NORTH AMERICA — Lying across the wide expanse of the Atlantic Ocean, was a new World waiting discovery and recognition. Europe was completely unaware of its existence for many centuries. Its discovery was destined to change the whole course of history and affect the fortunes of men and nations the world over. More than that, its discovery ushered in a whole new era of civilization, and marked the first faltering step towards the exploration and charting of all lands and waters of the world.

No discovery, before or since, has added more to man's opportunities and the wealth of the world; or played a more important part in shaping a world's destiny. Yet, its discoverer died in ignorance of his epoch-making contribution to the world. It remained for those who followed to prove the existence of a New World.

Landing on one of the Bahamas, how was Columbus to know that his quest for a new route to the East Indies had led him to an island outpost of two fabulous empires ? . . . now but a bare few hours by air travel from the sister continents of North and South America. In his wildest dreams Columbus could not have conceived of a land extending virtually from the North Pole to the South Pole, for a distance of some nine thousand miles.

We can imagine Balboa's thrill twenty-one years later, when he fought his way across the rocky Ithmus of Panama to gaze upon the Pacific. But, how was he to know that this narrow ribbon of tapering land joined two vast domains ? That, from where he stood, an unbroken expanse of land reached

northward for forty-five hundred miles, and actually spread out into a gigantic fan three thousand miles wide ? Also, that, to the south a similar, though lesser triangle of land, reached thousands of miles below the equator to the icy waters of the Antarctic ?

Today these are historical incidents of common knowledge, thanks to the intrepid discoverers, explorers and map-makers. We take their hard won glories for granted, and even forget the adventure and romance that has gone into the making of our geographical maps.

We must be constantly reminded that, of all the continents of the world, North America is the most favored for natural wealth, climate and position on the earth. Being situated between the two largest oceans has protected the people of North America from enemy invasion, and also enabled them to develop an extensive commerce. The millions of square miles of fertile soil and untold mineral wealth has provided a standard of living unknown elsewhere in the world. Hence, composed of peoples from all over the world, its inhabitants have enjoyed peace and plenty, without fear of their independent ways of life being encroached upon, or destroyed by jealous and covetous neighbors. We can be assured that such a fortunate people will not easily relinquish what they have come to hold so dear.

The principal geographical features of North America are its two mountain ranges and the intervening central plains. The high and rugged mountains to the westward extend from the tip of Alaska to the base of the Isthmus of Panama, or from the northern

to the southern extremity of the continent. These mountain ranges include the Coastal system that hugs the Pacific Coast, and the Rocky Mountains that branch out eastward and southward across the United States to become, in Mexico and Central America, the Sierra Madres. The Cascade Mountains, which farther south become the Sierra Nevada, are separate ranges that work inland from the coastal mountains. These diverging mountain chains in the east and west, form the bulwark for a number of high plateaus that lie between. The land adjoining the Cascade Mountains is the Columbia Plateau, while farther south lies the Colorado Plateau. In between is the arid region of the Great Basin. The Great Salt Lake is all that remains to reveal that this vast area was once a geologic lake.

In the east, extending from the Gulf of Saint Lawrence to the Gulf of Mexico is the Appalachian Range. These mountains are older and less rugged than the Rockies. Time has worn them down and rounded their peaks. On the side toward the Atlantic Ocean, they merge with the Piedmont Plateau, which slopes off into a coastal plain.

The great central plains that slope towards the center, and lie between the Rocky Mountain and Appalachian Highlands describe a giant "V" which extends from the Arctic Ocean to the Gulf of Mexico.

More varieties of climate prevail in North America than in any other land in the world. The greater part of the continent, however, enjoys a temperate and invigorating climate. The inhabitants of the far north must adjust themselves to the rigors of Arctic weather,

Spacious fields of wheat stacked for harvest are a frequent sight in the Prairie regions of Canada.

Canadian National Railroads

National Film Board of Canada

Fishing is the chief occupation in the Maritime Provinces of Canada.

Mexico endures sub-tropical temperatures, and Central America a tropical heat. Even from the east to west there is a wide variety of climate due to difference in altitude, and other conditions not affected by latitude.

To an airman soaring above the shifting panorama of North America, the realization must come that this is indeed a rich land of fertile soils, spreading forests, rolling plains, inland lakes, and mighty rivers. There is hardly an area of any size on the entire continent but contains, on the surface or beneath it, a species of natural wealth. On the western coast, the great Pacific Ocean, generally a protective barrier, separating most of North America from the shores of Asia, offers little promise of isolation at its far northwest corner. While eight thousand miles separate the peoples of China from the United States, Russia and Alaska almost meet at the Bering Strait, which is only fifty-seven miles wide.

ALASKA—Purchased from Russia in 1867 for a pittance of $7,200,000 and is still today the United States' most valued possession strategically. Although partially in the Arctic Circle, it is by no means the frozen and inhospitable land its latitude would suggest. Alaska has a wide area of equable climate. Along its mountainous and island-fringed coast, the warm Japanese Current keeps the temperature at all times above zero. This rises in the summer to a seasonal heat of 80°. These sections endure drenching rain, caused

by the condensation of warm winds striking the snow-capped peaks of the mountains. In the center of Alaska is a broad upland where grasses, flowers and mosses grow.

The Yukon River, rising in Canada, swings across Alaska for fifteen hundred miles, twelve hundred of which are navigable. Although frozen for two-thirds of the year, this river is a main artery of travel. Dog sled teams replace the large steamers during the months when it is ice-bound. A half million acres of land is cultivated in the Yukon Valley, and even though the growing season is short, the Arctic days provide long hours of sunshine.

First known as "Seward's Folly," Alaska justified its purchase within a few short years and has proved a veritable storehouse of treasure. Each year it produces more than twice its purchase price, in minerals alone.

The popular conception of the Arctic does, however, exist in the northern regions. Here the ground thaws only a few inches at the surface during the summer. Except for a few Eskimo and reindeer, there is comparatively no life or vegetation able to survive the rigors of the frigid climate.

While at one time Alaska was a remote and unexplored country, today with ever increasing population and extensive building and improvement of roads, development is steadily expanding.

The Aleutian islands are strung out in a broad arc off the tip of Alaska for a thousand miles and separate the Bering Sea

from the North Pacific. Numbering about one hundred and fifty islands, they are the tops of submerged mountains. Included in the purchase of Alaska, they have great strategic value as air bases and weather observing stations for the United States.

CANADA—The three thousand mile boundary between the United States and Canada is convincing proof that two great nations may live side by side in peace and harmony. For over a hundred years this boundary line —the longest in the world—has been free from fortification of any kind by either nation. In a world that has been repeatedly torn by war during the past century here is lasting evidence that national progress, pride and ambition can exist without adjoining countries being tempted to encroach on the other's domain.

Canada is the largest domain of the British Commonwealth. It extends from the icy waters of the Arctic to the borders of the United States, and from east to west its greatest distance is 3,700 miles. Its area is greater than that of the United States and nearly as large as the continent of Europe.

Canada is a vast diversified land of fertile plains, of mountains and rivers, and countless lakes. Over 6 per cent of the total is water area, affording ready power for her ever increasing industrial development. Like the United States it can be roughly divided into three sections; the eastern highlands, a great level central plain, and mountain ranges extending from the Rockies to the Pacific.

In the east the Appalachian region is a beautiful land of hilly or mountainous terrain with very heavily forested sections and fertile farm lands. Just west of the highlands lies the St. Lawrence Valley including the Ontario peninsula, the hub of Canada's in-

TWA Trans World Airline

A leading city of the Pacific Coast, Los Angeles has drawn its inhabitants from all parts of the United States.

North Carolina News Bureau

The American South contains unusually picturesque mountain scenery.

dustry. In this area, rich in minerals, forests, water power and fertile land, is the highest concentration of population. Moderate climate combined with valuable accessible resources have made this section of the greatest economic importance. Northwest of the Valley is the Canadian Shield, an area characterized by low hills, countless lakes connected by streams and rapids. Here is Canada's greatest store of resources, minerals, forests, furs and water power. In the interior Plains is the great wheat belt. In the west, parallel to the Pacific, is the magnificent mountain country formed by the Cordilleran Mountain System. In addition to minerals and valuable forests, this area, in the fertile valleys, produces much of Canada's fruit and vegetable crops.

Although primarily an agricultural country, Canada has developed rapidly in recent years as an industrial country. Lumbering is of great importance, which is to be expected, for the forests of Canada are among the largest in the world. Furs have been an important source of wealth since the early days of the Hudson's Bay Company, and the fishing grounds of Canada are the largest and most productive on earth. Wheat is the principal crop of the prairie provinces, and Canada is one of the biggest producers and exporters of this grain.

The provinces in the southern sections of

Canada enjoy much the same climate as exists in the Great Lakes regions of the United States. The southern parts of Ontario and Quebec have less severe winters, but the northern sections of these provinces have very severe winters, with short, hot summers. The prairies experience great extremes in temperature, while moderate rainfall in this region favors wheat production.

About half of the population is of British origin and one quarter is French. The remaining fourth is principally Russian, German, Austrian and Scandinavian. Some hundred thousand Indians live mostly on reservations.

UNITED STATES—In a little over one hundred and fifty years the United States of America has written an amazing chapter in history. In that brief period a wilderness has been tamed, and a powerful nation has arisen to take its place among the foremost countries of the world. A land populated by every race, creed and color, and a haven of refuge for the oppressed, its phenomenal growth has never been equalled. Far removed from the traditions and hampering fetters of the Old World, it has charted a new course in government. Its freedom loving people have devoted their energies to developing the riches that Nature has so lavishly supplied.

The United States has reached its present position of greatness because of a number of reasons. It is blessed with a climate that cannot be surpassed elsewhere in the world, and is rich in mineral wealth beyond that of any other country. With a coastline on three sides well supplied with harbors, it is ideally situated for trade with the rest of the world. Its rivers and lakes are navigable and give easy access into the interior of the country. The variety of climate and the fertility of the soil make a great diversity of crops possible.

Climate has made the people of the United States energetic, and Nature has endowed the land with more than enough to meet their needs. This country's way of life has provided the incentive for continually bettering the standards of living of its people. All this has brought continued economic, cultural and scientific progress.

The United States is the greatest manufacturing nation in the world, with half the population depending upon industry for a living. It has the finest systems of transportation and communication, including the great majority of the automobiles in the world. More than half the coal, and a quarter of the iron in the world, as well as large deposits of almost all important minerals are found here.

The three principal geographical features are a continuation of those in Canada. They are the eastern highlands, comprising the Appalachian Range, the broad central plains, and the Rockies and Coastal ranges in the Far West.

A closer study of the geography of the United States does much to explain the growth of the nation. For example, the stony

Gendreau

Gendreau

An attraction for all visitors to Mexico is Xochimilco's floating gardens.

The favorite sport of the Mexicans is the "corrida" or bullfight. Physical dexterity and fluid grace are requisites for this profession.

Publishers' Photo Service

The raising and export of indigenous fruit is an important activity in Central America.

soil of New England discouraged farming and caused the early settlers to turn to manufacturing and commerce. The swift streams furnished water power and the jagged coastline provided bays for harboring the ships from Europe. Farther south, the coastal plains widen out into broad stretches of fertile land, and the rivers are short and deep. This led to the development of the large plantations in the deep South, where the climate is favorable to crops that require long hot summers. Here the coastal plain includes half of Georgia, all of Florida, and extends along the Gulf of Mexico. It reaches into the interior as far north as southern Illinois.

The lake and prairie region of the upper Mississippi Valley is one of the most fertile in the world, and is linked by waterways with the East and South through the Great Lakes and the Mississippi River system. The Great Plains region, depending upon the nature of the topsoil and the amount of rainfall, is either grain or grazing country, with valuable deposits of oil in Texas and Oklahoma.

The great size of the country and the seemingly endless store of natural wealth, both above and below the surface of the earth, have been responsible for great waste in the past. Fortunately, strict conservation measures are now in force to protect the resources of the earth for future generations and to assure them an equal place in this "Land of Opportunity".

MEXICO—Beyond the southern border of the United States and across the Rio Grande, where North America begins to taper sharply to a point, lies Latin America. It is difficult to conceive of the contrast to be found beyond this man-made boundary with the rest of the continent. It is another world, with a totally different culture, another language, and traditions and customs which set it apart from its northern neighbors.

About one-fourth the area of the United States, Mexico swings south for about eleven hundred miles, ending in the narrow hook of the peninsula of Yucatan.

While half of Mexico lies in the torrid zone, its climate is determined more by elevation than latitude. Along the coast the weather is hot and humid, with luxuriant tropical vegetation. As the land rises the climate changes to temperate and the mountain peaks are snow-clad. Two mountain

chains, that are a continuation of those in the United States, converge and meet at the southern tip, leaving a flat tableland between. The average altitude of this plateau is about 6,500 feet. Mexico's highest concentration of population is here where the fertile land, ideal climate and favorable rainfall afford excellent conditions for agricultural crops. Although industrial development has increased rapidly in recent years and most of Mexico's wealth is derived from her mines and petroleum, the great majority of the people are still employed in agricultural pursuits. Except for the coastal plain bordering the Gulf of Mexico, mountains and plateaus occupy the greater part of Mexico. Lying in both the temperate and torrid zones allows the country to produce a greater

Bermuda News Bureau
The islands of the Caribbean depend largely on the tourist trade to support their economy.

Jamaica Development Board
Jamaica is the largest of the British West Indies possessions.

variety of crops than is possible in most other countries.

Mexico is a beautiful and picturesque country with ancient ruins of pyramids and temples still standing as mute evidence of a flourishing civilization that existed before the coming of the Spanish invaders in the early fifteenth century.

CENTRAL AMERICA—As North America

decreases in size from a land of magnificent distance to a slender neck of land where the Isthmus of Panama joins South America, the sizes of its nations shrink to even greater extent. In Central America a string of six small countries, Guatemala, Honduras, El Salvador, Nicaragua, Costa Rica and Panama, is confined to an area less than that of the State of Texas. Their total population does not equal that of New York City.

The Cordilleras, a continuation of the mountain chains starting far north in Alaska, extend the entire length of the land. Many of the peaks are volcanic and frequent eruptions occur. These mountains have formed many high and fertile plateaus which provide fine pasturage for livestock and rich soil for a diversity of crops. As in Mexico, the tropical climate of the lower regions is tempered by the elevation of the high plateaus. There are a number of harbors on both coasts, with the principal seaports on the Caribbean Sea. Most of the

rivers that flow into the Caribbean are navigable.

These agricultural nations have become increasingly important in the past few years. With the organizing of the Pan-American Union, the growth of air travel, and the fostering of a new spirit of co-operation between the republics of North and South America, Central America's future became one of promise. When global war shut off supplies of many important crops to the Western world from the East, it was found that here in the Americas could be grown many necessities that formerly had been imported from afar. Great variation in soils, rainfall, and terrain afford an enormous variety of tropical, semi-tropical and temperate crops. Experiments have successfully produced important quantities of spices, fibres, and essential oils for medicinal and industrial purposes that were introduced from the East. Among the important crops exported almost exclusively to the United States are bananas, natural rubber, coffee, rope fibres, cacao and sugar.

Although there is potential mineral wealth in most of the countries of Central America this resource, for the most part, has been unexploited. Much of the land is heavily forested and some of the world's most valuable woods such as mahogany, rosewood, teak and ebony are found here. However, only a very small part of the for-

ests have been as yet cut for commercial purposes.

ISLANDS OF THE CARIBBEAN—The

Caribbean Sea is a vital water link between the Americas and the West Indies. With the opening of the Panama Canal it took on added importance as a trade route for the ships of the world.

The island republics and colonies lying in the Caribbean have likewise become increasingly important with the passing years, both for their economic and strategic value.

The West Indies, numbering hundreds of islands, extend in a sweeping arc beginning near southern Florida and ending off the coast of Venezuela. Columbus named the islands, in the belief that he had reached India. Most of the islands, forming two main groups, the Greater and the Lesser Antilles, are mountainous. However, there is sufficient fertile land to afford a variety of tropical products. In general the climate is hot but is tempered by the sea breezes. All the islands are subject to tropical hurricanes and in many regions there are occasional volcanic eruptions.

With the greater part of the West Indies under the control of the United States and Great Britain, the islands enjoy advantages not usually possessed by small independent countries. Nearness to markets and the great manufacturing centers, and cheap ocean transportation are added advantages. As with the Central American republics, the West Indies have enjoyed increased production and trade with the importation of new crops from the East that are now grown throughout Middle America.

POLITICAL DIVISION	GOVERNMENT	MONETARY UNIT	PRINCIPAL LANGUAGES	PRINCIPAL RELIGIONS	MAJOR PRODUCTS
ALASKA	Territory of the U. S. ruled by congress and a territorial legislature jointly with a governor appointed by the President.	dollar	English	Protestant	Vegetables, hay and other forage crops; salmon, halibut, herring; lumber; gold, copper, coal, tin, silver, lead, zinc, antimony, mercury, platinum and petroleum; canned fish, paper and wood products.
ALBERTA PROVINCE	Lieutenant-Governor, cabinet, unicameral legislature.	dollar	English French	Protestant Roman Catholic	Wheat, oats, barley, rye, flax, hay, clover, fodder-corn; cattle, swine, sheep, poultry; lumber, fish, furs, wool, eggs; petroleum, gas, coal, gypsum, bituminous sands, clay, sulphur; meat packing; flour milling, oatmeal, biscuits and macaroni, dairy products, textiles, oil refineries, linseed oil.
BAHAMAS	British colony with governor, executive and legislative council and house of assembly.	pound	English	Roman Catholic and Protestant	Tomatoes, pineapples, okra, vegetables, citrus fruits, bananas, sisal;crawfish, shells; lumber; salt; handcraft products.
BARBADOS	British colony with governor, executive and legislative council and house of assembly.	B. W. I. dollar	English	Protestant	Sugar cane, cotton; flying fish; manjak (asphalt); sugar, molasses, rum, edible oil, margarine.
BERMUDA	British colony with governor, executive and legislative council and house of assembly.	pound	English	Protestant	Lily bulbs, onions, bananas, cabbage, tomatoes, beans; coral; fish; perfume.
BRITISH COLUMBIA PROVINCE	Lieutenant-Governor, cabinet, unicameral legislature.	dollar	English French	Protestant Roman Catholic	Wheat, oats, barley, potatoes, clover, apples, pears, cherries, peaches, grapes, other fruits, tobacco; cattle, sheep, swine, horses, poultry; furs; salmon, halibut, herring, cod, whaling; lead, copper, coal, zinc, gold, uranium, cadmium, silver, tungsten, aluminum; shipbuilding, saw mills, fish curing and packing, pulp, paper; slaughtering and meat packing, petroleum products; machinery; fruit and vegetable preparations.
BRITISH HONDURAS	British colony with governor, executive and legislative council.	Br. Honduras dollar	English and Spanish	Protestant and Roman Catholic	Rice, maize, beans, bananas, coconuts, citrus fruits, sugar cane; mahogany, chicle, pine, cedar; fish; rum, food products.
CANADA	Largest member of the British Commonwealth with a governor-general, prime minister and cabinet. Parliament consists of a senate and house of commons.	dollar	English French	Protestant Roman Catholic	(See individual provinces)
COSTA RICA	Republic with president, cabinet and one-house legislature.	colon	Spanish	Roman Catholic	Coffee, bananas, cocoa, abaca, sugar cane, maize, rice, tobacco; cattle; tuna; gold, silver; cigars and cigarettes, textiles, furniture and woodwork, sugar.
CUBA	Republic with president, vice-president, cabinet and a two-house legistlature.	peso	Spanish	Roman Catholic	Sugar cane, tobacco, coffee, pineapples, citrus fruits, bananas, henequen; cattle; cedar, mahogany and other woods; fish; chromite, iron, manganese, copper, nickel, asphalt; sugar, textiles, alcohol, molasses, chemicals, tobacco products, electrical goods, clothing.
CURACAO (NETH. ANTILLES)	Self-governing part of Netherlands Union with governor and one-house legislature.	guilder	Dutch and Papiamento	Protestant	Fish; dividivi (tannin), crude salt, phosphates; refined petroleum.
DOMINICAN REPUBLIC	Republic with president, cabinet and two house legislature.	peso	Spanish	Roman Catholic	Sugar cane, cacao, coffee, tobacco, bananas, rice, corn; cattle; lumber; gold; starch, alcohol, molasses, sugar, chocolate, meats, cigars, cigarettes, leather.
GREENLAND	An integral part of the Danish kingdom, with representation in Parliament.	krone	Danish and Greenlandic	Protestant	Grass for fodder; cod and other fish; sheep, furs; cryolite; processed fish, hides.
GUADELOUPE	Overseas department of France with a prefect and elective general council.	franc	French, French Patois	Roman Catholic	Sugar cane, bananas, coffee, cocoa, vanilla, cassava; fish; alcohol, rum.
GUATEMALA	Republic with a president, cabinet and one house legislature.	quetzal	Spanish	Roman Catholic	Coffee, bananas, sugar cane, rubber, chicle, cacao, abaca, cattle; mahogany and dye woods; essential oils; gold; textiles.
HAITI	Republic with a president, cabinet and a two house legislature.	gourde	Creole, French	Roman Catholic	Coffee, sugar, fig bananas, sisal, cotton, rice, cocoa; logwood; molasses, sisal products.
HONDURAS	Republic with a president, council of ministers and a one house legislature.	lempira	Spanish	Roman Catholic	Bananas, coffee, coconuts, tobacco, grapefruit, rice, henequen; mahogany; cattle; gold, silver.
JAMAICA	British colony with a governor, executive and legislative councils and house of representatives.	pound	English	Protestant, Roman Catholic	Sugar cane, bananas, tobacco, coconuts, cacao, pimentoes, coffee, ginger; bauxite; honey; logwood; rum, textiles, cigars.
LEEWARD ISLANDS	British colony with a governor and separate executive and legislative councils for each of the four island groups.	B. W. I. dollar	English	Protestant, Roman Catholic	Sugar cane, cotton, vegetables, limes, fruits; fish; barytes; sugar, molasses, rum, lime products, cotton lint, charcoal.
MANITOBA PROVINCE	Lieutenant-Governor, cabinet, unicameral legislature.	dollar	English French	Protestant Roman Catholic	Wheat, oats, barley, hay, clover, potatoes, sugar beets, honey; cattle, swine, poultry, fish, furs; lumber, pulp-wood; gold, copper, coal, zinc, silver, selenium, tellurium, cadmium, nickel, cobalt; meat packing, dairy products, railway shops, flour and feed mills, chemicals, clothing, cotton and jute bags.
MARTINIQUE	Overseas department of France with a prefect and elective general council.	franc	Creole, French	Roman Catholic	Sugar cane, cocoa, pineapples, bananas, coffee; rum, sugar.
MEXICO	Federative republic with a president, council of ministers and a two-house legislature.	peso	Spanish	Roman Catholic	Corn, wheat, beans, chick peas, sugar, bananas, barley, cotton, coffee, vegetables; cattle; henequen; fish; silver, petroleum, lead, gold, zinc, copper; textiles, sugar, alcohol, foundry products.
NEW BRUNSWICK PROVINCE	Lieutenant-Governor, cabinet, unicameral legislature.	dollar	English French	Roman Catholic Protestant	Potatoes, oats, mixed grains, hay, clover; cattle, swine, sheep, horses, poultry; limestone, granite, coal, gypsum; fish curing and packing; lumber, pulp, paper; shipbuilding and repairs, meat packing, wood working, furniture.

POLITICAL DIVISION	GOVERNMENT	MONETARY UNIT	PRINCIPAL LANGUAGES	PRINCIPAL RELIGIONS	MAJOR PRODUCTS
NEWFOUNDLAND AND LABRADOR PROVINCE	Lieutenant-Governor, cabinet, unicameral legislature.	dollar	English French	Roman Catholic Protestant	Sheep, cattle, dairying; furs; fish: cod, salmon, halibut, lobsters, herring, caplin, seals, whales; cod liver oil; newsprint, pulp, lumber; iron ore, lead, zinc, copper, limestone, fluorspar, cement, gold, gypsum, silver; fish processing, woodwork, furniture, shipbuilding, marine engines, fishing equipment, hydroelectric power.
NICARAGUA	Republic with a president, cabinet and a two-house legislature.	córdoba	Spanish	Roman Catholic	Coffee, sugar cane, sesame, corn, bananas, rice, cacao, cotton, beans; cattle; hardwoods; gold; silver; sugar, wood products.
NORTHWEST TERRITORIES	Administered by a Commissioner subordinate to the Governor-General and Minister of Resources and Development, Territorial Council.	dollar	English French	Protestant Roman Catholic	Gold, copper, silver, pitchblende, lead, salt, gypsum, uranium, cobalt, petroleum, cadmium; furs, fish, reindeer.
NOVA SCOTIA PROVINCE	Lieutenant-Governor, cabinet, unicameral legislature.	dollar	English French	Protestant Roman Catholic	Fruit, apples, cherries, plums, berries; hay, clover, oats, wheat, potatoes, turnips, alfalfa, barley, beets; cattle, sheep, dairying, poultry, horses, swine; lumber, wood-pulp, paper, christmas trees; Fish: lobsters, cod, haddock, mackerel, herring, halibut; coal, gypsum, iron, gold, manganese, barite, salt, silica, quartz, limestone, dolomite; fruits and vegetables, fish canning, shipbuilding, marine engines, steel.
ONTARIO PROVINCE	Lieutenant-Governor, cabinet, unicameral legislature.	dollar	English French	Protestant Roman Catholic	Oats, wheat, barley, mixed grains, rye, flax, potatoes, soy beans, hay, clover, fodder corn, alfalfa, vegetables, fruits, tobacco, sugar beets; swine, cattle, sheep, horses, poultry, dairy products, eggs; furs; fish; gold, silver, nickel, copper, cobalt, iron ore, zinc, petroleum, gas, asbestos, fluorspar; timber, pulp, paper, sawn lumber; automobiles, iron and steel, electrical apparatus, machinery, meat packing, textiles, leather, rubber goods, hydroelectric power flour and feed; chemicals, smelting, refining.
PANAMA	Republic with a president, two vice-presidents, and a one-house legislature.	balboa	Spanish	Roman Catholic	Bananas cacao, abaca, coconuts, rice, sugar cane, coffee, pineapples; cattle; hardwoods; gold; hides, sugar, wood products.
PRINCE EDWARD ISLAND PROVINCE	Lieutenant-Governor, cabinet, unicameral legislature.	dollar	English French	Protestant Roman Catholic	Oats, mixed grains, barley, wheat, potatoes, hay, clover, fruits, turnips, beets; swine, sheep, cattle, horses, poultry; Lumber; fish: lobsters, smelts, herring, cod, mackerel, oysters; furs (silver fox); wood products, printing and publishing, fish processing; castings, forgings, meat products, dairy products.
PUERTO RICO	A constitutional self-governing Commonwealth of the U. S., with a governor and an executive council.	dollar	Spanish English	Roman Catholic	Sugar cane, tobacco, fruits, pineapples, grapefruit, coconuts, coffee, cotton, livestock, vegetables; molasses, embroideries, rum, canned fruit and juice, alcohol, cordials, tobacco products.
QUÉBEC PROVINCE	Lieutenant-Governor, cabinet, unicameral legislature.	dollar	French English	Roman Catholic Protestant	Oats, barley, wheat, buckwheat, rye, flax, mixed grains, peas, beans, potatoes, turnips, beets, hay, clover, corn, alfalfa, fruits, maple products, cattle, swine, sheep, horses, poultry; butter, cheese; lumber, pulp, paper, fur farms; fish (cod, herring, mackerel, lobsters, salmon) gold, iron, titanium, asbestos, lime, dolomite, brucite, quartz, pyrite, copper, zinc, silver, chrome, molybdenum, cement, sand and gravel, limestone, clay, granite, non-ferrous metals; cottons, tobacco, clothing, chemicals, meat packing, petroleum products, cotton, yarn and cloth, railroal rolling stock, ship-building, brass and copper products, electrical goods, hydroelectric power.
ST. PIERRE AND MIQUELON	French territory with a governor, privy council and elective general council.	franc	French	Roman Catholic	Fish, silver fox; dried cod and cod liver oil; sienna earth, yellow ocher.
SALVADOR	Republic with a president and a one-house legislature.	colón	Spanish	Roman Catholic	Coffee, cotton, corn, tobacco, henequen, sugar cane, rice; balsam and other woods; gold, silver; cotton textiles, henequen bags, sugar.
SASKATCHEWAN PROVINCE	Lieutenant-Governor, cabinet, unicameral legislature.	dollar	English French	Protestant Roman Catholic	Wheat, oats, barley, rye, flax, potatoes, hay, clover, alfalfa; cattle, swine, sheep horses, poultry; fish, furs; gold, copper, lead, zinc, lignite, petroleum, gas, cadmium, silver, uranium, salt, sodium sulphate, selenium, tellurium, coal; flour, feed, meats, butter, cheese, eggs; beer, machinery, hydroelectric power, printing and publishing, aerated mineral water.
TRINIDAD AND TOBAGO	British colony with a governor and executive and legislative councils.	B. W. I. dollar	English	Roman Catholic, Protestant, Hindu	Coffee, cocoa, sugar cane, citrus fruits; cattle; petroleum, asphalt; rum, canned grapefruit juice, sugar.
UNITED STATES	Federal republic with a president, vice-president and two-house legislature.	dollar	English	Protestant, Roman Catholic Jewish	Corn, hay, tobacco, wheat, cotton, oats, soy beans, potatoes, barley, sorghums, peanuts, rye, rice, citrus fruits, fruits, sugar beets, sugar cane, vegetables, tree nuts, feed grains and hay; livestock; fish; lumber; petroleum, coal, cement, iron, natural gas, copper, sand and gravel, zinc, lead, stone, gold, silver, molybdenum, bauxite, phosphates, mica, sulphur; foods, transportation equipment, machinery, primary metal products, electrical machinery, textiles, chemicals, paper and wood products, beverages, dairy products.
VIRGIN ISLANDS (U. S.)	Territory of the U. S. with an appointed governor.	dollar	English Creole	Roman Catholic, Protestant	Sugar cane, vegetables, citrus fruits, coconuts; cattle; fish; rum, bay rum, bay oil, molasses, handicrafts, sugar, lime juice, hides, bitters.
WINDWARD ISLANDS	British colony with a governor. Each of the four islands has a separate executive and legislative council.	B. W. I. dollar	English	Roman Catholic, Protestant	Cocoa, sugar cane, nutmeg, sea island cotton, limes and other citrus fruits, coconuts, bananas, cassava; cattle; fish; sugar, bay rum, bay oil, bitters, hides, rum, molasses, copra, arrowroot starch, charcoal, spices, lime products.
YUKON TERRITORY	Administered by a commissioner subordinate to the Governor-General and Minister of Resources and Development, Territorial Council.	dollar	English	Protestant Roman Catholic	Gold, silver, lead, copper, coal; furs; timber; grains and vegetables.

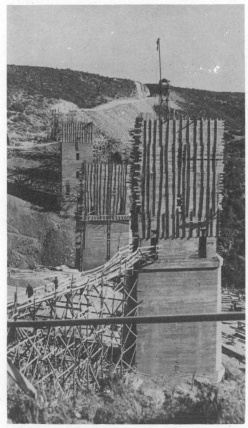

South America's roads undergo constant improvement.

Chile's coastal region extends for more than 2,500 miles along the Pacific. The country has many ports but its harbors cannot accommodate large ships.

SOUTH AMERICA—It is a common error to think of South America as being directly south of the United States. A glance at the globe will show that this is far from the truth. Except for the bulge to the west and the southern tip, all of South America is east of the Atlantic coast boundary of the United States. This places South America much closer to Africa than North America is to Europe. A theory has been advanced, though never proved, that at one time Africa and South America were joined.

Smaller than North America by nearly two million square miles, and representing one-seventh of the world's total land area, South America is the fourth largest continent.

With the equator crossing South America on a line with the Amazon River, two-thirds of this southern neighbor is in the tropics and the balance in the temperate zone. In common with other lands situated in the Southern Hemisphere, it has the further disadvantage of being far removed from the principal world markets. These factors, together with the history of the continent, explain why it has not developed as rapidly as the United States, although discovered at the same time. But in spite of the handicaps of climate, position and history, South America has an extensive trade with the United States and Europe. And, although for centuries the Spaniards robbed it of its buried treasures, South America still possesses great mineral wealth.

South of the Isthmus of Panama, the great line of mountains which extends the entire length of North America becomes the mighty Andes. Second only to the Himalayas, they follow the western coast to Cape Horn, rising steeply from the Pacific in long ranges of snow-capped peaks and wide plateaus. Mount Aconcagua is the highest peak in the Americas and rises to a height of twenty-three thousand feet. Several lesser peaks are active volcanos. To the south the range begins to narrow and the coast is bordered by a tattered fringe of islands clothed with pines and swept by fierce northwesterly winds.

On the east are two broad plateaus, the Guiana and Brazilian highlands, which might be compared with the Laurentian highlands and the Appalachian chain of North America. Between the eastern slope of the Andes and these plateaus lie broad lowlands. The grassy, tree dotted plains, or *llanos*, of the Orinoco Basin in Venezuela and Colombia, provide fine pasturage between the dry and rainy seasons. In the dry season they practically revert to desert. To the south are the dry plains, or *pampas*, of Northern Argentina, which is the great cattle country of the continent.

The Amazon—largest river system in the world—drains over one-third of the continent. This area is equal to two-thirds that of the United States. This mighty river is thirty-five hundred miles long and in places is over fifty miles wide. It flows through the densest tropical forest in the world and much of it is unexplored.

The La Plata River is actually the estuary for three rivers, the Parana, with a drainage area almost as large as that of the Mississippi, the Uruguay and the Paraguay. Buenos Aires, metropolis of the Southern Hemisphere is situated on the south bank of the La Plata 175 miles from the Atlantic. Buenos Aires is one of the world's most beautiful cities and important seaports. The above mentioned rivers drain Northern Argentina, Uruguay and Paraguay.

Other rivers of less importance are the São Francisco of Brazil, the Magdalena of Colombia, the Orinoco of Venezuela, and the Río Colorado of Argentina.

Lying in the Andes at an altitude of over twelve thousand feet is Lake Titicaca. With an area over half that of Lake Erie, it is the highest navigable lake in the world.

Much of Argentina and Chile are in southern latitudes that compare with the northern latitudes of the United States, but there are only sections where the climate is similar. Parts of Chile have a climate that compares with the Pacific coast states, and sections of Argentina and Uruguay are comparable to the east coast of the United States.

The heat is insufferable and the rainfall extremely heavy in the low Orinoco and Amazon Valleys. In the northern countries, while hot, the climate is tempered by the highlands. At the extreme southern tip the seasons are exactly the opposite of those in North America, but there is not the vari-

Moore McCormack Lines

Snowy mountain slopes provide ideal ski runs for winter vacationists in Argentina.

Pan-American-Grace Airways

Peru's cultural past is evident to all who visit her attractive cities.

ation in temperature. This is due to the influence of oceans and mountains.

The only important indentations on the Pacific are found along the rugged coast of southern Chile and the Gulf of Guayaquil in Ecuador.

The high temperature and humidity of the tropical regions, together with many insects and diseases, discourage the activity of white people and even sap the strength of the natives. Large areas of swamp and rugged mountains have made the development of transportation difficult and expensive. Only with the growth of air travel has it been possible for the Andean countries to contact one another with relative ease.

In the main, South America is sparsely settled, with the greatest density of population along the coasts. The original inhabitants were Indians, but, due to the early colonization by the Spanish and Portuguese, many of the present inhabitants are *mestizos*, a mixture of Indian and Spanish or Portuguese blood. The remainder is largely composed of Italian and German immigrants. Except in Brazil, where the official language is Portuguese, Spanish is spoken in all the other independent countries.

The three countries of Chile, Argentina and Uruguay, where there has been the largest European immigration, are making rapid industrial progress. The rest of South America is still largely agricultural. Most of the countries produce only one or two major products and there is little diversity of crops. Practically all exports are raw materials, while imports are manufactured goods.

With the exception of the three colonies of British, French and Dutch Guiana, all of South America is composed of independent républics. In spite of a common language and form of government there is little interchange between countries. In general they are more concerned with world trade than dealing with each other.

Since the early coming of the Spaniards, South America has continued to yield great stores of precious metals. The Andes are rich in minerals, and the eastern highlands contain iron, gold, and diamonds. Some coal is found in Brazil, Chile and Colombia, but not in great quantity. Water-power and oil are being utilized to make up for this lack.

Ecuador, Peru and Chile are all west coast countries, which, until the opening of the Panama Canal, were practically isolated from the rest of the world. Bolivia, having no outlet to the sea, moves nearly all of her exports through the seaports of Chile and Peru.

CHILE—Sometimes called the "Shoestring Republic," Chile stretches along the west coast for twenty-six hundred miles, from the borders of Peru to Cape Horn. It has a variety of climate ranging from frigid to torrid. This long, narrow and mountainous country is one of the most progressvie in South American. It is one of the three republics where there are more white people than natives. The other two are Argentina and Uruguay.

From north to south Chile is divided into three regions: the desert, a dry sub-tropical region which includes the coast, and a section that is forested. The greatest mineral region lies between Santiago and the Peru-

vian border. In the northern half of this area are the nitrate fields which have produced almost the entire world's supply of this important fertilizer. The nitrate beds located in the Pacific coastal desert (Atacama) were wrested from Peru during the War of the Pacific (1879-83) from which Chile emerged victorious. Chile's fame as a nitrate region has waned with the introduction of synthetic nitrate into world industry. The country is now seeking to stimulate the export of wine, honey and livestock. In the southern half there are deposits of copper, iron, gold and silver. Chile ranks next to the United States in the mining of copper and supplies about 20 per cent of the world's output.

PERU—This country is an extension of the narrow and arid coastal plain in northern Chile, with the Andes occupying fully half of the land. A densely wooded tropical region drops down in the east to meet the low plains of Brazil.

About a fourth of the population is white, most of whom are Spanish. The balance are *mestizos* (mixed) or Indians. Descendants of the ancient Incas, the Indians of Peru, are found principally living on the high mountain slopes of the Andes, and sailing their strange fiber craft on Lake Titicaca. These Indians have domesticated the llama and the alpaca, two animals which are native to this region, and which have never been raised successfully elsewhere. The llama is a sure-footed animal upon which the Indians depend for food, clothing and transportation. Used as a beast of burden in this lofty arid country, the llama, like the camel, can

Brazilian Government Trade Bureau
One of the most beautiful cities of South America, Rio is a fine example of urban planning.

Brazilian Government Trade Bureau
Fish abounds in South American rivers and coasts.

Brazilian Government Trade Bureau
Although in the torrid zone, Brazil's climate is tempered by rainfall, favorable winds and altitude.

go several days without water. The alpaca is too small to carry loads and is raised for its very long wool.

ECUADOR—Peru and Ecuador have a similar climate and topography except for the northern part of the coastal plain of Ecuador. This plain is as fertile as any area in South America and is the principal agricultural section of Ecuador. The principal crops are cacao and coffee, the former heading the articles of export. Ecuador's coffee has been increasing in importance since its cacao, blighted by witches'-broom, has suffered an appreciable decrease in export. Tagua, a substitute for ivory, is produced in

limited quantities. Ecuador is world-famous for its amazing variety of wild birds. The country contains one-fourth of all recorded species in South America.

BOLIVIA—Shut off from the sea by Chile and Peru, Bolivia is one of the most sparsely populated countries in the world. It consists of a high plateau in the southwest that is cold and dry, and wet tropical lowlands in the north and east. Though Bolivia's surface is three-fifths lowlands, the country includes one of the highest inhabitable regions in the world. The Andes spread out into two great chains of mountains which enclose a plateau nearly as high as the peaks themselves. Lake Titicaca, one of the highest of the larger lakes in the world, is situated on this plateau.

Bolivia ranks next to the Malay Peninsula and the Netherlands Indies in its tin deposits, and is well supplied with nearly all the known metals. Strangely enough, although having local supplies of coal, necessary in smelting, it is usually cheaper to import coal.

Lack of capital, the high cost of transportation, and the scarcity of labor, have retarded mining in all the countries of the Andes. Only the natives can do manual labor in the high altitudes and the people are not inclined toward mining. However, mining is the chief industry. Aside from tin, there is abundant amounts of gold, copper, bismuth, antimony, lead, zinc, wolfram and oil. Tobacco, wine and vanilla, together with quinine and rubber, are exported.

BRAZIL—Covering nearly half the continent and with half the population, Brazil lies almost entirely in the tropics. This re-

public is 10 per cent larger than the United States, and has three times the area of Argentina.

The Amazon and its tributaries have a total length of over nineteen thousand miles, of which thirteen thousand are navigable. This huge system extends through more than half the country's area.

The great plateau country, known as the Brazilian Highlands, lies in the south and east. It is composed of numerous mountain ranges and river valleys. Rio de Janeiro, the second largest city on the continent, is located in this region. Hemmed in by mountains and a wide bay, it has one of the finest and most beautiful harbors in the world.

Brazil at one time was the greatest rubber-producing country. Brazil has embarked on a program of intensified manufacturing. Silk, cotton and woolen mills have sprung up all over the eastern seaboard. Shoes and hats are becoming major products. Many paper mills are being built to utilize some of the billion acres of forests that cover half the land area. Its greatest mineral wealth has yet to be exploited, though one of the largest estimated deposits of iron ore in the world is now being developed. The country produces nearly fifty percent of the world's coffee. Efforts to do away with the one-crop system are gaining success and coffee is no longer the economic tyrant that it was. A growing cacao industry now ranks second in the world, while tobacco, rice, cotton and sugar are attaining commercial significance.

URUGUAY—This is the smallest republic in South America. It has a fine climate with

Pan-American World Airways

Inland lakes and quiet forests offer their charm to the natural serenity of the rural areas of South America.

the winds of the ocean modifying the temperature.

Since the Spanish brought sheep and cattle to the grassy plains of Uruguay in the 17th century, it has been a stock raising country. Today it is one of the leading meat producers of the world. Only a small percentage of the arable land is devoted to the raising of crops and it is limited in both minerals and manufacturing.

PARAGUAY—One of the two republics of South Amercia that is completely surrounded by other nations. Little has been done to develop its natural resources.

Most of the surface of western Paraguay is a low, swampy and unhealthy plain. The climate in the north is hot and unsuited to the white man. Most of the people live in the southern area east of the Paraguay River. It is a country of small villages, grazing, and farm lands, which depends upon the rivers for means of transportation.

Extending from Bolivia, across the western third of Paraguay, and south into Argentina, is the Gran Chaco, a great plain.

THE ARGENTINE REPUBLIC—The early colonists' anticipation of finding silver and gold in Argentina prompted them to name the country for the Latin word meaning silver. Although the colonists' search for great mineral wealth was in vain, the fertile soil and temperate climate have fostered the country's great economic progress. The Republic is the second largest of the South American countries.

The Gran Chaco, in the northern part, is a land of forests, lakes and swamps, which is largely unexplored. The grassy plains of the *Pampas* occupy a large area of Argentina. This cattle country and farm land extends from the Atlantic coast to the Andes in the west, and northwest to the highlands which reach into Brazil. The rich grazing lands, which have led to Argentina becoming a large exporter of meat and wool are in the center of the *Pampas;* the largest meat refrigerating plant in the world is at Buenos Aires.

Only about 10 per cent of the land is under cultivation, although it has been said that 80 per cent is capable of producing crops, grass or forests. An idea may be gained from this of the great possibilities for future development that lie ahead.

Argentina is an agricultural and commercial, rather than an industrial country. It has been hindered in the development of manufacture by a shortage of coal, the lack of water power, and an inadequate supply of minerals.

Descendants of the Spanish settlers are the leaders of the country, with most of the farm population consisting of Italians. Immigrants from the British Isles have taken to sheep raising, and many Germans have migrated to Argentina. Today half of the population is foreign-born or are descendants of immigrants.

NORTH COAST COUNTRIES—Colombia, Venezuela, and the British, French and Dutch Guianas, are all on the north coast.

COLOMBIA—The only South American country having a coastline along both the Atlantic and Pacific oceans. Half the country is high in the rugged Andes; the other half

Gendreau

Stockraising forms an important part of the economic life of South America.

Gendreau

Native handicraft display in Venezuela.

Pan-American-Grace Airways

The most cosmopolitan city of South America, Buenos Aires has been strongly influenced by Europe.

lies in unhealthy tropical plains. Three cordilleras of the Andes traverse in a parallel line from north and south which forms a barrier between the seacoast and the rich inland valleys. The chief source of welath is coffee. Colombian coffee is the finest in the world and the bean is jealously guarded. Ninety percent of the exported coffee is shipped to the United States. A type from the area around Medellin commands the highest price per pound in the world. Surpassed by Brazil in quantity, Colombia's coffee yields to none in quality. Next to coffee in export value is oil. The fields are to a large extent a continuation of those in Venezuela. Production has been over twenty million barrels

since World War II. Other resources include platinum, emeralds and coal.

VENEZUELA—One of the most productive oil regions in the world, is on the coast of the Caribbean. Easy access to this coast from the interior affords great possibilities for commercial and industrial development. Venezuela's land area is distinguished by its llanos or wide lowlands along the Orinoco River. The river is navigable for a course of 700 miles and is connected to the Amazon system by a canal. Coffee, chiefly from the basin of the Maracaibo, is second only to that of Colombia. A ranking producer of petroleum, Venezuela's exploitation of oil is fraught with difficulties which have never been successfully surmounted. Virgin forests cover the country and include about 600 species of wood. At Margarita is located a profitable pearl industry. Salt, asphalt, coal and gold figure as the main mineral resources.

THE GUIANAS—On the north coast of South America are the only European possessions on the continent. Their combined area is 178,000 square miles. The surface is composed of an alluvial plain at sea-level and another plain farther south which is distinguished by hills and forested mountains. The climate is tolerable except in the south where the northeast trade winds do not prevail. Though their topography is similar their economic importance varies greatly

from east to west. British Guiana, about the size of Great Britain, is the most highly developed. Dutch Guiana (Surinam) has no important industries except the mining of bauxite. French Guiana, the easternmost colony, is of little importance economically. Its sparse population and the excessive emphasis placed on the mining of gold has led to the neglect of its fertile soil. Mineral resources in the form of gold and diamonds are about equally divided among the three Guianas.

POLITICAL DIVISION	GOVERNMENT	MONETARY UNIT	PRINCIPAL LANGUAGES	PRINCIPAL RELIGIONS	MAJOR PRODUCTS
ARGENTINA	A republic with a president, vice-president, appointive cabinet, elective senate and house of deputies. In 1949 the constitution was revised greatly increasing the powers of the president.	peso	Spanish	Roman Catholic	Wheat, corn, oats, barley, linseed, rye, grapes and other fruit, tobacco, vegetables; yerba maté; cattle, sheep; quebracho, lumber; petroleum, natural gas, gold, lead, silver, tungsten; vegetable oils, wines, hides, wool, meats, textiles, metal products, vehicles and machinery, chemicals, wood and paper products, leather, clothing and shoes.
BOLIVIA	A republic with a president, vice-president, appointive ministers of state, and an elective senate and chamber of deputies.	boliviano	Spanish, Indian	Roman Catholic	Potatoes, corn, barley, quinoa, nuts, coca, vanilla, rubber, quinine; tin, zinc, lead, copper, silver, antimony, tungsten, sulphur, petroleum; cattle; textiles, flour, cement, tobacco products, hides, beer, earthenware.
BRAZIL	Federal republic with a president, vice-president, appointive secretaries of state, chamber of deputies and federal council.	cruzeiro	Portuguese	Roman Catholic	Coffee, corn, rice, cotton, cacao, sugar cane, cassava, beans, carnauba wax, medicinal plants, oranges, balata, tobacco, fibers, castor oil; livestock; timbo, brazil nuts; iron, manganese, gold, rutile, zirconium, diamonds, mica, bauxite, quartz, beryllium, chrome, tungsten, silver; foods, textiles, chemicals, pharmaceuticals, metallurgical products, paper and wood products, hides, vegetable oils, machinery.
CHILE	A republic with a president, vice-president, appointive cabinet of ministers of state, elective senate and chamber of deputies.	peso	Spanish	Roman Catholic	Wheat, potatoes, oats, rice, barley, corn, kidney beans, lentils, fruits; fish; livestock; copper, silver, nitrates, iodine, iron, sulphur, gold, manganese, coal; foods, textiles, leather, wood products, cement, chemicals and pharmaceuticals, wines and beer, wool.
COLOMBIA	A centralized federal republic with a president, vice-president, appointive cabinet, elective senate and house of representatives.	peso	Spanish	Roman Catholic	Coffee, sugar cane, corn, rice, root crops, cotton, bananas, cacao, wheat, tobacco, cinchona; cattle; rubber, fibers; petroleum, gold, silver, platinum, emeralds, salt; textiles, beer, sugar, cement, flour, tobacco products.
ECUADOR	A centralized republic with a president, vice-president, elective bi-cameral legislature of a senate and chamber of deputies and a council of state consisting of specified and elective representatives of various social, economic and governmental groups.	sucre	Spanish, Indian	Roman Catholic	Rice, cacao, coffee, bananas, rubber, kapok, cotton, tagua (ivory) nuts, cinchona; livestock; gold, petroleum, salt, balsa wood; textiles, toquilla (panama) hats, buttons, sugar, flour, shoes, beer and liquors, chemicals, pharmaceuticals, cement, soap, candles.
FALKLAND ISLANDS	British colony with a governor and an executive and a legislative council.	pound	English	Protestant, Roman Catholic	Forage crops, sheep; wool, skins, tallow, whale oil, whale-meat meal.
GUIANA, BRITISH	A British colony governed by a governor, and having a legislative council of elective members and nominated unofficial members.	B. W. I. dollar	English	Protestant	Sugar cane, rice, coconuts, coffee, citrus fruits, cacao; balata, rubber, green heart and other timber; livestock; bauxite, diamonds, gold; textiles, milled rice, beer and rum, lime rum and oil, sugar, woods, molasses, charcoal, matches.
GUIANA, FRENCH	Overseas department of France governed by a prefect, with an elective council-general and represented in the national assembly, the council of the republic and the assembly of the French Union.	franc	French	Roman Catholic	Rice, cacao, bananas, sugar cane, corn, cassava, woods; gold; hides, rosewood essence, shoes, rum, fish glue.
GUIANA, NETH. (SURINAM)	Self-governing part of the Netherlands Union with an appointed governor, an appointive council of ministers, an advisory council and an elective legislative body.	guilder	Dutch	Christian, Moslem, Hindu	Rice, citrus fruits, coconuts, coffee, bananas, sugar cane, cacao, balata, corn, tobacco; lumber; gold, bauxite; sugar, rum, plywood, molasses.
PARAGUAY	A centralized republic with a president, an appointed cabinet and a one-house legislature. The constitution of 1940 greatly increased the president's powers.	guarani	Spanish, Indian	Roman Catholic	Cotton, tobacco, sugar cane, rice, cassava, yerba maté, corn, citrus fruits; cattle, hides; lumber, quebracho; iron, manganese, copper; canned meats, vegetable oils, petit-grain oil, tobacco products.
PERU	A republic with a president, two vice-presidents, appointive cabinet and a two-house legislature.	sol	Spanish, Indian	Roman Catholic	Cotton, sugar, potatoes, barley corn, rice, wheat, coca, quinoa, cacao, tobacco, coffee, quinine, flax, rubber, balata, guano; fish; livestock; petroleum, lead, zinc, copper, silver, gold, vanadium; textiles, foodstuffs, cement, leather, wool, hides, pharmaceuticals, paper products, clothing, metal products.
URUGUAY	A republic governed (as of March, 1954) by a Federal Council, an appointed cabinet and a two-house elective legislature.	peso	Spanish	Roman Catholic	Wheat, corn, linseed, oats, sunflower seeds, peanuts, barley, rice, citrus fruits, peaches, grapes, vegetables, tobacco; sheep, cattle; gold; meat, hides, wool, textiles, leather, boots and shoes, wines.
VENEZUELA	A republic with a president, appointive cabinet, and elective two-house legislature.	bolivar	Spanish	Roman Catholic	Coffee, cacao, sugar cane, cotton, tobacco, coconuts, tonka beans; balata, dividivi, rubber; livestock; fish and pearls; petroleum, iron, gold, coal, copper, phosphates, magnesite, asphalt, salt, diamonds; textiles, leather, sugar, cement, wood products, foodstuffs, beverages, soap, tobacco products, meats, milk; refined petroleum.

The British Isles retain many landmarks of a by-gone age which bear mute testimony to its historical heritage.

TWA—Trans World Airline

British Travel Association

England's rolling countryside is specked with tiny cottages which augment the natural beauty of the landscape.

EUROPE—Eurasia is the world's largest land mass and includes both Europe and Asia. Europe occupies about a third of the western end of Eurasia, and, with the exception of Australia, is the smallest continent. It is the most densely populated for its size and no other continent has so many separate nations. Nearly all of these countries have distinctive customs and speak different languages. This does much to explain Europe's turbulent history.

Actually Europe is a huge peninsula, subdivided into a number of lesser peninsulas, caused by the oceans and inland seas which encroach upon it. Its irregular form, together with the mountain barriers, and the presence of important islands near the continent, have contributed to the growth of individual nations. Differences in language and customs have a natural tendency to arouse a strong nationalistic spirit. This keeps people apart and makes them suspicious of those with different customs, and who speak alien tongues. Among mountain people an independent spirit and love of freedom is even more pronounced.

In the northwest, two peninsulas are formed by the Baltic Sea. The countries of Norway and Sweden occupy the Scandinavian Peninsula. Denmark is on the Jutland Peninsula between the Baltic and North Seas. To the south, Portugal and Spain comprise the Iberian Peninsula. The peninsular boot of Italy thrusts out into the Mediterranean, and the Balkan Peninsula is surrounded by the Black Sea and the Adriatic, Ionian and Aegean Seas of the Mediterranean.

Great Britain is prevented from being a peninsula only by the narrow English Channel, and was once a part of the mainland. The entire course of history has been changed by this strip of water which made England an island. The same may be said for the Straits of Gibraltar separating Europe from Africa. But for this nine-mile passage, the Mediterranean would have had no outlet to the Atlantic.

Europe may be divided into five natural regions: (1) the Northwest Highlands, (2) the Central Plains, (3) the Central Highlands, (4) the Southern Mountains and Plateaus, and (5) the Southern Lowlands.

Most of the British Isles, a section of France, and a good part of the Scandinavian Peninsula are included in the Northwest Highlands. This is the coastal region with excellent harbors where men have made their living by the sea, and commerce has become most important. In those places where coal and iron are found it has led to an industrial life. This highland region enjoys a cool, temperate climate and people are energetic.

The great Central Plains extend from the British Isles to the Ural Mountains that separate Europe from Asia. These plains range from the tundra regions of the Far North to the Caspian Sea, the Caucasus Mountains, and the Black Sea of the Southeast. In the Southwest they reach into southern France. Within such an extensive area there are naturally great differences in climate. There is also great diversity of vegetation and the occupations of the people.

South of the Arctic tundra belt are extensive evergreen forests that reach westward to the Scandinavian Peninsula. In the grasslands to the south of the forests are large areas used for the growing of grain, and stock grazing is the chief occupation in the drier southeastern sections. This is the region of the dry and treeless steppes.

The Central Highlands include the plateau in central France and take in parts of Belgium, southern Germany, Austria, and the Czecho-Slovakian area. It is the region of forest, water-power, and varied mineral resources. The industrial districts of Central Europe are the outgrowth of the great deposits of coal and iron found here.

The impressive peaks of the Alps rise south of the Central Highlands, forming one of the many ranges of Southern Europe. The Apennines extend the length of Italy, and other ranges follow the eastern coast of the Adriatic through Yugoslavia and Albania to the southern tip of Greece. Spreading out to the east they include most of the Balkan Peninsula. To the north the Carpathian Mountains swing east and north around the valley of the Danube and then run northeast to almost circle the Plain of Hungary. Farther to the east, the Caucasus Mountains reach from the Black to the Caspian Sea. Separating France and Spain are the Pyrenees, and the Sierra Nevadas are in southern Spain bordering the Mediterranean.

The Alps are particularly famous for their scenic grandeur. The Sierra Nevadas and Carpathian Mountains are rich in mineral resources, and some of the world's greatest oil fields are in the Caucasus. The mountains of Italy lack valuable ores and have been largely stripped of their forests.

The Southern Lowlands of the Danube

British Travel Association
Scotland's lakes and hills are offset by the curious charm of her historical cities.

Danish Information Office
The sea-washed land of Denmark lies at the entrance of the Baltic endowing Danish seaports with excellent facilities for maritime commerce.

Valley and the Plain of Hungary represent some of the finest farming and grazing land in the world.

The extreme irregularity of the European coastline has been of great importance to the life of the people. With the North and Baltic Seas, the Mediterranean and Black Seas, penetrating far into the interior, only Central Europe and Eastern Russia are very far from the coast. Although the combined areas of South America and Africa are nearly five times that of Europe, the coastline of Europe is longer.

A majority of the great seaports of the world are in Western Europe. Its people have led the world in sea-faring.

Europe has a generally mild, temperate climate, particularly in the western areas, which are warmed by ocean currents and the winds blowing over these waters. Even the British Isles have a mild climate in spite of being in the same latitude as Labrador. Greater extremes of temperature exist in eastern Europe where these winds lose their moderating effect.

Due to the Alps blocking the cold north winds, and the influence of the warm waters of the Mediterranean, the southern shores of Europe enjoy a mild year-round climate. Excepting in eastern Europe, where the rainfall is light, there is generally sufficient moisture for agriculture.

An abundance of mineral resources, fine forests, rich farmlands, water-power, and the seas plentifully supplied with fish, have encouraged Europe's growth. An invigorating climate, waterways, harbors and access to the oceans of the world, have contributed to its commercial importance.

The climate and natural resources of each country have largely determined their individual occupations and prosperity.

GREAT BRITAIN AND NORTHERN IRELAND

—The British Isles and the British Commonwealth of Nations owe much of their commercial and industrial growth to the daring and initiative of their early mariners. Although we usually think of the British Isles as comprising Great Britain and Ireland, it actually consists of nearly five thousand islands. Within the small compass of the islands there is a considerable variety of topography.

In Northern Ireland there are many lakes, including the largest one of the island, Lough Neagh, as well as a range known as the Mourne Mountains. A large portion of the country consists of the basalt plateau of Antrim.

Northern Ireland, or Ulster, as the six counties are sometimes called, is the seat of a very extensive lace and linen industry. In County Down and County Antrim there are highgrade deposits of granite and bauxite which are being exploited. Shipbuilding is a major industry centered in the capital, Belfast.

In Scotland the three well-marked divisions stand out, the highlands, the southern uplands, and between these two, the central lowlands, into which four-fifths of the population is crowded. The lowlands contain the richest agricultural land, as well as the coal fields. They are penetrated by three great estuaries, the Firths of Tay and Forth on the east, and of Clyde on the west, so that communication coastwise or overseas is everywhere easy.

Scotland has some of the largest shipbuilding yards in the world on the Firth of Clyde. Sheep and cattle are raised in large numbers since the land is not well suited to agriculture.

The Welsh cliffy upland is flanked to the north and east by small coal fields, but the greatest field lies to the south. A belt of limestone running from Bill of Portland to Tees Bay, and bearing at many points valuable iron ores, serves as a rough boundary of industrial England, for to the south and east of it, apart from the metropolis, agricultural interests predominate. Lying to the west of the limestone band is the Devon-Cornwall peninsula, where great bosses of granite and slate form the famous moors.

Wales, after 700 years as a part of the English kingdom, retains its individuality and is nationalistic in speech, dress and customs. The Welsh language is Celtic, akin to the Gaelic of Ireland. It is the only speech of nearly one-tenth of the people.

Channel Islands, lying across the English Channel off the coast of Normandy, and Scilly Islands, lying southwest of Land's End, enjoy an almost complete freedom from frost and severe weather.

Because of the density of population Great Britain is far from self-sustaining and must depend upon the raw materials and products of other countries. This has led to the development of her world-wide commerce, a large part of which is carried on with her far-flung and numerous colonies. Agriculture is intensive with much importance placed on livestock. Many of the world's most valuable breeds of farm animals have been de-

The snow-encrusted northlands of Scandinavia force its northernmost inhabitants to lead nomadic existences.

Suomen-Matkat

veloped on English farms. This is exemplified by such names as Guernsey, Shropshire, Jersey, Hereford, Hampshire and Plymouth.

IRELAND—Except for coastal hills and mountains, the country is largely an ill-drained plain dotted with lakes and peat-bogs, and crossed by the sluggish Shannon. In the southwest is the beautiful Killarney Lakes region which attracts many tourists each year. Although little of the land is suitable for large scale agriculture, grass and fodder crops are abundant and provide stockraising needs which is the major industry of the country. The Shannon River, Royal Canal, and the Grand Canal provide an excellent inland waterway system of transportation. Shannon airport, near Limerick, is a major international airway terminal. Horse-breeding is the most famous of Irish farm industries. A prosperous tourist trade is developing.

NORWAY AND SWEDEN—With its saw-toothed coast, great fiords, and neighboring islands, it is natural that Norway, occupying the western part of the Scandanavian peninsula, would be a maritime country. Norway's long coast line, facing the Atlantic, is edged with lofty cliffs and seamed with deep fiords. Islands, countless in number, fringe the coast. Most of the country is a rocky, rugged and barren land, about 20 per cent of which is forested. The rivers are short and torrential, but provide the finest salmon fishing in Europe. The Kjolen Mountains which form the backbone of the peninsula separate Norway from Sweden. These mountains rise in many parts to over 6,000 feet, the highest peaks being over 8,000 feet.

Norway is the land of the "midnight sun". From Trondheim northward at least a part of the disk of the sun is visible from May through July. But the winter nights are 17 hours long and midday seems like twilight during the winter months. Another striking

Norwegian Travel Office

Norway, with its deep fiords and high cliffs, contain many placid scenes of captivating grace.

feature is that much of the area above the Arctic Circle is warmer than some regions further south. Northeast Norway is the warmest part of the country in the summer.

Sweden consists primarily of a table-land sloping from the Kjolen Range to the Baltic. No less than 8 per cent of the surface of Sweden is water, the immense number of lakes covering almost 15,000 square miles. The two largest, Vanern and Vattern, in the southern portion of the country, are connected by a system of canals. Besides the large number of small islands which fringe the coast, Sweden includes the two large Baltic islands of Gotland and Oland. Most of the people live in the southern part of their country while the Norwegians have settled chiefly near the fiords. Hydro-electric development is in an advanced stage in both countries.

In Sweden, iron deposits are among the richest in the world. Swedish steel is universally famous for its fine qualities. The making of machinery for export is a major industry. Swedish agriculture is in a very high state of development, and exports wheat, bacon and butter in large quantities. In forestry and sawmilling the nation has evolved such advanced methods that foreign technicians in the industry often go to Sweden to study logging and forestry. Nearly half of her exports are in pulp and paper products.

DENMARK—Denmark occupies a peninsula and numerous islands lying at the entrance to the Baltic. It is a lowland country characterized by many lakes, ponds and short rivers. Its sandy shores are shallow, with

lagoons shut in by shifting sand bars. Most of Denmark is farm land, about half of which is used for grazing. The Faeroe Islands produce fish, mutton and wool for the homeland.

Dairy farming is the country's chief industry, the products of which comprise nearly all her exports. Greenland, the largest island in the world, is Denmark's only possession.

ICELAND—The republic is an island in the north Atlantic consisting of a great tableland averaging 2,000 feet above sea level. Of its whole area barely a quarter is habitable. The surface is dotted by over 100 volcanic peaks. There are many boiling springs and the geysers are world-famous. It is too cold for agriculture but has rich grazing land for sheep and cattle.

FINLAND—Finland consists of a great plateau, ranging from 400 to 600 feet in elevation. The southern half of the plateau has about 25 per cent of its area occupied by thousands of shallow lakes, many of them linked by short natural or artificial channels, providing many miles of navigable waterways. Forests cover the greater part of the country which has led to lumbering, paper-making and the manufacture of woodenware. Over half the population is engaged in agricultural pursuits which are carried on under great difficulties.

THE NETHERLANDS—The tiny kingdom of the Netherlands, lacking natural resources has been largely a nation of seafarers for centuries. Along the canals, the meadows are often ten or twelve feet below the water line, and between the land and the sea at

The European peasant has long been a factor in the economic development of the Old World.

high tide there may be a difference of twenty-five feet or more. The land is protected by embankments and dikes, and it may be pictured as a great trough, the floor of which slopes down from east and southeast toward the North Sea. The rivers which flow across the country from the higher continent beyond, are at their mouths, frequently below the level of the sea, into which they have to be lifted by canals and locks across the dams or dikes. A large part of the land has been reclaimed from the sea and little by little it has become a fertile country.

BELGIUM—Smaller than Holland, Belgium is the most densely populated country in Europe. Situated between England, Holland, France and Germany, it is in the very center of industrial Europe. The country is well watered, and has two principal rivers, the Scheldt and the Maas. Four-fifths of the land is under cultivation, and although over half the people are engaged in either farming or stock raising the country still does not raise sufficient food to feed her people. Belgium's intensive industrialization has been at the expense of its agriculture, for the valley of the Sambre-Meuse, the chief industrial center, is also the richest farming land. Metals from the Katanga region of the Belgian Congo are intensifying industrial activities, and Belgium is regaining her prewar level of output. The textile industry is reviving also. The nation furnishes a great variety of farm products and is known for its world-famous breed of horses.

LUXEMBURG—The Grand Duchy of Luxemburg, smaller than the state of Rhode Island, is one of Europe's oldest states. An abundant store of iron ore has encouraged mining, smelting and some manufacturing. International trade of the duchy has been carried on through a customs union with Belgium.

Symbol of the "City of Light", the Eiffel Tower represents a capital that has known splendor, wealth and a long cultural tradition.

LIECHTENSTEIN—Only 27 square miles larger than San Marino, Liechtenstein is separated from Switzerland by the Rhine river and is bounded by Austria in the east. The population is largely German but Switzerland administers its postal and telegraph facilities, and its currency is Swiss. It also belongs to the Swiss customs union. The tillable soil, a long strip along the Rhine river, yields grapes, grains and pasturage for a small cattle industry.

FRANCE—France is largely an agricultural country where the farmers, instead of living on their farms, usually live in nearby villages. Although rich in minerals, it has lagged behind both England and Germany as an industrial country. The surface is diversified, but much of it is lowland, with a few level plains. In the center is a triangular plateau called the Auvergne Mountains, with a height of something over 3,000 feet. The Cevennes form the eastern edge of this plateau, and from them to the Vosges, the tableland continues. There is a mountainous area in Brittany, but the greatest heights are on the frontiers, the Jura, the Pyrenees, and the Alps separating it respectively from Switzerland, Spain and Italy. The Ardennes in the northeast are less lofty. The Seine drains the

north, the Loire and the Garonne the west, and the Rhone the east and south. France enjoys a delightful climate. Only in the region of the Alps is real winter encountered. Protected by the mountains to the north, the balmy area along the Mediterranean is a magnet that has drawn countless vacationers. Many semi-tropical plants and fruits are grown in this section. Indeed, France's greatest resource is her soil. Grape culture is by far the leading agricultural pursuit, for France produces a billion gallons of wine in a vintage year. Yet, the country imports millions of gallons. Textile production, particularly the silk industry centered around Lyons, is a valuable undertaking in the country; cotton mills are the leading producers of goods.

MONACO—The Principality of Monaco is one of the smallest states in the world. It possesses the administrative organs and institutions of larger nations in miniature. It has no taxes for it is supported by the gambling casino of Monte Carlo from which its own citizens are barred. The most striking feature of this 370 acre state is the Monagasque Acropolis on a headland 200 feet above the water. The Prince's Palace, a magnificent structure, is located on it. On the

Switzerland is a country whose imposing mountains and dense forests are a lure to tourists who come for relaxation and sport.

Swiss National Tourist Office

Austria State Tourist Dept.

Austria's small villages are nestled among the deep valleys of its mountainous countryside.

Mediterranean coast, surrounded by the Riviera of France, Monaco offers to the tourist auto-racing, skiing, bathing, sailing, and of course, gambling. There is also an oceanographic museum.

SWITZERLAND—This rugged little country is a completely land-locked republic nestling among the beautiful Alps. It has succeeded in maintaining its neutrality and independence while the rest of Europe engaged in costly and devastating wars. Between Lake Constance on the Rhine and Lake Geneve on the Rhone are Lakes Neuchatel, Zurich, Lucerne, Brienz, Thun, all of which drain to the Aar. Lake Geneve and Lake Constance each exceed 200 square miles in area. Many of Switzerland's mountains are permanently covered with snow. Capitalizing upon its wonderful mountain and lake scenery, and making the most of its limited resources, Switzerland has become one of the most prosperous of the smaller nations. With its snow-capped peaks rising from ten to fifteen thousand feet, it has been the playground of Europe for many years.

GERMANY—There are two natural regions in Germany, the northern plain and southern highlands. The former is the most extensive agricultural region. The land which borders Denmark is favorable to the grazing of cattle, and, in the northeast, large numbers of sheep and goats are raised. The minerals found in the central highlands have had the greatest influence upon the development of Germany in the last fifty years.

Except for ample supplies of coal and potash, Germany is deficient in natural resources. During the glacial period, sand was deposited over the plains region and as a result the soil is not naturally fertile. Only by intensive cultivation and the heavy use of fertilizers, made from potash, is much of the soil made productive. Germany's great scientific development has been largely the result of solving agricultural problems, and of searching for new uses to utilize the coal reserves.

Germany's only access to the ocean, and world trade, is through the Baltic and North Seas. To make the most of this she has developed a remarkable system of waterways. The Rhine rises in the Alps and flows through the fertile lowlands of western Germany to the border of Holland, and thence to the sea. The Elbe, Weser, and the Oder flow north across the low plain of Germany. The Oder empties into the Baltic. The Elbe and Weser flow into the North Sea. All three are navigable far inland for ocean-going vessels. The rivers, together with fifteen hundred miles of canals, form a network of waterways which provide cheap transportation.

AUSTRIA AND HUNGARY—Austria is characterized by its beautiful mountain scenery, over 90 percent of the land is classified as mountainous, which has contributed to development of one of its largest industries—tourist and resort trade. However, over 80 per cent of the land is productive and half of this is under cultivation. In contrast, Hungary is largely comprised of a low fertile plain. The country is primarily agricultural and is a great grain and wine producer.

CZECHOSLOVAKIA—This land-locked country contains strategic routes between north and south Europe of economic and political value. The country has two large mountain ranges, the Carpathian in the east and the Sudeten in the west. Czechoslovakia is famous for its subterranean caverns and its spas and mineral springs. The people are energetic and progressive and there are valuable forest resources, fertile soil and varied mineral deposits.

THE BALKANS—They include Rumania, Yugoslavia, Bulgaria, Albania, Greece and European Turkey. Located at the gateway to Asia, and on a natural route connecting the two continents, this region has been a battleground for centuries. Repeated invasions from various directions have resulted in a number of racial groups and religious beliefs. The rugged nature of the country has isolated the people into many rival factions with intense racial and national spirit.

YUGOSLAVIA consists essentially of a mountainous core, which stretches from the

The Italian peninsula possesses many fine harbors whose importance rivals those of the rest of Europe.

Both nature and time have combined to produce the bizarre interior of this cave in Yugoslavia.

Dinaric Alps in the northwest to the Balkan Mountains on the Bulgarian frontier. The only valley which cuts the mountains and forms a passageway is that of the Marava River, which with that of the Vardar, leads from Beograd to Thessalonike. Beyond the Sava-Danube, as far as the northern boundary, the land is low and swampy near the rivers, with a few minor elevations. The chief concentrations of people are around Zagreb and Beograd. Yugoslavia has recently experienced a crisis resulting from a boycott by the Cominform countries and the Soviet Union. Forced to turn to the West, the nation has signed trade agreements with several Western European states. Its greatest problem is the lack of communications between its regions. The more highly developed coastal areas have access to outside markets, but the distribution of economic aid further inland is hampered by the mountains which impose a rugged barrier between the provinces.

RUMANIA—In western Rumania the Carpathian Mountains from the northwest and the Transylvanian Alps from the southwest meet in the center to form a crescent. To the north and west of this crescent is the Transylvanian plateau; to the south and east are the plains of Moldavia and Walachia. The principal rivers are the Danube in the south which enters the Black Sea at Sulina, and the Prut in the northeast and the Siret in the southeast—both of which connect with the Danube.

BULGARIA—The country is hilly and well watered by numerous streams, of which the Isker, Struma and Maritza are the most important. Although nearly one-third of the country's area is in forests, only a small part of the wood is used commercially since about one-fourth of the forest area is completely unproductive. Many of the forests consist of scrub timber and a sizeable portion of the good forests are inaccessible. Eighty percent of Bulgaria's population is employed in agriculture, the chief crops being tobacco and cereals. Attar of rose and silk are important products.

ALBANIA—Albania is a mountainous country on the western side of the Peninsula. In the center, part of the plateau is cultivable, and in the south there is fertile alluvial soil with grazing land on the slopes.

GREECE—With a very long coast line on the Aegean and Ionian Seas, and a large number of islands, including Crete, Mitylene, Dodecanese and Chios, the area is generally mountainous. The mountains, though not very high, divide the country into a number of small districts, between which communication is difficult. It is the sea which links the different regions of Greece.

ITALY—Once the hub of the known world, Italy's importance declined as the age of exploration and discovery opened up the ocean routes of the world. Taking no part in this period of conquest and empire building,

she did not acquire colonies. Lacking unity she was in no position to demand her share of the rich prizes of newly discovered land being acquired by other European nations.

With the opening of the Suez Canal and tunnels through the Alps, her trade somewhat improved, but the absence of the necessary minerals prevented her from keeping pace with industrial development elsewhere in Europe.

The south slope of the Alps belongs to Italy. At the point where the Alps reach the Mediterranean, the Apennines begin. These mountains follow the length of Italy and form a rugged backbone which extends through the island of Sicily. The southern and western parts of the peninsula have been subjected to volcanic eruptions, and Vesuvius, Etna, and Stromboli are still active volcanoes. The chief lowlands are in the Po Valley with narrow coastal plains east and west of the Apennines. The majority of the people, and most of the agriculture and manufacturing, are located in the Po Valley. Consequently Northern Italy does not experience the poverty to be found in Southern Italy. It is from the south that most of the immigrants to the United States have come.

Italy's colorful history, scenery and balmy climate have attracted many tourists which has in some measure offset an unfavorable balance of trade.

SAN MARINO—San Marino is one of the oldest republics in the world and is the smallest. It has always been on good terms with its big neighbor, Italy, by whom it is surrounded. The state was founded in the fourth century by Marinius of Dalmatia, a stonecutter. Except for a few invasions, its liberty has been respected, even by Napoleon. During World War II it declared war

The coastal cities of Portugal draw heavily on the sea for their principal commodity.

A land of color and birthplace of Western culture, Greece, still posesses the remnants of a once glorious past.

against Germany and was occupied by the Germans and subsequently liberated by the British. Much of its revenue is obtained through the sale of its postage stamps issued for the benefit of collectors.

SPAIN AND PORTUGAL—

About three-fourths of the Iberian Peninsula is a granite plateau with a range of mountains dividing it in the center. The rivers that flow through this region through deep gorges block transportation and are unsuited for navigation, waterpower or irrigation. The dry climate, lack of water, a rugged land formation, poor soil and an absence of transportation have been great obstacles standing in the way of the economic development of both Spain and Portugal. A portion of the land in the valleys and plains has been made fertile through irrigation and farming is the main industry. Fishing is important along the Portugal coast, although a great part of the coast is too rugged for harbors. There are forests in most of the higher areas where half the world's supply of cork is produced.

ANDORRA—

Tiny Andorra is in the Pyrenees Mountains between France and Spain. It is not a republic, as is often supposed, but a joint dependency of France and the Bishops of Urgel in Spain. Its mountains are high and arid, and its valleys contain poor soil so that the people are nearly all engaged in pastoral pursuits. The one product of the soil is tobacco. Sheep-herding is the main industry, and the need of hay for winter forage further limits the use of soil for any other crop.

POLAND—

Poland was for many years a chiefly agricultural country but good supplies of coal, lead, iron and zinc have helped her industrial progress to such an extent that it is now almost equally industrial and agricultural. Most of the land is comprised of a plain, although there are low hills in the northeast in Pomerania. The lower regions of the Vistula have marshes, sand dunes and lakes. The central plain of Poland with an elevation of about 500 feet is traversed by great rivers, the most important being the Oder and the Vistula. Her strategic position near the Baltic Sea, and the lack of natural boundaries and barriers, have long made the people of this country, as well as those of the former Baltic States, the victims of stronger nations seeking an outlet to the sea.

U. S. S. R.—

Almost three times the size of the United States and comprising more than one-seventh of the world's land surface, the Union of Soviet Socialist Republics sprawls across two continents. Most of Russia is a great plain reaching from the Pacific to its western boundaries. Its position in northern latitudes and the absence of protecting barriers result in an extreme climate with long, cold winters. Vladivostok, on the Pacific coast, and the ports on the Arctic Ocean and Baltic Sea are closed by ice during the long winter months. Vladivostok, however, is kept open the year round by ice-breakers. In no part of the land is the rainfall heavy, and there are frequent and widespread droughts, which bring hunger and starvation to its people.

From the Black Sea in the south to the Arctic Ocean, and from the Baltic Sea to the Ural Mountains, which divide Asiatic Russia from European Russia, is a vast lowland. To the east of the Urals is Siberia, two-thirds of which is a flat, unbroken plain. In the far north the ground has been found to be frozen to a depth of over six hundred feet. This presents peculiar problems, if the government is to succeed with plans to mine the ores found there and industrialize this Arctic region. Here in the tundra country the moss, upon which the reindeer of the nomadic tribes feed, is often five feet thick.

South of the tundra belt is a great evergreen forest covering billions of acres, where lumbering and fur-trapping are the chief occupations.

Russia's supply of minerals is so great and widely scattered that the extent of many of the deposits is still unknown. There are immense reserves of coal in both European and Asiatic Russia. Copper, platinum, iron, gold, manganese and other minerals are found in the Urals. Some of the richest petroleum deposits in the world are located in the Baku region of the Caspian Sea.

Great strides have been made in industrial development, with the manufacture of iron and steel, machinery, textiles and leather goods in the lead.

In spite of climate, high cost of manufacture and difficulties of transportation, the U. S. S. R. is a country that is largely self-sustaining, and has become increasingly important industrially.

EUROPE

POLITICAL DIVISION	GOVERNMENT	MONETARY UNIT	PRINCIPAL LANGUAGES	PRINCIPAL RELIGIONS	MAJOR PRODUCTS
ALBANIA	A Soviet-type republic with president, prime minister, minister of foreign affairs and defense, and a one-house legislature.	lek	Albanian	Moslem, Orthodox, Roman Catholic	Corn, tobacco, wheat, flax, oats, barley, rye, rice, olives, fruit; cattle, sheep; fish; wool, hides; dairy products, furs; bitumen, salt, lignite, aluminum, petroleum, copper, chromite; flour, olive oil, cheese, cement, leather.
ANDORRA	A republic under the joint suzerainty of the French State and the Bishop of Urgel, with a council general of 24 elective members. Executive authority is vested in the First Syndic.	franc and peseta	Catalan	Roman Catholic	Tobacco, potatoes, barley; sheep, cattle; lumber.
AUSTRIA	The government consists of a president, chancellor and vice-chancellor, cabinet of ministers and a two-house assembly.	schilling	German	Roman Catholic	Rye, wheat, oats, barley, corn, potatoes, sugar beets, hops, grapes, rapeseed, flax, hemp, tobacco; iron, copper, lead, magnesite, graphite, coal, aluminum, petroleum, lignite, salt; timber, pulp, poultry and livestock; steel, machinery, machine tools, chemicals, textiles, paper, building materials, processed foods, leather.
BELGIUM	Constitutional, hereditary monarchy. King appoints a cabinet of ministers. Parliament consists of a senate and chamber of deputies.	franc	French and Flemish	Roman Catholic	Wheat, rye, oats, barley, potatoes, sugar beets, flax, tobacco, vegetables, fruit, hops, hemp, bulbs, livestock, fish; coal, iron, zinc, lead, copper, tin, silver; coke, steel, machinery, textiles, lace, glass, chemicals, uranium refining, sugar, margarine, cheese, vinegar, alcohol, beer, matches, paper, foods, beverages, wool, cut diamonds, dairy products.
BULGARIA	Soviet-type republic with a one-house legislature, which elects a presidium whose president is the nominal chief of state.	lev	Bulgarian	Eastern Orthodox	Wheat, corn, barley, oats, rye, tobacco, fruit, cotton, sugar beets, potatoes; livestock, silkworm cocoons; fish; coal, salt, bauxite, copper, iron, lead, manganese, silver, kaolin; tobacco products, attar of roses, sugar, flour, textiles, leather goods, shoes, lead concentrates, wines and spirits.
CZECHOSLOVAKIA	Soviet-type republic with a president and a one-house elective parliament.	koruna	Czech and Slovak	Roman Catholic	Wheat, rye, barley, oats, corn, hops, sugar beets, grapes, potatoes; poultry, livestock; timber; coal, lignite, iron, graphite, garnets, silver, copper, lead, salt, manganese, zinc; beer, spirits, malt, metals, munitions, machinery, iron and steel, porcelain, shoes, textiles, wood products, pulp and paper, sugar, leather, foods, chemicals, rubber products.
DENMARK	Constitutional, hereditary monarchy with a two-house, elective legislature and an appointive council of ministers.	krone	Danish	Protestant	Barley, mixed grains, oats, rye, wheat, potatoes, sugar beets; livestock, fish; clay; ships and transportation equipment, butter, bacon, eggs, cheese, milk, footwear, clothing, machines, chemicals, tobacco products, metal goods, leather goods, beverages; stone, earthenware and glassware, electrical goods.
FINLAND	A republic with a president, a one-house elective diet and appointive council of state.	marhka	Finnish and Swedish	Protestant	Hay, potatoes, wheat, oats, barley, rye, sugar beets, flax, hemp, vegetables; cattle, horses, sheep, pigs, poultry, reindeer; wood and timber; fish; copper; lumber, plywood, furniture, pulp and paper, cardboard, textiles, butter, eggs, cheese, flour, leather, chemicals, china and glass, foodstuffs.
FRANCE	A republic with a president, a two-house elective parliament and an appointive council of ministers.	franc	French	Roman Catholic	Sugar beets, potatoes, wheat, oats, barley, rye; corn, turnips, fruits, nuts, wine grapes, buckwheat; cattle, sheep, pigs, horses; fish; coal, iron ore, lignite, salt, bauxite, pyrites, potash salts, leeks, kaolin, natural gas, iron and steel, chemicals; silk, cotton, rayon, wool and linen, textiles; clothing, lace, perfumes and cosmetics, automobiles, machinery, dairy products, beet sugar, wines, porcelain, aluminum, foods, leather, spirits.
GERMANY	Country is divided between two governments — a democratic **Federal Republic of Germany** in the west and a Soviet-dominated **German "Democratic" Republic** in the east. **Federal Republic** has an elected federal diet and council who jointly elect the president. **German "Democratic" Republic** has a communist controlled legislative branch which selects the president, cabinet and prime minister.	East German and West German Deutsch mark	German	Protestant Roman Catholic	Wheat, rye, barley, oats, potatoes, sugar beets, fruits, hops; pigs, cattle, poultry, horses; fish; forest products; coal, lignite, iron, copper, potash, sulphur, salt, uranium, lead, zinc, fluor spar, gypsum, vanadium, aluminum; automobiles, steel, cement, diesel oil, gasoline, cotton yarn, woolen yarn, rayon fiber, beet sugar, beer, wines, optical instruments, sulphuric acid, sodium bicarbonate, chemicals.
GIBRALTAR	British Crown Colony administered by a governor, executive council, and a legislative council.	pound	English and Spanish	Roman Catholic	Fish for export and processing of commodities for local consumption.
GREAT BRITAIN: ENGLAND AND WALES	England is governed directly by the government of Great Britain and Northern Ireland. Executive power resides nominally in the Crown but actually in the prime minister and cabinet. Parliament consists of two houses.	pound	English and Welsh (Celtic)	Protestant	Potatoes, turnips, beets, oats, wheat, barley, rye, hay, beans, peas, cabbage, vetches, hops, fruits; sheep, cattle, pigs, horses, poultry; fish; coal, coke, gas, iron, copper, lead, nickel, tin, clay; dairy products, wool, cotton and linen textiles; electrical goods, vehicles, steel, scientific instruments, cutlery, foods and beverages, tobacco products, clothing and shoes, chemicals, pottery, china, machinery, locomotives, carpets, knitwear, lace, pharmaceuticals.

POLITICAL DIVISION	GOVERNMENT	MONETARY UNIT	PRINCIPAL LANGUAGES	PRINCIPAL RELIGIONS	MAJOR PRODUCTS
NORTHERN IRELAND	Ruled by a governor, a cabinet and a bicameral legislature.	pound	English and Gaelic	Protestant Roman Catholic	Potatoes, oats, flax, turnips, hay; cattle, sheep, pigs, poultry; basalt and igneous rocks, sand and gravel, grit and conglomerate, chalk, clays; linen, rayon, woolen goods, carpets, hosiery, cotton goods, shirts, collars, underwear, shipbuilding, aircraft, marine machinery, rope, tobacco, whiskey.
SCOTLAND	A secretary of state for Scotland in the British cabinet has in his charge four departments for Scotland (agriculture, education, health and home.) Authority in other matters is exercised by other members of the British cabinet.	pound	English and Gaelic	Protestant	Turnips, potatoes, wheat, barley, sugar beets, flax, vegetables, forage crops, fruits; sheep, cattle, pigs, horses; coal, iron ore, granite, sandstone, limestone, slate, lead, clay; steel, machinery, tools, locomotives, electronic equipment, linoleum, shipbuilding and repair, watches, clocks, jute, bagging, burlap, textiles, hosiery, thread, lace, carpet, yarn, chemicals, whiskey, ale, paper, bricks and other clay products, preserves, boots and shoes, furniture.
GREECE	A constitutional hereditary monarchy with a prime minister, cabinet of ministers and an elective assembly.	drachma	Greek	Greek Orthodox	Wheat, barley, corn, oats, rye, tobacco, currants, sultana raisins, olives, figs, grapes, cottonseed, sesame seed; sheep, goats, cattle, pigs, horses, mules; fish; iron ore, sulphur, emery, magnesite, zinc, lead, lignite, marble, bauxite; textiles, olive oil, foods, wines, chemicals, leather, wood and paper, metal products, machinery.
HUNGARY	A communist republic with a president and a presidential council selected by the national assembly.	forint	Hungarian	Catholic Protestant	Wheat, corn, rye, barley, oats, potatoes, sugar beets, tobacco, grapes and other fruits, peppers, hemp, flax; pigs, cattle, sheep, horses, poultry; fish; coal, lignite, petroleum, natural gas, iron ore, bauxite, manganese; flour, sugar, distilling, brewing, iron and steel, wines, textiles, paprika, chemicals, leather, metal products, wood and paper products.
ICELAND	A republic with a president, an elective, two-house legislature and an appointive cabinet of ministers.	krona	Icelandic	Protestant	Hay, potatoes, turnips, hothouse fruits and vegetables; sheep, poultry, horses, cattle; fish; dairy products, meats, animal and vegetable oils, hides, skins, leather, clothing, textiles, frozen fish, herring oil, herring meal.
IRELAND	A republic with a president, premier and an elective, two-house parliament.	pound	English and Gaelic	Roman Catholic	Hay, potatoes, turnips, fodder, beets, sugar beets, oats, wheat, barley, cabbage, rye, flax; cattle, sheep, pigs, horses, poultry; fish; coal, peat, gypsum; tobacco, dairy products, foodstuffs, beer, malt, clothing, meats, textiles, boots and shoes, wood and paper products.
ITALY	A republic with a president, a two-house, elective legislature and an appointive cabinet.	lira	Italian	Roman Catholic	Wheat, corn, oats, sugar, beets, potatoes, tomatoes, rice, olives, grapes, lemons and other fruits, hemp, tobacco, nuts; fish; sheep and goats, cattle, pigs, horses, donkeys; iron ore, sulphur, zinc, bauxite, lead, mercury, barite, copper, marble, manganese, lignite; textiles, chemicals, wines, automobiles and machinery, electrical goods, beet sugar, olive oil, cheese, clothing, processed foods.
LIECHTENSTEIN	A principality headed by a prince and an elective, one-house legislature.	Swiss franc	German	Roman Catholic	Grain, fruit, grapes, wood; cattle, pigs, chickens; cotton textiles, wine, leather, false teeth, pottery, wood-carving.
LUXEMBOURG	A grand duchy and hereditary, constitutional monarchy with an elective chamber of deputies and appointive minister of state and cabinet.	franc	Mosel-frankisch (German dialect)	Roman Catholic	Oats, potatoes, wheat, rye, grapes; livestock; iron ore, slate, gypsum, sand and gravel; iron, steel and metal working; chemicals, non-metallic minerals, beverages, tobacco, leather, wines, dairy products, quarrying.
MALTA	A self-governing colony of Great Britain with a governor, Lt. governor and an elective legislative assembly.	pound	Maltese and English	Roman Catholic	Wheat, barley, potatoes, onions, grapes and other fruits, cumin seed, cotton; goats, sheep, pigs, cattle; fish; lace, filigree, wine, footwear, beer, cigarettes, buttons, pipes, gloves.
MONACO	A principality. The prince's authority exercised through a state ministry and 3 government counsellors. The one-house legislative body is elective.	franc	French	Roman Catholic	Principal revenue derived from Monte Carlo gambling casino. Tobacco, postage stamps, perfume, liqueurs, olive oil, oranges.
NETHERLANDS	A constitutional, hereditary monarchy governed by the Queen, her ministers and a two-house legislature, partly elective and partly chosen by provincial councils.	guilder	Dutch	Roman Catholic Protestant	Potatoes, sugar beets, rye, wheat, oats, barley, flax, legumes, flower bulbs, seeds, vegetables, fruit; cattle, pigs, sheep, horses, poultry; fish; coal, petroleum, salt; leather, rubber, footwear, metal products, textiles, paper, building materials, chemicals, foods and beverages, clothing, shipbuilding, cheese and other dairy products, fertilizers, ceramics, cement, tobacco products.
NORWAY	A constitutional, hereditary monarchy headed by the king, his council of state and a two-house, elective legislature.	krone	Norwegian	Protestant	Hay, potatoes, oats, barley, wheat, rye, fruits, vegetables; dairy products, livestock; herring, cod and other fish; sulphur, iron, copper, zinc, silver, nickel, molybdenum; timber, pulp, cellulose, paper, canned foods, electro-chemical products, transportation equipment, salted, dried and canned fish, leather, basic metals, textiles, fertilizers, shipbuilding.

POLITICAL DIVISION	GOVERNMENT	MONETARY UNIT	PRINCIPAL LANGUAGES	PRINCIPAL RELIGIONS	MAJOR PRODUCTS
POLAND	A Soviet-type "People's Republic" headed by a one-party legislative Sejm which elects an executive Council of Ministers.	zloty	Polish	Roman Catholic	Potatoes, straw and hay, rye, sugar beets, mangolds, oats, barley, wheat, peas, beans, flax, hemp, rapeseed; livestock; fish; zinc, lead, coal, salt, iron ore, petroleum, natural gas, phosphates, lignite; iron and steel products, coke, foods and beverages, textiles, cement, lime, bricks, electrical goods, chemicals, wood, timber, paper, cellulose, leather and leather products, glass.
PORTUGAL	A "corporative republic" with a president, premier, and a one-house, elective legislature.	escudo	Portuguese	Roman Catholic	Wheat, corn, oats, barley, rye, rice, French beans, potatoes, grapes, olives; livestock; cork, lumber, resin; sardines, tuna and other fish; copper pyrites, coal, copper, tin, kaolin, cement, wolfram, sulphur, tungsten, iron; wines, olive oil, canned sardines, textiles, porcelain, tiles, embroideries, lace.
RUMANIA	A Soviet-type "People's Republic" with a five-member presidium, cabinet of ministers and a one-house legislature.	leu	Rumanian	Rumanian Orthodox	Wheat, barley, rye, corn, oats, potatoes, sugar beets, hemp, flax, grapes, fruits, tobacco; lumber; sheep, cattle, pigs, horses; petroleum, natural gas, salt, coal, lignite, iron and copper ores, gold, silver, bauxite, lead, manganese, zinc; flour, brewing and distilling, iron and steel, metal products, textiles, wood and paper products.
SAN MARINO	A republic with an elective, one-house legislature.	lira	Italian	Roman Catholic	Cattle, hides, wines, quarrying.
SPAIN	A nominal monarchy governed by a chief of state. The legislative Cortés prepares laws subject to the veto of the chief of state. A king is to be chosen by a regency council upon the death or incapacitation of the chief of state.	peseta	Spanish Catalan	Roman Catholic	Wheat, barley, potatoes, oranges, olives, oats, rye, rice, corn, peas, beans, grapes, onions, sugar beets, esparto, flax, hemp, pulse, cork, nuts; pigs, sheep, goats, donkeys, mules, horses, poultry; sardines, tuna, cod and other fish; coal, lignite, iron ore, lead, iron pyrites, potash, zinc, mercury, sulphur, copper; textiles, wines, olive oil, paper, cement, hides, preserved and canned fish and shellfish, paper products.
SWEDEN	A kingdom with a prime minister, council of state and a two-house, elective legislature.	krona	Swedish	Protestant	Hay, sugar beets, potatoes, fodder crops, oats, wheat, rye, barley; forest products, cattle, pigs, sheep, horses, poultry; fish; iron ore, sulphur, arsenic, zinc, copper, silver, gold, lead, manganese; lumber and wood products, machinery, textiles, iron and steel and metal goods, chemicals, dairy products, electric power, tobacco products, brick, porcelain and glass, shipbuilding, matches.
SWITZERLAND	A republic with a president, vice-president and a two-house, elective legislature.	franc	German, French, Italian, Romansch	Protestant Roman Catholic	Wheat, potatoes, sugar beets, rye, oats, barley, fruits, tobacco; livestock; salt, iron, manganese; dairy products, textiles, watches and clocks, chemicals, foods, wines, dyes, instruments.
TRIESTE	In July, 1955 the Free Territory of Trieste was dissolved as such. The city of Trieste and the area north remains under Italy and the area to the south remains under Yugoslavia.				
TURKEY	A republic with a president and a one-house, elective legislature.	pound	Turkish	Moslem	Tobacco, cereals, olives, cotton, figs, nuts, fruits; cattle, livestock; fish; chromium, iron ore, copper, coal, lignite, meerschaum, manganese; textiles, iron and steel, paper, rugs, olive oil.
U.S.S.R.	A federation of 15 socialist republics with authority vested in the Supreme Soviet, composed of two elective legislative chambers, whose chairman is the executive head of the government. The Communist party is the only legal party. It selects all candidates for election.	ruble	Russian, Ukrainian, White Russian, Uzbek, Tatar, Azerbaizhani, Georgian, Lithuanian, Armenian, Yiddish, Latvian, Mordvinian, Chuvash, Tadzhik, Esthonian, Kazakh.	Russian Orthodox	Wheat, rye, oats, barley, corn, sugar beets, sunflower seeds, cotton, forage crops, flax, hemp, potatoes, tobacco; cattle, sheep, goats, pigs, horses; lumber, furs; fish; coal, peat, petroleum, iron, lignite, copper, lead, zinc, nickel, aluminum, phosphates, manganese, gold, sulphur, potash, asbestos, platinum, salt, chromite; steel, machinery, textiles, sugar, flour, meats, automobiles, paper, synthetic rubber, foods, wines, chemicals.
VATICAN CITY	The Pope, who is elected for life by the cardinals of the Roman Catholic Church, exercises absolute legislative, executive and judicial power. He appoints a governor of the state and delegates diplomatic and judicial power.	lira	Italian Latin	Roman Catholic	
YUGOSLAVIA	A Soviet-type republic consisting of 6 republics with a central two-house, elective legislature.	dinar	Serbian-Croatian, Slovenian Macedonian	Eastern Orthodox Roman Catholic	Wheat, barley, rye, oats, corn, sugar beets, hemp, hops, opium, tobacco, flax, alfalfa, vegetables, fruits; sheep, cattle, pigs, goats, horses, poultry; coal, lignite, iron, copper, lead, salt, zinc, mercury, antimony, petroleum, bauxite, chrome, cement; lumber, textiles, foods, beverages, sugar, wood-distillates, wines.

Africa's varied topography lends itself to all sorts of livlihoods ranging from the industrial to the pastoral.

Many natural phenomena, like these hot springs, are present in Africa's terrain.

AFRICA—The term "sleeping giant," which has often been used in referring to China, can best be applied to Africa. This second largest continent is three times the size of China, and is richer in natural resources, but it has only one-third the population. Although two of the world's oldest civilizations once flourished along its northern shores in Egypt and Carthage, the rest of Africa long remained shrouded in mystery.

Joined to Asia by a land bridge at the Isthmus of Suez, and only separated from Europe by the narrow Strait of Gibraltar, it was not until the nineteenth century that Europe finally set about the conquest of the "Dark Continent." For centuries an unfavorable climate and natural barriers combined to guard its secrets and hold back development.

Almost midway of its length Africa is crossed by the equator. Being triangular in shape, this places most of the continent in unhealthy torrid regions. Added to this its coastline is steep and regular, and offers few places for ships to anchor. The rivers as regards navigability cannot be considered in the same light as the great rivers of Europe, Asia and the Americas. None, except the Nile and the Congo, has unimpeded entrance to the sea.

The deltas of the Niger and the Zambesi are choked by silt and, on nearly all, navigation is impeded by shoal or cataract. Nevertheless the Congo and the Nile with their tributaries have many thousands of miles of navigable waterways, as have the Niger, the Benue and the Zambesi.

To the north, the Sahara Desert proved an effective barrier of sand and intense heat, which for hundreds of years prevented any important exchange of ideas or trade between the white man of the north and the black man in the south. Extending from the Atlantic to the River Nile, and reaching from the Mediterranean to the Sudan, the dry Sahara is a region of desolation. What trade existed between Asia, Europe and Africa followed caravan routes which led from oasis to oasis. The only life to be found there is at these scattered oases.

It was only following the explorations of Livingstone, Stanley and others in the last century, that Europe became aware of the possibilities existing in Africa. Then, suddenly awakened to the great wealth that had been overlooked, the European powers rushed in to carve out vast empires. When they had finished only two sections remained which were not possessions or dependencies of the white man. Only the Republic of Liberia and the Kingdom of Ethiopia remained, where the native African had a voice in the government of his affairs. Later Egypt became an independent state, under the influence of the British, and the Union of South Africa acquired a dominion status in the British Commonwealth of Nations. Following the second World War, Libya also became an independent nation.

Africa is a great plateau, over four thousand miles long from north to south. The average height of the entire continent is over two thousand feet above sea level. Its loftiest peak is nearly twenty thousand feet high, while the Qattara Depression in the Libyan Desert sinks to four hundred feet below sea level.

The Atlas Mountains parallel the north coast of Africa, with their southern slopes dropping down to the Sahara. The Sudan Belt, which extends south from the Sahara to the Gold Coast and the Gulf of Guinea, is a lower region of hills, valleys and plains. To the southwest are the low Cameroon Mountains; and another chain in the eastern part follows the Red Sea.

In Eastern Africa, a ridge of highlands reaches below the equator to form a series of mountain ranges. It is here that the great lakes region is found. Only in North America are there lakes which compare to these in size. Unlike the mountain ranges of other continents, those of Africa do not follow a regular pattern. This, together with their location, provides an unusual drainage system. A mountain ridge separates the lakes that drain into the three great rivers, the Nile, the Congo and the Zambesi. This ridge dictates the direction of their courses, with the Nile flowing north toward the Mediterranean, the Congo twisting and turning to finally reach the Atlantic to the west, and the Zambesi flowing east to empty into the Indian Ocean. Each river follows a devious course through the mountains before finding a way over the edge of the plateau to reach the sea. This results in many falls and rapids which interrupt transportation. The Victoria Falls on the Zambesi, the rapids of the Congo, and the cataracts of the Nile are typical.

The Congo, winding through the gloomy depths of the fever-infested forests, is three thousand miles long. It is second only to the Amazon of South America in the volume of

POLITICAL DIVISION	GOVERNMENT	MONETARY UNIT	PRINCIPAL LANGUAGES	PRINCIPAL RELIGIONS	MAJOR PRODUCTS
ALGERIA	Consists of 12 overseas departments with a central elective assembly, governor-general and government council.	franc	Arabic French Berber	Mohammedan Roman Catholic Jewish	Wheat, barley, oats, corn, grapes, olives, tobacco, dates, figs, flax, pomegranates, prunes, apricots, legumes, potatoes; sheep, goats, cattle, mules, horses, pigs, camels; sardines, anchovies, tuna; forestry products; iron phosphates, zinc, petroleum; wine, olive oil, distilling, flour, carpet weaving, alcohol, cotton weaving, tobacco products, wool, cork.
ANGLO-EGYPTIAN SUDAN (now SUDAN)	A republic with a bicameral parliament and council of ministers. Executive power resides temporarily in a council of state.	Egyptian pound	Arabic Sudanese Hamitic languages English	Mohammedan Tribal religions	Cotton, cotton seed, gum arabic, Senna leaves and pods, groundnuts, sesame, millet, dates, dom nuts (vegetable ivory), wheat, shea nuts; sheep, goats, cattle, camels, asses; mahogany; hides and skins, ivory, gold, salt, trochus shell, mother-of-pearl.
ANGOLA	Portuguese overseas province with a governor general and district governors.	angolar	Bantu languages Portuguese	Tribal religions	Coffee, corn, sugar, palm oil and kernels, cotton, sisal, wax, tobacco; diamonds; whale oil, fish oil, sugar, palm oil,
ASCENSION ISLAND	Administered through the government of St. Helena by a resident magistrate and a Justice of the Peace.	pound	English	Protestant	
BASUTOLAND	British protectorate. Governed by a resident commissioner under High Commissioner for Basutoland, Bechuanaland and Swaziland.	pound	Bantu languages Afrikaans English	Tribal religions Christian missions	Corn, wheat, sorghum, barley, oats, beans, peas; cattle, sheep, goats, horses, donkeys, pigs, mules; wool, mohair.
BECHUANALAND	British protectorate. Governed by a resident commissioner under High Commissioner for Basutoland, Bechuanaland and Swaziland.	pound	Bantu languages Bushman English	Tribal religions Protestant	Kaffir, wheat and wheatmeal; cattle, sheep, goats, pigs; hides, gold.
BELGIAN CONGO	Belgian colony administered by a governor-general.	franc	Bantu languages French Flemish	Tribal religions Roman Catholic	Palm oil and kernels, cotton, coffee, oil cakes, copal, rice, groundnuts; rubber, manioc, fibers; copper, cement, coal, silver, cassiterite (tin), diamonds, gold, cobalt, radium, uranium, tantalum, zinc.
CAMEROONS	Under United Nations trusteeship, administered by Great Britain.	pound	Bantu and Sudanese languages	Mohammedan Tribal religions Christian	Cocoa, coffee, rubber, bananas, palm oil and kernels; cattle, goats, sheep, horses.
CAMEROUN	Under United Nations trusteeship, administered by France.	franc	Sudanese and Bantu languages Arabic French	Tribal religions Mohammedan Roman Catholic	Cocoa, palm kernels, bananas, caoutchouc, coffee, cacao, palm oil; timber; cattle, sheep, pigs, horses, asses; rubber, tobacco.
CANARY ISLANDS	Islands forming two provinces of Spain, governed by Cabildo Insular.	peseta	Spanish	Roman Catholic	Bananas, cochineal, potatoes, sugar cane, onions, fruits; fish; wine, sugar.
CAPE VERDE ISLANDS	Portuguese overseas province, ruled by a governor.	escudo	Portuguese	Roman Catholic	Coffee, castor beans, corn, fruit, grains, tobacco; goats, oxen, pigs, asses; hides, skins; preserved fish, salt, lime, sugar.
COMORO ISLANDS	An overseas territory of the French Union with an administrator, privy council and an elective general council.	franc	Arabic French	Mohammedan	Sugar cane, vanilla, rice, sweet potatoes, yams, copra, sisal, cacao, perfume plants; rum distilling.
DAHOMEY	Territory of Fr. West Africa with a governor and an elective representative assembly.	franc	Sudanese languages French	Tribal religions Mohammedan	Palm oil, shea nuts, groundnuts, cotton fiber, copra, castor oil, kapok, millet; gold, diamonds, bauxite, iron ore.
EGYPT	A republic under an interim government.	Egyptian pound	Arabic	Mohammedan Christian minorities	Cotton, barley, wheat, rice, sugar cane, onions, corn, millet, fruits, vegetables; sheep, goats, cattle, buffalo, donkeys, pigs, horses, mules; fish; petroleum, cement, phosphates, asbestos, chromite, cotton ginning, milling, pottery, perfume, soap.
ERITREA	Autonomous state federated with Ethiopia. Administered locally by a representative legislature.	Ethiopian dollar	Hamitic languages Arabic	Coptic Christian Mohammedan	Coffee, barley, sisal, bananas, legumes, gum arabic, wheat, tobacco, dates, dom nuts, senna; goats, sheep, camels, horses, mules, donkeys, cattle; hides, skins; fish-meal; pearls, mother-of-pearl; gold, salt, potassium salts, matting, matches, footwear.
ETHIOPIA	Kingdom with a king assisted by a council of ministers and a bicameral legislature. (See Eritrea).	Ethiopian dollar	Amharic Hamitic languages Arabic	Coptic Christian Mohammedan	Coffee, teff, barley, durra, wheat, cotton, sugar cane; cattle, sheep, goats, horses, mules; hides, skins; wax, gold, rocksalt.
FRENCH EQUATORIAL AFRICA	Overseas territory of France with a governor-general and an elective grand assembly representing the 4 constituent territories.	franc	Bantu and Sudanese languages Arabic French	Mohammedan Tribal religions Roman Catholic	Palm oil and kernels, coconuts, cotton, coffee, cocoa, groundnuts, kapok, butter; hides; timber, rubber, copal gum, wax; ivory, gold, copper, lead, zinc, diamonds.
FRENCH SUDAN	Territory of Fr. West Africa with a governor and an elective representative assembly.	franc	Sudanese languages Hamitic languages Arabic French	Mohammedan Tribal religions	Millet, rice, groundnuts, corn, sweet potatoes, cotton, manioc, tobacco, karite, shea nuts, yams, kopac, sisal; cattle, goats, sheep, horses, asses, camels; hides and skins; pottery, bricks, jewelry, weaving, leather, rice mills, soap.
FRENCH WEST AFRICA	Overseas territory of France with a governor-general and an elective grand assembly representing the 8 constituent territories.	franc	Sudanese and Hamitic languages Arabic French	Mohammedan Tribal religions Roman Catholic	Millet, rice, corn, cotton and fibers, nuts, oilseeds and oil, manioc, coffee, bananas, cocoa; cattle; gold, diamonds, iron ore, bauxite.
GAMBIA	Crown colony and protectorate of Great Britain administered by a governor, council and legislative assembly.	pound	Sudanese languages English	Mohammedan Tribal religions Christian	Groundnuts, palm kernels; hides and skins; beeswax.
GOLD COAST (GHANA)	Colony and protectorate of Great Britain administered by a governor and an executive council with legislative assembly.	pound	Sudanese languages English	Mohammedan Tribal religions Christian	Cocoa, palm oil and kernels, sorghum, millet, corn, yams, cassava, groundnuts, cotton.

POLITICAL DIVISION	GOVERNMENT	MONETARY UNIT	PRINCIPAL LANGUAGES	PRINCIPAL RELIGIONS	MAJOR PRODUCTS
GUINEA, FRENCH	Territory of Fr. West Africa with a governor and an elective representative assembly.	franc	Sudanese languages French	Tribal religions Mohammedan	Rice, groundnuts, palm oil and nuts, wax, honey, bananas, indigo, kola, orange products, coffee; cattle, sheep, goats, pigs; hides and skins; bauxite, iron ore, gold.
GUINEA, PORTUGUESE	Portuguese overseas province ruled by a governor.	escudo	Sudanese languages Portuguese	Tribal religions Roman Catholic	Rice, palm kernels and oil, wax, groundnuts; hides.
GUINEA, SPANISH	Spanish colony ruled by a governor.	peseta	Bantu languages Spanish	Tribal religions Roman Catholic	Cocoa, coffee, vegetables and fruit; wood.
IFNI	Spanish territory ruled by a sub-governor.	peseta	Berber Arabic Spanish	Mohammedan	Barley, alfalfa, corn, tomatoes, argan oil, wheat; fish.
IVORY COAST	Territory of Fr. West Africa with a governor and an elective representative assembly.	franc	Sudanese languages French	Tribal religions Mohammedan	Coffee, cocoa, bananas, manioc, corn, rice, yams, kola, coconuts, palm oil, groundnuts, cotton, millet, tobacco; mahogany, caoutchouc; sheep, cattle, goats, pigs; gold, diamonds, manganese, iron ore, ilmenite.
KENYA	Crown colony and protectorate of Great Britain administered by a governor, executive and legislative council.	East African shilling	Swahili English Sudanese Hamitic Bantu	Tribal religions Mohammedan	Sisal, wheat, tea, coffee, pyrethrum, cotton, corn, sugar cane, sesame, groundnuts, wattle; hides and skins; sodium carbonate, gold, kyanite, salt, silver, lime, bags, butter, sugar, sisal products.
LIBERIA	Republic with president, cabinet, senate and house of representatives.	Liberian dollar	English Sudanese languages	Christian Tribal religions Mohammedan	Rubber, rice, coffee, cassava, sugar cane, cacao, palm oil and kernels, piassava, groundnuts; rum; iron ore.
LIBYA	A constitutional monarchy with a bicameral legislature.	Libyan pound	Arabic	Mohammedan	Barley, wheat, olives, grapes, dates, almonds, figs, tobacco, esparto; goats, sheep, camels, cattle, donkeys, mules and horses; sponge and tuna fishing; matting, carpets, leather articles, embroidered fabrics.
MADAGASCAR	Overseas territory of France with a governor and an elective advisory council.	franc	French Malagasy and Bantu languages	Tribal religions Roman Catholic Protestant	Cassava, rice, corn, potatoes, coffee, sugar cane, haricot beans, groundnuts, sisal, castor oil, tobacco, raffia; cattle, pigs, goats, sheep; graphite, mica, gold, rock crystal, corundum, phosphates, agate; textiles, sugar and rice factories, tapioca.
MAURITANIA	Territory of Fr. West Africa with a governor and an elective representative assembly.	franc	Arabic Hamitic and Sudanese languages French	Mohammedan	Millet, gum, dates, corn, watermelons, wheat, henna; sheep and goats, cattle, camels, asses, horses; hides and skins; salt.
MAURITIUS	British colony ruled by a governor, an executive council and a legislative council.	rupee	English Hindustani French	Roman Catholic	Sugar, aloe fiber, rice, vanilla beans, hemp, sisal, groundnuts, tea, yams, manioc, pineapples, tobacco, coconuts; alcohol, molasses, rum, copra.
†MOROCCO, FRENCH ZONE	French protectorate governed by the Sultan of Morocco but subject to the effective control of a French resident-general.	Moroccan franc	Arabic Berber French	Mohammedan Roman Catholic Jewish	Wheat, barley, olives, almonds, citrus fruits, dates, beans, grapes, vegetables, linseed; cork, cedar; sheep, goats, cattle, asses, camels, horses, mules, pigs; fish; phosphate, iron ore, anthracite, manganese, lead, zinc, cobalt, copper, antimony; leather, carpets.
†MOROCCO, SPANISH (Southern Zone)	Spanish protectorate ruled by a sub-governor subordinate to the High Commissioner of Spanish Morocco.	peseta	Berber Arabic Spanish	Mohammedan	Barley; goats, camels; fish.
†MOROCCO, SPANISH	Spanish protectorate ruled in the name of the Sultan of Morocco by a khalifa whose administration is supervised by the High Commissioner of Spanish Morocco.	peseta	Arabic Spanish	Mohammedan Roman Catholic Jewish	Barley, sorghum, wheat, corn, beans, rye, rice; cork, cedar; goats, sheep, cattle, asses; fish; iron, lead, antimony.
MOZAMBIQUE	Portuguese overseas province ruled by a governor and a government council.	escudo	Bantu languages Portuguese	Tribal religions Roman Catholic	Sugar, corn, cotton, copra, sisal, cashew nuts, bananas, coffee, kapok, sorghum, manioc, beeswax, tea, tobacco, vegetable oils; mangrove bark, timber; oxen, goats, pigs, sheep, cattle; gold, silver, asbestos, uranium, bauxite, samerskite.
NIGERIA	A federated possession of Great Britain with a governor-general, a council of ministers and a federal house of representatives.	pound	Sudanese languages Arabic English	Mohammedan Christian	Palm oil and kernels, cacao, groundnuts, cotton, rubber, bananas, benni seeds, shea nuts, yams, cassava, corn, rice, fruits, millet, coffee; cattle, sheep, goats; hides and skins; timber; tin, coal, columbite, lead, gold, silver, zinc; cigarettes, soap, sugar.
NIGER	Territory of Fr. West Africa with a governor and an elective representative assembly.	franc	Sudanese Hamitic Arabic French	Mohammedan Tribal religions	Millet, manioc, groundnuts, rice, wheat, cotton, gum arabic, kapoc, kidney beans, corn, onions, sorghum, dates, sugar cane; goats, sheep, cattle, asses, camels, horses; hides and skins, leather; natron, sodium sulphate, salt.
NORTHERN RHODESIA	*British colony administered by a governor and executive and legislative council.	pound	Bantu languages English	Tribal religions	Corn, wheat, potatoes, tobacco, sorghum, millet, groundnuts, cassava, rice, beans, cow-peas, cotton; lumber; cattle and other livestock.
NYASALAND	*British protectorate administered by a governor and executive and legislative council.	pound	Bantu languages English	Tribal religions	Tobacco, tea, cotton, pulses, tung-oil, sisal, corn, cassava, wheat, rice, millet, groundnuts, rubber, beeswax; timber; goats, cattle, pigs, sheep; hides, skins, meat, ghee, soap; gold, mica, corundum.
PRINCIPE AND SÃO TOMÉ	Portuguese overseas province administered by a governor.	escudo	Bantu languages Portuguese	Tribal religions Roman Catholic	Cacao, coffee, coconuts, copra, palm oil, cinchona, bananas.
RÉUNION	French overseas department administered by a prefect and a council-general.	franc	French	Roman Catholic	Sugar, rum, vanilla, tapioca, essences, fruit and vegetable preserves.

* Member of new Federation of Rhodesia and Nyasaland.
†The French and Spanish protectorates in Morocco were dissolved in 1956. A unified and independent Morocco was re-established.

AFRICA

POLITICAL DIVISION	GOVERNMENT	MONETARY UNIT	PRINCIPAL LANGUAGES	PRINCIPAL RELIGIONS	MAJOR PRODUCTS
RUANDA—URUNDI	Under United Nations trusteeship, administered by Belgium and governed by a governor-general.	franc	Bantu languages Flemish French	Tribal religions Roman Catholic	Foods; cattle; hides.
ST. HELENA	British colony administered by a governor and advisory councils.	pound	English	Protestant	Hemp, lily bulbs, potatoes, tow, rope and twine, lace; sheep, goats, cattle, donkeys, poultry.
SENEGAL	Territory of Fr. West Africa with a governor and an elective representative assembly.	franc	Sudanese languages Arabic French	Mohammedan Tribal religions Roman Catholic	Millet, groundnuts, manioc, rice, corn, gum arabic, palm nuts, honey, sweet potatoes, sisal, indigo; sheep, goats, cattle, asses, horses; fish; titanium, zircon; brick, pottery, weaving, jewelry, oil cakes.
SEYCHELLES	A British colony ruled by a governor and a legislative and executive council.	rupee	English French	Roman Catholic	Coconuts, cinnamon, patchouli, copra, vanilla, corn; guano; salted fish, tortoise shell, calipee.
SIERRA LEONE	A British colony and protectorate ruled by a governor and a legislative and executive council.	pound	Sudanese languages English	Tribal religions Mohammedan Christian	Palm oil and kernels, kola nuts, ginger, piassava, groundnuts, cocoa; diamonds, iron ore, chrome ore.
SOMALILAND	Under United Nations trusteeship and administered by Italy with U. N. advisory council.	Somalo	Somali Arabic Italian	Mohammedan Roman Catholic	Sugar, cotton, tobacco, bananas, aromatic gums, resin, kapok, grains, beans; camels, goats, sheep, cattle; skins, hides; tunny, mother-of-pearl.
SOMALILAND, BRITISH	British protectorate ruled solely by governor.	Indian rupee East African shilling	Somali Arabic	Mohammedan	Millet, sorghum, corn; sheep, goats, camels, cattle; skins, hides; gums, salt.
SOMALILAND, FRENCH	Overseas territory of France with a governor and an elective advisory council.	Djibouti franc	Hamitic languages Arabic French	Mohammedan	Boats, sheep; salt.
SOUTHERN RHODESIA	*British dominion with governor and elective executive and legislative council.	pound	Bantu languages English	Tribal religions Protestant	Corn, tobacco, groundnuts, wheat, potatoes, citrus and other fruits; cattle, sheep, pigs, goats; meats, hides; gold, asbestos, chromite, coal; footwear, apparel, cigarettes, flour, groundnut oil, wood products.
SPANISH SAHARA	Spanish territory, consisting of Saguia el Hamra and Río de Oro, ruled by sub-governors.	peseta	Arabic Spanish	Mohammedan	Barley, corn; goats, sheep, camels; fish.
SWAZILAND	British protectorate governed by a resident commissioner under the High Commissioner for Basutoland, Bechuanaland and Swaziland.	pound	Bantu languages English	Tribal religions Christian missions	Tobacco, corn, groundnuts, kaffir-corn, wheat, oats, rye, barley, fruits; cattle, goats, sheep, pigs; butter; hides, skins; asbestos, gold, tin.
TANGANYIKA TERRITORY	Under United Nations trusteeship and administered by Great Britain. Ruled by a governor and a legislative and executive council.	East African shilling	Bantu languages Swahili English	Tribal religions Mohammedan Christian missions	Sisal, cotton, coffee, bananas, tobacco, papain, beeswax, grains, sugar; cattle, goats, sheep; hides, skins; wood, timber, wax, gum arabic; diamonds, gold, tin, mica, salt, camphor, tungsten.
†TANGIER	An international zone governed by an appointive administrator and an international assembly.	franc peseta	Arabic French Spanish English	Mohammedan Roman Catholic Jewish	Wheat, barley, chickpeas; soap, canned fish, essential oils.
TOGO (FRENCH)	Under United Nations trusteeship and administered by the Commissioner of the Republic assisted by advisory and legislative councils.	franc	Sudanese languages French	Tribal religions Mohammedan Roman Catholic	Palm oil and kernels, tapioca, cocoa, yams, coffee, plantains, corn, groundnuts, cotton, copra, kola, cassava, rubber; sheep, goats, pigs, cattle, asses, horses.
‡TOGOLAND	Under United Nations trusteeship and administered by Great Britain as part of the Gold Coast.	pound	Sudanese languages English	Tribal religions Mohammedan Christian	Cocoa, rice, cassava, yams, coffee, millet, corn, groundnuts, tobacco; mats, pottery.
TRISTAN DA CUNHA	Possession of Great Britain governed by an administrator and an island council responsible to St. Helena.	pound	English	Protestant	Potatoes, fruit; cattle, sheep; fish.
TUNISIA	A kingdom with a Bey (monarch) council of ministers and an assembly.	franc	Arabic French Berber	Mohammedan Roman Catholic	Wheat, barley, oats, corn, sorghum, beans, grapes, olives, citrus fruits, dates, alfa grass, almonds, oranges, shaddocks, pistachios, cork; sheep, goats, cattle, horses, asses, mules, camels, pigs; fish, sponges; flour milling, oil refining, wool spinning, pottery, leather, silk weaving; phosphates, iron ore, lignite, lead, zinc.
UGANDA	British protectorate controlled by governor but ruled subordinately by native kings and their assemblies.	East African shilling	Bantu and Sudanese languages English	Tribal religions Christian	Cotton, coffee, plantains, millet, cotton seed, tobacco, chilies, sugar cane, rubber; cattle, sheep, goats; hides, skins; tin; cigarettes.
UNION OF SOUTH AFRICA	British dominion with a governor general, cabinet, elective senate and house of assembly.	pound	Afrikaans English Bantu languages Bushman	Protestant Roman Catholic Mohammedan Hindu Buddhist	Corn, wheat, potatoes, oats, kaffir-corn, barley, tobacco, sugar cane, tea, citrus fruits, rye, groundnuts, grapes, pineapples; cattle, sheep, goats, pigs, horses, donkeys, mules; gold, coal, diamonds, copper, asbestos, manganese, lime, limestone, platinum, chrome, iron, silver, tungsten, mercury, ranadium, tin, antimony, silver, scheelite, talc; hides, wool, footwear, rubber, machinery, clothing, textiles, food, vehicles, printing, furniture, building materials,
UPPER VOLTA	Territory of Fr. West Africa with a governor and an elective representative assembly.	franc	Sudanese languages French	Tribal religions Mohammedan	Millet, groundnuts, corn, karite nuts and butter (shea nut), vegetables, rice, tapes, cotton, kapok, sesame, sorghum, tea; sheep, goats, cattle, asses, pigs; gold, manganese, copper, silver, chrome, lignite, iron.
ZANZIBAR	British protectorate nominally ruled by a sultan but under the effective control of a governor and a legislative and executive council.	East African shilling	Bantu languages Swahili English	Tribal religions Mohammedan Christian missions	Sisal, cotton, coffee, bananas, tobacco, papain, beeswax, grains, sugar; cattle, goats, sheep; hides, skins; wood, gum arabic; diamonds, gold, tin, mica, salt, camphor, tungsten.

* Member of new Federation of Rhodesia and Nyasaland.
†International Zone of Tangier was dissolved in 1956 and turned over to Morocco.
‡Joined to Gold Coast (Ghana) in 1957.

The cities along the coast of North Africa are crowded with market places and their exotic wares.

TWA—Trans World Airline

Except for the fertile soil of the Nile valley, Egypt's land is arid and unproductive.

TWA—Trans World Airline

water it empties into the sea. The Nile travels four thousand miles before reaching the Mediterranean, and today, as in ancient times, makes Egypt a habitable country. As the Nile winds slowly through the Sahara, the evaporation is so great that the river would dry up before reaching the sea were it not fed by rivers from the high Abyssinian Mountains. It is these waters of the Blue Nile which bring the great Nile floods and supply the water for irrigation to make of Egypt a fertile strip of land hemmed in by cliffs and burning sands. Africa's fourth large river, the Niger, while rising only one hundred and fifty miles from the ocean, flows twenty-five hundred miles before reaching the Atlantic.

Africa is a land of climatic contradictions. At the equator the temperature ranges from typical jungle weather at the lower levels, to a climate similar to that found well over a thousand miles to the north. This occurs in the high altitudes of the mountains. Along the Mediterranean, the weather compares with that of southern Europe. The weather in the Congo Basin is always hot and humid, although to the east, in the mountain and lake region, it is tempered by the higher altitudes. In the far south, around Capetown, the weather is mild and sunny like the climate of southern California. The same extremes exist in rainfall. At the equator it is excessive, with periods of torrential rains. Traveling north or south from this wet center there is less and less rain, with parts of the Sahara never getting a drop.

Plant life varies with the rainfall. The dense, matted tropical jungles, which are exceeded only in size by the forests of the Amazon, give way to grassy plains and open forests. The only vegetation in the Sahara is around the springs that nourish the oases. Because the hot winds of the south are blocked by the Atlas Mountains, the entire coastal area of North Africa from the Atlantic to the Nile River is agriculturally productive.

Africa is a strange mixture of white and black races. The four original races of Hamites and Semites, Negroes and Hottentots have become so intermingled that it is no longer possible to draw clear lines between racial groups. The Hamites and Semites of North Africa are white and Mohammedans. The Negroes and Hottentots are the black people of Central and South Africa. While probably members of the Negro race, the Hottentots have distinctive characteristics which put them in a class by themselves. These native tribes have a barbaric form of worship. The Sudanese, blackest of the Negroes, were sought by the early slave traders. For over three hundred years millions of these poor blacks were seized and transported to strange lands.

The slave trade was started by the son of a man who accompanied Columbus to America. Needing labor in her New World colonies to replace the Indian slaves, who preferred death to captivity, Spain granted each Spanish colonist the right to import twelve African Negroes. A year later the king of Spain bestowed a grant upon the Dutch allowing them to take four thousand slaves a year. Soon the "black ivory trade"

had grown to huge proportions, and It has been estimated that as many as two million slaves were removed from Africa in a single year.

In recent years Africa has been undergoing tremendous changes. Railroads, motor roads and airlines continue to reach out and draw distant points closer together. Modern engineering genius is overcoming the obstacles imposed by climate and land formation, and Africa is rapidly taking its place among the more fortunate continents.

TUNISIA—Battleground of World War II, is the most productive land in North Africa. Its fertile valleys produce grain and tropical fruits. Seat of ancient Carthage, it was once the wealthiest city of its time until Rome destroyed it during the Punic Wars.

LIBYA— Is relatively unprotected from the scorching desert winds and, consequently, the least valuable of North African regions. However, the coastal areas are cultivated with the aid of shade and irrigation.

EGYPT—In the heart of the Nile valley, has been one of the most productive regions in the world since recorded time. Recent dam construction regulating the flow of the Nile has increased the productivity of the soil. Agricultural methods are the same today as they were 6,000 years ago.

SUDAN (former Anglo-Egyptian)—Embracing the upper Nile basin to the borders of Uganda and Ethiopia, produces gum arabic

TWA—Trans World Airline
Modern methods of travel have made additional roads and bridges necessary in modern Africa.

Gendreau
Many races and a variety of languages and religions are represented within the boundaries of South Africa.

for the entire world. Cotton is raised in the fertile areas between the Blue and the White Niles. Dates, ivory and meat are also exported.

ETHIOPIA—The first country to be liberated by the Allies in World War II, has many undeveloped resources. Gold and platinum are mined. The Djimmah Province produces a fine, robust coffee. There is, as yet, only one railroad which leads out of the country. The Italians, true to the Roman tradition, built 4,340 miles of roads while they were occupying the country.

UGANDA—The Source of the Nile River. Much of the country is situated in the lofty mountains of East Africa. The climate is usually mild because of the altitude of the land.

KENYA—Eastern gateway to Central Africa abounds in big game. The lowlands bordering the Indian Ocean are fertile, the climate bearable. Western Kenya is a high plateau with isolated towering peaks, snow-capped the year 'round.

TANGANYIKA—Within its borders is Kilimanjaro, Africa's highest known peak located a few miles north of the equator. Tanganyika is famous as the gorilla country of Africa. Its jungle brims with wildlife, there-

by making it a paradise for big-game hunters.

NYASALAND—A British protectorate, lies along the west shore of Lake Nyasa. Semi-autonomous and self-supporting, it has a good system of roads and railways.

UNION OF SOUTH AFRICA comprises the Transvaal, Orange Free State, Natal and the Cape of Good Hope. Its northern areas contain many valuable minerals, chief of which is gold and diamonds. Most of the world's diamonds and half the world's gold are exported from this country.

NORTHERN RHODESIA—Crown Colony on the borders of the jungles of Central Africa and the wide plains of South Africa. Copper, lead and cattle comprise its principal forms of wealth. Victoria Falls, the world's highest, are on the Zambesi River in Northern Rhodesia.

SOUTHERN RHODESIA—Border region, is well suited to agriculture and European settlement. It possesses vast amounts of gold, asbestos and chrome.

ANGOLA or Portuguese West Africa, on Africa's west coast, is a huge treeless plain, arid in many places. Diamonds are mined, and recently coffee has been cultivated for export.

The grazing lands of Ruanda-Urundi have been added to the Belgian Congo, and a ten-year plan to develop the Congo region has been inaugurated. The Belgian Congo has the richest terrain in Africa. Metals, both common and rare, are imbedded in its soil.

The most important product of the Gold Coast is cacao. Some diamonds and gold are mined to a limited extent.

LIBERIA—Long unimportant economically, is presently producing rubber and coffee for export.

French colonies are located in most of West Africa. The areas from Dakar southward yield rubber, mahogany, ebony, cacao and coffee. The interior of West Africa merges with the Sahara Desert. A narrow savanna region stretches across the French lands to the headwaters of the Nile. This area contains some of Africa's large lakes and is the best suited for grazing. The great forests on its southern edge lead into the jungles of the Congo and Cameroons. The region is a habitat for a diversity of animal life including the leopard, lion and rhinoceros as well as some of the larger animals of the country.

MADAGASCAR—One of the world's largest islands, is located off the east coast of Africa. Graphite, copper and precious stones form a part of its mineral resources.

New Zealand Consulate

Modified by ocean currents, New Zealand's climate remains moderate.

Grendreau

Rapid strides in industrial growth have been made by many of Australia's port cities.

AUSTRALIA—This island continent of the South Seas is the smallest, and last to be discovered of all the continents.

The United States and Australia are nations of about the same age and size, and in other respects have much in common. The loss of America as a British Colony directly led to the settling of Australia. It was first claimed for the British Crown in 1788 as a settlement for British convicts who had previously been sent to America. Landing in a virgin country, the early pioneers of the two countries had to conquer the wilderness before creating a nation. In the process of so doing the people of both lands developed similar characteristics. In later years Australia even patterned its constitution after that of the United States.

But, whereas the United States became a melting pot for all the races and creeds in the world, Australia has been peopled almost entirely by British stock. Today 97 per cent of the population are descendants of British colonists, and 86 per cent are Australian born. Strict laws have confined immigration to the white race. Few of the natives who originally inhabited Australia remain. These aborigines are similar to the African Negro but not so intelligent, and are believed to be a separate race.

Almost half of Australia lies within the tropics, but being surrounded by great oceans, the continent has a mild climate throughout the year. Snow normally falls only in the high mountains in the winter.

Since the seasons are the reverse of those in the United States, this occurs in their winter months of June, July, and August.

Australia is said to be most level in surface and regular in outline of all the continents. There is an entire absence of towering mountains. The highest peak is only about seventy-three hundred feet above sea level. The mountains parallel the east coast, with, by far, the greater part of the continent a vast, irregular, and undulating plateau.

Australia can be regarded as falling into four well-defined regions: (1) The Great Plateau in the west extends over about half of the continent; (2) The Eastern Highlands follow along the whole of the eastern coastline, rarely exceeding a distance of a hundred miles inland; (3) The Central Basin is a lowland area much of which was once a sea-bed; and (4) the Coastal Plains, which form a rim surrounding most of the continent.

Despite rich coastal lands and an immense grazing area in the interior, much of this interior is unsuited for agriculture. It is a great arid region of desert and semi-desert which is sparsely settled and will never support a dense population. The heaviest rainfall is in the tropical regions of the north, and there is adequate moisture along the south coast and southern part of the highlands. Elsewhere there is insufficient rain. But for the presence of innumerable artesian wells scattered over wide areas, much more of the country would be without water. It is these wells that make stock-raising possible,

but because of its mineral content, the water is seldom used for agriculture or human use.

The major rivers of Australia are of two types—those which flow toward the coast and are similar to such rivers in other parts of the world; and the inland rivers which gradually lose their water as they flow away from the coastal regions. The headwaters of most of these inland rivers are in the Eastern Highlands.

The Murray River with its tributaries is the main river system and flows into the ocean on the south coast. The Gilbert, Norman and Flinders are the principal streams flowing into the Gulf of Carpentaria in the north. On the west the Murchison, Gascoyne, Ashburton and Fitzroy empty into the Indian Ocean.

The rivers which flow inland vary greatly in volume during the year. For long periods they are mere strings of waterholes, but during floods their waters spread out over the flat country for many miles. Most of their waters evaporate or soak into the ground before they flow very far. In the center of the continent the rivers flow into Lake Eyre when there is sufficient water in them, but generally they are merely beds of dry sand.

The lakes that appear to be scattered so liberally over the land are also a disappointment as they are little more than shallow basins that carry water only after rains.

Great Barrier Reef, the largest of all coral formations, follows the northeast coast for twelve hundred miles of Australia's twelve-thousand-mile coastline. Except in a few places this reef is impassable to ships, but it does provide an inner passage for coastal navigation. There are good harbors on the southeastern coast.

Wherever there is sufficient moisture for grass to grow, the land is especially adapted to grazing. This land has proved the most

Hawaii's fertile soil facilitates the growing of tropical fruits and sugar cane. Its pineapple cultivation accounts for 90% of the world's production.

The vast expanse of the Pacific Ocean contains thousands of uninhabited coral isles.

suitable in the world for raising sheep. Merino sheep, which produce a very fine quality of wool, comprise most of the flocks. The heavy fleece from these sheep exceeds that of breeds raised elsewhere, so, although Australia produces less than one-sixth of the world's sheep, the wool yield is more than a quarter of the world's requirement.

Lacking navigable rivers, most of the transportation is by railways. These have been of first importance in developing the country, but one great drawback of railroad transportation is that there are several gauges. During the last twenty-five years there has been a steady expansion of motor roads, and air routes are rapidly increasing.

In addition to the mainland and the island of Tasmania, Australia has extensive territorial interests. These comprise the Trust Territory of New Guinea, Papua, Nauru and Norfolk Island.

The Trust Territory of New Guinea includes the northeastern section of New Guinea, the Bismarck Archipelago, and the northern islands of the Solomon group. Scattered over a sea area of more than one million square miles, these islands are mountainous with limited coastal areas suitable for cultivation.

NEW ZEALAND—Two large islands and several small ones make up New Zealand. Situated about twelve hundred miles southeast of Australia, New Zealand is a lonely member of the British Commonwealth.

The two principal islands, North and South Island are separated by Cook Strait which is ninety miles wide. Close as they are to each other, these islands have little in common except that they are both mountainous. North Island is of volcanic origin and consists chiefly of forested hills and plateaus. South Island is more rugged with glaciers and snow-clad peaks that rival the Alps of Switzerland.

PACIFIC ISLANDS—The Pacific Islands fall into three major regions: Polynesia, Micronesia and Melanesia.

Polynesia, or "Many islands," consists of widely scattered groups and a few isolated islands forming a rough triangle. The Hawaiian Islands are at the northern point, twenty degrees north of the Equator. The Fiji Islands, at the western point of the triangle, are the meeting place of Polynesian and Melanesian cultures, the people being of mixed stock. The easternmost point lies in the Gambier group of the Tuamota Archipelago, although isolated Pitcairn Island, inhabited by Anglo-Tahitian descendants of the mutinous crew of the "Bounty," is generally included geographically. Within this area lies the most highly developed group of Pacific peoples, a mixture of white, black and yellow racial stocks, the Polynesians. Famous as navigators, they crossed the Pacific from Asia hundreds of years ago, and sailed their canoes eastward to their present homes. For the most part, the islands are mountainous, volcanic and covered with dense vegetation, often fringed by coral reefs. Along the equator and in the southeast, low coral atolls predominate, often only a few feet above sea level, and frequently torn by hurricanes.

The people, often easy-going to the point of idleness, are not always used in local production, some Chinese having been hired to do manual work. Famous for dancing and feasting, the generally happy Polynesians strive to maintain their early customs against the inroads of European traders, missionaries and government regulations.

In the western Pacific, for the most part north of the equator, lies Micronesia, or "little islands," confined to the Marianas, Carolines, Marshall Islands, and Gilbert and Ellice Islands. Except for the latter islands, they are mostly volcanic and coral-fringed, and are peopled by a light-skinned group—the latest arrivals in the Pacific. These inhabitants show more evidence of a recent black and yellow mixture.

The earliest inhabited area of the Pacific, New Guinea and the islands spreading to the southeast of it, is known as Melanesia, the "black islands." Of early Negroid stock, this area was generally by-passed by the later Polynesians and Micronesians, as settlement was already established. Melanesia is a rapidly developing area, rich in minerals as well as the usual coconuts. Today the people range from Europeanized workers in the plantations of New Caledonia and Fiji, and the missions of the New Guinea coast, to half-naked savages, often head-hunters and cannibals, in the higher regions of New Guinea.

POLITICAL DIVISION	GOVERNMENT	MONETARY UNIT	PRINCIPAL LANGUAGES	PRINCIPAL RELIGIONS	MAJOR PRODUCTS
AUSTRALIA	Member of the British Commonwealth of Nations with a governor-general, prime minister and cabinet. Parliament consists of a senate and house of commons.	Australian pound	English	Protestant Roman Catholic	(See individual States)
BISMARCK ARCHIPELAGO	A part of the territory of New Guinea administered by Australia as a U.N. trust territory.	Australian pound	Papuan English Chinese	Tribal religions Roman Catholic Protestant	Coconuts, cocoa, coffee, kapok, rubber, grains; cattle, goats, pigs; fish.
BONIN ISLANDS	Administered by the United States.	dollar yen	Japanese	Shinto-Buddhist	Vegetables, sugar, coca; poultry, pigs, cattle; fish.
CAROLINE ISLANDS	A group in the United States trust territory of the Pacific Islands and administered by a high commissioner.	dollar	Micronesian dialects Malayo-Polynesian languages	Tribal religions Protestant Roman Catholic	Copra, breadfruit, cassava, taro, sweet potatoes; pigs, cattle, poultry, fish; phosphates.
COOK ISLANDS	Territory of New Zealand administered by a resident commissioner.	New Zealand pound	Polynesian dialects English	Protestant Tribal religions	Citrus fruits, coconuts, copra, tomatoes, arrowroot, pineapples, breadfruit, taro, kumaras, plantains, yams; mother-of-pearl.
EASTER ISLAND (RAPA NUI)	Administered as part of Valparaíso province in Chile.	peso	Polynesian dialect Spanish	Roman Catholic	Plantains, sweet potatoes; fish; cattle, sheep; wool.
FIJI	British colony ruled by a governor with an executive and legislative council.	Fiji pound	English Fijian Hindustani Chinese	Protestant Roman Catholic Moslem Hindu	Sugar cane, coconuts, bananas, pineapples, rice, root vegetables, citrus fruits, cotton, rubber, castor oil seeds, taro, yams, cassava, sweet potatoes, groundnuts, pulses, corn, fodder crops, tobacco; cattle, pigs; tuna, bêche-de-mer, trochus shell; gold, silver; sugar, copra, coconut oil, soap, biscuits, molasses, paint, butter, ghee, candlenut oil.
GAMBIER ISLANDS	A group of islands in French Oceania governed from Tahiti.	franc	Polynesian dialects	Roman Catholic Tribal religions	Coconuts, copra, oranges, breadfruit; pearls, pearl shell, fish.
GILBERT AND ELLICE ISLANDS	British colony administered by a resident commissioner.	Australian pound	English Gilbertese Samoan	Tribal religions Protestant Roman Catholic	Coconuts, copra, phosphate of lime; pearl shell, fish; hats, mats.
GUAM	Territory of the United States administered by a governor and advisory and legislative bodies.	dollar	English Chamorro Spanish	Roman Catholic	Copra, coconut oil, corn, taro, bananas, citrus fruits, mangoes, papayas, breadfruit, sweet potatoes, cocoa, cassava, sugar cane, pineapples; cattle, pigs, poultry, buffalo.
HAWAII	Territory of the United States administered by a governor, a senate and a house of representatives.	dollar	English Japanese Hawaiian	Protestant Roman Catholic Buddhist	Sugar, pineapples, coffee, molasses, bananas, rice, flowers, cotton, tobacco; beef cattle, swine, sheep, poultry; hides, wood, stone, fish, printing, foodstuffs, ironworks, fertilizers, chemicals, clothing, fiber insulating board, handicrafts.
MARQUESAS ISLANDS	A group of islands in French Oceania administered from Tahiti.	franc	Marquesan French	Tribal religions Roman Catholic	Bananas, breadfruit, yams, bamboo, coconuts, sugar cane.
MARIANA ISLANDS	A group of islands in the United States trust territory of the Pacific administered by a high commissioner.	dollar	Micronesian dialects Spanish	Tribal religions	Fruits, corn, sweet potatoes, vegetables, breadfruit, cacao; fish; phosphates.
MARSHALL ISLANDS	A group of islands in the United States trust territory of the Pacific administered by a high commissioner.	dollar	Micronesian dialects	Tribal religions Protestant	Arrowroot, breadfruit, coconuts, pandanus, taro, vegetables, copra, bananas; poultry, pigs; fish.
NAURU	Trust territory of Great Britain, Australia and New Zealand. Administered by Australia.	Australian pound	English Micronesian Chinese	Protestant Roman Catholic	Phosphates; fishing; mats.
NEW CALEDONIA	French territory administered by a governor and advisory councils.	franc	Melanesian dialects French	Roman Catholic Tribal religions	Coconuts, copra, coffee, cotton, manioc, corn, tobacco, bananas, pineapples, wheat, rice, kauri logs; cattle, pigs, horses, goats, sheep, hides; guano, trochus shell; nickel, chrome, manganese, iron, cobalt, copper, lead, platinum; canned meat.
NEW HEBRIDES	British and French condominium administered by British and French resident commissioners.	Australian currency Bank of Indo-china Notes	Melanesian dialects Pidgin English English French	Tribal religions Protestant Roman Catholic	Coconuts, copra, cocoa, coffee, yams, taro, manioc, fruits; kauri pine; cattle, pigs; trochus shells.
NEW SOUTH WALES	Australian state with a governor, cabinet and a legislative council and assembly.	Australian pound	English	Protestant Roman Catholic	Wheat, rice, oats, corn, hay, potatoes, tobacco, sugar cane, grapes, bananas; sheep, cattle, horses, pigs, meats, dairy products, poultry, eggs; fish; timber; coal, silver, lead, zinc, sulphur, gold, tungsten, bismuth, antimony, cadmium, cobalt, titanium, zirconium, tin, platinum; steel, metal products, machinery, foods, beverages, tobacco, clothing, chemicals, paint, oil, grease, paper, printing, textiles, woodwork, baskets, bricks, pottery, glass, furniture, quarry products, skins, leather, rubber, precious metal, jewelry.
NEW ZEALAND	A member of the British Commonwealth with dominion status governed by a governor-general, cabinet and parliament.	New Zealand pound	English Maori	Protestant	Wheat, oats, barley, seeds, kauri, gum; sheep, cattle, pigs, horses; hides, skins; fish; gold, silver, coal, copper, limestone, manganese, iron, tungsten; dairy products, meats, wool, clothing, lumber, woodwork, furniture, electrical and radio goods, motor assembly, printing, publishing, biscuits, confections, footwear, rubber products, chemical fertilizers, tobacco products, brewing.

GAZETTEER OF THE WORLD
AUSTRALIA AND THE PACIFIC

POLITICAL DIVISION	GOVERNMENT	MONETARY UNIT	PRINCIPAL LANGUAGES	PRINCIPAL RELIGIONS	MAJOR PRODUCTS
NIUE	Dependency of New Zealand administered by a resident commissioner.	New Zealand pound	Melanesian and Polynesian dialects English	Protestant	Copra, sweet potatoes, bananas; hats, baskets.
NORFOLK ISLAND	Administered by Australia.	Australian pound	English	Protestant	Citrus, passion fruits, bananas, cherry guavas; hides; fish.
NORTH EAST (TERR. OF) NEW GUINEA	Trust territory of Australia governed by administrator of Papua.	Australian pound	Papuan Pidgin English English	Tribal religions Roman Catholic Protestant	Coconuts, copra, cocoa, dairying; timber; gold, silver, platinum; boat making.
NORTHERN TERRITORY	Australian territory governed by appointed administrator.	Australian pound	English Aboriginal dialects	Protestant Roman Catholic Tribal religions	Grains, groundnuts, cotton, millet, coconuts, vegetables, fruits; cattle, horses, sheep, goats, swine, donkeys, mules, camels; hides, skins; gold, silver, lead, tin, copper, nitrates, mica, wolfram, ochre, uranium, pearl shell, trapang.
PITCAIRN ISLAND	British colony administered by a chief magistrate responsible to the governor of Fiji.	Fiji pound	English Tahitian	Protestant (Seventh Day Adventist)	Fruits, vegetables, goats, poultry; handicraft.
PALAU ISLANDS	A civil administrative district in the Western Carolines and part of the United States Pacific trust territory.	dollar	Micronesian dialects	Tribal religions Christian	Coconuts, manioc, taro, pineapples, sweet potatoes, papayas; poultry, pigs, goats; fish; phoshate; handicrafts.
PAPUA TERRITORY	Australian colony governed by an administrator.	Australian pound	Papuan Pidgin English English	Tribal religions Protestant Roman Catholic	Coconuts, rubber, sweet potatoes, yams, taro, sago, rice, bananas, coffee, kapok, bamboo, sisal hemp, copra; shells; sponges; cattle, goats, poultry; gold, copper, manganese.
QUEENSLAND	Australian state with a governor, cabinet and a legislative council and assembly.	Australian pound	English	Protestant Roman Catholic	Sugar cane, wheat, sorghum, corn, barley, oats, potatoes, hay, pumpkins, tomatoes, peanuts, grapes, pineapples, citrus fruits, bananas, cotton, tobacco; sheep, cattle, pigs, horses, poultry, eggs, wool, meats, fish, dairy products; lead, zinc, coal, gold, silver, copper, tin, fluorspar, lumber, clothing, metal work, machinery, furniture, motor vehicles, paper, printing, sugar milling, wines, rum.
SAMOA, EASTERN	Possession of the United States with a governor and a bicameral legislature.	dollar	English Samoan	Protestant	Copra, taro, breadfruit, yams, bananas, arrowroot, pineapples, oranges; mats.
SAMOA, WESTERN	Under United Nations trusteeship administered by New Zealand.	New Zealand pound	Samoan English	Protestant Tribal religions	Copra, cocoa beans, bananas, taro; fish; pigs, poultry.
SOLOMON ISLANDS	A protectorate administered by a British resident commissioner.	Australian pound	Melanesian Pidgin English English	Tribal religions Protestant Roman Catholic	Copra, pigs, poultry; trochus shell, turtle shell, bêche-de-mer.
SOLOMON ISLANDS (NORTHERN)	Part of the territory of New Guinea and governed as an Australian trust territory.	Australian pound	Melanesian Pidgin English English	Tribal religions Protestant Roman Catholic	Coconuts, copra, bananas, yams, taro, fruits; trochus shell, green snail shell, rubber.
SOUTH AUSTRALIA	Australian state with a governor, cabinet and a legislative council and assembly.	Australian pound	English	Protestant Roman Catholic	Wheat, barley, oats, hay, grapes, fruits, vegetables, flax, gums, chicory, eucalyptus oil; sheep, cattle, horses, pigs, poultry, eggs, meats; hides, skins, wool, dairy products; iron, gypsum, salt, opals, talc, barite, clays, coal, uranium, pyrites, phosphates, gold, manganese, copper, steel, wines.
TASMANIA	Australian State with a governor, cabinet and a legislative council and assembly.	Australian pound	English	Protestant Roman Catholic	Oats, wheat, hay, peas, turnips, apples, barley, potatoes, hops; sheep, cattle, pigs, horses, poultry, eggs, meats, wool, dairy products; hides, skins; timber, paper, pulp; fish; zinc, lead, copper, tin, silver, limestone, gold, cadmium, osmiridium, phosphates, coal; refined metals, lumber, preserves, brick, tile, pottery, tanning, chemicals, cement, carbide, electrodes, furniture, agricultural tools, confections.
TOKELAU ISLANDS	An island territory of New Zealand administered by a high commissioner.	New Zealand pound	Samoan	Protestant Roman Catholic	Coconuts, fiber, taro, copra; pigs, chickens; fish; hats, mats.
TONGA	Kingdom under British protection ruled by queen with advisory bodies.	Tongan pound	Tongan English	Protestant Roman Catholic	Copra, bananas, fungus, candlenuts; pigs, cattle, goats.
TUAMOTU ARCHIPELAGO	Part of French Oceania governed from Tahiti.	franc	Polynesian dialects French	Tribal religions Roman Catholic	Copra, peals, pearl shell.
VICTORIA	Australian state with a governor, cabinet and a legislative council and assembly.	Australian pound	English	Protestant Roman Catholic	Wheat, oats, barley, potatoes, hay, raisins, currants, oranges; sheep, cattle, pigs, horses, poultry, eggs, meats, wool, dairy products; timber; coal, gold, limestone, titanium, antimony, potash, tin, bauxite; textiles, clothing, food processing, metal products, wines, wood work, machinery, vehicles, printing.
VOLCANO ISLANDS	Administered by the United States.	dollar yen	Japanese	Shintoist Buddhist	Sugar cane; fish; sulphur.
WESTERN AUSTRALIA	Australian state with a governor, cabinet and a legislative council and assembly.	Australian pound	English	Protestant Roman Catholic	Wheat, oats, barley, hay, potatoes, fruits, tobacco, grapes, vegetables; sheep, cattle, pigs, horses, poultry, eggs; wool, hides, skins; meats, dairy products; gold, coal, pyrite, lead, asbestos, silver, manganese, tin; timber; fish; food processing, clothing, wood work, machinery, vehicles, wines.
YAP	Administered by a civil administrator of the Palau district as a part of the United States Pacific trust territory.	dollar	Micronesian dialects	Tribal religions Christian	Coconuts, breadfruit, sweet potatoes, taro, manioc, vegetables; poultry, pigs; fish.

For centuries fishing has been the chief occupation of the people who live along the Sea of Galilee.

A rapid development of industry and commerce is forseeable in Israel's economic future.

ASIA—To say that this is the largest continent in the world gives no idea of its immensity. Covering one-third of the land area of the world, Asia is more than a million square miles larger than the combined areas of North and South America. It extends from the ice-bound regions of the Arctic Circle to the sun-burnt islands of the Tropics. It claims the highest and lowest elevations, as well as the wettest and driest areas in the world. Mount Everest is the highest and the Dead Sea the lowest. Assam is the wettest, and Northern Siberia the driest. Asia is the cradle of the earliest civilization and is now the home of over half the population of the world.

Man has drawn a line separating Asia from Europe but the only natural division is the low Ural Mountains and a depression extending from the mountains to the Caspian Sea. Only a man-made canal at the Isthmus of Suez separates Asia from Africa.

Washed by three oceans and a number of seas, Asia has a coast line over thirty thousand miles in length. Deep indentations along the irregular coast form seas, such as the Bay of Bengal and the Arabian Sea. Twisting and pointed peninsulas reach far out into the oceans. The shores are dotted with archipelagos and island groups. Among the island groups are Japan, the Philippines, and Indonesia, all of which have become as important as mainland countries.

The mountain ranges that sweep across Europe from west to east continue in long parallel lines through Asia. These mountain chains rise in height, first curving away from one another, and then closing in abruptly in a knot of massed mountains which has been referred to as "the roof of the world." Eastward, the awe-inspiring Himalayas reach to the plateau of Tibet, turn suddenly south through Indochina in long lines of deep, forested ravines, and disappear in a string of islands, drowned by the waters of the Indian Ocean. The Himalayas, covered with eternal snows and scored by mighty glaciers, are the highest mountains in the world. From Mount Everest, their loftiest peak, they drop steeply down to the low river plains below.

To the north of the mountains lies the great plain of Northern Asia, a continuation of the North European plain. Broken only by the Urals it sinks slowly to the frozen Arctic shore. To the south, in India and Arabia, are two low plateaus with steep sides, and the river lowlands of Mesopotamia and the Ganges plain.

This enormous continent is drained by many large rivers. Flowing toward the Arctic Ocean are the Ob, Yenisei and Lena Rivers. They are often blocked with ice for months and flood the surrounding country in thaw. In the east the silt carried down by the rivers has built the wide alluvial plains of China. The Hwang-ho, or Yellow River, flows into the Yellow Sea. Yellow is a sacred color, for this is the color of the silt deposited by the great river on the fertile plain, where crowded millions of Chinese grow their crops and find their livelihood. The Yangtse Kiang, or Blue River, rises in Tibet and passes through deep walls before winding sluggishly across the lowlands of China. These rivers often overflow in disastrous floods and have changed their courses many times.

The Ganges, Indus and Brahmaputra have built up the fertile lowlands of North India and are slowly extending it in broad, swampy deltas, out to sea.

Covering so many degrees of latitude, the climate of Asia would naturally show great variation. There are great extremes of cold and heat in the Siberian lowlands and Northern China. Great areas in the center of the continent, far from the sea, are dry; with tropical conditions prevailing in the south. The heaviest rainfall anywhere in the world is in some localities of Southeastern Asia and everywhere in the eastern region there is sufficient moisture for agriculture. In Assam, India, the rainfall averages about thirty-five feet a year.

There is every type of vegetation, ranging from tundra mosses in the extreme north to tropical plant life in the south. There are great stores of mineral wealth, but much of this is still undeveloped. Asia has been slow to awaken to the possibilities of an industrialized civilization.

Southwestern Asia is that section of the continent lying between India and the

TWA—Trans World Airline
Altered only slightly by a few modern buildings, Nazareth still rests in its ancient setting.

TWA—Trans World Airline
Flocks of sheep and goats are the economic mainstay of the Arab's life.

Aegean Sea. It is a rugged, mountainous country which includes the two desert plateaus of Iran and Arabia, and the rich lowlands of the Tigris and Euphrates valley.

Great nations flourished in Southwestern Asia several thousand years before the birth of Christ. Composed almost entirely of the white race, their civilizations contributed much to the early nations along the Mediterranean. Mongolian hordes invaded these lands in the thirteenth century, almost destroying the civilizations which they found. Growing in power, a mighty nation which spread into Africa and Europe came into being. The Turks are descendants of these war-like people.

TURKEY—Surrounded by mountains on three sides is a high, dry plateau which slopes to the fertile shores of the Mediterranean. Among the chief mountains are the Taurus range, stretching from the southwestern shore of the Aegean to the north of Syria, their principal peaks rising from 7,000 to 10,000 feet; the Bulgar Mountains rising over 10,000 feet; and the Ala Mountains, north of Seyhan, rising 8,000 to 10,000 feet high. The highest peak in the country is Mt. Ararat, 17,915 feet. Flowing into the Black Sea are the Coruh, the Yesil Irmak, the Kizil Irmak and the Sakariya. Into the Mediterranean flow the Seyhan and Ceyhan. In the east of Asia Minor are the headwaters of both the Euphrates and the Tigris as well as of the Araks.

ISRAEL—After 2,000 years the Jewish people realized their dream of an independent homeland with the establishment of the new state of Israel in 1948. Lying between Egypt and Jordan on the eastern shores of the Mediterranean, the country is a hot and arid land. The new nation's economy is based on the cultivation of citrus fruit for export made possible by extensive irrigation of the lands of Zionist sponsored settlements. Oil refining, chemical production and light industry are also important to the economy.

SYRIA AND LEBANON—The occupations of the people of these countries have not changed since Biblical times, and are similar to those of Turkey. Mostly agricultural, there is little mineral wealth, and manufacturing is largely for local markets. Lebanon is mainly mountainous with a fertile valley lying in the center between the Lebanon Mountains on the west coast and the Anti-Lebanon Mountains which form the eastern border between Lebanon and Syria. Syria consists largely of desert surrounded by mountains. In the northeast, the Euphrates flows across the desert and irrigates a valuable strip of agricultural land. Other fertile areas are found near Homs and Hama, both in the northwest, and Damascus and the Jebel Druze district in the southwest.

IRAQ—Once the site of the Babylonian Empire, the region of the Tigris and Euphrates is the "Fertile Crescent" of ancient times. The country is a great alluvial plain, bounded on the north by Kurdistan, on the east by Iran, on the south by the Persian Gulf, and on the west by the Syrian and Arabian Deserts. Northern Iraq has a valuable supply of oil which is piped to Haifa and Tripoli.

IRAN (Persia)—Most of the country is plateau, surrounded by mountain chains, except in the east where huge salt deserts are found. An extension of the mountain ranges, locally known as the Khorasan Mountains of the Hindu Kush, enters on the northeast from Afghanistan and merges into the Elburz Range south of the Caspian, the highest peak being Mt. Demavend. Except for narrow fertile areas along the Caspian Sea and Persian Gulf the land is too dry to sustain many people.

ARABIA—The Arabian Peninsula is a land composed almost entirely of desert, mostly of a barren and stony type, with an abundance of sand in the southeast. Besides scattered oases there are only a few small areas in Arabia with enough rainfall to permit the growing of crops. Saudi Arabia, which occupies the central two-thirds of the peninsula, has experimented with modern, mechanized methods of irrigation to improve farming conditions, and a modern railroad now reaches the interior from the Persian Gulf. The finest Arabian horses and camels are raised in the central highlands. Discovery of valuable oil reserves in the desert near the

One of the two chief ports of India, Bombay is a center for exported raw material and imported manufactures.

Representative of the fine architecture of India is the luxurious structure of the Taj Mahal.

Persian Gulf fostered new economic development, and many local sheikhs, or tribal rulers, have become suddenly rich. Pearling, once important in the Gulf, is now declining. In the mountain valleys of Yemen is the most fertile soil of the peninsula, and its Red Sea ports, such as Mocha and Hodeida handle its coffee and other exports, as well as pearls from nearby islands.

AFGHANISTAN—Barren tablelands, deep ravines and snow-covered mountains leave Afghanistan an unproductive land. Lying as a barrier between Siberia and India, it has been the scene of many invasions and conquests but the war-like Afghans have never

been completely vanquished. Cereals, fruits and vegetables are grown only in small areas under irrigation, and the fat-tailed sheep—a native of the country—furnishes meat and a butter substitute.

PAKISTAN—Pakistan is divided into two widely separated sections. The larger part, West Pakistan on the Arabian Sea, consists of the fertile Indus valley, the extremely rugged Northwest frontier and arid Baluchistan. Cereal raising and cotton production are concentrated in the Indus Valley which possesses one of the oldest and most efficient canal irrigation systems in the world. East Pakistan, on the Bay of Bengal, occupies the lower Ganges-Brahmaputra delta and the Assam highland foothills. This nation, while almost wholly Mohammedan in religion, is influenced politically and culturally not only by the Islamic world to the west but also the neighboring Hindu civilization of India.

INDIA—For over four thousand years, India has been at the mercy of marauding and conquering races. Unlike many lesser countries, who have successfully thrown off the yoke of oppression, India, until recently, has always been subject to foreign rule. As a result it is a confusion of races, castes, and religions, with a civilization ranging from the

highest type of culture to the most primitive. In 1947 India was granted independence and now takes her place among the important powers of the globe.

Except for the rocky slopes of the mountains, the soil is fertile and supports the largest agricultural population in the world. Like the farmers of France, a large majority of these people live in small villages surrounded by tilled fields. And, while primitive methods and equipment are used, surprisingly large crops are raised. Disastrous droughts, due to the vagaries of the weather, and the famines which followed, have been partially relieved by government sponsored irrigation works and the construction of railroads and motor roads.

SIKKIM, NEPAL AND BHUTAN—These three small independent states are shut off from the outside world by the Himalayas. Several of the world's highest mountains, including Mount Everest, are in southern Nepal. Their inhabitants are energetic people who raise cattle, wheat, rice, tobacco and spices which they export in exchange for necessary manufactured goods, sugar, oil, etc.

CEYLON—The island of Ceylon has been called the "Pearl of the Orient." Situated off the southern coast of India it is famous

Indonesia Information Office
The land surface of the Malay Peninsula is uneven and traversed by snow-capped peaks.

Much modernization in Indonesia has caused sharp contrasts between the old and new.
Indonesia Information Office

Indonesia Information Office
Asian art has been stimulated by many of the Eastern republics through the establishment of technical and cultural institutions.

for its tea, precious stones and tropical beauty. The broad coastal strip which surrounds the central mountains is, for the most part, fertile and produces a luxuriant vegetation. Although the climate is tropical, sea breezes temper the heat.

INDOCHINA—Included on this southeastern peninsula of Asia are a part of Burma, Thailand, Indochina and the Malayan Federation. Most of the peninsula is characterized by heavily forested valleys and mountain ridges of the Himalayas running the length of the land. This is the great rice-producing region, and most of the world's rubber comes from this area. The rainfall is heavy in the entire area and the land is very productive. In the dense forests are

valuable stands of prize woods, teak, ebony and other trees used for their wood or gum. Agriculture is the chief industry throughout the peninsula but there are many important deposits of valuable minerals. Modern methods of agriculture and mining have been introduced. Singapore, situated on an island at the extreme southern end of the peninsula, commands one of the most important sea routes in the world.

THE MALAY ARCHIPELAGO — The world's largest group of islands extends from Sumatra to the Philippine Islands off the coast of China, and includes many thousands of islands. With the exception of the Philippines, and parts of Timor, Borneo and New Guinea, the archipelago was ruled for

hundreds of years by the Netherlands.

INDONESIA—Colonization and development begun by the Dutch in the XVIIth century has resulted in the richest and most important island group in the world.

Most of the islands are mountainous and of volcanic origin. At one time they were a part of the mainland connecting Asia with Australia. Java is the most productive and highly developed of the East Indies. It is one of the most densely populated regions in the world. Much of the land is divided into native farms and large plantations. The plantation crops are chiefly for export.

Next to Greenland, New Guinea and Borneo are the largest islands in the world. Sumatra and Celebes are next in size in the East Indies. Much of the mineral wealth of these islands is yet untouched. Borneo is crossed almost in the middle by the equator and few white people occupy the island because of the humidity and heat. Petroleum is an important resource of Borneo, Sumatra and Java, and two small islands adjoining Sumatra have valuable deposits of tin. Bali, while one of the lesser islands, has been one of the most publicized, and is favored by tourists as a tropical paradise.

PHILIPPINE ISLANDS—Numbering over seven thousand islands, Philippines, like other islands of the Malay Archipelago, are the tops of drowned mountains protruding from the sea. There are well watered fertile plains between the mountains. Being near the equator the temperature is never very low. Although the days are warm, the nights are usually cool. Some of the many volcanoes in

The narrow streets of Peking are typical of China's crowded cities where the nation's trading and business are daily transacted.

Japan's development as a leading industrial nation has not effaced her customs and traditions.

the Philippines are still active and the islands are subject to earthquakes.

CHINA—Chinese civilization is of greater antiquity than any other existent world culture. It has shown great powers of survival and has possessed the ability to absorb all foreign influences without losing its own identity.

The Chinese people are patient, industrious, and have great physical endurance. They are among the world's best farmers, having grown more food for longer periods on the same land, without exhausting the soil, than any other people. They take naturally to mechanics and are fine traders and business men.

With the possible exception of Africa, China has the largest undeveloped natural resources in the world. There are rich deposits of coal, with China ranking second to the United States in total reserves. Iron ore reserves are large enough to meet its needs for many years to come. It is believed that China has one of the most valuable deposits of copper, and tin has been a leading mineral export.

China is a land of garden farmers and the soil is cultivated intensively. Few animals are raised, which conserves acreage for food crops. Hence the Chinese diet consists almost entirely of vegetable products. In a relatively mild climate people can subsist on less food than in a colder region. Rice is the most

important crop but almost every known crop is raised.

Inner Mongolia, Tibet and Sinkiang are outer provinces of China. Until the building of railroads and motor roads they were reached entirely by caravan routes. This region has extreme temperatures and is largely desert. The Great Wall was built to keep the Mongols out of China. Tibet, until recently opened up to British trade, excluded all foreigners. Sinkiang consists almost entirely of a desert basin.

MONGOLIAN REPUBLIC—This almost entirely pastoral country consists largely of an arid plateau composed mainly of the Gobi Desert. In the northwest are high mountains whose streams flow into numerous sizable lakes. The Mongolian people are almost entirely a nomadic race who wander from place to place seeking new pastures for their herds of cattle.

JAPAN—The chief feature of the country is its mountainous character, for each island has a mountainous backbone. Fujiyama, the highest mountain, reaches 12,395 feet. One of the most notable physical features is the Inland Sea or Japanese Mediterranean. It is almost entirely landlocked and surrounded by chains of volcanoes, of which few are now active. The climate is temperate and healthful, with abundant rainfall.

Only 20 per cent of the land can be cultivated and the balance is largely mountainous, with frequent destructive earthquakes and volcanic activity. While minerals have been a major factor in her industrial growth, Japan is not well supplied with them. The only large mineral deposits are coal and copper, with some gold, silver and lead. The petroleum produced falls far short of her needs.

The low standard of living and the small amount of land suitable for cultivation have made farming highly intensive. A large percentage of the farms are only an acre or two in size and most of the farmers are forced to carry on some other occupation to exist.

Manufacturing has risen rapidly in Japan with the production of textiles leading. Because of low wages and nearness to the Oriental market, Japan has been able to compete in cheaper goods to the disadvantage of other countries.

KOREA—Korea's strategic position between the Asiatic mainland and Japan has made it an historic pathway for invasion. Coveted at different times by China, Russia and Japan, she lost her independence early in the century to the Japanese Empire. During the second World War, Korea was promised her independence, but the end of the fighting brought her only division between the great powers and later renewed military conflict.

Physically and economically Korea is divided into two contrasting natural regions. The agricultural heart of the nation is south of the thirty-eighth parallel, producing chiefly rice and barley. North of the parallel, industry and mining of coal and iron predominate.

POLITICAL DIVISION	GOVERNMENT	MONETARY UNIT	PRINCIPAL LANGUAGES	PRINCIPAL RELIGIONS	MAJOR PRODUCTS
ADEN	British Crown colony administered by a governor and an executive and legislative council.	East African shilling	Arabic Hindu	Mohammedan	Salt, cigarettes, dhow building, fish cloth, dyeing, sesame oil, soap, sorghum, ship-bunkering.
ADEN PROTECTORATE	Ruled by native sultans and shieks advised by British political officers under a British agent.	East African shilling	Arabic	Mohammedan	Dates, gums, tobacco, fish oil, butter, wheat, barley, sesame, millet, sorghum, aloes, ghee; goats, sheep, camels, cattle.
AFGHANISTAN	A constitutional monarchy ruled by a king, a cabinet and a senate.	Afghani rupee	Afghan (Pushta) Persian	Mohammedan	Wheat, barley, millet, corn, sorghum, lentils, vegetables, fruits, nuts, castor beans, madder, asafetida, cotton, tobacco, fat-tailed sheep (karakul), camels, zebus; wool, skins; sheepskin, textiles, leather, carpets, rugs; gold, iron, lapis lazuli, coal, copper, lead, silver.
BAHRAIN	British protectorate ruled by an Arab sheik advised by a British political agent.	rupee	Arabic	Mohammedan	Pearl fishing, petroleum, boat building, fishing; reed mats, dates, lucerne; donkeys; textiles.
BHUTAN	Ruled by a Maharaja and advised by India in foreign relations.	rupee	Bhutanese (Tibetan dialect)	Lamaist Hindu	Rice, corn, millet, lac, wax, musk; elephants, ponies, chowries; cloth, baskets, mats, metalwork, guns, swords.
BRUNEI	A sultanate and British protectorate administered by a British resident.	Malagan dollar	Malay English	Mohammedan	Rice, sago, rubber, jelutong, cutch, sugar cane, tapioca, bananas, pineapples; timber; domestic birds, buffalo, pigs, cattle; petroleum, natural gas; boat building, cloth, brass and silverware.
BURMA, UNION OF	A republic with a president elected by a bicameral legislature.	kyat	Burmese Khaner Shan	Buddhist Tribal religions	Rice, sesame, peanuts, corn, cotton, millet, tobacco, sugar, beans, fruit, vegetables, pulses, rubber; teak wood, lumber; cattle, buffalo, pigs, goats, sheep; petroleum, silver, lead, zinc, tin, copper, tungsten, rubies, sapphires, amber, jade, nickel, gold, antimony, cobalt, salt; textiles, hides, matches, lacquer ware.
CAMBODIA	A kingdom with a national assembly.	riel	Khmer Tao	Buddhist	Rice, tobacco, kapok, cotton, pepper, coin, sugar, rubber; timber; cattle; fish; silk, cotton, textiles, pottery, rush mats, precious stones, phosphates.
CEYLON	British dominion ruled by a governor general, a prime minister, a cabinet and a bicameral legislature.	rupee	Singhalese Tamil	Buddhist Hindu	Tea, coconuts, rubber, rice, millet, tobacco, cacao, cinnamon, citronella, cloves, fruits, palmyra, fish; cattle, buffalo, goats, swine, sheep; graphite, plumbago, mica, ilmenite, monazite, iron ore; salt, pearls, zircon, glass sands, copra, plywood, leather, shoes, glass, steel, acetic acid, ceramics, quinine, strychnine, shark-liver oil, coconut oil, textiles.
CHINA: MAINLAND (COMMUNIST)	In 1949 the mainland of China came under Communist rule. In theory, governmental power resides in the National People's Congress and the State Council. In practice, power resides in the chairman of the Communist Party's Central Committee.	Chinese dollar	Chinese Mongol Turki	Confucianists Buddhists Taoists Mohammedan	Rice, wheat, sweet potatoes, corn, barley, millet, kaoliang, soybeans, cotton, tea, sugar cane, tobacco, peanuts, peas, beans, opium, tung, silk; pigs, oxen, sheep, goats, buffalo, donkeys, horses, mules, poultry; timber; fish; iron, coal, tungsten, tin, antimony, mercury, copper, lead, zinc, silver, salt, soda, gold, petroleum, bismuth, molybdenum; foodstuffs, textiles, chemicals, machinery, metal work, metallurgical products, bristles, cement, clothing, embroideries, ceramics.
CHINA: FORMOSA (NATIONALIST)	A republic whose supreme organ of government is the popularly elected National Assembly. The Assembly elects the president and vice-president. Legislative powers reside with the Legislative Yuan.	dollar	Chinese (Amoy dialect) Formosan	Confucianist Buddhist Taoist Christian Tribal religions	Rice, tea, sugar, sweet potatoes, ramic, jute, tumeric, pineapples, bananas, camphor; pigs, buffalo, cattle, goats, horses.
CHRISTMAS ISLAND	A part of Singapore colony administered by a district officer of the Malayan civil service.	Malayan dollar	Chinese Malay English	Confucianist Mohammedan	Phosphate of lime.
CYPRUS	British colony ruled by a governor with the assistance of an executive council.	pound	Greek Turkish	Greek Orthodox Mohammedan	Wheat, barley, oats, grapes, raisins, olives, fodder crops, potatoes, parobs, cotton, tobacco, linseed, hemp, flax, citrus fruits, bread beans, corn, sesame, melons; sponges, fish; sheep, goats, donkeys, cattle, pigs, horses, mules; copper pyrites, asbestos, chromite, gypsum, amber, copper concentrates; tobacco products, buttons, wines, spirits, false teeth, lace, gum, boots and shoes, dried fruits, cheese.
DAMÃO	Portuguese overseas province subject to government at Gôa and ruled by lieutenant-governor.	rupia	Portuguese Marathi	Hindu Roman Catholic Mohammedan	Salt, fish, rice, wheat, tobacco; palm-mat weaving.
DIU	Portuguese overseas province subject to government at Gôa and ruled by lieutenant-governor.	rupia	Portuguese Marathi	Hindu Roman Catholic Mohammedan	Salt; fish.
GÔA	Portuguese overseas province ruled by a governor assisted by executive and legislative councils.	rupia	Portuguese Marathi	Hindu Roman Catholic Mohammedan	Rice, cashew nuts, betel nuts, grains, vegetables, coconuts, mangoes; teak, bamboo, blackwood; fish; salt, manganese, asbestos, asphalt, guano, silica, coal, petroleum; sugar, textiles, distilling, dessicated coconut, tobacco products, rice milling, cocoa, coconut oil, embroideries.
HONG KONG	A British colony ruled by governor assisted by executive and legislative council.	Hong Kong dollar	Chinese English	Confucianist Buddhist Christian	Rice, sugar cane, peanuts, sweet potatoes; fish; poultry, pigs; kaolin, lead, iron, wolfram, granite, silver, cement; shipbuilding and repair; rape, rubber shoes, enameled hollow-ware, textiles, electric flashlights and batteries, preserved ginger.

ASIA

POLITICAL DIVISION	GOVERNMENT	MONETARY UNIT	PRINCIPAL LANGUAGES	PRINCIPAL RELIGIONS	MAJOR PRODUCTS
INDIA	An independent republic within the British Commonwealth with a president, cabinet and a bicameral legislature.	rupee	Indo-Aryan (Hindi, Bengali, Gujarati, Punjabi, Urdu) and Dravidian (Tamil, Kanarese, Telugan) English	Hindu Mohammedan Buddhist Animist Christian Sikh Jain Parsi	Rice, wheat, legumes, groundnuts, oilseeds, tea, tobacco, jute, cotton, rubber, coffee, sugar cane, barley, millet, corn; cattle, goats, buffalo, sheep, pigs; fish; coal, manganese, gold, petroleum, salt, mica, iron, copper, chromite, ilmenite, diamonds, silver, bauxite; textiles, shawls, carpets, jute manufacturers, wood-carving and metal work, leather, chemicals, shipbuilding, petroleum refining, sugar refining, cotton ginning, iron and steel mills, glass, soap, matches.
INDONESIA	Republic with president, cabinet and unicameral legislature.	rupiah	Indonesian (Malay, Javanese, etc.)	Mohammedan Tribal religions Christian Hindu	Rice, sugar cane, rubber, palm oil, tobacco, corn, coconuts, copra, cassava, sweet potatoes, groundnuts, soya beans, cotton, kapok, coffee, cinchona, cocoa, pepper, fruits, vegetables; cattle, buffalo; tin, coal, petroleum, bauxite, manganese; rubber goods, chemicals, shipyards, textiles, paper, breweries, glass, handicrafts.
IRAN	Constitutional monarchy governed by a shah, prime minister, cabinet and a bicameral legislature.	rial	Persian Arabic Kurdish	Mohammedan Parsi	Wheat, cotton, gums, opium, fruit, rice, barley, sugar beets, tobacco, tea, corn, millet, legumes, vegetables, nuts; sheep, goats, cattle, asses, horses, mules; fish; petroleum oil, redoxide, copper, sulphur, arsenic, coal, salt, marble, nickel, manganese, lead, cobalt, turquoise, iron ore; carpets, rugs, textiles, leather, glass, matches, chemicals, jute, tobacco products, oil refining, casings, wood, oils.
IRAQ	Kingdom with prime minister, cabinet and bicameral legislature.	dinar	Arabic Turkish Kurdish	Mohammedan	Dates, other fruits, barley, wheat, rice, tobacco, cotton, beans, corn, sorghum, sesame; sheep, goats, asses, camels, horses, buffalo; oil, salt, wool, textiles, cigarettes, distilling.
ISRAEL	Republic with president, prime minister, cabinet and elective unicameral legislature.	Israeli pound	Hebrew Arabic	Judaist Mohammedan	Dairy products, vegetables, eggs, fruits, green fodder, wheat, hay, barley, corn, durra; goats, sheep, cattle, camels, poultry; fish; textiles, clothing, foods, beverages, tobacco, diamond polishing, shoes, metal and woodwork, furniture, building materials, leather, dairy products, electrical products, paper, printing, false teeth, pharmaceuticals, chemicals, dyes, soap, radios, oil refining, wines.
JAPAN	The supreme power resides in the people. Legislative authority is in the elective Diet. A prime minister is the chief executive, the Emperor's duties being merely ceremonial.	yen	Japanese	Buddhist Shinto	Rice, wheat, barley, mulberry trees, potatoes, sweet potatoes, fruits, rape, vegetables, oats, tobacco, soy beans, tea, flax, hemp, camphor; timber, bamboo; horses, cattle, sheep, goats, pigs, rabbits; fish, agar, pearl oysters; silk worms; coal, pyrites, gold, copper, pyrethrum, manganese, silver, sulphur, chromite, zinc, salt, tin, lead, iron, petroleum; textiles, steel, paper, porcelain, earthenware, lacquer ware, vegetable oil, toys, slippers, shoes, machinery.
JORDAN	Kingdom with cabinet and bicameral legislature.	Jordan dinar	Arabic	Mohammedan	Wheat, barley, legumes, vegetables, fruits, olives; sheep, goats, camels; salt, phosphate, potash; wool, tobacco products, flour milling, building materials, olive oil.
KOREA	Divided into two parts by Armistice Line of August, 1953, pending final decisions of peace treaty. Communist "people's republic" in North Korea; South Korea headed by a president, a prime minister, a cabinet and a bicameral legislature.	hwan	Korean	Confucianist Buddhist Christian	Rice, barley, millet, wheat, soya beans, red beans, cotton, tobacco, hemp, ginseng, fruit, radishes; timber; draft cattle, pigs, horses, mules, donkeys, sheep, goats, rabbits; fish; gold, iron ore, coal, tungsten, copper, silver, graphite, salt, kaolin, talc, bismuth, flourite, minerals (N. Korea), textiles, fertilizer, chemicals, cement, heavy industries (N. Korea); textiles, cement, tobacco, silkworms, chemicals, machinery, metal, rubber, wood and paper and tobacco products (S. Korea).
KUWAIT	Independent kingdom protected by Great Britain and ruled by Arab sheik.	Indian rupee	Arabic	Mohammedan	Petroleum, shipbuilding (dhows), pearls, skins, wool.
LAOS	A kingdom with a national assembly.	kip	Khmer (Annamese) Lao	Buddhist	Rice, coffee, tea, citrus fruits, corn, cinchona, gum, benzoin, cardamon; stick-lac; teak; tin.
LEBANON	Independent republic governed by a president, cabinet and an elective legislature.	Lebanese pound	Arabic French	Christian Mohammedan	Wheat, barley, corn, potatoes, citrus and other fruits, onions, olives, tobacco (Latakia); goats, asses, cattle, buffalo, sheep, horses, mules; iron, lignite; textiles, cement, olive oil, tobacco products, soap, matches, petroleum refining, gasoline, leather.
MACAO	Portuguese overseas province ruled by a governor.	pataca	Chinese Portuguese	Confucianist Buddhist Taoist Christian	Fish; preserves, firecrackers, vegetable oil, cement, metal work, lumber, tobacco (processed), matches, wine.
MALAYAN FEDERATION	Federated protectorate of Great Britain whose rulers have delegated power and are assisted by executive and legislative councils.	Malayan dollar	Malay Chinese English	Mohammedan Confucianist	Rubber, rice, coconuts, pineapples, tapioca, pepper, spices, tobacco, fibers, gambier, vegetables, tea; buffalo, swine, oxen, goats, sheep; fish; guano, tin, coal, iron ore, bauxite, manganese, copra, palm oil, timber, gold, rubber products, gutta percha, wood products, canned pineapples, textiles.
MALDIVE ISLANDS	An independent sultanate, under British protection, with a bicameral legislature.	rupee	Singhalese Arabic Dravidian	Mohammedan	Coconuts, copra, coir, fruit, nuts; fish, cowries; cloth, mats, boats.
MONGOLIAN REPUBLIC	Communist republic administered by a cabinet and parliament.	Tugrik	Mongolian Russian	Lamaist Tribal religions	Stock raising (sheep, goats, cattle, horses, camels); milk, butter, cheese; wool, hides, skins, horns, bricks, machinery; coal, lead, gold.

POLITICAL DIVISION	GOVERNMENT	MONETARY UNIT	PRINCIPAL LANGUAGES	PRINCIPAL RELIGIONS	MAJOR PRODUCTS
NEPAL	An independent kingdom governed by a maharaja, prime minister and a bicameral legislature.	Nepalese rupee	Indo-Aryan languages Tibetan	Hindu Buddhist Lamaist	Rice, grains, jute, sugar cane, tea, vegetables, tobacco, cotton, potatoes, medicinal herbs; timber; cattle, hides, skins, ghee; iron, coal, copper, lead, zinc; cotton cloth, pottery, paper.
NEW GUINEA, NETHERLANDS	Status undetermined pending negotiations between Dutch and Indonesian Governments.	guilder	Papuan Dutch Negrito	Tribal religions	Sago, coconuts, sweet potatoes, wild nutmeg, mace, copra; bird of paradise plumes; petroleum.
NORTH BORNEO	British colony ruled by a governor and assisted by executive and legislative councils.	Malayan dollar	Malay Indonesian languages English Chinese	Tribal religions Mohammedan	Rubber, coconuts, copra, tobacco, manila hemp, sago, rice, cutch, sugar, pepper, kapok, groundnuts, derris root, vegetables; timber; fish.
OMAN AND MUSCAT	An independent sultanate.	rupee (official) Maria Theresa dollar	Arabic	Mohammedan	Dates, pomegranates, limes and other fruits, sugar cane; dried fish.
PAKISTAN	Self-governing republic of the British Commonwealth ruled by a president, cabinet and unicameral legislature.	Pakistani rupee	Indo-Aryan languages (Urdu, Bengali, Punjabi, etc.)	Mohammedan Hindu Christian Sikh	Rice, wheat, corn, jute, cotton, sugar cane, fruit, oilseeds, tobacco, tea, fibers; timber; cattle, goats, sheep, horses, camels, poultry; hides, skins, wool; fish; salt, copper, petroleum, chromite, gypsum, magnisite, sulphur, antimony; textiles, flour milling, cement, iron and steel foundries, sugar, leather, chemicals, glass, sportsgoods, handicrafts, surgical instruments.
PHILIPPINES	Republic governed by a president, cabinet and a bicameral legislature.	peso	Malayan languages (Tagalog, Visayan, etc.) English Spanish	Roman Catholic Mohammedan Tribal religions	Rice, sugar cane, copra, manila hemp (abacá), corn, tobacco, maguey, rubber, bananas, pineapples, mangoes, papaya, citrus fruits, other fruits; hogs, carabaos, cattle, horses, goats, sheep; fish; timber, gum resins, tan and dye barks, dye woods; gold, iron, copper, chromite, silver, manganese, asbestos, asphalt, guano, silica, coal, petroleum; sugar, textiles, distilling, dessicated coconuts, tobacco products, rice milling, cocoa, coconut oil, embroideries.
QATAR	Sheikdom under British protection.	rupee riyal	Arabic	Mohammedan	Dates; pearl fishing, dried fish; camels; petroleum.
RYUKYU IS.	Administered by the United States.	yen	Luchuan Japanese English	Animistic Shinto	Sweet potatoes, sugar cane, rice, fruits, mulberries; swine, cattle, goats, horses, poultry; silkworms; fish; Panama hats, textiles, lacquer, pottery, china, glassware, tiles.
SARAWAK	British colony administered by a governor and a executive and legislative council.	Malayan dollar	Malay Indonesian languages Chinese English	Mohammedan Tribal religions	Rice, rubber, sago, pepper, coconuts, pineapples, tobacco, coffee, fruits, vegetables; timber, rattan cane, guttas; buffalo, cattle, pigs, goats; fish; petroleum, gold, antimony, phosphate, cutch.
SAUDI ARABIA	Absolute monarchy, with premier and cabinet subject to veto power of king.	riyal	Arabic	Mohammedan	Dates, sorghums, wheat, rice, henna, coffee, fruits, nuts, vegetables, honey, gum, sesame oil; fish; camels, sheep, goats, cattle, donkeys, poultry, horses; hides, wool, clarified butter, charcoal, pottery, tile, salt, soap, weaving; petroleum, gold, pearls.
SIKKIM	A protectorate of India ruled by a maharaja and a council.	rupee	Nepali Tepcha Bhutia	Hindu Buddhist	Millet, corn, pulse, rice, fruits; cattle; woolen cloth.
SINGAPORE	British Crown colony administered by a governor, council of ministers and legislative assembly.	Malayan dollar	Chinese Malay Hindi English	Confucianist Buddhist Taoist Mohammedan Hindu Christian	Rubber, coconuts, fruits, vegetables, rice, coffee, tapioca, tobacco, sweet potatoes, pepper, pineapples; pigs, poultry, cattle; fish; tin, tin smelting, rubber milling, coconut milling, soap, beer, pineapple canning, biscuits, brick making, shipping, textiles, palm oil, cigarettes, gasoline, kerosene.
SYRIA	Republic ruled by a chief of state.	Syrian pound	Arabic Turkish Kurdish	Mohammedan Christian	Wheat, barley, sorghum, corn, cotton, lentiles, chickpeas, sesame, vegetables, olives, grapes, tobacco (Latikia); sheep, goats, cattle, donkeys, camels, horses, poultry; wool, hides, skins; gypsum; leather, textiles, food, tobacco, wine, flour.
THAILAND (SIAM)	Constitutional monarchy ruled by a king, prime minister and a legislative assembly.	baht	Thai Khmer	Buddhist Tribal religions	Rice, rubber, coconuts, tobacco, cotton, corn, beans; teak and other woods; bullocks, buffalo, horses, elephants; fish; tin, wolfram.
TIBET	Theocracy. Nominally independent but under effective Chinese Communist control. Religious affairs are directed by the Dalai Lama.	sang	Tibetan	Lamaist	Barley, wheat, pulse, corn, vegetables, rice; yaks, asses, sheep, goats, donkeys; hides, wool, furs, musk; borax, salt, gold; cult objects.
TIMOR, PORTUGUESE	Portuguese overseas province ruled by a governor.	escudo	Malay Portuguese	Mohammedan Tribal religions Roman Catholic	Coffee, copra, sandalwood, wax, cocoa; hides, shells.
TRUCIAL OMAN	Ruled by seven sheiks.	rupee riyal	Arabic	Mohammedan	Dates, grains, vegetables; fishing, pearl fishing.
VIETNAM	Divided in two parts by Armistice Line Sept. 1954. North of 17th parallel is Communist controlled "republic". South is a republic with a president and an assembly.	piaster	Khmer (Annamese) Lao	Buddhist	Rice, corn, sugar, tobacco, coffee, fruits, manioc, betel nuts, arrowroot, tea, cotton, areca nut, medicinal plants, cardamom, soya, rubber, copra, groundnuts, haricots, sweet potatoes, cinnamon; mulberries, silk; cattle, buffalo, pigs; lumber; gold, tin, copper, coal, zinc, iron, cement, limestone, calamine, tungsten, manganese, phosphate, lead, bauxite.
YEMEN	Independent kingdom.	riyal	Arabic	Mohammedan	Coffee, barley, wheat, millet, sesame; cattle, hides; fish.

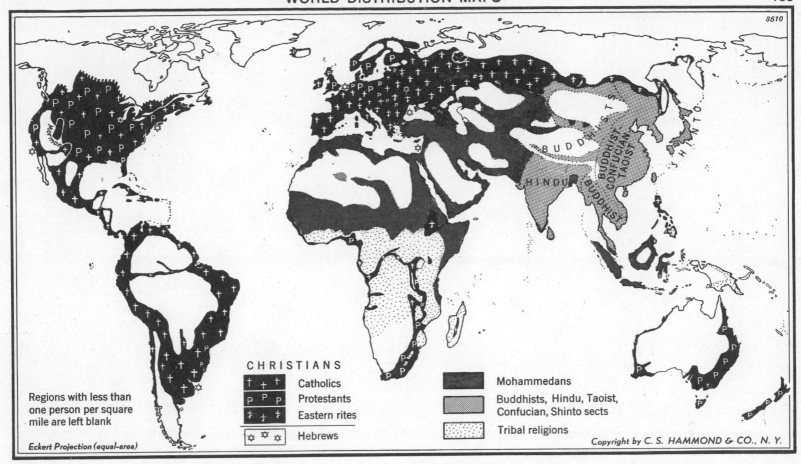

3510

CHRISTIANS

✝ ✝ ✝ Catholics

P P P Protestants

✝ ✝ ✝ Eastern rites

✡ ✡ ✡ Hebrews

Regions with less than one person per square mile are left blank

Mohammedans

Buddhists, Hindu, Taoist, Confucian, Shinto sects

Tribal religions

Eckert Projection (equal-area)

Copyright by C. S. HAMMOND & CO., N. Y.

RELIGIONS. *Most people of the Earth belong to four major religions: Christians, Mohammedans, Brahmans, Buddhists and derivatives. The Eastern rites of the Christians include the Greek Orthodox, Greek Catholic, Armenian, Syrian, Coptic and more minor churches. The lamaism of Tibet and Mongolia differs a great deal from Buddhism in Burma and Thailand. In the religion of China the teachings of Buddha, Confucius and Tao are mixed, while in Shinto a great deal of ancestor and emperor worship is added. About 11 million Hebrews live scattered over the globe, chiefly in cities and in the state of Israel.*

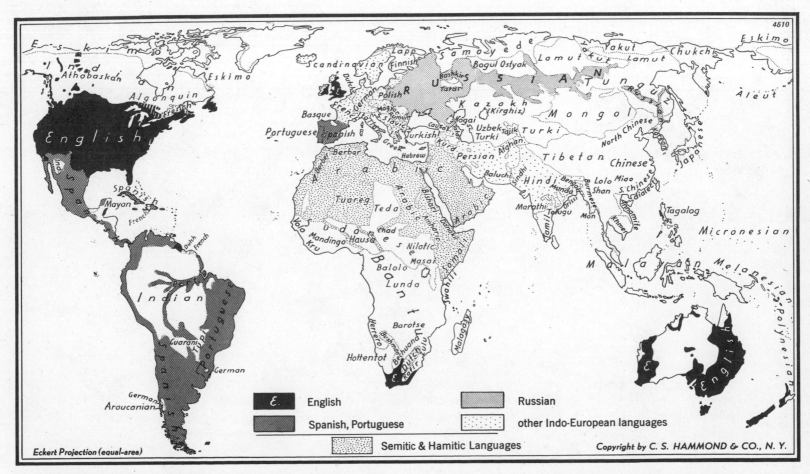

4510

E. English

Spanish, Portuguese

Semitic & Hamitic Languages

Russian

other Indo-European languages

Eckert Projection (equal-area)

Copyright by C. S. HAMMOND & CO., N. Y.

LANGUAGES. *Several hundred different languages are spoken in the World, and in many places two or more languages are spoken, sometimes by the same people. The map above shows the dominant languages in each locality. English, French, Spanish, Russian, Arabic and Swahili are spoken by many people as a second language for commerce or travel.*

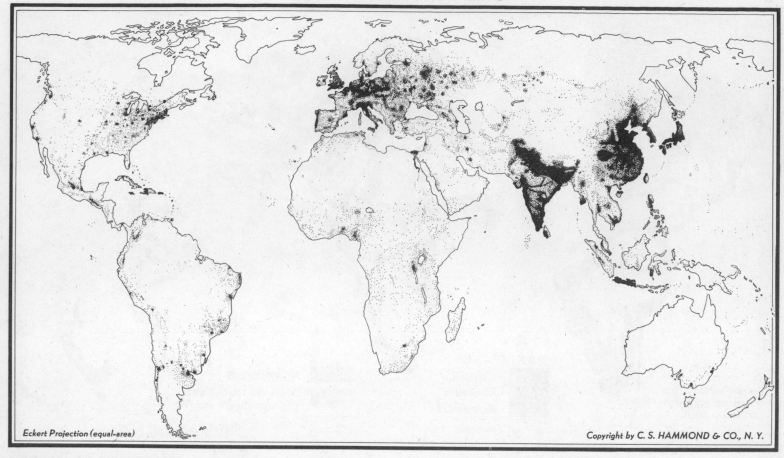

Eckert Projection (equal-area)   *Copyright by C. S. HAMMOND & CO., N. Y.*

DENSITY OF POPULATION. One of the most outstanding facts of human geography is the extremely uneven distribution of people over the Earth. One-half of the Earth's surface has less than 3 people per square mile, while in the lowlands of India, China, Java and Japan rural density reaches the incredible congestion of 2000-3000 per square mile. Three-fourths of the Earth's population live in four relatively small areas; Northeastern United States, North-Central Europe, India and the Far East.

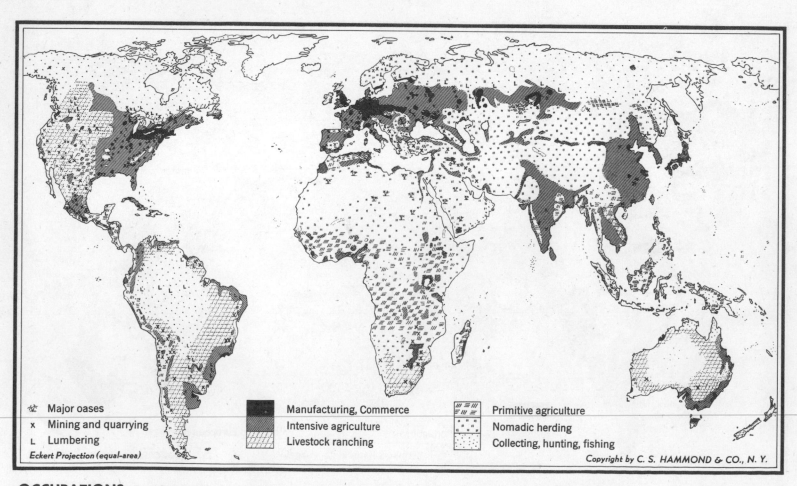

⚹ Major oases	■ Manufacturing, Commerce	▨ Primitive agriculture
x Mining and quarrying	▦ Intensive agriculture	▨ Nomadic herding
L Lumbering	▨ Livestock ranching	∴ Collecting, hunting, fishing

Eckert Projection (equal-area)   *Copyright by C. S. HAMMOND & CO., N. Y.*

OCCUPATIONS. Correlation with the density of population shows that the most densely populated areas fall into the regions of manufacturing and intensive farming. All other economies require considerable space. The most sparsely inhabited areas are those of collecting, hunting and fishing. Areas with practically no habitation are left blank.

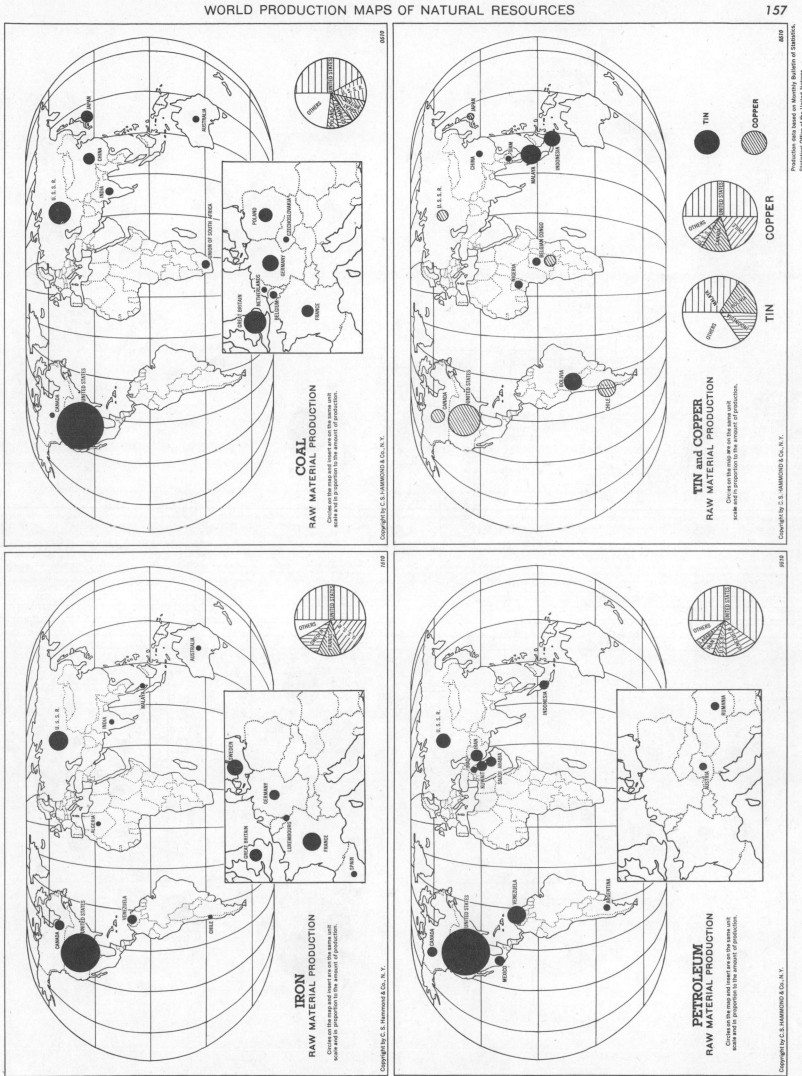

COAL
RAW MATERIAL PRODUCTION

Circles on the map and insert are on the same unit
scale and in proportion to the amount of production.

Copyright by C. S. HAMMOND & Co., N. Y.

TIN and COPPER
RAW MATERIAL PRODUCTION

Circles on the map are on the same unit
scale and in proportion to the amount of production.

Copyright by C. S. HAMMOND & Co., N. Y.

Production data based on Monthly Bulletin of Statistics,
Statistical Office of the United Nations.

IRON
RAW MATERIAL PRODUCTION

Circles on the map and insert are on the same unit
scale and in proportion to the amount of production.

Copyright by C. S. Hammond & Co., N. Y.

PETROLEUM
RAW MATERIAL PRODUCTION

Circles on the map and insert are on the same unit
scale and in proportion to the amount of production.

Copyright by C. S. HAMMOND & Co., N. Y.

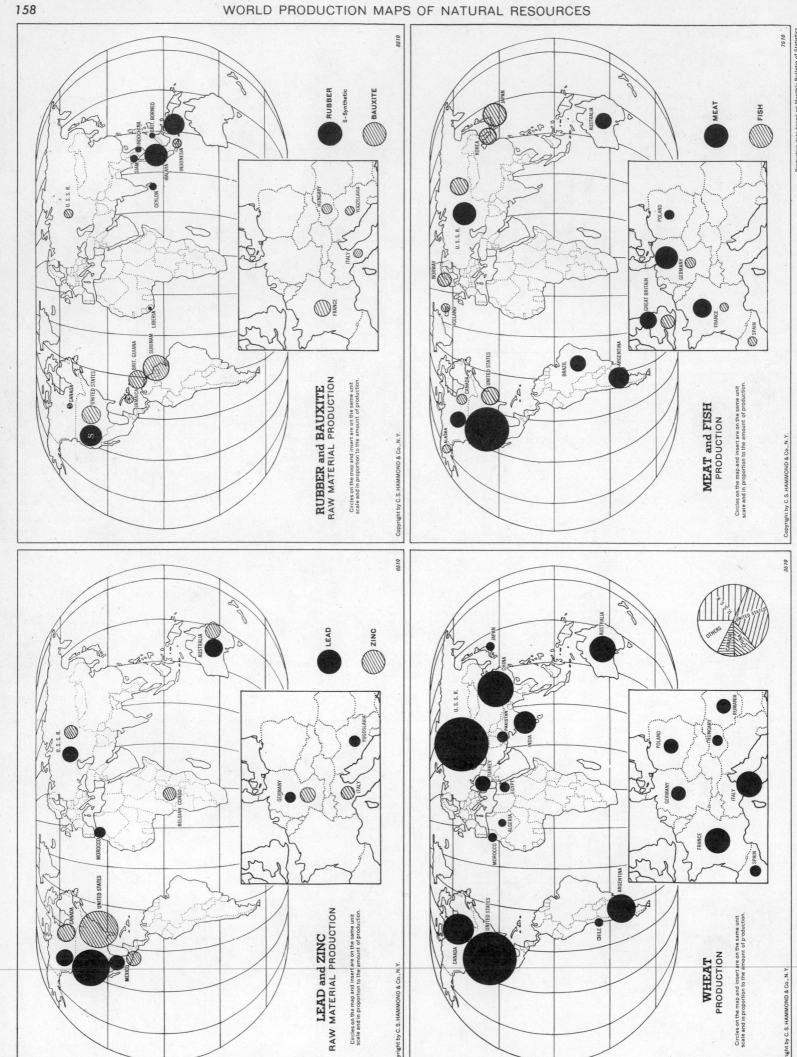

RUBBER and BAUXITE
RAW MATERIAL PRODUCTION

RUBBER
S—Synthetic
BAUXITE

Circles on the map and insert are on the same unit
scale and in proportion to the amount of production.

Copyright by C. S. HAMMOND & Co., N. Y.

8510

MEAT and FISH
PRODUCTION

MEAT
FISH

Circles on the map and insert are on the same unit
scale and in proportion to the amount of production

Copyright by C. S. HAMMOND & Co., N. Y.

7510

Production data based on Monthly Bulletin of Statistics,
Statistical Office of the United Nations.

LEAD and ZINC
RAW MATERIAL PRODUCTION

LEAD
ZINC

Circles on the map and insert are on the same unit
scale and in proportion to the amount of production.

Copyright by C. S. HAMMOND & Co., N. Y.

6510

WHEAT
PRODUCTION

Circles on the map and insert are on the same unit
scale and in proportion to the amount of production.

Copyright by C. S. HAMMOND & Co., N. Y.

3510

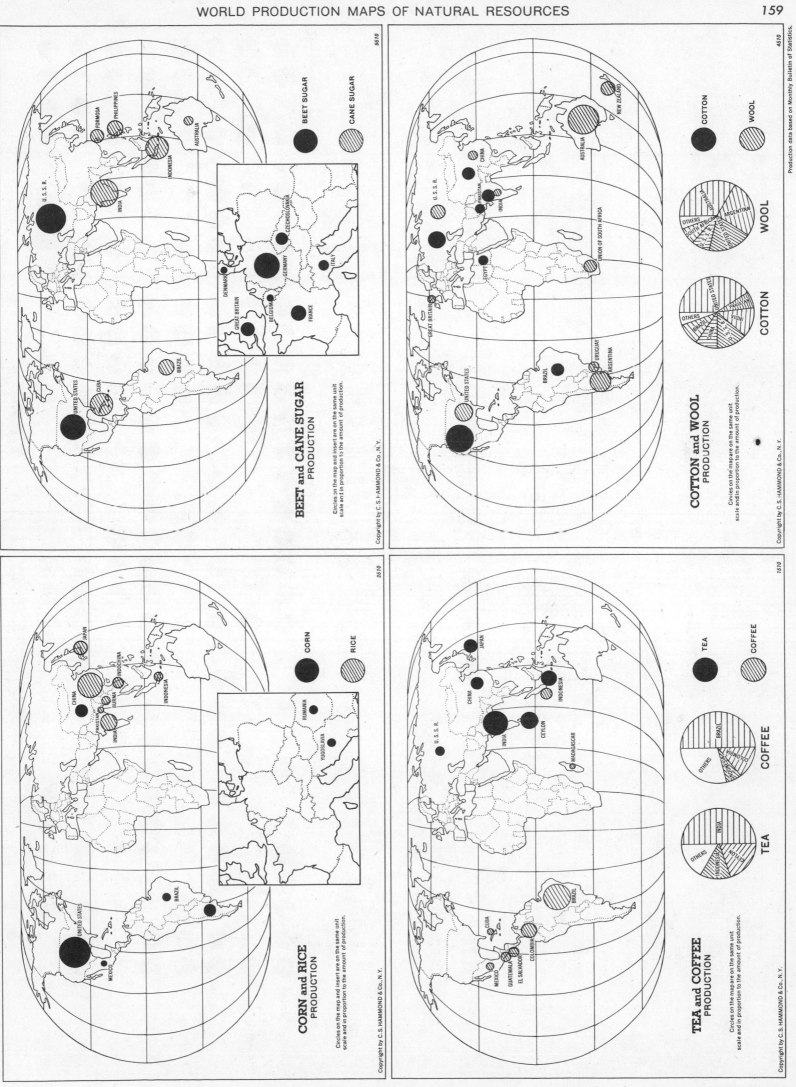

BEET and CANE SUGAR PRODUCTION

Circles on the map and insert are on the same unit scale and in proportion to the amount of production.

BEET SUGAR

CANE SUGAR

Copyright by C. S. HAMMOND & Co., N.Y.

9610

COTTON and WOOL PRODUCTION

Circles on the map are on the same unit scale and in proportion to the amount of production.

COTTON

WOOL

WOOL

COTTON

Production data based on Monthly Bulletin of Statistics, Statistical Office of the United Nations.

Copyright by C. S. HAMMOND & Co., N.Y.

4610

CORN and RICE PRODUCTION

Circles on the map and insert are on the same unit scale and in proportion to the amount of production.

CORN

RICE

Copyright by C. S. HAMMOND & Co., N.Y.

2610

TEA and COFFEE PRODUCTION

Circles on the map are on the same unit scale and in proportion to the amount of production.

TEA

COFFEE

COFFEE

TEA

Copyright by C. S. HAMMOND & Co., N.Y.

1610

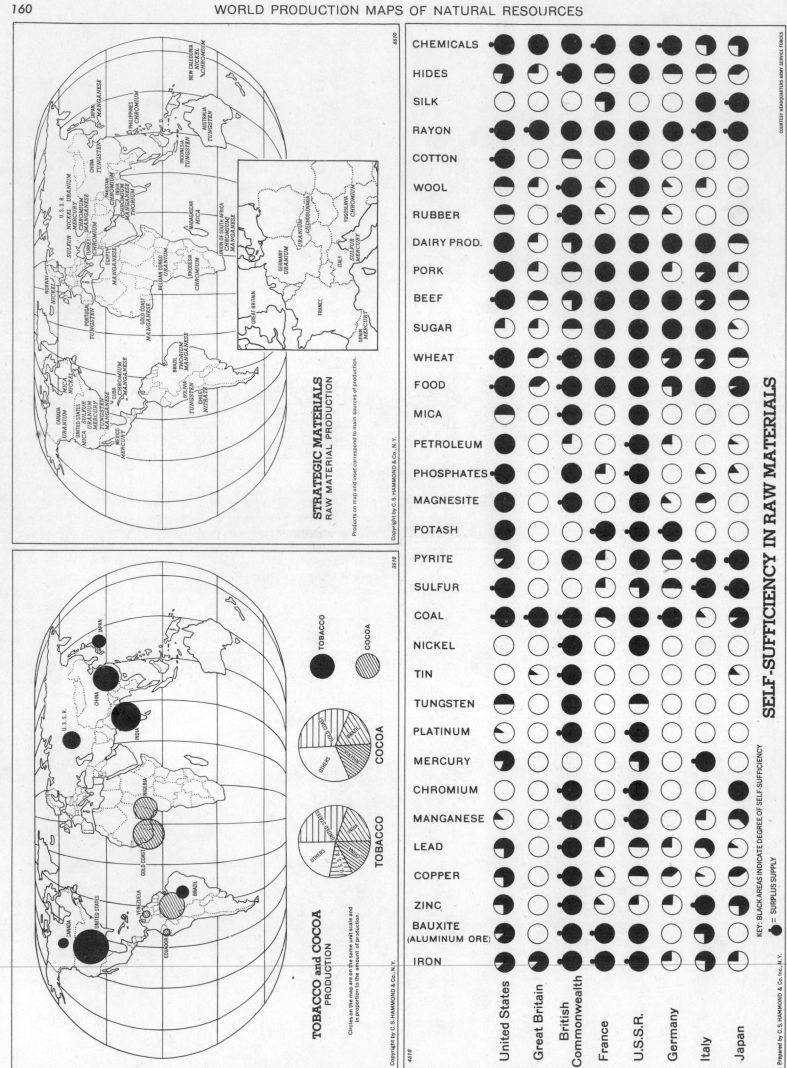

STRATEGIC MATERIALS
RAW MATERIAL PRODUCTION

Products on map and inset correspond to main sources of production.

Copyright by C. S. HAMMOND & Co., N. Y.

TOBACCO and COCOA
PRODUCTION

Circles on the map are on the same unit scale and in proportion to the amount of production.

Copyright by C. S. HAMMOND & Co., N. Y.

SELF-SUFFICIENCY IN RAW MATERIALS

KEY: BLACK AREAS INDICATE DEGREE OF SELF-SUFFICIENCY
= SURPLUS SUPPLY

CHEMICALS
HIDES
SILK
RAYON
COTTON
WOOL
RUBBER
DAIRY PROD.
PORK
BEEF
SUGAR
WHEAT
FOOD
MICA
PETROLEUM
PHOSPHATES
MAGNESITE
POTASH
PYRITE
SULFUR
COAL
NICKEL
TIN
TUNGSTEN
PLATINUM
MERCURY
CHROMIUM
MANGANESE
LEAD
COPPER
ZINC
BAUXITE (ALUMINUM ORE)
IRON

United States
Great Britain
British Commonwealth
France
U.S.S.R.
Germany
Italy
Japan

Prepared by C. S. HAMMOND & Co. Inc., N. Y.

COURTESY HEADQUARTERS ARMY SERVICE FORCES

MAN'S STORY IN MAPS

Through the ages mankind has penetrated further and further into the unknown and maps are the cumulative record of the history of his achievements, peaceful and warlike.

The animal kingdom, fish, fur and feather, travels and migrates; they, however, cannot record their adventures. But in prehistoric times Ug made scratches on a piece of stone or bark to show Og where he had killed his last mammoth and travelers and mariners long before and ever since the days of the Phoenicians, made records of their wanderings. The result of all these centuries of daring and fortitude and everlasting seeking for what lay over the hill is all here, illustrated in the most graphic known form in this collection of maps.

Regard the boundaries and frontiers separating the countries of today from one another; some the result of natural features (impassable mountain ranges or vast rivers); others holding their lines as the result of international intrigues and subtle diplomacies; still others the outcome of years of bloody warfare.

Think of the hardy souls, Cabot and Hendrik Hudson, Franklin, Peary, Scott and Byrd in the freezing Northlands and icy Antarctic. Think of Columbus, Vasco da Gama and Balboa; of Marco Polo, Sven Hedin and Younghusband in Asia. Maps were and are a vital part of the every day life of such men.

All of us have in us something of their spirit of "go—look—see." Some of us can do it for ourselves, some must do it vicariously. This section of maps will help in interpreting the story told by maps and will reawaken in all the spirit of adventure.

MAN'S STORY IN MAPS..

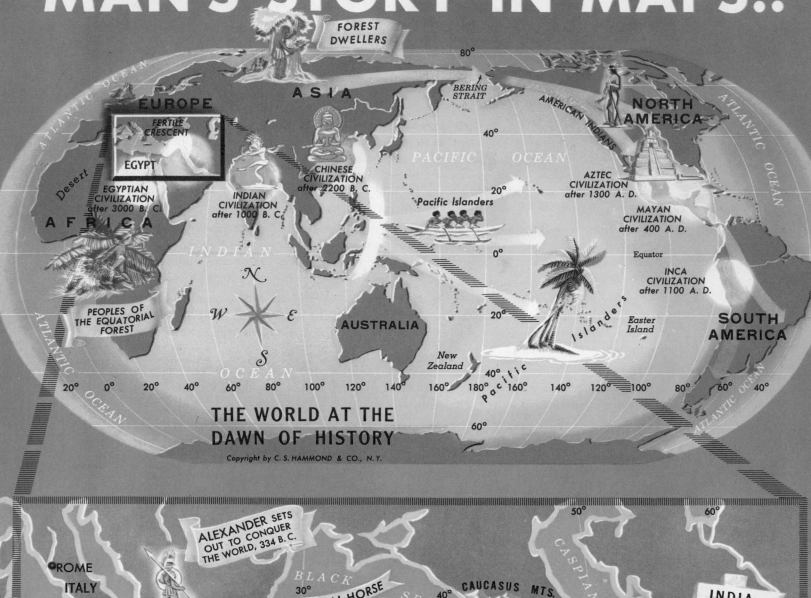

FOREST DWELLERS

ASIA

EUROPE

FERTILE CRESCENT

EGYPT

BERING STRAIT

NORTH AMERICA

AMERICAN INDIANS

Desert

EGYPTIAN CIVILIZATION after 3000 B. C.

INDIAN CIVILIZATION after 1000 B. C.

CHINESE CIVILIZATION after 2200 B. C.

PACIFIC OCEAN

AZTEC CIVILIZATION after 1300 A. D.

AFRICA

Pacific Islanders

MAYAN CIVILIZATION after 400 A. D.

INDIAN OCEAN

Equator

INCA CIVILIZATION after 1100 A. D.

PEOPLES OF THE EQUATORIAL FOREST

AUSTRALIA

Easter Island

Islanders

SOUTH AMERICA

New Zealand

Pacific

THE WORLD AT THE DAWN OF HISTORY

Copyright by C. S. HAMMOND & CO., N. Y.

ROME ITALY

ALEXANDER SETS OUT TO CONQUER THE WORLD, 334 B. C.

BLACK SEA

CAUCASUS MTS.

CASPIAN SEA

INDIA

THE TROJAN HORSE

GREECE ATHENS SPARTA

TROY

ISSUS

THE FERTILE CRESCENT

FIRST FARMERS

PERSIA

Euphrates

Tigris

SUSA

MEDITERRANEAN SEA

HOLY LAND

River

River

BABYLON

ULYSSES

JERUSALEM

ALEXANDRIA

MEMPHIS

MOUNT SINAI

HANGING GARDENS

ALEXANDER THE GREAT 356-323 B. C.

THE PYRAMIDS

E G Y P T

Sahara Desert

Nile River

Arabian Desert

TABLETS OF THE LAW

THE CRADLELAND OF CIVILIZATION

RED SEA

Scale of Miles

0 50 100 200 300 400 500

Copyright by C. S. HAMMOND & CO., N. Y.

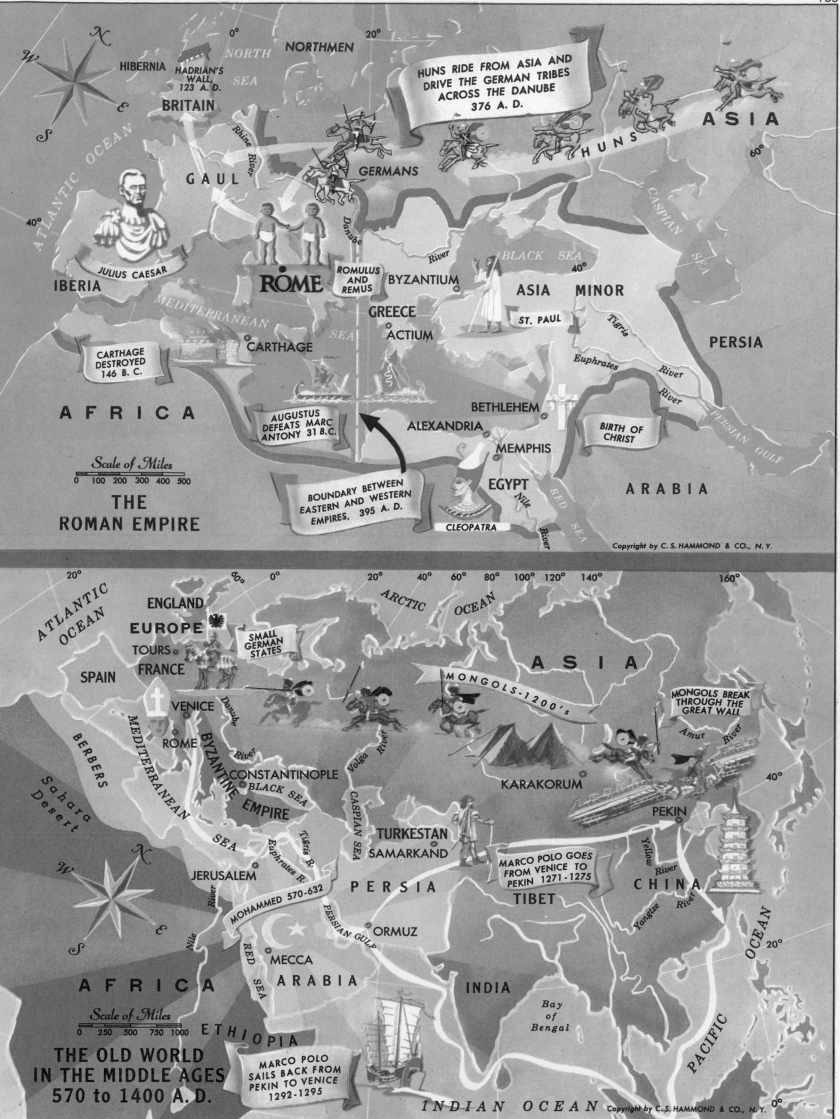

THE ROMAN EMPIRE

HIBERNIA

HADRIAN'S WALL, 123 A.D.

BRITAIN

NORTHMEN

NORTH SEA

GERMANS

HUNS RIDE FROM ASIA AND DRIVE THE GERMAN TRIBES ACROSS THE DANUBE 376 A.D.

HUNS

ASIA

ATLANTIC OCEAN

GAUL

Rhine River

Danube

JULIUS CAESAR

IBERIA

ROME

ROMULUS AND REMUS

BYZANTIUM

River

BLACK SEA

ASIA MINOR

CASPIAN SEA

GREECE

ACTIUM

ST. PAUL

Tigris

PERSIA

MEDITERRANEAN SEA

CARTHAGE

Euphrates

River

River

CARTHAGE DESTROYED 146 B.C.

BETHLEHEM

BIRTH OF CHRIST

AFRICA

AUGUSTUS DEFEATS MARC ANTONY 31 B.C.

ALEXANDRIA

MEMPHIS

PERSIAN GULF

Scale of Miles
0 100 200 300 400 500

BOUNDARY BETWEEN EASTERN AND WESTERN EMPIRES, 395 A.D.

EGYPT

Nile

ARABIA

CLEOPATRA

Red Sea

River

Copyright by C. S. HAMMOND & CO., N.Y.

THE OLD WORLD IN THE MIDDLE AGES 570 to 1400 A.D.

ATLANTIC OCEAN

ENGLAND

EUROPE

SMALL GERMAN STATES

ARCTIC OCEAN

ASIA

TOURS

FRANCE

SPAIN

VENICE

Danube River

MONGOLS—1200's

MONGOLS BREAK THROUGH THE GREAT WALL

ROME

BYZANTINE EMPIRE

CONSTANTINOPLE

BLACK SEA

Volga River

Amur River

BERBERS

MEDITERRANEAN SEA

CASPIAN SEA

KARAKORUM

PEKIN

Sahara Desert

Euphrates R.

Tigris R.

JERUSALEM

TURKESTAN

SAMARKAND

MARCO POLO GOES FROM VENICE TO PEKIN 1271-1275

Yellow River

CHINA

MOHAMMED 570-632

Nile River

PERSIA

TIBET

Yangtze River

PERSIAN GULF

ORMUZ

RED SEA

MECCA

ARABIA

INDIA

Bay of Bengal

PACIFIC OCEAN

AFRICA

Scale of Miles
0 250 500 750 1000

ETHIOPIA

MARCO POLO SAILS BACK FROM PEKIN TO VENICE 1292-1295

INDIAN OCEAN

Copyright by C. S. HAMMOND & CO., N.Y.

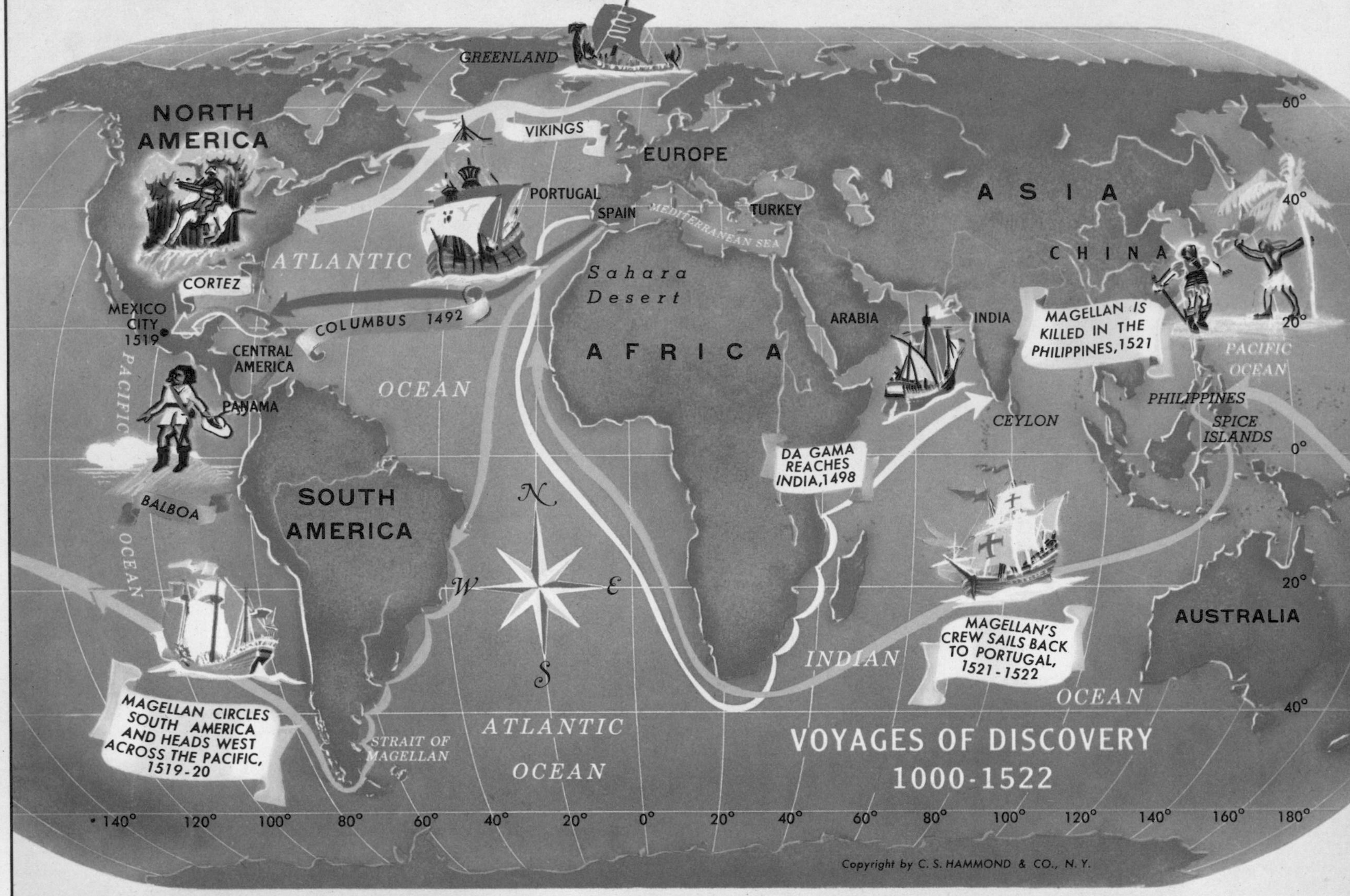

NORTH AMERICA

GREENLAND

VIKINGS

EUROPE

PORTUGAL

SPAIN

TURKEY

ASIA

CHINA

CORTEZ

ATLANTIC

MEXICO CITY 1519

COLUMBUS 1492

CENTRAL AMERICA

OCEAN

Sahara Desert

AFRICA

ARABIA

INDIA

MAGELLAN IS KILLED IN THE PHILIPPINES, 1521

PACIFIC OCEAN

PANAMA

PACIFIC OCEAN

BALBOA

SOUTH AMERICA

MEDITERRANEAN SEA

CEYLON

PHILIPPINES

SPICE ISLANDS

DA GAMA REACHES INDIA, 1498

N

W   E

S

INDIAN

MAGELLAN'S CREW SAILS BACK TO PORTUGAL, 1521-1522

AUSTRALIA

MAGELLAN CIRCLES SOUTH AMERICA AND HEADS WEST ACROSS THE PACIFIC, 1519-20

STRAIT OF MAGELLAN

ATLANTIC OCEAN

OCEAN

VOYAGES OF DISCOVERY
1000-1522

140° 120° 100° 80° 60° 40° 20° 0° 20° 40° 60° 80° 100° 120° 140° 160° 180°

Copyright by C. S. HAMMOND & CO., N. Y.

UNITED NATIONS 1945

CANADA CONFEDERATION
1867

THE WORLD WARS 1914-1918 & 1939-1945

MEDICAL & SCIENTIFIC RESEARCH

NORTH AMERICA

EUROPE

ASIA

RUSSIAN REVOLUTION 1917

JAPAN

CONSTITUTION OF THE UNITED STATES, 1789

SUEZ CANAL 1869

THE INDUSTRIAL REVOLUTION ABOUT 1800

AFRICA

ARABIA

INDIA

CHINA

PACIFIC OCEAN

CENTRAL AMERICA

PANAMA CANAL, 1914

ATLANTIC

OCEAN

STANLEY AND LIVINGSTONE 1871

ATOMIC BOMB 1945

INDIAN OCEAN

N

W   E

LATIN AMERICAN INDEPENDENCE AFTER 1800

SOUTH

AMERICA

ATOMIC ENERGY

S

AUSTRALIA

THE MODERN AGE
1700 TO THE PRESENT

ELECTRIC POWER, COMMUNICATION AND ELECTRONICS

SUPERSONIC TRAVEL

140° 120° 100° 80° 60° 40° 20° 0° 20° 40° 60° 80° 100° 120°

Copyright by C. S. HAMMOND & CO., N. Y.

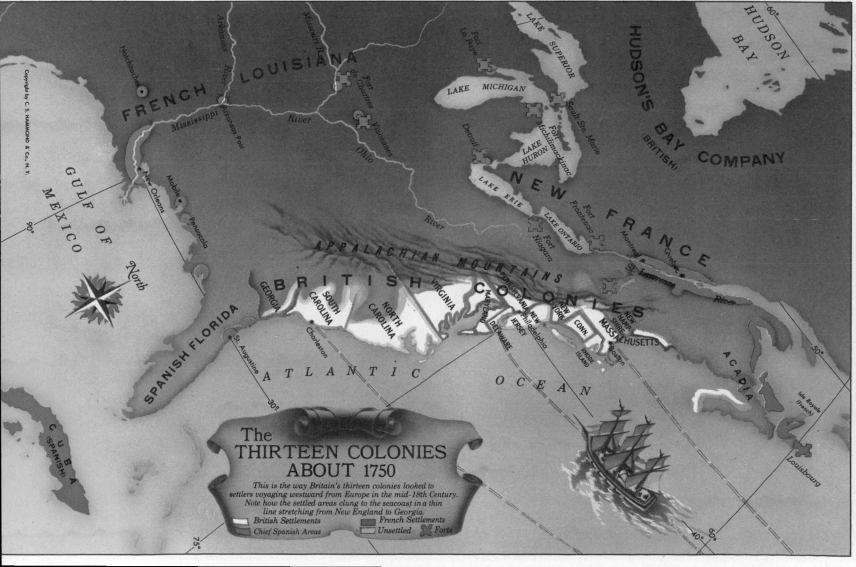

EUROPEAN EMPIRES IN AMERICA IN THE 17th CENTURY

This map shows the sections of North America under the control or influence of the Spanish, French, Dutch, Swedes and British in the Seventeenth Century. There were no clear boundaries, for each nation claimed areas held or claimed by others. The map shows North America as seen from the south, at a point over the Gulf of Mexico.

British
Spanish
Swedish
French
Dutch
Unclaimed or claims not established

Copyright by C. S. HAMMOND & Co., N. Y.

HUDSON BAY

NEWFOUNDLAND

PACIFIC OCEAN

Missouri River

LAKE SUPERIOR

LAKE MICHIGAN
LAKE HURON
LAKE ERIE
L. ONTARIO

Quebec

St. Lawrence River

Port Royal

Mississippi River

Plymouth

Ohio River

New Amsterdam

North

ATLANTIC OCEAN

Arkansas River

Santa Fe

Jamestown

Colorado River

Rio Grande

Mississippi River

St. Augustine

BERMUDA

GULF OF MEXICO

The THIRTEEN COLONIES ABOUT 1750

This is the way Britain's thirteen colonies looked to settlers voyaging westward from Europe in the mid-18th Century. Note how the settled areas clung to the seacoast in a thin line stretching from New England to Georgia.

British Settlements
French Settlements
Chief Spanish Areas
Unsettled
Forts

Copyright by C. S. HAMMOND & Co., N. Y.

FRENCH LOUISIANA

Nachitoches

Arkansas River

Missouri R.

Fort La Baye

LAKE SUPERIOR

HUDSON BAY

HUDSON'S BAY COMPANY (BRITISH)

Mississippi

Arkansas Post

River

Fort de Chartres

Vincennes

Ohio

LAKE MICHIGAN

Sault Ste. Marie

Fort Michilimackinac

Detroit

LAKE HURON

Fort Frontenac

NEW FRANCE

River

LAKE ERIE

LAKE ONTARIO

Fort Niagara

Montreal

Quebec

St. Lawrence River

GULF OF MEXICO

New Orleans

Mobile

Pensacola

North

APPALACHIAN MOUNTAINS

BRITISH COLONIES

SPANISH FLORIDA

GEORGIA

SOUTH CAROLINA

NORTH CAROLINA

VIRGINIA

MARYLAND

DELAWARE

PENNSYLVANIA Philadelphia

NEW JERSEY

NEW YORK

CONN.

RHODE ISLAND

MASSACHUSETTS

NEW HAMP.

Boston

ACADIA

St. Augustine

Charleston

ATLANTIC OCEAN

CUBA (SPANISH)

Isle Royale (French)

Louisbourg

THE UNITED STATES IN 1783

This map shows the new American republic as recognized by Great Britain in the Treaty of Peace, 1783.

Note that settlers were already leaving the original states for the West.

Copyright by C. S. HAMMOND & Co., N.Y.

Map labels:
CANADA (BRITISH)
LAKE SUPERIOR
LAKE HURON
LAKE MICHIGAN
LAKE ERIE
LAKE ONTARIO
THE NORTHWEST TERRITORY (Organized 1787)
Detroit
Fort Niagara
St. Lawrence River
Mississippi River
Missouri River
Ohio River
LOUISIANA (SPANISH)
UNITED STATES
NEW HAMPSHIRE
VERMONT State after 1791
NEW YORK
Mohawk Valley
MASSACHUSETTS
CONN. R.I.
PENNSYLVANIA
NEW JERSEY
DELAWARE
MARYLAND
VIRGINIA
WILDERNESS ROAD
Cumberland Gap
NORTH CAROLINA
SOUTH CAROLINA
GEORGIA
EAST FLORIDA (SPANISH)
WEST FLORIDA (SPANISH)
New Orleans
GULF OF MEXICO
CUBA (SPANISH)
ATLANTIC OCEAN
North
Area claimed by Spain

THE AMERICAN REVOLUTION

This map shows the major campaigns of the War of Independence. Note that the fighting began in Massachusetts ❶, and moved to the middle states. The war reached its turning point at Saratoga ❷, moved to the South, and ended at Yorktown ❸.

Copyright by C. S. HAMMOND & Co., N.Y.

Map labels:
HUDSON BAY
HUDSON'S BAY COMPANY (BRITISH)
CANADA (BRITISH)
NOVA SCOTIA (BRITISH)
LAKE SUPERIOR
LAKE MICHIGAN
LAKE HURON
LAKE ERIE
LAKE ONTARIO
St. Lawrence River
Quebec
Montreal
Fort Ticonderoga
Saratoga ❷
Concord Boston ❶
New York
Fort Niagara
Fort Pitt
Detroit
Fort Michilimackinac
Fort St. Joseph
Fort Edward Augustus
Vincennes
Cahokia
Kaskaskia
Ohio River
Clark's Expedition in the West 1778-9
THE THIRTEEN COLONIES
Trenton
Monmouth
Valley Forge
Philadelphia
Yorktown ❸
French fleet at Yorktown 1781
Guilford Court House
Moores Creek
Kings Mountain
Cowpens
Charleston
Savannah
FLORIDA (BRITISH)
SPANISH LOUISIANA
Mississippi River
Natchez
Baton Rouge
Mobile
New Orleans
GULF OF MEXICO
North
ATLANTIC OCEAN

Photo panel captions:
NORTH CHURCH
FORT TICONDEROGA
KINGS MOUNTAIN
CONCORD
SARATOGA
DELAWARE CROSSING
VALLEY FORGE
INDEPENDENCE HALL
GREENE'S CAMPAIGNS
YORKTOWN

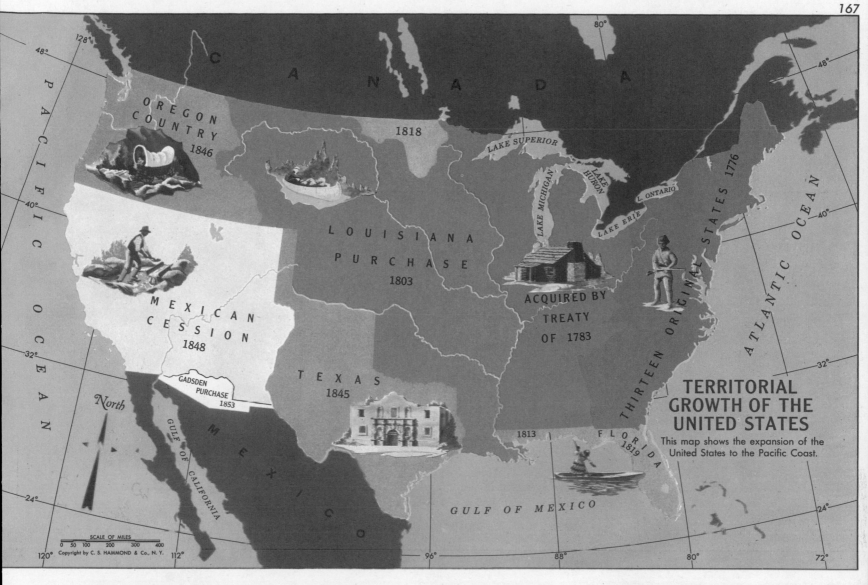

TERRITORIAL GROWTH OF THE UNITED STATES

This map shows the expansion of the United States to the Pacific Coast.

OREGON COUNTRY 1846

1818

LOUISIANA PURCHASE 1803

ACQUIRED BY TREATY OF 1783

THIRTEEN ORIGINAL STATES 1776

MEXICAN CESSION 1848

GADSDEN PURCHASE 1853

TEXAS 1845

FLORIDA 1813 1819

PACIFIC OCEAN

ATLANTIC OCEAN

GULF OF CALIFORNIA

MEXICO

GULF OF MEXICO

CANADA

LAKE SUPERIOR · LAKE MICHIGAN · LAKE HURON · LAKE ERIE · L. ONTARIO

North

SCALE OF MILES
0 50 100 200 300 400

Copyright by C. S. HAMMOND & Co., N. Y.

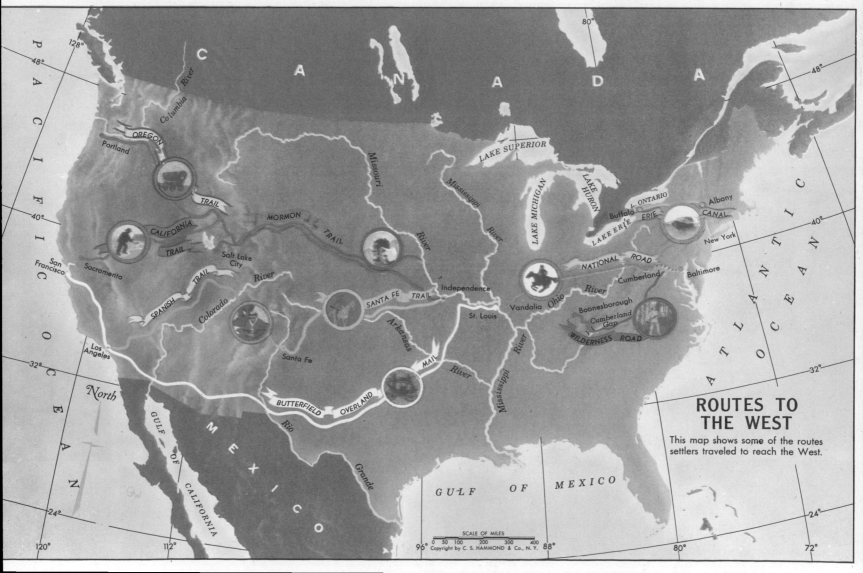

ROUTES TO THE WEST

This map shows some of the routes settlers traveled to reach the West.

Columbia River · Portland · OREGON TRAIL · CALIFORNIA TRAIL · Sacramento · San Francisco · Salt Lake City · SPANISH TRAIL · Colorado River · Los Angeles · MORMON TRAIL · Missouri River · SANTA FE TRAIL · Santa Fe · Arkansas River · BUTTERFIELD OVERLAND MAIL · Rio Grande · Independence · St. Louis · Mississippi River · Ohio River · Vandalia · NATIONAL ROAD · Cumberland · WILDERNESS ROAD · Boonesborough · Cumberland Gap · Baltimore · Buffalo · ERIE CANAL · Albany · New York

LAKE SUPERIOR · LAKE MICHIGAN · LAKE HURON · LAKE ERIE · L. ONTARIO

PACIFIC OCEAN · ATLANTIC OCEAN · GULF OF CALIFORNIA · MEXICO · GULF OF MEXICO · CANADA

North

SCALE OF MILES
0 50 100 200 300 400

Copyright by C. S. HAMMOND & Co., N. Y.

THE CONFEDERATE STATES OF AMERICA

This map shows the states that seceded and formed the Confederacy. The map shows North America as seen from the southwest, at a point over Mexico.

Copyright by C. S. HAMMOND & Co., N.Y.

Labels on the first map:

ATLANTIC OCEAN
North
BRITISH POSSESSIONS
HUDSON BAY
Mackenzie River
St. Laurence River
UNITED STATES
CONFEDERATE STATES
MEXICO
GULF OF MEXICO
CUBA
CARIBBEAN SEA
PACIFIC OCEAN
Rio Grande

MAINE, VERMONT, NEW HAMP., MASS, CONN, RHODE ISLAND, NEW JERSEY, NEW YORK, PENNSYLVANIA, DELAWARE, MARYLAND, Washington, Richmond, WEST VIRGINIA, VIRGINIA, NORTH CAROLINA, SOUTH CAROLINA, GEORGIA, FLORIDA, ALABAMA, MISSISSIPPI, TENNESSEE, KENTUCKY, OHIO, INDIANA, ILLINOIS, MICHIGAN, WISCONSIN, IOWA, MINNESOTA, MISSOURI, ARKANSAS, LOUISIANA, TEXAS, INDIAN TERRITORY, KANSAS, NEBRASKA TERRITORY, DAKOTA TERRITORY, COLORADO TERRITORY, NEW MEXICO TERRITORY, UTAH TERRITORY, NEVADA TERRITORY, WASHINGTON TERRITORY, OREGON, CALIFORNIA

LAKE SUPERIOR, LAKE HURON, LAKE MICHIGAN, LAKE ERIE, Ohio River, Missouri River, Colorado River, Mississippi River

---

THE STATES OF THE UNITED STATES

This map shows the states and the date each was admitted to the Union.

Note that many states were admitted in the same year or period.

Labels on the second map:

CANADA
PACIFIC OCEAN
ATLANTIC OCEAN
North
GULF OF CALIFORNIA
MEXICO
GULF OF MEXICO
LAKE SUPERIOR
LAKE HURON
L. MICHIGAN
LAKE ERIE
L. ONTARIO

WASHINGTON 1889 — Olympia
OREGON 1859 — Salem
MONTANA 1889 — Helena
NORTH DAKOTA 1889 — Bismarck
SOUTH DAKOTA 1889 — Pierre
MINNESOTA 1858 — St. Paul
WISCONSIN 1848 — Madison
MICHIGAN 1837 — Lansing
MAINE 1820 — Augusta
NEW HAMPSHIRE 1791 — Concord
VERMONT 1791 — Montpelier
MASS 1788 — Boston
RHODE ISLAND 1790 — Providence
CONN 1788 — Hartford
NEW YORK 1788 — Albany
IDAHO 1890 — Boise
WYOMING 1890 — Cheyenne
NEBRASKA 1867 — Lincoln
IOWA 1846 — Des Moines
ILLINOIS 1818 — Springfield
INDIANA 1816 — Indianapolis
OHIO 1803 — Columbus
PENNSYLVANIA 1787 — Harrisburg
NEW JERSEY 1787 — Trenton
DELAWARE 1787 — Dover
MARYLAND 1788 — Annapolis
WEST VIRGINIA 1863 — Charleston
VIRGINIA 1788 — Richmond
NEVADA 1864 — Carson City
UTAH 1896 — Salt Lake City
COLORADO 1876 — Denver
KANSAS 1861 — Topeka
MISSOURI 1821 — Jefferson City
KENTUCKY 1792 — Frankfort
TENNESSEE 1796 — Nashville
NORTH CAROLINA 1789 — Raleigh
CALIFORNIA 1850 — Sacramento
ARIZONA 1912 — Phoenix
NEW MEXICO 1912 — Santa Fe
OKLAHOMA 1907 — Oklahoma City
ARKANSAS 1836 — Little Rock
MISSISSIPPI 1817 — Jackson
ALABAMA 1819 — Montgomery
GEORGIA 1788 — Atlanta
SOUTH CAROLINA 1788 — Columbia
TEXAS 1845 — Austin
LOUISIANA 1812 — Baton Rouge
FLORIDA 1845 — Tallahassee

Legend:
1776-1790 Thirteen original states
1791-1819
1820-1850
1851-1876
1877-1912

SCALE OF MILES
0 50 100 200 300 400

Copyright by C. S. HAMMOND & Co., N.Y. 72

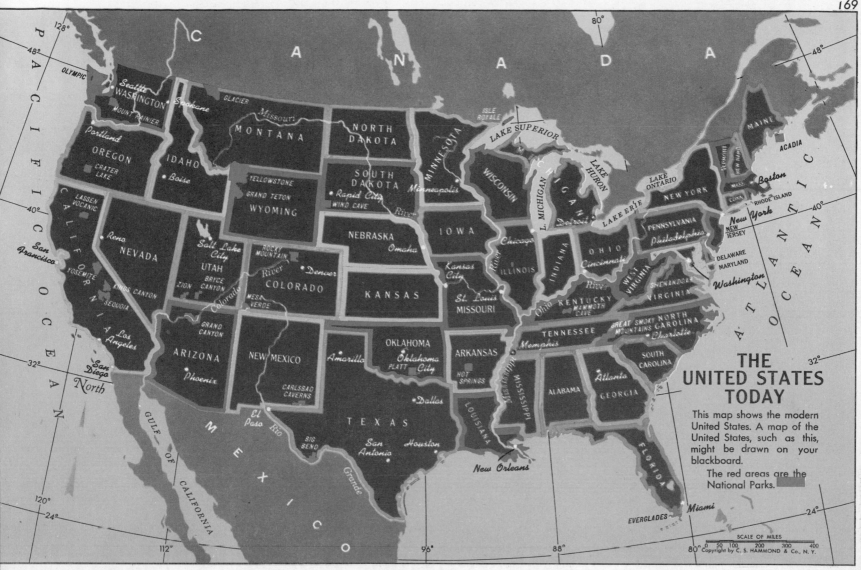

THE UNITED STATES TODAY

This map shows the modern United States. A map of the United States, such as this, might be drawn on your blackboard.

The red areas are the National Parks.

SCALE OF MILES
0 50 100 200 300 400
Copyright by C. S. Hammond & Co., N. Y.

THE UNITED STATES AND OVERSEAS POSSESSIONS

The United States and its overseas possessions. The dates appearing after the names of the overseas possessions refer to the year of their acquisition by the United States.

Philippine Islands–acquired 1898 –independent 1946

Copyright by C. S. HAMMOND & Co., N. Y.

FACTS ABOUT OUR

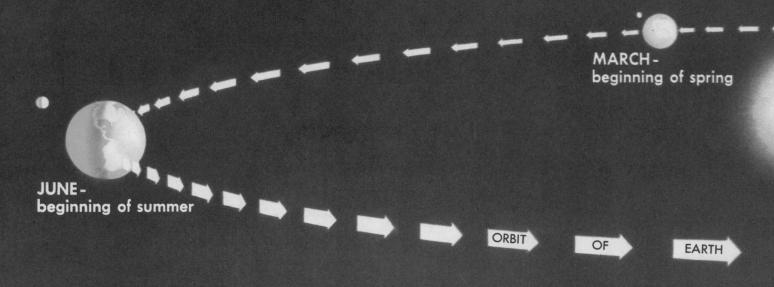

MARCH-
beginning of spring

JUNE-
beginning of summer

ORBIT   OF   EARTH

This picture shows the trip our earth takes around the sun every year. The circular path that it follows in *revolving* around the sun is known as its *orbit*.

HOW WE KNOW THE EARTH IS ROUND...

HORIZON

We know that our earth is round because we can see a ship go out of sight as it sails under the horizon.

NIGHT AND DAY

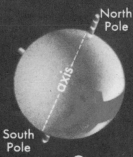

North Pole

axis

South Pole

Our earth turns or *rotates* on its *axis* once every 24 hours. We are carried by the spinning earth from daylight into darkness and, about 12 hours later, into daylight again.

Earth

The sun is much larger than the earth. This is how our earth would look if it were placed next to the sun.

EARTH...

Our earth receives its *light* and *heat* from the sun.

The moon *revolves* around the earth in its own *orbit.*

DECEMBER –
beginning of winter

SEPTEMBER –
beginning of fall

JULY
Summer

Winter

JANUARY
Winter

Summer

The top half of the globe, or the *Northern Hemisphere,* leans toward the sun in summer making the period of daylight longer. The sun's rays, shining straight down on the earth, heat the land. In winter, the top half leans away from the sun making the days shorter and the land colder. The bottom half, or the *Southern Hemisphere,* has seasons that are just the opposite.

JULY

JANUARY

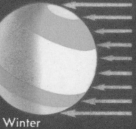

FRIGID ZONE
always cold
Arctic Circle

NORTH TEMPERATE ZONE
seasons change

Tropic of Cancer

TORRID ZONE
-- Equator --
always hot

Tropic of Capricorn

SOUTH TEMPERATE ZONE
seasons change

Antarctic Circle
FRIGID ZONE

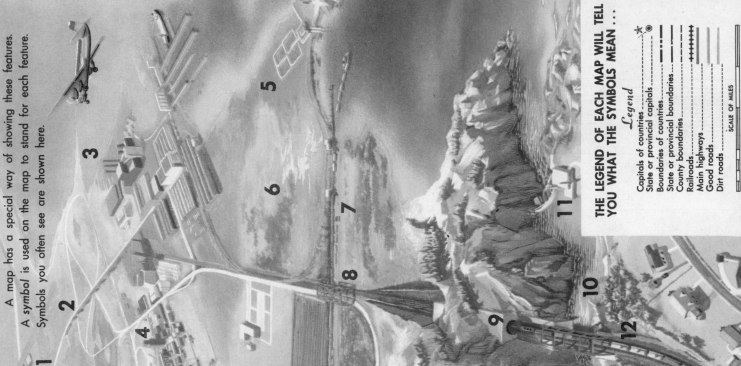

1. AIRPORT	2. ROADS	3. COASTLINE	4. TOWNS AND CITIES	5. SAND OR DESERT	6. MARSH OR SWAMP	7. CANAL	8. BRIDGE	9. TUNNEL	10. RIVERS	11. DAM	12. RAILROADS	COUNTRIES, STATES, PROVINCES OR COUNTIES

A map has a special way of showing these features.
A symbol is used on the map to stand for each feature.
Symbols you often see are shown here.

THE LEGEND OF EACH MAP WILL TELL YOU WHAT THE SYMBOLS MEAN . . .

Legend

Capitals of countries
State or provincial capitals
Boundaries of countries
State or provincial boundaries
County boundaries
Railroads
Main highways
Good roads
Dirt roads

SCALE OF MILES

0 1 2 3 4   8   12   16

WHAT A MAP IS . . .

A *map* is like a picture of the earth taken from high in the air.

A *globe* is the only true map of the earth because it shows us the roundness of the earth. A globe shows us all the lands and seas in their true shapes and positions. A globe is really a model or small copy of our earth.

A *doll* is a model of a person.

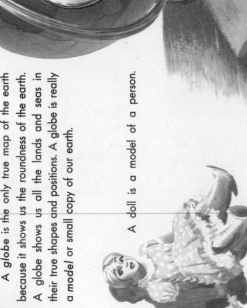

A *toy airplane* is a model of a real airplane.

NATURAL FEATURES

MAN-MADE FEATURES

ROUTES

A map can show us many things that are located upon the earth. A few of them are shown here.

HOW TO USE A MAP...

TO FIND YOUR WAY: You should turn the map so that N on the compass rose will point north. When this is done the position of the features on the map will be the same as on the earth.

Map of Harbor Area

2. A map tells you how far away, or the *distance*, one object is from another. You can find distance in the following ways.....

DRAWING COMPASS

RULER

TRANSFER TO BAR SCALE

Scale of Feet

Copyright by C. S. HAMMOND & CO., N. Y.

A MAGNETIC COMPASS

The needle of a compass points toward north.

The compass-rose tells you where north is located on your map.

WHAT A MAP DOES...

1. A map tells you in which *direction* one object or place is from another.

You can find direction on the ground in the following ways.....

YOUR SHADOW: At noon, if you face the sun, you are looking south. Your shadow will point *north*. If you raise your arms, your right arm will point west and your left arm will point east.

THE NORTH STAR: If you face the North Star, you are facing north.

NORTH STAR

BIG DIPPER

The two pointer stars of the Big Dipper point to the North Star.

WHAT SCALE MEANS...

The maps on this page will show you how you see how scales, all of the same length, can stand for different distances.

If you drew a plan or map of your schoolroom the same size or scale as the actual room, it would be too big to use.

If you drew the plan or map somewhat smaller, it still would be too large to use easily.

A still smaller plan or map could be drawn to a convenient size or scale.

We do this by making a small length, such as an inch, stand for a large one, such as a foot or a mile. This diagram shows one inch equaling a foot.

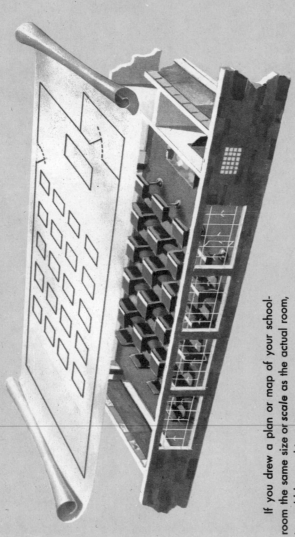

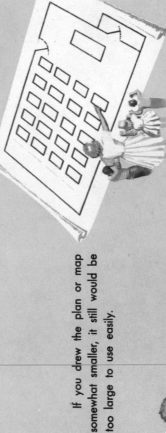

1 FOOT

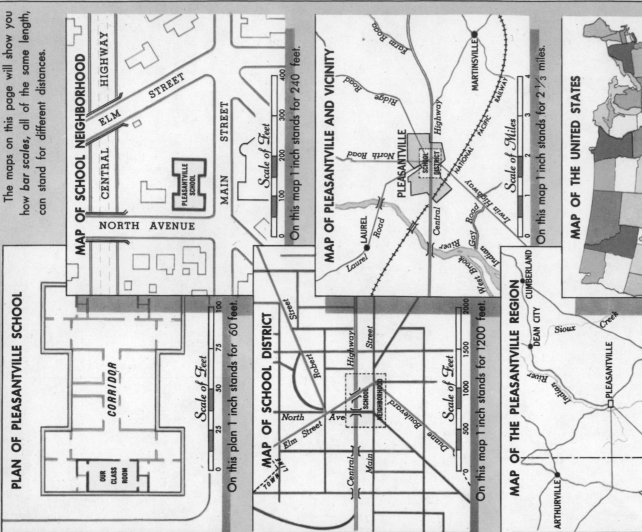

PLAN OF PLEASANTVILLE SCHOOL

OUR CLASS ROOM

CORRIDOR

Scale of Feet

0   25   50   75   100

On this plan 1 inch stands for 60 feet.

MAP OF SCHOOL NEIGHBORHOOD

NORTH AVENUE

HIGHWAY

ELM STREET

CENTRAL

MAIN STREET

PLEASANTVILLE SCHOOL

Scale of Feet

0   100   200   300   400

On this map 1 inch stands for 240 feet.

MAP OF SCHOOL DISTRICT

TOWN LINE

Robert Street

North

Elm Street

Street Ave.

Central

Main

Highway

Street

SCHOOL

NEIGHBORHOOD

Dunne Boulevard

Scale of Feet

0   500   1000   1500   2000

On this map 1 inch stands for 1200 feet.

MAP OF PLEASANTVILLE AND VICINITY

Farm Road

Ridge Road

North Road

NATIONAL PACIFIC RAILWAY

MARTINSVILLE

PLEASANTVILLE

SCHOOL DISTRICT

Highway

Laurel Road

LAUREL

West Brook

Indian Brook

River

Gay Road

Central

Irwin Highway

Scale of Miles

0   1   2   3   4

On this map 1 inch stands for 2 1/3 miles.

MAP OF THE PLEASANTVILLE REGION

CUMBERLAND

DEAN CITY

Sioux Creek

BORDERTOWN

Indian River

PLEASANTVILLE

JUNCTION CITY

ARTHURVILLE

EDMUND

Scale of Miles

0   50   100   150   200

On this map 1 inch stands for 117 miles.

MAP OF THE UNITED STATES

Scale of Miles

0   400   800   1200   1600

On this map 1 inch stands for 936 miles.

PROJECTION: CHANGING A GLOBE INTO A FLAT MAP

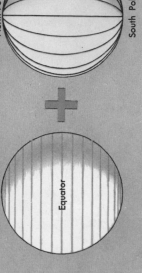

North Pole

South Pole

We can peel a globe as we can peel an orange. However, a map separated in this manner is difficult to use.

A better way to make a world map is to project the features of the round globe onto a flat surface. We do something like this when we make shadow pictures on the wall with our hands.

When placed together they form a *grid* which helps to find the location of any place on earth.

Latitude—imaginary lines that extend around the globe in the same direction as the equator.

Longitude—imaginary half-circles that extend from the North Pole to the South Pole.

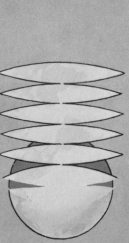

Greenland as it appears on the world map shown at the right.

Greenland as it appears on a globe.

All flat maps show some areas stretched out of size or shape. Here is an example of a distorted area on a flat map.

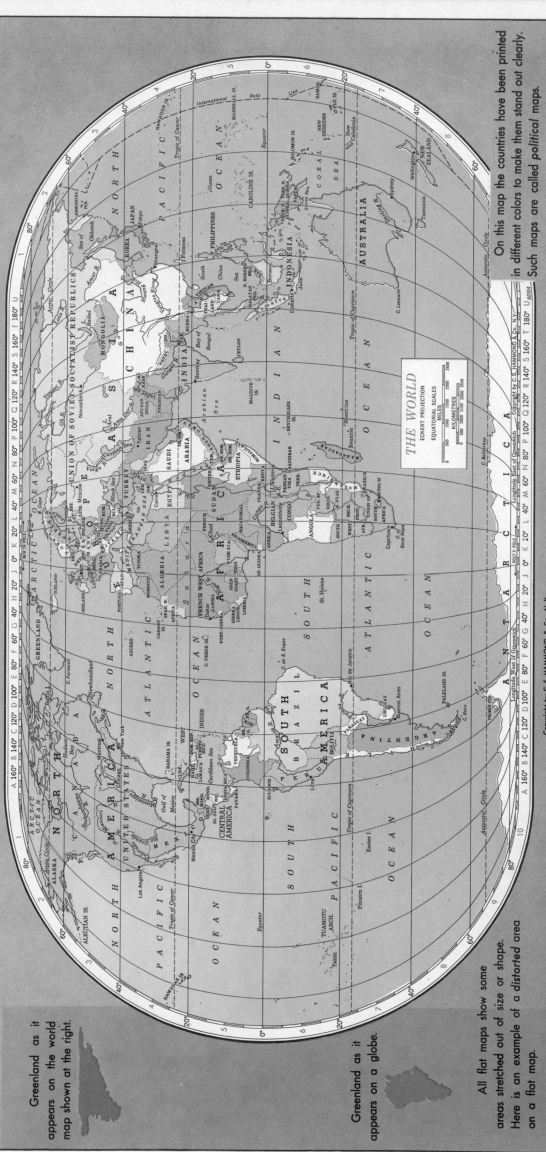

THE WORLD
ECKERT PROJECTION
EQUATORIAL SCALES
MILES

KILOMETRES

On this map the countries have been printed in different colors to make them stand out clearly. Such maps are called *political* maps.

Copyright by C. S. HAMMOND & Co., N. Y.

CONTOURS: WHAT THEY ARE... HOW TO USE THEM...

Some maps show highlands and lowlands. There are many ways of doing this on a map. One important way of showing the height and shape of land on a map is by means of *contour lines*. A contour is a line drawn on a map to connect all points that are the same height or *altitude* above the sea.

Sea-level means the level of the ocean. We start measuring from sea-level because it is the same all over the world.

If you made a clay model of the mountain shown above and sliced it into layers of the same thickness, the cuts would show on the surface as lines or *contour lines*.

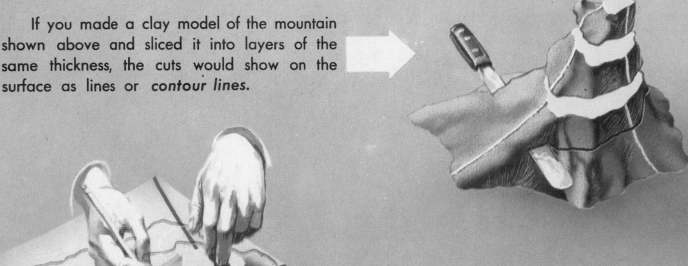

If you traced the outline of each layer on a piece of paper, your drawing would look something like this. Contour lines spaced closely together indicate a steep slope. Lines spaced far apart indicate a gentle slope.

A finished contour map may appear as...

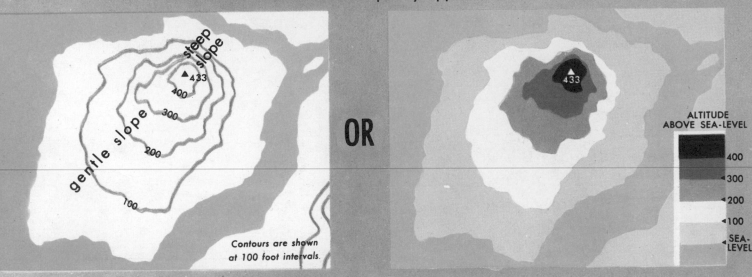

OR

Contours are shown at 100 foot intervals.

ALTITUDE ABOVE SEA-LEVEL

400
300
200
100
SEA-LEVEL

Lines with altitudes given in feet.

Colored areas with an altitude scale

EARTH AND SOLAR SYSTEM

Elements of the Solar System

PRINCIPAL LAKES AND INLAND SEAS

PLANETS	DISTANCE FROM SUN IN MILES MAXIMUM	MINIMUM	PERIOD OF REVOLUTION AROUND SUN IN DAYS	DIAMETER IN MILES	DENSITY (EARTH=1)
Sun	....	....	....	865,390	0.26
Mercury	43,404,000	28,599,000	87.87	3,009	0.68
Venus	67,730,000	66,814,000	224.70	7,575	0.94
Earth	94,560,000	91,446,000	365.26	7,927	1.00
Mars	154,936,000	128,476,000	686.98	4,216	0.71
Jupiter	507,289,000	460,465,000	4,332.59	88,698	0.24
Saturn	936,637,000	837,655,000	10,759.20	75,060	0.12
Uranus	1,868,930,000	1,700,745,000	30,685.93	30,878	0.25
Neptune	2,820,610,000	2,773,510,000	60,187.64	27,700	0.41
Pluto	4,585,000,000	2,753,000,000	90,470.23	3,600 approx.	0.7

Dimensions of the Earth

Superficial area	196,950,000	sq. miles
Land surface	57,510,000	" "
North America	8,500,000	" "
South America	6,814,000	" "
Europe	3,872,000	" "
Asia	16,990,000	" "
Africa	11,500,000	" "
Australia	2,974,581	" "
Water surface	139,440,000	" "
Atlantic Ocean	31,830,000	" "
Pacific Ocean	63,801,000	" "
Indian Ocean	28,356,000	" "
Arctic Ocean	5,440,000	" "
Equatorial circumference	24,902	miles
Meridional circumference	24,860	"
Equatorial diameter	7,926.677	"
Polar diameter	7,899.988	"
Equatorial radius	3,963.34	"
Polar radius	3,949.99	"
Volume of the Earth	260,000,000,000	cubic miles
Mass, or weight	6,592,000,000,000,000,000,000	tons
Mean distance from the Sun	92,897,416	miles

The Moon, the only satellite of the Earth, from which her mean distance is 238,857 miles, occupies an average period, in her revolution round the earth, of 29 days, 12 hours, 44 minutes, 3 seconds; her diameter is 2,160 miles, and her mean density 0.60.

	AREA IN SQ. MILES
Caspian Sea	163,800
Lake Superior	31,820
Lake Victoria	26,828
Lake Aral	24,900
Lake Huron	23,010
Lake Michigan	22,400
Lake Tanganyika	12,700
Lake Baikal	12,150
Great Bear Lake	12,000
Great Slave Lake	11,170
Lake Nyasa	11,000
Lake Erie	9,940
Lake Winnipeg	9,398
Lake Ontario	7,540
Lake Ladoga	7,100
Lake Balkhash	6,700
Lake Tchad (Chad)	6,500
Lake Onega	3,765
Lake Titicaca	3,200
Lake Nicaragua	3,100
Lake Athabaska	3,058
Reindeer Lake	2,444
Issyk-kul	2,276
Vänern	2,149
Lake Urmia	1,795
Great Salt Lake	1,700
Lake Albert	1,640
Lake Van	1,453
Lake Peipus	1,400
Lake Tana	1,219
Lake Bangweulu Approx.	1,000
Vättern	733
Dead Sea	405
Lake Balaton	266
Lake Geneva	225
Lake Constance	208
Lough Neagh	153
Lake Garda	143
Lake Neuchâtel	83
Lake Maggiore	82
Lough Corrib	71
Lake Como	56
Lake Lucerne	44½
Lake Zürich	34

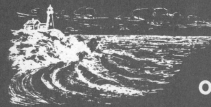

OCEANS AND SEAS OF THE WORLD

GREAT SHIP CANALS

	AREA IN SQ. MILES	GREATEST DEPTH FEET	VOLUME IN CUBIC MILES
Pacific Ocean	63,801,000	35,400	162,870,600
Atlantic Ocean	31,830,000	30,246	75,533,900
Indian Ocean	28,356,000	22,968	69,225,200
Arctic Ocean	5,440,000	17,850	4,029,400
Mediterranean Sea	1,145,000	15,197	1,019,400
Bering Sea	876,000	13,422	788,500
Caribbean Sea	750,000	23,748	2,298,400
Sea of Okhotsk	590,000	11,070	454,700
East China Sea	482,000	10,500	52,700
Hudson Bay	475,000	1,500	37,590
Japan Sea	389,000	13,242	383,200
North Sea	222,000	2,654	12,890
Red Sea	169,000	7,254	53,700
Black Sea	165,000	7,200	....
Baltic Sea	163,000	1,506	5,360

	LENGTH IN MILES	DEPTH IN FEET
Baltic-White Sea, U.S.S.R.	141	....
Suez, Egypt	100.76	34
Albert, Belgium	81	16.5
Moscow-Volga, U.S.S.R.	80	18
Kiel, Germany	61	37
Göta, Sweden	54	10
Panama, Canal Zone, U.S.A.	50.72	41
Houston, U.S.A.	50	36
Amsterdam-Rhine, Netherlands	45	41
Beaumont-Port Arthur, U.S.A.	40	32
Manchester, England	35.5	28
Chicago Sanitary and Ship, U.S.A.	30	22
Welland, Canada	27.6	25
Juliana, Netherlands	21	11.8
Chesapeake-Delaware, U.S.A.	19	27
Cape Cod, U.S.A.	13	25
Lake Washington, U.S.A.	8	30
Corinth, Greece	4	26.25
Sault Ste. Marie, U.S.A.	1.6	24.5
Sault Ste. Marie, Canada	1.4	18.25